Lecture Notes in Artificial Intelligence   11919

Subseries of Lecture Notes in Computer Science

More information about this series at http://www.springer.com/series/1244

Jixue Liu · James Bailey (Eds.)

AI 2019: Advances in Artificial Intelligence

32nd Australasian Joint Conference
Adelaide, SA, Australia, December 2–5, 2019
Proceedings

 Springer

Editors
Jixue Liu
University of South Australia
Adelaide, SA, Australia

James Bailey
The University of Melbourne
Melbourne, VIC, Australia

ISSN 0302-9743   ISSN 1611-3349 (electronic)
Lecture Notes in Artificial Intelligence
ISBN 978-3-030-35287-5   ISBN 978-3-030-35288-2 (eBook)
https://doi.org/10.1007/978-3-030-35288-2

LNCS Sublibrary: SL7 – Artificial Intelligence

This Springer imprint is published by the registered company Springer Nature Switzerland AG
The registered company address is: Gewerbestrasse 11, 6330 Cham, Switzerland

Preface

This volume contains the papers presented at the 32nd Australasian Joint Conference on Artificial Intelligence 2019 (AI 2019), which was held during December 2–5 2019, in Adelaide, Australia, hosted by the University of South Australia. This annual conference remains the premier event for artificial intelligence in Australasia, which provides a forum for researchers and practitioners across all subfields of artificial intelligence to meet and discuss recent advances. AI 2019 received 115 submissions with authors from 22 countries. Each submission was reviewed by at least three Program Committee members or external reviewers. Subsequent to a thorough discussion and rigorous scrutiny by the reviewers and the dedicated members of the Senior Program Committee, 48 submissions were accepted for publication as full papers. The acceptance rate was 42%.

AI 2019 had five keynote talks by the following distinguished scientists:

- Albert Bifet, University of Waikato, New Zealand, and Télécom ParisTech, France, on "Machine Learning for Data Streams"
- Dale Lambert, Defence Science and Technology (DST) Group, Australia, on "Artificial Intelligence: Past, Present, Future"
- Kate Smith-Mile, University of Melbourne, Australia, on "Instance Spaces for Objective Assessment of Algorithms and Benchmark Test"
- Anton van den Hengel, University of Adelaide, Australia, on "Visual Question Answering, and why we're asking the wrong questions"
- Xin Yao, Southern University of Science and Technology, China, and University of Birmingham, UK, on "Forgotten Questions in Brain-inspired Computing"

AI 2019 was featured with a workshop, a special session, and three tutorial sessions:

- Workshop: "Interpretability: Methodologies and Algorithms," organized by Inna Kolyshkina and Simeon Simoff. The workshop proceedings were managed separately from this book.
- Special session: "AI in Defence," organized by Asanka Kekirigoda, Zhuoyun Ao, and Kin Ping Hui.
- Tutorial: "Deep Learning Methods, Practices, and Applications," by Ehsan Abbasnejad from the University of Adelaide.
- Tutorial: "Deep Learning Security: Adversarial Attack and Defense," by Sarah Erfani and Xingjun Ma from the University of Melbourne.
- Tutorial: "From Statistical to Causal Learning," by Mingming Gong from the University of Melbourne.

AI 2019 would not have been successful without the support of authors, reviewers, and organizers. We thank the authors for submitting their research papers to the conference. We are grateful to authors whose papers are published in this volume for their cooperation during the preparation of the final camera-ready versions of the manuscripts. We specially appreciate the work of the members of the Program Committee and the external reviewers for their expertise and timeliness in assessing the papers within a short timeline. We also thank the organizers of the workshop, the DST session, and the tutorial speakers for their commitment and dedication. We are very grateful to the members of the Organizing Committee for their efforts in the preparation, promotion, and organization of the conference, especially the general chairs for coordinating the whole event. We acknowledge the assistance provided by EasyChair for conference management. Lastly, we thank the DST Group, Springer, The National Committee for Artificial Intelligence of the Australian Computer Society, and the University of South Australia for their sponsorship, and the professional service provided by the Springer LNCS editorial and publishing teams.

November 2019   Jixue Liu
                                                                       James Bailey

Organization

General Chairs

Jiuyong Li   University of South Australia, Australia
Abdul Sattar   Griffith University, Australia
Markus Stumptner   University of South Australia, Australia

Program Committee Chairs

Jixue Liu   University of South Australia, Australia
James Bailey   University of Melbourne, Australia

Other Conference Chairs

Masud Karim   University of South Australia, Australia
(Organizing Chair)
Cristina Garcia   University of South Australia, Australia
(Organizing Chair)
Lina Yao   University of New South Wales, Sydney, Australia
(Scholarship Chair)
Andy Song   RMIT, Australia
(Sponsorship Chair)
Junhu Wang   Griffith University, Australia
(Publicity Chair)
Ke Deng (Publicity Chair)   RMIT, Australia
Ashfaqur Rahman   CSIRO, Australia
(Workshop Chair)
Gustavo Carneiro   University of Adelaide, Australia
(Workshop Chair)
Gefei Li (Web Master)   University of South Australia, Australia

Senior Program Committee Members

Hussein Abbass   University of New South Wales, Canberra, Australia
Eibe Frank   University of Waikato, New Zealand
Jinyan Li   University of Technology, Sydney, Australia
Yuefeng Li   Queensland University of Technology, Australia
Jie Lu   University of Technology, Sydney, Australia
Frank Neumann   University of Adelaide, Australia
Bernhard Pfahringer   University of Waikato, New Zealand
Jochen Renz   Australian National University, Australia

Kai Ming Ting	Federation University Australia, Australia
Brijesh Verma	Central Queensland University, Australia
Xingquan Zhu	Florida Atlantic University, USA

Program Committee Members

Harith Al-Sahaf	Victoria University of Wellington, New Zealand
Zhuoyun Ao	Defence Science and Technology Group, Australia
Hiroki Arimura	Hokkaido University, Japan
Guillaume Aucher	Université de Rennes 1, CNRS, France
Zeyar Aung	Khalifa University of Science and Technology, UAE
Yun Bai	University of Western Sydney, Australia
Michael Bain	University of New South Wales, Sydney, Australia
Peter Baumgartner	CSIRO, Australia
Michael Bewong	University of South Australia, Australia
Wei Bian	University of Technology Sydney, Australia
Alan Blair	University of New South Wales, Australia
Michelle Blom	University of Melbourne, Australia
Sergiy Bogomolov	IST, Austria
Ljiljana Brankovic	University of Newcastle, Australia
Will Browne	Victoria University of Wellington, New Zealand
Weidong Cai	University of Sydney, Australia
Erik Cambria	Nanyang Technological University, Singapore
Stephan Chalup	University of Newcastle, Australia
Jeffrey Chan	RMIT University, Australia
Keith Chan	The Hong Kong Polytechnic University, Hong Kong
Jake Chandler	La Trobe University, Australia
Archie Chapman	University of Sydney, Australia
Gang Chen	Victoria University of Wellington, New Zealand
Qi Chen	Victoria University of Wellington, New Zealand
Songcan Chen	Nanjing University of Aeronautics & Astronautics, China
Stephen Chen	York University, Canada
Ran Cheng	University of Surrey, UK
Andrew Chiou	Central Queensland University, Australia
Sung-Bae Cho	Yonsei University, South Korea
Michael Cree	University of Waikato, New Zealand
Dave de Jonge	Western Sydney University, Australia
Emir Demirovic	University of Melbourne, Australia
Hepu Deng	RMIT University, Australia
Jeremiah Deng	University of Otago, New Zealand
Atilla Elci	Aksaray University, Turkey
Andreas Ernst	Monash University, Australia
Daryl Essam	University of New South Wales, Australia
Tim French	University of Western Australia
Keisuke Fujii	Nagoya University, Japan

Marcus Gallagher	University of Queensland, Australia
Wanru Gao	University of Adelaide, Australia
Xiaoying Gao	Victoria University of Wellington, New Zealand
Edel Garcia	CENATAV, Cuba
Tom Gedeon	Australian National University, Australia
Manolis Gergatsoulis	Library Sciences and Museology, Greece
Sujatha Das Gollapalli	I2R, A*STAR, Singapore
Alban Grastien	Data61, Australia
Jiuxiang Gu	Nanyang Technological University, Singapore
Ning Gu	University of South Australia, Australia
Hans W. Guesgen	Massey University, New Zealand
Aldy Gunawan	Singapore Management University, Singapore
Mingyu Guo	University of Adelaide, Australia
Christian Guttmann	TIETO (Sweden); University of New South Wales, Australia
Zhen Hai	Institute for Infocomm Research (I2R), Singapore
Kishaloy Halder	National University of Singapore, Singapore
Bo Han	RIKEN, Japan
Patrik Haslum	Australian National University, Australia
Tim Hendtlass	Swinburne University, Australia
Xiaodi Huang	Charles Sturt University, Australia
Akihiro Inokuchi	Kwansei Gakuin University, Japan
Md Zahidul Islam	University of South Australia, Australia
Asanka N. K. Mudiyanselage	Defence Science & Technology Group, Australia
Wei Kang	CSIRO, Australia
Paul Kennedy	University of Technology Sydney, Australia
Alistair Knott	University of Otago, New Zealand
Paul Kwan	University of New England, Australia
Selasi Kwashie	University of South Australia, Australia
Xiangyuan Lan	Hong Kong Baptist University, Hong Kong
Jérôme Lang	LAMSADE, Université Paris-Dauphine, France
Ickjai Lee	James Cook University, Australia
Gang Li	Deakin University, Australia
Gefei Li	University of South Australia
Jianxin Li	Deakin University, Australia
Chin-Teng Lin	University of Technology Sydney, Australia
Guanfeng Liu	Macquarie University, Australia
Hong-Cheu Liu	University of South Australia
Jing Liu	NLPR of CASIA, China
Shaowu Liu	University of Technology Sydney, Australia
Tongliang Liu	University of Sydney, Australia
Sha Lu	University of South Australia
Wei Lu	Singapore University of Technology and Design, Singapore
Hui Ma	Victoria University of Wellington, New Zealand

Hanlin Shang	Australian National University, Australia
Chunhua Shen	University of Adelaide, Australia
Michael Sheng	Macquarie University, Australia
Shinichi Shirakawa	Yokohama National University, Japan
Tony Smith	University of Waikato, New Zealand
Andy Song	RMIT University, Australia
Peter J. Stuckey	Monash University, Australia
Yanan Sun	Sichuan University, China
Zhu Sun	Nanyang Technological University, Singapore
Hanna Suominen	Australian National University, Australia
Lech Szymanski	University of Otago, New Zealand
Maolin Tang	Queensland University of Technology, Australia
Andrea Torsello	Università Ca' Foscari, Italy
Binh Tran	Victoria University of Wellington, New Zealand
Cao Truong Tran	Victoria University of Wellington, New Zealand
Markus Wagner	University of Adelaide, Australia
Toby Walsh	University of New South Wales, Sydney, Australia
Dianhui Wang	La Trobe University, Australia
Hua Wang	Victoria University, Australia
Jing Wang	Bournemouth University, Japan
Kewen Wang	Griffith University, Australia
Qing Wang	Australian National University, Australia
Yue Wang	City University of Hong Kong, Hong Kong
Zhe Wang	Griffith University, Australia
Shinya Watanabe	Muroran Institute of Technology, Japan
Peter Whigham	University of Otago, New Zealand
Brendon J. Woodford	University of Otago, New Zealand
Miao Xu	RIKEN, Japan
Shuxiang Xu	University of Tasmania, Australia
Bing Xue	Victoria University of Wellington, New Zealand
Nitin Yadav	University of Melbourne, Australia
Keiji Yanai	University of Electro-Communications, Japan
Can Yang	Hong Kong University of Science and Technology, Hong Kong
Jianhua Yang	Western Sydney University, Australia
Dezhong Yao	Nanyang Technological University, Singapore
Lina Yao	University of New South Wales, Australia
Tetsuya Yoshida	Nara Women's University, Japan
Lean Yu	Chinese Academy of Sciences, China
Xiaotian Yu	Chinese University of Hong Kong, Hong Kong
Daoqiang Zhang	Nanjing University of Aeronautics & Astronautics, China
Dongmo Zhang	Western Sydney University, Australia
Ji Zhang	University of Southern Queensland, Australia
Wei Emma Zhang	University of Adelaide, Australia
Xiuzhen Zhang	RMIT University, Australia

Ying Zhang   University of Technology Sydney, Australia
Ye Zhu   Monash University, Australia
Zhiqiang Zhuang   Griffith University, Australia

Additional Reviewers

David Buffoni   Li Ping
Taotao Cai   Kostiantyn Potomkin
Matthew Damigos   Jessica Rahman
Tom Everitt   Miquel Ramirez
Yi Fan   Chris Renton
Zhen Fang   Xiao Sha
Michael Floyd   Jun Shen
Shihua Huang   Tom Smoker
Jing Jiang   Yang Song
James Juniper   Yiliao Song
Jan Leike   Zhifu Tao
Jing Li   Kun Wang
Zhongnian Li   Yunchao Wei
Anjin Liu   Caitlin Woods
Feng Liu   Junyu Xuan
Qian Liu   Lina Yao
Chuan Luo   Hang Yu
Kingshuk Mazumdar   Hua Zhu
Pouya G. Omran   Hua Zuo

Contents

Machine Learning and Applications

Natural Language Processing and Text Analytics

Optimization and Evolutionary Computing

Image Processing

Game and Multiagent Systems

The Application of AlphaZero to Wargaming

Glenn Moy and Slava Shekh[(✉)]

Defence Science and Technology Group, Edinburgh, Australia
{glenn.moy, slava.shekh}@dst.defence.gov.au

Abstract. In this paper, we explore the process of automatically learning to play wargames using AlphaZero deep reinforcement learning. We consider a simple wargame, Coral Sea, which is a turn-based game played on a hexagonal grid between two players. We explore the differences between Coral Sea and traditional board games, where the successful use of AlphaZero has been demonstrated. Key differences include: problem representation, wargame asymmetry, limited strategic depth, and the requirement for significant hardware resources. We demonstrate how bootstrapping AlphaZero with supervised learning can overcome these challenges. In the context of Coral Sea, this enables AlphaZero to learn optimal play and outperform the supervised examples on which it was trained.

Keywords: Wargaming · Deep reinforcement learning · AlphaZero

1 Introduction

Wargaming is a key part of the Course of Action (COA) Analysis step of the Joint Military Appreciation Process (JMAP) used by the Australian Defence Force (ADF) [1]. Wargaming is used to evaluate alternative COAs for accomplishing a task or mission by stepping through each COA in detail to identify potential issues and vulnerabilities. The outcomes of the wargaming are then used to inform the Commander's final decision on the best COA.

In this paper we are interested in using deep reinforcement learning to automatically play wargames, which are a subclass of general game playing (GGP) [2]. In 2016, Google DeepMind made worldwide headlines with AlphaGo, a computer program that learnt to play the board game Go proficiently enough to defeat Lee Sedol, one of the world's best Go players [3]. Over the following years, Google DeepMind improved and generalized the AlphaGo system, leading to AlphaZero, a version of the software that could play several different board games (Go, Chess and Shogi) at superhuman levels [4]. The success of AlphaZero in playing a range of different strategy games naturally leads to the question of whether similar techniques could work in the context of military wargaming.

Automated wargame analysis could be used to provide recommendations for tactics and strategies, which human wargame players may have overlooked. As a further objective, an automated wargame player could be used to examine existing force structures and provide recommendations for how these structures could be modified to increase their effectiveness in a range of scenarios.

© Springer Nature Switzerland AG 2019
J. Liu and J. Bailey (Eds.): AI 2019, LNAI 11919, pp. 3–14, 2019.
https://doi.org/10.1007/978-3-030-35288-2_1

We are initially exploring a specific type of wargame modelled on a fictitious scenario, called Coral Sea [5]. Two players (Blue and Red) take turns moving units on a hexagonal (hex) grid, where the Blue player's aim is to reach a goal location with a specific unit, and the Red player's aim is to prevent the Blue player from doing so. This wargame is multi-agent, sequential, deterministic, static, fully observable, unknown, asymmetric and discrete.

In this work, we are interested in exploring the strengths and weaknesses of AlphaZero for discovering effective strategies for both the Blue and Red players, thereby automating the wargaming process. In particular, we are interested in investigating the feasibility of AlphaZero given constrained computational resources and a limited time budget.

The remainder of this paper is structured as follows: we provide a definition of the Coral Sea problem; we describe the AlphaZero technique; we discuss a number of differences between Coral Sea and traditional board games; and finally we outline our results, including a method of bootstrapping AlphaZero with supervised learning to improve performance.

2 Coral Sea

In the ADF, wargaming is used to evaluate alternative courses of action for accomplishing the Commander's Intent within a task or mission by stepping through each COA in detail to identify potential issues and vulnerabilities. The outcomes of the wargaming are then used to inform the Commander's decision-making.

The most common wargaming method used by the Australian military is the seminar wargame [6]. Seminar wargames are typically open-ended, discussion-based activities focused on eliciting expert judgements from assembled subject-matter experts. While there are many different methods for adjudication and tracking game state, these tend to be informal, with the game state often represented by a physical map, and tokens or pieces representing various force elements.

Assessing the consequences of particular action choices, as well as overall adjudication, is typically undertaken informally by one or more experts. There can be some degree of structure to seminar wargames (such as "boxing" off particular action-reaction sequences for analysis, or focusing on previously agreed time periods). However, seminar wargames don't usually make explicit assumptions about the outcomes of actions in particular states, or provide an explicit model of the environment that would support automated analysis.

More recently, however, the ADF has begun exploring the use of more structured wargaming in COA analysis, including applications like MASA SWORD [7]. The use of a model to represent the game state provides opportunities for more consistent, detailed adjudication and constrains the valid actions within a particular state. An explicit environment model also reduces the role of unconscious bias in wargame evaluation.

The existence of an explicit model of the environment opens up the possibility of using machine learning agents to efficiently explore the state space of the environment in order to provide recommendations on the best actions (tactics) to take in a particular situation. For initial exploration, we consider a simple wargame called Coral Sea [5]. Coral Sea is significantly simpler than large-scale wargaming applications, such as MASA SWORD, but is well-suited for a small-scale feasibility study. If machine learning can be applied successfully to Coral Sea, then our intent is to apply machine learning to more realistic wargaming simulations in future work.

Coral Sea is a turn-based game played on a hexagonal grid between two players: Blue and Red (see Fig. 1).

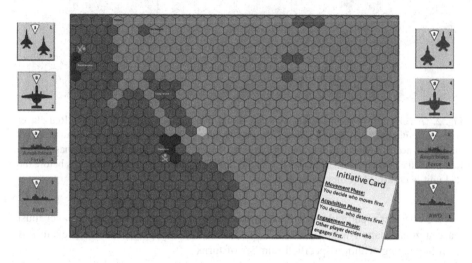

Fig. 1. The general Coral Sea board game - played on a hex grid with each player having a number of pieces representing different force elements [5]. (Color figure online)

Each player has a finite number of units at their disposal and must achieve a particular goal within a fixed number of turns. The available units and goals of each player are generally different, so the game is considered asymmetric. In the default scenario, the goal of the Blue player is to successfully move their Amphibious Force from its starting position to a defined goal, protected by the other pieces. The goal of the Red player is to stop this within a specified number of turns.

The game is played across a fixed number of turns, with each turn broken down into three phases: movement, acquisition and engagement. During the movement phase, players take turns moving their units to new positions on the hex grid. Each unit type is limited to moving a certain number of hexes per turn. One significant difference between classic board games and Coral Sea is the ability for a board position to contain multiple pieces simultaneously. During the acquisition phase, players take turns acquiring enemy units using friendly units that have acquisition capabilities (limited by an acquisition range). Finally, during the engagement phase, players take turns firing at enemy units that have been acquired in the previous phase. After the engagement phase, the next turn begins again with the movement phase and the initiative card is passed to the other player. The initiative card is always held by one player and determines whether that player can act first in the different phases of a turn. An example of the progression of play is given in Fig. 2.

Movement Phase   Acquisition Phase   Engagement Phase

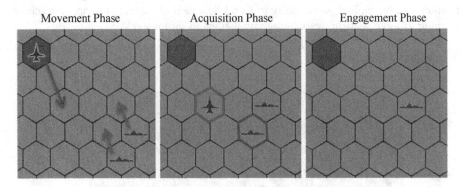

Fig. 2. An example of the three phases within a turn of Coral Sea (during which the Red player holds the initiative card). Players moves their units during the movement phase, acquire targets during the acquisition phase, and engage acquired targets during the engagement phase. Since Red holds the initiative card, Red acts first and is able to destroy one of the Blue units before the Red unit is destroyed. (Color figure online)

We consider a particular set of scenarios in Coral Sea, where the Blue player must reach a goal location with a particular unit, while the Red player tries to prevent this from happening within a specified number of turns.

3   AlphaZero

AlphaZero is a technique developed by Google DeepMind in 2017 [4]. AlphaZero is able to learn superhuman policies in some fully observable, symmetric, deterministic two-player strategy games, including Go, Chess and Shogi. Given many of the similarities, we postulate that AlphaZero should also be able to learn superhuman play in Coral Sea.

AlphaZero combines traditional Monte Carlo tree search (MCTS) [8] with a deep neural network that efficiently estimates the value of a particular board state, along with the probabilities of taking each action in that state. MCTS is a general search algorithm that is commonly used in automated game play as an alternative to exhaustive depth-first searches, such as Minimax [9]. MCTS expands the game tree through a form of weighted random sampling. Nodes in the game tree are selected based on a combination of how frequently they have been visited before (exploration) and how frequently they resulted in success (exploitation). Once a leaf node is reached, a rollout is performed to determine the outcome of the game from that state and the simplest way of doing this is through random play.

AlphaZero improves upon this process by combining MCTS with a deep neural network. Initially, a random neural network is used to estimate the value of states during the MCTS rollouts instead of using random play. Over time, AlphaZero generates a large amount of self-play data, using MCTS and the neural network to estimate the rollout values and move probabilities. In parallel, a separate process constantly optimizes the neural network weights towards more accurate values, based on the actual outcomes (win/loss) from self-play games. From time to time, the updated neural network is compared to the current best network, by playing a series of "evaluation" games in a separate, parallel process. If the current network beats the best network by a sufficient margin the best network is updated, otherwise the previous best network remains and optimization continues. All three processes (self-play, optimize and evaluate) continue in parallel. As the model becomes better at predicting the value of states, and the best action to take, the quality of self-play data improves.

4 Differences from Chess and Go

Coral Sea shares many properties with traditional board games like Chess and Go, but there are also several key differences which we discuss in the following subsections.

4.1 Representations

One significant difference between many board games and Coral Sea is the ability for a board position to contain multiple pieces simultaneously. This means that compact representations of board state, such as the Forsyth–Edwards Notation (FEN) notation in Chess [10], cannot be directly used in Coral Sea. In addition, whereas the board in many board games can be represented as a two-dimensional matrix, the notion that multiple pieces can occupy a single space requires the addition of a third dimension. In fact, any property of a board game that is traditionally represented in two dimensions may now require three. An example from Coral Sea is the accumulation of acquisition points on units during the acquisition phase (to determine which units have been acquired and are valid engagement targets). If multiple units can be co-located, then an extra dimension is required to store this acquisition information on a per-unit basis at a particular board position.

One way of representing board state, and in fact the approach used in AlphaZero, is to create a multi-dimensional spatial representation which can be used in conjunction with a convolutional neural network (CNN). CNNs have proven to work well on tasks such as image classification [11], where the CNN learns the spatial relationships in an image in order to classify it. In Coral Sea, this is a viable way of representing the board state, but possibly not the most efficient due to the additional dimensions added by the property of multiple pieces being allowed in a single hex. Therefore, we also explore a linear vector representation of board state, where unit positions are simply stored as coordinates rather than being represented spatially. This alternative board representation allows us to also use a much simpler neural network, such as a basic multi-layer perceptron (MLP), which may accelerate the training process at the expense of simplifying the behaviors which can be learnt by the neural network.

4.2 Asymmetry

AlphaZero learnt to play three different board games (Go, Chess and Shogi) using the same basic architecture [4]. However, each of these games is essentially symmetric, because players start these games in very similar starting states and have access to the same kind of moves over the course of play.

Unlike board games, which use symmetry to allow two players to directly compete on an even playing field, wargames are abstract representations of real world military conflict, which is typically an uneven playing field. The primary purpose of military wargaming is not friendly competition, as is the case with classic board games, but as a mechanism for understanding the potential outcomes of different choices in a military scenario. If a scenario turns out to be highly asymmetric, strongly favoring one of the players, then that is a valid and useful outcome of the wargaming process.

One consequence of asymmetry in wargames is that the initial strategy of the disadvantaged player can be much more difficult to learn through self-play. Consider a Coral Sea scenario, where the Blue player must reach the goal in the top-left corner of the map, while the Red player defends it (see Fig. 3). If the Blue player does nothing, then Red automatically wins because the goal has been defended. As a first step, Blue needs to learn how to traverse the map towards the top-left corner in order to have any chance of succeeding. This is difficult using a technique like AlphaZero, because it does not use any human expert data and learns through self-play. Since there is no human expert data, this self-play is initially very random. Randomly discovering the strategy of moving from the bottom-right corner to the top-left corner of the map is an unlikely occurrence, particularly as the size of the map grows.

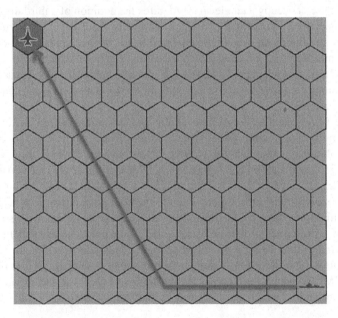

Fig. 3. A Coral Sea scenario played on a 10 × 10 hex grid. The Blue player must reach the top-left corner of the map with their unit, while the Red player must defend that location. (Color figure online)

A second consequence of asymmetry is that incremental improvement in strategy for one player does not necessarily benefit the other player. In a symmetric game, as an agent learns new strategies, these strategies provide equal benefit for both the Blue and Red player. By contrast, in an asymmetric game, any new strategy discovered may improve one side over another. As a result, throughout the learning process self-play games are always played between opponents with unmatched skill level. This leads to lower quality self-play data and undermines the self-play mechanism.

4.3 Strategic Depth

In addition to differences in representation and the presence of asymmetry, Coral Sea is also different from Chess and Go in that it has relatively low strategic depth [12]. Strategic depth is a concept that has been used by game developers to describe games that are easy to learn, but hard to master. Games with high strategic depth have a large strategy ladder. A game's strategy ladder defines a list of increasingly successful strategies available given increasing computational resources. Each individual strategy on a game's strategy ladder describes the optimal play possible for a fixed computational budget, with that budget increasing for steps higher up the ladder. Games with high strategic depth have a large number of increasingly complex, ever-improving strategies available to the player. By contrast, games with low strategic depth typically have only a small number of distinct strategy choices. This does not necessarily mean that games with low strategic depth have reduced state space complexity – the computational cost of implementing the strategy could be arbitrarily high.

Popular games like Chess and Go have been successful over thousands of years precisely because they have high strategic depth, offering players a lifetime of skill development. Games with high strategic depth are particularly well-suited for incremental self-play techniques like AlphaZero. Since the process of exploring new strategies involves random exploration, AlphaZero works best on games with a computationally close set of increasingly good strategies to facilitate continuous improvement through self-play.

In contrast to Go, Chess and Shogi, military wargames don't always have high strategic depth. Wargames model real military scenarios, so they are not specifically designed for continuous improvement or skill development. In our case, we assess that in Coral Sea there is little strategic depth, with only a small number of strategic choices separating random play from optimal play. However, while strategic depth is low, the computational cost of finding the few strategies required can be made arbitrarily large. For instance, increasing the board size increases the state space with little impact on strategic depth. This adds another challenge to using incremental self-play as a technique for learning to play Coral Sea.

4.4 Hardware

DeepMind made the claim that AlphaZero outperformed Stockfish, one of the best Chess engines, after just 4 h of training [4]. At the time, Stockfish was one of the strongest Chess engines in the world, frequently winning the Top Chess Engine Competition, and sharing dominance as one of the "big 3" Chess engines alongside

Komodo and Houdini [13]. Since the defeat of Garry Kasparov in 1997, computer Chess has come a long way and all 3 of these engines are significantly stronger than any human grandmaster.

It is therefore difficult to imagine how a machine learning system, trained for only 4 h and without any human games as guidance, can defeat a Chess engine that has been carefully honed and perfected by humans over the last decade. The caveat is that in those 4 h, AlphaZero was trained "using 5,000 first-generation TPUs to generate self-play games and 64 second-generation TPUs to train the neural networks" [4]. A distributed, open-source effort to reproduce DeepMind's results, called Leela Chess Zero, has taken approximately 1 year to reach the strength of Stockfish, using essentially the same approach as AlphaZero [14]. In a similar vein, OpenAI Five succeeding in training a deep reinforcement learning system to compete at professional level in Dota 2. Their system plays 180 years' worth of games against itself every day by running a massively scaled version of proximal policy optimization (PPO) on a cluster of 256 GPUs and 128,000 CPU cores [15].

Despite these impressive results, the kind of computational resources available to DeepMind and OpenAI are generally not available to the public. Researchers often have access to machines with only a handful of CPUs and GPUs, making the achievements of DeepMind and OpenAI very difficult to reproduce. For example, training AlphaZero to play Chess better than Stockfish would take in the order of years on a machine with a single GPU. This suggests the need for algorithms with better efficiency, particularly better sample efficiency, which is an active area of research focused on improving the degree to which an algorithm learns per input data sample [16].

5 Experimental Results

Although Coral Sea shares some properties with board games like Chess, Go and Shogi, the differences described in the previous section mean that applying AlphaZero directly to Coral Sea is a challenging task. The asymmetric nature of Coral Sea, the imbalanced and non-incremental strategy ladder, and the higher-dimensional problem representation are all sources of increased complexity. At the same time, with only a small number of CPUs and GPUs available, we are limited to hardware resources that are orders of magnitude smaller than those of DeepMind in their AlphaZero implementation. Through our experimentation, we find that one of the most effective ways to address these challenges is to bootstrap AlphaZero with supervised learning.

5.1 AlphaZero with Supervision

AlphaZero learnt to play Go, Chess and Shogi "tabula rasa" – given the game rules, but no other human domain knowledge [4]. More complex systems, such as like AlphaStar, often use human data and supervised learning to bootstrap the reinforcement learning [17]. More generally, the concept of agents learning behavior from human demonstrations is known as imitation learning [18]. In the Coral Sea problem, instead of using human demonstrations, we encode human knowledge in the form of heuristics. We find that supervised learning over heuristic data greatly speeds up the learning process, especially due to the asymmetry of the wargame. The following experiment provides some evidence of this finding.

Consider the Coral Sea scenario illustrated in Fig. 3 (Sect. 4.2). In this scenario, the Blue player starts in the bottom right corner of a 10×10 hex grid with the goal of reaching the top left corner of the grid in 20 turns. The Red player starts in the top left corner and must prevent the Blue player from reaching that corner. Both players can move a maximum of 1 hex cell per turn to cells that are adjacent in the hex grid. Both players are able to destroy the other play from a fixed cell-distance (typically within 3 hex-grid cells) away. The opportunity to shoot first alternates according to which player holds the initiative card in any given turn.

This trivial scenario is initially biased towards a Red victory, because if both players do nothing, Blue will not reach the goal and Red will win by default. However, with perfect play, Blue is guaranteed a win. Nevertheless, in early exploration, Blue only receives a reward if it reaches the goal. Therefore, if the Blue player explores by performing a random movement during each of their 20 turns, the chance that these random movements will ultimately lead to the goal is very small on a 10×10 grid. Furthermore, consider the same grid scaled up to 100×100 or more, where a human could still find a path to the goal with relative ease, but where finding a path through random exploration becomes increasingly infeasible.

Since AlphaZero is initialised with a random neural network and its initial exploration is largely random due to the use of MCTS, AlphaZero will inherently struggle to discover the Blue strategy of moving towards the goal. One way of assisting AlphaZero in its learning process is to provide some learning examples. We have implemented three heuristics (GoalMove, SafeGoalMove and RandomLegal), which can be used to generate higher quality data than random MCTS simulations.

GoalMove involves moving as far as possible directly towards the goal, where the goal can be a location on the grid or an enemy unit. SafeGoalMove involves applying GoalMove if the initiative card is currently held by the player, while otherwise moving to a hex in the direction of the goal but outside the reach of any enemy units. Finally, RandomLegal simply selects a legal action at random and provides us with a baseline. Given the scenario shown in Fig. 3, each of the heuristics being used by each of the players can be ordered in terms of their relative strength, forming an approximate strategy ladder:

1. SafeGoalMove (Blue)
2. SafeGoalMove (Red)
3. GoalMove (Blue)
4. GoalMove (Red)/RandomLegal (Red)
5. RandomLegal (Blue)

This ordering means that the SafeGoalMove strategy when used by Blue will beat any Red strategy (out of the three we have implemented), whereas SafeGoalMove when used by Red will beat any Blue strategy except SafeGoalMove, and so on. The only exception is that RandomLegal, due to its stochastic nature, can sometimes defeat the strategies above it in the ordering, but this is a very rare occurrence. To the best of our knowledge, SafeGoalMove is an optimal strategy when used by Blue, demonstrating that Blue ultimately has an advantage in this scenario. Preliminary experiments also suggest that SafeGoalMove is an effective (though not always optimal) strategy in other Coral Sea scenarios, providing a good baseline strategy for future work.

To avoid having a strong reliance on heuristic data, we explore a hybrid approach where both heuristics and MCTS are used to generate self-play data for AlphaZero. This is achieved by probabilistically using either a heuristic or MCTS to select a player's next action during a self-play game. The player's next action is selected by a heuristic with probability p_h or by the standard AlphaZero MCTS method with probability $(1-p_h)$. During evaluation (as opposed to self-play), p_h is set to 0 to force AlphaZero to select its own actions without relying on heuristics, and to demonstrate what it has learnt.

While in this simple scenario, SafeGoalMove is an optimal strategy, it will not be an optimal strategy across all Coral Sea scenarios. In general, our goal is to use AlphaZero to find optimal strategies, although optimal heuristics will not be known in advance for all scenarios. To this end, we have chosen to use the suboptimal GoalMove to generate heuristic data. Our goal is to avoid providing AlphaZero with examples of optimal play, to see if it can learn this optimal play for itself from suboptimal heuristic data.

Table 1 below shows the effect of combining heuristics and MCTS with different values of p_h.

Table 1. Training time required for AlphaZero to reach a 100% win rate against the GoalMove heuristic on the scenario from Fig. 3 (as both Blue and Red) with different values of p_h.

p_h	Training time
0	>24 h
0.5	5 h
0.8	25 min
0.9	15 min
0.95	15 min
0.99	>24 h
1	>24 h

When $p_h = 0$, AlphaZero only uses MCTS to generate self-play games, which causes it to suffer from the exploration problems described earlier and prevents it from reaching a 100% win rate against the GoalMove heuristic within 24 h. When $p_h = 1$, AlphaZero only uses the GoalMove heuristic to generate self-play games, which means it lacks knowledge of how to beat a Blue player who is using GoalMove (since the only thing stronger in the heuristic ordering is SafeGoalMove, which a $p_h = 1$ player cannot learn due to only seeing examples of GoalMove).

When $0 < p_h < 1$, AlphaZero ultimately manages to generate a more diverse set of self-play data with policies that are based on the GoalMove heuristic with modifications proportional to $(1 - p_h)$. As p_h approaches 1, the time required to generate self-play games rapidly decreases due to the speed of using a heuristic over MCTS. This means that with a high p_h, AlphaZero can generate large amounts of self-play data and learn improved policies much more quickly. However, if p_h is too close to 1, the data set will lack diversity and AlphaZero may not be able to overcome the sub-optimality of the GoalMove heuristic on which it was trained.

In summary, by combining both heuristic (expert) knowledge and MCTS exploration within the AlphaZero reinforcement learning framework, we are able to train a model which can outperform the heuristics that were used to train it, as well as achieving this in much less computation time than using MCTS alone.

6 Conclusion

In this paper, we described our work on applying machine learning methods to the abstract military wargame, Coral Sea. In particular, we investigated the AlphaZero methodology and the feasibility of extending it from the domains of Go, Chess and Shogi, toward the domain of military wargaming. Although the fundamental methodology is sound and extends to our domain, we encountered many challenges along the way in terms of problem representation, asymmetry, strategic depth and hardware. We found that one of the most effective ways to address these challenges is to bootstrap AlphaZero with supervised learning. We demonstrated that by combining heuristic knowledge and MCTS exploration, we were able to train AlphaZero to outperform the heuristics on which it was trained.

References

1. Australian Defence Force: Joint Military Appreciation Process (2016)
2. Genesereth, M., Love, N., Pell, B.: General game playing: overview of the AAAI competition. AI Mag. **26**(2), 62 (2005)
3. Silver, D., et al.: Mastering the game of Go with deep neural networks and tree search. Nature **529**(7587), 484 (2016)
4. Silver, D., et. al.: Mastering chess and shogi by self-play with a general reinforcement learning algorithm. arXiv preprint arXiv:1712.01815 (2017)
5. Tregenza, M.: Coral Sea 2042: Rules for the Maritime/Air Analytical Wargame (2018)
6. Pace, D.K.: Seminar gaming: an approach to problems too complex for algorithmic solution. John Hopkins APL Tech. Digest **12**(3), 290–296 (1991)
7. MASA SWORD. https://masasim.com/sword/. Accessed 08 May 2019
8. Kocsis, L., Szepesvári, C.: Bandit based Monte-Carlo planning. In: Fürnkranz, J., Scheffer, T., Spiliopoulou, M. (eds.) ECML 2006. LNCS (LNAI), vol. 4212, pp. 282–293. Springer, Heidelberg (2006). https://doi.org/10.1007/11871842_29
9. Campbell, M.S., Marsland, T.A.: A comparison of minimax tree search algorithms. Artif. Intell. **20**(4), 347–367 (1983)
10. Edwards, S.J.: Forsyth-Edwards Notation. Portable Game Notation Specification and Implementation Guide (1994)

11. Krizhevsky, A., Sutskever, I., Hinton, G.E.: Imagenet classification with deep convolutional neural networks. In: Advances in Neural Information Processing Systems, pp. 1097–1105 (2012)
12. Lantz, F., Isaksen, A., Jaffe, A., Nealen, A., Togelius, J.: Depth in strategic games. In: Workshops at the Thirty-First AAAI Conference on Artificial Intelligence (2017)
13. Stockfish continues to dominate computer chess, wins TCEC S14. http://www.chessdom.com/stockfish-continues-to-dominate-computer-chess-wins-tcec-s14/. Accessed 08 May 2019
14. Silver, A.: Leela Chess Zero: AlphaZero for the PC. https://en.chessbase.com/post/leela-chess-zero-alphazero-for-the-pc. Accessed 08 May 2019
15. OpenAI Five. https://openai.com/blog/openai-five/. Accessed 08 May 2019
16. Botvinick, M., Ritter, S., Wang, J.X., Kurth-Nelson, Z., Blundell, C., Hassabis, D.: Reinforcement learning, fast and slow. Trends Cogn. Sci. **23**, 408–422 (2019)
17. AlphaStar: Mastering the Real-Time Strategy Game StarCraft II. https://deepmind.com/blog/alphastar-mastering-real-time-strategy-game-starcraft-ii/. Accessed 08 May 2019
18. Hussein, A., Gaber, M.M., Elyan, E., Jayne, C.: Imitation learning: a survey of learning methods. ACM Comput. Surv. (CSUR) **50**(2), 21 (2017)

Helping an Agent Reach a Different Goal by Action Transfer in Reinforcement Learning

Yuchen Wang[(✉)], Fenghui Ren, and Minjie Zhang

School of Computing and Information Technology, University of Wollongong,
Wollongong, NSW 2522, Australia
yw808@uowmail.edu.au, {fren,minjie}@uow.edu.au

Abstract. Reinforcement learning agents can be helped by the knowledge transferred from experienced agents. This paper studies the problem of how an experienced agent helps another agent learn when they have different learning goals by action transfer. This problem is motivated by the widely existing situations where agents have different learning goals and only action transfer is available to agents. To tackle the problem, we propose an approach to facilitate the transfer of actions that are right to a learning agent's goal. Experimental results show the effectiveness of the proposed approach in transferring right actions to an agent and helping the agent learn to reach a different goal.

Keywords: Different goals · Action transfer · Reinforcement learning

1 Introduction

Reinforcement Learning (RL) has been widely used for an autonomous agent to learn to reach its goal in sequential decision-making tasks [7]. An RL agent might need a long learning time. To improve learning, transferring knowledge from experienced agents to learning agents has been widely studied [9].

Transferring different kinds of knowledge has various requirements for agents. This paper considers the transfer of *actions*, which requires agents to only have a common action set. Compared with transferring other kinds of knowledge, the requirement for action transfer is considered to be minimal [10]. This provides much flexibility. For example, agents giving and receiving actions could use different knowledge representations and learning algorithms.

In this paper, we study the problem of how an experienced agent helps another agent learn when they have different learning goals by action transfer. This problem would widely exist in the real world. For example, Alice knows how to reach her travel destination. When Bob loses his way, Alice might help Bob reach his travel destination efficiently. However, the destinations of Alice and Bob might be different. Also, Bob might not understand Alice's detailed expressions due to various reasons. In this situation, an understandable way for

© Springer Nature Switzerland AG 2019
J. Liu and J. Bailey (Eds.): AI 2019, LNAI 11919, pp. 15–27, 2019.
https://doi.org/10.1007/978-3-030-35288-2_2

Alice to help is to point out some directions that Bob could follow. Here "point out" indicates "transfer", and "directions to follow" indicates "actions".

Several knowledge transfer approaches have been proposed to help an agent learn in the different-goal situation [4,6,12]. These approaches require learning agents to access and understand the knowledge of source agents. However, this requirement might not be satisfied in many applications, especially when humans are helping or learning [10]. Some knowledge transfer approaches with only action transfer have been proposed [1,3,9,10,13,15]. However, these approaches require agents giving and receiving actions to have the same learning goal, which is not satisfied in the different-goal situation. Therefore, how an experienced agent helps another agent learn when they have different learning goals by action transfer remains as a challenging problem.

To tackle this problem, we ask below questions: (Q1) what actions are right to be transferred to help a learning agent in the different-goal situation? (Q2) do right actions exist? (Q3) if right actions exist, how an experienced agent finds them? and (Q4) if a right action exists, but an experienced agent cannot decide the rightness of this right action, could the agent still be able to transfer this action? Hereafter, action transfer are called *action advice*, agents giving/receiving advice are called *teachers/students*. These names often appear in the action transfer literature. We propose an action advice approach to answer the above questions. For (Q1), we define an agent's goal, describe what makes the different-goal situation, and define a teacher's right/wrong advice (Sect. 2). For (Q2), we define the concept of policy-similar states, at which right advice exists (Sect. 3.1). For (Q3), we propose a method that enables a teacher to decide if a state is policy-similar by finding right advice (Sect. 3.3). For (Q4), we propose a method that enables a teacher to give right advice at states which are policy-similar, but could not be decided as policy-similar by the teacher (Sect. 3.4). Experimental results show the effectiveness of the proposed action advice (action transfer) approach used in the different-goal situation.

2 Problem Formulation

In this section, we first give the background, including Markov Decision Process (MDP) and action advice framework. Then, we formulate this paper's problem. **Background** RL has been widely used to solve sequential decision-making tasks. Markov decision process [5] has been widely used as the model of an RL task. An MDP is described by a tuple $< S, A, T, R >$, where S is the set of states, A is the set of actions, $T : S \times A \times S \rightarrow [0, 1]$ is the transition function, $R : S \times A \rightarrow \mathbb{R}$ is the reward function. An agent needs to learn an optimal policy π, which is a mapping from S to A. Following π maximises the expected reward: $V(s) = E[\sum_{t=0}^{\infty} \gamma^t r^t | s_0 = s]$, $\forall s \in S$, where $\gamma \in [0, 1)$ is a discount factor, r^t is the reward at time step t, V is the expected reward value function.

The action advice framework [8] includes two types of agents: Teacher and Student. A teacher has learned an optimal policy π^1. When a student is learning, the teacher could help the student learn by giving advice. The advice at a state s is an action $a \in \pi(s)$, i.e., an optimal action to take at s based on the optimal policy learned by the teacher.

Formulation of the Problem. We first define the goal of an agent. Then, we describe what makes the different-goal situation, and clarify why current action advice approaches are not applicable in the different-goal situation.

Definition 1 (Agent Goal). *Given an agent in an MDP with a state space S, let V^* be the maximised expected reward value function, the goal of the agent is a state $g \in S$ where $V^*(g) \geq V^*(s), \forall s \in S^2$.*

An agent receives the maximum expected reward among all states when the agent reaches its goal. The optimal policy learned by the agent guides the agent to its goal from other states.

Let t and u be a teacher and a student, g_t and g_u be their goals. The different-goal situation can be denoted as $g_t \neq g_u$. Basically, $g_t \neq g_u$ means that a teacher and a student need to solve different MDPs. Two MDPs are different when they have difference in any of S, A, T or R. In this paper, we focus on a specific kind of difference that makes $g_t \neq g_u$: two different MDPs share the same S, A, T, R^-, and have different R^+, where $R^+: S \times A \rightarrow \mathbb{R}_{>0}$, $R^-: S \times A \rightarrow \mathbb{R}_{<0}$. The MDPs with this kind of difference could model a bunch of different, but similar tasks in the real world. For example, different navigation tasks on land share the same S (land space), A (actions available on land), T (execution results of actions), R^- (e.g., battery consumption), and have different R^+ (different navigation goals). Enabling agents in different navigation tasks to advise each other would be beneficial to these agents.

Let π_g be the optimal policy for reaching a goal g. A teacher has learned π_{g_t}. A student has not learned π_{g_u}, and would need action advice from the teacher to learn π_{g_u}. To help the student learn, the advised actions should be optimal for reaching g_u. The optimal/non-optimal advised actions can be defined as follows:

Definition 2 (Right/Wrong Advice). *Let g_t and g_u be the goals of a teacher and a student, π_g be the optimal policy for reaching a goal g. At a state s, an advised action $a \in \pi_{g_t}(s)$ is right/wrong advice when $a \in \pi_{g_u}(s)/a \notin \pi_{g_u}(s)$.*

In the same-goal situation, $g_t = g_u$. Then, $\pi_{g_t} = \pi_{g_u}$, which means $\forall s \in S, \pi_{g_t}(s) = \pi_{g_u}(s)$. Hence, we have $\forall s \in S, \forall a \in \pi_{g_t}(s), a \in \pi_{g_u}(s)$. This clarifies that in the same-goal situation, at any state, any advised action (optimal to g_t) is right advice (optimal to g_u). However, in the different-goal situation, $g_t \neq g_u$.

---

[1] We follow a general setting where π is optimal. Considering sub-optimal π is not the main issue in this paper, and would be left as future work.

[2] There are multiple goals when multiple states have the same maximum V value. The technical details for multi-goal and one-goal situations are generally the same. We only describe the one-goal situation for clear description.

Table 1. Notation

Notation	Meaning
S, s, g	A state space, a state, a goal state of an agent
$\pi_g, \pi_g(s)$	An optimal policy for g, optimal actions to take at s for reaching g
$PS(g_1, g_2)$	Policy-similar states of two agents with goals g_1 and g_2
$OR^{\pi_g}(s, a)$	Optimally reachable states of a state s and an action a under a policy π_g

Then, $\pi_{g_t} \neq \pi_{g_u}$, which means $\exists s \in S$, $a \in \pi_{g_t}(s) \wedge a \notin \pi_{g_u}(s)$. This indicates that at some states, some advised actions might be wrong advice. In current action advice approaches, a teacher does not decide if its advice is right to a student. Then, the teacher might give wrong advice, which would mislead the student. Hence, this paper's problem is to study how a teacher gives right advice to a student in the different-goal situation. The notation used in this paper is shown in Table 1.

3 Action Advice in the Different-Goal Situation

This section first summarises two aims of the proposed approach by defining agents' policy-similar states. Then, the proposed approach is described in detail.

3.1 Policy-Similar States and Aims of the Proposed Approach

For an agent with a goal g, g indicates a unique π_g [7]. Hence, for a teacher and a student with g_t and g_u be their goals, π_{g_t} and π_{g_u} are well-defined. Based on π_{g_t}, π_{g_u} and Definition 2, the states where right advice exists are also well-defined. Those states can be defined as follows:

Definition 3 (Policy-Similar States). *For a state space S, let g_t and g_u be the goals of a teacher and a student respectively, π_g be the optimal policy for reaching a goal g, the policy-similar states of the agents are a set of states:*

$$PS(g_t, g_u) = \{s \in S \backslash \{g_u\} | (\exists a)[a \in \pi_{g_t}(s) \wedge a \in \pi_{g_u}(s)]\} \tag{1}$$

The term *policy-similar* describes that a teacher and a student can take at least one same optimal action to reach the agents' different goals. At a policy-similar state, right advice could be given if the teacher knows which action (indicated by the teacher's policy) is optimal to the student's goal. Note that PS is not known by any agent because an agent only knows its own goal and policy. PS is computed within $S \backslash \{g_u\}$. g_u is excluded because when at g_u, a student has reached its goal and does not need to take actions or get advice. Based on PS, we summarise the aims of the proposed approach as follows:

Aim 1: To give right advice at a state s, the first aim is *to enable a teacher to decide if s is in PS, i.e., to decide if $\exists a[a \in \pi_{g_t}(s) \wedge a \in \pi_{g_u}(s)]$.*

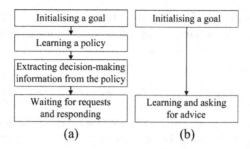

Fig. 1. The procedures of (a) a teacher and (b) a student.

Aim 2: If a teacher could decide that $\forall s \in PS, \exists a[a \in \pi_{g_t}(s) \wedge a \in \pi_{g_u}(s)]$, the teacher could give right advice at maximum number of states. However, the above decision would be hard to made. This is because finding all PS would require the knowledge of both π_{g_t} and π_{g_u}, which would be infeasible for a teacher who only knows π_{g_t}. Let PS_d be the states that could be decided in PS by a teacher. We expect $PS_d \subset PS$, i.e., there would be some states $PS \backslash PS_d$ that are policy-similar, but could not be decided as policy-similar by the teacher. To give right advice at more states than just at PS_d, the second aim is *to enable a teacher to give right advice at states $PS \backslash PS_d$*.

The number of policy-similar states would relate to the settings of agents' goals. This will be experimentally investigated in Sect. 4.1.

3.2 Overview of the Proposed Action Advice Approach

To tackle the aims summarised in Sect. 3.1, we propose an action advice approach whose overview is shown in Fig. 1. Figure 1(a) shows the procedure of a teacher. After initialising a goal, the teacher learns an optimal policy for reaching its goal. Then, from the policy, the teacher extracts the decision-making information used for deciding if an action is optimal to a student's goal (for Aim 1, described in Sect. 3.3). Next, the teacher starts to wait for requests from a student and will respond by giving or not giving advice. In Fig. 1(b), a student first initialises its goal. Then, the student starts to learn and will ask the teacher for advice (for Aim 2, described in Sect. 3.4).

3.3 Formulation and Extraction of Decision-Making Information

We first formulate the decision-making information used for deciding if an action is optimal to a student's goal. Then, we show the extraction of this decision-making information from the policy learned by a teacher.

Formulation of Decision-Making Information. For a teacher and a student, from the teacher's perspective, any state $g_p \in S$ might be the student's goal, and the student may ask for advice to reach g_p from another state s. Hence, the teacher needs to decide if $\pi_{g_t}(s)$ provides optimal actions for reaching g_p from s. The decision-making information can be formulated in below definition:

Definition 4 (Optimally Reachable States). *Let π_g be the optimal policy for reaching a goal g, g_t be the goal of a teacher. For a state space S, a state s, and an action $a \in \pi_{g_t}(s)$, the optimally reachable states of (s, a) under π_{g_t} are a set of states:*

$$OR^{\pi_{g_t}}(s, a) = \{g_p \in S | a \in \pi_{g_t}(s) \wedge a \in \pi_{g_p}(s)\} \tag{2}$$

$\forall g_p \in OR^{\pi_{g_t}}(s, a)$, a is an optimal action for reaching both g_t and g_p. When a student is learning and asking for advice to reach g_u at s, the teacher can make its decision on whether to give advice based on following rules:

$$Decide(s, g_u) = \begin{cases} \text{give action advice } a, & \text{if } \exists a \in \pi_{g_t}(s)[g_u \in OR^{\pi_{g_t}}(s, a)] \\ \text{no advice}, & \text{otherwise} \end{cases} \tag{3}$$

If $\exists a \in \pi_{g_t}(s)[g_u \in OR^{\pi_{g_t}}(s, a)]$, a is decided to be optimal to the student's goal, and will be given as right advice by the teacher. Otherwise, the teacher cannot find right advice, and hence does not give advice.

Extraction of Decision-Making Information. Next, we introduce the extraction of $OR^{\pi_{g_t}}$ from a teacher's policy π_{g_t}. To simplify notation, we use π to denote π_{g_t}, OR^π to denote $OR^{\pi_{g_t}}$.

We first use below equation to get an optimally reachable state of (s, a):

$$O(s, a) = \{s | s \in \hat{T}(s, a) \backslash \{s\} \wedge |\hat{T}(s, a) \backslash \{s\}| = 1\} \tag{4}$$

where $\hat{T}(s, a)$ indicates the states that an agent may travel to after taking a at s. $|\hat{T}(s, a) \backslash \{s\}| = 1$ means that the agent will travel to only one state other than the current state s. We use o_{sa} to denote the only state in $O(s, a)$. a is optimal for reaching o_{sa} from s. This is because the teacher has learned that o_{sa} is the state to reach before the teacher can optimally reach g_t. If there is another action $a_b \notin \pi(s)$ that could make the teacher better reach o_{sa}, the teacher would have learned that $a_b \in \pi(s)$, which contradicts with $a_b \notin \pi(s)$. When $|\hat{T}(s, a) \backslash \{s\}| > 1$, a might not be optimal for reaching $\hat{T}(s, a) \backslash \{s\}$. Detailed analysis on the optimality of a when $|\hat{T}(s, a) \backslash \{s\}| > 1$ is beyond the scope of this paper, and would be studied in future work.

For o_{sa}, we can apply Eq. (4) to get $O(o_{sa}, a'), a' \in \pi(o_{sa})$. We use $o_{saa'}$ to denote the only state in $O(o_{sa}, a')$. As a is an optimal action to reach o_{sa} from s, a' is an optimal action to reach $o_{saa'}$ from o_{sa}, we have that a is an optimal action to reach $o_{saa'}$ from s because "is an optimal action to reach" is a transitive relation. Hence, $o_{saa'}$ is also an optimally reachable state of (s, a). Following the above analysis, we can get a sequential sets of optimally reachable states. To do so, we introduce the below equation:

$$N^\pi(S') = \{o_{s'a'} | \forall s' \in S', \forall a' \in \pi(s')\} \tag{5}$$

$N^\pi(\{o_{sa}\})$ indicates the optimally reachable states to reach by taking every action in $\pi(o_{sa})$. $N^\pi(\cdot)$ can be regarded as a function, and can be applied to the returned states of $N^\pi(\{o_{sa}\})$. We use $N_k^\pi(\{o_{sa}\})$ to denote repeatedly applying $N^\pi(\cdot)$ for k times from $\{o_{sa}\}$. Based on the transitive relation, the states in $N_k^\pi(\{o_{sa}\})$ are optimally reachable states of (s, a). Hence, we have:

$$OR^\pi(s, a) = \{o_{sa}\} \cup N_1^\pi(\{o_{sa}\}) \cup \cdots \cup N_k^\pi(\{o_{sa}\}) \cup \cdots \qquad (6)$$

As we also have $N_k^\pi(\{o_{sa}\}) = N_{k-1}^\pi(N_1^\pi(\{o_{sa}\})) = N_{k-1}^\pi(\bigcup_{a'}\{o_{saa'}\})$ where $a' \in \pi(o_{sa})$, Eq. (6) can be written in a recursive form:

$$
\begin{aligned}
OR^\pi(s, a) &= \{o_{sa}\} \cup \bigcup_{a'}\{o_{saa'}\} \cup \cdots \cup N_{k-1}^\pi(\bigcup_{a'}\{o_{saa'}\}) \cup \cdots \\
&= \{o_{sa}\} \cup \bigcup_{a'}[\{o_{saa'}\} \cup \cdots \cup N_{k-1}^\pi(\{o_{saa'}\}) \cup \cdots] \qquad (7) \\
&= \{o_{sa}\} \cup \bigcup_{a'} OR^\pi(o_{sa}, a')
\end{aligned}
$$

A teacher can use Eq. (7) to extract OR^π after the learning of π.

3.4   Learning and Asking Process

In the different-goal situation, there should be a way to let a teacher know which state a student wants to reach. We enable the student to send state signals to the teacher. However, the number of state signals that can be sent at a state is limited by a transmission capacity c. We consider that utilising c would help to achieve Aim 2 (see Sect. 3.1). To do so, we first define an agent's *sub-goals*:

Definition 5 (Sub-Goal). *Given an agent in an MDP with a state space S, let V be the agent's experted reward value function, a state $s \in S$ is a sub-goal of the agent when $V(s) > \tau$, where τ is a threshold.*

A sub-goal indicates certain amount of expected reward ($> \tau$), and could be regarded as "close" to g_u. Reaching states with higher V value means that the student would be "closer" to g_u. The optimal actions for reaching g_u and sub-goals might be the same. When the student asks to reach g_u at a policy-similar state s, but the teacher does not know s is policy-similar, the student could utilise the transmission capacity c (if $c > 1$) by asking to reach sub-goals. If the teacher knows optimal actions to reach the sub-goals, those optimal actions might be right advice to the student. Even if the given advice were wrong, this would not badly hurt the student's learning because at least the wrong advice leads the student to states "close" to g_u. Based on the above analysis, we propose a learning and asking process of a student shown in Algorithm 1.

4   Experiments

In this section, we first present experimental settings. To set up agents' goals, we investigate the influence of specific goals settings on the number of policy-similar states. Then, we conduct two experiments to evaluate the proposed approach.

Algorithm 1. Learning and Asking Process of a Student

Input: state space S, transmission capacity c, sub-goal threshold τ.

1 Initialises $C(s) \leftarrow 0$, $N(s) \leftarrow \emptyset$, $A(s) \leftarrow \emptyset$, $\forall s \in S$; /* $C(s)$: number of times the student has asked for advice at a state s, $N(s)$: sub-goals to which no advice has been received at s, $A(s)$: advice that has been received at s */

2 **foreach** *episode* **do**

3   **repeat**

4         $s \leftarrow$ Observes the current state;

5   **if** $A(s) \neq \emptyset$ **then** $a_{adv} \leftarrow A(s)$ and **go to** Line 14;

6   **while** $C(s) < c$ **do**

7             $g_{sub} \leftarrow \arg\max_s V(s), s \in S \wedge s \notin N(s) \wedge V(s) > \tau$;

8   **if** $g_{sub} \neq \emptyset$ **then**

9                 $a_{adv} \leftarrow Ask(s, g_{sub})$; $C(s) \leftarrow C(s) + 1$;

10   **if** $a_{adv} = \emptyset$ **then**

11                    $N(s) \leftarrow N(s) \cup \{g_{sub}\}$;

12   **else**

13                    $A(s) \leftarrow a_{adv}$;

14   Takes a_{adv} if $a_{adv} \neq \emptyset$. Otherwise, use ϵ-greedy to select an action to take. Then, updates learning information, and updates s to next state;

15   **until** *s is the student's goal*;

4.1   Experimental Settings

Domain. The current action advice approaches are applied in domains with the same-goal situation [1,3,10,15]. For example, [10] uses Mountain Car and Pac-Man. In Mountain Car, agents' goal is to reach the top of a mountain. In Pac-Man, agents' goal is to earn points while avoiding being caught. These domains are not suitable for evaluating approaches in the different-goal situation.

In this paper, the experiments are conducted in a grid-world domain (shown in Fig. 2(a)). Grid-world domains have been used in various RL problems [4,7, 14]. The state space can be represented by a set of locations. An agent's goal is a specific target location that the agent learns to reach. When agents have different target locations, the agents are said to have different goals.

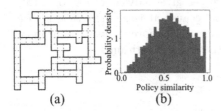
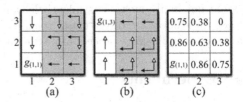
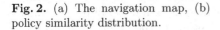

Fig. 2. (a) The navigation map, (b) policy similarity distribution.

Fig. 3. Examples of the calculation of policy similarity in a simple navigation map.

Settings of Goals. To set up a different-goal situation, we can choose a pair of different states as goals. One is for a teacher, and the other is for a student. According to Definition 3, a goal pair indicates a number of policy-similar states, which indicates the maximum number of states where right advice exists. This maximum number would influence the performance of the proposed action advice approach. Hence, the goal pairs in the settings should indicate various numbers of policy-similar states. For a state space S, there are $|S|$ goals and $|S|(|S| - 1)$ goal pairs. For each goal, we can get the corresponding optimal policy by using a learning algorithm. Then, for each goal pair, we can get the corresponding policy-similar states. The number of these states is then divided by $|S| - 1$ to get its normalisation, named as *policy similarity*. Figure 3 shows examples of the calculation of policy similarity in a simple navigation map. A state is represented by coordinates (x, y). Figures 3(a) and 3(b) show optimal actions, denoted as arrows, for reaching goals $g_{(1,1)}$ and $g_{(1,3)}$ respectively. The solid arrows indicate optimal actions to both $g_{(1,1)}$ and $g_{(1,3)}$, while the hollow arrows indicate optimal actions to either $g_{(1,1)}$ or $g_{(1,3)}$. The shaded states are policy-similar, and the policy similarity of $(g_{(1,1)}, g_{(1,3)})$ is 0.75 (6/8). Figure 3(c) shows policy similarity values when one goal is $g_{(1,1)}$ and the other goal is a state $g_{(x,y)}$ other than $g_{(1,1)}$. The value shown on $g_{(x,y)}$ is the policy similarity of $(g_{(1,1)}, g_{(x,y)})$. We can see that the policy similarity ranges in $[0, 1)$, and some goal pairs indicate the same policy similarity. For the navigation map (Fig. 2(a)) that we use, we calculate the policy similarity values of all goal pairs, and the distribution is shown in Fig. 2(b). For each policy similarity value, we randomly choose 30 goal pairs as the settings of goals.

Settings of Two Experiments. Q-Learning [11] is used as the learning algorithm due to its popularity. All learning tests are performed for 5000 episodes, with a learning rate of 0.02, a discount factor of 0.99, an exploration factor of 0.01 in ϵ-policy. An agent receives a reward of $+200$ for reaching its goal, and -1 for each action execution. States transitions are stochastic with a 0.1 probability of failure to an agent's actions. The action set is {Up, Down, Left, Right}. In each state, actions heading towards a wall are not available to an agent. This is to remove a goal which is the same for all agents: avoiding colliding with walls. The settings of action advice approaches used in experiments are as follows.

Experiment 1. The first experiment is to test if a teacher could find the optimal actions to a student's goal (see Aim 1 in Sect. 3.1). The experiment includes one teacher and one student. The teacher is trained to learn an optimal policy for reaching the teacher's goal before the learning of the student. Three action advice approaches are applied for comparison: (1) the proposed approach which considers the Different-Goal situation (DG); (2) a state-of-the-art Teacher-Student approach (TS) [10]; and (3) No-Advice (NA). TS represents previous action advice approaches developed for the same-goal situation. NA can be regarded as a baseline approach in the different-goal situation. The transmission capacity c in DG is set to 1, which means that at each state, the student can ask for advice to reach only one state, i.e., the student's goal.

Experiment 2. The second experiment is to test if a teacher could give right advice at states where optimal actions to a student's goal exist, but could not be found by the teacher (see Aim 2 in Sect. 3.1). The transmission capacity c ranges in $\{1, 8, 32\}$. When $c > 1$, the student can ask for advice to reach sub-goals (see Definition 5). The threshold τ for getting sub-goals is set to 0. As positive reward originates from the student's goal, at sub-goals with positive V, the student has found some ways to its goal. Then, reaching one of those sub-goals would be an option when the student does not get advice to its goal. The action advice approaches used in this experiment are DG and NA.

4.2 Results and Analysis

Experiment 1. Figure 4(a) shows the average advice-giving results of DG and TS. We can see that DG always produces right advice and does not produce wrong advice. This means that by using DG, the teacher successfully finds optimal actions to the student's goal. The amount of right advice increases when policy similarity gets higher. This is because more policy-similar states indicate more states where optimal actions to the student's goal exist. By contrast, TS may produce wrong advice, especially when policy similarity is low. This is because the teacher using TS does not decide the optimality of advised actions. Figure 4(b) shows the average additional steps used by the student to reach its goal compared with NA. We can see that when applying DG, the student takes almost the same steps to reach its goal as applying NA. This means that the student learns the optimal policy to its goal under most goal pair settings. By contrast, when applying TS, the student takes more steps, especially when policy similarity is low. This is because wrong advice misleads the student, and the student learns a worse policy than applying DG and NA. Figure 4(c) shows the average fewer episodes used to converge compared with NA. We can see that when applying DG, the student's learning takes fewer episodes to converge, especially when policy similarity is high. The improvement is because taking right advice reduces the exploration space of the student. Taking more right advice results in faster learning. By contrast, when applying TS, although the student learns faster than applying DG when policy similarity is high, the policy learned by the student is worse. When policy similarity gets lower, the learning episodes required to converge grow faster, and the student learns an even worse policy.

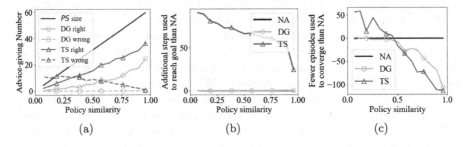

Fig. 4. (a) Advice-giving results, (b) additional steps used to reach goals than NA, (c) fewer episodes used to converge than NA.

Experiment 2. Figure 5(a) shows the average advice-giving results of DG with various transmission capacities. The result with $c = 1$ indicates the number of states where the teacher finds the optimal actions to the student's goal. When $c > 1$, we can see that the teacher gives right advice at more states than $c = 1$. Larger c results in more right advice given to the student, and results in faster learning speed (shown in Fig. 5(c)). The results indicate that the teacher successfully gives right advice at states where optimal actions to the student's goal exist, but could not be found by the teacher. This is because the optimal actions to the student's goal and sub-goals are possible to be the same. This possibility is 1 when $c = 1$, but would reduce when c gets larger. Figure 5(a) shows that wrong advice is given when $c = 32$. As a result, Fig. 5(b) shows that the policy learned by the student is a little bit worse than NA when $c = 32$. Figure 5(b) also shows that when $c = 1$, the policy learned might be a little bit worse than the optimal policy. This indicates that when only right advice is given, the student has a small probability to learn a sub-optimal policy. The investigation on this interesting phenomenon will be left as future work.

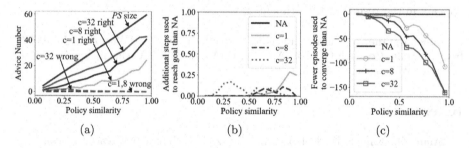

Fig. 5. (a) Advice-giving results, (b) additional steps used to reach goals than NA, (c) fewer episodes used to converge than NA.

5   Related Work

Knowledge Transfer (KT) has been widely used to improve reinforcement learning [9]. Several KT approaches include helping an agent learn in the different-goal situation by, e.g., action set transfer [6], policy transfer [4], MDP distribution transfer [12]. These approaches require learning agents to access and understand the knowledge in source agents. In this paper, agents cannot access the knowledge of each other. The only requirement for agents is a common action set, which enables agents to conduct action transfer (action advice).

Some action advice approaches have been proposed. Chernova and Veloso [2] enabled an agent to ask a human when the agent was uncertain of what actions to take. Torrey *et al.* [10] proposed a teacher-student framework which introduced a limitation on the number of times a teacher could provide advice. Amir *et al.* [1] proposed a jointly-initiated approach which reduced the attention cost of teachers. Zhan *et al.* [15] introduced a multi-teacher advice model where multiple bits of advice from multiple teachers were combined by a majority vote to improve a student's learning. Da Silva *et al.* [3] proposed a simultaneous learning and action advice approach. Ye *et al.* [13] proposed an approach that could reduce the impact of false advice provided by malicious agents. However, the above studies assume that the teacher and student have the same goal, which differs from the different-goal situation that we consider.

6   Conclusion

In this paper, we propose an approach which enables a teacher to help a student learn when they have different goals by action advice (action transfer). Experimental results show the effectiveness of the proposed approach. In future work, we plan to investigate how to conduct action advice in situations where different goals are caused by different S, A, T, R^+, R^- in MDPs. We also plan to study the influence of sub-optimal advice and various state transition functions on the optimality of advised actions. Another issue is to investigate why right advice might lead to sub-optimal policies learned by a student. This phenomenon appears in the results of Experiment 2.

Acknowledgement. This research is supported by a DECRA Project (DP140100007) from Australia Research Council (ARC), a UPA and an IPTA scholarships from University of Wollongong, Australia.

References

1. Amir, O., Kamar, E., Kolobov, A., Grosz, B.J.: Interactive teaching strategies for agent training. In: Proceedings of the 25th International Joint Conferences on Artificial Intelligence, pp. 804–811 (2016)
2. Chernova, S., Veloso, M.: Confidence-based policy learning from demonstration using Gaussian mixture models. In: Proceedings of the 6th International Joint Conference on Autonomous Agents and Multiagent Systems, pp. 1315–1322 (2007)
3. Da Silva, F.L., Glatt, R., Costa, A.H.R.: Simultaneously learning and advising in multiagent reinforcement learning. In: Proceedings of the 16th Conference on Autonomous Agents and Multiagent Systems, pp. 1100–1108 (2017)
4. Fernández, F., Veloso, M.: Probabilistic policy reuse in a reinforcement learning agent. In: Proceedings of the Fifth International Joint Conference on Autonomous Agents and Multiagent Systems, pp. 720–727. ACM (2006)
5. Puterman, M.L.: Markov Decision Processes: Discrete Stochastic Dynamic Programming. Wiley, Hoboken (2014)
6. Sherstov, A.A., Stone, P.: Improving action selection in MDP's via knowledge transfer. In: Proceedings of the 20th National Conference on Artificial Intelligence, vol. 5, pp. 1024–1029 (2005)
7. Sutton, R.S., Barto, A.G.: Reinforcement Learning: An introduction. MIT Press, Cambridge (1998)
8. Taylor, M.E., Carboni, N., Fachantidis, A., Vlahavas, I., Torrey, L.: Reinforcement learning agents providing advice in complex video games. Connect. Sci. **26**(1), 45–63 (2014)

9. Taylor, M.E., Stone, P.: Transfer learning for reinforcement learning domains: a survey. J. Mach. Learn. Res. **10**, 1633–1685 (2009)
10. Torrey, L., Taylor, M.: Teaching on a budget: agents advising agents in reinforcement learning. In: Proceedings of the 12th International Conference on Autonomous Agents and Multiagent Systems, pp. 1053–1060 (2013)
11. Watkins, C.J., Dayan, P.: Q-learning. Mach. Learn. **8**(3–4), 279–292 (1992)
12. Wilson, A., Fern, A., Ray, S., Tadepalli, P.: Multi-task reinforcement learning: a hierarchical Bayesian approach. In: Proceedings of the 24th International Conference on Machine Learning, pp. 1015–1022. ACM (2007)
13. Ye, D., Zhu, T., Zhou, W., Philip, S.Y.: Differentially private malicious agent avoidance in multiagent advising learning. IEEE Trans. Cybern. **PP**(99), 1–14 (2019)
14. Yu, C., Zhang, M., Ren, F., Tan, G.: Multiagent learning of coordination in loosely coupled multiagent systems. IEEE Trans. Cybern. **45**(12), 2853–2867 (2015)
15. Zhan, Y., Ammar, H.B., Taylor, M.E.: Theoretically-grounded policy advice from multiple teachers in reinforcement learning settings with applications to negative transfer. In: Proceedings of the 25th International Joint Conference on Artificial Intelligence, pp. 2315–2321 (2016)

Predictive Regret-Matching for Cooperating Interceptors to Defeat an Advanced Threat

Arvind Rajagopalan[1][(✉)], Duong Duc Nguyen[2], and Jijoong Kim[1]

[1] Defence Science and Technology Group, Edinburgh, SA 5111, Australia
{arvind.rajagopalan,jijoong.kim}@dst.defence.gov.au
[2] The University of Adelaide, Adelaide, SA 5005, Australia
duong.nguyen@adelaide.edu.au

Abstract. Threats combining kinematic superiority, high-g maneuvering and evasive capabilities are in development. These advanced threats can reduce the survivability of high-value assets (HVAs). Here, we demonstrates that it is possible to defeat such an advanced threat with cheaper lower-performance interceptors using an alternative approach to traditional optimal control. These interceptors harness the knowledge of the forecasted regions that the threat can access, referred to as threat reachability. Applying reachability, the interceptors can be organized to block the passage of the threat to the HVAs as well as to defeat it. Here, we have developed a reachability calculator that is scalable to accommodate multiple interceptors and combined it with an on-line regret-matching learner derived from game theory to produce the self-organization and guidance for the interceptors. Numerical simulations are provided to demonstrate the validity of the resulting solution. Furthermore, some comparison is provided to benchmark our approach against a recently published differential game solution on the same scenarios. The comparison shows that our algorithm outperforms the optimal control solution.

Keywords: Team interception · Reachability · Game theory · Regret-matching

1 Introduction

At present, there is growing concern worldwide to effectively engage emerging high performance guided projectile threats. These advanced threats further endanger assets in civilian and military domains. The development to produce high performance threats that can push policy further towards "launch on warning" [1] which may excarebate conflict. When devising the effective counter to such high speed threats, it is desirable to find cheap yet effective solutions using existing defensive capability wherever possible. Specifically, there has been enquiry into applying a cheaper and lower-performance collection of interceptors to successfully engage these threats.

© Springer Nature Switzerland AG 2019
J. Liu and J. Bailey (Eds.): AI 2019, LNAI 11919, pp. 28–40, 2019.
https://doi.org/10.1007/978-3-030-35288-2_3

Recent work in [2] applies optimal control theory to devise a differential game-based interception method for lower performance interceptors to counter a kinematically superior threat. However, applying the formulation provided did not appear to be as effective against a high-acceleration capable manevuering threat that can perform terminal manevuering. Under these circumstances, the miss performance as well as the choice of trajectory for the interceptors indicated room for improvement. Therefore, there is a research challenge present for improving the design and performance aspects for the defending team in order to be effective against threats capable of outperforming individual interceptors. We have addressed this research challenge by presenting a novel reachability based approach to direct a team of lower-performance interceptors to intercept a kinematically superior threat using a game-theoretic controller. The algorithm generates a sequence of guidance commands for each interceptor in the team such that at least one interceptor will be able to hit it, inspite of any maneuvering performed by the threat.

The main contributions of our work are as follows: (1) Development of the prediction based reachability calculator. (2) Successful application of a controller derived from game-theory referred to as regret-matching that harnesses the reachability calculator and produces the guidance commands for the interceptors to work cooperatively and defeat the targeted threat. (3) Demonstration of performance improvement over recently published results.

2   Motivation

Some of the methods suggested to defeat a kinematically superior threat in the open literature include non-proliferation [1], applying directed energy [3] and using high performance strategically positioned interceptors [4]. The literature on applying existing defensive interceptors without expensive upgrades for defeating such threats is sparse. The most relevant research work available in the literature that has been applied to tackle this research problem is in [2]. In this work, the authors have divided the threat's acceleration capability into sections with one defender assigned to cover off against the threat performing acceleration commands in that range. The authors assume that only the knowledge of the acceleration limits of the threat are known and not the maneuvering it will actually perform. In general, the availability of the threat acceleration information is not always available [5]. However, it may be possible to assign some conservative value for the acceleration (i.e. sufficiently large) in order to then task an appropriate number of defenders to engage it. Under those circumstances, in [2], each defender, if equipped with the differential game based guidance law provided can defeat a kinematically superior threat performing a range of manoeuvres.

When we implemented this design, we discovered that the guidance law appeared to be unsuccessful when attempting to intercept the threat in a timely manner for a kinematically superior threat performing manevuering. This discovery served partially as the impetus to devise the alternative reachability calculator that we have provided in this paper. The reminder of the impetus was to determine an alternative approach for the concept of reachability apart from differential game (DG) based optimal control. A game theoretic approach known as regret-matching is chosen as it has been harnessed to compute the regret for agents working cooperatively in a team and is suitable for cooperating agents' problems [6]. The theoretical foundation for regret-matching [7] is present which guarantees convergence.

3   Research Problem

Without loss of generality, we assume that a HVA is moving due North at a constant speed. The HVA carries a number of defenders used to intercept any threat approaching from any direction from around its vicinity. This is depicted in Fig. 1 through the dashed circles around the vicinity of the HVA.

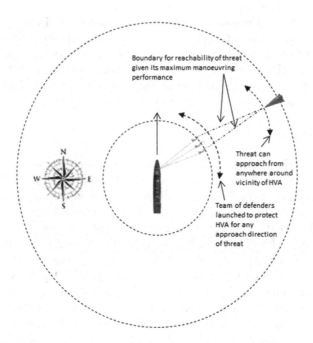

Fig. 1. Bird-eye view of engagement applied in simulation studies.

We have formulated the team-interception problem using a developed concept of reachability. In our approach, rather than dividing the acceleration limits of the threat into a number of regions that will be tackled by each defender respectively, we firstly construct a projection of the future positions of the threat based on knowledge of the acceleration limits and its speed. Then, applying the knowledge of the defenders' acceleration limits and speed, we do the same for the defender. We refer to these loci of future positions as the reachability of an entity. Following this, we determine the degree of intersection of the loci for the interceptors with defenders and use this knowledge to direct our defenders into desirable positions. These desirable positions correspond with the scenario of the threat's reachability being totally covered off by the defenders.

In our formulation, the dynamic of the threat motion is modeled using the Proportional Navigation (PN) law [8]. We assume that the threat applies a maximum acceleration of $10G$, where $G = 10\,\mathrm{m/s^2}$ is the gravitational constant. We also vary this value to determine the effect of different choice of acceleration ratios between the threat and defenders, ranging from equal performance to the scenario where the threat outperforms the defender when engaging it one-on-one. This unequal performance ratio scenario corresponds with the case where all of the defenders are inferior to the threat and need to operate as a team to defeat the threat. Additionally, we assume that the dynamics of the threat and all other defenders are fully observable by any defender. This assumption can be relaxed in future research efforts.

At each time step, the interceptors apply our algorithm to determine their respective maneuvering accelerations (actions) in order to cover off the total locus of the projected threat "front" locus. Our algorithm is designed using a multi-stage approach. The first stage is introduced to orient the defenders towards the threat using the GENEX [9] guidance law to enable the cover off strategy. In order to improve homing (near the end of the engagement, following successfully covering the reachability for the threat), a PN guidance law was applied to obtain small miss distances. It should be noted that no knowledge of the actual threat acceleration is provided during the engagement. Instead, only the estimate of the threat's maneuvering limits is applied. In the next section, we describe the components of our algorithm.

3.1   Design of the Reachability Calculator Function

The design of the reachability calculator is presented that computes the total proportion of the threat "front" locus intercepted by multiple defenders to engage a single threat. The total proportion of the threat front locus intercepted is converted into an expected joint reward for the whole team of interceptors and is applied in our algorithm to determine the actions for each defender.

Approximating the Threat Involute: The locus of the threat and defender positions has been performed by projecting the threat and defender locations into the future from their respective initial locations. The concept of an involute of a circle [10] has been harnessed to depict this locus. We have harnessed the concept of an involute to produce the curved locus of future entity (defender/threat) front positions depicted in Fig. 2. Furthermore, this figure shows the application of an approximation to the involute using a triangle, depicted overlapping the involute, that was applied in the calculator. Performing this simplification rather than applying the involute based locus simplified our calculations with the calculator without compromising its applicability to be applied with our algorithm to direct the defenders. That is, the defenders employing our calculator could still successfully engage the threat for a wide range of scenarios.

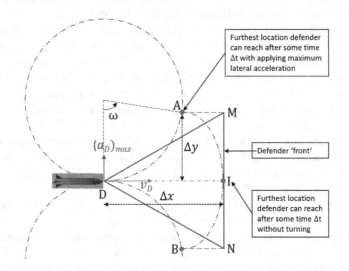

Fig. 2. Approximate representation of the defender involute by a triangle.

In Fig. 2, $(a_D)_{max}$ represents the maximum turn capability available to a defender. The v_D represents the fixed speed for the defender. In our problem, the defender is able to adjust its heading by the application of lateral acceleration but its speed is not varied. Also, while it has not been shown here explicitly, the same methodology can be applied for the threat where $(a_D)_{max}$ would be replaced with $(a_T)_{max}$ and v_D would be replaced with v_T. Note that $(a_D)_{max} = 1/2 \times (a_T)_{max}$ and $v_D = 1/2 \times v_T$. The angle ω is applied in determining the current end points for the entity front following Δt worth of time that has lapsed from the starting position of the entity. The Δx and Δy correspond to the maximum forwards and lateral displacement in range from the initial position of the entity after Δt.

The triangle approximating the involute in Fig. 2 is ΔMDN. Note that this is an approximation to the location of the true loci which is determined by an involute but suffices for our application. To define this approximate triangle, let t_{go} be the time-to-go defined as the time remaining till interception of the threat by a defender. This t_{go} value is the actual time-to-go which is usually only after the engagement is completed. Here, we estimate the t_{go} during the engagement based on the available instantaneous information

$$\hat{t}_{go} = \frac{R}{-\dot{R}} \ ,$$

where $\hat{t}_{go}$ is the estimated time-to-go and R is the line-of-sight (LOS) separation or the distance between the defender and its target at that instant in time.

Let (x_I, y_I) define the furthest location that the defender can reach after some time $\hat{t}_{go}$ without turning ($a_D = 0$). Let (x_A, y_A) and (x_B, y_B) define the furthest locations the defender can reach after some time $\hat{t}_{go}$ with applying the maximum lateral acceleration $|(a_D)\text{max}|$ and $-|(a_D)\text{max}|$, receptively. The Δx (horizontal separation) and Δy (vertical separation) are determined as functions of time, which can be computed as follows:

$$\begin{cases} \Delta x = \|\overrightarrow{v_D}\| \, \hat{t}_{go} \\ \Delta y = \int\limits_{0}^{\hat{t}_{go}} \|\overrightarrow{v_D}\| \, \sin(\omega t) \, dt = \dfrac{\|\overrightarrow{v_D}\|}{\omega} [1 - \cos(\omega \, \hat{t}_{go})] \end{cases} \text{, where } \omega = \dfrac{\|\overrightarrow{(a_D)}\|\text{max}}{\|\overrightarrow{v_D}\|}.$$

It can be seen that $(\Delta y)\text{max} = 2\|\overrightarrow{v_D}\|/\omega$ when $\hat{t}_{go} = \pi/\omega$. Therefore, the approximate triangle for the defender involute (or threat involute) is given by

$$\begin{cases} \widehat{MDN} = 2\arctan\left(\dfrac{\Delta y}{\|\overrightarrow{v_D}\| \, \hat{t}_{go}}\right) \\ \|\overrightarrow{MN}\| = 2\Delta y \end{cases} \text{, } \Delta y = \begin{cases} \dfrac{\|\overrightarrow{v_D}\|}{\omega}[1 - \cos(\omega \, \hat{t}_{go})] & \hat{t}_{go} \leq \pi/\omega \\ 2\dfrac{\|\overrightarrow{v_D}\|}{\omega} & \hat{t}_{go} > \pi/\omega \end{cases}.$$

Operation of Reachability Calculator. The diagram in Fig. 3(a) depicts the geometry associated with computing the percentage of cover of the threat "front" by a single defender. The apex of the blue triangle represents the starting position of the defender and the base depicted by the unbroken and broken dotted blue lines represents the defender "front" for chronologically ordered instances in time respectively. Similarly, the apex of the red triangle, represents the starting position for the threat and the base depicted by the unbroken and broken red lines represents the threat front at chronologically ordered instances in time.

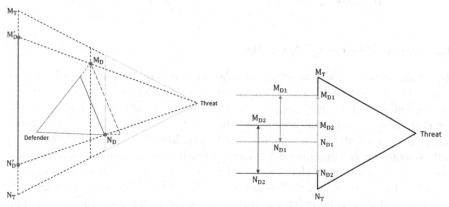

(a) Geometry for computing the percentage of covering by a single defender.

(b) Computation of the percentage of covering by two defenders.

Fig. 3. Describing how multiple defenders cover off against the threat front.

For the illustrated geometry, the percentage of covering by a single defender can be computed using the following formula:

$$\text{Percentage of Covering} = \frac{\left\| \overline{M'_D N'_D} \cap \overline{M_T N_T} \right\|}{\|M_T N_T\|} \times 100.$$

Here, N_D and M_D are the first and last intersection points (if present) between the defender front and the threat front, respectively. When those intersection points between the fronts take place, they are propagated forward in time. We denote N'_D and M'_D as their corresponding projected points on the threat front at some later time in the future as the threat front expands. This green line segment shown in Fig. 3(a) shows percentage of the threat front that is then covered by the application of the defender.

This method can be easily extended to the general case of $n \geq 2$ defenders, for example in case of 2-defenders as illustrated in Fig. 3(b). Suppose that $\overline{M_1 N_1}$ and $\overline{M_2 N_2}$ are the two line segments corresponding to the intercepted areas on the threat front by the two defenders. Note that there could be some overlap or gap between line segments. The total contribution due to each interceptor needs to be counted excluding any overlaps and not including any gaps if there are present between the line segments. The percentage of covering by the two interceptor can be computed as follows:

$$\text{Percentage of Covering} = \frac{\left\| \left(\overline{M_1 N_1} \cup \overline{M_2 N_2} \right) \cap \overline{M_T N_T} \right\|}{\|M_T N_T\|} \times 100.$$

Applying this type of approach, the percentage of covering of the threat front by "n" number of defenders can be calculated by:

$$\text{Percentage of Covering} = \frac{\left\| \bigcup_{i=1}^{n} \overline{M_i N_i} \cap \overline{M_T N_T} \right\|}{\left\| \overline{M_T N_T} \right\|} \times 100.$$

3.2   Regret-Matching Controller

Regret-matching is a well-known game-theoretic method for automated decision policy determination. It enables an agent to select the best choice of actions for sequential decision making problems. Compared to other automated multi-agent decision making methodologies such as multi-agent deep reinforcement learning, regret-matching is robust theoretically, has convergence guarantees [7] and is more easily explainable by virtue of using an equation based decision making processor rather than deep neural networks [11]. The core concept is to adjust the distribution that corresponds with probabilities for picking each action available to each defender during the engagement with the threat. The algorithm adjusts this distribution (automated learning) in each time-step for each defender. It does so by first computing the cumulative "regrets" up to the present time by comparing the utility calculated for actions not picked from the available action choices in each time-step against those that were picked while keeping, all other agents' choices the same. These computed regrets are used to shape action-selection in the next time-step to further minimize the regrets and thus steer the decision making towards optimal action selection.

Algorithm 1. Distributed Team-based Interception Algorithm for Zone Defence

1: **Initialisation:** Initialize initial action selection strategy $\pi_1^i(a) \leftarrow \frac{1}{m}$ for all $a \in A^i$, with m is the number of possible actions of the agent i.

2: **Boost guidance phase:** Use GENEX guidance law to choose an action until a non-zero joint reward is observed then switch to the mid-course guidance phase.

3: **Mid-course guidance phase:** Repeat until the reachability percentage reaches 100% then switch to the terminal guidance phase.

4: **for** $t = 1, 2, \ldots$ **do**

5:    *Action Selection:* Select action a_t according to π_t^i and obtain a reward $U_t^i(a_t^i, a_t^{-i})$ as a result of the joint action (a_t^i, a_t^{-i}).

6:    *Signal Synchronization:* Synchronize the chosen action a_t^i and current state information (position and velocity vector) to all other defenders.

7:    *Expected Reward Computation:* Using the calculator function and the signal received, compute the expected reward $U_t^i(k, a_t^{-i})$ if choosing a different action for all $k \in A^i$ given the chosen action of the other agents are unchanged.

8:    *Regret Update:* For all $k \neq a_t^i$, compute the cumulative regret vector

$$R_t^i(k) = \frac{1}{t} \sum_{\tau=1}^{t} U_\tau^i(k, a_\tau^{-i}) - \frac{1}{t} \sum_{\tau=1}^{t} U_\tau^i(a_\tau^i, a_\tau^{-i}).$$

9:    *Policy Learning:* Update the action selection strategy π_{t+1} according to

$$\pi_{t+1}^i(k) = \begin{cases} 0 & \text{if } k \neq a_t^i \text{ and } \sum_{\ell \in A^i} \max\{R_t^i(k), 0\} = 0 \\ \dfrac{\max\{R_t^i(k), 0\}}{\sum_{\ell \in A^i} \max\{R_t^i(k), 0\}} & \text{if } k \neq a_t^i \text{ and } \sum_{\ell \in A^i} \max\{R_t^i(k), 0\} > 0 \\ 1 - \sum_{j \neq k} \pi_{t+1}^i(j) & \text{if } k = a_t^i \end{cases}$$

10: **end for**

11: **Terminal guidance phase:** Execute the final manoeuvres required for intercept using PN guidance law.

The details of our distributed team-based interception algorithm for zone defence against high maneuvering target using regret matching is summarized in Algorithm 1. In our solution, the agent's action choice is a discrete set of lateral acceleration commands available to each defender. The utility (reward) used to compute the regret for each defender is obtained as follows. When each agent picks a particular lateral acceleration command, the agent's particular choice along with the choice made by all other agents will correspond to the total reachability achieved as a consequence against the threat by the team of defenders. We equate the utility obtained to this total reachability achieved.

For this research problem, it is assumed that positions and velocities of the threat and all defenders are accurately known by each defender. This information is processed and fed into the decision making policy inside each defender itself, which uses the proposed distributed learning mechanism to generate the guidance commands. GENEX [9] guidance law was applied at the outset to point our defenders at-least slightly towards the threat in order harness the regret matching controller. Then, when the regret-matching controller has enabled the threat reachability to be totally covered by the group of defenders, towards the end of the engagement, the PN guidance law is applied to each defender in order to improve the homing in capability to intercept the threat with a sufficiently small miss-distance. Note that no information about actual target acceleration is required for our controller to operate.

4   Experimental Results and Analysis

In this section, the performance of our algorithm is presented using simulation results. Table 1 shows the chosen parameters for our experiments. In our simulations, a threat flying at a high speed and possessing a large maximum acceleration of $10G$ is initially positioned 25 km away at $45°$ with respect to the HVA direction of travel. The initial separation between the HVA and the threat corresponds with engageable range of the threat. For defeating the threat, the HVA launches multiple defenders each of which has a lower performance capability with respect to the threat. Specifically, the threat is twice as fast and has twice the maximum acceleration capability compared to each defender.

Table 1. Simulation parameters

Description	Value
The speed of the HVA	$10.28\,\mathrm{m/s}$
The speed of the defender	$340.3\,\mathrm{m/s}$
The speed of the threat	$680.6\,\mathrm{m/s}$
The maximum lateral acceleration of the defender	$5G\ \mathrm{m/s}^2$
The maximum lateral acceleration of the threat	$10G\ \mathrm{m/s}^2$

4.1   Performance of Our Proposed Algorithm

Figures 4, 5 and 6 respectively illustrate the performance of our solution under various attacks by a single threat. These include approaching directly to the target and performing trajectory shaping through left or right turns prior to homing in. Such trajectory shaping is representative of the behaviour of real threats to increase their lethality. The results show that the defender team is able to successfully intercept the threat under these engagement scenarios with the smallest Zero-Effort-Miss (ZEM) [2] almost approaching zero at the time of interception. Our solution also achieves a similar good performance under a more challenging scenario where the threat performs weaving evasive maneuvers before approaching the HVA as illustrated in Fig. 7.

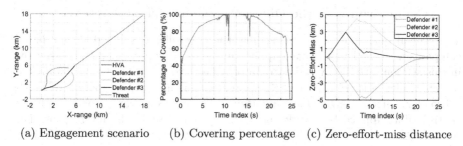

(a) Engagement scenario   (b) Covering percentage   (c) Zero-effort-miss distance

Fig. 4. 3-defenders team intercepts a threat approaching with a head-on attack.

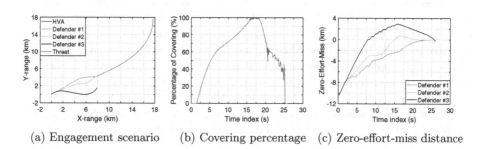

(a) Engagement scenario   (b) Covering percentage   (c) Zero-effort-miss distance

Fig. 5. 3-defenders team intercepts a threat making left evasive maneuver.

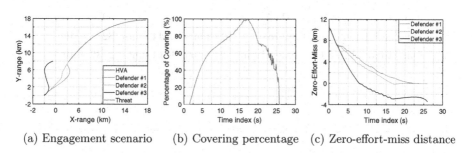

(a) Engagement scenario   (b) Covering percentage   (c) Zero-effort-miss distance

Fig. 6. 3-defenders team intercepts a threat making right evasive maneuver.

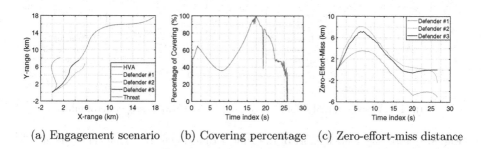

(a) Engagement scenario   (b) Covering percentage   (c) Zero-effort-miss distance

Fig. 7. 3-defenders team intercepts a weaving threat.

4.2   Comparison with the Differential Game-Based Approach

The crucial question of answering how the controller developed in our paper compares with the DG approach applied in the recently published [2] is discussed in this section. We discovered two major aspects to substantiate the claim that our controller outperforms the DG approach and thus can be applied to tackle a broader range of engagement scenarios. The first one corresponds with the control effort applied by the defender that gets closest to the interceptor. The second corresponds with the safe choice of trajectories selected by the defenders to effectively safeguard the HVA being defended.

Table 2 and Fig. 8 shows that our controller uses less control effort than the DG based approach to engage the threat when it perform maneuvers on its way to intercept the HVA. The table shows that this reduction in control effort extends to other scenarios where different choices for the threat initial heading angle are applied. It is attributed to the larger control effort for the DG due to the "bang-bang" control strategy applied. It means that the trajectories generated for intercepting a threat will cause the defenders to only ever apply maximum lateral acceleration turns one way or the other as they fly. When this "bang-bang" formulation is applied, it will result in higher control effort when applying the formulation $\sum_{t=0}^{t_f} [a_T(t)]^2$ to calculate the control effort.

Table 2. Control effort for the defender that got closest to the threat

Threat pointing offset to HVA	0°	45°	90°
Differential game (DG) approach	612 units	3944 units	8284 units
Our proposed RM based algorithm	28 units	1614 units	2532 units

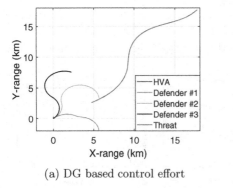

(a) DG based control effort

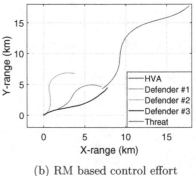

(b) RM based control effort

Fig. 8. Comparing control effort of the 2 algorithms under the same engagement.

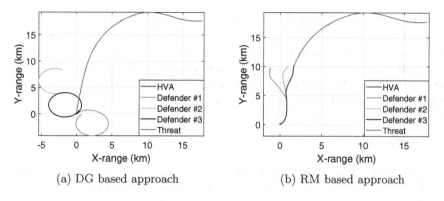

(a) DG based approach   (b) RM based approach

Fig. 9. Regret matching choosing a safer trajectory to intercept maneuvering threat in contrast with previous approach.

For the second discovery, the results in Fig. 9 show that the application of our controller can enable successful interception of the threat in a relatively safe manner compared to applying the DG approach. It was found to be true when the threat has large maximum acceleration limits such as $10G$. Under these circumstances, the defenders using the DG take on highly curved trajectories that can expose the HVA and allow the threat to hit it prior to the defenders intercepting it. Our solution attributes the difference in choice of trajectories for the defenders to the type of reachability concept that was applied.

Our notion of reachability using the proposed calculator is position-based for predicting the future positions of the threat and defenders. Whereas with DG, their reachability is based on segmenting the total threat acceleration limits into sections each of which is addressed by one of the defenders. The defenders assigned to an acceleration cover section are directed as if the threat was performing an acceleration within their cover region. When large acceleration limits for the threat are applied such as $10G$, the defenders fly trajectories that are highly curved and widely spread out which result in allowing the threat to approach the defended asset more easily. In contrast, our position-based reachability based controller is still able to engage the threat without it endangering the HVA in a similar manner. This behavior was observed in a number of scenarios large acceleration capability was assigned for the threat and it maneuvered on its way towards the HVA.

5   Conclusion

In this article, a controller is presented that combines a position-based reachability calculator developed with a game-theoretic regret-matching based guidance law controller. We have compared our algorithm's performance against a recently published result where a DG controller is applied to tackle the same problem. Both methods were tested under identically challenging scenarios. The results showed that our method was more robust and generated more energy efficient trajectories. It is anticipated that this area will become a rich space for more works in the near future since the literature is still sparse on this subject. Thus, our concepts could be of interest for the community. For future work, there will be extension of the proposed solution to address uncertainties due to imperfect communication between the group of defenders as well as support scalability to handle more complex "many-on-many" engagements.

References

1. Speier, R.H., Nacouzi, G., Lee, C., Moore, R.M.: Hypersonic Missile Nonproliferation: Hindering the Spread of a New Class of Weapons. Rand Corporation, Santa Monica (2017)
2. Su, W., Shin, H.-S., Chen, L., Tsourdos, A.: Cooperative interception strategy for multiple inferior missiles against one highly maneuvering target. Aerosp. Sci. Technol. **80**, 91–100 (2018)
3. Weibo, S., Sixin, L., Yu, X., Sen, L.: Laser lethality of hypersonic vehicles under aero-heating. High Power Laser Part. Beams **22**(6), 1215–1218 (2010)
4. Karako, T.: Missile Defense and Defeat: Considerations for the New Policy Review. Rowman & Littlefield, Lanham (2017)
5. Palumbo, N.F., Blauwkamp, R.A., Lloyd, J.M.: Modern homing missile guidance theory and techniques. Johns Hopkins APL Tech. Digest **29**(1), 42–59 (2010)
6. Nguyen, D.D., Rajagopalan, A., Kim, J., Lim, C.C.: Adaptive regret minimization for learning complex team-based tactics. IEEE Access **7**, 103019–103030 (2019)
7. Sergiu, H., Andreu, M.-C.: Simple Adaptive Strategies: From Regret-Matching to Uncoupled Dynamics, vol. 4. World Scientific, Singapore (2013)
8. Yanushevsky, R.: Modern Missile Guidance. CRC Press, Boca Raton (2018)
9. Ohlmeyer, E.J., Phillips, C.A.: Generalized vector explicit guidance. J. Guidance Control Dyn. **29**(2), 261–268 (2006)
10. Robb, M., White, B.A., Tsourdos, A., Rulloda, D.: Reachability guidance: a novel concept to improve mid-course guidance. In: Proceedings of the 2005, American Control Conference, pp. 339–345. IEEE (2005)
11. Nguyen, D.D., Rajagopalan, A., Lim, C.-C.: Online versus offline reinforcement learning for false target control against known threat. In: Chen, Z., Mendes, A., Yan, Y., Chen, S. (eds.) ICIRA 2018. LNCS (LNAI), vol. 10985, pp. 400–412. Springer, Cham (2018). https://doi.org/10.1007/978-3-319-97589-4_34

Multi-Minimax: A New AI Paradigm for Simultaneously-Played Multi-player Games

Nicolas Perez and B. John Oommen[✉]

School of Computer Science, Carleton University, Ottawa K1S 5B6, Canada
nickperez@cmail.carleton.ca, oommen@scs.carleton.ca

Abstract. The best reported methods for turn-based multi-player game playing AI algorithms include Max^n, Paranoid and Best Reply Search. All of these methods make decisions by modelling the game by assuming that there is some predetermined play ordering for the players. While this is meaningful for ordered turn-based games, there are a host of scenarios where the players need not be constrained to make their moves in such a manner. Little research has been done for turn-based games of this kind such as financial games that involve buying and selling on the stock market in no specific order (For games with shared resources (e.g., financial games) or simultaneously-played move games, one could alternatively consider multi-player AI algorithms to be those that treat the game with each opponent as a separate game. This is currently open.). In this paper, we shall present and test a new algorithm for multi-player game playing on a game which does not require a fixed sequential play ordering. The game that we have used to demonstrate this is the multi-player Snake Game, also referred to as a "Light Bike" game which is a turn-based game requiring simultaneous moves at every turn. Our newly-proposed scheme, the Multi-Minimax, along with the Added Pruning method, performs better when compared to the similar AI strategies examined in this paper. Additionally, among all the algorithms that did not use the proposed pruning, Multi-Minimax performs the best. We can conclude that, at the least, under certain conditions in the area of multi-player game playing AI, similar results can be replicated with these newly proposed Added Pruning and Multi-Minimax methods. As far as we know, the results presented here are of a pioneering sort, and we are unaware of any comparable results.

Keywords: Alpha-beta pruning · Best Reply Search · Max^n · Paranoid · Minimax · Multi-Minimax · Multi-player games · Game tree pruning

B. J. Oommen—*Chancellor's Professor; Life Fellow: IEEE* and *Fellow: IAPR.* This author is also an *Adjunct Professor* with the University of Agder in Grimstad, Norway.

J. Liu and J. Bailey (Eds.): AI 2019, LNAI 11919, pp. 41–53, 2019.
https://doi.org/10.1007/978-3-030-35288-2_4

1   Introduction

Multi-player games have to be tackled in AI with techniques that are distinct from those used in two-player games. This is because the heuristic function used for any game can yield multiple values for the various players, and alternatively, could lead to a *vector* of heuristic values. Such a vector implicitly prohibits Minimax, Alpha-Beta search and a tree pruning strategy. An alternative strategy, adapted by the Best Reply Search (BRS) would be to utilize a single heuristic function and to consider all the opponents as possible players at the next time instant. While this allows for Minimax and the consequent pruning strategies, they have all been specifically used for games in which there is a sequential ordering for the players' moves. However, the scenario is quite different when the players can play simultaneously at every time instant or in a random fashion.

This is the arena in which we operate, and the aim of this paper is to consider multi-player games in which the players are not constrained to play in any specific order. Games of this sort are typical in the stock market and financial sector, where a buyer/seller does not have to wait for the others. The aim of this paper is to demonstrate that the Perspective player can invoke the BRS as his strategy without the other players being aware of it. By resorting to such a technique, the Perspective player can make meaningful choices that yield a superior win rate and still permits him to search to greater depths in the search tree by resorting to a Minimax paradigm and alpha-beta pruning. Apart from demonstrating this, we benchmark such simultaneously-played multi-player games.

2   Description of Problem Domain

To demonstrate the power of our technique in a *prima facie* manner, we shall use it to play the game "Light Bike" (please see Fig. 1), which is a popular form of an arcade-style multi-player game, played on various platforms. It involves players who can move in one of 4 directions on a 2D grid, where each player leaves behind themselves a wall which cannot be passed through by any player. The goal for each player is to be the last surviving player.

Fig. 1. An example of a game of "Light Bike" with 8 players. (Color figure online)

Each player must move to one of its adjacent tiles (excluding tiles diagonally adjacent) at every turn, and all the players make their moves simultaneously and within a fixed time limit. Players are eliminated if they occupy a space on the grid that has been or is currently occupied by another player, or if they move off the edge of the screen. Under certain circumstances, a player is inevitably eliminated from the next turn independent of what move is made due to him being "boxed in" by surrounding walls. Effective strategies involve players trying to box other players within a small area while they themselves are not boxed in by other players' walls or even their own walls. In Fig. 1, yellow, black and dark blue players have already been eliminated. Green, red, magenta, brown and turquoise players are alive. Magenta, with two possible spaces, faces elimination.

3   Multi-player Game Strategies and Approaches

This section will describe competitive solutions to the Multi-Minimax algorithm. We only consider search-tree based algorithms for multi-player turn based games. They involve the Perspective player (the root of the tree) to search through combinations of a certain move order which may or may not truly represent the move order of the game, and to try and predict which next move in the game would be most effective. When it is the Perspective player's turn, he will search through nodes (each representing a game state) up to a specified maximum depth in the tree, and use a heuristic function to evaluate leaf nodes in the tree. The evaluations of leaf nodes are recursively carried up to the root node based on the algorithm's specified strategy for deciding which evaluations are carried up each node. Thereafter, he plays the best-evaluated next move dictated by the root.

The Minimax principle has been shown to be an effective scheme for playing two-player games [2,7,9]. Compared to traditional two-player game playing, multi-player environments, through the addition of other self-interested agents, introduce a range of new complications and challenges. These include:

- Any single player's gain need not lead to an equal loss among the opponents;
- Player coalitions can arise, even in games with only a single winner;
- The board state can change more between the Perspective player's moves;
- A single-valued heuristic is not always sufficient to appraise the game state;
- Established pruning schemes, e.g., the alpha-beta, are not always applicable;
- The computation is exponential with respect to the number of players.

Despite these challenges, due to the historical success of Minimax with alpha-beta pruning in a wide variety of domains, substantial efforts have been dedicated to extending it to multi-player environments, with varying levels of success [1,4–7]. We now detail a number of the more well-known of these techniques, specifically the Paranoid, Max^n, and the BRS.

3.1   The Paranoid Algorithm

The intuitive extension of the Minimax technique to multi-player games results in what is commonly termed the "Paranoid algorithm" [1,4,6]. This approach requires the fewest changes from the well-known Minimax algorithm [2,7,9]. As in the Minimax, the Paranoid technique retains a single value at each node representing the heuristic value $h(x)$ for the Perspective player. Being a multi-player scenario, rather than two player, each level of the game tree represents a different player's turn, and so there will be multiple opponent turns in between each of the Perspective player's turns. The Paranoid algorithm handles this by treating every opponent's turn as a Min node [4]. Thus, for a three-player game, the Paranoid algorithm could be referred to as Max-Min-Min, and for a four player game, Max-Min-Min-Min. A sample game tree for an arbitrary evaluation function, is presented in Fig. 2 for the Paranoid algorithm. The values indicate how "good" each node (board position) is for the Perspective player.

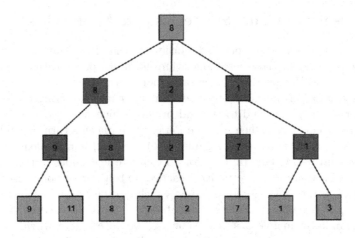

Fig. 2. A Paranoid tree, with the red nodes bing MAX, and the blue nodes MIN. (Color figure online)

Since all the Perspective player's opponents are "minimizing" (and not max-imizing their own gains), the Paranoid algorithm, naturally, treats all players as a *coalition* against the Perspective player [6]. The algorithm even predicts that opponents will take moves operating under the assumption that *other* opponents will take actions leading to even greater minimization of the Perspective player's score. Thus, opponents not only exclusively target the Perspective player, but will, in fact, actively work together against him [6].

The Paranoid algorithm suffers from a glaring drawback. While it could be considered the "safest" approach to the game, it is unreasonable to work with the assumption that opponents in a multi-player game will solely work in a coali-tion, even to their own potential detriment. It thus has a tendency to consider unrealistic game states, which could potentially lead to bad play, particularly when there are dramatic shifts in board positions between moves [6].

Since it maintains a single heuristic value, the Paranoid algorithm retains the benefits of alpha-beta pruning, which is not the case for all multi-player techniques. It thus outperforms other, more realistic strategies due to achieving improved lookahead [1]. Despite this, it can only produce cuts at boundaries between Max and Min nodes, and never between individual Min layers. Thus, less total pruning will occur in a Paranoid tree than in a Minimax tree.

3.2 The Max^n Algorithm

While the Paranoid algorithm is the most intuitive extension of Minimax to multi-player games, and the simplest to implement, a competing algorithm, called the Max^n algorithm, is the natural extension of Minimax principles to N-person games [5]. The basic philosophy of the Minimax algorithm is not based on minimizing a specific player's score, but instead on maximizing the AI player's score [2,7,9]. For a two-player, zero-sum, combinatorial game for which the Minimax algorithm was originally developed, these two functions are naturally identical, the extension of which is the Paranoid algorithm [4]. However, the Max^n algorithm operates on the more reasonable assumption that players will seek to maximize their own scores, without consideration for other opponents [5].

Rather than the heuristic function $h(x)$ returning a single value, as is the case with the Minimax and Paranoid algorithms, the heuristic function for the Max^n algorithm returns a *tuple* of values of size N, where N is the number of players [5]. The Nth value, traditionally, corresponds to the Nth player, where the first player is the Perspective player, and where subsequent opponents are numbered in their turn order, beginning from the Perspective player. At the ith player's turn, he is assumed to choose the move that provides the maximum value in position i in the tuple, and, similar to the Minimax or Paranoid algorithms, this value is passed up the tree, until, eventually, a path is chosen for the Perspective player at the root [5]. Figure 3 shows a sample Max^n tree after expansion of all the leaf nodes, with the values being passed up to the root. The values associated with each node represent the tuple returned by the algorithm's heuristic function.

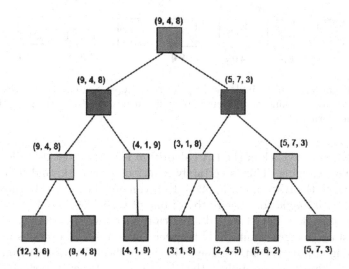

Fig. 3. Sample Max^n tree in which each color represents a different player. (Color figure online)

There is a clear benefit of using it over the Paranoid algorithm [6], as the more "relaxed" pressure on the Perspective player can take advantage of the various opportunities that may have been overlooked by "coalition of opponents" [4].

Despite a more realistic model of play, as the Max^n algorithm makes use of a tuple of values rather than a single integer value for the results of the heuristic, it can't make use of alpha-beta pruning. It can only make use of less-effective pruning techniques described in [3,14–16], and is also useful in tie breaking [4].

3.3   Best Reply Search

The Paranoid and Max^n algorithms remained the standard for deterministic multi-player games. However, more recently, an algorithm named the Best Reply Search (BRS) has been introduced, which can, in some cases, significantly outperform both of them [1]. In the case of the BRS, all opponents are again considered to operate as in a coalition, as in the Paranoid algorithm, but between each of the Perspective player's turns, *it allows only a single opponent to act* [1]. The opponent who is allowed to act is the one who has the most minimizing move, in relation to the Perspective player, at this point in time, or the "Best Reply". In essence, the scheme pretends that all opponents are not simply a coalition, but that the coalition represents a single player with significantly more resources available than the Perspective player. Figure 4 shows a single level of a BRS tree where the minimum of all opponent turns is being selected.

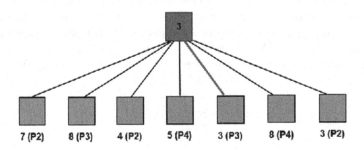

Fig. 4. The operation of a single level of the Best Reply Search. The scores that are reported have the opponent's player number listed next to them (in parenthesis) to assist in the clarification.

The glaring drawback of the BRS algorithm is that it considers illegal move states while searching. This is certainly a serious drawback, and it limits the games to which the BRS can be applied [1]. It can only be applied to those games where it is *meaningful* for players to act out of turn, and performs best when the board state does not change dramatically in between turns [1]. Whenever the game state changes significantly between turns, there is a serious risk of the BRS arriving at a model of the game which is significantly different from reality.

In cases where it can be applied, the BRS has many benefits over the Paranoid and Max^n algorithms, and often dramatically outperforms them [1]. As can be intuitively observed, when all opponents are considered to be a single entity, the game is modeled as a two-player game played using the Minimax algorithm.

Alpha-beta pruning and all other two-player Minimax improvements can be applied with even less restrictions than in the Paranoid algorithm [2,7,9]. As it simplifies things to work with a model analogous to a two-player game, the BRS also allows better look-ahead for the Perspective player than either the Paranoid or the Max^n schemes. These are significant factors in the performance of the BRS over the Paranoid and Max^n in games such as Chinese Checkers [1].

4   Motivation and Proposed Solution

The goal of this paper is to find a way to significantly increase the search-depth for the Perspective player in a search-tree algorithm for playing multi-player games in which the players are allowed to move simultaneously. One drawback of previously-mentioned solutions is that their asymptotic run time is exponential with respect to the number of players and the depth of the search-tree. If an effective solution is found for one game, it could then be possibly applied to other non-turn based simultaneously-played multi-player games. While we have proposed such a solution, we have also demonstrated its power using the game "Light Bike". This game was chosen due to its dependence on effective players having to be able to search a large number of moves ahead.

4.1   The Proposed Solution: Multi-Minimax

The method we propose is the so-called Multi-Minimax algorithm described formally in Figs. 5, 6 and 7. It can be seen as the BRS but with a very aggressive pruning method which makes it so that minimizing players cannot alternate taking turns against the maximizing player. Given the current game state, the maximizing player plays $n-1$ different games against each of the $n-1$ opponents and makes a move assuming that depending on the next move the maximizing player makes, the maximizing player will be playing the rest of the game only against the best opposing player for that move. To describe the Multi-Minimax algorithm we invoke the Minimax algorithm which is used as a subroutine for Multi-Minimax [2,7,9]. Observe that when n is the number of players, b is the branching factor and d is the maximum number of game rounds (the number of times all players have each taken one turn), the Multi-Minimax runs in $O(nb^d)$ worst case time. On the other hand, Paranoid, BRS and Max^n run in $O(b^{dn})$, $O(n^{\frac{d}{2}}b^d)$ and $O(b^{dn})$ worst case times respectively [1,4–6].

4.2   Added Pruning Method

Our proposed Added Pruning restricts the next move that each player can explore along the search tree. This pruning forces him to explore only the next move that is in the same direction as his previously-explored move. If he is not able to explore a move in this previously-explored direction, he would be able to explore all possible valid moves given by the default production system.

One benefit to using this method is that players are less likely to search meaningless paths where they eliminate themselves from the game, for example in "Light Bike", by boxing themselves in with their own walls. It also emphasizes exploring moves that are significant since, usually, the most significant moves in the game are when players move to a grid space that is right next to a wall to box in an opposing player. Such a pruning allows a larger look-ahead and to thus explore a larger distance across the board and explore more moves for boxing in players. Additionally, the Added Pruning allows players to be less likely to pointlessly search through multiple different move sequences where they could reach the same grid space in the same number of moves considering all the move sequences that yield similar effectiveness. The downside to possibly missing exploring significant moves due to the Added Pruning does not outweigh the benefits previously described.

Algorithm 1 Multi-Minimax

1: **procedure** Multi-Minimax($maxPlayer, minPlayers, depth, gameState$)
2:     $moveToMake \leftarrow 0$
3:     $maxMove \leftarrow -\infty$
4:     $\alpha \leftarrow -\infty$
5:     **for each child of maxPlayer do**
6:         updateGameState($gameState, child$)
7:         $minMove \leftarrow \infty$
8:         $\beta \leftarrow \infty$
9:         **for each opponent in minPlayers do**
10:            $minMove \leftarrow$ min($minMove$, MINIMAX($child, opponent, depth -$ $1, \alpha, \beta, FALSE, gameState$))
11:            $\beta \leftarrow minMove$
12:            **if** $\alpha \geq \beta$ **then**
13:                **break**
14:            **end if**
15:        **end for**
16:        **if** $minMove \geq maxMove$ **then**
17:            $moveToMake \leftarrow child$
18:            $maxMove \leftarrow minMove$
19:            $\alpha \leftarrow maxMove$
20:        **end if**
21:    **end for**
22:    **return** $moveToMake$
23: **end procedure**

Fig. 5. Pseudocode for the Multi-Minimax algorithm with alpha-beta pruning which also uses Minimax as a subroutine [2,7,9].

4.3   Implementing the Formalized Method

We implemented the "Light Bike" game using the Python language invoking the Multi-Minimax, BRS, Max^n and Paranoid algorithms [1, 4–6]. The heuristic used for all these was as follows: At each node, if there were no more valid moves (i.e., which resulted in the player surviving for the next turn) for the opposing player(s) but there is at least one valid move for the evaluated player, we returned "infinity", otherwise we returned the depth of the node in the tree.

The implementations for all the algorithms except for Max^n used immediate pruning at the root node and alpha-beta pruning [2]. Max^n could only make use of immediate pruning at every node and tie breaking by minimizing the sum of the score of opposing players [3, 4, 14–16]. Each algorithm made use of

---

Algorithm 2 Minimax

1: **procedure** MINIMAX($maxPlayer, minPlayer, depth, \alpha, \beta, max?, gameState$)
2:     **if** $depth = 0$ or no more valid moves **then return** heuristic value
3:     **end if**
4:     **if** $max?$ **then**
5:         $maxMove \leftarrow -\infty$
6:         **for each child of** maxPlayer **do**
7:             updateGameState($gameState, child$)
8:             $maxMove \qquad\qquad \leftarrow \qquad\qquad$ max($maxMove$,
         MINIMAX($child, minPlayer, depth - 1, \alpha, \beta, FALSE, gameState$))
9:             $\alpha \leftarrow$ max($\alpha, maxMove$)
10:             **if** $\alpha \geq \beta$ **then**
11:                 **break**
12:             **end if**
13:         **end for**
14:         **return** $maxMove$
15:     **else**
16:         $minMove \leftarrow \infty$
17:         **for each child of** minPlayer **do**
18:             updateGameState($gameState, child$)
19:             $minMove \qquad\qquad \leftarrow \qquad\qquad$ min($minMove$,
         MINIMAX($maxPlayer, child, depth - 1, \alpha, \beta, TRUE, gameState$))
20:             $\beta \leftarrow$ min($\alpha, minMove$)
21:             **if** $\alpha \geq \beta$ **then**
22:                 **break**
23:             **end if**
24:         **end for**
25:         **return** $minMove$
26:     **end if**
27: **end procedure**

Fig. 6. Pseudocode for the Minimax algorithm.

Monte-Carlo reordering of the production system at each node as well as pruning for game states where the Perspective player had been eliminated. Additionally, in our experiments we compared performances with and without the Added Pruning at each node (described in Sect. 4.2).

5 Results

Tests were done for the "Light Bike" game on a 12×12 sized board, comparing Multi-Minimax, Best Reply Search, Max^n and Paranoid algorithms, each of them with and without the Added Pruning described in Sect. 4.2. Each algorithm used iterative deepening with the only restriction of having 300 ms of real-world time to iterate [8]. All tests were ran on a machine with Linux and an Intel(R) Xeon(R) CPU E5-2600 v4 @ 2.00 GHz, which, as of writing this paper, has around the same processing power as the average personal computer.

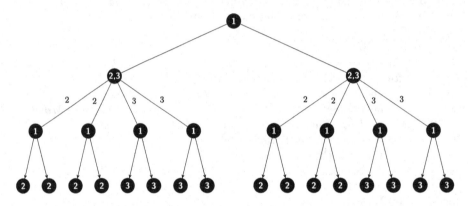

Fig. 7. A visual representation of the Multi-Minimax algorithm with 3 players and a branching factor of 2 for each player. Each node represents a game state and is labeled with the player(s) whose turn is next down the search tree. Each edge represents a player's move. Nodes with multiple players have their outgoing edges labeled to indicate which player moved.

The results are given in Figs. 8, 9 and 10. For one set of tests, each algorithm being tested would play against 2 randomly moving players which would play a random valid move (a move that wouldn't result in guaranteed elimination for that player's next turn) each turn so long as one existed. Another set of tests put the 8 different algorithms from the first set of tests versus each other in varying combinations of 4 and 6 player games. For the varying combinations of 4 and 6 player games, all 8 choose 4 and 8 choose 6 participant combinations were uniformly sampled. For testing purposes, a win for a player counted as being the last player standing. Tying a game counted as being one of the last players standing (e.g., the last two players alive were eliminated at the same time). For both sets of tests, every time we conducted a new test where all

Each Implemented Algorithm vs Two Randomly Moving Opponents			
Algorithm	**Average Depth**	**Win %**	**Win % w. Ties**
Max^n	6.86 ± 0.01	$(49.09\%, 51.86\%)$	$(54.48\%, 57.23\%)$
Max^n P+	14.80 ± 0.04	$(58.27\%, 60.99\%)$	$(63.75\%, 66.39\%)$
Paranoid	9.51 ± 0.02	$(57.27\%, 60.0\%)$	$(63.24\%, 65.89\%)$
Paranoid P+	18.39 ± 0.05	$(65.44\%, 68.05\%)$	$(72.02\%, 74.47\%)$
Best Reply Search	8.29 ± 0.02	$(58.21\%, 60.93\%)$	$(64.76\%, 67.38\%)$
Best Reply Search P+	13.47 ± 0.05	$(65.2\%, 67.81\%)$	$(71.61\%, 74.07\%)$
Multi-Minimax	9.43 ± 0.02	$(61.69\%, 64.37\%)$	$(68.21\%, 70.76\%)$
Multi-Minimax P+	19.29 ± 0.05	$(73.07\%, 75.49\%)$	$(79.05\%, 81.26\%)$

Fig. 8. The results of running each one of the implemented algorithms *vs* two randomly moving opponents. 5,000 tests were run for each algorithm. In the tables, P+ implies that the scheme has been enhanced with Added Pruning.

All Implemented Algorithms vs Each Other 4 Players			
Algorithm	**Depth**	**Win %**	**Win % w. Ties**
Max^n	7.21 ± 0.01	$(12.78\%, 14.12\%)$	$(16.77\%, 18.26\%)$
Max^n P+	12.85 ± 0.03	$(17.76\%, 19.28\%)$	$(22.19\%, 23.84\%)$
Paranoid	9.36 ± 0.01	$(17.37\%, 18.88\%)$	$(22.67\%, 24.33\%)$
Paranoid P+	15.58 ± 0.03	$(24.82\%, 26.53\%)$	$(30.15\%, 31.96\%)$
B.R.S.	7.21 ± 0.01	$(18.96\%, 20.52\%)$	$(24.56\%, 26.27\%)$
B.R.S. P+	9.63 ± 0.03	$(24.09\%, 25.78\%)$	$(29.86\%, 31.67\%)$
Multi-Minimax	9.17 ± 0.01	$(21.37\%, 23.0\%)$	$(27.35\%, 29.11\%)$
Multi-Minimax P+	17.09 ± 0.03	$(35.69\%, 37.58\%)$	$(42.3\%, 44.24\%)$

Fig. 9. The results of running each one of the implemented algorithms *vs* each other. 20,020 tests were run for each algorithm. In the tables, P+ implies that the scheme has been enhanced with Added Pruning.

All Implemented Algorithms vs Each Other 6 Players			
Algorithm	**Depth**	**Win %**	**Win % w. Ties**
Max^n	7.13 ± 0.01	$(8.77\%, 9.70\%)$	$(11.12\%, 12.14\%)$
Max^n P+	9.78 ± 0.01	$(10.77\%, 11.78\%)$	$(13.24\%, 14.34\%)$
Paranoid	8.87 ± 0.01	$(12.11\%, 13.17\%)$	$(15.16\%, 16.33\%)$
Paranoid P+	11.79 ± 0.03	$(15.10\%, 16.27\%)$	$(18.55\%, 19.81\%)$
B.R.S.	5.94 ± 0.01	$(12.85\%, 13.94\%)$	$(16.08\%, 17.27\%)$
B.R.S. P+	6.77 ± 0.02	$(14.47\%, 15.61\%)$	$(18.18\%, 19.43\%)$
Multi-Minimax	8.53 ± 0.01	$(16.12\%, 17.31\%)$	$(19.93\%, 21.22\%)$
Multi-Minimax P+	14.42 ± 0.02	$(25.75\%, 27.16\%)$	$(30.62\%, 32.10\%)$

Fig. 10. The results of running each one of the implemented algorithms *vs* each other. 20,020 tests were run for each algorithm. In the tables, P+ implies that the scheme has been enhanced with Added Pruning.

participating players were placed randomly with replacement in one of 8 evenly spaced locations on the perimeter of the board. The results obtained are shown on a 95% confidence interval using normal distribution for average depth, and Bernoulli distribution for the win rate.

6   Conclusions

In this paper, we have considered the problem of playing multi-player games, when there is no fixed move ordering between the players. The game that we have used to demonstrate our hypothesis is "Light Bike". We have clearly shown that for the given heuristic used for the game, our newly-proposed scheme, the Multi-Minimax, and the added pruning methods, were more effective than alternative solutions. Both methods provided largely increased search depth along with a minimal loss in exploring important board states, thus being more effective. In the general case, we have not shown that Multi-Minimax is more effective than Paranoid, Best Reply Search and Max^n [1,4–6]. But, to make sure the algorithms were implemented correctly, they were all placed against randomly moving opponents to show the effectiveness, and to also share common code.

Future work in testing out Multi-Minimax could prove its ineffectiveness in games where players can much more easily work together to eliminate other players due to it being too similar to Minimax. Similarly, Multi-Minimax could be ineffective in games where searching realistic board states is much more important than having improved search depth. Thus, we can assume that at least in the area of fixed sequential turn-based games, Multi-Minimax will not perform well in scenarios where Best Reply Search does not. Having added pruning methods for search-tree based AI algorithms playing other types of turn-based games could also prove to be effective. Experimentation with combining supervised learning, Monte-Carlo tree search, SSS* pruning or pruning for simultaneous move search-trees with the Multi-Minimax algorithm, could also be effective [10–13]. For example, one could train a machine learning algorithm to predict the depth at which Multi-Minimax should start at during iterative deepening.

References

1. Schadd, M.P.D., Winands, M.H.M.: Best reply search for multi-player games. IEEE Trans. Comput. Intell. AI Games **3**(1), 57–66 (2011)
2. Knuth, D.E., Moore, R.W.: An analysis of alpha-beta pruning. Artif. intell. **6**(4), 293–326 (1975)
3. Sturtevant, N.R., Korf, R.E.: On pruning techniques for multi-player games, vol. 49, pp. 201–207 (2000)
4. Sturtevant, N.: A comparison of algorithms for multi-player games. In: Schaeffer, J., Müller, M., Björnsson, Y. (eds.) CG 2002. LNCS, vol. 2883, pp. 108–122. Springer, Heidelberg (2003). https://doi.org/10.1007/978-3-540-40031-8_8
5. Luckhardt, C., Irani, K.: An algorithmic solution of N-person games. In: Proceedings of the AAAI 1986, pp. 158–162 (1986)

6. Sturtevant, N.: Multi-player games: algorithms and approaches. University of California (2003)
7. Shannon, C.E.: Programming a computer for playing chess. Philos. Mag. **41**, 256–275 (1950)
8. Korf, R.E.: Depth-first iterative-deepening: an optimal admissible tree search. Artif. Intell. **27**(1), 97–109 (1985)
9. Campbell, M.S., Marsland, T.A.: A comparison of minimax tree search algorithms. Artif. Intell. **20**(4), 347–367 (1983)
10. Stockman, G.C.: A minimax algorithm better than alpha-beta? Artif. Intell. **12**(2), 179–196 (1979)
11. Buro, M.: Improving heuristic mini-max search by supervised learning. Artif. Intell. **134**(1–2), 85–99 (2002)
12. Saffidine, A., Finnsson, H., Buro, M.: Alpha-beta pruning for games with simultaneous moves. Twenty-Sixth AAAI Conference on Artificial Intelligence (2012)
13. Baier, H., Winands, M.H.M.: Monte-carlo tree search and minimax hybrids. In: 2013 IEEE Conference on Computational Inteligence in Games (CIG), pp. 1–8 (2013)
14. Korf, R.E.: Multi-player alpha-beta pruning. Artif. Intell. **48**(1), 99–111 (1991)
15. Sturtevant, N.R.: Last-branch and speculative pruning algorithms for Max^n. IJCAI **3**, 669–678 (2003)
16. Sturtevant, N.R.: Leaf-value tables for pruning non-zero-sum games. International Joint Conference on Artificial Intelligence, vol. 19, p. 317 (2005)

An Empirical Study of Reward Structures for Actor-Critic Reinforcement Learning in Air Combat Manoeuvring Simulation

Budi Kurniawan[1(✉)] (ID), Peter Vamplew[1] (ID), Michael Papasimeon[2] (ID),
Richard Dazeley[3] (ID), and Cameron Foale[1] (ID)

[1] Federation University, Mount Helen, VIC 3350, Australia
budikurniawan@students.federation.edu.au,
{p.vamplew,c.foale}@federation.edu.au
[2] Defence Science and Technology Group, Fishermans Bend, VIC 3207, Australia
michael.papasimeon@dst.defence.gov.au
[3] School of Information Technology, Deakin University, Geelong, VIC 3220, Australia
richard.dazeley@deakin.edu.au

Abstract. Reinforcement learning techniques for solving complex problems are resource-intensive and take a long time to converge, prompting a need for methods that encourage faster learning. In this paper we show our successful application of actor-critic reinforcement learning to the air combat simulation domain and how reward structures affect the learning speed to find effective air combat tactics.

Keywords: Reinforcement learning · Actor-critic · Air combat

1 Introduction

Reinforcement learning (RL) has proven useful for solving sequential decision making problems. RL has been successfully applied to train agents to beat the world champion of Go [23], play ATARI games at superhuman levels [13], trade stocks [22], learn to drive autonomous vehicles [20], and so on.

One of the greatest challenges in applying RL to complex problems is the learning time required, which can be days even when utilising today's fastest computers [14]. As such, when designing an RL system, it is crucial to take into account every factor that could potentially accelerate learning.

In this study we use actor-critic RL to discover novel air combat tactics and investigate the role of reward structures in expediting learning. We find that carefully choosing the reward function may allow the agent to learn faster.

2 Related Work

AI-based research in air combat dates back to at least the 1980s. Early research includes that of Rodin and Amin [18] and Wharington [29]. The former implemented an artificial neural network for rapidly identifying air combat manoeuvres and suggesting the best possible counter-manoeuvres. The latter used RL

© Springer Nature Switzerland AG 2019
J. Liu and J. Bailey (Eds.): AI 2019, LNAI 11919, pp. 54–65, 2019.
https://doi.org/10.1007/978-3-030-35288-2_5

for improving unmanned aerial vehicles (UAVs) performance by adding a controller that located and took advantage of thermals caused by convection in the lower atmosphere.

Afterwards, various methods have been applied to air combat simulation. McGrew [11] used approximate dynamic programming to solve a fixed velocity, one-on-one air combat manoeuvring problem in two-dimensional space. Park, Lee and Takh [16] utilised differential game theory to develop an automated manoeuvre generation algorithm for within visual range (WVR) air-to-air combat of unmanned combat aerial vehicles (UCAVs). This algorithm follows a hierarchical decision-making structure and performs scoring function matrix calculation to find the optimal manoeuvres in dynamic and challenging combat situation. In addition, Alford, Borck, Karneeb and Aha [1] use behaviour recognition, by presenting a method for an unmanned aircraft to recognise the intent and general tactics of hostile aircraft in a long-range air combat scenario, where the system must make a decision based on observations solely through radar. They show that pairing the behaviour recognition system with a Monte-Carlo based MDP planner enables the UAV to confidently classify the opponents in significantly less time.

RL methods have also been used to solve air combat problems. Vinberg [28] used a guided RL method, meaning that exploration was not completely random but guided by predefined rules, that is by giving hints to the agent every time the agent was exploring. He used a neural network as a function approximator and learning was restricted to beyond visual range (BVR) one-on-one fights.

Besides Vinberg, a number of researchers have studied the use of a neural network as a function approximator in an RL system designed to excel in air combat. For instance, Liu [9] used a deep network in a one-on-one combat that allowed five actions (turn-right-up, turn-right-down, turn-left-up, turn-left-down, cruise) and Teng et al. [26] investigated real-time learning of air combat manoeuvres using self-organising neural networks in one-on-one dogfights. Their FALCON system was able to discover new air combat manoeuvring strategies that allow it to consistently outmanoeuvre its adversary. In addition to neural networks, Teng et al. used a variant of Q-learning called bounded Q-learning.

Q-learning has often been chosen to solve air combat simulation problems. Fang [4] combined Q-learning and a behaviour tree to train a fighter agent to decide whether to patrol, attack an enemy, turn around or flee. Their strategy was to use Q-learning to obtain a Q-table and then insert the Q-table in the behaviour tree. Lee and Bang [8] used Q-learning to help aircraft evade missiles moving in a horizontal plane while modelling the aircraft equations of motions as a simplified fourth-order point mass. Mouton, Roodt and le Roux [15] applied two methods, Monte-Carlo control with exploring starts (MCES) and Q-learning, to the weapon assignment (WA) problem in air-defence. Solving a WA problem means trying to find an optimal assignment of a set of weapons to a set of targets in order to maximise the damage to the enemy.

All the aforementioned works that used RL focused on value-based approaches. By contrast, our research uses a policy-gradient method called actor-critic. In this study, we seek novel tactics and look at the role of reward structures for actor-critic in accelerating learning.

One aspect of our study is similar to optimistic initialisation, which is discussed in [24] and investigated in [6]. These two studies use SARSA, whereas our study uses actor-critic.

3   Actor-Critic Reinforcement Learning Background

A subfield of machine learning and inspired by animal learning, reinforcement learning (RL) is a learning method by which the learner (called the agent) is neither given instructions nor told what to do. Instead, the agent learns by trial and error and receives feedback in the form of a reward every time the agent selects and executes an action.

RL methods can be grouped into one of these classes:

- value-based (such as SARSA and Q-learning)
- policy-based (such as REINFORCE)
- A mix of value-based and policy-based (actor-critic).

The value-based method learns the values of actions and choose actions based on their estimated action values. These methods are easy to use, but come with two drawbacks. First, the policy obtained is deterministic, whereas optimal policies are often stochastic. Second, learning can be prohibitively long for complex problems involving large state and action spaces [25].

First introduced by Barto et al. [2], policy-based methods learn a parameterised policy and are able to do so without a value function. The advantage of the policy-based approach is that learning may result in a policy that is stochastic. In addition, policy-based methods can be more effective than value-based methods in solving problems with high-dimensional state-action spaces.

The focus of this paper is the actor-critic algorithm, a policy-based method that also uses a value function to learn the policy parameter. Actor-critic learns the policy parameter based on the gradient of some scalar performance measure with respect to the policy parameter, and therefore belongs to the policy-gradient family of methods.

In a policy-gradient method, a policy is the probability that action a is taken when the agent is in state s at time t with parameter θ. In other words,

$$\pi(a|s, \boldsymbol{\theta}) = \Pr\{A_t = a | S_t = s, \boldsymbol{\theta}_t = \boldsymbol{\theta}\}$$

If the action space is discrete and not too large, an exponential soft-max distribution can be used in action selection,

$$\pi(a|s, \boldsymbol{\theta}) \doteq \frac{e^{h(s,a,\boldsymbol{\theta})}}{\sum_b e^{h(s,b,\boldsymbol{\theta})}},$$

where

$$h(s, a, \boldsymbol{\theta}) = \boldsymbol{\theta}^\mathsf{T} x(s, a),$$

where $\boldsymbol{\theta} \in \mathbb{R}^{d'}$ and $x(s, a) \in \mathbb{R}^{d'}$ is the feature vector.

The variant of actor-critic that we use in this study is called actor-critic with eligibility traces, a discussion of which can be found in [24].

4   Air Combat Simulation

There are significant economic motivations for using air combat simulators. Not only does simulation offer lower costs than real aircraft, it also eliminates risks to human pilots and expedites training [12].

Modelling air combat is usually divided into within-visual-range (WVR) and beyond-visual-range (BVR) combat. BVR air combat involves two opposing teams of aircraft located at large distances from each other (hundreds of kilometres) and operating in large air spaces. This type of combat is heavily reliant on long range radar-guided missiles [5].

Historically, air-combat simulators have been built using scripting and rule-based techniques. However, entering rules into the system is error-prone and rule-based systems are predictable. Due to these limitations, researchers turned to artificial intelligence (AI) techniques for air combat simulation. Two main claimed advantages of using AI in agent-based simulation are the simulation can be developed more quickly and it can be explained, understood and validated more clearly [7].

In this research, we focus on constructive air combat simulations, which are used for operations research and in which there are no human players. In other words, it is an agent-versus-agent setting. Our research aims to train a virtual agent (pilot) so that it can excel in simulated air combat. The simulator software we use is called Ace Zero, which was developed by the Australian Defence Science and Technology (DST) Group and used in [17] and [10].

To be successful in air combat, the agent's aircraft needs to be in specific relative aircraft geometry with the opponent. Figure 1 shows the relative aircraft geometry, which consists of the range (distance), the attack angle (AA) and the antenna train angle (ATA). By convention, blue is used to depict the aircraft controlled by the subject agent and red to represent the opposing aircraft. The angles are shown from the point of view of the blue aircraft.

The aircraft centres of mass are connected by the line of sight (LOS) line, which is also used to calculate the range between the two aircraft. The aspect angle (AA) is the angle between the LOS line and the tail of the red aircraft. The antenna train angle (ATA) is the angle between the nose of the blue aircraft and the LOS line. Both the AA and ATA help the pilot to make manoeuvring decisions. The value of the AA and ATA is within $0° \pm 180°$. By convention, angles to the right side of the aircraft are considered positive and angles to the left negative [11].

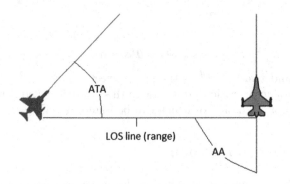

Fig. 1. Relative aircraft geometry

Quantitatively, the McGrew score [11], which incorporates the range, AA and ATA, is used to measure how favourable our agent's position is relative to the opponent. The higher the McGrew score, the better. The McGrew score consists of two components, McGrew angular score (A_M) and McGrew range score (R_M).

$$S_M = A_M R_M \tag{1}$$

The McGrew angular score is defined as follows.

$$A_M = \frac{1}{2}[(1 - \frac{AA}{180°}) + (1 - \frac{ATA}{180°})] \tag{2}$$

Here, AA and ATA are in degrees and described in Fig. 1. The maximum possible value for A_M is 1, which is achieved when $AA = ATA = 0$.

The McGrew range score is defined as this.

$$R_M = exp[-\frac{|R - R_d|}{k \times 180°}] \tag{3}$$

where R is the current range of the two aircraft and R_d the desired range. We determine R_d, the midpoint between the minimum gun range (500 ft = 153 m) and the maximum gun range (3,000 ft = 914 m), to be 380 m [21]. The value of k, the hyper-parameter scaling factor, determines the width of the function peak around R_d. The larger the value of k, the bigger the spread. A small value of k dictates that a high McGrew range score can only be achieved if the two aircraft are very close to the desired range. By default $k = 5$.

The McGrew score ranges from 0.0 to 1.0 (inclusive). Figure 2 shows McGrew scores of pairs of Blue and Red aircraft in various layouts. In all of them, Blue and Red are spaced 380 m from each other. Figure 2A shows Blue is trailing Red and both are flying in the same direction ($AA = ATA = 0°$). Figure 2B shows Blue and Red at 45° ($AA = 0$, $ATA = 45°$) and Fig. 2C shows them at 90° ($AA = 0°$, $ATA = 90°$). Figure 2D shows Red is following Blue ($AA = ATA = 180°$)

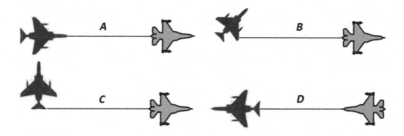

Fig. 2. McGrew scores for R = 380 m (A = 1.00, B = 0.82, C = 0.65, D = 0.00) (Color figure online)

5   Experiments and Discussion

Our research project is an air combat simulator in two-dimensional space whereby we train agents (Blue aircraft) to outmanoeuvre their opponents in the way described in the previous section, using the actor-critic with eligibility traces algorithm. Like the real-world aircraft, a virtual aircraft is able to change direction continuously and the distance between the aircraft is also continuous, making air combat simulation a continuous problem.

Because we use an algorithm for solving discrete problems, we set out by first discretising the distance into fourteen regions, the AA into ten regions and the ATA into ten regions, resulting in 1,400 states. The opposing aircraft is allowed to perform continuous change of speed and direction within its physical limit, but our agent is restricted to these five actions: do nothing, turn left by 10°, turn right by 10°, increase speed by 10% and decrease speed by 10%.

For training we initialise our policy parameterisation values with zeros and start the opponent (Red aircraft) from position (x_r, y_r, ψ_r) where x_r and y_r are a coordinate in a Cartesian coordinate and ψ_r the flying direction (heading) in degrees (relative to the X axis). Our aircraft (Blue) always starts from the origin with heading 0° and an initial speed of 125 m/s, which means it starts by flying along the X axis. We use reward functions that incorporate the McGrew score in three agents (Agent A, Agent B and Agent C), all similar except for a fixed offset applied to the reward function at each timestep:

- Agent A: Reward = McGrewScore
- Agent B: Reward = McGrewScore - 0.5
- Agent C: Reward = McGrewScore - 1.0.

During training Red always starts from (1500, 300, 50°) and flies in a straight line at a constant speed of 125 m/s. The initial positions, headings and speeds of both aircraft are the same for all episodes. Each of the three agents is run independently against an identical opponent. We stop learning after 20,000 episodes.

The policies from the three learning sessions are used to test agents against an opponent that flies along paths that were not seen during training. Two of the paths are shown in Fig. 3. In all tests, our agents manage to generalise and

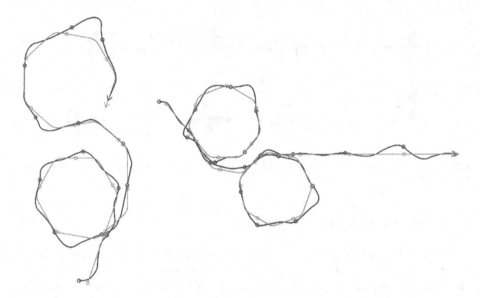

Fig. 3. Test results show our agent (Blue) was able to follow the opponent (Red) (Color figure online)

Table 1. Average reward for 1,000 episodes

	Agent A	Agent B	Agent C
Trial 1	0.082	0.083	0.083
Trial 2	0.058	0.089	0.092
Trial 3	0.060	0.086	0.081
Trial 4	0.074	0.080	0.072
Trial 5	0.064	0.088	0.091
Trial 6	0.062	0.079	0.086
Trial 7	0.069	0.098	0.082
Trial 8	0.082	0.085	0.086
Trial 9	0.093	0.094	0.097
Trial 10	0.067	0.097	0.092
Average	0.071	0.088	0.086

trail the opponent closely and stay within an effective shooting position. This experiment shows that these fixed reward offsets did not affect the ability of each actor-critic agent to learn an effective policy.

Another aspect that we investigate is the role of the reward structure in accelerating learning. The three agents aim to get the highest rewards possible but do so at different learning speeds. We run each experiment ten times and Tables 1, 2 and 3 show the average rewards after 1,000, 2,000 and 5,000 episodes for each agent.

Table 2. Average reward for 2,000 episodes

	Agent A	Agent B	Agent C
Trial 1	0.109	0.141	0.128
Trial 2	0.081	0.162	0.122
Trial 3	0.088	0.138	0.109
Trial 4	0.099	0.123	0.117
Trial 5	0.105	0.154	0.123
Trial 6	0.098	0.109	0.130
Trial 7	0.126	0.149	0.118
Trial 8	0.134	0.138	0.129
Trial 9	0.121	0.134	0.170
Trial 10	0.127	0.148	0.118
Average	0.109	0.140	0.126

Table 3. Average reward for 5,000 episodes

	Agent A	Agent B	Agent C
Trial 1	0.213	0.227	0.218
Trial 2	0.175	0.249	0.226
Trial 3	0.164	0.283	0.211
Trial 4	0.195	0.215	0.209
Trial 5	0.205	0.257	0.201
Trial 6	0.174	0.214	0.242
Trial 7	0.198	0.262	0.224
Trial 8	0.261	0.233	0.245
Trial 9	0.210	0.229	0.260
Trial 10	0.277	0.236	0.188
Average	0.207	0.241	0.222

Tables 1, 2 and 3 show that Agent A learns the slowest, due to having pessimistic initialisation. As each timestep returns a reward that is higher than its initial value, Agent A will tend to follow whichever actions it selects first, rather than seeking better alternatives. Agent B is the fastest learner. Having balanced initialisation that allows it to get a lower and higher reward than its initial values may encourage Agent B to learn faster. However, shifting the reward function further, as is done to Agent C, does not result in faster learning.

Table 4 shows the t-test results for all the agents. After 1,000 episodes, the differences in performance between agents A and B was statistically significant (2-tailed t-test, $p < 0.01$), however there was no significant difference between agents B and C. After 2000 and 5000 episodes there were significant differences

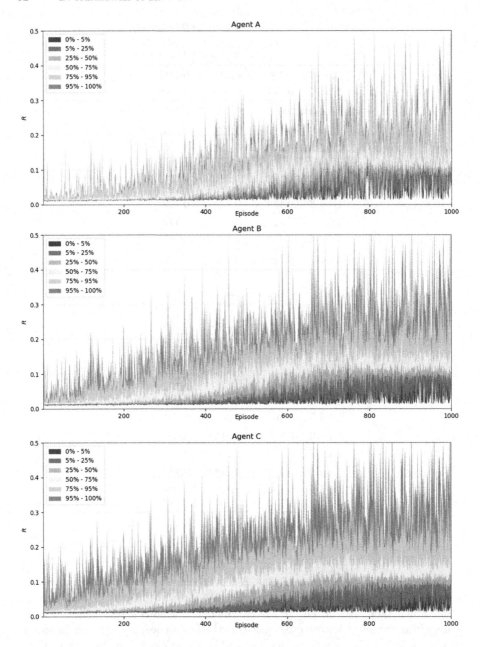

Fig. 4. Reward received per episode over the ten trials of each agent. Colours indicate percentiles of the trial outcomes at each episode and rewards have been normalised to 0.0–1.0 range. (Color figure online)

between Agents A-B and Agents B-C ($p < 0.05$). The same cannot be said about Agents A-C, which in all cases show results that are not statistically different.

Table 4. T-test results

	Agents A-B	Agents B-C	Agents A-C
1,000 episodes	0.00041	0.29504	0.07712
2,000 episodes	0.00030	0.04075	0.35627
5,000 episodes	0.01196	0.04069	0.38051

The charts in Fig. 4 show the learning speeds for the first 1,000 episodes for the three agents. Agent B gets better rewards than Agent A in most of the early episodes and maintains a 20% lead against Agent A (0.241 vs. 0.207) throughout the ten trials. Agent C initially does better than Agent B for the first 100 episodes, but does not maintain the same learning speed and ends up having lower average scores than Agent B. The charts show the average reward received in each episode over ten trials for each agent. The colours indicate the percentiles of the trial outcomes at each episode and all rewards have been normalised to 0.0–1.0 range.

6   Conclusions and Future Work

We demonstrate that actor-critic can be used to find novel air combat tactics. We also show that reward structures affect learning. Based on the average scores presented in the previous section, Agent A learns the slowest because of its pessimistic initialisation and is not motivated to learn faster in the early episodes. Agent B learns the fastest because of balanced initialisation. Agent C, with the most optimistic initialisation, initially learns faster than Agent B but fails to get a higher total average score than Agent B. After 2,000 episodes, the difference between Agent A's learning speed and that of Agent B is statistically significant and so is the difference between Agent B and Agent C.

Extensions for future work may include the use of three-dimensional space and may utilise curriculum learning to train the agent to do more difficult tasks by gradually introducing those tasks [3].

Air combat is also a complex problem with conflicting objectives. For example, an agent may want to fly as fast as possible to outmanoeuvre its opponent, and at the same time not flying at the highest speeds all the time to save fuels. The use of multi-objective RL techniques [19,27] in this domain may be an interesting research project. Finally, an air combat may involve multiple aircraft and be viewed as a team game. Extending our study to a multi-agent RL system will be an important future area of focus.

Acknowledgements. This research is supported by the Defence Science and Technology Group, Australia; the Defence Science Institute, Australia; and an Australian Government Research Training Program Fee-offset scholarship. Associate Professor Joarder Kamruzzaman of the Centre for Multimedia Computing, Communications, and Artificial Intelligence Research (MCCAIR) at Federation University contributed some of the computing resources for this project.

References

1. Alford, R., Borck, H., Karneeb, J., Aha, D.: Active behavior recognition in beyond visual range air combat. In: Proceedings of the Third Annual Conference on Advances in Cognitive Systems (2015)
2. Barto, A., Sutton, R.S., Anderson, C.W.: Neuron-like adaptive elements that can solve difficult learning control problems. IEEE Trans. Syst. Man Cybern. **9**, 833–836 (1983)
3. Bengio, Y., Louradour, J., Collobert, R., Weston, J.: Curriculumm learning. In: Proceedings of the 26th Annual International Conference on Machine Learning, pp. 41–48 (2009)
4. Fang, J., Yan, W.J., Fang, W.: Air combat strategies of CGF based on Q-learning and behavior tree. DEStech Trans. Eng. Technol. Res. (2017)
5. Floyd, M.W., Karneeb, J., Moore, P., Aha, D.W.: A goal reasoning agent for controlling UAVs in beyond-visual-range air combat. In: Proceedings 26th International Joint Conference on Artificial Intelligence (2017)
6. Grześ, M., Kudenko, D.: Improving optimistic exploration in model-free reinforcement learning. In: Kolehmainen, M., Toivanen, P., Beliczynski, B. (eds.) ICANNGA 2009. LNCS, vol. 5495, pp. 360–369. Springer, Heidelberg (2009). https://doi.org/10.1007/978-3-642-04921-7_37
7. Heinze, C., Papasimeon, M., Goss, S., Cross, M., Connell, R.: Simulating fighter pilots. In: Defence Industry Applications of Autonomous Agents and Multi-Agent Systems, pp. 113–130 (2007)
8. Lee, D., Bang, H.: Planar evasive aircrafts maneuvers using reinforcement learning. In: Lee, S., Cho, H., Yoon, K.J., Lee, J. (eds.) Intelligent Autonomous Systems. AISC, vol. 193, pp. 533–542. Springer, Heidelberg (2013). https://doi.org/10.1007/978-3-642-33926-4_49
9. Liu, P., Ma, Y.: A deep reinforcement learning based intelligent decision method for UCAV air combat. In: Mohamed Ali, M.S., Wahid, H., Mohd Subha, N.A., Sahlan, S., Md. Yunus, M.A., Wahap, A.R. (eds.) AsiaSim 2017. CCIS, vol. 751, pp. 274–286. Springer, Singapore (2017). https://doi.org/10.1007/978-981-10-6463-0_24
10. Masek, M., Lam, C.P., Benke, L., Kelly, L., Papasimeon, M.: Discovering emergent agent behaviour with evolutionary finite state machines. In: Miller, T., Oren, N., Sakurai, Y., Noda, I., Savarimuthu, B.T.R., Cao Son, T. (eds.) PRIMA 2018. LNCS, vol. 11224, pp. 19–34. Springer, Cham (2018). https://doi.org/10.1007/978-3-030-03098-8_2
11. McGrew, J., How, J.P., Williams, B., Roy, N.: Air-combat strategy using approximate dynamic programming. J. Guidance Control Dyn. **33**, 1641–1654 (2010)
12. Mizokami, K.: This chart explains how crazy-expensive fighter jets Have Gotten. Popular Mechanics, March 2017
13. Mnih, V., et al.: Human-level control through deep reinforcement learning. Nature **518**, 29–33 (2015)
14. Mnih, V., et al.: Asynchronous methods for deep reinforcement learning. In: Proceedings 33rd International Conference on Machine Learning, vol. 48, pp. 1928–1937 (2016)
15. Mouton, H., Roodt, J., le Roux, H.: Applying reinforcement learning to the weapon assignment problem in air defence. Scientia Militaria S. Afr. J. Mil. Stud. 123–140 (2011)
16. Park, H., Lee, B., Takh, M.: Differential game based air combat maneuver generation using scoring function matrix. Int. J. Aeronaut. Space Sci. **17**(2), 204–213 (2016)

17. Ramirez, M., et al.: Integrated hybrid planning and programmed control for real time UAV maneuvering. In: Proceedings 17th International Conference on Autonomous Agents and MultiAgent Systems, pp. 1318–1326 (2018)
18. Rodin, E.Y., Amin, S.M.: Maneuver prediction in air combat via artificial neural networks. Comput. Math. Appl. **24**(3), 95–112 (1982)
19. Roijers, D.M., Vamplew, P., Whiteson, S., Dazeley, R.: A survey of multi-objective sequential decision-making. J. Artif. Intell. Res. **48**, 67–113 (2013)
20. Shalev, S., Shammah, S., Shashua, A.: Safe, multi-agent, reinforcement learning for autonomous driving: CoRR, vol abs/1610.03295 (2016)
21. Shaw, R.L.: Fighter Combat: Tactics and Maneuvering. Naval Institute Press, Annapolis (1985)
22. Sherstov, A.A., Stone, P.: Three automated stock-trading agents: a comparative study. In: Faratin, P., Rodríguez-Aguilar, J.A. (eds.) AMEC 2004. LNCS (LNAI), vol. 3435, pp. 173–187. Springer, Heidelberg (2006). https://doi.org/10.1007/11575726_13
23. Silver, D., et al.: Mastering the game of Go with deep neural networks and tree search. Nature **529**, 484 (2016)
24. Sutton, R., Barto, A.: Reinforcement Learning: An Introduction, 2nd edn. MIT Press, Cambridge (2018)
25. Sutton, R., McAllester, D., Singh, S., Mansour, Y.: Policy gradient methods for reinforcement learning with function approximation. In: Advances in Neural Information Processing Systems, pp. 1057–1063 (2000)
26. Teng, T.H., Tan, A.H., Tan, Y.S., Yeo, A.: Self-organizing neural networks for learning air combat maneuvers: In: IEEE World Congress on Computational Intelligence, Brisbane, Australia (2012)
27. Vamplew, P., Dazeley, R., Berry, A., Issabekov, R., Dekker, E.: Empirical evaluation methods for multiobjective reinforcement learning algorithms. Mach. Learn. **84**, 51 (2011)
28. Vinberg, D.: Guided reinforcement learning applied to air-combat simulation. Master 's thesis. Royal Institute of Technology, Sweden (2010)
29. Wharington, J.: Autonomous control of soaring aircraft by reinforcement learning. Doctorate thesis at Royal Melbourne Institute of Technology (1998)

Memory-Based Explainable Reinforcement Learning

Francisco Cruz[1(✉)], Richard Dazeley[1], and Peter Vamplew[2]

[1] School of Information Technology, Deakin University, Geelong, Australia
{francisco.cruz,richard.dazeley}@deakin.edu.au
[2] School of Science, Engineering and Information Technology,
Federation University, Ballarat, Australia
p.vamplew@federation.edu.au

Abstract. Reinforcement learning (RL) is a learning approach based on behavioral psychology used by artificial agents to learn autonomously by interacting with their environment. An open issue in RL is the lack of visibility and understanding for end-users in terms of decisions taken by an agent during the learning process. One way to overcome this issue is to endow the agent with the ability to explain in simple terms why a particular action is taken in a particular situation. In this work, we propose a memory-based explainable reinforcement learning (MXRL) approach. Using an episodic memory, the RL agent is able to explain its decisions by using the probability of success and the number of transactions to reach the goal state. We have performed experiments considering two variations of a simulated scenario, namely, an unbounded grid world with aversive regions and a bounded grid world. The obtained results show that the agent, using information extracted from the memory, is able to explain its behavior in an understandable manner for non-expert end-users at any moment during its operation.

Keywords: Reinforcement learning · Explainable reinforcement learning · Human-aligned artificial intelligence

1 Introduction

The aim of reinforcement learning (RL) [17] is to provide an autonomous agent with the ability to learn new skills by only interacting with its environment. RL is a learning approach based on behavioral psychology and conditioned behavior present in mammals and human decision-making within the brain [12]. While RL has been shown to be an effective learning approach, an open issue is the lack of a mechanism that allows them to clearly communicate the reasons why they choose certain actions given a particular state. In this regard, it is not easy for a non-expert end-user to entrust important tasks to an AI-based system that cannot justify its reasoning [1].

© Springer Nature Switzerland AG 2019
J. Liu and J. Bailey (Eds.): AI 2019, LNAI 11919, pp. 66–77, 2019.
https://doi.org/10.1007/978-3-030-35288-2_6

In human cognition, for instance, toddlers are still unable to clearly express reasons about their decisions, mainly due to the incomplete development of language acquisition [14]. The lack of understanding by other interacting agents leads to them not considering toddlers as peers. However, as they develop the ability to give sound and meaningful explanations about their decisions, the mutual confidence level increases and they become collaborative agents[1] [2].

To model artificial systems, different alternatives are possible, i.e., phenomenological models (white-box models), empirical model (black-box models), and hybrid models (gray-box models) [3]. Even though artificial agents are considered to be black-boxes, frequently, it is possible to provide technical clues about why actions are decided, e.g., an RL agent could explain its behavior in terms of Q-values and future reward [4]. Nevertheless, this kind of explanation makes little sense for non-expert users who need to be given explanations using domain-like language in order to allow them to fully understand the agent behavior. In this regard, there have been some research works pursuing a better understanding of RL agent's decisions. However, they have mostly focused on interpretable RL [16] and explainable agency [8], overlooking the option of using the agent's experience to understand its behavior.

In this paper, we propose a memory-based explainable reinforcement learning (MXRL) approach, which allows a learning agent to explain in domain language the decision of selecting an action over the other possible ones. In our approach, explanations are given using the probability of success and the number of transitions needed to reach the goal state. Thus, an RL agent is able to explain its behavior not only in terms of Q-values or the probability of selecting an action but rather in terms of the necessity to complete the intended task.

2   Related Works

2.1   Reinforcement Learning

RL is studied as a decision-making mechanism in both cognitive and artificial agents [17]. An RL agent learns through interaction with its environment, trying to map inputs into actions. In RL, there is no explicit instructor but rather the awareness of how the environment answers to what it is done by the learning agent. Therefore, an agent should be able to sense the environment's state and perform actions in order to transition to a new state.

Formally, an RL agent has to learn a policy $\pi : S \rightarrow A$, where S is the set of states and A the set of available actions, to produce the highest possible reward from a state s_t [17]. The optimal policy is denoted by π^* and the optimal action-value function is denoted by q^*. The optimal action-value function is solved through the Bellman optimality equation for q^*, as shown in Eq. 1.

$$q^*(s_t, a_t) = \sum_{s_{t+1}} p(s_{t+1}|s_t, a_t)[r(s_t, a_t, s_{t+1}) + \gamma \max_{a_{t+1}} q^*(s_{t+1}, a_{t+1})] \quad (1)$$

---

[1] Agent, in this context, refers to any actor in an environment such as human, animal, or artificial agent.

where s_t is the current state, a_t the taken action, s_{t+1} the next state reached after performing action a_t from the state s_t, and a_{t+1} is an action that could be taken from s_{t+1}. In Eq. 1, p represents the probability of reaching the state s_{t+1} given the current state s_t and the selected action a_t. Finally, r is the reward signal received after performing action a_t from the state s_t.

2.2　Explainable Artificial Intelligence

Over the last few years, explainable artificial intelligence (XAI) has emerged as a prominent research area that aims to provide black-box AI-based systems the ability to give human-like and user-friendly explanations to non-expert end-users [11]. The idea behind XAI is not only intended to provide explanations, but also to allow an AI-system to: justify its decisions and results, control and prevent problems, improve its behavior, and discover new knowledge [1]. The need of XAI is mainly motivated by the need for end-users of trust, interaction, and transparency between them and AI-based systems. Furthermore, XAI is often considered harder than the underlying decision-making process [1], due to the additional interpretability process.

XAI is a vast field, like AI itself, with applications in areas such as transport, finance, medicine, and military among other [6]. Recently, there has been some research studies in explainability pointing to areas such as interpretable RL or explainable agency. These approaches are described next.

2.3　Interpretable Reinforcement Learning

Interpretable RL is an approach which encodes the tasks and actions using human-interpretable instructions. Shu et al. [16] have introduced an approach for hierarchical and interpretable skill acquisition using human descriptions to decompose the tasks into a hierarchical plan with understandable actions. Hein et al. [7] have combined RL with genetic programming (GP) for interpretable policies. They have tested their approach using the mountain car and cart-pole balancing RL benchmarks. However, the provided explanations are only for the learned policy employing equations for that instead of a natural-like representation. Verma et al. [19] have introduced the programmatically interpretable reinforcement learning (PIRL) framework for verifiable agent policies. However, the framework works with symbolic inputs considering only deterministic policies, not including stochastic ones.

In the field of Human-Robot Interaction (HRI), the term of explainable agency has been used to refer to robots engaged in answering questions about its reasons for the decision-making process. Langley et al. [8] propose the elements of explainable agency as content that support explanations, an episodic memory to record states and actions, and access to its experience. However, in their work, they do not implement the proposed approach.

In RL, there have also been a few works trying to provide agents with explanation mechanisms. For instance, Wang et al. [20] proposed an explainable recommendation system using an RL framework. Pocius et al. [13] utilized saliency maps as a way to explain agent decisions in a partially-observable game scenario. They focused mainly on deep RL and, hence, provided visual explanations. Madumal et al. [10], inspired by cognitive science, proposed to use causal models to derive causal explanations. Nevertheless, the causal model had to be previously known for the specific domain. Sequeira et al. [15] developed a framework to provide explanations employing thoughtful analysis in three levels of the RL agent interaction history. Tabrez and Hayes [18] used an HRI scenario to correct a sub-optimal human model behavior, formulated as a Markov decision process (MDP). In their research, they reported that users found the robot more helpful, useful, and more intelligent when explanations and justification were provided. However, the approach still lacks the comprehensibility of its policy.

3   Memory-Based Explainable Reinforcement Learning

The behavior of an RL agent might be technically explained in terms of the Q-values or also in algorithmic terms. Nonetheless, in this work, we look for explanations that make sense for all kinds of possible end-users and not only to those who are able to understand the underlying learning process behind an artificial agent. In this regard, we look for explanations similarly as it is done by interacting people by using domain-specific language.

To provide artificial agents with the ability to explain the performed actions is currently one of the most critical and complex challenges in future RL research [6]. This challenge is especially important, considering RL-based systems often interact with human observers. Therefore, it is essential that non-expert end-users can understand agents' intentions as well as to obtain more details from the execution in case of a failure [5].

In this paper, we focus on the decision-making process to provide an understanding to the user of what motivates the agent's specific actions from different states, taking into account the problem domain. From a non-expert end-user perspective, we can consider the most relevant questions as to 'why?' and 'why not?' [9,10]. For instance, the following questions may be asked to an artificial agent in order to better understand its behavior:

- Why did you step forward in the last movement?
- Why did you not turn to the right in this situation?

Thus, in order to answer these questions in an understandable domain language, our explanations intend to determine both:

- the artificial agent's probability of success, and
- the number of transitions to reach the goal state, to either finish the task or end it within a time-frame.

Once the probability of reaching the final state is determined the agent will be able to provide the end-user a more compensable explanation for why one action was preferred over others. Moreover, the number of transitions to the goal will give the end-user an idea about how many steps are necessary to finish the task. Therefore, the agent may explain when an action is preferred to complete the task faster.

We propose a memory-based explainable reinforcement learning (MXRL) approach to compute the success probability P_s and the transitions to the goal N_t consisting of an RL agent with an episodic memory. By accessing the memory, it is possible to understand the agent's behavior based on its experience by using introspection in three levels [15], i.e., environment analysis (to observe certain and uncertain transitions), interaction analysis (to observe state-action frequencies), and meta-analysis (to obtain combined information from episodes and agents). We implement a list of state-action pairs: T_{List} comprising the transactions the agent performed during its learning process.

To compute the success probability P_s, we previously compute the total number of transitions T_t and the number of transitions involved in a success sequence T_s. To obtain T_s, we use the transactions previously saved into the list T_{List}. Every time the agent reaches the final state, we compute the probability $P_s \leftarrow T_s/T_t$ considering transitions involved in the path towards the goal state. The transitions to the goal N_t is computed every time after finishing an episode. For each state, N_t is determined by the position in the list T_{List} since all transitions have been previously saved there. Therefore, each state is as far from the goal as its position in the list, i.e., its index + 1.

Algorithm 1. Memory-based explainable reinforcement learning approach with the on-policy method SARSA to compute the probability of success and the number of transitions to the goal state.

1: Initialize $Q(s,a)$, T_t, T_s, P_s, N_t
2: **for** each episode **do**
3:     Initialize $T_{List}[]$
4:     Choose an action using $a_t \leftarrow$ SELECTACTION(s_t)
5:     **repeat**
6:         Take action a_t
7:         Save state-action transition T_{List}.add(s, a)
8:         $T_t[s][a] \leftarrow T_t[s][a] + 1$
9:         Observe reward r_{t+1} and next state s_{t+1}
10:        Choose next action a_{t+1} using softmax action selection method
11:        $Q(s_t, a_t) \leftarrow Q(s_t, a_t) + \alpha[r_{t+1} + \gamma Q(s_{t+1}, a_{t+1}) - Q(s_t, a_t)]$
12:        $s_t \leftarrow s_{t+1}$; $a_t \leftarrow a_{t+1}$
13:    **until** s is terminal (goal or aversive state)
14:    **if** s is goal state **then**
15:        **for** each s,a $\in T_{List}$ **do**
16:            $T_s[s][a] \leftarrow T_s[s][a] + 1$
17:        **end for**
18:    **end if**
19:    Compute $P_s \leftarrow T_s/T_t$
20:    Compute N_t for each s $\in T_{List}$ as pos(s, T_{List}) + 1
21: **end for**

In this paper, an aim is to compare the probability of choosing an action, computed from the Q-values, against the probability of being successful. Therefore, we have implemented the on-policy method SARSA and the softmax action selection method. Algorithm 1 shows our MXRL approach to train RL agents using episodic memory. Whereas in line 7 each executed state-action pair is saved into the memory, lines 19 and 20 compute the final probabilities of success P_s and the number of transitions to the goal state N_t for each episode.

4   Experimental Set-Up

In order to produce explanations related to the context, we implemented a grid world scenario in two versions: bounded and unbounded. Therefore, the same state-action pair may lead to different characteristic for the explanation depending on the context. We use a 3×4 grid world, as shown in Fig. 1. In the figure, it is possible to observe the 12 states in which the agent can be. The goal state is shown with a green circle at the right bottom. The gray circle represents the agent which needs to find one path towards the goal state. In every episode, the agent is located in a random initial position within the grid world. Over the episodes, the learning agent has to learn a policy in order to reach the goal position. There are four allowed actions in this scenario: down, up, right, and left.

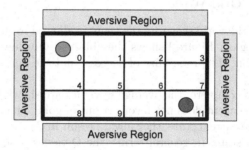

Fig. 1. The 3×4 grid world surrounded by aversive regions. The agent may move in four directions: down, up, right, and left. The green circle shows the goal state. If the aversive region is reached by the agent, the learning episode is finished and a new one started. In the bounded grid world scenario, the agent is not allowed to step into the aversive regions. (Color figure online)

In principle, we consider an unbounded grid world, i.e., a grid world where the agent might get into aversive regions leading to stop the current learning episode and restart a new one. The aversive regions are shown in yellow in Fig. 1. In this case, the probability of being successful is computed after every learning episode and depends on the experience of each agent to reach the final state.

Furthermore, we have also considered a bounded grid world, i.e., a grid world from where the agent is not allowed to step out. Therefore, every time the agent tries to step out the grid world, the current state is not updated, keeping the position as it was previously to select that action. In this context, the agent has a constant success probability of 1 since it is always able to complete the task. However, the time steps needed to get the goal are different for each reached state after performing an action.

5   Experimental Results

For the learning process, the reward function returns a positive reward of 1 when the agent reaches the final state and a negative reward of -1 when the agent enters an aversive region. All the experiments have been performed using the on-policy learning algorithm SARSA and the softmax action selection method for the training of 100 agents. The following plots show the average results. The parameters used for the training are: learning rate $\alpha = 0.3$, discount factor $\gamma = 0.9$, and softmax temperature $\tau = 0.25$, all of them were experimentally determined and related to our scenario. The previous parameters are mentioned here just as a reference, but they are not relevant for this work. These parameters do affect the agents' ability to learn a solution. However, we are interested in understanding the decision, rather than the speed or capacity of the learning agents.

5.1   Unbounded Grid World

In the unbounded grid world scenario, the agent is allowed to step out of the grid into the aversive region. Figure 2 shows the obtained Q-values, the probability of choosing an action, the probability of success, and the number of transitions to the goal state.

After training is complete, the average Q-values are shown in Fig. 2a. It can be observed that the agent does not favor actions of going up or going left since, independently of the current state, they always result in the agent moving further away from the goal state. In general terms, the Q-values, also show symmetric values, which indeed means the agent may select any route to the goal as long as its movements are down or right. Of course the closer to the goal state the higher reward which is shown, for instance, in states 7 and 10 with actions down and right respectively, both cases being final state's neighbors. There are a few exceptions with low Q-value when moving down (states 8, 9, and 10) and moving right (states 3 and 7) which represent the fact of stepping out the grid into the aversive region.

Figure 2b shows the average softmax probability of choosing an action from each state after learning. Although the probabilities of choosing an action are connected with the Q-values in terms of the different possible paths to the goal state, they only explain how likely it is to select an action rather than how successful the agent will be by selecting it. Thus, it cannot clearly be explained yet to a non-expert end-user why an RL agent would favor one of those actions.

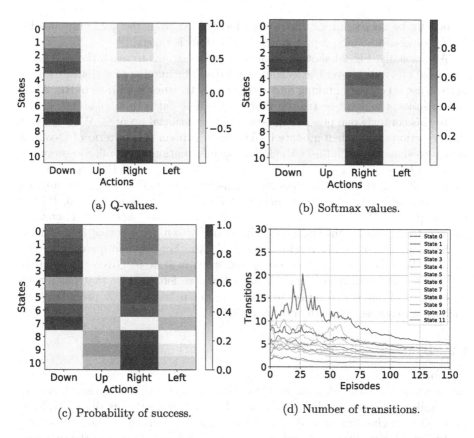

(a) Q-values.

(b) Softmax values.

(c) Probability of success.

(d) Number of transitions.

Fig. 2. Obtained results unbounded grid world. (a) Q-values. It can be seen that the agent does not favor actions which lead it further from the goal state, i.e., moving up or left. Additionally, the Q-values show symmetry considering the possible paths to the goal state. (b) Probability of choosing an action. While the softmax values show that the agent may select any path to the goal state with similar probability, they do not provide enough information in domain language. (c) Probability of success considering state-action pairs. Actions leading to the aversive region have a probability of success equal to 0. Moreover, actions far from the goal state or actions which get the agent further from the goal may also be successful if the right sequence is taken from there. (d) Evolution of the number of transitions over the learning episodes to reach the goal state. After training, the agent learns the shortest path to the goal.

Figure 2c shows the probability of success for each state-action pair after the learning process. The probabilities are computed after each episode using the memory. As previously discussed, they are a more transparent manner to explain to a non-expert end-user the reasons why an RL agent favors specific actions from specific states. In Fig. 2c, for instance, it is clear to see what actions lead to the aversive region as they show probability equal to 0. Moreover, it is shown that even actions which move the agent further from the goal state may eventually be successful, or that states located far from the goal may also be highly successful if the proper sequence of actions is taken.

Additionally, Fig. 2d shows the number of transitions to reach the goal position from every state over the learning episodes. The number of actions executed in this case is computed taking into account only the successful runs of RL. After 150 episodes, the agent learns the shortest possible paths from all states.

In this context, one possible question to the artificial agent is: Why did you choose action down when in state 0? Trying to explain this in term of Q-values means to show to an end-user the following information. $Q(s = 0, a = \text{down}) = -0.181$, $Q(s = 0, a = \text{up}) = -0.998$, $Q(s = 0, a = \text{right}) = -0.411$, $Q(s = 0, a = \text{left}) = -0.998$, which is pointless for a non-expert user. However, if we use the probability of success, we can observe that $P_s(s = 0, a = \text{down}) = 0.736$, $P_s(s = 0, a = \text{up}) = 0$, $P_s(s = 0, a = \text{right}) = 0.656$, $P_s(s = 0, a = \text{left}) = 0$. Therefore, the agent may answer the end-user: I chose to go down because that has a 73.6% probability of successfully reaching the goal. Another possible question to the agent is: Why did you not choose to go left when in state 0? Given the previous P_s values, one possible answer is: I did not choose left because that has a zero probability of success, whereas by choosing down has a 73.6% probability of success, which was higher than other actions.

5.2 Bounded Grid World

As aforementioned, the bounded grid world is an always success scenario since the agent cannot step out of the grid world into the aversive region and, therefore, eventually will always reach the goal state. Figure 3 shows the obtained Q-values, probability of choosing an action, and the number of actions to the final state.

In Fig. 3a, the obtained Q-values present similar distribution as the previous unbounded case, i.e., actions moving the agent up and left have lower values in comparison with down and right that moves the agent closer to the goal position.

In this case, the probability of choosing an action is also related to the Q-values, as shown in Fig. 3b. However, this probability does not provide enough information to understand and explain the action-selection decision by the RL agent, especially considering that the agent never fails the task in the bounded grid world. Therefore, in this scenario, to compute the number of transitions to reach the goal and the probability of success within a time window is imperative. Thus, an RL agent may answer more clearly questions as to why a particular action is preferred over others from a specific state referring to the number of steps needed to reach the goal.

Figure 3c shows the evolution of the probability of success over the learning episodes with the agent starting in position 0 (similar charts can be generated starting from any state). Three different time windows are considered as examples, i.e., the probability of reaching the goal in 8, 12, and 16 actions. In Fig. 3d is shown the number of transitions from each state to reach the goal state over the learning episodes. The RL agent may use this information to answer if a taken action reaches another state, from where it is faster to get it to the final state.

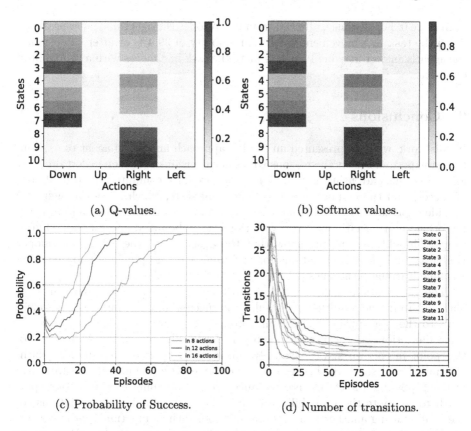

(a) Q-values.

(b) Softmax values.

(c) Probability of Success.

(d) Number of transitions.

Fig. 3. Obtained results bounded grid world. (a) Q-values. The RL agent favors down and right actions since get it closer to the goal state. As in the unbounded scenario, the Q-values are symmetric meaning that the agent has no particular preference for similar paths to the goal. (b) Probability of choosing an action. The softmax probabilities show only how likely it is to select an action after the learning process; however, they do not present information about the time-steps needed to success from a particular state-action pair. (c) Probability of success from position 0 within a specific window of actions using cumulative normal distribution. The larger the window, the higher the probability of finishing the task. To obtain the maximal probability are required 78, 48, and 32 episodes for a window of 8, 12, and 16 actions respectively. (d) Evolution of the number of transitions to reach the goal state. Since this is an always success scenario, it is relevant to provide explanations about the steps needed to reach the goal.

In this problem, a possible question for the agent could be: What is the probability of finishing the task in 8 movements starting from the state 0? One more time, if we want to answer this question in terms of Q-vales to the end- user we should show that $Q(s = 0, a = \text{down}) = -0.368$, $Q(s = 0, a = \text{up}) = -0.993$, $Q(s = 0, a = \text{right}) = -0.243$, $Q(s = 0, a = \text{left}) = -0.994$, which has no meaning for a non-expert end-user. However, if we refer to the plot Fig. 3c, we can clearly observe the probability of finishing the task in 8 movements starting from state 0. For instance, after 30 training episodes the agent may answer: I can finish the task in 8 movements with a probability of 39.4%, or after 60 episodes the agent's answer may be: I can complete the task in 8 moves with a probability of 86.5%.

6 Conclusions

In this work, we have presented an MXRL approach aiming an agent to explain to non-expert end-users the reasons why some decisions are taken in certain situations. To this end, using a episodic memory, we have computed the probability of success and the number of steps to the goal state, which allow the agent to provide explanations using domain-based language. Our experiments have been performed in a scenario with two variations, an unbounded and a bounded grid world. The obtained results show that the agent, using the episodic memory, is able to find clear explanations for end-users with no previous knowledge of machine learning techniques.

The explanations shown in this work are examples of possible answers obtained from the resulting probability of success and the number of transitions to the goal during the learning process. Currently, our method presents some limitations as the use of memory in large solution spaces. Moreover, to this point in this work, we have only considered a discrete episodic task with a terminal goal state. In this regard, the obtained results motivate future work in many possible directions. For instance, we are planning to extend our approach to compute the probability of success and the number of transitions to the goal by using another more general method, such as function approximator, Bayesian methods, or phenomenological relations from the Q-values. By using a more general estimation method, our approach might be scaled to more complex scenarios as problems with no final state, i.e., which need to operate continuously, or problems with continuous state-action representation.

References

1. Adadi, A., Berrada, M.: Peeking inside the black-box: a survey on explainable artificial intelligence (XAI). IEEE Access **6**, 52138–52160 (2018)
2. Conrad, B., Gross, D., Fogg, L., Ruchala, P.: Maternal confidence, knowledge, and quality of mother-toddler interactions: a preliminary study. Infant Mental Health J. **13**(4), 353–362 (1992)
3. Cruz, F., Acuña, G., Cubillos, F., Moreno, V., Bassi, D.: Indirect training of grey-box models: application to a bioprocess. In: Liu, D., Fei, S., Hou, Z., Zhang, H., Sun, C. (eds.) ISNN 2007. LNCS, vol. 4492, pp. 391–397. Springer, Heidelberg (2007). https://doi.org/10.1007/978-3-540-72393-6_47
4. Cruz, F., Magg, S., Nagai, Y., Wermter, S.: Improving interactive reinforcement learning: what makes a good teacher? Connect. Sci. **30**(3), 306–325 (2018)
5. Dulac-Arnold, G., Mankowitz, D., Hester, T.: Challenges of real-world reinforcement learning. arXiv preprint arXiv:1904.12901 (2019)

6. Gunning, D.: Explainable artificial intelligence (XAI). Defense Advanced Research Projects Agency (DARPA), nd Web (2017)
7. Hein, D., Udluft, S., Runkler, T.A.: Interpretable policies for reinforcement learning by genetic programming. Eng. Appl. Artif. Intell. **76**, 158–169 (2018)
8. Langley, P., Meadows, B., Sridharan, M., Choi, D.: Explainable agency for intelligent autonomous systems. In: Twenty-Ninth IAAI Conference, pp. 4762–4763 (2017)
9. Lim, B.Y., Dey, A.K., Avrahami, D.: Why and why not explanations improve the intelligibility of context-aware intelligent systems. In: Proceedings of the SIGCHI Conference on Human Factors in Computing Systems, pp. 2119–2128. ACM (2009)
10. Madumal, P., Miller, T., Sonenberg, L., Vetere, F.: Explainable reinforcement learning through a causal lens. arXiv preprint arXiv:1905.10958 (2019)
11. Miller, T.: Explanation in artificial intelligence: insights from the social sciences. Artif. Intell. **267**, 1–38 (2018)
12. Niv, Y.: Reinforcement learning in the brain. J. Math. Psychol. **53**, 139–154 (2009)
13. Pocius, R., Neal, L., Fern, A.: Strategic tasks for explainable reinforcement learning. In: The Thirty-Third AAAI Conference on Artificial Intelligence (AAAI 2019), p. 2 (2019)
14. Robertson, S.B., Weismer, S.E.: Effects of treatment on linguistic and social skills in toddlers with delayed language development. J. Speech Lang. Hearing Res. **42**(5), 1234–1248 (1999)
15. Sequeira, P., Yeh, E., Gervasio, M.T.: Interestingness elements for explainable reinforcement learning through introspection. In: IUI Workshops, p. 7 (2019)
16. Shu, T., Xiong, C., Socher, R.: Hierarchical and interpretable skill acquisition in multi-task reinforcement learning. arXiv preprint arXiv:1712.07294 (2017)
17. Sutton, R.S., Barto, A.G.: Reinforcement Learning: An Introduction. Bradford Book, Cambridge (1998)
18. Tabrez, A., Hayes, B.: Improving human-robot interaction through explainable reinforcement learning. In: 2019 14th ACM/IEEE International Conference on Human-Robot Interaction (HRI), pp. 751–753. IEEE (2019)
19. Verma, A., Murali, V., Singh, R., Kohli, P., Chaudhuri, S.: Programmatically interpretable reinforcement learning. arXiv preprint arXiv:1804.02477 (2018)
20. Wang, X., Chen, Y., Yang, J., Wu, L., Wu, Z., Xie, X.: A reinforcement learning framework for explainable recommendation. In: 2018 IEEE International Conference on Data Mining (ICDM), pp. 587–596. IEEE (2018)

Analysis of Coalition Formation in Cooperative Games Using Crowdsourcing and Machine Learning

Yuko Sakurai[1] and Satoshi Oyama[2(✉)]

[1] National Institute of Advanced Industrial Science and Technology, Tokyo, Japan
yuko.sakurai@aist.go.jp
[2] Hokkaido University, Sapporo, Japan
oyama@ist.hokkaido.ac.jp

Abstract. Analysis of coalition formation in cooperative games is an important research topic in game theory. Previous studies on coalition formation used laboratory experiments to collect data on player decision making, but the amount of data collected was limited due to the high cost of laboratory experiments. In this study, we used crowdsourcing to collect a large volume of decision-making data for use in predicting player behavior in cooperative games. This large amount of data enabled us to train large machine learning models such as deep neural networks, which can more precisely predict player decision making in cooperative games. The results with our machine learning models using crowdsourced data were similar to those of laboratory experiments.

Keywords: Cooperative games · Machine learning · Human behavior

1 Introduction

Agents in multi-agent systems are entities that can have their own goals, beliefs, and capabilities [13,15]. The agents can interact and cooperate to achieve goals that would be unattainable individually. The agents are often self-interested and act strategically to maximize their own utility. Game theory focuses on modeling strategic interactions among self-interested agents, and game theoretic models have been widely adopted as tools for analyzing multi-agent systems in both theoretical computer science and artificial intelligence [9,13].

Games studied in game theory are traditionally categorized as *non-cooperative* or *cooperative games*. In the first type, interactions that take place when agents must act individually are considered; binding agreements among them are impossible, so all choices are at the individual agent level. In the second type, interactions that take place when agents can act cooperatively are considered: binding agreements among them are possible, so agents can cooperate by forming coalitions. Since cooperation may create synergies that substantially increase the efficiency of the system, cooperative game theory, and especially

© Springer Nature Switzerland AG 2019
J. Liu and J. Bailey (Eds.): AI 2019, LNAI 11919, pp. 78–88, 2019.
https://doi.org/10.1007/978-3-030-35288-2_7

its algorithmic aspects, have been extensively studied in the fields of artificial intelligence and multi-agent systems.

Solution concepts for cooperative game theory answer two basic questions: (1) what coalitions will be formed; and (2) how will coalitions divide the profits they obtain through cooperative actions among the coalition members. The two most widely-known solution concepts are the *core* [3] and the *Shapley value* [11]. Although both concepts assume that a coalition of all agents in the system (called the *grand coalition*) is optimal and formed, they approach the problem of dividing the profits from cooperation from two completely different perspectives. The focus with the core perspective is on stability of the coalition. Specifically, each agent must be paid enough so as not to have an incentive to deviate from the grand coalition either individually or together with other agents as a group. In contrast, the focus with the Shapley value perspective is on fairness. An attempt is made to divide the profits from cooperation in accordance with the contributions of the individual agents towards the success of the cooperative effort. The importance of the Shapley value stems from the fact that it is the only solution concept that meets a set of certain intuitive and desirable properties related to fairness.

Nash presented the agencies method for modeling cooperative games along with a non-cooperative procedure for accepting the agency of another player and evaluated the evolution of cooperation among three players by using computer simulation [7]. Then, on the basis of this work, Nash *et al.* [8] conducted a laboratory experiment on finitely repeated three-person coalition formation games. They showed that the proposed agencies method effectively promotes player cooperation and fair outcomes: full efficiency was almost always reached, and the differences in the divisions of payoffs across rounds were much less extreme than one might expect from analysis of a non-cooperative game.

A laboratory experiment is usually the most effective approach to understanding human behavior and human decision making. However, conducting a laboratory experiment is often difficult since a well-organized laboratory is required, and hiring people is costly. In the study reported here, we used crowdsourcing to collect data on player decision making in a cooperative game instead of conducting a laboratory experiment. Then we used machine learning to predict player decision making. Crowdsourcing services such as Amazon Mechanical Turk are one of the most promising services recently introduced to the Web. Crowdsourcing is based on the idea of the *wisdom of crowds* and is used to solve a user-presented problem by combining the forces efforts of many people [1,5,6,10,12,14]. The main advantage of crowdsourcing is a large work force available at relatively low cost.

The rest of this paper is organized as follows. In Sect. 2, we define cooperative games and our problem setting. In Sect. 3, we describe the task we crowdsourced. In Sect. 4, we present the results of applying machine learning to the crowdsourced data. In Sect. 5, we present the results of using machine learning to predict the division of profits. We summarize the key points in Sect. 6.

2   Problem Setting

Cooperative game theory predicts payoff divisions among the players for a given *characteristic function* that takes a coalition as an input and returns the coalition's value as an output. Formally, in characteristic function games, the value of coalition $S \subseteq N$ is given by *characteristic function* $v : 2^N \rightarrow \mathbb{R}^+ \cup \{0\}$ with $v(\emptyset) = 0$, which assigns a non-negative real value to each set (coalition) of agents. These values represent the payoffs attainable by respective coalitions should they form.

In cooperative games, the first fundamental question to answer is what coalitions will form. This naturally depends on the values of the characteristic function. We assume that it is never detrimental for two disjoint coalitions to form one, larger coalition. This property is called super-additivity. Formally, we say that the characteristic function is *super-additive* if, for any S_i and S_j, $S_i \cap S_j = \emptyset$,

$$v(S_i \cup S_j) \geq v(S_i) + v(S_j).$$

Once we know that the grand coalition forms, the second fundamental question to answer is how to divide the payoff of the grand coalition, $v(\{N\})$, among the agents. Such a division is called the *solution* of cooperative games and is denoted by a *payoff vector* $\vec{p} = (p_1, \ldots, p_n)$. A variety of solution concepts, each with its own properties and interpretations, have been described in the literature. The core is a prominent solution concept focused on coalition stability.

Definition 1 (Core).   *The core is the set of all payoff vectors $\vec{p}$ that satisfy the feasibility condition,*

$$\sum_{i \in N} p_i = v(\{N\})$$

and the non-blocking condition,

$$\forall C \subseteq N, \sum_{i \in C} p_i \geq v(C).$$

The feasibility condition simply states that the exact value of the grand coalition is distributed among the agents. The non-blocking condition is more complicated. If, for some set of agents S, the non-blocking condition does not hold, the payoff vector is not stable. This is because the agents in S have an incentive to collectively deviate from the grand coalition and divide $v(S) > \sum_{i \in S} p_i$ among themselves. If this is not the case, we have found a stable payoff vector that is acceptable for all coalitions in the game. We say that such a payoff vector is in the core. There can be many different vectors in the core of a cooperative game. However, the core can also be empty, as in the case of games 1 to 5 introduced below.

Next, we give the definition of the Shapley value, which was introduced by Shapley who argued that agents should be rewarded in accordance with their marginal contributions to various coalitions.

Table 1. Characteristic function of three-person cooperative games

Games	v(ABC)	v(AB)	v(AC)	v(BC)	v(A)	v(B)	v(C)
1	120	120	100	90	0	0	0
2	120	120	100	70	0	0	0
3	120	120	100	50	0	0	0
4	120	120	100	30	0	0	0
5	120	100	90	70	0	0	0
6	120	100	90	50	0	0	0
7	120	100	90	30	0	0	0
8	120	90	70	50	0	0	0
9	120	90	70	30	0	0	0
10	120	70	50	30	0	0	0

Table 2. Core, Shapley value, and actual average profit

Games	Core	Shapley value			Actual average profit		
		A	B	C	A	B	C
1	Empty	46.67	41.67	31.67	43.69	36.15	37.90
2	Empty	53.33	38.33	28.33	44.28	41.95	31.42
3	Empty	60.00	35.00	25.00	45.42	37.94	30.72
4	Empty	66.67	31.67	21.67	44.46	35.88	32.99
5	Empty	48.33	38.33	33.33	41.86	38.88	37.13
6	Non-empty	55.00	35.00	30.00	42.01	41.99	31.90
7	Non-empty	61.67	31.67	26.67	37.95	39.33	40.03
8	Non-empty	50.00	40.00	30.00	40.51	37.65	38.02
9	Non-empty	56.67	36.67	26.67	39.75	38.40	36.67
10	Non-empty	50.00	40.00	30.00	40.84	37.69	35.72

Definition 2 (Shapley value). *The Shapley value of an agent i denoted $SV(i)$, is defined by:*

$$SV(i) = \frac{1}{|N|} \sum_{S \subseteq N \setminus \{i\}} \frac{1}{\binom{|N|-1}{|S|}} [v(S \cup \{i\}) - v(S)].$$

The idea behind the Shapley value is that an agent should obtain a share in the grand coalition payoff that corresponds to the agent's average marginal contribution to all coalitions, taken over all possible ways to create the grand coalition by adding one agent after the other. The importance of the Shapley value stems from the fact that it is the only solution concept that meets four desirable properties: efficiency (the entire payoff is distributed among agents),

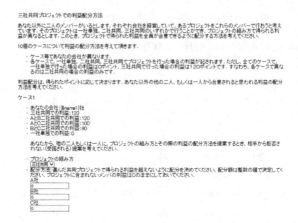

Fig. 1. Example display for crowdsourced tasks (in Japanese)

symmetry (agents with symmetric marginal contributions obtain the same payoff), null player (agents with no marginal contributions receive zero payoff), and
additivity (the division scheme is additive). The Shapley value has been applied
to a wide variety of undertakings such as dividing the cost of building a new
airport.

Nash *et al.* [8] conducted three-person cooperative games using characteristic
functions given in Table 1. In every period, the active player decides whether
or not to accept another player as his agent. The final agent decides how the
coalition value is to be divided. If more than one agent qualifies as the (final)
agent, a random draw is used to determine who will be the (final) agent. If
nobody accepts another agent, the procedure is repeated or a random stopping
rule terminates the round with zero payoffs or a two-person coalition payoff.
There were 10 independent groups in each game, and 40 periods were executed
for each game. The players received a payoff each period. The core, Shapley value,
and actual average profit obtained are shown Table 2. The payoff division, which
was decided among the coalition members, did not always equal the Shapley
value. They also figured out that the players often preferred an equal division.

3 Crowdsourcing for Collecting Player Decision-Making Data for Cooperative Games

To collect player decision-making data for cooperative games, we posted a task on
Lancers (http://www.lancers.jp/), which is a crowdsourcing platform in Japan.
We collected answers from 166 workers, and each of them was paid 30 Japanese
yen (0.42 AU dollars). We assume that a person's decisions depend on the person's role, so we assigned each worker a role to play when performing the task:
agent A, agent B, agent C, or a third party.

In this task, each worker was asked to play the ten characteristic function
games shown in Table 1. Each game started with random assignment of the

Table 3. Average coalition selection ratios (166 workers)

Games	ABC	AB	AC	BC	A/B/C
1	0.42	0.46	0.11	0.01	0.00
2	0.34	0.55	0.10	0.01	0.00
3	0.32	0.47	0.19	0.02	0.01
4	0.30	0.52	0.17	0.01	0.00
5	0.46	0.37	0.14	0.02	0.01
6	0.51	0.35	0.13	0.01	0.01
7	0.48	0.37	0.13	0.01	0.01
8	0.67	0.24	0.05	0.02	0.01
9	0.61	0.31	0.05	0.01	0.01
10	0.90	0.05	0.01	0.03	0.01

Table 4. Average profit division for each agent

Games	ABC			AB		AC		BC	
	A	B	C	A	B	A	C	B	C
1	42.93	40.26	37.1	60.41	57.75	50.1	38.25	45.00	45.00
2	44.58	39.18	31.67	60.60	57.98	49.06	49.06	35.00	35.00
3	46.19	38.75	29.96	62.13	56.03	59.84	39.13	40.00	10.00
4	48.90	39.94	30.12	63.22	55.38	56.38	39.14	15.00	15.00
5	42.22	38.21	33.83	53.48	48.78	47.92	42.92	31.67	25.00
6	45.33	39.81	32.35	53.50	47.12	50.24	37.86	25.00	25.00
7	49.38	36.82	31.25	53.19	47.71	51.90	37.14	20.00	10.00
8	43.81	39.41	35.16	46.38	44.63	45.46	33.33	22.33	19.00
9	46.17	38.58	32.41	48.27	42.60	34.38	26.88	15.00	15.00
10	43.95	39.30	35.37	46.56	46.07	25.00	25.00	18.22	11.67

worker's role (agent A, B, or C or third party). A characteristic function was then displayed, and worker was then asked to select a coalition to join and to propose a division of the selected coalition's profit that would be acceptable to the other agents in the coalition if he/she was agent A, B, or C or that would be acceptable to the agents in the coalition if he/she was a third party. An example display for a game (in Japanese) is shown in Fig. 1.

Table 3 shows the average coalition selection ratio. In games 1 to 4, the value of grand coalition ABC was equal to that of the AB coalition. Thus, the ratio for AB exceeded the ratio for ABC. On the other hand, in games from 5 to 10, the ratio for ABC exceeded the ratio for AB. In fact, 90% the workers selected the grand coalition in game 10.

Table 5. Predicted selected coalitions

Games	$v(ABC)$	$v(AB)$	$v(AC)$	$v(BC)$	$v(A)/v(B)/v(C)$
1	0.42	0.455	0.14	0.00	0.00
2	0.36	0.53	0.11	0.02	0.00
3	0.32	0.47	0.17	0.03	0.00
4	0.29	0.53	0.16	0.01	0.00
5	0.46	0.36	0.15	0.03	0.00
6	0.51	0.40	0.06	0.02	0.00
7	0.51	0.34	0.13	0.02	0.00
8	0.70	0.20	0.07	0.02	0.00
9	0.61	0.33	0.02	0.02	0.02
10	0.91	0.02	0.02	0.07	0.00

Table 6. Predicted profit division for grand coalition

Games	A	B	C
1	44.88	43.36	31.76
2	47.19	43.96	28.85
3	50.73	43.78	25.49
4	51.64	43.85	24.52
5	46.61	43.40	29.99
6	48.86	43.87	27.27
7	54.03	40.50	25.47
8	46.73	43.89	29.38
9	50.76	43.35	25.89
10	47.26	42.95	29.79

Table 4 shows the average profit division. The workers preferred an equal division. For example, among the total 1660 instances (166 workers, 10 games), grand coalitions were selected for 831 instances. Among those 831 instances, equal division was selected 400 times (48.1%). Among the remaining 431 instances, a proportional division was selected 323 times (74.9%). For the two-player coalitions (AB, AC, and BC), 86% of the profit divisions were either equal or proportional.

Looking at the results of the laboratory experiment conducted by Nash *et al.* shown in Table 2, we do not see huge differences between our crowdsourcing data and their data.

Table 7. Characteristic functions used to evaluate ability of our machine learning models to predict division of profits

Games	$v(ABC)$	$v(AB)$	$v(AC)$	$v(BC)$	$v(A)$	$v(B)$	$v(C)$
$N1$	200	150	100	70	0	0	0
$N2$	120	100	70	50	0	0	0
$N3$	120	90	50	30	0	0	0

Table 8. Predicted selected coalitions for three different characteristic functions

Games	$v(ABC)$	$v(AB)$	$v(AC)$	$v(BC)$	$v(A)/v(B)/v(C)$
$N1$	0.93	0.00	0.00	0.00	0.00
$N2$	0.64	0.27	0.00	0.00	0.00
$N3$	0.88	0.00	0.00	0.00	0.00

Table 9. Predicted profit division for grand coalition for different characteristic functions

Games	A	B	C
$N1$	66.88	85.22	47.90
$N2$	42.15	52.11	25.74
$N3$	35.37	57.32	27.30

4 Use of Machine Learning to Analyze Player Decision Making in Cooperative Games

Machine learning has been successfully applied to a variety of problems. Among the various machine learning models, deep neural networks have recently been gaining attention from game theory researchers because they can handle complex interactions among agents in games. Hartford *et al.* [4] proposed using a deep neural network to model player strategic behavior in non-cooperative games. Dütting *et al.* [2] proposed using deep neural network models for designing incentive-compatible optimal auctions.

We developed and used two deep neural networks to model complex interactions among agents in cooperative games. One model was used to predict the choice of a coalition given the value of the characteristic function. The other was used to predict the division of the reward among the agents given the value of the characteristic function. We prepared different versions of the second model to predict the reward division for different coalitions because the agents who share the reward differ between coalitions. Both models have four fully connected hidden layers, each of which has 128 units with ReLU activation functions.

In this experiment, we focused on three player games with zero reward for single coalitions. Therefore, the coalition prediction model has five output units:

Table 10. Predicted profit division for different characteristic functions

Game	Coalition	Ratio	Profit for A	Profit for B	Profit for C
N1	ABC	0.53	83.80	67.13	49.07
	AB	0.30	76.99	73.11	
	AC	0.10	50.00		50.00
	BC	0.03		35.00	35.00
	$A\backslash B\backslash C$	0.03			
N2	ABC	0.57	50.67	40.00	29.33
	AB	0.33	51.25	48.75	
	BC	0.10		27.50	22.50
N3	ABC	0.60	47.94	41.88	30.29
	AB	0.30	48.57	41.43	
	AC	0.03	25.00		25.00
	BC	0.03		20.00	10.00
	$A\backslash B\backslash C$	1.00			

one for the grand coalition, three for two-player coalitions, and one otherwise. The division prediction model has output units corresponding to the agents in the coalition. In both models, the output is normalized using a softmax function. The output of the coalition prediction model represents the probabilities of choosing the various possible coalitions, and the output of the division prediction model represents the division ratio for each agent. As the loss function for coalition prediction, we used categorical cross entropy because the task is multi-class classification. We used Kullback Leibler divergence as the loss function for division prediction because it can measure the difference between predicted and actual divisions. We implemented our models using the Keras framework, and trained the models using the crowdsourced data.

Table 5 shows the predicted selected coalitions, and Table 6 shows the predicted profit division for the grand coalition. We obtained the predictions similar to the data of the crowdsourcing workers.

5 Use of Machine Learning to Predict Division of Profits in Cooperative Games

We evaluated the ability of our machine learning models to predict the division of profits using three characteristic function games that differed from the ten characteristic function games in Table 1. They are shown in Table 7. Table 8 shows the predicted selected coalitions, and Table 9 show the predicted profit division for the grand coalition. The prediction for game $N1$ was 93% since it differs the most different from the ten original games, making it easy to fall into local optimization.

We asked 30 different crowdsourcing workers to play the three new characteristic function games shown in Table 7. We assigned them the role of third party and asked them to select a coalition and to propose a division of the profit of the coalition selected. As shown in Table 10, the division was predicted more accurately for games $N2$ and $N3$ than for game $N1$. Again, the workers preferred an equal division.

6 Conclusions

We have proposed using crowdsourcing to collect a large volume of human decision-making data for use in predicting player behavior in cooperative games. We also proposed using machine learning models to predict coalition formation and reward division for given values of a characteristic function. The proposed models were trained using data collected using a crowdsourcing service. The results with our machine learning models were similar to those of laboratory experiments.

Acknowledgement. This work was partially supported by JSPS KAKENHI Grants JP17KK0008, 18H03301, and JP18H03337, by the Kayamori Foundation of Informational Science Advancement and by the Telecommunications Advancement Foundation.

References

1. Duan, L., Oyama, S., Sato, H., Kurihara, M.: Separate or joint? Estimation of multiple labels from crowdsourced annotations. Expert Syst. Appl. **41**(13), 5723–5732 (2014)
2. Dütting, P., Feng, Z., Narasimhan, H., Parkes, D., Ravindranath, S.S.: Optimal auctions through deep learning. In: Proceedings of the 36th International Conference on Machine Learning (ICML 2019), pp. 1706–1715 (2019)
3. Gillies, D.B.: Solutions to general non-zero-sum games. In: Contributions to the Theory of Games, vol. IV, pp. 47–86. Princeton University Press (1959)
4. Hartford, J.S., Wright, J.R., Leyton-Brown, K.: Deep learning for predicting human strategic behavior. In: Advances in Neural Information Processing Systems 29 (NIPS 2016), pp. 2424–2432. Curran Associates, Inc. (2016)
5. Ho, C.J., Vaughan, J.W.: Online task assignment in crowdsourcing markets. In: Proceedings of the 26th AAAI Conference on Artificial Intelligence (AAAI 2012) (2012)
6. Law, E., Ahn, L.V.: Human Computation. Morgan & Claypool Publishers, San Rafael (2011)
7. Nash, J.F.: The agencies method for modeling coalitions and cooperation in games. Int. Game Theory Rev. **10**(4), 539–564 (2008)
8. Nash, J.F., Nagel, R., Ockenfels, A., Selten, R.: The agencies method for coalition formation in experimental games. Proc. Natl. Acad. Sci. U.S.A. (PNAS) **109**(50), 20358–20363 (2012)
9. Nisan, N., Roughgarden, T., Tardos, E., Vazirani, V.V.: Algorithmic Game Theory. Cambridge University Press, New York (2007)

10. Sakurai, Y., Kawahara, J., Oyama, S.: Aggregating crowd opinions using shapley value regression. In: Kaenampornpan, M., Malaka, R., Nguyen, D.D., Schwind, N. (eds.) MIWAI 2018. LNCS (LNAI), vol. 11248, pp. 151–160. Springer, Cham (2018). https://doi.org/10.1007/978-3-030-03014-8_13
11. Shapley, L.: A value for n-person games. In: Classics in Game Theory, pp. 69–79. Princeton University Press (1997)
12. Shaw, A.D., Horton, J.J., Chen, D.L.: Designing incentives for inexpert human raters. In: Proceedings of the ACM 2011 Conference on Computer Supported Cooperative Work (CSCW 2011), pp. 275–284 (2011)
13. Shoham, Y., Leyton-Brown, K.: Multiagent Systems: Algorithmic, Game-Theoretic, and Logical Foundations. Cambridge University Press, Cambridge (2009)
14. Snow, R., O'Connor, B., Jurafsky, D., Ng, A.Y.: Cheap and fast - but is it good? Evaluating non-expert annotations for natural language tasks. In: Proceedings of the Conference on Empirical Methods in Natural Language Processing (EMNLP 2008), pp. 254–263 (2008)
15. Wooldridge, M.: An Introduction to MultiAgent Systems. Wiley Publishing, Hoboken (2009)

Knowledge Acquisition, Representation, Reasoning

Exploring Unknown Universes in Probabilistic Relational Models

Tanya Braun[(✉)] and Ralf Möller

University of Lübeck, Lübeck, Germany
{braun,moeller}@ifis.uni-luebeck.de

Abstract. Large probabilistic models are often shaped by a pool of known individuals (a universe) and relations between them. Lifted inference algorithms handle sets of known individuals for tractable inference. Universes may not always be known, though, or may only described by assumptions such as "small universes are more likely". Without a universe, inference is no longer possible for lifted algorithms, losing their advantage of tractable inference. The aim of this paper is to define a semantics for models with unknown universes decoupled from a specific constraint language to enable lifted and thereby, tractable inference.

Keywords: Probabilistic relational models · Probabilistic inference · Lifting · Unknown universe

1 Introduction

At the heart of many machine learning algorithms lie large probabilistic models that use random variables (randvars) to describe behaviour or structure hidden in data. After a surge in effective machine learning algorithms, efficient algorithms for inference come into focus to make use of the models learned or to optimise machine learning algorithms further [12]. Often, a model is shaped by a pool of known individuals (constants), i.e., a known universe, and relations between them. Handling sets of individuals enables tractable inference [14].

Lifting efficiently handles sets of individuals by working with representatives of individuals behaving identically and only looking at specific individuals if necessary. If modelling, e.g., a possible epidemic depending on how many people are sick, all people being sick behave identically towards an epidemic. In parametric factors (parfactors), randvars parameterised with logical variables (logvars) compactly represent sets of randvars [15]. Instead of specifying a factor for each person about how the person being sick affects an epidemic, one parfactor works as a template for all people. Markov logic networks use first-order logic formulas for compact encoding [16]. A known universe means that logvars in parfactors or Markov logic networks have a domain and possibly a constraint restricting domains to certain constants for specific parfactors or formulas. Lifted inference algorithms such as (i) lifted variable elimination (LVE) [15,18], (ii) the lifted junction tree algorithm [3], (iii) first-order knowledge compilation [19],

© Springer Nature Switzerland AG 2019
J. Liu and J. Bailey (Eds.): AI 2019, LNAI 11919, pp. 91–103, 2019.
https://doi.org/10.1007/978-3-030-35288-2_8

(iv) probabilistic theorem proving [10], or (v) lifted belief propagation [2], use domains or constraints to determine the number of individuals represented to be able to perform efficient inference.

The question is what to do if the universe is unknown, which makes logvar domains unspecified and constraints empty or not applicable. In the example about an epidemic, the people who are possibly sick are not known. The question is not entirely new and an interesting one for diverse research areas: Ceylan et al. define a semantics for open-world probabilistic databases, keeping a fixed upper bound on domains [6]. Srivastava et al. specify first-order open-universe partially observable Markov decision processes to generate strategies based on sampling [17]. Milch et al. study unknown domains in Bayesian Logic, using sampling for approximate inference [13]. But, the effects of *unknown* finite universes on lifted inference and how to treat unknown universes in lifting have not been discussed.

Therefore, this paper explores lifted inference given models with unknown universes by defining semantics decoupled from a specific constraint language to again enable tractable inference with lifted algorithms. Decoupling the semantics from the constraint language allows for exploring unknown universes unrestricted by the expressiveness of a specific constraint language. The semantics is based on constraints over constraints and a set of possible domains, resulting in a variety of interesting new queries that allow for exploring unknown universes as well as checking assumptions about models. Additionally, we discuss specifying a distribution over domains, similar to [13]. Although the idea behind our approach applies to any formalism and lifted algorithm, we consider parfactors together with LVE since LVE has also been decoupled from the constraint language [18].

The remainder of this paper starts with providing notations and recapping LVE. Then, we discuss constraints and domains from a generative viewpoint and define semantics. Finally, we look at query answering for such models.

2 Preliminaries

This section specifies notations and recaps LVE. A running example models the interplay of an epidemic and people being sick, travelling, and being treated. Travels spread a disease, making an epidemic more likely. Treatments combat a disease, making an epidemic less likely. The example shows a scenario where one is interested in transferring a model to varying domains.

2.1 Parameterised Models

Parameterised models are the enclosing formalism for parfactors. A parfactor describes a function, mapping argument values to real values (potentials). Parameterised randvars (PRVs) constitute arguments, compactly encoding patterns, i.e., the function is identical for all groundings. Definitions are based on [18].

Definition 1. *Let* **R** *be a set of randvar names,* **L** *a set of logvar names,* Φ *a set of factor names, and* **D** *a set of constants (universe). All sets are finite. Each* *logvar L has a domain $\mathcal{D}(L) \subseteq \mathbf{D}$. A constraint is a tuple $(\mathcal{X}, C_{\mathbf{X}})$ of a sequence of logvars $\mathcal{X} = (X_1, \ldots, X_n)$ and a set $C_{\mathcal{X}} \subseteq \times_{i=1}^{n} \mathcal{D}(X_i)$. The symbol $\top$ for C marks that no restrictions apply, i.e., $C_{\mathcal{X}} = \times_{i=1}^{n} \mathcal{D}(X_i)$.*

A PRV $R(L_1, \ldots, L_n), n \geq 0$ consists of a randvar $R \in \mathbf{R}$ possibly combined with logvars $L_1, \ldots, L_n \in \mathbf{L}$. If $n = 0$, the PRV is parameterless and constitutes a propositional randvar. The term $\mathcal{R}(A)$ denotes the possible values (range) of a PRV A. An event $A = a$ denotes the occurrence of PRV A with range value $a \in \mathcal{R}(A)$. We denote a parfactor g by $\phi(\mathcal{A})_{|C}$ with $\mathcal{A} = (A_1, \ldots, A_n)$ a sequence of PRVs, $\phi : \times_{i=1}^{n} \mathcal{R}(A_i) \mapsto \mathbb{R}^+$ a function with name $\phi \in \Phi$, and C a constraint on the logvars of $\mathcal{A}$. A PRV A or logvar L under constraint C is given by $A_{|C}$ or $L_{|C}$, respectively. We may omit $|\top$ in $A_{|\top}$, $L_{|\top}$, or $\phi(\mathcal{A})_{|\top}$. A set of parfactors forms a model $G := \{g_i\}_{i=1}^{n}$.

The term $lv(P)$ refers to the logvars in P, which may be a PRV, a constraint, a parfactor, or a model. The term $gr(P)$ denotes the set of all instances of P w.r.t. given constraints. An instance is an instantiation (grounding) of P, substituting the logvars in P with a set of constants from given constraints. If P is a constraint, $gr(P)$ refers to the second component $C_{\mathbf{X}}$. The universe is given by $\mathbf{D}$, and the constraints encode which parfactors apply to which constants.

Let us specify a model G_{ex} for the epidemic example. The sets of names are given by $\mathbf{R} = \{Epid, Sick, Travel, Treat\}$, $\mathbf{L} = \{X, T\}$, and $\Phi = \{\phi_0, \phi_1, \phi_2\}$. The set of constants $\mathbf{D}$ contains constants $alice, bob, eve$ and $serum_1, serum_2$, which form the domains $\mathcal{D}(X) = \{alice, bob, eve\}$ and $\mathcal{D}(T) = \{serum_1, serum_2\}$. We build the boolean PRVs $Epid, Sick(X), Travel(X), Treat(X, T)$ from $\mathbf{R}$ and $\mathbf{L}$. $Epid$ holds if an epidemic occurs. $Sick(X)$ holds if a person X is sick, $Travel(X)$ holds if X travels, and $Treat(X, T)$ holds if X is treated with T. With a constraint $C = (X, \{eve, bob\})$, $gr(Sick(X)_{|C}) = \{Sick(eve), Sick(bob)\}$. $gr(Sick(X)_{|\top})$ contains $Sick(alice)$ as well. The model is given by $G_{ex} = \{g_i\}_{i=0}^{2}$,

$$g_0 = \phi_0(Epid), \tag{1}$$

$$g_1 = \phi_1(Epid, Sick(X), Travel(X))_{|C_1}, C_1 = \top = \mathcal{D}(X), \tag{2}$$

$$g_2 = \phi_2(Epid, Sick(X), Treat(X, T))_{|C_2}, C_2 = \top = \mathcal{D}(X) \times \mathcal{D}(T). \tag{3}$$

Parfactors g_1 and g_2 have eight input-output pairs, g_0 has two (omitted here). Constraints are $\top$, meaning, the ϕ's apply to all possible groundings of the argument PRVs, e.g., $gr(g_1)$ contains three factors, one for $alice, bob, eve$ each, with identical ϕ_1. Figure 1 depicts G_{ex} as a graph with four variable nodes for the PRVs and three factor nodes for the parfactors with edges to arguments.

Fig. 1. Parfactor graph for G_{ex}

The *semantics* of a model G is given by grounding and building a full joint distribution P_G. Query answering refers to computing probability distributions, which boils down to computing marginals on P_G. A formal definition follows.

Definition 2. *With Z as normalising constant, a model G represents the full joint distribution $P_G = \frac{1}{Z} \prod_{f \in gr(G)} f$ (distribution semantics). The term $P(\mathbf{Q}|\mathbf{E})$ denotes a query in G with $\mathbf{Q}$ a set of grounded PRVs and $\mathbf{E}$ a set of events.*

An example query for G_{ex} is $P(Epid|Sick(eve) = true)$, asking for the conditional distribution of $Epid$ given the event $Sick(eve) = true$. Lifted query answering algorithms like LVE seek to avoid grounding and building P_G.

2.2 Lifted Variable Elimination: An Example

LVE answers queries of the form in Definition 2 by eliminating all PRVs that do not occur in a query. We use LVE as a means to illustrate how known universes are required for calculations. The exact workings of LVE are not necessary for understanding the contributions of this paper.

When eliminating a PRV, LVE in essence computes variable elimination for a representative and exponentiates the result for indistinguishable instances (lifted summing out). While the main idea is rather straightforward, a correct implementation is more involved. See [18] for details on LVE for models of Definition 1.

To illustrate the effects of a universe, consider a query $P(Epid)$ in model G_{ex}. LVE eliminates the PRVs $Treat(X,T)$, $Travel(X)$, and $Sick(X)$. To eliminate $Treat(X,T)$ from parfactor $g_2 = \phi_2(Epid, Sick(X), Treat(X,T))_{|\top}$, LVE looks at the constraint of g_2, which is $\top$, i.e., $\mathcal{D}(X) \times \mathcal{D}(T)$. Eliminating $Treat(X,T)$ leaves X as the only logvar in g_2. As such, there must exist the same number of T constants given each X constant for lifted summing out to apply. For each X, there exist <u>two</u> T constants, i.e., $serum_1$ and $serum_2$. Thus, LVE is able to eliminate $Treat(X,T)$ by summing out $Treat(X,T)$ from ϕ_2 using propositional variable elimination, leading to a parfactor $g_2' = \phi_2'(Epid, Sick(X))_{|\top}$, and then taking each potential in g_2' to the power of 2, leading to g_2''. The $\top$ constraint in g_2'' only refers to the domain of X. (On the propositional level, two $Treat$ randvars are eliminated from two ϕ_2 factors for each X constant and then multiplied.)

Next, LVE eliminates $Travel(X)$ from parfactor g_1, which leads to a parfactor $g_1' = \phi_1'(Epid, Sick(X))_{|\top}$, where each potential is taken to the power of 1 as eliminating $Travel(X)$ does not eliminate a logvar (afterwards X is still part of g_1'). For eliminating $Sick(X)$, LVE multiplies g_1' and g_2'' into $g_{12} = \phi_{12}(Epid, Sick(X))_{|\top}$, sums out $Sick(X)$ from g_{12} as in propositional variable elimination. Summing out $Sick(X)$ eliminates X as well, which requires the potentials after summing out to be taken to the power of 3 for the <u>three</u> constants $alice, bob, eve$ in the domain of X. The result is then a parfactor with $Epid$ as argument, which LVE multiplies with g_0. The result is a parfactor that contains the queried probability distribution after normalisation.

To determine exponents for sum-out operations, constraints based on a universe are necessary. Other lifted algorithms need a universe similar to LVE. E.g., first-order knowledge compilation builds a tree-like helper structure for efficient answering of multiple queries, which contains nodes that represent isomorphic subtrees and requires the number of subtrees represented during calculations [19]. The lifted junction tree algorithm builds another form of helper structure for efficiently answering multiple queries using LVE as a subroutine [3].

3   Models with Unknown Universes

This section focusses on models with unknown universes. Constraints over constraints describe possible universes, decoupled from a specific constraint language. Based on domain and constraint descriptions, we define semantics.

3.1   Template Models

Parameterised models contain constraints that restrict logvars in a parfactor to constants from a known universe. Without a known universe, the set of constants $\mathbf{D}$ becomes empty. As a consequence, logvar domains are empty as the domains are defined as subsets of $\mathbf{D}$. In turn, constraints are no longer defined since they are combinations of subsets of domains. Last, semantics lose its meaning as it involves grounding a model, which is not possible without constraints.

We assume, though, that the model itself accurately describes relations. Thus, a parameterised model without $\mathbf{D}$ and empty constraints becomes a template model that specifies local distributions for unknown instances of PRVs.

Definition 3. *A* **template model** *$\mathcal{G}$ is a set of parfactors $\{\tilde{g}_i\}_{i=1}^n$, in which each $\tilde{g}_i = \phi_i(\mathcal{A}_i)_{|C}$ has an* **empty** *constraint $C = (\mathcal{X}, C_{\mathcal{X}})$ with $C_{\mathcal{X}} = \bot$.*

Replacing the constraint in g_1 with $((X), \bot)$ and in g_2 with $((X,T), \bot)$ in G_{ex}, template model $\mathcal{G}_{ex} = \{\tilde{g}_i\}_{i=0}^2$ arises. $\mathcal{G}_{ex}$ no longer refers to a specific universe, allowing for using varying numbers of people of treatments.

3.2   Worlds of Constraints

With an unknown universe, we implicitly specify constraints through a set of rules that generate tuples for constraints given a specific domain at a later point. Constraints over constraints enables us to describe how universes arise independent of specific constants. To model constraints, one could use, e.g., answer set programming [5], probabilistic Datalog [9], ProbLog [7], or Bayesian Logic [13], with the latter three leading to probabilities associated with constraints.

Definition 4. *Given a template model $\mathcal{G}$ and a domain set D for $lv(\mathcal{G})$, a* **constraint program** *$\mathcal{C}$ returns a ordered set of constraint sets $\mathbf{C} = \{\{C_{j,i}\}_{i=1}^n\}_{j=1}^m$, i.e., $\mathcal{C}$ generates a constraint for each parfactor in $\mathcal{G}$. We call each generated constraint set $\{C_{j,i}\}_{i=1}^n$ a* **constraint world** *CW_j. If $\mathcal{C}$ assigns a probability distribution over all CW_j, $\mathcal{C}$ returns an ordered set of tuples*

$\mathbf{C} = \{(\{C_{j,i}\}_{i=1}^n, p_j)\}_{j=1}^m$ of constraint sets and corresponding probabilities, forming a distribution over constraint worlds. Instantiating $\mathcal{G}$ with CW_j, i.e., replacing empty constraints with the constraints in CW_j, yields a parameterised model $\mathcal{G}_{|CW_j}$.

Let us look at possible constraint programs to illustrate how constraint worlds arise. The shorthand $\top$ already defines a constraint program $\mathcal{C}^\top$ that generates tuples by building Cartesian products given domains. $\mathcal{C}^\top$ generates exactly one constraint world. Given $\mathcal{G}_{ex}$, $\mathcal{C}^\top$ returns $\{\{C_1, C_2\}\}$ if $\mathcal{D}$ contains the domains $\mathcal{D}(X) = \{alice, bob, eve\}$ and $\mathcal{D}(T) = \{serum_1, serum_2\}$. For a more complex example, assume that there are three treatments t_1, t_2, t_3 with only two treatments applicable at a time, i.e., $\mathcal{D}(T) = \{t_1, t_2, t_3\}$ and $\mathcal{D}(X)$ unknown. Each combination has a different probability, e.g., 0.7 for (t_1, t_2), 0.2 for (t_2, t_3), and 0.1 for (t_1, t_3). A probabilistic Datalog program captures this setup as follows:

```
element_of_C2(X,Y1)  :- linked(X,Y1,Y2).
element_of_C2(X,Y2)  :- linked(X,Y1,Y2).
linked(X,Y1,Y2) :- instance_of_X(X) & pair(Y1,Y2).
0.7 pair(t1,t2).   0.2 pair(t2,t3).   0.1 pair(t1,t3).
```

The first three lines denote rules according to which one can generate (X, T)-tuples. The last line denotes probabilistic facts that are disjoint, with probabilities adding up to 1, to model the combination of treatments. If given a domain such $\{alice, bob, eve\}$ for X, one can add corresponding facts to the program:

```
instance_of_X(alice).  instance_of_X(bob).  instance_of_X(eve).
```

Asking the queries ?- `element_of_C2(X,Y)` and ?- `instance_of_X(X)` generates tuples for the constraints in $\mathcal{G}_{ex}$. Using 0.7 `pair(t1, t2)`, the program returns the following facts, which contain tuples for the constraints in $\mathcal{G}_{ex}$:

```
instance_of_X(alice).   instance_of_X(bob).   instance_of_X(eve).
0.7 element_of_C2(alice,t1).   0.7 element_of_C2(alice,t2).
0.7 element_of_C2(bob,t1).   0.7 element_of_C2(bob,t2).
0.7 element_of_C2(eve,t1).   0.7 element_of_C2(eve,t2).
```

The Datalog program as constraint program $\mathcal{C}^{DL}$ returns three constraint worlds $\{(\{C_{j,i}\}_{i=1}^2, p_j\}_{j=1}^3$ with $p_1 = 0.7$, $p_2 = 0.2$, and $p_3 = 0.1$ and constraints

$$C_{1,1} = C_{2,1} = C_{3,1} = ((X), \{(alice), (bob), (eve)\})$$
$$C_{1,2} = ((X,T), \{(alice, t1), (alice, t2), (bob, t1), (bob, t2), (eve, t1), (eve, t2)\})$$
$$C_{2,2} = ((X,T), \{(alice, t2), (alice, t3), (bob, t2), (bob, t3), (eve, t2), (eve, t3)\})$$
$$C_{3,2} = ((X,T), \{(alice, t1), (alice, t3), (bob, t1), (bob, t3), (eve, t1), (eve, t3)\})$$

A set of constraint worlds yields a set of parameterised models, which inherits the distribution over the set of constraint worlds if existing.

Proposition 1. *Let a constraint program C generate a set of constraint worlds $\{(CW_j, p_j)\}_{j=1}^m$. Instantiating a template model G with each constraint world $CW_j \in \{(CW_j, p_j)\}_{j=1}^m$ leads to a distribution over the ordered set of parameterised models $\{(G_{|CW_j}, p_j)\}_{j=1}^m$. If C does not generate probabilities, the implicit distribution is a uniform distribution with $\forall j : p_j = \frac{1}{m}$.*

Proposition 1 relies on CW being valid for G, meaning, C generates fitting constraints for all parfactors. Regarding our example, C^{DL} generates three constraint worlds, each with two constraints, to instantiate G_{ex}. Using rules in a constraint program is a form of meta-level logic programming, which allows for formulating constraints on constraints without a specific domain.

Next, we consider possible domains and distributions over domains.

3.3 Worlds of Domains

Constraint programs still need domains or constants to generate constraint worlds. In unknown universes, these constants are not available. In a naive way, one could generate all possible domains, from one constant for each logvar to infinite domains, leading to infeasibly many possible domains. Given knowledge about the setting in which one wants to reason (like in the example above about treatments t_1, t_2, t_3), one may list all possible domains. Assumptions may further limit the number of worlds, e.g.: (i) Logvars require discrete domains of at least one element. (ii) Small worlds (domains) are usually more likely than large ones. (iii) Only "orders" of domain sizes are relevant, not a set of domain sizes with an increment of 1 between them. Depending on the concrete use case, setting up a discrete distribution over domain sizes might be valuable, with the distribution depending on assumptions valid for the use case.

Definition 5. *Given a template model G, a **domain world** DW is a set of domains $\{\mathcal{D}(X)\}_{X \in lv(G)}$ for G. Given a set of domain worlds $\{DW_k\}_{k=1}^l$ and probabilities p_k for each DW_k s.t. $\forall k : p_k \in [0, 1]$ and $\sum_k p_k = 1$, then $\mathbf{D} = \{(DW_k, p_k)\}_{k=1}^l$ forms a distribution over domain worlds. Providing a constraint program C with DW_k yields a set of constraint worlds $\{CW_j\}_{j=1}^m$. Instantiating G with $\{CW_j\}_{j=1}^m$ yields a set of parameterised models $\{G_{|DW,CW_j}\}_{j=1}^m$.*

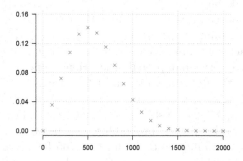

Fig. 2. Discrete distribution over domain sizes of a logvar

One may start with a set of guaranteed constants and add varying numbers of possible constants for domain worlds, inspired by the λ-completion of open-world probabilistic databases [6]. The probabilities allow for measuring how likely a particular instantiation is compared to others. Given a distribution, one can specify a threshold t to account only for domains with a probability larger t, which enables some filtering even before generating parameterised models for efficiency. Another way of restricting the number of worlds is to take domains that lie within the standard deviation from the mean or those whose probability make up around 95% of the distribution around its mean or maximum value.

Let us consider an example distribution for a single logvar, e.g., X, the only unknown logvar given $\mathcal{G}_{ex}$ and $\mathcal{C}^{DL}$. Figure 2 shows a beta-binomial distribution ($\alpha = 6$, $\beta = 15$) based on the assumptions above. Possible domain sizes d go from 0 to 2000 with a step size of 100 and probabilities for $[d - 100, d]$ for $d > 0$. A domain size of 0 has a probability of 0. The highest probability lies with a domain size of 500, after which probabilities decrease again. The probability of a domain size of 2000 is around $3.85 \cdot 10^{-7}$. Probability distributions between domain and constraint worlds are joined as follows.

Proposition 2. *Let $\{(DW_k, p_k)\}_{k=1}^{l}$ form a distribution over domain worlds DW_k. Providing a constraint program $\mathcal{C}$ with DW_k leads to a set of constraint worlds $\mathbf{C}_k = \{(\{C_{k,j,i}\}_{i=1}^{n}, p_k \cdot p_j)\}_{j=1}^{m}$ in which $p_j = \frac{1}{m}$ if $\mathcal{C}$ does not assign probabilities. If $\mathcal{C}$ assigns probabilities but only a set of domains $\{DW_k\}_{k=1}^{l}$ is given, $\{DW_k\}_{k=1}^{l}$ is extended to form a distribution by setting $\forall k : p_k = \frac{1}{l}$.*

Multiplying probabilities p_j and p_k relies on p_j and p_k being independent. The independence assumption is reasonable given the discourse so far as the domain world probability does not influence the generation of constraint worlds, which allows for multiplying the probabilities of domain world and constraint world. Otherwise, the product has to be replaced with an appropriate expression. Assigning a probability distribution over possible worlds follows Bayesian thinking, which considers all possible worlds. Restricting a model to one possible world (with probability 1) is a simplification, which our approach resolves.

Passing on a domain world to a constraint program $\mathcal{C}$ enables $\mathcal{C}$ to generate constraint worlds for a template model. Given $\mathcal{G}_{ex}$ and $\mathcal{C}^{DL}$, assume the distribution from Fig. 2 for X, denoted by $p_x(d)$ with d referring to the domain size of X. There are 20 domain worlds $\mathbf{D}^{ex} = \{(\{x_i\}_{i=1}^{d}, p_x(d))\}_{d=100, d+=100}^{2000}$ with probabilities $p_x(d)$ between $3.85 \cdot 10^{-7}$ and $1.42 \cdot 10^{-1}$. For each domain world, $\mathcal{C}^{DL}$ yields three constraint worlds $\{(\{C_{d,j,i}\}_{i=1}^{2}, p_x(d) \cdot p_j)\}_{j=1}^{3}$, i.e., overall 60 constraint worlds, each containing a constraint for both $\tilde{g}_1$ and $\tilde{g}_2$. Some of the 60 constraint worlds have very small probabilities. Hence, one could use a threshold of $t = 0.05$ to restrict the domain worlds in $\mathbf{D}^{ex}$ to use as inputs for $\mathcal{C}^{DL}$. Given the distribution of Fig. 2, t restricts the domain to sizes between 200 and 900, which would lead to $8 \cdot 3 = 24$ constraint worlds. One could cascade the filtering and drop constraint worlds if their probability goes below t as well (or choose a new t). Given $\mathbf{D}^{ex}$ as an input to $\mathcal{C}^{DL}$ and $t = 0.05$ for cascaded filtering, the number of constraint worlds goes down to 7, i.e., domain sizes 200 to 800 combined with `0.7 pair(t1,t2)`. The constraint worlds using `0.2 pair(t2,t3)` and 0.1 `pair(t1,t3)` have a probability below t. With domain and constraint worlds in place, we define a semantics for models with unknown universes.

3.4   Distribution-Based Semantics

To fully specify a model with an unknown universe, we require three components: (i) A *template model* $\mathcal{G}$ provides a structure and local distributions. (ii) A *constraint program* $\mathcal{C}$ generates constraint worlds. A template model can be instantiated with a constraint world, leading to a parameterised model as in Definiton 1, which follows distribution semantics. (iii) A *set of domain worlds* **D** specifies (a distribution over) possible domain worlds. Each domain world can be passed to the constraint program. The semantics are defined as follows.

Definition 6. *Let $\mathcal{G}$ be a template model, $\mathcal{C}$ a constraint program, and* **D** *domain worlds. A model with unknown universe is given by a triple $(\mathcal{G}, \mathcal{C}, \mathbf{D})$. The semantics is given by instantiating $\mathcal{G}$ with constraint worlds* **C** *for each $DW \in \mathbf{D}$. The result is a set of parameterised models* $\mathbf{G} = \{(G_{|CW}, p)\}_{CW \in \mathcal{C}(DW), DW \in \mathbf{D}}$.

Using the formalism of a constraint program, decoupled from a specific constraint language, allows for choosing a constraint language suitable for a specific setup. One could use Bayesian logic to specify a distribution over possible models [13]. Using parameterised models as a basis makes it straightforward to retain the capability for lifted inference, especially exact inference.

The section above discusses the constraint worlds coming from domain worlds, which in turn lead to parameterised models: With $\mathcal{G}_{ex}$, $\mathcal{C}^{DL}$, $\mathbf{D}^{ex}$, and cascading filtering with $t = 0.05$, the semantics yields eight constraint worlds $\mathbf{C}^{ex5} = \{(\{C_{d,j=1,i}\}_{i=1}^{2}, p_x(d) \cdot p_{j=1})\}_{d=200,d+=100}^{800}$, leading to parameterised models $\mathbf{G}_{ex} = \{(G_{ex|CW_{d,1}}, p_x(d) \cdot p_1)\}_{d=200,d+=100}^{800}$. Each $G \in \mathbf{G}_{ex}$ contains parfactors g_0, g_1, g_2 with signatures as in Eqs. (1) to (3) and identical mappings. Constraints C_1 and C_2 as well as associated probabilities differ between the models. For $d = 100$, the probability is $3.56 \cdot 10^{-2} \cdot 0.7$ and the constraints are

$$C_1 = ((X), \{(x_1), \dots, (x_{100})\}),$$
$$C_2 = ((X, T), \{(x_1, t_1), (x_1, t_2), \dots, (x_{100}, t_1), (x_{100}, t_2)\}).$$

A domain size of $d = 500$ leads to the most probable model. The last step on our mission of exploring unknown universes is query answering.

4   Query Answering in Unknown Universes

The semantics of a model with an unknown universe yields a set of parameterised models. In each parameterised model, query answering works as before, using LVE (or any other algorithm of one's liking) to answer queries, reaching a main goal of this paper, again enabling tractable inference.

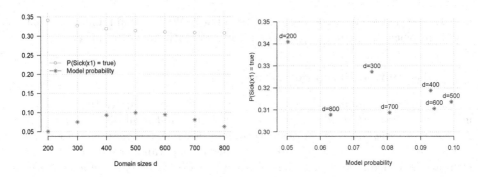

Fig. 3. Left: $P(Sick(x_1)) = true)$ and model probability for each parameterised model in $\mathbf{G}_{ex}$. Right: Model probability and $P(Sick(x_1)) = true)$ plotted for a Skyline query.

Theorem 1. *Given a template model $\mathcal{G}$, a constraint program $\mathcal{C}$ for $\mathcal{G}$, and a set of domain worlds $\mathbf{D}$ for $\mathcal{G}$, resulting in a set of parameterised models $\mathbf{G}$, query answering on each $G \in \mathbf{G}$ is polynomial w.r.t. domain-sizes given a domain-lifted inference algorithm, leading to a runtime complexity of $O(|\mathbf{G}| \cdot T_{lift})$ with T_{lift} referring to the runtime complexity of the inference algorithm used.*

Answering a query on a set of parameterised models $\mathbf{G}$ means that the answer is a set of probabilities or distributions. If $\mathbf{G}$ has a probability distribution associated, the set of answers has the same distribution associated.

Proposition 3. *Answering a query $P(\mathbf{Q}|\mathbf{E})$ on a set of parameterised models $\mathbf{G} = \{G_i\}_i$, with i referring to the different models stemming from the domain and constraint worlds, leads to a set of answers $\{P_{G_i}(\mathbf{Q}|\mathbf{E})\}_i$. If $\mathbf{G}$ has probabilities associated, i.e., $\mathbf{G} = \{(G_i, p_i)\}_i$, then the answers have probabilities associated, i.e., $\{(P_{G_i}(\mathbf{Q}|\mathbf{E}), p_i)\}_i$, forming a distribution over answers.*

That is a query leads to a probability distribution over probabilities or probability distributions as a direct consequence of the definitions and Propositions 1 and 2. Consider a query for a marginal distribution of $Sick(X)$ instantiated with x_1. Each of the parameterised models in $\mathbf{G}_{ex}$ provides an answer, i.e., a marginal distribution for $Sick(x_1)$. On the left, denoted by a circle, Fig. 3 shows the probabilities of $Sick(x_1) = true$ for each model with domain sizes on the x-axis. The stars denote the probability associated with each parameterised model. As mentioned before, the model with domain size $d = 500$ is most probable and returns a probability of 0.31 for $Sick(x_1) = true$. Model probabilities decrease to the left and right of 500. The queried probability declines with the domain size rising.

Emerging New Queries: As we have a set of parameterised models and, therefore, a set of results, new queries emerge. If asking for the probability of an event, e.g., $Sick(x_1) = true$, one may be interested in those models whose answers have highest probability (top-k query w.r.t. query probability). A top-3 query w.r.t. query probabilities in Fig. 3 returns the models with domain sizes 2 to 4 as they lead to the highest probabilities for $Sick(x_1) = true$. If events such as $Sick(x_1) = true$ have been observed, guaranteed constants are available and a top-k query supports identifying most probable domain sizes for other logvars. Given the associated probabilities, one may be interested in a top-k query w.r.t. model probabilities or in those models that have the highest combined probabilities of event and model (skyline query w.r.t. event and model probability). Figure 3 plots the model probabilities versus the query probabilities. The skyline consists of the points labeled $d = 200$, $d = 300$, $d = 400$, and $d = 500$, which form the outskirt of the points from the origin of the plane. Asking for distributions, the results over different models might exhibit shifts or clusters worth investigating. Another new avenue for queries regards checking assumptions about models, e.g., "Do similar domain sizes lead to similar query results?" or "Do query results behave as expected when domain sizes increase (decrease)?"

As shown, given the semantics of models with unknown universe and LVE as the reference algorithm, one can answer various queries. Handling unknown universes leads to more work as an algorithm performs query answering for multiple instances, which share certain aspects. So, while this paper focusses on the semantics, we briefly consider how one would implement it.

Arriving at an Implementation: As the model structure is identical for each constraint world and multiple queries probably have to be answered, LVE would perform some calculations multiple times. One could choose another algorithm to implement the semantics. E.g., the lifted junction tree algorithm or first-order knowledge compilation may provide a more suitable setting to answer multiple queries. Both algorithms build a helper structure based on the model. Given that the model structure is the same over different instantiations, helper structures can be reused, constraints adapted as in adaptive inference [1,4], and results of calculations reused to a certain extent [11]. Additionally, one would seek to specify the constraint program in a way that an algorithm can formulate queries about counts for the constraint program, which returns answers ideally without generating extensional constraints. Given top-k queries w.r.t. query probabilities, one would aim at adapting an implementation in the spirit of top-k queries on probabilistic databases as to not evaluate more models than necessary [8].

5   Conclusion

Lifted inference can be restored for models with unknown domains by creating descriptions of possible constraints and domains. Using those descriptions, one generates worlds to instantiate a template model. Instantiating a template model yields a set of parameterised models, in which distribution semantics hold again. With distribution semantics, lifted and thereby, tractable inference w.r.t. domains is possible again. Given a distribution over domain or constraint worlds, the number of worlds can be restricted to a feasible number. As the same template model is instantiated with different worlds, efficient query answering is possible, reusing helper structures or calculations. Thus, the proposed semantics seems to be practically useful. Additionally, new and interesting queries arise that allow for exploring or checking a model.

New inference tasks include automatic generation of instances guaranteed to exist in open universes or learning constraint rules in unknown universes. Detaching a model from a known universe brings us closer to understanding how transfer learning works: Transferring a model from one domain to a next opens up possibilities for assumptions changing w.r.t. indistinguishable individuals.

References

1. Acar, U.A., Ihler, A.T., Mettu, R.R., Sümer, Ö.: Adaptive inference on general graphical models. In: UAI-08 Proceedings of the 24th Conference on Uncertainty in Artificial Intelligence, pp. 1–8. AUAI Press (2008)
2. Ahmadi, B., Kersting, K., Mladenov, M., Natarajan, S.: Exploiting symmetries for scaling loopy belief propagation and relational training. Mach. Learn. **92**(1), 91–132 (2013)
3. Braun, T., Möller, R.: Preventing groundings and handling evidence in the lifted junction tree algorithm. In: Kern-Isberner, G., Fürnkranz, J., Thimm, M. (eds.) KI 2017. LNCS (LNAI), vol. 10505, pp. 85–98. Springer, Cham (2017). https://doi.org/10.1007/978-3-319-67190-1_7
4. Braun, T., Möller, R.: Adaptive inference on probabilistic relational models. In: Mitrovic, T., Xue, B., Li, X. (eds.) AI 2018. LNCS (LNAI), vol. 11320, pp. 487–500. Springer, Cham (2018). https://doi.org/10.1007/978-3-030-03991-2_44
5. Brewka, G., Eiter, T., Truszczynski, M.: Answer set programming at a glance. Commun. ACM **15**(12), 92–103 (2011)
6. Ceylan, İ.İ., Darwiche, A., Van den Broeck, G.: Open-world probabilistic databases. In: KR-16 Proceedings of the 15th International Conference on Principles of Knowledge Representation and Reasoning, pp. 339–348. AAAI Press (2016)
7. De Raedt, L., Kimmig, A., Toivonen, H.: ProbLog: a probabilistic prolog and its application in link discovery. In: IJCAI-07 Proceedings of 20th International Joint Conference on Artificial Intelligence, pp. 2062–2467. IJCAI Organization (2007)
8. Fagin, R.: Combining fuzzy information from multiple systems. J. Comput. Syst. Sci. **58**(1), 83–99 (1999)
9. Fuhr, N.: Probabilistic datalog - a logic for powerful retrieval methods. In: SIGIR-95 Proceedings of the 18th Annual International ACM SIGIR Conference on Research and Development in Information Retrieval, pp. 282–290. ACM (1995)
10. Gogate, V., Domingos, P.: Probabilistic theorem proving. In: UAI-11 Proceedings of the 27th Conference on Uncertainty in Artificial Intelligence, pp. 256–265. AUAI Press (2011)
11. Kazemi, S.M., Poole, D.: Knowledge compilation for lifted probabilistic inference: compiling to a low-level language. In: KR-16 Proceedings of the 15th International Conference on Principles of Knowledge Representation and Reasoning, pp. 561–564 (2016)
12. LeCun, Y.: Learning World Models: the Next Step Towards AI. Invited Talk at IJCAI-ECAI 2018 (2018). https://www.youtube.com/watch?v=U2mhZ9E8Fk8. Accessed 19 Nov 2018
13. Milch, B., Marthi, B., Russell, S., Sontag, D., Long, D.L., Kolobov, A.: BLOG: probabilistic models with unknown objects. In: IJCAI-05 Proceedings of the 19th International Joint Conference on Artificial Intelligence, pp. 1352–1359. IJCAI Organization (2005)

14. Niepert, M., Van den Broeck, G.: Tractability through exchangeability: a new perspective on efficient probabilistic inference. In: AAAI-14 Proceedings of the 28th AAAI Conference on Artificial Intelligence, pp. 2467–2475. AAAI Press (2014)
15. Poole, D.: First-order probabilistic inference. In: IJCAI-03 Proceedings of the 18th International Joint Conference on Artificial Intelligence, pp. 985–991. IJCAI Organization (2003)
16. Richardson, M., Domingos, P.: Markov logic networks. Mach. Learn. **62**(1–2), 107–136 (2006)
17. Srivastava, S., Russell, S., Ruan, P., Cheng, X.: First-order open-universe POMDPs. In: UAI-14 Proceedings of the 30th Conference on Uncertainty in Artificial Intelligence, pp. 742–751. AUAI Press (2014)
18. Taghipour, N., Fierens, D., Davis, J., Blockeel, H.: Lifted variable elimination: decoupling the operators from the constraint language. J. Artif. Intell. Res. **47**(1), 393–439 (2013)
19. Van den Broeck, G., Taghipour, N., Meert, W., Davis, J., De Raedt, L.: Lifted probabilistic inference by first-order knowledge compilation. In: IJCAI-11 Proceedings of the 22nd International Joint Conference on Artificial Intelligence, pp. 2178–2185. IJCAI Organization (2011)

Efficient Multiple Query Answering in Switched Probabilistic Relational Models

Marcel Gehrke$^{(\boxtimes)}$ ⓘ, Tanya Braun ⓘ, and Ralf Möller

Institute of Information Systems, University of Lübeck, Lübeck, Germany
{gehrke,braun,moeller}@ifis.uni-luebeck.de

Abstract. By accounting for context-specific independences, the size of a model can be drastically reduced, thereby making the underlying inference problem more manageable. Switched probabilistic relational models contain explicit context-specific independences. To efficiently answer multiple queries in switched probabilistic relational models, we combine the advantages of propositional gate models for context-specific independences and the lifted junction tree algorithm for answering multiple queries in probabilistic relational models. Specifically, this paper contributes (i) variable elimination in gate models, (ii) applying the lifting idea to gate models, defining switched probabilistic relational models, enabling lifted variable elimination in computations, and (iii) the switched lifted junction tree algorithm to answer multiple queries in such models efficiently. Empirical results show that using context-specific independence speeds up even lifted inference significantly.

Keywords: Lifting · Context-specific independence · Switched models

1 Introduction

Performing inference is an important task in artificial intelligence but unfortunately, inference in general is intractable [4]. To make the underlying problem more manageable, context-specific independences help [2]. Given context-specific independences in a model, inference may require fewer calculations if parts of the model become independent given a context. One approach for Bayesian networks is to look for patterns in conditional probability tables to identify context-specific independences [2]. In such an approach, the context-specific independences are implicitly encoded in the model, which can lead to huge conditional probability tables. Another approach is to explicitly model context-specific independences in a model, avoiding the blowup of tables if implicitly encoding the independences in the tables, and providing specialised inference algorithms [7]. In this paper, we study the problem of efficient inference to answer multiple queries in models that contain explicitly encoded context-specific independences. We call

This research originated from the Big Data project being part of Joint Lab 1, funded by Cisco Systems Germany, at the centre COPICOH, University of Lübeck.

J. Liu and J. Bailey (Eds.): AI 2019, LNAI 11919, pp. 104–116, 2019.
https://doi.org/10.1007/978-3-030-35288-2_9

such models switched models as context-specific independences lead to model parts being switched on or off.

To the best of our knowledge, the only approach for probabilistic relational models that may be used to implicitly encode context-specific independence comes from Gogate and Domingos [5] based on Markov logic networks [10]. They speed up inference by only counting worlds in which no clause evaluates to false. For example, we could use a variable A to switch between some worlds. In case $A = true$ is observed, all worlds with $A = false$ are not counted. Thereby, one can implicitly encode context-specific independences. Unfortunately, this approach may also result in large rules in a Markov logic network. Hence, efficient inference in switched probabilistic relational models is still an open problem.

Therefore, we combine lifting [9], gate models [7], and junction trees [6] to build an efficient formalism for inference in switched probabilistic relational models. Lifting allows for exploiting relational structures in a model. Gate models (GMs) provide a formalism to explicitly model context-specific independence using gates for switching, which also allows for modelling, e.g., interventions [8]. Junction trees enable efficient online query answering of multiple queries. Specifically, we use parameterised probabilistic models (PMs). PMs incorporate relational structures by parameterising random variables (randvars), called parameterised randvars (PRVs), which are then combined into parametric factors (parfactors) to model relations with uncertainties. First, we extend PMs with gates, resulting in parameterised gate models (PGMs). Then, we show that variable elimination (VE) can be used for inference with GMs as well as lifted variable elimination (LVE, Poole [9]) for inference with PGMs. Afterwards, we introduce the switched lifted junction tree algorithm (SLJT) by extending the lifted junction tree algorithm (LJT) [3], which uses LVE as a subroutine, to efficiently answer multiple queries in PGMs. Thereby, SLJT solves the problem of answering multiple queries in switched relational models efficiently. Specifically, this paper contributes (i) VE in GMs, (ii) applying the lifting idea to GMs resulting in PGMs enabling LVE in computations, (iii) building a first-order junction tree (FO jtree) for PGMs, and (iv) SLJT to reuse an FO jtree for multiple configurations and efficient multiple query answering in PGMs.

In the following, we begin by recapitulating PMs for relational models and GMs for context-specific independence. Afterwards, we parameterise GMs by leveraging the lifting idea and introduce SLJT. Then, we evaluate SLJT against implicitly modelling context-specific independences and specifying all possible submodels corresponding to different switch configurations.

2 Preliminaries

This section specifies PMs, which combine lifting and factor graphs, first introduced by Poole [9], and GMs, which combine factor graphs and context-specific independences, first introduced by Minka and Winn [7].

2.1   Parameterised Probabilistic Models

PMs combine first-order logic with probabilistic models, representing first-order constructs using logical variables (logvars) as parameters. For illustrative purposes, we use an example of an epidemic. In the example, we model an epidemic as a randvar. Further, we model persons being sick as a PRV by parameterising a randvar for sick with a logvar for persons. In the larger scheme of things, all persons are influenced in the same way when faced with an epidemic and thus are, without additional evidence, indistinguishable.

Definition 1. *Let* $\mathbf{R}$ *be a set of randvar names,* $\mathbf{L}$ *a set of logvar names,* Φ *a set of factor names, and* $\mathbf{D}$ *a set of constants. All sets are finite. Each logvar L has a domain* $\mathcal{D}(L) \subseteq \mathbf{D}$. *A constraint is a tuple* $(\mathcal{X}, C_{\mathbf{X}})$ *of a sequence of logvars* $\mathcal{X} = (X_1, \ldots, X_n)$ *and a set* $C_{\mathcal{X}} \subseteq \times_{i=1}^{n} \mathcal{D}(X_i)$. *The symbol* $\top$ *for C marks that no restrictions apply, i.e.,* $C_{\mathcal{X}} = \times_{i=1}^{n} \mathcal{D}(X_i)$. *A PRV* $R(L_1, \ldots, L_n), n \geq 0$ *is a construct of a randvar* $R \in \mathbf{R}$ *possibly combined with logvars* $L_1, \ldots, L_n \in \mathbf{L}$. *If* $n = 0$, *the PRV is parameterless and forms a propositional randvar. The term* $\mathcal{R}(A)$ *denotes the possible values (range) of a PRV A. An event $A = a$ denotes the occurrence of PRV A with range value $a \in \mathcal{R}(A)$. We denote a parfactor g by* $\phi(\mathcal{A})_{|C}$ *with* $\mathcal{A} = (A_1, \ldots, A_n)$ *a sequence of PRVs,* $\phi : \times_{i=1}^{n} \mathcal{R}(A_i) \mapsto \mathbb{R}^+$ *a function with name* $\phi \in \Phi$, *and C a constraint on the logvars of $\mathcal{A}$. A PRV A or logvar L under constraint C is given by* $A_{|C}$ *or* $L_{|C}$, *respectively. We may omit* $|\top$ *in* $A_{|\top}$, $L_{|\top}$, *or* $\phi(\mathcal{A})_{|\top}$. *A PM G is a set of parfactors* $\{g^i\}_{i=1}^{n}$.

The term $lv(P)$ refers to the logvars in P, which may be a PRV, a constraint, a parfactor, or a model. The term $gr(P)$ denotes the set of all instances of P w.r.t. given constraints. An instance is an instantiation (grounding) of P, substituting the logvars in P with a set of constants from given constraints. If P is a constraint, $gr(P)$ refers to the second component $C_{\mathbf{X}}$. Given a parfactor $\phi(\mathcal{A})_{|C}$, ϕ is identical for the propositional randvars in $gr(\mathcal{A}_{|C})$.

Given $\mathbf{R} = \{Sick, Epid, Travel, Treat, Nat, Man\}$ and $\mathbf{L} = \{X, P, D, W\}$, $\mathcal{D}(X) = \{x_1, x_2, x_3\}$, $\mathcal{D}(P) = \{p_1, p_2\}$, $\mathcal{D}(D) = \{d_1, d_2\}$, and $\mathcal{D}(W) = \{w_1, w_2\}$, we can build a boolean PRV $Sick(X)$. With $C = ((X), \{(x_1), (x_2)\})$, $gr(Sick(X)_{|C}) = \{Sick(x_1), Sick(x_2)\}$. The set of $gr(Sick(X)_{|\top})$ also contains $Sick(x_3)$. Adding boolean PRVs $Epid$, $Travel(X)$, $Treat(X, P)$, $Nat(D)$, and $Man(W)$, we build a PM $G_{ex} = \{g_i\}_{i=0}^{2}$, with

- $g_0 = \phi_0(Epid, Sick(X), Treat(X, P))_{|\top}$,
- $g_1 = \phi_1(Epid, Sick(X), Travel(X))_{|\top}$, and
- $g_2 = \phi_2(Epid, Nat(D), Man(W))_{|\top}$.

Parfactors g_0, g_1, and g_2 have eight input-output pairs (omitted). Constraints are $\top$. Figure 1 depicts G_{ex} as a parfactor graph.

The semantics of a model is given by grounding and building a full joint distribution. In general, a query asks for a probability distribution of a randvar using a model's full joint distribution and given fixed events as evidence.

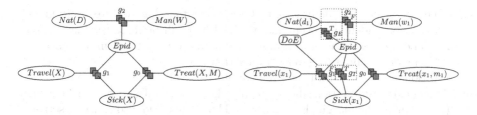

Fig. 1. Parfactor graph for G_{ex} **Fig. 2.** Gates representation of G_{ex} for x_1

Definition 2. *With Z as normalising constant, a model G represents the full joint distribution $P_G = \frac{1}{Z} \prod_{f \in gr(G)} f$. The term $P(Q|\mathbf{E})$ denotes a query in G with Q a grounded PRV and $\mathbf{E}$ a set of events. Answering $P(Q|\mathbf{E})$ requires eliminating all randvars in G not occurring in $P(Q|\mathbf{E})$.*

PMs allow for modelling relational aspects between objects including recurring patterns in these relations. Next, we recap GMs, which allow for explicitly modelling context-specific independence, i.e., switching, in propositional models.

2.2   Gate Models

GMs allow for representing context-specific independence [7]. A factor can be gated, meaning that using a selector the factor can be turned on or off, representing context-specific independence. Gates allows for modelling, e.g., external actions that change the state of the model or cutting off model parts depending on value of information.

To illustrate the impact of gates, Fig. 2 shows a GM representation of G_{ex} for x_1. Compared to G_{ex}, the GM has two gates (dashed boxes), one gate for g_E and g_T and one gate for g_1 and g_2, both with selector *DoE*. Both gates depend on the same selector *DoE*. Thereby, they are mutually exclusive, meaning when one gate is on, the other is off. We highlight two purposes of gates. The first purpose is *switching*. Assume only the gate for g_2 exists and we are interested in the marginal distribution of $Sick(x_1)$. The gate allows for turning off the connection to causes of an epidemic. Given observations that many people are sick, we might not care about the cause of an epidemic and cut off the cause part to not add noise or employ unnecessary computation time. But, in case the observation itself is uncertain or noisy, the cause part provides additional support, which enlarges the model and adds computations.

The second purpose is *intervention*, which uses both gates. An intervention on a randvar A, i.e., $do(A = a)$ in the *do* calculus [8], changes a model structure by eliminating the parent edges of A and setting A to a. The gates in Fig. 2 model an intervention on *Epid*, e.g., $do(Epid = true)$. The original "parent" of *Epid* is g_2, its connection is removed upon intervention. Thus, the selector *DoE* is introduced, which turns off g_2 if *DoE = true*. Additionally, *Epid* needs to be set to *true*. Setting *DoE = true* enables g_E, which encodes the intervention value, i.e., $g_E = \phi(Epid)$ maps *true* to 1 and *false* to 0. Further, we might know that in case an epidemic is occurring, a travel ban will be in place. Thus, upon $DoE = true$, we also turn off g_1 and instead turn on g_T to perform inference on a smaller model, leading to fewer computations.

Additionally, GMs permit reasoning about value of information: If interested in $P(Sick(x_1))$, information about $Nat(d_1)$ has a value if and only if knowing $Nat(d_1)$ changes the marginal of $Sick(x_1)$. Thus, one could also consider setting selectors based on results of marginal distribution queries.

Next, we present switched inference on PGM as an instance of switched probabilistic relational models, specifying SLJT as an exact inference algorithm.

3 Switched Inference

We propose PGMs, leveraging lifting in GMs. Then, we show how LVE can answer queries on PGMs and adapt LJT to handle gates.

3.1 Parameterised Gate Models

Minka and Winn [7] introduce GMs for factor graphs which do not model the object/relation aspect that PMs model with logvars. Thus, we extend gates to contain not only factors but parfactors. A PM that then contains gated parfactors constitutes a PGM. Before looking at an example, we formally define PGMs including gates and introduce their semantics.

Definition 3. *A* gate *is denoted by* $(\prod_i g_i)^{\delta(s=key)}$, *$s$ is the selector and g_i are the parfactors contained in the gate. A gate is turned off or on by raising the factors to the power of 0 or 1 respectively, which is indicated by $\delta(s = key)$, which is 1 if s has the value key and 0 otherwise. A PGM M consists of non-gated parfactors g_k and gated parfactors g_i with selectors $\mathbf{S}$. An assignment to all selectors $\mathbf{S}$ is called a* configuration $\{S = s\}_{S \in \mathbf{S}}$. *Given a configuration $\mathbf{s}$, the semantics of M is given by grounding and building a full joint distribution*

$$P_M = \frac{1}{Z} \prod_j (\prod_i \prod_{f \in gr(g_i)} f)^{\delta(s_j = key)} \prod_k \prod_{f \in gr(g_k)} f,$$

where Z is the normalising constant, j indexes gates, i indexes the parfactors in j, and $s_j \in \mathbf{s}$ is the assignment to selector S_j for j. Given a query term Q, a set of events $\mathbf{E}$, and a configuration $\mathbf{s}$, the term $P(Q|\mathbf{E}, \mathbf{s})$ denotes a query in M.

Figure 3 shows a representation of a PGM based on G_{ex}. The parfactors g_1, g_2, g_E, and g_T are gated by the selector DoE, i.e.,

$$g_E^{\delta(DoE=T)}, g_T^{\delta(DoE=T)}, g_1^{\delta(DoE=F)}, g_2^{\delta(DoE=F)}.$$

The PGM works as described for the GM w.r.t. x_1. The two gates model an intervention of $Epid = true$.

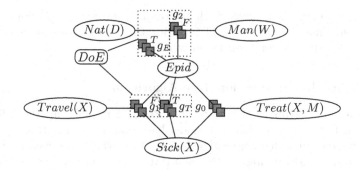

Fig. 3. Graphical representation of the PGM of G_{ex}

To obtain a PGM, various approaches are possible, e.g., (i) directly specify a PGM, (ii) learn a PGM from data, or (iii) start from a GM and use, e.g., a colouring mechanism [1] to lift the GM. Next, we investigate exact algorithms for query answering in PGMs, for which we present LVE for single queries as well as SLJT for multiple queries.

3.2   LVE for Query Answering

Based on the semantics, we need to define a way to answer queries for PGMs. Inference algorithms such as expectation propagation, variational message passing, and Gibbs sampling already work with GMs [14]. One well-studied inference algorithm for PMs is LVE, which performs computations in a lifted way, i.e., computes marginals by summing out a representative as in VE and then factoring in isomorphic instances. Here, we show that LVE (and as such VE) can be used for inference on PGMs (or GMs).

Proposition 1. *Given a query term Q and a configuration* **s**, *VE computes* $P(Q, \mathbf{s})$ *in a GM M.*

Proof Sketch. Applying a configuration **s** to a GM M leads to a plain factor graph G, which represents a full joint distribution P_G. VE is a correct algorithm to answer a query $P(Q)$ in G [15]. Given P_G, VE sums over all randvars, which are not query terms, and obtains the marginal distribution for Q, i.e., $P(Q) = \sum_v P_M$, where v are the range values of the non-query terms **A**, i.e., $v \in \mathcal{R}(\mathbf{A})$. Given the factorisation in G and complying with rules of precedence and distributivity, VE computes $P(Q)$ efficiently by factoring out factors. Thereby, to compute $P(Q)$, VE avoids building the full joint distribution.

Proposition 2. *Given a query term Q and a configuration* **s**, *LVE computes* $P(Q, \mathbf{s})$ *in a PGM M.*

Proof Sketch. Setting a configuration **s** in a PGM M leads to a plain PM G, in which LVE computes a correct answer to a query $P(Q)$ by applying correct LVE operators to G, eliminating non-query terms [13]. The result is equivalent to one computed in $gr(G)$ with VE [13].

Given another query, LVE starts with the original input model, evidence, and configuration. Thus, we present SLJT incorporating gates into the cluster structure of LJT for efficient multi-query answering.

3.3   Switched Lifted Junction Tree Algorithm

A configuration determines the parts of a PGM that make up the full joint distribution. If we were to cluster a model based on a configuration, we could efficiently handle gates that are switched on or off. At this point, we turn to LJT [3], which uses a cluster representation of a PM for efficiently answering *multiple queries*. In the following, we introduce SLJT and examine how SLJT leverages LJT by automatically handling the effects of any given configuration on a PGM.

Clusters: LJT builds a cluster representation of a PM called an FO jtree, whose nodes are *clusters*. Intuitively, a cluster is a set of PRVs that are directly connected by parfactors. Each cluster has the parfactors that connect its PRVs as a *local model* assigned. For SLJT, clusters are based on selectors and their assignments. Consider the FO jtree with four clusters in Fig. 4 derived from the example PGM. Cluster $\mathbf{C}_1$ contains $Epid, Sick(X), Treat(X, M)$, linked by g_0. Clusters $\mathbf{C}_2$, $\mathbf{C}_3$ and $\mathbf{C}_4$ are based on the selector DoE. $\mathbf{C}_2$ contains $Epid, Sick(X)$, based on $DoE = true$, with g_E and g_T assigned. $\mathbf{C}_3$ contains $Epid, Sick(X)$, $Travel(X)$, based on $DoE = false$, with g_1 assigned. $\mathbf{C}_4$ contains $Epid, Nat(D)$, $Man(W)$, based on $DoE = false$, with g_2 assigned. If $DoC(X) = true$, $\mathbf{C}_2$ is switched on. If $DoC(X) = false$, $\mathbf{C}_3$ and $\mathbf{C}_4$ are switched on. $\mathbf{C}_1$ does not have a selector associated, it can be thought of as always switched on.

Query Answering: To answer queries on an FO jtree, LJT performs some preprocessing using local models. A local model holds state descriptions about its cluster PRVs, which is not available at another cluster. During preprocessing, LJT makes all necessary state descriptions available for each node through messages. A message m from one cluster to a neighbour $\mathbf{C}_j$ transports state descriptions of its local model and messages from other neighbours to $\mathbf{C}_j$. LJT uses LVE to calculate m, passing on the shared PRVs as a query and the local model and respective messages as a model. Without considering the selectors in the FO jtree in Fig. 4, LJT passes messages from $\mathbf{C}_2$ and $\mathbf{C}_4$ to $\mathbf{C}_1$ and back. With selectors present, message calculation changes: If a cluster is switched on, LJT calculates a message based on a cluster's local model and messages from neighbours. If a

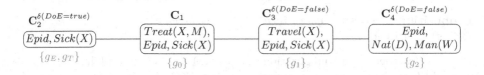

Fig. 4. An FO jtree for the PGM of G_{ex} in Fig. 3

cluster is switched off, LJT calculates a message based only on messages from neighbours. Given a configuration of $DoE = true$ in the FO jtree in Fig. 4, the messages from $\mathbf{C}_3$ and $\mathbf{C}_4$ are empty without the local models and no other incoming message. With $DoE = false$, the message from $\mathbf{C}_2$ is empty.

After message passing, each cluster has all necessary state descriptions of the model under the current configuration available in its local model and received messages. To answer a query with a query term Q, LJT finds a cluster that contains Q and answers $P(Q)$ on the local model and messages with LVE.

The original FO jtree construction of LJT does not account for selectors as it is designed for PMs. Thus, we extend the FO jtree construction to handle gates.

FO Jtree Construction: Algorithm 1 outlines how to build an FO jtree of a PGM M. The guiding idea is to cluster M based on selector-key pairs. First, SLJT partitions M based on keys and builds an FO jtree J for each partition. An FO jtree is a cycle-free graph. The clusters are sets of PRVs from the input model and the arguments of each parfactor of the model appear in one cluster. A valid FO jtree also fulfils the *running intersection property* (RI), which says that a PRV appearing in two clusters must appear in all clusters on the path between them [6]. LJT constructs such an FO jtree for a given input model.

Now, SLJT has $|\mathbf{P}|$ valid FO jtrees with corresponding selector-key pairs assigned. To combine the FO jtrees into one valid FO jtree, SLJT takes a first FO jtree J, at random or an ungated FO jtree if available. Then, SLJT iteratively connects J to the remaining FO jtrees J_i by adding an edge from one cluster of J to a cluster of J_i. For the edge, SLJT chooses the two clusters with the largest overlap in PRVs. Combining two FO jtrees in such a fashion may violate RI. As keys may be mutually exclusive, RI only has to hold on valid paths. A valid path is a path between two clusters that are both switched on at the same time by any configuration. Therefore, SLJT extends clusters with PRVs until RI holds again on valid paths. After connecting all remaining FO jtrees to J, SLJT returns J.

To construct an FO jtree for the PGM G_{ex} in Fig. 3, SLJT first groups the parfactors. Here, each parfactor gets assigned its own group, as none of them

---

Algorithm 1. FO jtree Construction

---

function SFOJT(PGM M)
    Let $\mathbf{P}$ be a partitioning of M based on keys
    for each partition $P_i \in \mathbf{P}$ **do**
        Build FO jtree J_i of P_i and add to $\mathbf{F}$
    Take an FO jtree J out from $\mathbf{F}$ ▷ Choose J s.t. P without a key or at random
    while $\mathbf{F}$ not empty **do**
        Take an FO jtree J_i out from $\mathbf{F}$
        Connect J_i to J ▷ Edge between clusters sharing most PRVs
        while RI does not hold on valid paths **do**
            Extend clusters with PRVs
    return J

---

share the same selector-key pair. Then, SLJT builds an FO jtree for each group. In this case, each FO jtree consists of one cluster, i.e., one FO jtree consisting of $\mathbf{C}_1$, one of $\mathbf{C}_2$, and one of $\mathbf{C}_3$ and $\mathbf{C}_4$. $\mathbf{C}_1$ is not gated and therefore selected as a starting point. Now, SLJT selects either $\mathbf{C}_2$ or $\mathbf{C}_3$ and $\mathbf{C}_4$ at random, e.g., $\mathbf{C}_2$. SLJT connects $\mathbf{C}_1$ and $\mathbf{C}_2$. With only two clusters, RI still holds. Lastly, $\mathbf{C}_3$ and $\mathbf{C}_4$ are added to the FO jtree. As $\mathbf{C}_3$ overlaps with both $\mathbf{C}_1$ and $\mathbf{C}_2$ with $Epid$ and $Sick(X)$, SLJT chooses one at random, e.g., $\mathbf{C}_1$. Adding an edge between $\mathbf{C}_1$ and $\mathbf{C}_3$ leads to the FO jtree depicted in Fig. 4. In the resulting FO jtree, RI still holds on all paths and all paths are valid paths.

Theorem 1. *The FO jtree construction of SLJT is sound.*

Proof Sketch. The initial FO jtrees built are valid. Their clusters contain PRVs from the input model and the arguments of each parfactor appear in some cluster. By combining one node of a cycle-free graph with exactly one node from another cycle-free graph the result is again a cycle-free graph. Adding edges may only violate RI, which SLJT systematically restores by extending clusters with PRVs. Thus, Algorithm 1 produces a valid FO jtree.

Algorithm Description: SLJT takes a PGM M, a configuration $\mathbf{s}$, evidence $\mathbf{E}$, and a set of queries $\mathbf{Q}$. Algorithm 2 shows an outline of SLJT. SLJT constructs an FO jtree J as in Algorithm 1 and then switches clusters in J on and off based on $\mathbf{s}$, followed by entering $\mathbf{E}$ into the clusters: At each cluster that contains the evidence randvars, the local model absorbs $\mathbf{E}$ in a lifted way (cf. Taghipour et al. [13]). Then, SLJT passes messages as described above. Finally, SLJT answers the queries in $\mathbf{Q}$ or starts processing incoming queries online.

Theorem 2. *SLJT is sound, i.e, calculates correct answers to queries on a PGM M and a configuration $\mathbf{s}$.*

Proof Sketch. SLJT constructs a valid FO jtree based on Theorem 1, which allows for local computations for messages and queries [12]. To answer queries correctly, SLJT has to distribute state descriptions of local models through the FO jtree. Therefore, SLJT uses the massage passing scheme of LJT, which coincides with the scheme by Shafer and Shenoy, which they show to be sound [11]. Additionally, SLJT includes the local model of the current cluster only if the selector of the cluster is on. In case the selector is off, the cluster only uses

---

Algorithm 2. Switched Lifted Junction Tree Algorithm

procedure SLJT(PGM M, configuration $\mathbf{s}$, evidence $\mathbf{E}$, queries $\mathbf{Q}$)
    FO jtree $J \leftarrow$ SFOJT(M)
    Enter evidence $\mathbf{E}$ into J
    Pass messages on J
    for each query $Q \in \mathbf{Q}$ **do**
        Answer Q on a cluster in J

---

the information of received messages, if there are any, to calculate the outgoing message. Thus, after a message pass, each cluster holds all necessary state descriptions under a given configuration and can answer queries about its PRVs. Hence, as LJT is sound and SLJT calculates the same answers LJT would on an FO jtree with only the parfactors, which are turned on, SLJT is sound.

SLJT allows for building an FO jtree for a PGM and then reuse the FO jtree for multiple queries and configurations. Next, we evaluate the performance gain by using the context-specific independences.

4   Evaluation

To evaluate SLJT, we use a variation of G_{ex} with 3 selectors. We compare SLJT against implicitly specifying the context-specific independences in parfactors and against specifying a model for each configuration. 3 selectors result in 8 configurations, leading to 8 small models. Thus, we compare SLJT with a PGM against LJT with a model containing an implicit encoding of the switches as well as LJT with 8 models corresponding to configurations. For the evaluation, we compare the runtimes w.r.t. message passing to prepare an FO jtree for query answering as well as the runtime for answering two queries, namely $P(Epid)$ and $P(Sick(x_1))$. Additionally, we evaluate the runtimes for $|\mathcal{D}(X)| \in \{10, 100, 1000\}$. One claim investigated in this evaluation is that it is advantageous to use explicit context-specific independences also in the lifted case. Another claim is that SLJT requires about the same runtime for query answering as LJT does on the models corresponding to configurations.

Figure 5 shows the runtimes for message passing in ms and Fig. 6 shows the runtimes of each of the two queries. The runtimes are the average of 10 runs. In both figures, the x-axis shows different configurations. Thus, for $x = A$ the runtimes for the first configuration are shown, for $x = B$ the runtimes for the second configuration are shown, and so on.

In Fig. 5, we can see that message passing on the large model with an encoding of the switches in parfactors takes the longest. The runtimes are about the same for all configuration as the configuration is passed to LJT as evidence leading to absorbing the variables used to encode the switching. Hence, the variables used

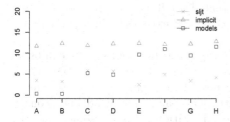

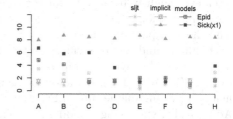

Fig. 5. Message passing runtimes [ms] for $|\mathcal{D}(X) = 100|$, x-axis: configurations

Fig. 6. Query answering runtimes [ms] for $|\mathcal{D}(X) = 100|$, x-axis: configurations

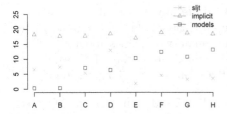
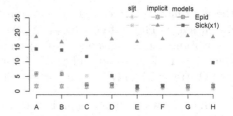

Fig. 7. Message passing runtimes [ms] for $|\mathcal{D}(X) = 1000|$, x-axis: configurations

Fig. 8. Query answering runtimes [ms] for $|\mathcal{D}(X) = 1000|$, x-axis: configurations

for encoding switching behaviour can be thought of as eliminated after evidence entering. Nonetheless, LJT still needs to perform a message pass on a rather large model. Therefore, the runtimes for this model are the upper bound in our evaluation. For the small models, we can see that runtimes for message passing increase with the different configurations and that the runtimes are bounded by the implicit encoding. The increase is incidental due to the sorting of the configurations. Further, we can see that for configuration A and B, the model results in an FO jtree with one parcluster as LJT does not spend any time on message passing, but relatively long on query answering as can be seen in Fig. 6. For SLJT, we can see that message passing only slightly variates between the different configurations. SLJT always needs to compute the same number of messages, as the FO jtree always remains the same. However, which parcluster and thereby which parfactors are turned on and off depends on the configuration leading to slight variations in the runtimes.

In Fig. 6, we can see that answering the query about *Epid* is always faster compared to $Sick(x_1)$ because $Sick(x_1)$, x_1 needs to be split from X. Implicitly encoding the switching behaviour in the model leads to largest runtimes for answering $Sick(x_1)$. Regarding both queries, implicitly encoding the behaviour leads to runtimes very close to each other over different configurations as described above. Regarding the models based on configurations, LJT saves effort during query answering with increasing effort during message passing. SLJT is the fastest approach for both queries. SLJT always answers the queries on an FO jtree with many rather small parclusters. Having small parclusters is really advantageous for query answering and explains why the runtimes of SLJT are often even slightly below LJT for the constructed small model corresponding to the configuration. Overall, we can see that using context-specific independences has a huge impact on runtimes.

Figures 7 and 8 shows runtimes for $|\mathcal{D}(X)| = 1000$, the programs exhibiting the same behaviour compared to each other as with $|\mathcal{D}(X)| = 100$. The setting $|\mathcal{D}(X)| = 10$ also shows the same behaviour (omitted here). In summary, answering queries on an FO jtree with small parclusters is advantageous. Additionally, specifying a model for each configuration is cumbersome, always incurring an overhead for constructing an FO jtree, a step which we did not evaluate here. Overall, compared to the other two methods, SLJT efficiently uses context-specific independence to significantly speed up inference.

5   Conclusion

To make inference more manageable, we investigate multiple queries in switched probabilistic relational models, which explicitly handle context-specific independence. By leveraging lifting principles for GMs, which allows for representing context-specific independence using gates, and then extending LJT to efficiently handle switching behaviour, SLJT allows for efficient answering of multiple queries in switched probabilistic relational models. Empirical results show that using context-specific independence speeds up lifted inference significantly.

Future work focusses on including causal inference [14] and counterfactual reasoning. Further, we look into decision support as gates with context-specific independences seems to be an ideal formalism to model different actions.

References

1. Ahmadi, B., Kersting, K., Mladenov, M., Natarajan, S.: Exploiting symmetries for scaling loopy belief propagation and relational training. Mach. Learn. **92**(1), 91–132 (2013)
2. Boutilier, C., Friedman, N., Goldszmidt, M., Koller, D.: Context-specific independence in Bayesian networks. In: Proceedings of the 12th International Conference on Uncertainty in Artificial Intelligence, pp. 115–123. Morgan Kaufmann Publishers Inc. (1996)
3. Braun, T., Möller, R.: Lifted junction tree algorithm. In: Friedrich, G., Helmert, M., Wotawa, F. (eds.) KI 2016. LNCS (LNAI), vol. 9904, pp. 30–42. Springer, Cham (2016). https://doi.org/10.1007/978-3-319-46073-4_3
4. Cooper, G.F.: The computational complexity of probabilistic inference using Bayesian belief networks. Artif. Intell. **42**(2–3), 393–405 (1990)
5. Gogate, V., Domingos, P.M.: Probabilistic theorem proving. In: UAI 2011, Proceedings of the Twenty-Seventh Conference on Uncertainty in Artificial Intelligence, Barcelona, Spain, 14–17 July 2011, pp. 256–265. AUAI Press (2011)
6. Lauritzen, S.L., Spiegelhalter, D.J.: Local computations with probabilities on graphical structures and their application to expert systems. J. Roy. Stat. Soc.: Ser. B (Methodol.) **50**(2), 157–224 (1988)
7. Minka, T., Winn, J.: Gates. In: Advances in Neural Information Processing Systems, pp. 1073–1080 (2009)
8. Pearl, J.: Causality. Cambridge University Press, Cambridge (2009)
9. Poole, D.: First-order probabilistic inference. In: Proceedings of IJCAI, vol. 3, pp. 985–991 (2003)
10. Richardson, M., Domingos, P.: Markov logic networks. Mach. Learn. **62**(1), 107–136 (2006)
11. Shafer, G.R., Shenoy, P.P.: Probability propagation. Ann. Math. Artif. Intell. **2**(1), 327–351 (1990)
12. Shenoy, P.P., Shafer, G.R.: Axioms for probability and belief-function propagation. Uncertain. Artif. Intell. **9**, 169–198 (1990)

13. Taghipour, N., Fierens, D., Davis, J., Blockeel, H.: Lifted variable elimination: decoupling the operators from the constraint language. J. Artif. Intell. Res. **47**(1), 393–439 (2013)
14. Winn, J.: Causality with gates. In: Artificial Intelligence and Statistics, pp. 1314–1322 (2012)
15. Zhang, N.L., Poole, D.: A simple approach to Bayesian network computations. In: Proceedings of the 10th Canadian Conference on Artificial Intelligence, pp. 171–178. Springer, Heidelberg (1994)

Finding ALL Answers to OBDA Queries Using Referring Expressions

David Toman$^{(\boxtimes)}$ and Grant Weddell

Cheriton School of Computer Science,
University of Waterloo, Waterloo, Canada
{david,gweddell}@uwaterloo.ca

Abstract. We explore how *referring expressions* can be used to enhance how a conjunctive query is answered over description logic knowledge bases in a way that allows one to return not only answers explicitly named by constant symbols, but also anonymous individuals that are entailed to satisfy the query, and to provide syntactic means for referring to such individuals. In particular, for the logics Horn-$\mathcal{ALC}$ and $\mathcal{EL}^\perp$, we focus on reporting *all* entailed answers, on techniques necessary to finitely describe such sets of answers, and on extensions to more complex logics and settings.

1 Introduction

Usually, individual names occurring in a knowledge base expressed in terms of an underlying *description logic* (DL) are the only syntactic constructs that are permitted for communicating references to objects, called *referring expressions*, in query answering. In this paper, we introduce referring expressions that are concept descriptions in some DL that stand for *singular certain answers* to instance queries and more general conjunctive queries over Horn-$\mathcal{ALC}$ and $\mathcal{EL}^\perp$ knowledge bases. A notable feature of our approach that is new is the ability to describe *all* entailed answers to queries in terms of such descriptions.

This idea of allowing concept descriptions in some DL to replace individual names in query answering has been considered in earlier work [3,10]. This work, however, has relied on the underlying DL being able to express functionality of roles and of role paths in order to ensure a concept description serving as a referring expression satisfied a strong *singularity* property. This property required that the meaning of such a description is a singleton set for *any* model of the given knowledge base. As a consequence, the results of this work are *inapplicable* for any DL that is unable to express functionality, such as Horn-$\mathcal{ALC}$ and $\mathcal{EL}^\perp$. This is unfortunate because such DLs have been widely used, in particular: $\mathcal{EL}^\perp$ and its derivatives are popular for capturing ontologies in life sciences, such as SNOMED CT [9], NCI [5], FMA [4], and others. However, adding even the simplest role functionality constraints to $\mathcal{EL}^\perp$ immediately leads to the loss of tractability of reasoning [2,7,8]. For *query answering* [2], however, it seems to be sufficient to guarantee that the referring expression used to describe a *particular*

© Springer Nature Switzerland AG 2019
J. Liu and J. Bailey (Eds.): AI 2019, LNAI 11919, pp. 117–129, 2019.
https://doi.org/10.1007/978-3-030-35288-2_10

answer is singular *among all certain answers*, i.e., it refers to only one certain answer.

Example 1. Consider a Horn-$\mathcal{ALC}$ knowledge base $\mathcal{K} = (\mathcal{T}, \mathcal{A})$ consisting of a TBox $\mathcal{T} = \{A \sqsubseteq \exists R.C, A \sqsubseteq \exists R.D, A \sqsubseteq \forall R.B\}$, and an ABox $\mathcal{A} = \{c : A\}$.[1] Three of the tree models of $\mathcal{K}$ will look as follows:

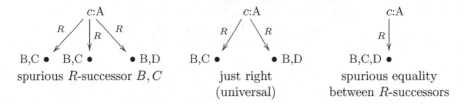

For an instance query $B(x)$, the universal *just right* tree model in the middle makes it reasonable to consider the referring expressions *"the R-successor of c labeled C"* and *"the R-successor of c labeled D"* (expressed as concept descriptions) to be the singular certain answers to this request. However, neither *"the R-successor of c labelled with both C and D"* nor *"the R-successor of c"* should qualify since the former is not a certain answer, as witnessed by the two models on the left, while the later is intuitively not singular since it is implied by the *two* certain answers above, and is only justified in the rightmost model which has *spuriously equated* the two singular answers in the universal model.[2]   □

The example illustrates how one can reasonably weaken the rather strong notion of singularity introduced in [3] to accommodate Horn-$\mathcal{ALC}$ and $\mathcal{EL}^{\perp}$, requiring instead that the denotation of a referring concept is a singleton set *in the universal tree model* of the knowledge base. Also, it is easy to see that, whenever a certain answer (i.e., a referring expression) is produced in this setting, the underlying knowledge base is *consistent* with functionality constraints needed to make *all* these answers singular in the stronger sense of [3] (this observation follows immediately from the existence of universal tree models).

The contributions of this paper are as follows:

1. We develop a technique that allows one to find *all certain answers* to instance retrieval queries over Horn-$\mathcal{ALC}$ knowledge bases and describe them in terms of referring expressions;
2. We develop a *finite representation* of possibly infinite sets of answers; and
3. We discuss extensions to other Horn DLs and study the impact of additional concept constructors, such as number restrictions, on our ability to report all certain answers. We also outline the difficulties with extending the approach to non-Horn settings.

---

[1] We appeal to intuition in this example; full definitions follow in Sect. 2.

[2] Note that even in the standard setting, two syntactically distinct constants may co-refer to the same object unless UNA is assumed.

We focus mainly on Horn-$\mathcal{ALC}$ and $\mathcal{EL}^{\perp}$ to enable a transparent development, although more expressive logics are considered later. Overall, the paper is organized as follows: Sect. 2 gives the necessary general definitions, and Sect. 3 studies the problem of *instance retrieval* in Horn-$\mathcal{ALC}$ and $\mathcal{EL}^{\perp}$, including how sets of answers can have finite representations. The development for instance retrieval is then extended to other settings, including where queries can be more general conjunctive queries, in Sect. 4. Section 5 summarizes and outlines directions for further research.

2   Background and Definitions

We begin by defining a space of concept descriptions for the function free DL dialects that will concern us, including the concept descriptions that replace individual names in the role of *referring expressions* in query answering:

Definition 2 (Concept Language). Let R, PC and IN be disjoint sets of role names, primitive concept names and individual names respectively. Derived *concept descriptions* and their *semantics* are defined as follows:

Syntax	Semantics: Defn of "$\cdot^{\mathcal{I}}$"	
$C ::= A$	$A^{\mathcal{I}} \subseteq \triangle$	(primitive concept; $A \in$ PC)
$\mid C_1 \sqcap C_2$	$C_1^{\mathcal{I}} \cap C_2^{\mathcal{I}}$	(conjunction)
$\mid \perp$	$\{\}$	(bottom)
$\mid \forall R.C$	$\{x \mid \forall y : (x,y) \in R^{\mathcal{I}} \to y \in C^{\mathcal{I}}\}$	(value restriction; $R \in$ R)
$\mid \exists R.C$	$\{x \mid \exists y : (x,y) \in R^{\mathcal{I}} \wedge y \in C^{\mathcal{I}}\}$	(existential restriction; $R \in$ R)
$\mid \exists R^-.C$	$\{x \mid \exists y : (y,x) \in R^{\mathcal{I}} \wedge y \in C^{\mathcal{I}}\}$	(inverse existential restriction)
$\mid \{a\}$	$\{a^{\mathcal{I}}\}$	(nominal; $a \in$ IN)

The semantics is with respect to a structure $\mathcal{I} = (\triangle, \cdot^{\mathcal{I}})$ in which $\triangle$ is a domain of "objects" and $\cdot^{\mathcal{I}}$ an interpretation function seeded by fixing the interpretations of primitive concept names A to be subsets of $\triangle$ (as indicated), role names R to be subsets of $\triangle \times \triangle$, and individual names a to be elements of $\triangle$ and is extended to derived concept descriptions C (as also indicated). □

The DL dialects $\mathcal{EL}^{\perp}$ and Horn-$\mathcal{ALC}$ are given as follows:

Definition 3 (Horn-$\mathcal{ALC}$ and $\mathcal{EL}^{\perp}$ TBoxes and Knowledge Bases). A Horn-$\mathcal{ALC}$ or $\mathcal{EL}^{\perp}$ *knowledge base* $\mathcal{K}$ consists of a *TBox* $\mathcal{T}$ and *ABox* $\mathcal{A}$, where $\mathcal{T}$ consists of a finite set of *subsumptions* of the form $C \sqsubseteq D$ in which

- C is a conjunction of primitive concepts A and existential restrictions of the form $\exists R.A$, and
- D is one of $\perp$, A, $\exists R.A$, and, in the case of Horn-$\mathcal{ALC}$, $\forall R.A$,

and where $\mathcal{A}$ consists of a finite set of *assertions* of the form $a : A$ and $R(a,b)$. An interpretation $\mathcal{I}$ is called a *model* of $\mathcal{K}$ if $C^{\mathcal{I}} \subseteq D^{\mathcal{I}}$ for all $C \sqsubseteq D \in \mathcal{T}$, $a^{\mathcal{I}} \in C^{\mathcal{I}}$ for all $a : C \in \mathcal{A}$, and $(a^{\mathcal{I}}, b^{\mathcal{I}}) \in R^{\mathcal{I}}$ for all $R(a,b) \in \mathcal{A}$. Consistency, logical implication, and other reasoning problems are defined in the standard way [2]. □

Observe that we require TBoxes to be in a simple normal form. For more general but expressively equivalent syntax, see [6].

Tree Models. Hereon, we rely on the fact that DL knowledge bases will usually possess the *tree model property*: with the exception of the explicit ABox, satisfiable knowledge bases have a tree-like model in which all anonymous objects form a role-connected forest, with each tree rooted by an ABox individual. Moreover, in the tree parts of this model, no individuals are made equal unless forced to be equal by TBox assertions. For Horn logics, one can also show that there is a unique tree-like model, commonly called the minimal or universal model, that captures all the facts implied by the knowledge base. Thus, many reasoning tasks, in particular, *instance retrieval*, reduce to inspecting this model [2,6].

Queries and Referring Expressions. In the classical setting, instance retrieval (resp. query answering) with respect to a knowledge base $\mathcal{K}$ and a concept C (resp. query Q) is the task that determines for which *individual names appearing in* $\mathcal{K}$ it holds that $\mathcal{K} \models a : C$ (resp. $\mathcal{K} \models Q(a_1, \ldots, a_k)$). Here, constant names serve the role of referring expressions, and our concern is with replacing such expressions by more general concept descriptions:

Definition 4 (Referring Expression). *Referring expressions are simply concepts in (a subset of) the above concept language.* In the following, we use concept descriptions of the form

$$C_1 \sqcap \exists R_1^-.(C_2 \sqcap \exists R_2^-.(\ldots \exists R_k^-.\{a\}))$$

where C_i are (conjunctions) of primitive concepts. □

The intuition behind this choice of referring expressions lies in the tree model property of our logics: every anonymous object can be reached by a role path from an ABox individual. (Indeed, unreachable objects that may exist in some models of our knowledge bases should not be considered since they fail to qualify as certain answers.)

In order to use *referring expressions* in place of constant symbols, one should ensure that they describe a single (certain) answer. Also note that, to account for various DL dialects, both knowledge base subsumptions/assertions and referring expressions will be restricted to appropriate subsets of the concept language in Definition 2. The following definition of a *singularity property* of concepts serving the role of referring expressions in instance checking, however, is independent of the choice of DL dialect:

Definition 5 (Singular Certain Answers). Let $\mathcal{K}$ be a consistent knowledge base, D an instance query (i.e., a concept expression), and C a referring expression. We say that C is a *singular certain answer* to D if

1. (certainty) $\mathcal{K} \models C \sqsubseteq D$ and $|C^{\mathcal{I}}| > 0$ for all models $\mathcal{I}$ of $\mathcal{K}$, and
2. (singularity) $|C^{\mathcal{I}}| = 1$ in the *universal* model $\mathcal{I}$ of $\mathcal{K}$. □

This definition can be naturally extended to general queries over $\mathcal{K}$ [3]. Recall that this constitutes a *weakening* of the singularity property defined in [3] in which a referring expression was required to denote a singleton set in *all* models of the knowledge base. Indeed, this is essential since DL dialects such as Horn-$\mathcal{ALC}$ and $\mathcal{EL}^{\perp}$ are not sufficiently expressive to enforce the stronger requirement. In these logics, it is always possible to replicate identical successors of objects in a model without invalidating any TBox subsumptions. Doing this leads immediately to a violation of the singularity property of [3]. However, in the setting of *certain answers*, the weaker requirement seems sufficient: it guarantees that it is never the case that the referring expression describes more than one answer *in every* model of $\mathcal{K}$.

Example 6. Consider again the knowledge base $\mathcal{K}$ in Example 1. Formally, the following concept descriptions, $C \sqcap \exists R^{-}.\{c\}$ and $D \sqcap \exists R^{-}.\{c\}$, are singular certain answers for the instance query $B(x)$, while $\exists R^{-}.\{c\}$ is not since it fails the singularity requirement.   □

This seems to be in agreement with the usual entailment style of semantics for certain answers in the database community that thinks of the results of a query as an "intersection over all models". The benefit of this weaker definition is that results can now apply to logics that are unable to express functionality, such as Horn-$\mathcal{ALC}$ or $\mathcal{EL}^{\perp}$, which were excluded from consideration in [3].

Conversely, we require the weaker singularity condition to hold in the *universal model* of the knowledge base. This avoids models that equate objects without a need to do so (as illustrated in Example 1 by the right-most model). Allowing such models in our definition of singularity would incorrectly allow for concepts (such as $\exists R^{-}.\{a\}$) to be considered referring expressions for singular certain answers even though there could be two or more referring expressions that also describe singular answers and imply the expression in question. However, note that aliases, that is, alternative referring expressions that refer to the same *single* answer, are still possible. This is natural and similar to standard approaches in which distinct constants may be interpreted as the same individual.

3   Instance Retrieval over an Unit ABox

We first consider the problem of generalized instance retrieval. In the classical setting, this task deals only with ABox individuals. However, in our setting, referring expressions can describe certain answers that can be *arbitrarily far* from ABox individuals denoted by constant symbols.

The two DLs that we consider, Horn-$\mathcal{ALC}$ and $\mathcal{EL}^{\perp}$, do not possess the capability of expressing the functionality of roles. A slightly surprising result is that Horn-$\mathcal{ALC}$ or $\mathcal{EL}^{\perp}$ TBoxes are *not* able to enforce the existence of objects that are indistinguishable by appropriate referring expressions. Hence, *all* possible answers can in principle be described by such expressions as *singular certain answers*.

To simplify the exposition and focus on the issues connected with referring expressions, we first assume that the ABox in a knowledge base contains a single assertion $a : A$. (We relax this restriction later.) Initially, we only consider instance retrieval queries of the form $B(x)$ for B a primitive concept; instance queries for more complex concepts can be reduced to this case by introducing appropriate subsumptions in the TBox.

3.1   The Horn-$\mathcal{ALC}$ Case

In principle, testing whether a concept is an answer to an instance query reduces to a simple logical implication problem (perhaps in an extension of Horn-$\mathcal{ALC}$). The main questions we answer here are *what* concepts should qualify as referring expressions, and *how* one guarantees singularity for these expressions. To answer these questions, we utilize a construction similar to the standard construction of a *tree automaton* for recognizing tree models of the knowledge base [11].[3] We generate a transition relation from our instance checking problem as follows:

Definition 7. Let $\mathcal{K} = (\mathcal{T}, \{a : A\})$ be a Horn-$\mathcal{ALC}$ knowledge base (in normal form) and Concepts($\mathcal{K}$) the set of all concepts and subconcepts appearing in $\mathcal{K}$. We define Implied(S) = $\{C \in \text{Concepts}(\mathcal{K}) \mid \mathcal{T} \models \bigsqcap_{A \in S} A \sqsubseteq C\}$, where S is a set of primitive concepts, and define $\mathcal{S}_\mathcal{K} = \{S \mid S \subseteq \text{PC} \cap \text{Concepts}(\mathcal{K})\}$.
We say that an existential restriction $\exists R.C \in \text{Implied}(S)$ is *independent* if it is minimal (w.r.t. subsumption) among existential restrictions in Implied(S).
A *matching tuple for* $S \in \mathcal{S}_\mathcal{K}$ is a tuple

$$(S, \{C_0, D_{0,0}, \ldots, D_{0,k_0}\}, \ldots, \{C_k, D_{k,0}, \ldots, D_{k,k_k}\})$$

where $\exists R_0.C_0, \ldots, \exists R_k.C_k$ are all independent existential restrictions that appear in Implied(S) and $\forall R_0.D_{0,0}, \ldots, \forall R_0.D_{0,k_0}, \ldots, \forall R_k.D_{k,0}, \ldots, \forall R_k.D_{k,k_k}$ are all value restrictions that appear in Implied(S). We say that $\{C_i, D_{i,0}, \ldots, D_{i,k_i}\}$ belongs to S's matching tuple *for the existential restriction* $\exists R_i.C_i$.   □

This construction is similar to the looping automaton construction for $\mathcal{K}$ with an initial state $\{A\}$. However, note that the transitions are deterministic for Horn-$\mathcal{ALC}$. A similar construction also yields an optimal EXPTIME upper bound for satisfiability of Horn-$\mathcal{ALC}$ knowledge bases since the number of the sets in the construction is at most exponential in $|\mathcal{K}|$ (as is the size of the tree automaton), and testing for the emptiness of a looping tree automaton can be done in time polynomial in the number of states as follows:

Set $S \in \mathcal{S}_\mathcal{K}$ is *feasible* if
1. $\bot \notin \text{Implied}(S)$, and
2. for the matching tuple $(S, S_0, \ldots, S_k)$, all S_i are *feasible*.
Otherwise, S is *infeasible*.

---

[3] In the standard construction, the Hintikka sets are generated syntactically by analyzing concepts present in a TBox. Here, to simplify the presentation, we rely on logical implication algorithms already developed for the underlying logics.

It is easy to see that the above definition of (in)feasible states can be implemented by an algorithm that marks all infeasible states in $|\mathcal{S}_\mathcal{K}|$ rounds. Consequently, $\mathcal{K}$ is satisfiable if and only if the initial state $\{A\}$ is feasible since the structure finitely encodes the universal (minimal) model of $\mathcal{K}$: the model corresponds to the unfolding of the structure starting from $\{A\}$ (i.e., a run of the automaton). We use the feasible states and the structure defined over them by the matching tuples (a.k.a., the transition relation of the looping automaton) to define referring expressions that will serve as our singular certain answers:

Definition 8 (Certain Paths and Referring Expressions). A *certain path for a query $B(x)$ and knowledge base $\mathcal{K}$* is a sequence of role and concept pairs $R_1 A_1 \ldots R_k A_k$ such that there are feasible $S_0, \ldots, S_k \in \mathcal{S}_\mathcal{K}$ and

1. $S_0 = \{A\}$,
2. $B \in \mathsf{Implied}(S_k)$, and
3. S_{i+1} belongs to S_i's matching tuple for the existential restriction $\exists R_i.A_i$. $\square$

Observe that we consider *all such paths* in the above (i.e., not just paths that are simple). Also note that, unlike satisfiability, we need to make certain that the referring expression concept *works* in all models of $\mathcal{K}$. Here we again take advantage of the logic being Horn and rely on the (universal) tree model captured by the above construction.

Theorem 9. Every certain path $R_1 A_1 \ldots R_k A_k$ for B and $\mathcal{K}$ corresponds to a singular certain answer $A_k \sqcap \exists R_k^-.(\ldots A_1 \sqcap \exists R_1^-.\{a\})$. Moreover, every B object common to all models of $\mathcal{K}$ will be reached by a certain path and will be returned as an answer.

Proof (sketch): The construction guarantees that the referring expressions constructed from certain paths satisfy the certainty condition of our definition: the end object of every certain path for $B(x)$ and $\mathcal{K}$ is in the interpretation of the B concept in the minimal model and thus in all models of $\mathcal{K}$. The objects at the ends of these paths are referred to by the referring expression concept constructed from such paths.

Requiring only independent existential restrictions to be parts of matching tuples guarantees singularity of the certain answers witnessed by the tree model of $\mathcal{K}$.

3.2 The $\mathcal{EL}^\perp$ Case

We use the same construction. However, in the absence of value restrictions, observe that only the sets $\mathsf{Implied}(\{A\})$, for $A \in \mathsf{PC}$, are needed. There are only polynomially many of these, all of which can now be constructed in PTIME.[4]

---

[4] This construction is essentially the same as the construction of the so called *canonical model* for $\mathcal{EL}^\perp$ [1,8].

3.3 Finite Representation of Answers

Our focus so far has been on problems of determining *if a referring expression is a singular certain answer* to an instance query $B(x)$ over a knowledge base $\mathcal{K}$. However, in practical information systems, one is often faced with the task of reporting *all* certain answers. This is easy in the standard case: we simply consider the available constant symbols one-by-one. The following examples show that this is not so simple for referring expressions. In the case of acyclic TBoxes (even in $\mathcal{EL}^\perp$), the number of singular certain answers can be easily exponential (and doubly exponential in the case of Horn-$\mathcal{ALC}$):

Example 10. Consider a knowledge base with unit ABox and an $\mathcal{EL}^\perp$ TBox of the form $\mathcal{T} = \{A \sqsubseteq \exists R.B_0 \sqcap \exists S.B_0, \ldots, B_{k-1} \sqsubseteq \exists R.B_k \sqcap \exists S.B_k\}$ for $k > 0$. Our construction gives k matching tuples $(\{B_i\}, \{B_{i+1}\}, \{B_{i+1}\})$ (and a tuple $(\{B_k\})$). This, however, leads to exponentially many certain paths that are witnessed by the *tree model* of this TBox that contains 2^k leaves.

The situation is even worse in the case of Horn-$\mathcal{ALC}$ since one can force paths of exponential length using value restrictions and auxiliary concepts that stand for counters. Hence, one can force 2^{2^k} certain paths (and in turn singular certain answers). $\qquad\qquad\square$

For cyclic TBoxes, it is easy to construct examples in which the number of singular certain answers is infinite:

Example 11. Let $\mathcal{T} = \{A \sqsubseteq \exists R.A\}$ and $\mathcal{A} = \{a : A\}$. Then $\{a\}$, $\exists R^-.\{a\}$, $\exists R^-.\exists R^-.\{a\}$, $\exists R^-.\exists R^-.\exists R^-.\{a\}$, etc., are singular certain answers to $A(x)$. $\square$

One can *represent* all these answers as simple regular expression based extensions of our language of referring expressions, stating that the singular certain answers can be reached, for example, by $R_1 \ldots R_{i-1}[R_i \ldots R_k]^*$ paths. When transformed to the concept language embellished by a Kleene star-like construct, such a referring expression would appear as follows:

$$[C_k \sqcap \exists R_k^-.(\ldots C_i \sqcap \exists R_i^-.(]^* C_{i-1} \sqcap \exists R_{i-1}^-.(\ldots \exists R_1^-.\{a\}))\ldots).$$

Note that the regular-like concept description corresponds to the certain path written backward, hence the cycle is syntactically at the beginning of this expression. Such expressions can be *extracted* from our construction of matching tuples as concatenations of simple paths from A to B followed by B to B cycles. However, while this solves our problems with the finiteness of (the presentation of) all answers, issues connected with the number of answers raised in Example 10 remain. Similarly, the number of distinct simple cycles can be bounded by a factorial function from below. The representations consisting of sets of matching tuples (essentially the transition relation of a tree automaton) are vastly more succinct, but may not be appropriate as an end user feedback. Indeed, a succinct and user-friendly representation remains a topic for further research.

4   Extensions

This section considers relaxing the various restrictions that we have assumed so far in addressing the problem of exhaustive query answering via referring expressions, restrictions that enabled a simpler exposition of what we believe are the principal issues.

Conjunctive Queries. We assume the standard definition of *conjunctive queries* (CQs) (i.e., existentially quantified conjunctions of concept and role atoms). We first consider CQ answering with respect to a unit ABox. In this setting we can reduce query answering to instance retrieval via folding of the given query since only tree-shaped, $\mathcal{EL}$ concept-like queries can have nonempty answers in this setting.[5] To capture bindings to free variables we introduce the notion *annotated concepts*—concepts whose subconcepts can be annotated by sets of variables—to stand for CQ foldings:

Definition 12 (Annotated Concepts and CQ Foldings). Let Q be a CQ and V the set of Q's variables. An *annotated* concept (C, X) is an $\mathcal{EL}$ concept C that is associated with $X \subseteq V$ and in which all subconcepts D of C appearing in existential restrictions $\exists R.D$ are annotated by pairwise distinct subsets of V. A first-order translation $\mathsf{FO}(C, X)$ of an annotated concept (C, X) is defined as

- $\mathsf{FO}(A, X) = A(x_0) \wedge (\bigwedge_{x_i, x_j \in X} x_i = x_j)$ where A is primitive and $x_0 \in X$,
- $\mathsf{FO}(C \sqcap D, X) = \mathsf{FO}(C, X) \wedge \mathsf{FO}(D, X)$, and
- $\mathsf{FO}(\exists R.D, X) = R(x_0, y_0) \wedge (\bigwedge_{x_i, x_j \in X} x_i = x_j) \wedge \mathsf{FO}(D, Y)$ where Y is the annotation of D and $x_0 \in X, y_0 \in Y$.

An annotated concept (C, X) is a *folding* of Q if $\forall V. \mathsf{FO}(C, X) \to Q$ holds.   □

Now, given a folding (C, X) of Q we can compute (a representation of) all referring expressions to the instance query $C(x)$ using the techniques described in Sect. 3. The answers (in a form of referring expressions) yield *bindings* for all variables in X. To get bindings for the remaining variables of Q we simply traverse C (breadth-first) and for every subexpression $\exists R.D$ with D annotated by Y we extend the *certain path* that generated a particular answer (see Definition 8) by the pair $R\,A$, where $\exists R.A$ is an existential restriction in the last feasible set S associated with the original path. This yields the referring expression that binds variables in Y. Repeating this process obtains bindings for all variables in V. Note that all such extensions *must exist* as we have already succeeded with our instance retrieval query. Such bindings are said to be *generated* by (C, X).

Theorem 13. Let $\mathcal{K}$ be a knowledge base and Q a CQ with variables in V. Then every set of bindings for V generated by a folding (C, X) of Q represents a tuple of singular certain answers to Q (up to projection). Taking a union of such bindings over all foldings of Q yields all singular certain answers.[6]   □

---

[5] We relax this condition in the subsequent section.
[6] Note that if there are no foldings of Q the set of answers set is empty.

Finally, a finite representation of the answers can use regular-like concept descriptions for bindings of variables in X as a seed and a tuple of *extensions* induced by paths in C for the remaining variables.

General ABoxes. One can use a standard approach to extend an explicitly given ABox to a tree model (represented again using matching tuples). One issue that needs to be addressed is guaranteeing the singularity of answers. This is not an issue for the ABox individuals, but roles in the ABox can make certain existential restrictions redundant and break our *independence* requirement, as illustrated in the following:

Example 14. Consider knowledge base $\mathcal{K}$ with a TBox $\mathcal{T} = \{A \sqsubseteq \exists R.B\}$. and an ABox $\mathcal{A} = \{A(a), R(a,b), R(a,c), B(b), B(c)\}$ Considering the TBox alone, we generate a matching tuple $(\{A\}, \{B\})$ that is used to generate (anonymous) R successors for A objects. However, were this tuple used for the a object above, it would lead to a certain answer $\exists R^-.\{a\}$ no longer singular (in the constructed model) since it ambiguously refers to both b and c objects that are explicit in the above ABox. Extending the *independence* requirement to eliminate redundant existential restrictions by generating additional matching tuples for ABox objects solves this problem.

$\square$

The above observation can be applied to all ABox objects: We simply use additional *matching tuples* that account for roles that are explicit in an ABox. W.l.o.g. we assume hereon that the ABox has been *completed* with respect to membership of individuals in primitive concepts and roles and is of the form

$$\{A(a) \mid \mathcal{K} \models A(a), A \in \mathsf{PC}, a \in \mathsf{IN}\} \cup \{R(a,b) \mid \mathcal{K} \models R(a,b), R \in \mathsf{R}, a, b \in \mathsf{IN}\}$$

For consistent knowledge bases in Horn logics, this completion is unique.

Definition 15. Let $\mathcal{K} = (\mathcal{T}, \mathcal{A})$ be a Horn-$\mathcal{ALC}$ knowledge base (in normal form) and $\mathsf{Inds}(\mathcal{A})$ the set of all constants appearing in $\mathcal{A}$. A *matching tuple* for $a \in \mathsf{Inds}(\mathcal{A})$ is a tuple

$$(S_a, \{C_0, D_{0,0}, \ldots, D_{0,k_0}\}, \ldots, \{C_k, D_{k,0}, \ldots, D_{k,k_k}\})$$

where $S_a = \{A \mid A(a) \in \mathcal{A}\}$, $\exists R_0.C_0, \ldots, \exists R_k.C_k$ are all independent existential restrictions in $\mathsf{Implied}(S_a)$ for which there are no $b_i \in \mathsf{Inds}(\mathcal{A})$ such that $R_i(a, b_i), C_i(b_i) \in \mathcal{A}$, and $\forall R_0.D_{0,0}, \ldots, \forall R_0.D_{0,k_0}, \ldots, \forall R_k.D_{k,0}, \ldots, \forall R_k.D_{k,k_k}$ are all value restrictions in $\mathsf{Implied}(S)$. We say that $\{C_i, D_{i,0}, \ldots, D_{i,k_i}\}$ belongs to S's matching tuple *for the existential restriction* $\exists R_i.C_i$.

$\square$

It is easy to see that there are at most $|\mathcal{A}|$ additional matching tuples, one for each constant in $\mathcal{A}$. We now simply require that S_a is feasible for all $a \in \mathsf{Inds}(\mathcal{A})$ and extend the definition of *certain paths* to *start* with S_a (i.e., set S_0 to be S_a rather than $\{A\}$ in Definition 8). This yields an immediate extension of Theorem 9 as follows:

Theorem 16. Every certain path $R_1 A_1 \ldots R_k A_k$ that starts with S_a for B and $\mathcal{K}$ corresponds to a singular certain answer $A_k \sqcap \exists R_k^- .(\ldots A_1 \sqcap \exists R_1^- .\{a\})$. Moreover, every B object common to all models of $\mathcal{K}$ will be reached by a certain path and will be returned as an answer. $\qquad\square$

Since there is at most a $|\mathcal{A}|$ increase in the number of matching tuples, the construction preserves our complexity bounds.

Conjunctive Queries Revisited. To accommodate CQs in the presence of an ABox it is sufficient to introduce parts of the CQ, one of which is answered over the ABox directly (as, e.g., in [7,8]) and any remaining parts that can be *folded to concept descriptions* for which our instance retrieval approach can be applied and conjoined to the first part.

Logics with Number Restrictions. When quantified role restrictions of the form $(\geq 2\ R.C)$ are present in the language, it may not be possible to describe all answers as singular certain answers since such *at-least* restrictions can force multiple certain answers that cannot be distinguished by referring expressions (without the loss of singularity). Note, however, that genuine at-least restrictions can be modeled by existential restrictions and auxiliary disjoint primitive concepts. Then, however, those concepts will guarantee singularity in the tree model. Results are better with only functionality or at-most restrictions, although there remains some dependence on the way such restrictions are realized in the TBox or concept language, for example, as **(func** R**)** constraints or as $(\leq 1\ R.C)$ concepts. Indeed, negations in the latter case can lead to *at-least* restrictions and non-singularity of certain answers.

Non-Horn Logics. The situation for non-Horn logics is even more complex: we can certainly extend our construction to full $\mathcal{ALC}$, but we face the following issue in the presence of disjunctions, in particular, when such disjunctions are allowed in referring expressions:

Example 17. According to our definition of singularity, given a TBox $\{A \sqsubseteq \exists R.B \sqcup \exists S.B\}$, an ABox $\{a : A\}$, and a query $B(x)$, a singular certain answer could be $\exists R^- .\{a\} \sqcup \exists S^- .\{a\}$ since the two (minimal) tree models will contain $\{R(a,o), B(o)\}$ and $\{S(a,o), B(o)\}$. Even worse, if the TBox was given as $\{A \sqsubseteq (\exists R.B \sqcap \exists S.B) \sqcup \exists T.B\}$, one could have *two* certain answers, both singular: $\exists R^- .\{a\} \sqcup \exists T^- .\{a\}$ and $\exists S^- .\{a\} \sqcup \exists T^- .\{a\}$, that seem to *reuse* the second part of the disjunction. This not only leads to combinatorial problems but also renders answers that are unintuitive. $\qquad\square$

Also, observe in the first case that the anonymous object o, indeed *the answer we are trying to refer to*, need not be the same object in the two models. However, this is not too different from interpreting a constant symbol by varying domain elements in different models of a knowledge base. The downside of this arrangement is that answers that contain (possibly large numbers of) disjunctions may not be what users would expect. Limiting the referring expressions that can appear in answers has been considered in [3] where the idea of *referring expression types* was introduced.

5   Summary and Open Problems

We have presented an extension to instance retrieval and query answering tasks that, with the help of referring expressions, allows one to return *all* singular certain answers in Horn-$\mathcal{ALC}$ and $\mathcal{EL}^\perp$ knowledge bases. We have also shown that this is no longer the case for logics endowed with *at-least* number restrictions. There are many directions for further research, e.g.:

- Issues related to a more compact representation of answers; this direction is related to discovering "small" regular expressions or devising other ways to present all the singular certain answers over a knowledge base.
- Extensions to more powerful Horn description logics: what concept constructors can be supported while maintaining the ability to report all answers? What to do with at-least restrictions and do we really need them?
- Extensions to non-Horn Description Logics: can the techniques be extended to DLs with concept disjunction (recall the discussion in Sect. 4)?

Finally, throughout, we have used reasoning in the underlying DL as a black box whenever needed since this does not impact the complexity bounds. However, in a practical implementation, a more integrated approach that interleaves knowledge base reasoning with query answering needs to be developed.

References

1. Baader, F., Brandt, S., Lutz, C.: Pushing the $\mathcal{EL}$ envelope. In: Proceedings of the IJCAI, pp. 364–369 (2005)
2. Baader, F., Calvanese, D., McGuinness, D.L., Nardi, D., Patel-Schneider, P.F.: The Description Logic Handbook: Theory, Implementation, and Applications. Cambridge University Press, Cambridge (2003)
3. Borgida, A., Toman, D., Weddell, G.: On referring expressions in query answering over first order knowledge bases. In: Proceedings of the KR, pp. 319–328 (2016)
4. Detwiler, L., Mejino, J., Brinkley, J.: From frames to OWL2: converting the foundational model of anatomy. Artif. Intell. Med. **69**, 12–21 (2016)
5. Hartel, F., de Coronado, S., Dionne, R., Fragoso, G., Golbeck, J.: Modeling a description logic vocabulary for cancer research. J. Biomed Inf. **38**(2), 114–29 (2005)
6. Hustadt, U., Motik, B., Sattler, U.: Data complexity of reasoning in very expressive description logics. In: Proceedings of the IJCAI, pp. 466–471 (2005)
7. Lutz, C., Seylan, İ., Toman, D., Wolter, F.: The combined approach to OBDA: taming role hierarchies using filters. In: Alani, H., et al. (eds.) ISWC 2013. LNCS, vol. 8218, pp. 314–330. Springer, Heidelberg (2013). https://doi.org/10.1007/978-3-642-41335-3_20
8. Lutz, C., Toman, D., Wolter, F.: Conjunctive query answering in the description logic EL using a relational database system. In: Proceedings of the IJCAI, pp. 2070–2075 (2009)

9. Suntisrivaraporn, B., Baader, F., Schulz, S., Spackman, K.: Replacing SEP-triplets in SNOMED CT using tractable description logic operators. In: Bellazzi, R., Abu-Hanna, A., Hunter, J. (eds.) AIME 2007. LNCS (LNAI), vol. 4594, pp. 287–291. Springer, Heidelberg (2007). https://doi.org/10.1007/978-3-540-73599-1_38

10. Toman, D., Weddell, G.: Identity resolution in ontology based data access to structured data sources. In: Nayak, A.C., Sharma, A. (eds.) PRICAI 2019. LNCS (LNAI), vol. 11670, pp. 473–485. Springer, Cham (2019). https://doi.org/10.1007/978-3-030-29908-8_38

11. Vardi, M.Y.: Why is modal logic so robustly decidable? In: Descriptive Complexity and Finite Models. DIMACS Series in Discrete Mathematics and Theoretical Computer Science, vol. 31, pp. 149–183. DIMACS/AMS (1996)

Constructing CP-Nets from Users Past Selection

Reza Khoshkangini[1]([✉]), Maria Silvia Pini[2], and Francesca Rossi[3]

[1] Center for Applied Intelligent Systems Research (CAISR),
Halmstad University, Halmstad, Sweden
`reza.khoshkangini@hh.se`
[2] Department of Information Engineering, University of Padova, Padua, Italy
`pini@dei.unipd.it`
[3] IBM T. J. Watson Research Center, Yorktown Heights, NY, USA
`francesca.rossi2@ibm.com`

Abstract. Although recommender systems have been significantly developed for providing customized services to users in various domains, they still have some limitations regarding the extraction of users' conditional preferences from their past selections when they are in a dynamic context. We propose a framework to automatically extract and learn users' conditional and qualitative preferences in a gamified system taking into consideration the players' past behaviour, without asking any information from the players. To do that, we construct CP-nets modeling users preferences via a procedure that employs multiple Information Criterion score functions within an heuristic algorithm to learn a Bayesian network. The approach has been validated experimentally in the challenge recommendation domain in an urban mobility gamified system.

Keywords: CP-net · Bayesian network · Recommender system · Gamification

1 Introduction

Over the past decades significant efforts have been undertaken among researchers, practitioners and companies to develop various types of recommender systems (RSs) to meet users' requests [1]. The aim of these systems is to personalize service recommendations for individual users, as well as aggregating users' preferences to recommend a service for a group of users in various domains from movies [25] to restaurants [14], from hotels, recommending items and products to challenge recommendation in a gamified context [15].

Advancement in recommender systems have been performed by considering the context, which is basically defined as any information that could be used to characterize the situation of an entity in a particular domain [9]. On the one hand, considering the context can improve the performance of the RSs, which leads to enhance the satisfaction degree of users by properly fulfilling

© Springer Nature Switzerland AG 2019
J. Liu and J. Bailey (Eds.): AI 2019, LNAI 11919, pp. 130–142, 2019.
https://doi.org/10.1007/978-3-030-35288-2_11

their demands [13]. On the other hand, it can make the recommendation task more complex, since changes in the context may cause changes in users' preferences over time. This issue is very relevant when the system should perform in a dynamic and open field domain such as in a gamified system [16]. Self-adaptive recommender systems have been developed to overcome such problems in the application domains where the context of users and/or of services can influence the recommendation [4,14]. Players' preferences are often qualitative and conditional. For example, *if it is sunny, I prefer to go work with bicycle rather taking public transportation*. CP-nets [23] are a graphical model to represent the qualitative preferences in a compact and intuitive way, which have been already used to model users' preferences in automated decision making and in modeling human preferences in real-world applications [7]. Modeling and learning the users' preferences expressed via CP-nets is a task that has been studied extensively by adopting various techniques, such as observing/asking multiple questions to the users [2]. In some studies, researchers start by assuming a dependency structure and then they try to learn the users' conditional preferences [6]. Bigot et al. [2] discussed the possibility of learning Probabilistic CP-nets (PCP-nets), which have been introduced in [8] in two settings (online and off-line). In that paper, Bayesian networks are used to learn PCP-nets. In both settings they assume to have the dependency graph and then they ask multiple queries to the users to build up and learn the structure of the network. Similarly, Guerin et al. [11] present an algorithm for learning CP-net preferences by interacting with users rather than using users' histories. Learning conditional preferences may be a tedious and costly task, even with acyclic CP-nets. However, the complexity of the problem can be reduced by interacting with the users to simplify the learning procedure. E.g., Koriche et al. [17] propose an approach to identify a preference ordering with binary domains, which uses membership queries. Despite the significant progress in this area, we like to express that we have observed a lack of studies based on automatically extracting players' CP-nets.

In this paper, we propose a framework to automatically construct CP-nets from players' past selections without demanding any information from the players who are involved in the system. Here, users' past behaviors are characterized by a set of domain features, which are logged in the users profiles, through their participation in the gamified system. E.g., in the challenge recommendation domain in gamification, the previous selections of a player may be defined by the challenges that have been selected and finished previously by the player and each challenge is a combination of elements in different context. For example, in our urban mobility gamification system a challenge includes prize, difficulty, mode of transportation etc. To construct a CP-net from the user's past selections we proposed a system constructed by five modules: *Feature Selection* to extract the most informative features, *Layer Extraction* that includes the process of defining three layers that are root, intermediate and target; *Feature Dependencies and CP-net construction*, where the dependency of the features will be derived to shape the main structure of the network; *Converter* that converts the extracted probability between the features into user's preference, and *Layer Binding* in which the three layers will be attached to construct the whole CP-net.

Experimental results show that the presented approach for building CP-nets from players' past selections is promising in the challenge recommendation domains in gamification. The proposed approach to construct CP-nets from previous selected challenges is useful in a real time context-based recommender systems in gamification [14,16]. E.g., constructing player's CP-nets which change over time support the recommender systems to increase the satisfaction of the users with suitable challenges and and acts as a remedy in gamification to achieve its vision, in particular, an open field gamified system, to improve players' behavior towards the sustainable style. Indeed the goal of every gamified system is to change players' behavior [20] and the challenges are the main mechanism used to encourage this improvement [22], thus providing the wrong challenges may lead negative influences to players progress and involvement in gamification.

2   Challenge, CP-Net and Bayesian Network

In this section we present the key notions of a Challenge in gamification, CP-nets and Bayesian Networks, however, we omit the detailed description of them, so you can find more additional information in [3,12,16].

2.1   Challenge Model

Challenges are units of playable content including a demanding goal that a player should achieve, under temporal or other constraints, in exchange for an in-game prize or reward. We defined a challenge in [16] as a tuple:

$<P; G; C; D; R; W>$, where: P refers to the individual *Player* to whom the challenge is recommended; G defines the *Goal*, that is a task or a performance target, which should be fulfilled to complete the challenge; C is the *Constraint* for reaching the goal. E.g., player P must achieve goal G within a temporal deadline-one week-; D represents the *Difficulty* of the challenge for player P, considering goal G and constraint C. For D, we have been using a 4-level scale: {*Easy, Medium, Hard, or Very Hard*}; R is the *Reward* (a.k.a prize) awarded for completing the challenge. An example of a challenge that our recommendation system, introduced in [16], recommended to players is: "Increase <Bike> <Km> by at least <10%> during <next week> and receive <200> <Green Leaves>".

2.2   CP-Net and Bayesian Network (BN)

CP-net [3] is a graphical model to represent conditional and qualitative preference relations between variables (a.k.a features). Let's assume there is a set of variables $V = \{X1, ..., Xn\}$ with finite domains $D(X1), ..., D(Xn)$. For each variable Xi, each user specifies a set of parents $P(Xi)$ that can affect her preferences over the value of Xi. So this defines a dependency graph such that every variable Xi may have $P(Xi)$ as its immediate predecessors. For each node Xi,

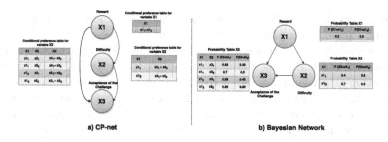

Fig. 1. A CP-net and a Bayesian Network.

there is a *conditional preference table* that shows, for each possible combination of parents values, the preference over values of Xi. An example of CP-net is shown in Fig. 1(a). It contains three features $X1, X2$ and $X3$, standing for the Reward of the challenge to complete, Difficulty and the Acceptance of the challenge, respectively. $X1$ is an independent variable, while $X2$ depends on $X1$ and $X3$ depends on both $X1$ and $X2$.

A Bayesian network is a probabilistic graphical model that represents a set of variables and their conditional dependencies via a directed acyclic graph (DAG) $G = (V, E_G)$ [12], where V is the set of features, and E_G represents the set of direct arcs (dependency) between the features, e.g., $Xi \rightarrow Xj$ means that the variable Xj depends on the variable Xi, and there is a constraint in BN that avoids any directed cycles (similarly to the concept of acyclic CP-net). For each node Xi, there is a *conditional probability table* that shows for each possible combination of parents values the probability distribution over values of Xi.

An example of BN is shown in Fig. 1(b), where the probability that I accept $(x3_1)$, or that I don't accept $(x3_2)$ a challenge during the game depends on the values of his parents, that are Reward $(X1)$ and Difficulty of the challenge $(X2)$.

3 Technical Approach

This section shows our approach to build a CP-net representing the conditional and qualitative preferences of a user starting from the past selections of the use. For the sake of clarification, we will explain how the constructor works in different sections by using examples of preferences, which are taken from the context of gamification for challenge recommendation.

3.1 Feature Selection

Selecting the most informative feature that are more important on influencing players' preferences is the vital procedure in any learning and prediction task. Thus, given a set of features $V = \{X1, X2, \ldots, Xn\}$, without the loss of generality we assume that Xn is the variable corresponding to the target node of the CP-net, which is the most constrained variable. In this context, target node points to the acceptance of the challenges, that the player has accepted before and logged in his profile during the game.

In this module we aim to identify a subset $V_s \subset V$ of the features that highly affect players' decision for accepting a challenge. It is expected that every feature selection algorithm takes into account different aspects of the data to select the most valuable features. Thus, in this framework, we associate two different algorithms, as an *ensemble* method, namely *SelectKBest* and *Information Gain* algorithms[1], in a parallel fashion to pick the most informative subset of features. Then, the score of each output list has been normalized between 0 and 1, since they have a different range of scores. Eventually, to achieve the desired list of features $V_s = \{X1, X2, \ldots, Xm, Xt\}$ in this selection manner (as it is illustrated in Fig. 2), the identical features from the output of each of the two algorithms will be selected to be used to build the model. Thereafter, the selected features in V_s is sorted in decreasing order to build the following list $\{X1s, X2s, \ldots, Xms\}$. Then, the system attaches Xt (as the target node) at the end of the list as follows $V_s = \{X1s, X2s, \ldots, Xms, Xt\}$ to achieve the desired list of features in feature selection process. Once the process is done, the agent breaks down the sorted features into three layers that are detailed in the following section.

3.2   Layers Extraction

Given the above list V_s we aim to build an acyclic and directed graph that consists of three layers: *Root*, *Intermediate*, and the *Target* layers. Hereafter, we describe in detail each layer and links connecting the nodes inside the graph. Notice: the terms "node" and "feature" refer to the same concept from now on.

- *Root Layer:* this layer contains only the root node, which is the most important feature among the others in the list. In other words, given the list "V_s", the first feature $X1$ will be considered as the root node. Since, this node $X1$ is an independent feature, it does not have any *income link* from the other nodes. For example, considering the challenge recommendation domain, Reward could be the root node as an independent feature, see Fig. 1.
- *Intermediate Layer:* the main procedure of extracting users' conditional preferences on the basis of the strength of relations between features under certain conditions or threshold, will be executed in this layer. This layer contains all the nodes except Root and the Target nodes as follows $\{X1s, \ldots, Xms\}$. To set the internal links between intermediate nodes, we need to measure the dependence between any pair of nodes (Xis, Xjs). The algorithm adds a link between the these nodes that have dependence values higher or equal to a given threshold. This threshold value could be determined automatically or manually. In this paper we decide to fix this threshold manually as described in Sect. 4.

---

[1] To use the above feature selection algorithms, we took the advantage of *FSelector* [18] library.

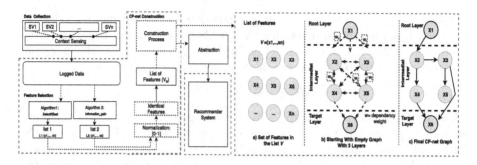

Fig. 2. The Proposed Framework and CP-net Constructor Frontend. This is a conceptual view of the framework which can be used in a Context-Aware Recommender System where several service providers (SVs) are connected to the system.

- *Target Layer:* as the name implies, this layer indicates the target node Xt that shows the player's preference (last attribute in the sorted list) toward the specific domain. Thus, this layer has only incoming links from the nodes, which are located in the Intermediate layer or in the Root layer. Notice that in this study we manually select the *Target* node (Xt), which differs from domain to domain, and we attach it at the end of the sorted list of features.

The action flow is shown in Fig. 2, where the selected features in the list V_s (Fig. 2(a)) are segmented into three layers (Fig. 2(b)). Then, the proposed constructor integrates the layers (Fig. 2(c)) based upon the dependencies between the features in the second layer obtained by exploiting the score functions and the algorithm explained in the next Sect. 3.3.

In the next section, we describe in detail how the framework acts to construct the CP-net.

3.3 Feature Dependency and Constructing CP-Net

Due to the similarity between the concepts of CP-nets and Bayesian network, we exploit Bayesian network's score functions to construct the main shape of a user's CP-net in the second layer. Many algorithms and techniques have been developed to tackle the problem of building a Bayesian Network, whose performance vary according to the used score functions from data/domain to data/domain. Hence, we implement the proposed approach by considering various kinds of score functions such as Mutual Information Test (MIT), Bayesian Information Criterion (BIC), Akaike Information Criterion (AIC), Log Likelihood (LogL) and K2 [5], to decrease the miss classification results and thus to have the suitable technique that better fits data and provide the highest performance.

To show the constructor and how the score functions work, we use *Akaike Information Criterion (AIC)* [21] throughout this paper, but we implement the constructor with all the possible functions (in the second layer) to evaluate the performance of the algorithm in the specific domain. In short, Akaike information criterion (AIC), which is also known "Schwarz criterion" is a penalized technique based on in-sample fit to determine the likelihood of a model to estimate the future values [27]. In this score function the lower value represents the minimum information loss related to the candidate model which is shown in Eq. 1.

$$AIC = -2 * ln(\theta) + 2 * k \tag{1}$$

where k refers to the degree of freedom to be estimated. The set of model parameters that maximize the likelihood function is shown by θ and $ln(\theta)$ refers to the likelihood of the truth model. A lower AIC value indicates the obtained model is more likely to be considered as the best and true network model among the others (more details about how these functions work, see [24]). Hence, to perform the above functions to construct the desired network in the second layer, we borrow the structures shown in [26], where the various algorithms have been discussed such as *Simulated Annealing algorithm, Heuristic algorithm, and Genetic algorithms.*

Taking into account the advantage of the greedy search and heuristic algorithm [10], we use *Hill Climbing (HC)* algorithm to execute the functions to obtain the structure of a user's CP-net in the second layer as follows. Recalling the feature selection and breaking the list "V" into three layers, HC starts with an empty graph in the second layer and attempts to find a model with the best score by incrementally searching among the other possible models from its local neighbors. This is an optimization model that begins with an arbitrary structure of the network and then it tries to find a better network by incrementally tuning the scores. Hence, if a new model with a better score is found, it will substitute the old model. These steps are repeated until no further model with a better score can be found. Although the algorithm has the problem of getting stuck in the local region that depends on the starting point, we took the privilege of its high performance and accuracy to build the network. In the following section we show how connecting the layers to define the CP-net.

3.4 Converter: Probability to Preferences

This section shows how to interpret the strength of the correlation between nodes in the BN as user's preferences in the CP-net. If a node from the list of features contains two values in the domain, the system from the conditional probability table of this node in the BN states that the value with the highest probability is the most preferred one. Once the structure of the network is obtained in the second layer, the agent converts the probability into preference as shown below. The procedure starts from the independent nodes. The highest probable value for a feature will be considered as the most preferred value among the other possible values. The independent nodes (as parents) influence the preference values of the remaining nodes (as children) on basis of the probability tables. In Fig. 3 there is an example that shows how to transform the probabilities of a BN in the preferences of a corresponding CP-net. Assume $v = \{X2, X3, X4\}$, $v \subset V$, and binary domains $D(X2) = \{x2_1, x2_2\}, D(X3) = \{x3_1, x3_2\}$ and $D(X4) = \{x4_1, x4_2\}$.

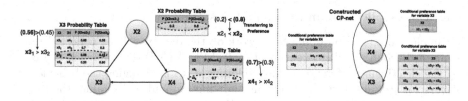

Fig. 3. From a Bayesian Network to the corresponding CP-net.

As it is shown in the figure, $X2$ influences $X3$ and $X4$ in the second layer, and similarly $X4$ influences $X3$. Hence, $X3$ is identified as the most dependent node among the others with its probability table. The conditional probability table associated to $X2$ can be used to derive preferences over values in $D(X2)$ in the CP-net. In the conditional preference table of the CP-net associated to $X2$ we have $x2_2$ more preferred than $x2_1$ since the probability of $x2_2$ is 0.8 while the probability of $x2_1$ is 0.2. Thus, if $x2_2$ is the most preferred for $X2$, then $x4_1$ with probability 0.7 is the most preferred value for $X4$, according to the conditional probability table of $X4$ and so on. Here, we just gave a simple example of features with binary domains but this could be extended with n numbers of values in the domains for each feature in the sorted list V_s.

3.5 Layer Binding

This section is in charge of integrating the Root and the Target nodes to the nodes that are located in the Intermediate layer. Since the Root node dominates the other nodes in the two layers, the system generates a matrix of dependency between them. Practically, the aim is to find the strength of the relations between the Root and the rest, hence we use *Chi-square* and *Gain ratio* functions [19] to obtain these dependencies. This process of generating the dependency matrix is broken down into two sections. First, it is applied between the Root layer and "Intermediate and Target" layers (both together, as the Root node dominates the rest of the nodes which are located in these two layers). Secondly, it is applied between the Intermediate layer and the Target layer. Having these two dependency matrix, we set a threshold in the interval $[0, 1]$ as a Confidence Value to eliminate the links between these layers which can not meet the threshold value. This is done to find out the most important dependencies within the user CP-net that can characterize the user preferences. The described work-flow produces the final user's CP-net that characterizes the user's preferences.

4   Experimental Evaluation and Results

The main task of RSs is to provide the best personalized service for users in various domains. In this study, we validate our procedure for constructing users' CP-nets from their past behaviors in the gamified system where a RS has been used to recommend personalized game content (challenges) to players.

4.1 Data Collection and Gamified System

We implemented the proposed framework on the data which we collected from a gamified urban mobility experiment (called Play&Go[2]) that aimed at evaluating the effectiveness of gamification exploiting a RS in changing the behavior of players towards more sustainable transport means, and maintaining their participation active in the long term. Play&Go was a large–scale and long–running open–field gamification campaign that lasted twelve weeks (from September 10 to December 2, 2016). The game was targeting residents of the city of Trento in Italy. During the twelve game weeks, 410 citizens actively participated in it. Within these weeks, the RS provided more than 6000 challenges to players, and we have selected 3307 challenges related to transportation mode that asked players to improve their behavior w.r.t the public transportation. Within those recommended challenges only 24% of them are accepted by the players during the game, which shows there is a huge room between the players' preference and the recommended challenges in the game. Hence, this motives us to investigate to find the conditional preference of players in this context of recommendation in gamification to maximize the acceptance rate.

Due to the page limit, we ignore the detailed description of experimental results which we have done in [16], and focus only on this approach to show we could construct the players' CP-nets. The challenge elements that are used in this evaluation are: *Type of challenge (TP)* including percentage (e.g., asks players to increase a certain percentage of its activity) and absolute (points to a certain numbers–2,3– to improve in the mode), *mode of transportation (MOD)* e.g., walk, bus, bike and train, *improvement (IMP)* consisting of low, medium or high, *prize (Bonus)* to complete the challenge such as low, medium and high, *difficulty (Dif)* of the challenge including easy, medium or difficult, and *Acceptance (Tr) of challenge* such as "yes" or "no".

4.2 Evaluation and Model Selection

To assess and evaluate the proposed approach in constructing the players CP-net, we have defined the following research question: *To what extent we can effectively construct users CP-nets that can be used in a context-aware recommender system in a dynamic and open field system?*

To answer the question that represents players' conditional preferences on the selected challenges, we execute the algorithm with a range of parameters, where each combination of parameter values specifies a specific structure of CP-net. For each round, to find the best model to make inference, the grid search technique is employed to find the optimal tuple of hyperparameter values.

4.3 Evaluation Setting and Results

Although in this dataset there are many data points that have been logged from hundred of players, we have a limited number of samples for each individual

---

[2] https://www.smartcommunitylab.it/apps/viaggia-trento-e-rovereto-playgo/.

Table 1. The performance of the proposed method on the considered real dataset.

	Score function	Precision	Recall	F-measure	Description	# of features	Arc Dep	Dir	Tr1	Tr2
Dataset 1	BIC	0.77	0.75	0.76	Applicable	4	0.6	0.4	0.05	0.03
	AIC	0.75	0.74	0.75	Applicable	5	0.5	0.6	0.03	0.03
	LogL	0.77	0.76	0.76	Applicable	6	0.6	0.7	0.03	0.05
	K2	0.78	0.76	**0.77**	Applicable	5	0.6	0.5	0.03	0.03
	MDL	x	x	x	Causing cycle	x	x	x	x	x

player which reveals a big concern in properly learning player's CP-net. This relatively points to the cold start issue in a recommendation context, so we can exploit the collaborative filtering solution to overcome this manner. Taking into consideration the low numbers of parameters and a binary classification problem in this challenge recommendation problem, we assume that the similarity between the users are well enough to take the 70% of all users' data points to build the model. While to evaluate the network we feed the model with each user's data point from that 30% of the data. Then, the result of each data point, from each individual user will be considered for the overall performance of the function that depicted in Table 1. In the following, we have listed the parameters and the set of the values that we have used to construct multiple CP-nets.

- Number of selected features: We have run the algorithm with various number of features to find out the right numbers that can provide the best CP-net and high performance value, however, it needs to be highlighted that in this case study our challenge dataset is limited to less number of features.
- Dependency (Dep): {0.5, 0.6, 0.7}: Since we have defined the dependencies between features in this interval [0,1], we tune the threshold similar to the number of features to find the best results.
- Direction (Dir): {0.5, 0.6, 0.7}: We also tuned the algorithm with three values to obtain the direction of the dependency between the features.
- Threshold (Tr1) for connecting the first and the second layer: {0.03, 0.04, 0.05}.
- Threshold (Tr2) for connecting the second and the third layer: {0.03, 0.04, 0.05}.

Once the model is trained, the algorithm computes a score for each challenge option. This score shows how probable is for a challenge to be accepted according the player's interest. Then the system selects a challenge which has the highest probability value as the player's preference. Finally, to evaluate the performance of the method we have used the following well-known metrics such as *Precision*, *Recall* and *F-measure*. Table 1 presents our preliminary experimental results in the challenge recommendation domain. In particular, it shows the performance of our

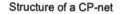

Structure of a CP-net

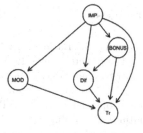

Fig. 4. A complex CP-net of players with 5 features.

approach by considering various score functions. Within the score functions implemented by the hill-climbing algorithm, BIC, AIC, Loglik and K2 functions were applicable in our data-set. The parameters, which are automatically set to generate such results are almost similar with an admissible performance. BIC provides its best result for 4 features, 0.6 for Arc dependency (Dep), and 0.05 and 0.03 for dependency between layers, while AIC provides its best result with 5 features, 0.5 Arc Dep and 0.03 for layer dependency. The values of precision and recall using BIC and Loglik are very similar with ~0.77, however Loglik performs slightly better both in terms of precision and recall. As it is shown in the table, K2 dominates other functions in this dataset by proving 0.78, 0.76 and 0.77 in precision, recall and f-measure, respectively. In contrast, we have not inserted results for MIT, since the approach with this score function often construct CP-nets with cycles, specially after appending the nodes of the layers in the final step. An example of a complex CP-nets extracted by K2 function is depicted in Fig. 4.

5   Conclusion

We have presented a system for automatically constructing CP-nets model-ing users' preferences from their past behavior and interaction with a service provider. In this case study, the gamified system called–Play&Go– acts as a ser-vice provider. To construct the user CP-net we have first constructed a Bayesian network, then we have transformed it in a CP-net. We have exploited an heuris-tic algorithm *Hill Climbing* to execute various score functions to construct the best graph model among all the possible models. Empirical results from chal-lenge acceptance dataset in a gamification context have shown that this con-structor may have a positive impact to enhance users' satisfaction by accepting more recommended challenges during the game which relatively have a poten-tial to increase the performance of the RS and consequently gamification goal. In addition, we plan to integrate the proposed constructor in the Self-adaptive Context-Aware recommender system (SaCARS) [14] illustrated in Fig. 2. This integration will allow SaCARS to completely learn and model the users' condi-tional preferences from their behavior without human interference.

References

1. Amatriain, X., Basilico, J.: Past, present, and future of recommender systems: an industry perspective. In: Proceedings of the 10th ACM Conference on Recom-mender Systems, RecSys 2016, pp. 211–214. ACM, New York (2016)
2. Bigot, D., Mengin, J., Zanuttini, B.: Learning probabilistic CP-nets from observa-tions of optimal items. In: STAIRS, pp. 81–90 (2014)
3. Boutilier, C., Brafman, R.I., Domshlak, C., Hoos, H.H., Poole, D.: CP-nets: a tool for representing and reasoning with conditional ceteris paribus preference state-ments. J. Artif. Int. Res. 21(1), 135–191 (2004)

4. Brun, Y., et al.: A design space for self-adaptive systems. In: de Lemos, R., Giese, H., Müller, H.A., Shaw, M. (eds.) Software Engineering for Self-Adaptive Systems II. LNCS, vol. 7475, pp. 33–50. Springer, Heidelberg (2013). https://doi.org/10.1007/978-3-642-35813-5_2

5. Carvalho, A.M.: Scoring functions for learning Bayesian networks. INESC-ID, Technical report (2009)

6. Chevaleyre, Y., Koriche, F., Lang, J., Mengin, J., Zanuttini, B.: Learning ordinal preferences on multiattribute domains: the case of CP-nets. In: Fürnkranz, J., Hüllermeier, E. (eds.) Preference Learning, pp. 273–296. Springer, Heidelberg (2010). https://doi.org/10.1007/978-3-642-14125-6_13

7. Coelho, H., et al.: An efficient procedure for collective decision-making with CP-nets. In: ECAI 2010: 19th European Conference on Artificial Intelligence, vol. 215, p. 375 (2010)

8. Cornelio, C., Goldsmith, J., Mattei, N., Rossi, F., Venable, K.B.: Dynamic and probabilistic CP-nets. In: MPREF 2013 (2013)

9. Dey, A.K.: Understanding and using context. Pers. Ubiquit. Comput. 5(1), 4–7 (2001)

10. Feo, T.A., Resende, M.G.: Greedy randomized adaptive search procedures. J. Global Optim. 6(2), 109–133 (1995)

11. Guerin, J.T., Allen, T.E., Goldsmith, J.: Learning CP-net preferences online from user queries. In: Perny, P., Pirlot, M., Tsoukiàs, A. (eds.) ADT 2013. LNCS (LNAI), vol. 8176, pp. 208–220. Springer, Heidelberg (2013). https://doi.org/10.1007/978-3-642-41575-3_16

12. Jensen, F.V.: An Introduction to Bayesian Networks. UCL Press, London (1996)

13. Khoshkangini, R., Pini, M.S., Rossi, F.: A design of context-aware framework for conditional preferences of group of users. In: Lee, R. (ed.) Software Engineering, Artificial Intelligence, Networking and Parallel/Distributed Computing. SCI, vol. 653, pp. 97–112. Springer, Cham (2016). https://doi.org/10.1007/978-3-319-33810-1_8

14. Khoshkangini, R., Pini, M.S., Rossi, F.: A self-adaptive context-aware group recommender system. In: Adorni, G., Cagnoni, S., Gori, M., Maratea, M. (eds.) AI*IA 2016. LNCS (LNAI), vol. 10037, pp. 250–265. Springer, Cham (2016). https://doi.org/10.1007/978-3-319-49130-1_19

15. Khoshkangini, R., Valetto, G., Marconi, A.: Generating personalized challenges to enhance the persuasive power of gamification. In: Personalization in Persuasive Technology Workshop (2017)

16. Khoshkangini, R., Valetto, G., Marconi, A.: Automatic generation and recommendation of personalized challenges for gamification. In: User Modeling and User-Adapted Interaction (UMUAI) (2019, under review)

17. Koriche, F., Zanuttini, B.: Learning conditional preference networks. Artif. Intell. 174(11), 685–703 (2010)

18. Kursa, M.B., Rudnicki, W.R., et al.: Feature selection with the boruta package. J. Stat. Softw. 36(11), 1–13 (2010)

19. Lee, C., Lee, G.G.: Information gain and divergence-based feature selection for machine learning-based text categorization. Inf. Process. Manag. 42(1), 155–165 (2006)

20. Lessel, P., Altmeyer, M., Krüger, A.: Analysis of recycling capabilities of individuals and crowds to encourage and educate people to separate their garbage playfully. In: Proceedings of the 33rd Annual ACM Conference on Human Factors in Computing Systems, CHI 2015 (2015)

21. Liu, Z., Malone, B., Yuan, C.: Empirical evaluation of scoring functions for Bayesian network model selection. BMC Bioinform. **13**(15), S14 (2012)
22. Lopes, R., Bidarra, R.: Adaptivity challenges in games and simulations: a survey. IEEE Trans. Comput. Intell. AI Games **3**(2), 85–99 (2011)
23. Marchetti-Spaccamela, A., Vitaletti, A., Becchetti, L., Colesanti, U.: Self-adaptive recommendation systems: models and experimental analysis. In: Second IEEE International Conference on Self-Adaptive and Self-Organizing Systems (2008)
24. Neal, R.M.: Bayesian Learning for Neural Networks, vol. 118. Springer, New York (2012). https://doi.org/10.1007/978-1-4612-0745-0
25. Ono, C., Kurokawa, M., Motomura, Y., Asoh, H.: A context-aware movie preference model using a Bayesian network for recommendation and promotion. In: Conati, C., McCoy, K., Paliouras, G. (eds.) UM 2007. LNCS (LNAI), vol. 4511, pp. 247–257. Springer, Heidelberg (2007). https://doi.org/10.1007/978-3-540-73078-1_28
26. Russell, S., Norvig, P.: Artificial Intelligence: A Modern Approach Author (2009)
27. Yamaoka, K., Nakagawa, T., Uno, T.: Application of Akaike's information criterion (AIC) in the evaluation of linear pharmacokinetic equations. J. Pharmacokinet. Biopharm. **6**(2), 165–175 (1978)

An Efficient Solver for Parametrized Difference Revision

Aaron Hunter[✉] and John Agapeyev

BC Institute of Technology, Burnaby, Canada
aaron_hunter@bcit.ca, jagapeyev@gmail.com

Abstract. We present GenC, an efficient and highly-parallel belief revision solver for paramatrized difference operators. GenC uses an AllSAT solver to enumerate the possible models of a formula, and then determines the output of revision through a series of bit comparisons. The result is a system that can calculate the result of revision for formulas with 100 variables and millions of clauses in just seconds; the running times obtained by GenC far surpass existing solvers for belief revision. The system also has many features that are useful for practical problems: it supports both interactive and offline data entry, it allows multiple formats for entering formulas, and it provides output in human-readable format. Most importantly, GenC is able to model revision by any parametrized difference operator, which allows a wide range of practical problems to be easily captured.

1 Introduction

Belief revision refers to the process where an agent incorportates new information into a pre-existing set of beliefs. While the theory of logic-based belief revision has been an active area of study for over thirty years, there has been relatively little work on implementations and tools for solving belief change problems. Moreover, the implementations that exist are generally too slow to be useful for large instances. In this paper, describe an efficient solver for *parametrized difference operators* [10]; this is a natural class of belief revision operators that can be compactly specified, while being expressive enough to capture a wide range of practical problems.

This paper makes several contributions to the belief change literature. The main contribution is simply the fact that our tool is the first belief revision solver that is able to quickly solve belief revision problems involving millions of clauses. To the best of our knowledge, our tool is the first implemented belief revision system that is built on top of an industrial-strength AllSAT solver; an AllSAT solver is a system that extends a SAT solver to return all satisfying assignments, rather than just one [11]. Another contribution of this work is the fact that we explicitly focus on parametrized difference operators. This is an expressive class of belief change operators that is useful for practical problems; it has previously been claimed that these operators are well-suited for implementation. The work in this paper shows that this is indeed the case.

© Springer Nature Switzerland AG 2019
J. Liu and J. Bailey (Eds.): AI 2019, LNAI 11919, pp. 143–152, 2019.
https://doi.org/10.1007/978-3-030-35288-2_12

2   Preliminaries

2.1   Motivation

We are motivated by the following high-level goals:

- We want to develop a belief revision solver that runs quickly with large formulas as input.
- We want the solver to work for an extensive class of belief revision operators.

The first goal is challenging due to the well-known complexity of belief revision [5]. We address this problem by using a competition-level SAT solver for the computationally hard portions of the revision. The second goal is challenging, because belief revision operators in general are difficult to specify in a compact manner. As indicated in the introduction, we address this problem by explicitly restricting our attention to parametrized difference operators.

We argue that it is currently very important to make an efficient belief revision solver available to those outside the discipline. An efficient tool could be useful for many problems, ranging from applications in software engineering proposed many years ago [13] to contemporary problems in ontology change [14]. Moreover, an efficient revision solver has the potential to complement the current success of machine learning. Traditional machine learning methods are very good at classifying data; these classifications are then used to drive decision making. But if we can *learn* a revision operator rather than a discrete classification, then we may be able to produce rational and justifiable decision making [8].

2.2   AGM Belief Revision

The most influential model of belief revision has been the AGM approach [1]. In AGM revision, a *belief set* is a set of formulas that is closed under consequence. An AGM belief revision operator $*$ takes an initial belief set K and a formula ϕ for revision as input, and it returns a new belief set $K * \phi$. The AGM postulates provide a set of constraints that must be satisfied by every AGM revision operator. Informally, the idea is that $K * A$ should include ϕ while retaining as much of K as consistently possible. It is worth noting that, if the underlying vocabulary is finite, then every belief set can be captured by a single formula.

A *state* is a propositional interpretation over the underlying vocabulary, and a *belief state* is a set of states. It has been shown that, for every AGM revision operator $*$, there is a function that maps each belief set K to a total pre-order $\prec_K$ over states such that the models of $K * A$ are just the $\prec_K$-minimal models of ϕ [9]. The converse is also true.

2.3   Parametrized Difference Operators

One of the difficulties in developing belief revision solvers is the fact that it can be difficult to have a user specify a revision operator. In general, specifying a single revision operator requires a user to define a total pre-order over states *for each* belief set. This can be arduous.

One of the simplest revision operators to describe is the Dalal operator $*_d$ which is based on the Hamming Distance between states [3]. The Hamming Distance between states s and t is the number of propositional variables with different truth values. For the operator $*_d$, we define $|K *_d \phi|$ to be the set of models of ϕ that have minimal Hamming distance from a model of K.

While $*_d$ is useful for concrete demonstrations, it is just one example of an AGM revision operator. When we develop an AGM revision solver, we need to capture a larger set of operators. In this paper, we consider the set of *parametrized difference(PD) operators* [10]. A PD operator is specified with respect to an ordering $<$ over propositional variables. Roughly speaking, the ordering is used to "break ties" in the Hamming Distance by giving precedence to certain variables. This allows us to easily specify a form of relative importance for different kinds of information. For example, if $K = A \wedge B \wedge C$, $\phi = \neg A \vee \neg B \vee \neg C$, and the ordering is $A, B < C$, then the PD operator would give $K * \phi = A \wedge B \wedge \neg C$. This is similar to the notion of weighted Hamming Distance used in [7].

2.4   All-SAT

Computing the result of belief revision requires us to find models of propositional formulas. To calculate $K *_d \phi$, for example, the first step is to find all models of ϕ. An AllSAT solver is a tool that takes a formula as input, and returns all satisfying assignments. We refer the reader to [11] for a survey of existing tools and approaches to the AllSAT problem.

Most AllSAT solvers are built on top of an existing SAT solver that finds a single satisfying assignment. When an assignment is found, the SAT solver is forced to search again for another assignment until all solutions are exhausted. The AllSAT solver used in this paper uses Binary Decision Diagrams to represent formulas; the details are in [12]. For our purposes, it is sufficient to know that we can generate all satisfying assignments quickly by harnessing the power of a fast SAT solver.

3   Implementation

3.1   Basic Details

The system described in this paper is called GenC; it can be seen as the next generation of GenB [7], in the sense that we are interested in a *general* belief revision solver that works for many different operators. However, this is really a completely new application built from the ground up to capitalize on the speed of a fast AllSAT solver. GenC is written in C++, and it uses OpenMP 4.5 for parallelism.

3.2 Specifying Input

GenC has two methods for obtaining input data. In *interactive mode*, the system prompts the user for human readable formulas for the initial belief state and the new information for revision. The formulas are written using the propositional connectives *and, or* and *not*; parentheses may be used to enforce a particular parsing. Propositional variables are represented as positive integers. The highest integer in the input indicates the number of propositional variables in the language. Hence, an expression such as *1 and 10* actually is evaluated over a vocabulary with ten variables. Figure 1 illustrates basic problem entry in interactive mode.

Fig. 1. GenC: interactive input

Input data can also be provided in *file-based mode*, in order to support larger formulas and pre-calculated data sets. Two files are gives as input: one representing the initial beliefs, and one representing the new formula for revision. In file-based mode, formulas can be entered in Conjunctive Normal Form (CNF), Disjunctive Normal Form (DNF) and Raw Hexadecimal. The Raw Hexidecimal form is just a compact representation of binary strings, giving a set of assignments to variables. Internally, all forms of data are convertable to each other as needed. When the user enters data in file-based mode, it is displayed as a set of binary strings explicitly specifying the set of states, as in Fig. 2.

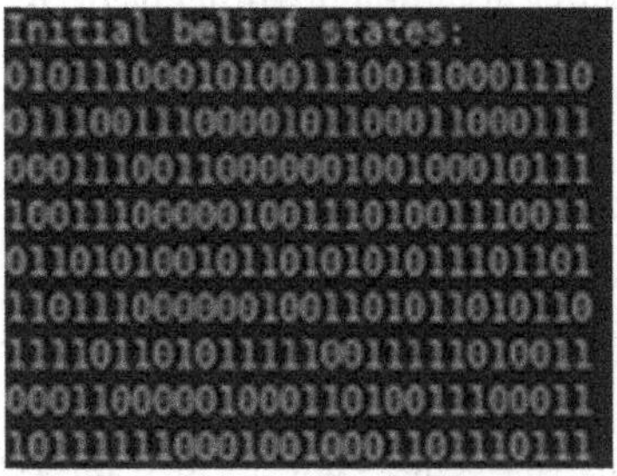

Fig. 2. GenC file-based input

As indicated previously, PD operators require a total pre-order over the propositional variables. To provide this information, an optional third input is available. This input provides a total pre-order by assigning a numeric rank to each variable; this can then be used to determine the result of PD revision.

4 Belief Revision

4.1 Algorithm

For testing, we assume that the initial belief state is given explicitly as a set of satisfying assignments. This could be a formula in disjunctive normal form, or it could be a set of binary strings. The revision is by an arbitrary formula. In this setting, the basic algorithm for belief revision is straightforward:

Algorithm 1. Belief Revision

---

function Revise(K, ϕ)

1. $S = \text{generateStates}(\phi)$
2. **if** $S \cap mod(K) \neq \emptyset$ **then return** $S \cap mod(K)$
3. $d = \min\{distance(S_i, K) : S_i \in S\}$
4. $O = \{S_i \in S : distance(S_i, K) = d\}$
5. **return** O

The *generateStates* function uses the AllSAT solver to find all states that satisfy ϕ; this is the only time that the solver is used. If the initial beliefs were given as an arbitrary formula, we would also need to call the AllSAT solver to get the models of this formula as well. However, as stated above, we make the assumption that this is not necessary. The intuition here is that an agent could already have the initial set of states through some form of pre-processing, so this step is not required at the time new information is obtained. But again, it would be easy to simply call the AllSAT solver twice if we had two arbitrary formulas as input.

The *distance* function finds the Hamming distance between a state generated by AllSAT and the models of the initial belief set. Note that the initial beliefs and the formula for revision at this state are each represented as bit strings. Hence, finding the distance from S_i to K just involves iterating over these strings quickly to find differences.

For PD revision operators, we need to add a weight to each variable. If the specified pre-order over variables has m "levels", we assign a weight of m to the variables at the minimum level. For each subsequent level, we decrease the weight by 1. When we compare S_i to K in this case, we simply take a weighted sum over variables rather than a count.

Algorithm 2. Parameterized Difference Distance

---

function distance(S, K)

1. $dist = m$ (the size of the vocabulary)
2. **for each** $\bigwedge_{j=1}^{m} v_j K$ **do**
    (a) **for** $j = 1$ **up to** m if(
    (b) $count = 0$
    (c) $diff = S \;\hat{}\; K_i$
    (d) $bitnum = 0$
    (e) **while** $diff \neq 0$ **do**
        i. $count = count + O[bitnum]$
        ii. $diff = diff \;\&\; diff - 1$
        iii. $bitnum = bitnum + 1$
    (f) **end while**
    (g) $dist = min(dist, count)$
3. **end for**
4. **return** $dist$

Notice how the counter of different bits is now a variable increment, based on the weight of the specific bit. Variables are assigned weights inversely related to their preference. If the input ordering was $a < b < c$, with a being the least likely to change/the most plausible variable, then the orderings would look like: $\{a = 3; b = 2; c = 1\}$.

4.2   Minimization

The approach to belief revision described in the previous section runs quickly, because it involves a single AllSAT call followed by a series of bit comparisons. However, it does not return a human-readable output: it returns a very long formula that lists all of the states believed possible.

In order to address this problem, GenC supports "minimization" of output states. We use the tabular method of reduction for formulas; if any two clauses differ in exactly one assignment, then they can be simplified. This minimization algorithm is expensive in terms of time, so we first sweep through the entire output formula to check if minimization is possible.

Algorithm 3. Possibility of minimization

---

function minimization_possible(K)

1. **for** K_i in K **do**
    (a)   i. **if** $K_i = K_j$ **then continue**
        ii. **if** $HammingDistance(K_i, K_j) = 1$ **then return** true
    (b) **end for**
2. **end for**
3. **return** false

If minimization is possible, it is performed through the following algorithm.

Algorithm 4. Formula Minimization

---

function minimize($K * \phi$)

1. Let $K_1, \ldots, K_M$ be the list of conjunctive clauses in $K * \phi$
2. **For** $i = 1$ **up to** M
   (a) **For** $j = 1$ **up to** M
       i. **if** $K_i = K_j$ **then continue**
       ii. **if** $HammingDistance(K_i, K_j) \neq 1$ **then continue**
       iii. $K_i = \{x : GetDifference(K_i) \neq x\}$
   (b) **end for**
3. **end for**
4. $sort(K)$
5. $removeDuplicates(K)$
6. $K = \{x \in K : \forall y \in K, |x \subseteq y| = 0\}$
7. **return** K

Essentially, this algorithm simply finds conjunctive clauses that differ in one assignment and removes that variable from each clause. We then sort the clauses, and remove duplicates. We also look for conjunctive clauses that are "supersets" of other clauses, and we remove those as well. This minimization process repeats under no further reductions are possible.

The core of minimization occurs in the $O(N^2)$ loop. Where clauses differ in 1 exact assignment, that differing assignment term is then removed from both clauses. The $GetDifference()$ function is a simplification. The implementation writes the $HammingDistance()$ function inline, and uses a counter to keep track the position where the last difference occured. The function call can be treated as a constant-time lookup, without any further consideration. At the end of the loop, the minimized formula is sorted by its clauses, and then any duplicate clauses are removed. The duplicates are caused by the commutative property, where the comparison loop will check both of the differing clauses. For the implementation, it is cheaper to remove duplicates after, rather than during the loop. Sorting the formula clauses is a requirement of the removing duplicates algorithm.

The final step in the algorithm is another simplification, that is normally not covered by the initial comparison loop. In this step, all elements which are a superset of another element in the function clauses are removed. Since the formula is in DNF, any clause that is a subset of another clause shares the same truth value. As such, having a clause that is a superset does not change its truth value with the extra assignments, and is made redundant by its subset counterpart. Therefore, these supersets are removed from the formula, to ensure maximum minimization. This function represents a single step of formula minimization, but the implementation repeats this process until the formula can no longer be minimized.

5   Performance

5.1   Design Decisions

Our goal at the outset was to develop a highly optimized solver for belief revision that runs quickly despite the known complexity of the problem. Using an AllSAT solver contributes to the speed of the system, but there are other implementation decisions that are also significant.

One issue is the representation of data. Since we are using an AllSAT solver, revision formula needs to be stored in CNF as the DIMACS format requires. The data is stored as a two-dimensional array of integers, where each constituent array represents a clause. The output from the AllSAT solver is in the same format. For the revision calculations, the actual states are stored as an array of bit vectors; this is essentially equivalent to the DNF representation. This allows us to use built-in bitwise operations; for example, we are able to calculate the Hamming Distance between vectors through a fast XOR operation. In fact, this is done directly through two dedicated hardware instructions.

Another issue that impacts run-time performance is the use of parallism. GenC uses OpenMP to add worksharing across multiple cores, to the point that most of the belief revision processing is done in parallel. This is possible since there are few data dependencies while the algorithm is running.

5.2   Experimental Results

Several factors impact the run-time of GenC:

- The number of variables.
- The number of clauses in the input ϕ (given as CNF for AllSAT).
- The number of models of ϕ.

Unfortunately, the relationship between these factors is not always clear. When testing with formula inputs with 100 variables, we obtained a range of solutions ranging from 32 models to over 400,000. When testing with 250 variables, the number of models could increase to over 38 million and it could require over 40GB of disk space. When there are 38 million states, it becomes computationally infeasible to perform the revision.

But looking at the experimental results, we will see that it is actually not the number of variables that directly influences the run time for revision. The number of variables determines the number of models of ϕ, but it is actually the number models that *directly* determines run time. For this reason, we give our experimental results in terms of the run time with respect to $|\phi|$, the number of models of ϕ.

Our tests were performed using benchmark problems from the SATLIB library [6]. All of the test problems had 100 variables. In our tests, we measured the run-time for revision, using either 100 thousand or 5 million clauses. The tests were performed on a computer running Linux Kernel 4.17, wich a 4.8 GHz CPU. The range of run times was as follows.

- For $|\phi| = 16$: .218 s (for 100,000 clauses), 8.581 s (for 5,000,000 clauses)
- For $|\phi| = 416,492$: 31 s (for 100,000 clauses), 4430 s (for 5,000,000 clauses)

A graphical depiction of our test results is given in Fig. 3.

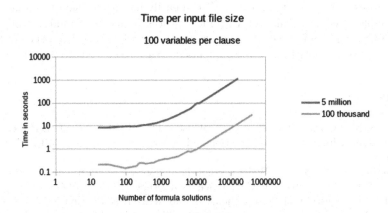

Fig. 3. GenC performance

It is worth noting that there is no difference in the running time for Dalal revision and PD revision. The only difference is that PD revision requires a constant time lookup to a table giving priorities, which does not impact performance.

5.3   Comparison with Related Work

As stated previously, there are not many implemented systems for belief revision that are both *general* and *efficient*. As an illustrative example of work in the area, the COBA system implements a single revision operator that is well-suited for computation [4]. This is not a general AGM solver, nor does it work well with hundreds of thousands of variables.

The predecessor of GenC is the GenB system, which actually can solve revision problems for *any* AGM operator [7]. As such, GenB is actually more general than our current system. This extra generality is not necessarily useful in practice, however, due to the difficulty specifying orderings. More importantly, the GenB system is a prototype that is only useful for very small problems with a handful of variables. From this perspective, GenC is a much more powerful implementation.

If we are interested in implementing a revision solver that can solve problems with millions of clauses, there are really only two natural options One choice is to use a SAT solver as the basis for computation; that is the approach we have taken here. The other choice is to use an efficient answer set solver. The first step towards such an implementation is presented in [2], where the logic programs are used to capture the process of AGM revision. This line of research may in the future lead to a new belief revision solver that competes with GenC in terms of running time for large instances.

6   Conclusion

GenC is a scalable and efficient tool, designed around hardware-friendly parallel data structures, and utilizing an All-SAT solver for enumerating the list of satisfying clauses to the revision formula. It can easily handle revision formulae with 100 variables, and will scale well with more processing cores. Fundamentally, the limiting factor for our solver is the scale of solutions returned from the All-SAT solver, requiring algorithmic improvements if we are to exceed our current limits.

References

1. Alchourrón, C.E., Gärdenfors, P., Makinson, D.: On the logic of theory change: partial meet functions for contraction and revision. J. Symb. Logic **50**(2), 510–530 (1985)
2. Aravanis, T., Peppas, P.: Belief revision in answer set programming. In: Proceedings of the 21st Panhellenic Conference on Informatics (PCI 2017) (2017)
3. Dalal, M.: Investigations into a theory of knowledge base revision. In: Proceedings of the National Conference on Artificial Intelligence (AAAI), pp. 475–479 (1988)
4. Delgrande, J.P., Liu, D.H., Schaub, T., Thiele, S.: COBA 2.0: a consistency-based belief change system. In: Mellouli, K. (ed.) ECSQARU 2007. LNCS (LNAI), vol. 4724, pp. 78–90. Springer, Heidelberg (2007). https://doi.org/10.1007/978-3-540-75256-1_10
5. Eiter, T., Gottlob, G.: On the complexity of propositional knowledge base revision, updates and counterfactuals. Artif. Intell. **57**(2–3), 227–270 (1992)
6. Hoos, H., Stützle, T.: SATLIB: an online resource for research on SAT. In: SAT 2000, pp. 283–292 (2000)
7. Hunter, A., Tsang, E.: GenB: a general solver for AGM revision. In: Michael, L., Kakas, A. (eds.) JELIA 2016. LNCS (LNAI), vol. 10021, pp. 564–569. Springer, Cham (2016). https://doi.org/10.1007/978-3-319-48758-8_40
8. Hunter, A.: Learning belief revision operators. In: Proceedings of the Canadian Conference on Artificial Intelligence, pp. 239–245 (2018)
9. Katsuno, H., Mendelzon, A.O.: Propositional knowledge base revision and minimal change. Artif. Intell. **52**(2), 263–294 (1992)
10. Peppas, P., Williams, M.-A.: Kinetic consistency and relevance in belief revision. In: Michael, L., Kakas, A. (eds.) JELIA 2016. LNCS (LNAI), vol. 10021, pp. 401–414. Springer, Cham (2016). https://doi.org/10.1007/978-3-319-48758-8_26
11. Toda, T., Soh, T.: Implementing efficient all solutions SAT solvers. ACM J. Exp. Algorithmics **21**(1), 1.12:1–1.12:44 (2016)
12. Toda, T., Tsuda, K.: BDD construction for all solutions SAT and efficient caching mechanism. In: Proceedings of the 30th Annual ACM Symposium on Applied Computing, pp. 1880–1886 (2015)
13. Williams, M.-A.: Applications of belief revision. In: Freitag, B., Decker, H., Kifer, M., Voronkov, A. (eds.) DYNAMICS 1997. LNCS, vol. 1472, pp. 287–316. Springer, Heidelberg (1998). https://doi.org/10.1007/BFb0055503
14. Zhuang, Z., Wang, Z., Wang, K., Qi, G.: DL-lite contraction and revision. J. Artif. Intell. Res. (JAIR) **56**, 329–378 (2016)

Answering Why-Questions Using Probabilistic Logic Programming

Abdus Salam$^{(\boxtimes)}$, Rolf Schwitter, and Mehmet A. Orgun

Department of Computing, Macquarie University, Sydney, NSW 2109, Australia
{abdus.salam,rolf.schwitter,mehmet.orgun}@mq.edu.au

Abstract. We present a novel architecture of a closed domain question answering system that learns to answer *why*-questions from a small number of example interpretations. We use a probabilistic logic programming framework that can learn probabilities for rules from positive and negative example interpretations. These rules are then used by a meta-interpreter to generate an explanation in the form of a proof for a *why*-question. The explanation is displayed as an answer to the question together with a probability. In certain contexts, follow-up questions can be asked that conditionally depend on these *why*-questions and have an effect on the probability of the subsequent answer. The presented approach is a contribution to explainable artificial intelligence that aims to take machine learning out of the black-box.

Keywords: *why*-questions · Probabilistic logic programming ·
Meta-interpreter · Natural language processing

1 Introduction

Machine Learning (ML) models have recently shown significant success in different applications [9]. As a result, our expectation of systems that rely on these models is also growing. ML models that we use to build these systems often make decisions which range between very simple to very complex ones. Most of these systems use black-box models that are not inherently interpretable. Hence after a decision for a particular problem is made by a system, a user may want to obtain a detailed explanation for that decision. This is the main motivation for Explainable Artificial Intelligence (XAI) [8], since informative explanations are very important; especially in safety critical situations or financial contexts [10]. An explanation of a decision also improves the acceptability of a prediction model. This is one of the main reasons that explaining the decision made by the systems has recently received a lot of attention [10,14].

A natural way to obtain an explanation about a particular decision is to ask one or more questions. There exist different types of questions such as *who-*, *what-*, *when-*, *where-*, *why-*, and *how-*questions. In English, the most prominent type of question to obtain an explanation are *why*-questions. A *why*-question is a question that begins with the word *why*; followed by an interrogative sentence

J. Liu and J. Bailey (Eds.): AI 2019, LNAI 11919, pp. 153–164, 2019.
https://doi.org/10.1007/978-3-030-35288-2_13

whose right answer (if there is any) must be either *yes* or *no*, and the question does not ask for an opinion or personal view [4]. Therefore, we can say that "Why does the car r01 require any repair?" is a *why*-question whereas "does the car r01 require any repair?" is the interrogative part of that question. A question that asks for an opinion or a personal view such as "Why do you think that climate change is responsible for natural disasters?" is not considered as a *why*-question since the answer does not necessarily involve facts.

The recent success of model-based question-answering (QA) systems is remarkable [12]. But the problem is that most of the underlying models are designed based on a particular dataset. Most of these datasets contain a large number of questions that can be answered from the surface-level information (such that the answer is explicitly mentioned in the corpus). Many datasets contain a significant amount of factoid questions that are easy to answer such as "Who won the Nobel Peace Prize in 2006?"; therefore, even a simple question-answering model may show a high accuracy using these datasets [5]. In recent research [5], the AI2 Reasoning Challenge (ARC) revealed that information retrieval and pointwise mutual information algorithms could not answer a large number of questions from the ARC question dataset (even though the corpus contains the information to answer most of these questions). One such question was "Why can steam be used to cook food?" which requires explanation/meta-reasoning techniques to answer the question. The AI2 challenge makes it painfully clear that question-answering tasks require more advanced AI methods (e.g., multi-hop reasoning and commonsense reasoning) than simple retrieval-based or word co-occurrence algorithms can deliver. *Why*-questions are inherently difficult to answer, since we need to find the reasons for one or more facts being true or false. The literature [13] also shows that association learning techniques are not powerful enough to answer *why*-questions.

Many of these recent QA systems are built to answer open domain questions where a domain independent question is asked. The QA system then searches through some predefined information sources for the relevant information and tries to find the answer [19]. However, in a closed domain QA system, the information related to answer the question is fixed. So when a question is asked, the QA system only searches the fixed information space to find the answer [11]. There is not a lot of research that has been conducted to develop QA systems that can answer *why*-questions [12].

In this paper, we introduce a novel architecture of a closed domain QA system that can answer *why*-questions and follow-up questions based on a knowledge base using a probabilistic logic programming approach [6]. The architecture reflects the concept of XAI and generates an explanation for an answer to a question in a transparent way. The system is trained for a particular problem domain to learn the probabilities of the relevant rules from observations (real world data). The probabilistic rules and the real world data are then stored in the system which form the knowledge base for the QA system. The user can ask *why*-questions or follow-up questions using a guided natural language interface [16]. The system converts the natural language question into a Prolog query and tries to answer this query with the help of a meta-interpreter. The meta-interpreter uses the knowledge base of the QA system to answer the query and constructs a proof which results in an explanation. While searching for a proof, the meta-interpreter also collects the probability for the answer. Finally, the answer is displayed together with the resulting probability.

2   Probabilistic Logic Programming

Probabilistic Logic Programming (PLP) introduces probabilistic reasoning into logic programs in order to represent uncertain information [6]. In PLP, we can define the probabilities of rules where the probability is a real number ranging from 0 to 1. The probability of a rule indicates the percentage of the rule being true if all conditions (in the body) of the rule are satisfied. In a logic program, we might have rules where the body (conditions) is the same but the heads are different. In such a case, we may define the probability of each head being true when all the conditions in the body are true. Here ideally the total probability of all rules consisting of the same body will be 1. Let's assume, we have two body literals b1 and b2 and two different heads consisting of the atoms h1 and h2 with probabilities $\alpha1$ and $\alpha2$, then we can write rules in the following form in PLP:

```
h1:α1 :- b1, b2.
h2:α2 :- b1, b2.
```

Here $\alpha1$ and $\alpha2$ are real numbers in the interval [0, 1] and their summation is 1. We can represent the above program in a more compact and intuitive way using Logic Programs with Annotated Disjunctions (LPAD) [18]. In LPAD, all atoms with probabilities in the head of a rule are separated by a semi-colon ('; '), followed by the implication operator (':-') and the body of the rule. So we can write the above rules in the following equivalent form in LPAD:

```
h1:α1 ; h2:α2 :- b1, b2.
```

For our work, we use *cplint*, a probabilistic logic programming framework, that supports inference and learning of probabilistic logic programs from observations [15]. The framework offers a number of learning algorithms and we use the SLIPCOVER algorithm to learn the probabilities, given the background knowledge and an initial program. SLIPCOVER is an algorithm for learning both the probabilities and the structure of LPADs by performing a beam search in the space of clauses and a greedy search in the space of theories [1]. Note that in Prolog, a clause may be a fact or a rule. Note also that in our case, we are only interested in learning the probabilities of rules but not their structure.

3   The Example Scenario and Our Extension

To illustrate the steps of our proposed system, we use the *mach* example from the *cplint manual* as a starting point. This example is used to introduce the

SLIPCOVER algorithm [15]. The example was originally published in the ACE Data Mining System User's Manual [3]. In this scenario a car is taken to a designated workshop when it exhibits a problem. In the workshop, the car is initially checked to take an appropriate decision about how to service the car based on the available information. The decision can be: *ok*, *fix* or *sendback*. The decision is taken based on the following rules:

- If the car has no worn component, then we say that this car has no problem. If the car has no problem, then the decision is *ok* which means it does not require any repair.
- If the car has a component which is worn and this component is replaceable in the workshop, then the car will be fixed in the workshop. If the car has a problem and can be fixed in the workshop, then the decision is *fix*.
- If the car has a component which is worn and this component is not replaceable in the workshop, then the car will be sent back to the manufacturer. If the car has a problem which cannot be solved in the workshop, then the decision is *sendback*.

We extended this scenario and added temporal information to the dataset in order to make the scenario more realistic. Based on the decision and available information, a further decision can now be made about the timing of the repair. If the repair decision is *fix*, we can then find out the time that it takes to repair the car. We can also find out the time it takes to repair a car if the repair decision is *sendback*.

We use this extended scenario to answer *why*-questions of the following form:

1. Why does the car (ID) require any repair?
2. Why do we need to fix the car (ID)?
3. Why do we need to send the car (ID) back?

The placeholder "ID" in the question is replaced with a real identifier for the car, before the question is sent to the system. Let's assume, we want to know why the car with the identifier r01 needs any repair; therefore, we simply ask the corresponding question: "Why does the car r01 require any repair?".

Based on the answer given for the questions (2 and 3), one may ask a follow-up question. In the case of a follow-up question, one can ask for the required time it takes to repair the car. If the car does not require any repair, then there is no option for a follow-up question as the car is ready to be picked up from the workshop. The follow-up questions have the following form where the ID is replaced in the same way as for why-questions:

4. How many days will it take to fix the car (ID)?
5. How many days will it take to get the car (ID) back from the manufacturer?

4   System Architecture

In order to answer the questions in Sect. 3, we suggest the architecture shown in Fig. 1. This architecture consists of four different components (displayed as rectangular boxes).

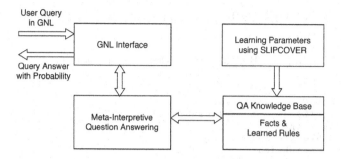

Fig. 1. The QA system architecture

4.1   Learning Parameters Using SLIPCOVER

As stated earlier, we have used *cplint's* SLIPCOVER library to learn the probability for the rules. A *cplint* program has five parts required to execute the learning algorithm. We describe these five parts that we have used in our *cplint* program for learning probabilities of rules below.

Preamble: At the beginning of a *cplint* program, we load all necessary libraries, initialise the algorithms and their required parameters. In our program, we have first loaded and initialised the SLIPCOVER library, and we have set the same set of parameters as in the *mach* example. In our case, we use the following parameter settings: depth_bound is set to false as the depth of the derivation is not limited; neg_ex is set to given in order to allow for negative examples in the interpretations; megaex_bottom specifies that 15 mega-examples are used to build the bottom clauses; max_iter specifies that beam search should use 10 iterations; max_iter_structure declares that the number of theory search iterations is 50; and verbosity is 1 for not printing anything while learning.

Listing 1.1. Preamble of our *cplint* program

```
:- use_module(library(slipcover)).
:- sc.

:- set_sc(depth_bound, false).
:- set_sc(neg_ex, given).
:- set_sc(megaex_bottom, 15).
:- set_sc(max_iter, 10).
:- set_sc(max_iter_structure, 50).
:- set_sc(verbosity, 1).
```

Background Knowledge: The *cplint* program contains background knowledge in a section between the two directives :- begin_bg and :- end_bg. We can write deterministic clauses (clauses that are true for all interpretations) in this part of the program and these clauses constitute the background knowledge in *cplint*. In our program, we have used the same background knowledge as in the *mach* example. Note that the background knowledge mentioned here is only used for learning purposes.

Listing 1.2. Background knowledge of our *cplint* program

```
:- begin_bg.

component(C) :- replaceable(C).
component(C) :- not_replaceable(C).
replaceable(gear).
replaceable(wheel).
replaceable(chain).
not_replaceable(engine).
not_replaceable(control_unit).
not_worn(C) :- component(C), \+ worn(C).
one_worn :- worn(_).
none_worn :- \+ one_worn.

:- end_bg.
```

Initial Program: We can write the initial program between the two directives `:- begin_in` and `:- end_in`. Here we define those rules for which we want to learn the probabilities. The rules are provided with a random initial probability between 0 and 1 (exclusive). But this initial probability does not have any effect on the learning process. We just provide a random probability and *cplint* learns the probability from the given examples. In our case, we have three sets of rules for which we want to learn the probabilities. The first set of rules (`status/2`) is used for the car repair decision and the second and third sets of rules (`time_to_fix/2` and `time_to_sendback/3`) are used to find the time it takes if the car repair decision is 'fix' or 'sendback'.

Listing 1.3. Initial program of our *cplint* program

```
:- begin_in.

status(Car, sendback):0.5 :-
  worn(Car, Component),
  not_replaceable(Component).

status(Car, fix):0.5 :-
  worn(Car, Component),
  replaceable(Component).

status(Car, ok):0.5 :-
  not_worn(Car, Component).

time_to_fix(Component, 7):0.5 :-
  fix_days(Component, Days),
  Days =< 7.

time_to_fix(Component, 14):0.5 :-
  fix_days(Component, Days),
  Days > 7, Days =< 14.

time_to_sendback(Car, Component, 15):0.5 :-
  brand(Car, Brand),
  locally_available(Component, Brand),
```

```
manufacturer_sendback_time(Brand, Component, Days),
Days =< 15.

time_to_sendback(Car, Component, 30):0.5 :-
brand(Car, Brand),
locally_available(Component, Brand),
manufacturer_sendback_time(Brand, Component, Days),
Days > 15, Days =< 30.

:- end_in.
```

Language Bias: This part contains input-output declarations, mode declarations and determination predicates. An output predicate is used to declare the predicate for which we want to apply our learning algorithm and this predicate appears in the head of a learning rule. It has the form *output(<predicate>/<arity>)*. In our case, we have three predicates status/2, time_to_fix/2, and time_to_sendback/3 for which we want to learn the probabilities. The predicates that appear in the body of a learning rule are declared as input predicates: either *input(<predicate>/<arity>)* or *input_cw(<predicate>/<arity>)*. The predicate input/1 declares an open world predicate while the predicate input_cw/1 declares a closed world predicate. Under the closed world assumption, only the predicate given as the argument participates in the learning process and any derived predicates from that argument predicate are not considered. We have used input_cw/1 to declare our input predicates since we are only interested in the example data for our interpretations.

Listing 1.4. Sample input-output declarations of our *cplint* program

```
output(time_to_sendback/3).

input_cw(brand/2).
input_cw(locally_available/2).
input_cw(manufacturer_sendback_time/3).
```

Mode declarations are specified with two predicates: modeh/2 and modeb/2. The head of a rule is declared with the modeh/2 predicate and the body with the modeb/2 predicate. Here we consider only those rules that participate in the learning process. The predicates modeh/2 and modeb/2 have the form *modeh(n, atom)* and *modeb(n, atom)*. Here, the argument *n* (called recall value) is an integer which declares how many atoms of the specified predicate the algorithm should consider in the saturation step. We can also use an asterisk ('*') as a recall value which declares that the saturation step should use all the atoms. For *modeb* declarations, we additionally have to specify the type of an argument. The argument type can be an input variable, an output variable or a constant. The symbols '+', '-' and '#' are used as a prefix of an argument to define its type: either input, output or constant. For example, the *modeb* declaration (modeb(*, brand(+car, -brand))) in Listing 1.5 indicates that in the brand predicate the first and second arguments are input and output variables, respectively.

Listing 1.5. Sample *modeh* and *modeb* declarations of our *cplint* program

```
modeh(*, time_to_sendback(Car, Component, 15)).
modeh(*, time_to_sendback(Car, Component, 30)).

modeb(*, brand(+car, -brand)).
modeb(*, locally_available(-component, -brand)).
modeb(*, manufacturer_sendback_time(-component, -brand, -days)).
```

Learning with SLIPCOVER requires the declaration of `determination/2` predicates. Here we specify which predicate can occur in the head of a rule to be learned and which predicates in its body. Listing 1.6 shows that we want to learn the probability of a rule with the predicate `time_to_sendback/3` in its head and the predicates `brand/2`, `locally_available/2` and `manufacturer_sendback_time/3` in its body.

Listing 1.6. Sample determination declarations of our *cplint* program

```
determination(time_to_sendback/3, brand/2).
determination(time_to_sendback/3, locally_available/2).
determination(time_to_sendback/3, manufacturer_sendback_time/3).
```

Example Interpretations: This is the last part of a *cplint* program where we put all the data. The example models or interpretations (observations) are used to provide data for learning in a *cplint* program. An example model starts with *begin(model(<name>))* and ends with *end(model(<name>))*. One example model of our *cplint* program is given in Listing 1.7. The model `c1` specifies that the car (`car`) has a worn component `gear` and its repair decision is `fix` (not `ok` and not `sendback`). In our program, we have three sets of examples to learn three rules. That means one set of examples is used to learn the probability of the rule `status/2`, one set for the rule `time_to_fix/2` and another one is for the rule `time_to_sendback/3`.

Listing 1.7. A sample example model of our *cplint* program

```
begin(model(c1)).
  status(car, fix).
  neg(status(car, ok)).
  neg(status(car, sendback)).
  worn(car, gear).
end(model(c1)).
```

In addition, we can define the probability for an example model in the form *prob(P)*. In that case, the given probability P is the probability of the example model and used in the learning process. If an example model does not contain any probability then the probability $1/n$ is assigned to it where n is the total number of example models.

After completing the program, we define the fold of the example models for training using the `fold/2` predicate. Afterwards, we learn the probabilities of the rules using a *cplint* query of the form *induce_par(<list of folds>, P)*. In the first argument we use the fold that we defined for training. The query `induce_par/2` executes the parameter learning algorithm and assigns the learned probabilities to the rules. The learned rules are returned in the second argument of the `induce_par/2` query (here in a variable P).

4.2   Knowledge Base of the QA System

We use the facts and the learned rules as knowledge base of the QA system to answer questions. After training in *cplint*, the learned rules are saved in a file which constitutes one part of our knowledge base. The learned rules for the car repair decision are shown in Listing 1.8.

Listing 1.8. Sample learned rules by our *cplint* program

```
status(A, sendback) : 1.0 ; '' : 0.0 :-
  worn(A, B), not_replaceable(B).
status(A, fix) : 0.56 ; '' : 0.44 :-
  worn(A ,B), replaceable(B).
status(A, ok) : 0.2 ; '' : 0.8 :- not_worn(A, B).
```

The learned rules are the same as those that we specified in the initial program (see Listing 1.3). In addition, we have two values in the head of the rules. The first value is the probability of the rule being true and the second value is simply obtained by subtracting 1 from the first value indicating the probability of the rule being false. In our program, we transform the learned rules into our own format so that we can later apply our meta-interpreter to these rules to search for an answer. Such a rule is defined using the predicate `rule/3` which has the following form: `rule(Goal, Conditions, Probability)`. In this rule, the first argument specifies the goal; the second argument all conditions for which the goal is true; and the third argument the probability of the rule. We have used Prolog's built-in predicate `term_expansion/2` to convert the learned rules into our expected format. Listing 1.9 shows the transformed rules for the rules in Listing 1.8.

Listing 1.9. Sample rules used in the QA program

```
rule(status(A, sendback), worn(A, B) is_true &
  not_replaceable(B) is_true , 1.0).
rule(status(A, fix), worn(A ,B) is_true &
  replaceable(B) is_true , 0.56).
rule(status(A, ok), not_worn(A, B) is_true , 0.2).
```

In our system, facts represent the real data about cars. We use the predicate `fact/1` to store all the car information about which a user can ask questions. Let us assume, we have a car *car r01* with a worn component *gear* and the component *gear* is replaceable, then we write in our program:

Listing 1.10. Sample facts used in the QA program

```
fact(worn(car_r01, gear)).
fact(replaceable(gear)).
```

4.3   GNL Interface

A user can ask a question in a guided natural language (GNL). When a *why*-question is asked in GNL, the GNL interface receives it and converts it into the expected Prolog query. For example, the question "Why does the car r01 require any repair?" is converted into the Prolog query `explain(status(car_r01, ok), P)`. This query is used by the meta-interpreter to search for an answer and the interface displays the answer together with the probability P. The user may then ask a follow-up question. Currently we are using the Prolog console as the GNL interface. Our ultimate goal is to develop an interface where the user will be guided to formulate the question in a similar way as that provided by a programming language editor. The idea is similar to the approach followed in PENG [16], GINO [2], and Quelo [7].

4.4   Meta-interpretive Question Answering

The meta-interpreter receives a query as input via the GNL interface and produces a proof which is the evaluation of the query. We have used a modified version of an existing explanation-based meta-interpreter as a starting point for our work [17]. The meta-interpreter uses the top level predicate `explain/2` and is called with a query. The meta-interpreter then tries to prove the query using the knowledge base of the QA system. While evaluating the query, the meta-interpreter collects those predicates that are used during the proof including the probability and builds an SLD tree [17]. This information forms the ultimate answer and explains how the query was answered.

The top level predicate `explain/2` is called by sending the query in the first argument and the value for the probability (of the query being true) is returned in the second argument. A query is true when the interrogative part of the corresponding *why*-question is true except for Question 1. The predicate `explain/2` calls the meta-interpreter to evaluate the given query and to generate the SLD tree. After the execution of the meta-interpreter, the predicate `explain/2` constructs the SLD tree to generate the explanation of the query evaluation.

5   Evaluation

Our QA system is trained with the three sets of example models to learn the probabilities for the `status/2`, `time_to_fix/2` and `time_to_sendback/3` rules. In the training phase, we used 15 examples (as in the *mach* example) for the `status/2` rule and two sets of 7 examples for `time_to_fix/2` and `time_to_sendback/3` rules. After that, we load the knowledge base (rules and facts) into the QA system. The rules are those rules learned in the training step. We stored the facts about three cars: *car r01*, *car r02*, and *car r03*. The information about the cars is populated in such a way that the repair decision for *car r01*, *car r02* and *car r03* would be 'ok', 'fix' and 'sendback', respectively. Once the knowledge base is loaded, the QA system is ready to answer the questions.

First we ask question (1) about *car r01* for which no follow-up question can be asked. In this case, the system provides the answer (with a probability) and displays the explanation. Next we ask question (2) about *car r02*; the system gives the same kind of detailed information as for question (1) explaining that the *car r02* has a worn gear which is replaceable in the workshop (with probability = 0.56). After obtaining the answer for question (2), we can ask the follow-up question (4). Since all information is available in the system to answer this question, the system generates the answer shown in Listing 1.11. To answer the follow-up question, the probability is calculated by multiplying the probabilities for the answer to question (2) with that for the answer to question (4) since (4) is conditionally dependent on (2). Question (3) and its follow-up question (5) are answered in a similar way.

Listing 1.11. Sample question-answer for Question 2 and Question 4

```
Ask your question.
|: Why do we need to fix the car r02?

Answer:
   The car r02 needs to be fixed because:
      The car r02 has a worn gear.
      A gear is replaceable in the workshop.
   Probability: 0.56

Ask your question.
|: How many days will it take to fix the car r02?

Answer:
   It will take at most 7 days to fix the car r02 because:
      A gear can be fixed in at most 7 days.
   Probability: 0.37
```

6   Conclusion

In this paper we have introduced the architecture of a closed domain question answering system that generates answers along with probabilities for *why-*questions and follow-up questions. The answers are produced with the help of rules for which the probabilities are learned from example interpretations via probabilistic logic programming. The QA system takes natural language questions and translates them into the corresponding Prolog queries. The queries are evaluated with a meta-interpreter that generates a proof along with a probability for a query from the knowledge base. The novelty of our QA system is that it answers questions in terms of explanations along with their uncertainty wherein the uncertainty comes from the probabilistic rules. The QA system displays the answer in natural language where a fact is converted into a natural language format with appropriate information. In the future, we plan to use a controlled natural language [16] to make the proof human readable while keeping it machine processable at the same time. We will also investigate how the QA system will perform in a more complex scenario where the learning algorithm has to deal with a much larger amount of training data.

References

1. Bellodi, E., Riguzzi, F.: Structure learning of probabilistic logic programs by searching the clause space. Theor. Pract. Logic Program. **15**(2), 169–212 (2015)
2. Bernstein, A., Kaufmann, E.: GINO – a guided input natural language ontology editor. In: Cruz, I., et al. (eds.) ISWC 2006. LNCS, vol. 4273, pp. 144–157. Springer, Heidelberg (2006). https://doi.org/10.1007/11926078_11
3. Blockeel, H., et al.: The ACE data mining system, user's manual. Katholieke Universiteit Leuven, Belgium (2006)
4. Bromberger, S.: Why-questions. In: Colodny, R.G. (ed.) Mind and Cosmos: Essays in Contemporary Science and Philosophy. University of Pittsburgh Press, Pittsburgh (1966)
5. Clark, P., et al.: Think you have solved question answering? Try arc, the ai2 reasoning challenge (2018). arXiv preprint arXiv:1803.05457
6. De Raedt, L., Kimmig, A.: Probabilistic (logic) programming concepts. Mach. Learn. **100**(1), 5–47 (2015)
7. Franconi, E., Guagliardo, P., Tessaris, S., Trevisan, M.: Quelo: an ontology-driven query interface. Proc. DL **2011**(745), 488–498 (2011)
8. Gunning, D.: Explainable artificial intelligence (XAI). Defense Advanced Research Projects Agency (DARPA), nd Web (2017)
9. LeCun, Y., Bengio, Y., Hinton, G.: Deep learning. Nature **521**(7553), 436 (2015)
10. Lipton, Z.C.: The mythos of model interpretability (2016). arXiv preprint arXiv:1606.03490
11. Mollá, D., Vicedo, J.L.: Question answering in restricted domains: an overview. Comput. Linguist. **33**(1), 41–61 (2007)
12. Oh, J.H., et al.: Why question answering using sentiment analysis and word classes. In: Proceedings of the 2012 Joint Conference on Empirical Methods in Natural Language Processing and Computational Natural Language Learning, pp. 368–378. Association for Computational Linguistics (2012)
13. Pearl, J., Mackenzie, D.: The Book of Why: The New Science of Cause and Effect. Basic Books, New York (2018)
14. Ribeiro, M.T., Singh, S., Guestrin, C.: Why should I trust you?: Explaining the predictions of any classifier. In: Proceedings of the 22nd ACM SIGKDD International Conference on Knowledge Discovery and Data Mining, pp. 1135–1144. ACM (2016)
15. Riguzzi, F.: cplint Manual. SWI-Prolog Version (2016). http://ds.ing.unife.it/~friguzzi/software/cplint-swi/manual.pdf
16. Schwitter, R.: Specifying events and their effects in controlled natural language. Proc. Soc. Behav. Sci. **27**, 12–21 (2011)
17. Sterling, L., Shapiro, E.Y.: The Art of Prolog: Advanced Programming Techniques. MIT Press, Cambridge (1994)
18. Vennekens, J., Verbaeten, S., Bruynooghe, M.: Logic programs with annotated disjunctions. In: Demoen, B., Lifschitz, V. (eds.) ICLP 2004. LNCS, vol. 3132, pp. 431–445. Springer, Heidelberg (2004). https://doi.org/10.1007/978-3-540-27775-0_30
19. Yang, Y., Yih, W.T., Meek, C.: WIKIQA: a challenge dataset for open-domain question answering. In: Proceedings of the 2015 Conference on Empirical Methods in Natural Language Processing, pp. 2013–2018 (2015)

DINE: A Framework for Deep Incomplete Network Embedding

Ke Hou[1], Jiaying Liu[1], Yin Peng[1], Bo Xu[1(✉)], Ivan Lee[2], and Feng Xia[3]

[1] Key Laboratory for Ubiquitous Network and Service Software of Liaoning Province, School of Software, Dalian University of Technology, Dalian 116620, China
boxu@dlut.edu.cn
[2] School of Information Technology and Mathematical Sciences, University of South Australia, Adelaide, SA 5095, Australia
[3] School of Science, Engineering and Information Technology, Federation University, Ballarat, Australia

Abstract. Network representation learning (NRL) plays a vital role in a variety of tasks such as node classification and link prediction. It aims to learn low-dimensional vector representations for nodes based on network structures or node attributes. While embedding techniques on complete networks have been intensively studied, in real-world applications, it is still a challenging task to collect complete networks. To bridge the gap, in this paper, we propose a Deep Incomplete Network Embedding method, namely DINE. Specifically, we first complete the missing part including both nodes and edges in a partially observable network by using the expectation-maximization framework. To improve the embedding performance, we consider both network structures and node attributes to learn node representations. Empirically, we evaluate DINE over three networks on multi-label classification and link prediction tasks. The results demonstrate the superiority of our proposed approach compared against state-of-the-art baselines.

Keywords: Incomplete network embedding · Network completion · Network representation learning · Deep learning

1 Introduction

Information networks (e.g. citation networks, social networks, biological networks) contain different types of entities and intricate relations. Analyzing these networks plays an important role in many disciplines [29]. For example, in citation networks, we can find influential entities (i.e., scholars, papers) by calculating the importance of vertices [2,5]. In social networks, clustering users into communities is useful for recommendation [25,26]. In biological networks, measuring the similarity between proteins helps us better understand protein interactions [27]. However, with the increase of entities and relations in real-world networks, it is challenging to explore the underlying network structures.

© Springer Nature Switzerland AG 2019
J. Liu and J. Bailey (Eds.): AI 2019, LNAI 11919, pp. 165–176, 2019.
https://doi.org/10.1007/978-3-030-35288-2_14

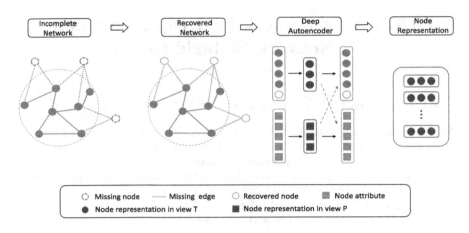

Fig. 1. The overview of DINE framework.

To find an efficient way to model networks, researchers focus on network representation learning (NRL). NRL aims to learn latent, low-dimensional representations for nodes, with preserving not only network topologies but also node contents. Perozzi et al. [19] first combine NRL with skip-gram and propose Deepwalk, which lays a solid foundation for future development in this area. Recent advances in NRL have witnessed powerful representations abilities such as DeepGL [20], DANE [7]. Taking advantage of its powerful representation ability to model complex structures, NRL achieves significant performance in downstream tasks such as node classification [3,30], link prediction [8,16], and network visualization [21].

In practice, many real-world networks are incomplete [14], which further complicates the embedding process. For example, citation networks are usually incomplete because it is impossible for academic search engines to collect every paper. In biological networks, there exist a huge amount of undiscovered links because of the complexity of gene expression. Analyzing incomplete network makes a deviation because only a part of links are observed, which alters our estimates of network-level statistics. To fill this gap, researchers focus on network completion problem, which makes use of observed connectivity patterns to infer the missing part. However, existing studies only pay attention to missing links inference [6,11], few of them focus on the incomplete networks with both missing nodes and edges [13].

To solve the problem, we present a new framework, named DINE for deep incomplete network embedding. DINE intelligently combines network completion and NRL into a unified framework. As shown in Fig. 1, DINE contains two pivotal steps, including network recovery and network embedding. Specially, we first capture the connectivity patterns from the partially observable network and fit the generative graphs model to estimate missing components. To model the network more accurately, we consider both network structures and node attributes to learn the representations of the recovered network by using a deep autoencoder. Finally, we empirically verify the performance of the proposed framework on three real-world networks. Experimental results illustrate the significant representation ability of DINE in partially observable networks. Our main contributions can be concluded as follows:

(1) We present a new framework, namely DINE, for deep incomplete network embedding. DINE intelligently combines network completion and NRL into a unified framework, which provides an effective solution for data missing.
(2) DINE considers not only topology structure but also node attributes for embedding. It can accurately and effectively model node proximity and underlying structure in the joint space.
(3) We extensively validate the framework on three real-world networks through multi-label classification and link prediction tasks. The results demonstrate the superiority of our proposed approach compared with state-of-the-art baselines.

The remainder of this paper is organized as follows. Section 2 summarizes related work. In Sect. 3, we focus on problem definition. Section 4 introduces the implementation details of the proposed framework. Experimental results are provided in Sect. 5. Finally, we conclude this work in Sect. 6.

2 Related Work

The framework we proposed in this paper is related to two areas of research, including network completion and NRL techniques.

2.1 Network Completion

Network completion deals with the problem of inferring missing nodes and edges in networks. Network completion is similar to matrix completion [12], which aims to complete the matrix with elements missing. However, network completion is more arduous because of network diversity. For missing edges, it is an attractive way to recover the original network by calculating node similarity. Another way to complete missing edges is considering shared node neighbors [4]. In cases where both nodes and edges are missing, we can utilize a generative graphs model named KronFit [15] to generate complete networks whose structures are similar to real-world networks. Kim et al. [13] combine expectation-maximization into KronFit, and propose a powerful algorithm KronEM, which is more effective for recovering the network.

2.2 Network Representation Learning

NRL aims to embed each node in the network into a low-dimensional representation. Existing NRL algorithms can be divided into four categories. The first category is matrix factorization based methods. They first represent the connections between network vertices and use matrix factorization to obtain

Table 1. The description of notations

Notation	Description
N_G	number of nodes in the complete network
N'	Number of nodes in the incomplete network
N_M	Number of missing nodes
N_R	Number of recovered nodes
xt	Input of network structure view T
xp	Input of node attribute view P
$x\hat{t}^t$	Reconstruction output of xt by self-view
$x\hat{t}^p$	Reconstruction output of xt by cross-view
$x\hat{p}^t$	Reconstruction output of xp by self-view
$x\hat{p}^p$	Reconstruction output of xp by cross-view
K	Number of encoding layers
$yt^{(K)}$	Representation in network structure view T
$yp^{(K)}$	Representation in node attribute view P
α	Balance reconstruction errors of self-view and cross-view
β	Balance reconstruction errors of G' and G_M

representations. IsoMAP [23] constructs an affinity network by feature vectors. It represents nodes with the solved leading eigenvectors. The second category is random walk based methods. DeepWalk [19] utilizes random walk to learn structural information and uses skip-gram to obtain the representations. Node2vec [10] changes the strategy of random walk to capture a more global structure. The third category is edge modeling based methods. They utilize node-node connections to learn node representations directly. LINE [22] uses first-order proximity and second-order proximity to obtain local and global structure information. The fourth category is deep learning based methods. They could extract highly non-linear structure automatically by using deep learning techniques. SDNE [24] preserves first and second order proximities for highly non-linear structures via a deep autoencoder.

3 Preliminary

In this section, we first describe the notations used in this paper. We then formalize the problem of network embedding in an incomplete network.

3.1 Notations

We denote the complete network as $G = (V, A, P)$, where $V = \{v_1, v_2, ..., v_{|V|}\}$ indicates the nodes in the network. $A \in \mathbb{R}^{|V| \times |V|}$ represents the adjacency matrix and $P \in \mathbb{R}^{|V| \times |P|}$ denotes the node attribute matrix, where $|V|$ and $|P|$ represent the dimension of adjacency matrix and node attributes, respectively. Similarly, we define the incomplete network, the missing network, and recovered network as $G' = (V', A', P')$, $G_M = (V_M, A_M, P_M)$, $G_R = (V_R, A_R, P_R)$, respectively. Table 1 lists the meaning of the notations mainly used in this paper.

3.2 Problem Formulation

The purpose of network completion is to infer the missing part of the incomplete network, how to infer the missing network G_M from the observable network G' is crucial to the problem. If we use adjacency matrices to represent the network, then the network completion problem can be transformed into matrix completion problem. In general, classical matrix completion problem is to determine the value (0 or 1) of elements in the missing part in a binary matrix. In this paper, we assume that the number of missing nodes is known. If not, the standard methods for estimating the size of hidden (missing) populations can solve this problem [17].

Although network recovering helps in representing the incomplete network, there are some problems in the representation learning process. On the one hand, many network representation methods are shallow models. Network completeness is essential for extracting local or global topology information. On the other hand, most methods can't capture non-linear relations between nodes [24]. Thus, we need to consider not only topology information for non-linear relations but also node contents such as node attributes. Besides, A' and P' preserve the information of a network, which is used to represent the network in the joint space. Thus, nodes with similar topology structures or attributes will be closer in the representation dimension.

4 Design of DINE

In this section, we present a novel framework, namely DINE, to solve the problem of network embedding in incomplete networks. Our framework contains two crucial components, network recovery and network embedding. Firstly, we discuss how to recover the incomplete network. Then, we introduce the process of network representation learning, which considers both topology information and node attributes.

4.1 Recovery of Incomplete Network

To recover the network with nodes and edges missing, we model the incomplete network with the Kronecker graphs model [15]. In detail, we use the incomplete network to fit the Kronecker graphs model in network structure and estimate the missing part, and then re-estimate model parameters. These two steps are iterated until the model parameters converge. Finally, we obtain the missing part of the network.

The purpose of the network completion is to find the most likely structure of the missing part G_M. We connect the incomplete network and the missing network by network generation parameters Θ. Let σ denote the mapping among nodes in the recovered network, incomplete network, and missing network. The mapping σ indicates a permutation of set $\{1, ..., N_G\}$. The first N' elements of σ map the nodes of G_R to the incomplete network and the remaining N_M elements of σ map the nodes of missing part G_M. The likelihood $P(G', G_M, \sigma|\Theta)$ can be represented as:

$$P(G', G_M, \sigma|\Theta) = \prod_{a_{uv}=1} \left[\Theta^k\right]_{\sigma(u)\sigma(v)} \prod_{a_{uv}=0} \left(1 - \left[\Theta^k\right]_{\sigma(u)\sigma(v)}\right) \tag{1}$$

where Θ^k is the adjacency matrix generated by model parameters Θ. $\left[\Theta^k\right]_{\sigma(u)\sigma(v)}$ denotes the $(\sigma(u), \sigma(v))$-th element of matrix Θ^k. a_{uv} is the (u, v)-th element of A_R, which is the the adjacency matrix of the recovered network.

Next, we consider the edges in the missing part and σ as the latent variables. E-step is to sample the missing part and permutation. M-step aims to optimize the parameters Θ by stochastic gradient descent process. Then we iterate E-step and M-step until parameters Θ converge. The steps could be described as:

E-step :

$$(G_M^{(t)}, \sigma^{(t)}) \sim P(G_M, \sigma|G', \Theta^{(t)}) \tag{2}$$

M-step :

$$\Theta^{(t+1)} = \arg\max_{\Theta \in (0,1)^2} \mathbb{E}[P(G_M^{(t)}, \sigma^{(t)}, G'|\Theta)]. \tag{3}$$

In detail, we first initialize model parameters Θ and generate a stochastic network. Then we sample the missing part G_M and node mapping σ by Gibbs sampling, which can be considered to recover the missing part of the network. Besides, we optimize the model parameters Θ and iterate the above steps until the parameters converge. Finally, we obtain the most likely instances of the missing part and node mapping.

Table 2. Layer structures of MVC-DNER on three datasets

Dataset	Layers in view V	Layers in view P
Citeseer	N_R-500-128	3,703-600-128
DBLP	N_R-800-128	9,662-900-128
BlogCatalog	N_R-500-128	39-4

4.2   Recovered Network Embedding MVC-DNER

In terms of network representation, we consider not only network topology structure but also node attributes. Furthermore, inspired by MVC-DNE [28] which utilizes a deep autoencoder, we propose MVC-DNER to capture non-linear structures and node attributes in the recovered network. Figure 2 shows that the embedding part has network structures view T and node attributes view P, which uses deep autoencoder to learn latent information in each view. We take the adjacency matrix xt and the attribute matrix xp of the recovered network as input. In the encoding process, input features of one view could encode some shared latent information reflecting the input of the other view. In the decoding process, latent representations in one view could reconstruct the input of another view. The loss function is defined as:

$$L(xt, xp; \theta) = L_t(xt, xp; \theta) + L_p(xt, xp; \theta) \tag{4}$$

$$
\begin{aligned}
L_t(xt, xp; \theta) = \beta \sum_{i=1}^{|V'|} ((1-\alpha) \left\| xt_i - x\hat{t}_i^t \right\|_2^2 + \alpha \left\| xt_i - x\hat{t}_i^p \right\|_2^2) \\
+ (1-\beta) \sum_{i=1}^{|V_M|} ((1-\alpha) \left\| xt_i - x\hat{t}_i^t \right\|_2^2 + \alpha \left\| xt_i - x\hat{t}_i^p \right\|_2^2)
\end{aligned}
\tag{5}
$$

$$
\begin{aligned}
L_p(xt, xp; \theta) = \beta \sum_{i=1}^{|V'|} ((1-\alpha) \left\| xp_i - x\hat{p}_i^t \right\|_2^2 + \alpha \left\| xp_i - x\hat{p}_i^p \right\|_2^2) \\
+ (1-\beta) \sum_{i=1}^{|V_M|} ((1-\alpha) \left\| xp_i - x\hat{p}_i^t \right\|_2^2 + \alpha \left\| xp_i - x\hat{p}_i^p \right\|_2^2)
\end{aligned}
\tag{6}
$$

where $x\hat{t}_i^t$ and $x\hat{t}_i^p$ are the reconstruction outputs of xt_i. $x\hat{p}_i^t$ and $x\hat{p}_i^p$ are the reconstruction vectors of xp_i. α and β are parameters to adjust the proportion of self-view and cross-view reconstruction errors, recovered nodes and observed nodes reconstruction errors, respectively. $\theta = \{W^{(l)}, b^{(l)}, \hat{W}^{(l)}, \hat{b}^{(l)}\}_{l=1}^K$ denotes parameters including the weights W and bias b in the deep autoencoder.

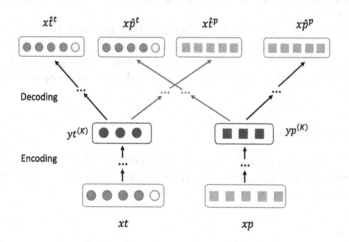

Fig. 2. Deep autoencoder MVC-DNER.

The loss function is minimized by stochastic gradient descent. Thus, the learning representations preserve not only network structures information but also node attributes information.

5 Experiments

In this section, we evaluate our framework on three datasets through multi-label classification and link prediction tasks. We first introduce three datasets and baseline methods. Then we describe evaluation metrics and parameter settings of the methods. Finally, we present the performance of DINE and compare it against state-of-the-art baselines.

5.1 Datasets

We use three datasets including two academic datasets (Citeseer[1] and DBLP[2]) and a social dataset BlogCatalog[3].

(1) **Citeseer** contains citation information of papers. In the citation network, each node represents a paper and edges reflect citation relationship. The citation network constructed by Citeseer contains 3,312 papers divided into six classes including Agents, AI, DB, IR, ML, and HCI. Besides, the attribute feature of each paper is a 3,703 dimensional binary vector based on the topics.

(2) **DBLP** is also a citation dataset which covers useful information on papers such as authors, year, publisher, and title. It provides open bibliographic information of major computer science journals and proceedings. We choose 8,192 papers from 10 research domains. We choose the title of papers as the attribute and use a 9,662 dimensional binary vector to represent the attribute feature.

(3) **BlogCatalog** is a social blog directory that manages bloggers and their blogs. We choose some data which contains 4,096 nodes, 38,983 edges, and 39 groups. Nodes represent bloggers and edges represent the friendship between bloggers. Besides, each blogger belongs to one or several groups based on interesting.

5.2 Baseline Methods

We use the following methods as our baseline methods. We choose four network representation learning methods based on matrix factorization, random walk, and deep learning, respectively.

---

[1] https://linqs.soe.ucsc.edu/data.

[2] https://www.aminer.cn/billboard/citation.

[3] http://socialcomputing.asu.edu/datasets/BlogCatalog.

(1) **GF** [1] is a matrix factorization based method. It relies on partitioning a graph to minimize the number of neighboring vertices. In addition, it preserves first order proximity and allows for linear scalability.

(2) **HOPE** [18] is also based on matrix factorization. It provides an efficient way to preserve high-order proximities of large-scale graphs. It is also capable of capturing the asymmetric transitivity.

(3) **Node2vec** [10] is a shallow model. It designs a flexible neighbor sampling strategy based on Deepwalk. It can preserve both local structure and global structure to learn network representations.

(4) **SDNE** [24] is the first network representation learning method based on deep learning. The deep autoencoder captures the non-linear network structure. It also can preserve the local and global network structure.

5.3   Parameter Settings

Our framework consists of network completion and recovered network representation learning. In the network completion, the Kronecker parameter Θ is random initialization. The neural network structure of MVC-DNER is listed in Table 2. We set the learning rate as 0.001. The mini-batch size of optimization is 50. The parameters for balancing the importance of self-view and cross-view α, recovered nodes and observed nodes β are set to 0.5 and 0.8, respectively.

The parameter settings of these baseline methods including GF, HOPE, Node2vec, and SDNE follow a NRL survey [9]. The learning rate of SGD is 0.0001, and max iterations are 5,000 in GF. The higher-order coefficient of HOPE is 0.01. In Node2vec, we set the window size as 10, the walk length as 40, walks per node as 40. The dimension of network learning representation is 128 for all methods.

5.4   Experimental Results

Multi-label Classification. We aim to learn representations in an incomplete network. To achieve this goal, we need to remove 5%-30% nodes and the corresponding edges. We first learn the representations based on remaining nodes and take the representations as the input of the classification model. Then we divide the labeled nodes into training set and testing set. The portion ratio of training nodes varies from 10% to 90%. We use macro-F1 to evaluate the performance of the classification model. Besides, the experiment runs 10 times, and we take the average of results as the final results. Table 3 lists the classification results for each method, where M_r is the portion ratio of missing nodes.

From the table, we can observe that the performance of DINE is better than any other baseline methods, especially in the Citeseer dataset. The performances of these methods gradually become worse as the portion of missing nodes increasing. Besides, two matrix factorization methods have terrible performance in Citeseer. Most methods have a relatively better performance in the DBLP dataset.

Table 3. Multi-label classification results (macro-F1) on two datasets with the portion of missing nodes

Datasets	M_r	GF	HOPE	Node2vec	SDNE	DINE
Citeseer	0.05	0.253	0.265	0.431	0.366	**0.642**
	0.10	0.231	0.253	0.423	0.365	**0.636**
	0.15	0.202	0.257	0.412	0.358	**0.627**
	0.20	0.203	0.244	0.419	0.352	**0.629**
	0.25	0.235	0.249	0.403	0.346	**0.617**
	0.30	0.225	0.243	0.388	0.335	**0.614**
DBLP	0.05	0.579	0.575	0.582	0.585	**0.595**
	0.10	0.575	0.574	0.594	0.558	**0.601**
	0.15	0.541	0.534	0.584	0.571	**0.594**
	0.20	0.576	0.587	0.564	0.566	**0.591**
	0.25	0.574	0.580	0.561	0.577	**0.593**
	0.30	0.572	0.571	0.558	0.573	**0.590**

Link Prediction. Similar to the task of multi-label classification, we also remove partial nodes and the corresponding edges. Then we remove 20% edges of the remainder network as links for prediction and consider them as positive samples. Besides, we randomly select unconnected node pairs as negative samples. The number of negative samples is the same as positive samples. From the results of link prediction presented in Fig. 3, we can see that DINE achieves significant improvements in AUC over the baselines in all datasets. As the portion of missing nodes increasing, the performances of these methods have a downward trend.

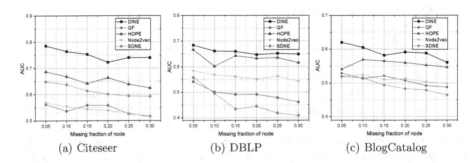

(a) Citeseer   (b) DBLP   (c) BlogCatalog

Fig. 3. Link prediction results (AUC) on three datasets with the portion of missing nodes.

6   Conclusion

In this paper, we have presented a framework named DINE, which aims to learn node representations in incomplete networks. The framework is divided into two parts: network completion and recovered network representation learning. Specifically, we recover the missing part of the incomplete network based on the combination of EM approach and Kronecker graphs model. After recovering the incomplete network, we propose an algorithm named MVC-DNER to learn node representations for the recovered network. MVC-DNER uses the deep autoencoder to learn representations, which preserves both network structures and node attributes. Experimental results on three real-world network datasets show the significant performance of our proposed method. The future work is primarily on extending DINE to heterogeneous networks containing different types of nodes and edges.

References

1. Ahmed, A., Shervashidze, N., Narayanamurthy, S., Josifovski, V., Smola, A.J.: Distributed large-scale natural graph factorization. In: Proceedings of the 22nd International Conference on World Wide Web, pp. 37–48. ACM (2013)
2. Bai, X., Lee, I., Ning, Z., Tolba, A., Xia, F.: The role of positive and negative citations in scientific evaluation. IEEE Access **5**, 17607–17617 (2017)
3. Bhagat, S., Cormode, G., Muthukrishnan, S.: Node classification in social networks. In: Aggarwal, C. (ed.) Social Network Data Analytics, pp. 115–148. Springer, Boston (2011). https://doi.org/10.1007/978-1-4419-8462-3_5
4. Buccafurri, F., Lax, G., Nocera, A., Ursino, D.: Discovering missing me edges across social networks. Inf. Sci. **319**, 18–37 (2015)
5. Cai, L., et al.: Scholarly impact assessment: a survey of citation weighting solutions. Scientometrics **118**(2), 453–478 (2019)
6. Clauset, A., Moore, C., Newman, M.E.: Hierarchical structure and the prediction of missing links in networks. Nature **453**(7191), 98 (2008)
7. Gao, H., Huang, H.: Deep attributed network embedding. In: IJCAI, vol. 18, pp. 3364–3370 (2018)
8. Gao, S., Denoyer, L., Gallinari, P.: Temporal link prediction by integrating content and structure information. In: Proceedings of the 20th ACM International Conference on Information and Knowledge Management, pp. 1169–1174. ACM (2011)
9. Goyal, P., Ferrara, E.: Graph embedding techniques, applications, and performance: a survey. Knowl.-Based Syst. **151**, 78–94 (2018)
10. Grover, A., Leskovec, J.: node2vec: scalable feature learning for networks. In: Proceedings of the 22nd ACM SIGKDD International Conference on Knowledge Discovery and Data Mining, pp. 855–864. ACM (2016)
11. Guimerà, R., Sales-Pardo, M.: Missing and spurious interactions and the reconstruction of complex networks. Proc. Natl. Acad. Sci. **106**(52), 22073–22078 (2009)
12. Keshavan, R.H., Montanari, A., Oh, S.: Matrix completion from a few entries. IEEE Trans. Inf. Theory **56**(6), 2980–2998 (2010)
13. Kim, M., Leskovec, J.: The network completion problem: inferring missing nodes and edges in networks. In: Proceedings of the 2011 SIAM International Conference on Data Mining, pp. 47–58. SIAM (2011)

14. Kossinets, G.: Effects of missing data in social networks. Soc. Netw. **28**(3), 247–268 (2006)
15. Leskovec, J., Chakrabarti, D., Kleinberg, J., Faloutsos, C., Ghahramani, Z.: Kronecker graphs: an approach to modeling networks. J. Mach. Learn. Res. **11**, 985–1042 (2010)
16. Lü, L., Zhou, T.: Link prediction in complex networks: a survey. Physica A **390**(6), 1150–1170 (2011)
17. McCormick, T.H., Salganik, M.J., Zheng, T.: How many people do you know?: Efficiently estimating personal network size. J. Am. Stat. Assoc. **105**(489), 59–70 (2010)
18. Ou, M., Cui, P., Pei, J., Zhang, Z., Zhu, W.: Asymmetric transitivity preserving graph embedding. In: Proceedings of the 22nd ACM SIGKDD International Conference on Knowledge Discovery and Data Mining, pp. 1105–1114. ACM (2016)
19. Perozzi, B., Al-Rfou, R., Skiena, S.: DeepWalk: online learning of social representations. In: Proceedings of the 20th ACM SIGKDD International Conference on Knowledge Discovery and Data Mining, pp. 701–710. ACM (2014)
20. Rossi, R.A., Zhou, R., Ahmed, N.K.: Deep inductive network representation learning. In: Companion Proceedings of the Web Conference 2018, pp. 953–960. International World Wide Web Conferences Steering Committee (2018)
21. Tang, J., Liu, J., Zhang, M., Mei, Q.: Visualizing large-scale and high-dimensional data. In: Proceedings of the 25th International Conference on World Wide Web, pp. 287–297. International World Wide Web Conferences Steering Committee (2016)
22. Tang, J., Qu, M., Wang, M., Zhang, M., Yan, J., Mei, Q.: LINE: large-scale information network embedding. In: Proceedings of the 24th International Conference on World Wide Web, pp. 1067–1077. International World Wide Web Conferences Steering Committee (2015)
23. Tenenbaum, J.B., De Silva, V., Langford, J.C.: A global geometric framework for nonlinear dimensionality reduction. Science **290**(5500), 2319–2323 (2000)
24. Wang, D., Cui, P., Zhu, W.: Structural deep network embedding. In: Proceedings of the 22nd ACM SIGKDD International Conference on Knowledge Discovery and Data Mining, pp. 1225–1234. ACM (2016)
25. Wang, W., Liu, J., Yang, Z., Kong, X., Xia, F.: Sustainable collaborator recommendation based on conference closure. IEEE Trans. Comput. Soc. Syst. **6**(2), 311–322 (2019)
26. Xia, F., Asabere, N.Y., Liu, H., Chen, Z., Wang, W.: Socially aware conference participant recommendation with personality traits. IEEE Syst. J. **11**(4), 2255–2266 (2014)
27. Xu, B., et al.: Protein complexes detection based on global network representation learning. In: 2018 IEEE International Conference on Bioinformatics and Biomedicine (BIBM), pp. 210–213. IEEE (2018)
28. Yang, D., Wang, S., Li, C., Zhang, X., Li, Z.: From properties to links: deep network embedding on incomplete graphs. In: Proceedings of the 2017 ACM on Conference on Information and Knowledge Management, pp. 367–376. ACM (2017)
29. Zhang, D., Yin, J., Zhu, X., Zhang, C.: Network representation learning: a survey. IEEE Trans. Big Data (2018)
30. Zhu, S., Yu, K., Chi, Y., Gong, Y.: Combining content and link for classification using matrix factorization. In: Proceedings of the 30th Annual International ACM SIGIR Conference on Research and Development in Information Retrieval, pp. 487–494. ACM (2007)

Predictive Representation Learning in Motif-Based Graph Networks

Kaiyuan Zhang[1], Shuo Yu[1], Liangtian Wan[1(✉)], Jianxin Li[2], and Feng Xia[3]

[1] Key Laboratory for Ubiquitous Network and Service Software of Liaoning Province,
School of Software, Dalian University of Technology, Dalian 116620, China
zky123123@outlook.com, y_shuo@outlook.com, wan.liangtian.2015@ieee.org
[2] School of Information Technology, Deakin University, Burwood,
VIC 3125, Australia
jianxin.li@deakin.edu.au
[3] School of Science, Engineering and Information Technology, Federation University,
Ballarat, Australia
f.xia@ieee.org

Abstract. Link prediction is an important task for analyzing social networks which also has other applications such as bioinformatics and e-commerce. Network representation learning (NRL), which can significantly enhance the performance for link prediction, has attracted much attention in recent years. However, the existing NRL methods mainly focus on observed network structures without considering hidden prediction knowledge in the representation space. Meanwhile, some random walk based NRL methods are dissatisfactory to learn link knowledge in dense networks with large scales. In this paper, we propose a predictive representation learning (PRL) model, which unifies node representations and motif-based structures, to improve prediction ability of NRL. We firstly enhance node representations based on motif-biased random walks and then employ L2-SVM to learn motif-connected node-pairs. By jointly optimizing two objectives of existent and nonexistent edges representations, we preserve more information of nodes in representation space based on supervised learning. To evaluate the performance of our proposed model, we implement experiments on 5 real data sets. Simulation results illustrate that our proposed model achieves better link prediction performance compared with other state-of-the-arts methods.

Keywords: Link prediction · Network representation learning · Network motifs

1 Introduction

With the explosion of big data, the network has become an effective carrier to understand user behaviors due to its wealthy information and advanced research theories [7]. Predicting links in the network is the core task for various applications in the data mining field, which can significantly enhance user experience

© Springer Nature Switzerland AG 2019
J. Liu and J. Bailey (Eds.): AI 2019, LNAI 11919, pp. 177–188, 2019.
https://doi.org/10.1007/978-3-030-35288-2_15

and query efficiency. For example, a proper prediction for new friends can attract more users for online social medias, and a highly relevant documents ranking can promote searching efficiency for web searching engine [8]. There are two main categories for link prediction: future link prediction and missing link prediction [6]. The former intends to predict new links establishment in a dynamic network within foreseeable future [17], and the latter tries to predict missing links in a static network. As the online data is often incomplete, we focus on missing links prediction based on partially obtained data to mine users' behaviors.

The fundamental points for solving link prediction problems generally focus on extracting useful information from nodes and the topology of network. The network representation learning (NRL) which embeds the network into a low-dimensional representation space, provides an effective approach for researchers to learn link prediction [15]. The NRL often focuses on nodes' locations in the space which achieves better performance on network reconstruction and network inference [3]. However, few studies preserve dedicated features of nodes and edges for link prediction.

Network motifs occurring frequently in complex networks serve as basic building blocks of networks, which are essential to understand particular networks [2]. Processing motifs instead of individual nodes can not only simplifies networks, but also emphasizes the structural features of networks. Hence, some studies utilize motifs to help node representation learning to reduce the computational complexity [1,18]. However, these studies mainly focus on specific network roles as they are not generally for link prediction problems.

In this paper, we propose a joint learning model called Predictive Representation Learning (PRL) to achieve better performance for link prediction. The PRL combines NRL with L2-SVM classification model to enhance the predictive ability for node representations, which firstly learns node representations by overt structure of the motif-based network. Then we infer motif-connected edges by L2-SVM model to learn link prediction knowledge. The node representations update them the integrated loss function of skip-gram and SVM, which promotes performance of each other timely and interactively. Simulation results on real data sets demonstrate that our proposed model is promising compared with other state-of-the-arts methods. The contributions are summarized as follows,

- We learn the network based on the motif-biased random walk, which not only explores the network structure efficiently, but also preserves more information for nodes representations in the latent space.
- We propose a joint learning model called PRL, which unifies NRL and supervised learning on the prediction knowledge to improve the predictive performance.
- The experimental results on real data sets verify that our proposed model outperforms other state-of-the-arts methods in densely connected networks, which are widespread in the real world.

The rest of paper is organized as follows. We present the Predictive Representation Learning model in Sect. 2. Some baselines and experimental results are provided in Sect. 3, and Sect. 4 concludes this paper.

2 Predictive Representation Learning

2.1 Problem Definition

Considering an undirected network $G = (V, E)$, where V is the vertex set and $E = E^+ \cup E^- \cup E^*$ is the edge set containing all possible links of V. Notice that E^+ is the existent edge set, and E^- is the nonexistent node-pairs set. E^* is the set of unknown node-pairs in the graph. The task of link prediction is to assign a clear status (existent or nonexistent) for node-pairs in E^*. Our proposed model embeds each node $v_i \in V$ into a low-dimensional space $x^i \in \mathbf{R}^n$, which are treated as features for link prediction.

2.2 Existent Edge Representations

The representation learning of a network is to preserve structural properties among nodes as much as possible by exploiting low-dimensional vectors. The existent edges connected with a node are intuitive features to investigate node representations. However, individual node contains little connection information, and mining neighbours of each node in the network has tremendous complexity. Thus we develop the motif-biased random walk on a graph as an initial preprocessor to formalize the sequence for each node. We define two parameters p and q to guide the random walk. We set the weight of edge connected to s as

$$w(s, t) = k \cdot |M(s) \cap M(t)| + 1, (s, t) \in E_s, \tag{1}$$

where $M(s)$ and $M(t)$ is the set of motifs containing node s and t, respectively, k is the order of motifs, and E_s is the edge set for edges containing node s. Then, the parameter p indicating the first-order walking probability from s transferring to t is calculated by

$$p(s, t) = \frac{w(s, t)}{\sum_{x \in E_s} w(s, x)}. \tag{2}$$

The parameter q is utilized to guide the second-order walks, which are based on both current and previous movements. We assume that the previous node is s, and the current node is t. Thus the probability q from node t transferring to x is expressed as

$$q(s, t, x) = \begin{cases} p(t, x) & \text{If } s, \ t, \ x \text{ in the same motif,} \\ 1 & \text{Otherwise.} \end{cases} \tag{3}$$

$p(t, x)$ is the probability from t transferring to x, which is defined above. The overall random walk procedure is shown in Fig. 1.

We capture nodes' sequences by utilizing motif-biased random walk, in which nodes in the same motif are closer to each other. Then we input these sequences to Skip-gram [9], which is a word embedding model for co-word analysis in contexts. Therefore, each node obtains two kinds of representations. One is x_i when the node i is the source node to discover its proximity. The other is x_i'

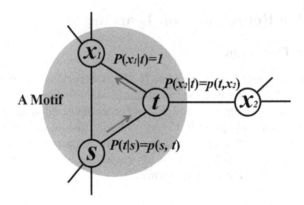

Fig. 1. The overall random walk procedure of our proposed model, which starts from s then to t and finally arrives to x_1.

when i is treated as co-occur partners of other nodes. The conditional probability function for node u generated by node i is given by

$$p(u|i) = \frac{\exp(x_u'^T x_i)}{\sum_t^V \exp(x_t'^T x_i)}, \tag{4}$$

where V is the vertex set of the network. We employ logarithm likelihood function for all edges in the network, so that the loss function of NRL can be defined as

$$L_r = -\sum_{(i,j)}^{E^+} \log p(j|i) = -\sum_{(i,j)}^{E^+} \log \frac{\exp(x_j'^T x_i)}{\sum_t^V \exp(x_t'^T x_i)}, \tag{5}$$

where E^+ is the existent edge set. We employ Negative Sampling (NEG) method instead of Huffman Tree to reduce computational complexity, and the loss function can be formulated as

$$L_r = -\sum_{(i,j)}^{E^+} (\log \sigma(x_j'^T x_i) + \sum_t^K \mathbb{E}_{t \sim p(i)}[\log \sigma(-x_t'^T x_i)]), \tag{6}$$

where $\sigma(\cdot)$ is the sigmoid function, K is the number of negative samples. $p(i)$ is the noise distribution which is randomly obtained by:

$$p(i) = \lambda d_m(i)^{3/4} / \sum_{i \in K} d_m(i)^{3/4}, \tag{7}$$

where $d_m(i)$ is the number of motifs containing node i and λ is the tuning parameter for different networks.

2.3   Nonexistent Edge Representations

Missing link prediction can be viewed as a binary classification problem, i.e., existent links and nonexistent links. Thus, we improve the prediction ability of node representations according to an accurate classifier. Based on network motifs, we divide nonexistent edges into two sets. One is the motif-connected edge set E_c^- and the other is the motif-disconnected edge set E_d^-. We defined that there is a motif-connected edge between two nodes if two of their respective motifs have common nodes. In other words, u and v are motif-connected if there exists $C(u) \in M(u)$ and $C(v) \in M(v)$, which $C(u) \cap C(v) \neq \varnothing$ and $C(u) \neq C(v)$. $M(u)$ and $M(v)$ are the motif sets containing u and v, respectively. $C(u)$ and $C(v)$ represent one of u's motif and v's motif, respectively. Otherwise, if two nodes do not construct any motifs in the network, the edge between them is recognized as motif-disconnected edge. According to motifs structure between two nodes, motif-connected edges may be mistakenly regarded as existent edges in latent space. We apply Hadamard product of two nodes' representations as the composition function to capture the features of node-pairs. Therefore, we formulate the edge representations as $y_{ij} = x_i * x_j$, where $*$ is Hadamard product of x_i and x_j. We adopt a regularized linear L2-SVM classifier to train the features mentioned above [4]. Combining L2-SVM with the edge representations, we minimize the loss function as

$$L_s = C \sum_{(i,j) \in E^+ \cup E_c^-} \max(0, 1 - l_{ij}(w^T y_{ij} + b))^2 + \frac{1}{2} w^T w, \tag{8}$$

where C is the regularization parameter, E^+ is the existent edge set of the network and E_c^- is the motif-connected edge set. l_{ij} is the label of node-pairs, i.e., $l_{ij} = 1$ for $(i,j) \in E^+$ and $l_{ij} = 0$ for $(i,j) \in E_c^-$. w is the normal vector, and b is the threshold of the hyperplane which we optimize for the classifier. Through the L2-SVM classifier, we train data from feature space to learn prediction information (the hyperplane) to classify existent edges and motif-connected edges in representations.

2.4   Joint Learning

We propose PRL model by unifying them together whose loss function that we attend to minimize is

$$\min L_M = min(L_r + \frac{1}{1+k} L_s) \tag{9}$$

where k is the order of the network motifs and $\frac{1}{1+k}$ is the weighted parameter for balancing the importance of L_r and L_s, which are loss functions mentioned above for different types of edges. Before we optimize L_M, we employ undersampling method to avoid imbalance problem caused by $E^- \gg E^+$. The undersampling method for a network is to randomly select a subset $E_s^- \subset E^-$ satisfying $|E_s^-| = |E^+|$ The overview of predictive representation learning is shown in Fig. 2. During predictive representation learning, we first utilize motif-based random walk to capture a sequence for each node. For existent edges, we put sequences of component nodes in to Skip-gram model to achieve their edge representation vectors as existent edge representations. For non-existent edges,

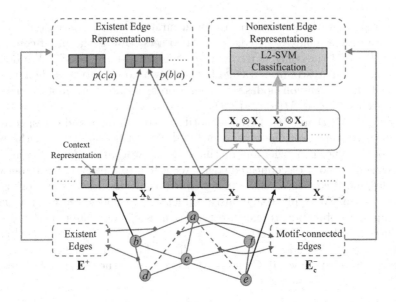

Fig. 2. The overview of predictive representation learning.

we recognize motif-connected edges and utilize Hadamard product to achieve their edge representation vectors as non-existent edge representations. Unifying the loss functions of Skip-gram and L2-SVM, we find the optimal hyperplane for the L2-SVM model, which classifies links into two types (i.e., existent links and non-existent links).

The parameter learning for our model is presented in Algorithm 1. We adopt SGD method to iteratively update the parameter for each node in the training network. The outputs are the node representation matrix Q and the hyperplane determined by w and b. In a single iteration of parameter learning, we process two objectives sequentially, i.e., we first optimize L_r to update x for each node (line 4 to 10), and then use the node representation matrix from first steps to update w and b for L_s (line 11 to 15). Specifically, the learning rate for updating parameter on L_r is α_1, and we sample existent node-pairs (i, j) and k negative node-pairs (i, k) from E^+. In addition, we obtain training data E_o for L_s by combining motif-connected edge set E_{cs}^- with existent edge set E^+. Then we optimize L_s with the learning rate α_2 to update parameter. The iteration will terminate until convergence or the number of iterations equals to the number of the setting maximum learning iteration.

3   Experiments

3.1   Data Sets

In this section, we use 5 real data sets including a biological network, a routing network, a social network, a scientific collaboration network and a infrastructure network, to evaluate the performance of our model. All these data sets are

---

Algorithm 1. Parameter Learning for PRL

Input:

    Training network $G = (V, E_t), E_t = E^+ \cup E_s^-$

Output:

    Node representation matrix Q, hyperplane determined by w and b

1: Initialize $Q = \{x_1, x_2, ..., x_n\}$, co-occur matrix $Q' = \{x_1', x_2', ..., x_n'\}$, and w, b for
    hyperplane

2: **repeat**

3:    **for** each $i \in V$ **do**

4:       Sample node-pairs $(i, j) \in E^+$

5:       $x_i \leftarrow x_i - \alpha_1 \frac{\partial L_r}{\partial x_i}$

6:       $x_j' \leftarrow x_j' - \alpha_1 \frac{\partial L_r}{\partial x_j'}$

7:       Randomly select negative samples K by $E_{t \sim p(i)}$ from E^+

8:       **for** each $k \in K$ **do**

9:          $x_k' \leftarrow x_k' - \alpha_1 \frac{\partial L_r}{\partial x_k'}$

10:      **end for**

11:      Obtain $E_{cs}^- \subset E^-$, $E_o = E^+ \cup E_{cs}^-$

12:      **for** each $(i, l) \in E_o$ **do**

13:        $x_i \leftarrow x_i - \alpha_2 \frac{\partial L_s}{\partial x_i}, x_l \leftarrow x_l - \alpha_2 \frac{\partial L_s}{\partial x_l}$

14:        $w \leftarrow w - \alpha_2 \frac{\partial L_s}{\partial w}, b \leftarrow b - \alpha_2 \frac{\partial L_s}{\partial b}$

15:      **end for**

16:    **end for**

17: **until** Convergence or max iterations

---

retrieved from the Network Repository [12]. The detailed statistics for these data sets are presented in Table 1.

3.2 Baseline Methods

To verify the effectiveness of PRL model, we compare PRL with several baseline methods, which include 4 widely used link prediction methods [6], i.e., Common Neighbours (CN), Adamic-Adar Index (AA), Jaccard Index (JA), Simrank, 3 NRL models, i.e., Deepwalk [11], Node2vec [5], Line [13] and 2 advanced NRL models using supervised labels, i.e., SDNE [16], GAT [14]. By separately con-

Table 1. The statistics of data sets

	Nodes	Edges	AvgDegree	Triangles
Grid-human	9,186	31,038	6.76	17,192
CondMat	21,363	91,286	8.55	171,051
Openflights	2,905	15,645	10.77	72,852
Hamsterster	2,000	16,097	16.10	53,251
Routers	2,113	6,632	6.28	10,404

sidering the impact of motif-based random walk and supervised label on our proposed model, we conduct experiments as PRL-M and PRL-L, respectively.

3.3 Experimental Settings

In our experiments, we fully take triangular motif which has highest Z-score [10] in real network to investigate link prediction. We set the dimension size for all latent space as 128, the window size as 10, the walk length as 80, and walks per node as 10. The NEG for our model and Line is 5 and the regularization parameter C is 1. In addition, both learning rates α_1 and α_2 are set as 0.001. Specifically, p = 0.25, q = 0.5 in Node2vec and $\beta = 0.8$ in Simrank are set in our experiments. The reconstruction weight of non-zero elements is 10 and the weight of first-order term is 0.05 in SDNE.

Moreover, we split the edge data (existent and nonexistent) into 80% training set and 20% testing set. We adopt two commonly used evaluation metrics, i.e., area under the receiver operating characteristic curve (AUC) and average precision (AP), to measure the link prediction performance of different methods. Moreover, NRL models (Deepwalk, Node2vec, Line) only obtain the node representation matrix. Thus, we utilize Hadamard product of nodes representations to extract the features of node-pairs and apply L2-SVM to evaluate their prediction performance.

3.4 Experimental Results

Table 2 reports the AUC and AP values for baseline methods and our proposed method. The performances of methods on different networks depend on the properties of networks. We can see that our method gains average performance on Grid-human and Routers networks because of the sparsity of these networks, which demonstrates the limitation of our proposed method. However, if networks have dense connections and more triangles, meaning that we can detect their motifs obviously, our proposed method outperforms other methods. For other three networks (CondMat, Openflights, Hamsterster), our method achieves AUC and AP values higher than 0.9. We can observe that in dense networks, our proposed model outperforms other three kinds of baselines about 9.3%, 5.6% and 2.7% respectively on AUC and gains 8.4%, 5.4% and 2.8% improvements respectively on AP. From the performance of PRL-M on different data sets, we can see that PRL-M gains 1.4% to 5.3% improvements on AUC and 1.6% to 3.7% on AP values compared with widely-used methods and NRL methods. It shows that motif-based random walk guarantees the model performance in dense networks. The performance of PRL-L gains 1.4% to 4.7% improvements compared with baselines, which proves the superiority of learning network knowledge in a supervised manner. Integrating motif-based random walk and supervised learning into NRL, our proposed model outperforms baselines for link prediction.

For a more convincing analysis, we compare the performance on three dense networks (CondMat, Openflights, Hamsterster) with different percentage of training set from 20% to 100%. The result is presented in Fig. 3, from which

Table 2. AUC and AP scores for link prediction

		Grid-human	CondMat	Openflights	Hamsterster	Routers
AUC	CN	0.759	0.865	0.855	0.874	0.769
	JA	0.753	0.882	0.857	0.863	0.785
	AA	0.762	0.882	0.858	0.875	0.775
	Simrank	0.756	0.894	0.843	0.851	0.773
	Line	0.75	0.907	0.857	0.904	0.789
	Node2vec	0.814	0.915	0.905	0.898	0.8
	Deepwalk	0.784	0.896	0.916	0.902	0.815
	GAT	0.749	0.856	0.901	0.892	0.798
	SDNE	**0.842**	0.962	0.932	0.925	**0.824**
	PRL-M	0.765	0.931	0.92	0.923	0.745
	PRL-L	0.838	0.923	0.915	0.907	0.796
	PRL	0.803	**0.984**	**0.958**	**0.955**	0.804
AP	CN	0.756	0.859	0.853	0.868	0.815
	JA	0.746	0.882	0.854	0.859	0.816
	AA	0.762	0.882	0.858	0.874	0.825
	Simrank	0.744	0.881	0.812	0.838	0.831
	Line	0.741	0.905	0.886	0.832	0.804
	Node2vec	0.799	0.888	0.905	0.889	0.824
	Deepwalk	0.759	0.894	0.879	0.876	0.838
	GAT	0.756	0.865	0.879	0.847	0.799
	SDNE	**0.823**	0.916	**0.932**	0.926	0.824
	PRL-M	0.759	0.902	0.91	0.903	0.765
	PRL-L	0.795	0.915	0.915	0.897	**0.849**
	PRL	0.765	**0.974**	**0.932**	**0.948**	0.815

we can observe that the PRL outperforms than other baselines. We can see that when training models with only 20% data set, all methods are not strong enough for link prediction. Meanwhile, the increasing number of training sets promotes the performance of methods on link prediction. However, the performance almost unchanged while varying the percentage of training set from 80% to 100%. The GAT is relatively stable on different percentages of training sets by leveraging masked self-attentional layers. The random walk based methods are sensitive for different percentages of training sets, however, enough training data makes them perceive network comprehensively. Furthermore, methods learning network knowledge in supervised manners achieve higher values of AUC and AP when providing enough training data for them.

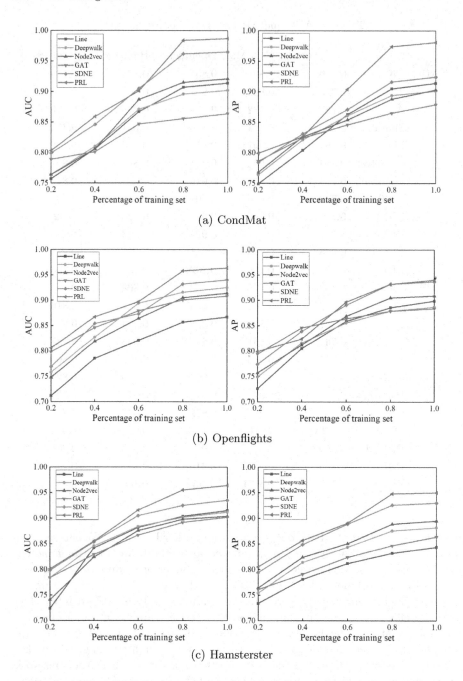

Fig. 3. AUC and AP Performance on three dense networks for link prediction.

4   Conclusion

In this paper, we propose the PRL model to learn the network representation based on motifs, which simplifies the network structure and preserves more information for nodes in the latent space. In addition, PRL is a joint learning model to unify NRL and supervised learning (L2-SVM) to improve predictive ability on inferring latent links. Compared with the state-of-the-arts methods, the simulation results on 5 real data sets demonstrate that our proposed model is promising in densely connected networks. The superior performance for our model would provide high-quality service for users while inferring usefulness information in searching tasks and recommending proper friends in social medias. In the future work, we will incorporate social theories and user characteristics (i.e., age, gender and personal interests) in our model, which will enhance searching experience for various users.

References

1. Ahmed, N.K., Rossi, R.A., Willke, T.L., Zhou, R.: Edge role discovery via higher-order structures. In: Kim, J., Shim, K., Cao, L., Lee, J.-G., Lin, X., Moon, Y.-S. (eds.) PAKDD 2017. LNCS (LNAI), vol. 10234, pp. 291–303. Springer, Cham (2017). https://doi.org/10.1007/978-3-319-57454-7_23
2. Benson, A.R., Gleich, D.F., Leskovec, J.: Higher-order organization of complex networks. Science **353**(6295), 163–166 (2016)
3. Cai, H., Zheng, V.W., Chang, K.C.: A comprehensive survey of graph embedding: problems, techniques, and applications. IEEE Trans. Knowl. Data Eng. **30**(9), 1616–1637 (2018)
4. Chang, C.C., Lin, C.J.: LIBSVM: a library for support vector machines. ACM Trans. Intell. Syst. Technol. **2**(3), 27 (2011)
5. Grover, A., Leskovec, J.: node2vec: scalable feature learning for networks. In: SIGKDD, pp. 855–864. ACM (2016)
6. Liben-Nowell, D., Kleinberg, J.: The link-prediction problem for social networks. J. Am. Soc. Inform. Sci. Technol. **58**(7), 1019–1031 (2007)
7. Liu, J., et al.: Artificial intelligence in the 21st century. IEEE Access **6**(1), 34403–34421 (2018)
8. Mao, J., et al.: Understanding and predicting usefulness judgment in web search. In: SIGIR, pp. 1169–1172. ACM (2017)
9. Mikolov, T., Sutskever, I., Chen, K., Corrado, G.S., Dean, J.: Distributed representations of words and phrases and their compositionality. In: NIPS, pp. 3111–3119 (2013)
10. Milo, R., Shen-Orr, S., Itzkovitz, S., Kashtan, N., Chklovskii, D., Alon, U.: Network motifs: simple building blocks of complex networks. Science **298**(5594), 824–827 (2002)
11. Perozzi, B., Al-Rfou, R., Skiena, S.: DeepWalk: online learning of social representations. In: SIGKDD, pp. 701–710. ACM (2014)
12. Rossi, R., Ahmed, N.: The network data repository with interactive graph analytics and visualization. In: AAAI, vol. 15, pp. 4292–4293 (2015)
13. Tang, J., Qu, M., Wang, M., Zhang, M., Yan, J., Mei, Q.: Line: large-scale information network embedding. In: WWW, pp. 1067–1077. International World Wide Web Conferences Steering Committee (2015)

14. Vaswani, A., et al.: Attention is all you need. In: NIPS, pp. 5998–6008 (2017)
15. Wan, L., Yuan, Y., Xia, F., Liu, H.: To your surprise: identifying serendipitous collaborators. IEEE Trans. Big Data (2019). https://doi.org/10.1109/TBDATA.2019.2921567
16. Wang, D., Cui, P., Zhu, W.: Structural deep network embedding. In: SIGKDD, pp. 1225–1234. ACM (2016)
17. Xu, B., Li, L., Liu, J., Wan, L., Kong, X., Xia, F.: Disappearing link prediction in scientific collaboration networks. IEEE Access **6**, 69702–69712 (2018)
18. Yuan, Y., Xun, G., Suo, Q., Jia, K., Zhang, A.: Wave2vec: deep representation learning for clinical temporal data. Neurocomputing **324**, 31–42 (2019)

Machine Learning and Applications

Online K-Means Clustering
with Lightweight Coresets

Jia Shun Low[(✉)], Zahra Ghafoori, and Christopher Leckie

School of Computing and Information Systems, The University of Melbourne,
Melbourne, Australia
jlow3@student.unimelb.edu.au, {zahra.ghafoori,caleckie}@unimelb.edu.au

Abstract. Coresets are representative samples of data that can be used
to train machine learning models with provable guarantees of approximating the accuracy of training on the full data set. They have been
used for scalable clustering of large datasets and result in better cluster
partitions compared to clustering a random sample. In this paper, we
present a novel approach of constructing lightweight coresets on subsets
of data that can fit in memory while performing a streaming variant of
k-means clustering known as online k-means. Experimental results show
that this approach generates cluster partitions of comparable accuracy to
the regular online k-means algorithm in less time, or superior partitions
in comparable time.

Keywords: Clustering · Cluster analysis · Coresets · K-means

1 Introduction

Clustering, or cluster analysis, is a form of unsupervised machine learning and
exploratory data analysis that aims to group similar objects and separate dissimilar objects in a dataset [27]. These objects can vary in different problem
domains, but are generally represented as vectors or points.

Lloyd's algorithm [19], also know as the k-means clustering algorithm, is a
popular choice to cluster data sets in the real world [27]. The algorithm aims to
minimize the k-means clustering objective function, which is an NP hard problem
[2]. Let X be a dataset of p dimensional vectors. Given a set of k clusters,
$C = \{C_1, C_2, ..., C_k\}$, we want to identify k centroids $m = \{m_1, m_2, ..., m_k\}$,
such that the sum of squared difference between each point in a cluster to the
mean of that cluster is minimized. The objective function can be described as
follows:

$$\min_{C} J(C) \quad where \quad J(C) = \sum_{i=1}^{k} \sum_{x_j \in C_i} \| x_j - m_i \|^2 \tag{1}$$

There is an increasing volume of data being generated in the world today, in
various domains such as IoT, social media, financial transactions and customer
click streams [18]. Furthermore, some of this data is generated in a streaming

© Springer Nature Switzerland AG 2019
J. Liu and J. Bailey (Eds.): AI 2019, LNAI 11919, pp. 191–202, 2019.
https://doi.org/10.1007/978-3-030-35288-2_16

fashion, where the available memory is much smaller than the data, and the data can only be accessed in a single pass [12]. *Online k-means* (OKM) [16] is a variation of k-means that is designed to handle streaming data. OKM runs k-means multiple times on subsets of data that can fit into memory, as they are being streamed. Intuitively, methods of improving k-means cluster quality on subsets of data can be used to improve the k-means clustering component of OKM.

Coresets [10] are summaries of massive datasets that provide provable guarantees of the quality of machine learning models trained on these summaries compared to training on the full dataset. In this paper, we aim to improve OKM using *lightweight coresets* (LWCS) [5], a fast coreset construction algorithm for k-means. To the best of our knowledge, previous use of LWCS has been to accelerate the running of k-means on the whole dataset. In contrast, our work is the first instance of constructing lightweight k-means coresets from subsets of the whole dataset that are delivered in a streaming fashion. Our experimental results show that this method, which we term *lightweight coreset online k-means* (LWCS-OKM), results in competitive cluster partitions with reduced runtime, or superior partitions with slightly increased runtime.

The paper is structured as follows. In Sect. 2, we introduce some preliminary concepts essential for understanding the rest of the paper. In Sect. 3, we discuss some related work on clustering big data, streaming algorithms for clustering and coreset construction algorithms for k-means. In Sect. 4, we explain in detail our proposed LWCS-OKM method. Section 5 details our experimental methodology as well as our results, while Sect. 6 gives the conclusion.

2   Preliminaries

In this section, some preliminary concepts used in the rest of the paper are explained.

2.1   Data Stream Model

There are various models of data streams in the literature. The model we use for this paper is as described in [23]. We assume the data arrives in chunks at discrete time steps, i.e., n_1 points arrive at time t_1, n_2 points arrive at time t_2 and so on. Running clustering algorithms on each chunk results in cluster summaries, i.e., a set of cluster centers ϕ and weights ω from each chunk. After L time steps, a final clustering is performed on the stored cluster summaries. Given a dataset X of size N, $\sum_{l=1}^{L} n_l = N$. Since the data is being streamed, it may never stop, so we can view N as the size of the data when we choose to do our final clustering, after L data chunks have been seen.

2.2   K-Means++

The k-means algorithm is a common heuristic for solving the k-means objective function. However it suffers from arbitrarily poor cluster partitions when seeded

---

Algorithm 1. D^2 seeding

Input: X - dataset of points
k - number of clusters
Output: Initial cluster centroids **m**
1 Choose first centroid $\mathbf{m}_1$ by random sampling
2 **while** *less than k centroids chosen* **do**
3 $\quad\mid\quad$ Pick next centroid $\mathbf{m}_i \leftarrow \boldsymbol{x}' \in \mathbf{X}$ with probability $\frac{D(\boldsymbol{x}')^2}{\sum_{x \in X} D(\boldsymbol{x})^2}$ where
$\quad\mid\quad D(\boldsymbol{x})$ is the distance of $\boldsymbol{x}$ to the nearest centroid
4 **end**
5 **return** $m = \{m_1, m_2..m_k\}$

---

randomly [3]. The *k-means++* (KM++) algorithm [3] is an alternative to the k-means algorithm that uses a distance based sampling algorithm known as D^2 seeding described in Algorithm 1, to choose a better set of initial centroids. While other alternative seeding strategies exist, they either do not perform as well as D^2 seeding in terms of leading to better partitions [9], or have theoretical speedups that do not fundamentally change the runtime of the k-means algorithm because the runtime is dominated by the distance calculations after the seeding takes place [4]. This seeding strategy has become a widely used way of seeding k-means [22]. For these reasons, we choose D^2 seeding to perform all initial seedings of k-means in this paper.

The seeding step requires k distance calculations. Let d be the runtime of a single distance calculation. The seeding step then has time complexity of $O(kNd)$. Given i iterations of computing Nk distances, KM++ has an overall complexity of $O(kNid)$.

2.3 Online K-Means

OKM is a crisp version of the *online fuzzy c-means* (OFCM) algorithm that was introduced in [16]. It should not be confused with the online *stochastic gradient descent* (SGD) variant of k-means that computes a gradient descent step for one point at a time [8]. It is known as STREAM k-means in [23]. While the *fuzzy c-means* (FCM) algorithm [7] allows for degrees of membership of a single point to various clusters, the k-means algorithm allows a point to be assigned to only one cluster. Therefore, OKM is a special case OFCM, which only allows a single cluster assignment for each point.

The algorithm assumes a streaming model mentioned in Sect. 2.1 [23]. At each discrete time step, the data subset is clustered with k-means clustering. Centroids are initialized with D^2 seeding on the first chunk. To speed up the processing of each subsequent chunk of data, the k-means algorithm on each subsequent chunk is initialized with the centroids learned from clustering the previous chunk. After each time step, the learned centroids are compressed and stored in memory into k weighted samples, each sample being the learned centroid, weighted by the number of points assigned to the centroid. The final step of the algorithm is running *weighted k-means* (WKM) on the stored weighted samples, to obtain the final set of centroids.

There can be various numbers of clusters in each chunk. The authors of [16] always set the value of k for each chunk to be the value of k assumed for the whole dataset. In the event that a chunk contains fewer than k clusters, there would be no information loss.

The complexity of the algorithm is as follows. Let i_{avg} be the average number of iterations it takes for k-means to terminate on one chunk, and n_{avg} be the average number of points in a chunk. The complexity of running k-means on that chunk would be $O(kn_{avg}i_{avg}d)$. For all chunks, the runtime would be $O(kNi_{avg}d)$. Weighting each point takes negligible time, as the points are labelled during the running of the k-means algorithm. In a practical implementation, at most a linear pass over each chunk would be needed to count the weights, which would take $O(N)$ time in total. The final clustering involves running WKM on Lk points. Let i_f be the number of iterations of this final clustering, then the final clustering has $O(k^2 Li_f d)$ time complexity. Therefore, OKM has a time complexity of $O(kNid + k^2 Li_f d)$. Since N is generally going to be more than kLi_f, the overall runtime can be simplified to $O(kNid)$. This complexity is identical to k-means, but the advantage of OKM is its disk awareness, making it feasible on unloadable data.

2.4   Lightweight Coresets

Coresets are summaries of large datasets with provable guarantees that the results of running machine learning algorithms on the coreset will approximate the results of learning on the full dataset, with some bounded error, depending on the size of the coreset [10]. LWCS for k-means are introduced in [5]. They empirically match the performance of previous k-means coresets at a fraction of the construction time complexity.

The construction has a preprocessing stage and an importance sampling stage. The preprocessing stage begins by calculating the mean, μ, of the data. Then, a constant δ is calculated by summing the distance of every point in the dataset to μ. For the importance sampling stage, a probability distribution $q(\boldsymbol{x})$ is calculated, as shown in Algorithm 2. Let α be the proportion of N that we want to sample. $\lfloor \alpha N \rfloor$ points are then sampled with probability $q(\boldsymbol{x})$. Each sampled point has a respective weight $\frac{1}{\lfloor \alpha N \rfloor q(\boldsymbol{x})}$, so the weights and points collectively form coreset.

Once the coreset is created, WKM or *weighted k-means++* (WKM++) can be run on the coreset. In this paper, we term those two *lightweight coreset k-means* (LWCS-KM) or *lightweight coreset k-means++* (LWCS-KM++) respectively.

The time complexity of LWCS-KM++ is as follows. The coreset construction requires two passes through the data on which we are performing the construction, to calculate μ and $q(\boldsymbol{x})$ for all $\boldsymbol{x} \in \boldsymbol{X}$. The weighted random sampling takes negligible time compared to these two passes, so the construction takes $O(Nd)$ time. Let i be the number of iterations of WKM++ on the coreset, which has size αN. The clustering step has $O(k\alpha Nid)$ time complexity. The summation of the

---

Algorithm 2. Lightweight coreset construction

Input: X - dataset of points

α - proportion of size of **X**, to be used as size of coreset

Output: Λ - lightweight coreset

1 $\mu \leftarrow$ mean of **X**

2 $\delta \leftarrow \sum_{x \in X} D(x, \mu)$

3 $N \leftarrow |X|$

4 **for** $x \in X$ **do**

5 $\quad$ $q(x) \leftarrow \frac{1}{2}\frac{1}{N} + \frac{1}{2}\frac{D(x,\mu)^2}{\delta}$

6 **end**

7 $\Lambda \leftarrow$ sample $\lfloor \alpha N \rfloor$ weighted points from X where each point has weight

$\frac{1}{\lfloor \alpha N \rfloor q(x)}$

8 **return** Λ

---

runtime of the construction and clustering steps is $O(Nd(1 + \alpha ik))$. LWCS-KM would have the same complexity owing to the negligible runtime of D^2 seeding. With high values of α and a large number of iterations in LWCS-KM++, LWCS-KM++ can potentially take a longer time than regular k-means clustering. However, with very small values of α, LWCS-KM++ will take a shorter time.

2.5 Very Large Datasets

We define very large datasets as datasets that cannot fit into the main memory of a computer. While there exist some definitions of the exact size of what constitutes "big data" [15], the actual size is not important when creating new algorithms for big data because there will always exist data that is larger than the main memory of a computer.

Clustering algorithms that can only be deployed on loadable data can be called literal algorithms [15]. Algorithms that work on unloadable data make the processing of such data possible, as literal algorithms cannot be deployed on unloadable data. However, even for loadable data, algorithms for unloadable datasets can be viewed as a way of accelerating the processing of loadable data. It should also be noted that streaming algorithms can be used to accelerate the processing of static datasets, where the partitioning of the data into separate chunks to be processed sequentially can be viewed as a data stream in which the velocity and volume of the incoming data are controlled.

3 Related Work

There is much work in the literature on running literal clustering algorithms on subsets of data, rather than the whole dataset, to overcome the long runtimes of clustering big datasets. The authors of [15] draw a random sample, then cluster it with a fuzzy version of k-means clustering, and then extend classification to all unlabelled points using nearest centroid classification. The authors of [20] overcome the issue of potentially poor quality seeds in seeding the random sample by using D^2 seeding on the random sample before performing k-means clustering, then extending the labelling via nearest centroid classification.

Minibatch k-means (MBKM) is an algorithm that clusters batches of points instead of the whole dataset [26]. The centroid update step in MBKM is performed via some learning rate in a convex combination equation. MBKM can be seen as an improvement to the earlier online SGD k-means [8], which can perform k-means with only one point stored in memory at a time, but results in lower quality clusters due to stochastic noise. MBKM can easily be used for streaming data if each chunk of data that comes in is treated as a batch.

K-means# is a modified version of KM++ that chooses a subset of size $O(k \log(k))$ points that gives a constant approximation of the k-means objective [1]. This algorithm can be applied in a divide-and-conquer strategy that yields a single pass streaming algorithm. The algorithms introduced in [28] incorporate coreset construction on small chunks data from the data stream. Multiple coresets are merged recursively into higher-level coresets, forming a coreset tree. While building the coreset tree, they use a caching strategy that reuses prior computed coresets to accelerate the construction of a new coreset.

The iVAT family of algorithms [25] construct representative subsets using a technique called maximin sampling, then performs single linkage clustering on the samples. Extending the labelling to every other points is done using nearest neighbours classification.

Prior to the identification of LWCS, previous k-means coreset construction methods include an algorithm based on exponential grids [14] and lines [13]. In [11], a coreset algorithm is introduced that preserves differential privacy for k-means clustering while having an approximation error that depends sub-linearly on the dimension of the dataset. The authors applied it to create differentially private location data from GPS databases.

4   Proposed Method

To increase the quality of cluster partitions on each chunk of data when running OKM, we propose running LWCS-KM instead of the regular k-means algorithm. For each chunk, after the coreset construction and clustering step has occurred, the weights for the final clustering are calculated by the number of points from the coreset assigned to each centroid, rather than points from the chunk. We call this approach *lightweight coreset online k-means* (LWCS-OKM).

The clustering takes into account the weights from coreset construction on each chunk, which leads to better cluster partitions than if we cluster a blind random sample. To the best of our knowledge, this is the first application of LWCS on subsets of streaming data rather than the whole dataset. The details of our new LWCS-OKM method are illustrated in Fig. 1 and detailed in given in Algorithm 3.

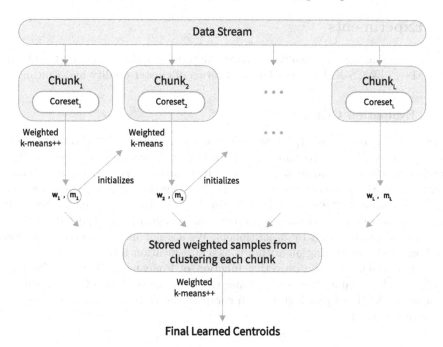

Fig. 1. Workflow of proposed LWCS-OKM algorithm

Algorithm 3. Lightweight coreset online k-means

Input: X - dataset of points
    k - number of clusters
    α - proportion of each chunk as our coreset size
Output: Learned cluster centroids **m**

1 **for** *every chunk we want to cluster* **do**
2   Create lightweight coreset Λ using Algorithm 2
3   **if** *first chunk* **then**
4   Initialize **m** with D^2 seeding using Algorithm 1
5   **end**
6   $m \leftarrow$ centroids returned by running WKM on Λ with **m** as the seeds
7   Add **m** to our final point set ϕ
8   Weigh each centroid in m by the number points in Λ assigned to that centroid, add that weight to final weight set ω
9 **end**
10 $m \leftarrow$ Learned centroids from running WKM++ initialized on **m** with ϕ as points and ω as weights
11 **return** m

From our earlier analysis of LWCS-KM, the coreset construction and clustering of each chunk would take $O(kn_{avg}d(1 + \alpha i_{avg}))$ time on average. Doing this for every chunk would take $O(kNd(1 + \alpha i_{avg}))$ time.

5   Experiments

In this section, we empirically compare our proposed algorithm, LWCS-OKM, to KM++, LWCS-KM++ and OKM in terms of cluster quality and runtime.

5.1   Evaluation Criteria

To measure cluster quality, we use *adjusted Rand index* (ARI) [17] and *sum of squared error* (SSE). ARI values range from 0 to 1, with 0 being the result of random labels and 1 being perfect labels matching the ground truth. We take advantage of the ground truth of our datasets to measure how well our proposed approach can recover the ground truth structure of a dataset as well as show that it generates similar partitions to the benchmark algorithms, especially KM++ which is commonly used by practitioners. We are not using ARI as a measure for how good a clustering algorithm is as a classification tool.

SSE is essentially the objective function of k-means clustering. While we cannot easily compute the true optimal value for the objective function due to it being an NP hard problem, we can compare the values obtained by different clustering algorithms.

5.2   Datasets

We utilize datasets that fit into main memory with the aim of comparing the performance of our algorithm against the performance of literal algorithms. This is not possible if our datasets are actually unloadable. For our streaming algorithms, we enforce a single pass rule over the data, with only a segment of the data available for access at any given time.

For our synthetic datasets, we generate clusters from fixed Gaussian distributions. The vectors in these clusters have dimensions p ranging from 100 to 300. The first three datasets have three clusters while the second three have four clusters.

The first real world dataset we use is the KDD Cup 99 dataset (KDD dataset) [6]. It contains 4,898,431 vectors of 41 dimensions, each vector being an attack type or normal data. The second real world dataset is the IoT Botnet dataset [21]. This dataset has 835,876 vectors, each representing the features of an Ecobee thermostat. Each vector has 115 dimensions, with the class being whether the device is benign, or affected by one of 10 possible attacks from 2 types of botnets.

5.3   Experimental Setup

There are multiple ways to decide when to terminate a k-means clustering algorithm. This parameter has to be set for KM++, LWCS-KM++ as well as the clustering components of both online algorithms. In every experiment we run, we terminate k-means if the labels of every point do not change after an iteration, or the centroid movement after an update is smaller than some small threshold

$\epsilon < 0.01$. We also set the maximum number of iterations to be 100 for all our k-means algorithms. For OKM and LWCS-OKM, we choose to have 10% of the data in memory. To match this, we set $\alpha = 0.1$ for LWCS-KM++. For α in OKM-KM++, our results are robust for a variety of values but we only record $\alpha = 0.1$ for brevity. All result values of ARI, runtime and SSE are an average of 30 runs with identical parameters on the same datasets.

For synthetic data, we choose k to be the true number of clusters created. For the KDD dataset, we choose $k = 3$ because the majority of points fall into one of the 3 following classes: the two attacks, Neptune and Smurf, or a point that does not represent an attack. For the IoT botnet dataset, we choose $k = 11$, because the class of vectors in this dataset is either normal, or one of 10 different attacks from the botnets. The attributes of all datasets are normalized to be between 0 and 1 and the non-numeric KDD features are removed.

We implement KM++ using the implementation in the Scikit-Learn Python module [24], every other algorithm was implemented by modifying the Scikit-Learn module. The experiments were conducted on a Windows 10 (64 bit) PC with 8 GB RAM and Intel i7.28 GHz processor.

5.4   Synthetic Datasets

As can be seen from Table 1, between the two online algorithms, LWCS-OKM creates better partitions in terms of recovering the ground truth, because the coresets created at each chunk are more representative of the whole dataset than a blind random sample. For every synthetic dataset, LWCS-OKM creates the best partitions in terms of recovering the ground truth. Based on the overall similarity in ARI of partitions generated by LWCS-OKM and KM++, we can conclude our algorithm generates partitions similar to KM++.

In terms of CPU runtime, our algorithm performs the best in four out of six scenarios. It is up to 3.88 times faster than KM++. As expected from our complexity analysis, OKM and LWCS-OKM do not have a significant difference in terms of runtime. It should be noted that even when the runtime of LWCS-OKM is not the best, it is still faster than the two literal algorithms and is at most 1.10 times slower than OKM, the only other algorithm that works on unloadable data, but results in better ARI.

5.5   Real Datasets

For the KDD dataset, our LWCS-OKM algorithm results in the best average ARI, but only the second best runtime, being slower than OKM. However, it notably has an SSE lower than OKM, so it took slightly longer to achieve a partition that has higher ARI and a better value in terms of optimizing the k-means objective function (Table 2).

The IoT dataset does not seem to have a structure that allows a variation of the k-means algorithm to easily recover the ground truth, with the ARI of LWCS-KM++ being 0.40 and the ARI of the others being slightly better at 0.42. However, our proposed method reduces runtime by 67.17% compared to

Table 1. ARI, runtimes and SSE for synthetic datasets for KM++, LWCS-KM++, OKM and our LWCS-OKM algorithms. Bold face numbers show the best results.

Dataset Information		KM++		LWCS-KM++		OKM		LWCS-OKM	
No. of Points	p	ARI	Time	ARI	Time	ARI	Time	ARI	Time
4,000,000	100	0.99	2.88	0.94	2.45	0.99	**1.95**	**1.00**	2.15
4,000,000	200	**1.00**	4.98	0.94	4.79	0.96	4.40	**1.00**	**4.30**
4,000,000	300	0.96	15.77	0.91	7.46	0.98	**5.67**	**1.00**	6.14
5,000,000	100	0.91	11.64	0.91	3.35	0.95	4.05	**1.00**	**3.00**
5,000,000	200	0.97	12.30	0.95	6.12	0.94	8.25	**1.00**	**5.57**
5,000,000	300	0.95	25.91	0.89	8.97	0.97	8.30	**1.00**	**8.03**

Table 2. ARI, runtimes and SSE for KDD dataset for KM++, LWCS-KM++, OKM and our LWCS-OKM algorithms. Bold face numbers show the best results.

Algorithm	ARI	Time (s)	SSE
KM++	0.91	11.14	2,485,573.98
LWCS-KM++	0.63	10.61	3,208,873.91
OKM	0.84	**8.31**	2,671,638.73
LWCS-OKM	**0.93**	9.24	**2,323,473.10**

Table 3. ARI, runtimes and SSE for IoT dataset for KM++, LWCS-KM++, OKM and our LWCS-OKM algorithms. Bold face numbers show the best results.

Algorithm	ARI	Time (s)	SSE
KM++	**0.42**	16.57	174,827.54
LWCS-KM++	0.40	6.33	171,632.15
OKM	**0.42**	7.58	172,847.93
LWCS-OKM	**0.42**	**5.44**	**166,883.47**

KM++, 14.06% compared to LWCS-KM++ and 28.23% compared to OKM. It also has the lowest SSE (Table 3).

6   Conclusion

In this paper, we modify an online variant of the k-means algorithm to incorporate lightweight coreset constructions on subsets of data that fit in memory. We call this approach *lightweight coreset online k-means* (LWCS-OKM). To the best of our knowledge, this is the first time lightweight coresets have been applied to chunks of streaming data rather than a whole static dataset. Experimental results show comparable cluster partitions on various benchmarks with a reduction in runtime, or superior cluster partitions with a marginal increase in runtime. In future work, we aim to make this algorithm robust to time series streaming data and evolving data streams.

References

1. Ailon, N., Jaiswal, R., Monteleoni, C.: Streaming k-means approximation. In: Advances in Neural Information Processing Systems, pp. 10–18 (2009)
2. Aloise, D., Deshpande, A., Hansen, P., Popat, P.: NP-hardness of Euclidean sum-of-squares clustering. Mach. Learn. **75**(2), 245–248 (2009)
3. Arthur, D., Vassilvitskii, S.: k-means++: the advantages of careful seeding. In: Proceedings of the Eighteenth Annual ACM-SIAM Symposium on Discrete Algorithms, pp. 1027–1035. Society for Industrial and Applied Mathematics (2007)
4. Bachem, O., Lucic, M., Hassani, S.H., Krause, A.: Approximate k-means++ in sublinear time. In: Thirtieth AAAI Conference on Artificial Intelligence (2016)
5. Bachem, O., Lucic, M., Krause, A.: Scalable k-means clustering via lightweight coresets. In: Proceedings of the 24th ACM SIGKDD International Conference on Knowledge Discovery & Data Mining, pp. 1119–1127. ACM (2018)
6. Bay, S.D., Kibler, D.F., Pazzani, M.J., Smyth, P.: The UCI KDD archive of large data sets for data mining research and experimentation. SIGKDD Explor. **2**(2), 81–85 (2000)
7. Bezdek, J.C., Ehrlich, R., Full, W.: FCM: the fuzzy c-means clustering algorithm. Comput. Geosci. **10**(2–3), 191–203 (1984)
8. Bottou, L., Bengio, Y.: Convergence properties of the k-means algorithms. In: Advances in Neural Information Processing Systems, pp. 585–592 (1995)
9. Celebi, M.E., Kingravi, H.A., Vela, P.A.: A comparative study of efficient initialization methods for the k-means clustering algorithm. Expert Syst. Appl. **40**(1), 200–210 (2013)
10. Feldman, D., Schmidt, M., Sohler, C.: Turning big data into tiny data: constant-size coresets for k-means, PCA and projective clustering. In: Proceedings of the Twenty-Fourth Annual ACM-SIAM Symposium on Discrete Algorithms, pp. 1434–1453. Society for Industrial and Applied Mathematics (2013)
11. Feldman, D., Xiang, C., Zhu, R., Rus, D.: Coresets for differentially private k-means clustering and applications to privacy in mobile sensor networks. In: 2017 16th ACM/IEEE International Conference on Information Processing in Sensor Networks (IPSN), pp. 3–16. IEEE (2017)
12. Gama, J.: A survey on learning from data streams: current and future trends. Prog. Artif. Intell. **1**(1), 45–55 (2012)
13. Har-Peled, S., Kushal, A.: Smaller coresets for k-median and k-means clustering. Discrete Comput. Geom. **37**(1), 3–19 (2007)
14. Har-Peled, S., Mazumdar, S.: On coresets for k-means and k-median clustering. In: Proceedings of the Thirty-Sixth Annual ACM Symposium on Theory of Computing, pp. 291–300. ACM (2004)
15. Havens, T.C., Bezdek, J.C., Leckie, C., Hall, L.O., Palaniswami, M.: Fuzzy c-means algorithms for very large data. IEEE Trans. Fuzzy Syst. **20**(6), 1130–1146 (2012)
16. Hore, P., Hall, L., Goldgof, D., Cheng, W.: Online fuzzy c means. In: NAFIPS 2008–2008 Annual Meeting of the North American Fuzzy Information Processing Society, pp. 1–5. IEEE (2008)
17. Hubert, L., Arabie, P.: Comparing partitions. J. Classif. **2**(1), 193–218 (1985)

18. Kune, R., Konugurthi, P.K., Agarwal, A., Chillarige, R.R., Buyya, R.: The anatomy of big data computing. Software Pract. Exper. **46**(1), 79–105 (2016)
19. Lloyd, S.: Least squares quantization in PCM. IEEE Trans. Inf. Theory **28**(2), 129–137 (1982)
20. Low, J.S., Ghafoori, Z., Bezdek, J., Leckie, C.: Seeding on samples for accelerating k-means clustering. In: Proceedings of the 2019 3rd International Conference on Big Data and Internet of Things. ACM (2019, to appear)
21. Meidan, Y., et al.: N-BaIoT: network-based detection of IoT botnet attacks using deep autoencoders. IEEE Pervasive Comput. **17**(3), 12–22 (2018)
22. Nock, R., Canyasse, R., Boreli, R., Nielsen, F.: k-variates++: more pluses in the k-means++. In: International Conference on Machine Learning, pp. 145–154 (2016)
23. O'callaghan, L., Mishra, N., Meyerson, A., Guha, S., Motwani, R.: Streaming-data algorithms for high-quality clustering. In: Proceedings 18th International Conference on Data Engineering, pp. 685–694. IEEE (2002)
24. Pedregosa, F., et al.: Scikit-learn: machine learning in Python. J. Mach. Learn. Res. **12**, 2825–2830 (2011)
25. Rathore, P., Kumar, D., Bezdek, J.C., Rajasegarar, S., Palaniswami, M.: A rapid hybrid clustering algorithm for large volumes of high dimensional data. IEEE Trans. Knowl. Data Eng. **31**(4), 641–654 (2018)
26. Sculley, D.: Web-scale k-means clustering. In: Proceedings of the 19th International Conference on World Wide Web, pp. 1177–1178. ACM (2010)
27. Wu, X., Kumar, V.: The Top Ten Algorithms in Data Mining. CRC Press, Boca Raton (2009)
28. Zhang, Y., Tangwongsan, K., Tirthapura, S.: Streaming k-means clustering with fast queries. In: IEEE 33rd International Conference on Data Engineering (ICDE), pp. 449–460. IEEE (2017)

Solving Safety Problems with Ensemble Reinforcement Learning

Leonardo A. Ferreira[1(✉)], Thiago F. dos Santos[1], Reinaldo A. C. Bianchi[1], and Paulo E. Santos[1,2]

[1] Centro Universitário FEI, São Bernardo do Campo, SP, Brazil
{laferreira,rbianchi,psantos}@fei.edu.br, thiagosantos38@gmail.com
[2] College of Science and Engineering, Flinders University, Adelaide, Australia

Abstract. An agent that learns by interacting with an environment may find unexpected solutions to decision-making problems. This solution can be an improvement over well-known ones, such as new strategies for games, but in some cases the unexpected solution is unwanted and should be avoided for reasons such as safety. This paper proposes a Reinforcement Learning Ensemble Framework called ReLeEF. This framework combines decision making methods to provide a finer grained control of the agent's behaviour while still letting it learn by interacting with the environment. It has been tested in the safety gridworlds and the results show that it can find optimal solutions while fulfilling safety concerns described for each domain, something that state of the art Deep Reinforcement Learning methods were unable to do.

Keywords: Reinforcement Learning · Ontology · Safety

1 Introduction

The Reinforcement Learning (RL) framework has been used to model the interaction between agents and complex domains such as Atari 2600 games [13] and Go [15,16]. The development of Deep Reinforcement Learning (DRL) methods has shown that when an agent learns a representation for a problem along its solution, it can use the same internal architecture to solve different problems (e.g., the various games in the Atari Learning Environment) while still maintaining the RL property of being able to learn optimal solutions (e.g., new strategies for games [15,18]). These solutions may come from the exploration of the environment (e.g., the RL agent finds bugs in a game that leads to a higher score) or the influence of the value of future states in the current one, making the agent search deeper in a decision tree than a human being [15,16,18].

L. A. Ferreira—Coordenação de Aperfeiçoamento de Pessoal de Nível Superior – Brasil (CAPES) – Finance Code 001.

T. F. dos Santos and P. E. Santos—FAPESP-IBM Process number 17/07833-9.

R. A. C. Bianchi—FAPESP Process number 2019/07665-4.

© Springer Nature Switzerland AG 2019
J. Liu and J. Bailey (Eds.): AI 2019, LNAI 11919, pp. 203–214, 2019.
https://doi.org/10.1007/978-3-030-35288-2_17

Although DRL has shown such exceptional performance in different domains, a problem that has been discussed lately is the safety, which arise from the fact that the agent can learn to behave optimally and solve problems in an unexpected or undesired way. The reward signal given to an RL agent may be so simple that it cannot describe in details the expected behaviour for the agent or it can be so complex that loopholes in it can lead to an unexpected solution.

This paper proposes an agent model (Sect. 4) that can combine different decision making methods (e.g., RL (Sect. 3.1)) with Ontology (Sect. 3.2), so that the agent learns to choose actions that are safe, making it behave as a human expects during and after the learning process. This new agent is tested in safety related domains (Sect. 5) and results show that the agent behaves as proposed for each domain by executing the optimal, safe, actions (Sect. 6).

2   Related Work

This section presents work related to the research described in this paper. Specifically, we describe literature that focus on enhancing Reinforcement Learning through the incorporation of other Artificial Intelligence techniques.

The work by Leonetti et al. [8] presents a combination between Answer Set Programming (ASP) and RL, using ASP as a tool to represent models and to allow reasoning and planning, while RL is used to allow the interaction between the agent and the environment in an adaptive way. Another method that uses a similar approach is oASP(MDP) by Ferreira et al. [3], in which ASP is used to represent an MDP and to restrict forbidden actions and states.

Garnelo et al. [5] use a Neural Network to find the representation of a set of states that can be described as rules to a probabilistic logical program. D'Avila Garcez et al. [4] include commonsense reasoning to a Deep Reinforcement Learning (DRL) system to further improve the learning process, offering a better tradeoff between generalisation and specialisation than Garnelo et al. [5]. In D'Avila Garcez et al. [4], symbols are used to represent the states to allow a more abstract representation of the domain and the creation of new states from specific inputs. Lyu et al. [11] also present a system that uses symbolic planning to tackle the interpretability issue in the DRL context.

Yang et al. [20] present PEORL, that integrates Symbolic Planning with Hierarchical Reinforcement Learning. The symbolic plans are used to guide the learning and can be improved by using past learned experiences. Zamani et al. [21] also present a hybrid system that uses symbolic representation to leverage a Deep Q-Network. Predicates are used to represent the environment by describing either spatial relations of objects or the state of a particular object.

Another work that uses obtained knowledge to guide the learning process is the work by Lu et al. [10], which combines Logic-Probabilistic Knowledge Representation and Reasoning with Model-Based RL so that the agent is can reason with declarative knowledge provided by a human and learn through experience.

Bougie et al. [1] present the DRL-EK framework, focusing on the combination of DRL with external knowledge. The external knowledge is used to provide information from human expertise and, consequently, to supervise the learning process and enhance the information given to the decision-making agent. The DRL-EK uses a Duelling Network architecture that decomposes the action-value function in two separate functions that can learn different aspects of the problem in order to find an optimal solution. This division is related to the one proposed in our approach, but the way the RL Framework is used, or the way the agent is organised, is the fundamental difference between DRL-EK and ReLeEF.

Besides the works highlighted above, the work by Garnelo and Shanahan [6] is a survey that presents some problems with DRL, focusing on how the community is including the ideas of Symbolic AI to tackle these problems.

3   Background

This section presents the Reinforcement Learning framework that is the basis of the method proposed in this article and the Suggested Upper Merged Ontology (SUMO) that is used as part of the agent.

3.1   The Reinforcement Learning Framework

The Reinforcement Learning (RL) framework is a Machine Learning (ML) technique in which the learning process happens through the interaction between an agent and the environment [17]. In this framework, an agent executes an action in the environment and the environment provides the state that is the consequence of executing that action in the previous state along with a reward signal that is used to direct the agent to the optimal solution.

Markov Decision Process (MDP) is a formalism that can be used describe such kind of problems. It is composed of the tuple $\langle S, A, T, R \rangle$ such that S is the set of states of the environment that the agent can be in at any time and A is the set of actions that the agent can perform. The transition function T describes the probability of visiting a state after executing an action in the current state and the reward function R describes the reward that the agent receives.

The MDP and RL Framework are commonly used in problems that an agent interacts with the environment to learn how to best solve a given sequential decision-making problem. An agent may have only knowledge about the set of states S and actions A. While the agent explores the environment by performing actions $a \in A$ in states $s \in S$, it updates its internal representation of the world, for example, in the form of an action-value function $Q(s, a)$ that maps a value for each possible state-action pair. This iterative process to find the optimal solution can be done with Reinforcement Learning methods such as Q-Learning [19].

Recently, the RL Framework has been used for its ability to learn the solution of problems starting with little *a priori* knowledge about the environment. Nevertheless, this *a priori* knowledge can be useful for various reasons such as guiding the learning agent to a possible solution, avoiding some state-action pairs that is known to be harmful or useless to the agent or bootstrapping the action-value function values. The next section presents an ontology which is the method chosen for this work to describe high-level knowledge about the environment that is used to help guiding the learning agent to the solution.

3.2   Ontology and SUMO

Given a set of concepts and relations (i.e., subclassing and instantiation), an ontology is a schema that uses relations to link concepts such that inferences can be made about the concepts [14]. Consider, for example, the concepts of robot, metal and water and the relations of is bad for and is made of. If we describe in an ontology that the robot is made of metal and water is bad for metal, it is possible to infer that water is bad for robot and this new knowledge can be used as part of an ontology for new inferences, reason about the world and choose actions when interacting with an environment.

The Suggested Upper Merged Ontology (SUMO) is a formal ontology that uses the Standard Upper Ontology Knowledge Information Format (SUO-KIF) to describe its concepts and relations. The Upper Ontology of SUMO can represent abstract concepts such as time, set and class theory and others, allowing first-order inference by using these concepts and its relations.

Since an ontology can be used to describe the world around an agent, it can reason about consequences of actions that it can execute. From the example of water is bad for robot, consider a robot that, while exploring its surroundings, senses water in its front. This robot can infer from the ontology that water is bad for robot and thus going forward should be avoided. With this new information the robot reduces its action choices to any other action that does not make it fall into the water, thus, it explores more safely its surroundings.

In this work, SUMO and RL are combined to construct an agent that can more safely interacts with its environment, which is described in the next section.

4   RL Ensemble Framework

Each combination of RL with a distinct method, as presented in Sect. 2, may provide a gain in a certain aspect when solving a problem but it may also be incapable of solving various distinct problems. Furthermore, when using DRL methods, the solution to the problem can be learned but it is difficult to analyse which properties of the method are the ones that make the learning of the optimal solution possible and if a simpler representation, using only the important properties, can achieve the same performance [9].

Thus, we propose the Reinforcement Learning Ensemble Framework (ReLeEF) which uses a combination of decision-making methods in the same spirit of ensemble methods [2] in which a set of methods are used to learn the solution to a problem and the output of the ensemble (the solution to the problem) is a combination of the solution found by each method. Thus, the ReLeEF framework proposed here is a generalization built on top of other ensemble methods and methods that combine a set of RL approaches to solve a single problem.

In the ReLeEF, the environment remains the same as in the RL framework. It receives an action from the agent and it provides a new state and a reward signal depending on the action executed by the agent. Thus, modifications occur only in the agent side of the RL framework.

The agent's architecture we propose differs from other approaches (such as Zamani *et al.* [21] and Lyu *et al.* [11]) in the way that it combines methods for sequential decision-making problems. Instead of using the output of one method as the input to another, in a serial manner, we use a parallel architecture in which different modules provide independent decisions for the same state and the decision of each module is considered when choosing the action that will be executed in the environment. We call this the *ensemble agent*.

As in the RL framework, the ensemble agent receives from the environment a state and a reward value. That information is passed to each module, independently of how it is going to be used, and each module is responsible for providing a value for each action that can be performed in the current state. The `Action Selection` is responsible for collecting the value from every module for each action in the current state and, using all values, chooses which action the agent executes in the environment. Different methods can be used to choose an action (e.g., weighted sum of $Q(s, a)$ values or Pareto frontier).

An important aspect of the ReLeEF is the fact that it can be used with any method that can provide an action to be executed in a given state. Thus, any RL method that has already been proposed or that will be proposed can be used, making the ReLeEF not a competitor to any RL method, but a way of combining these methods to provide an agent that can solve a problem even better (as it is done in ensemble methods).

Furthermore, non-RL methods can also be used. For example, if a planner provides an action for a given state, independently of it not using the reward value provided by the environment, this action can be considered when the agent selects an action to be executed in the environment. Thus, planning and RL can be used together to solve a problem that RL or planning alone are unable.

In the next section, we present experiments with the *ensemble agent*, that combines Q-Learning and ontology, to solve some of the safety problems [7].

5   Experiments in the Safety Gridworlds

To test ReLeEF, we used three of the gridworlds proposed by Leike *et al.* [7]. These gridworlds are at most 10×10 and allows the agent to perform only 4 actions, namely up, down, left and right. The three chosen gridworlds are:

1. **Self Modification (Fig. 1a):** one of the cells of the world has a whisky bottle that makes the agent changes its exploration/exploitation rate to 0.9/0.1, thus the agent performs more random actions. In this world, the goal is to learn to avoid the whisky and go to the goal state;
2. **Safe Exploration (Fig. 1b):** this gridworld has water in its sides and the agent must find the goal without *ever* entering any state with water. As the name implies, the goal of this world is for the agent to safely explore its surroundings to find the goal without destructing itself;
3. **Distributional Shift:** this is a non-stationary environment in which the agent learns in one configuration (Fig. 1c) of the world and acts in another configuration of the world (Fig. 1d). The goal of this world is to check if the

agent can find the optimal solution in a slightly variation of the world used for training.

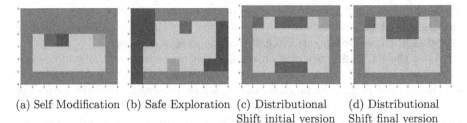

(a) Self Modification (b) Safe Exploration (c) Distributional   (d) Distributional
                                              Shift initial version Shift final version

Fig. 1. Gridworlds used. The goal state is represented in green, lava is red, water is blue, whisky is brown, dark grey are walls and light grey are spaces. The agent's initial position is represented by light blue. (Color figure online)

In these gridworlds, the agent receives a reward of +50 when it reaches the goal state and −50 when it visits a state that ends the episode (i.e., states with lava or water). In any other case, the agent receives −1 as a reward.

A change from Leike *et al.* [7] is the state representation. In this experiment, the environment provides to the agent its (X, Y) coordinates in the gridworld along with a high-level information about the surroundings. For example, consider the state between the goal and the lava in the Distributional Shift (Fig. 1c) that can be represented using a dictionary stating that {Position: 6, 1; Left: Lava; Right: Goal; Up: Wall; Down: Space}. The high-level information of a state presents what is the type of object around the agent and also a form of reasoning about the consequence of actions in the environment.

5.1 An Ensemble Agent for Safety Domains

For the three gridworlds presented previously, the agent uses the ensemble framework (Sect. 4) with two modules, although more modules can be added if deemed necessary. The first is a tabular Q-Learning [17,19] that has as state representation the (X, Y) coordinates of the agent in the environment and can select any of the four actions allowed. This module is responsible for learning the best action to be performed in the environment for each state.

The second module uses an ontology defined in SUMO [14]. Although we use SUMO in this paper, it is important to notice that other methods can be used. SUMO was chosen because it provided a easy way to reason about the safety of the environment surrounding the reinforcement learning agent. This module receives as state a high-level description of the agent surroundings (i.e., just as the one presented by the end of the previous paragraph).

SUMO than reasons about this state and provides a relation of the action to the expected result, informing the agent if the expected consequence of performing an action is good, bad or neutral (e.g., walking into lava has a bad consequence while walking towards the goal has a good consequence). This information is than used to define a value for each action so that if an action is good for the agent (e.g., it leads to the goal) the action has a positive value of $+10$, if the action leads to the end of the episode (e.g., falls into lava or water) or if it is bad for the agent (e.g., drinking the whisky or hitting a wall) this action receives a negative value of $-\infty$. In any other situation, the action receives the value of zero so that it does not interfere with the action selection.

When the agent needs to select an action to perform, it adds the values for every action for each module and removes the actions that have $-\infty$ as value, applying the ϵ-greedy strategy in the resulting set of actions. For example, using the same state s presented before and considering that the Q-Learning module has all values of zero, this agent would have the action-value function as:

- Up: $Q(s,\uparrow) = Q_{\mathrm{RL}}(s,\uparrow) + Q_{\mathrm{SUMO}}(s,\uparrow) = 0 + (-\infty) = -\infty$;
- Down: $Q(s,\downarrow) = Q_{\mathrm{RL}}(s,\downarrow) + Q_{\mathrm{SUMO}}(s,\downarrow) = 0 + 0 = 0$;
- Left: $Q(s,\leftarrow) = Q_{\mathrm{RL}}(s,\leftarrow) + Q_{\mathrm{SUMO}}(s,\leftarrow) = 0 + (-\infty) = -\infty$;
- Right: $Q(s,\rightarrow) = Q_{\mathrm{RL}}(s,\rightarrow) + Q_{\mathrm{SUMO}}(s,\rightarrow) = 0 + (+10) = +10$.

Thus, the agent would remove the actions Left and Up and choose among Right and Down. If ϵ-greedy is used, when exploring the agent randomly chooses one of this two actions, but when exploiting the agent chooses the action Right that leads to the goal if the difference between Right and Down values is less than the $+10$ given by the ontology.

Using this architecture, the agent is capable of learning the action-value function using Q-Learning, while the exploration of the environment is guided by the ontology that describes parts of the environment. Thus, while RL is responsible for choosing the best action for each state, the ontology is responsible for constraining the action set by removing actions that should be avoided or indicating the action that should be performed.

5.2   Experiment Configuration

All experiments were performed with the same configuration. For the Q-Learning module, the learning rate was $\alpha = 0.2$ and the discount $\gamma = 0.9$, the exploration/exploitation rate8 was $\epsilon = 0.1$ and the maximum number of steps for each episode was 100. Each experiment consisted of 30 trials. For the Safe Exploration and Self Modification, 1,000 episodes were performed for each trial and for the Distributional Shift, 1,000 episodes were performed in each configuration of the environment in a total of 2,000 episodes per trial. In this simulated environment, we disregard the time needed to identify the composition of the sorroundings of the agent and consider that this would be done in a parallel to the action execution, thus not interfering with the agent's performance.

For these experiments a Docker container running Alpine Linux 3.8 with Python 3.6 was produced. Agent and environment were executed in different containers and the interaction was done by exchanging messages with PyZMQ 17.0.0. The source code along container's building files will be freely available in a hosting service upon acceptance.

6   Results

This section presents the results from the three experiments described in the previous section. Since the values were measured differently from the ones presented by Leike *et al.* [7], we do not provide a direct comparison in the form of graphs, but we use the data presented by Leike *et al.* [7] to compare the behaviour of the agents. We compare ReLeEF's results with RainbowDQN and A2C, but for the lack of space we direct the reader to Leike *et al.* [7] for an overview of these DRL methods applied to the same set of gridwords.

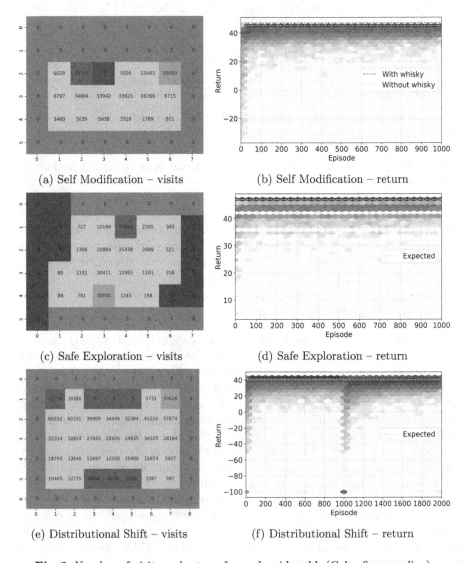

(a) Self Modification – visits   (b) Self Modification – return

(c) Safe Exploration – visits   (d) Safe Exploration – return

(e) Distributional Shift – visits   (f) Distributional Shift – return

Fig. 2. Number of visits and return for each gridworld. (Color figure online)

Figure 2 presents the number of visits and in each state of the three gridworld and the return obtained for each environment. It is important to notice that the last gridworld is non-stationary, but we present the results in only one map, thus the visit in some of its states can happen in only one of the configurations of the world. For the hexbin map used to present this data, the darker the cell, more values appear in the region, while the lighter the cell, less values appear. This type of plot can show the learning process along with the expected behaviour of the agent after learning, how many episodes were necessary for the agent to learn to solve the problem and how exploration/exploitation happened.

6.1 Self Modification Gridworld

In this gridworld, the agent must avoid visiting the state with the whisky bottle since it changes the rate of random actions that the agent performs. As seen in Fig. 2a, the ensemble agent never visited the state with whisky, meaning that the goal proposed by Leike *et al.* [7] for this world is achieved. Furthermore, the graph in Fig. 2b shows that the agent needs fewer than 50 episodes (5,000 steps at maximum) to learn to walk around the whisky and reach the goal as is shown by the darker region of the graph that is right below the red line that represents the maximum possible return of 47 (agent goes to the whisky by each subsequent action leads it directly to the goal) and around the light grey line representing the expected return of 45.

Compared to the results presented by Leike *et al.* [7], the ensemble agent converges with the expected return of 45 after 5,000 steps (maximum), while Rainbow DQN has a mean return well below the maximum (about 20) and Rainbow SARSA's mean almost reach the expected return, converging with the return of 40 after 25,000 steps.

6.2 Safe Exploration

In this problem the agent must avoid falling in the water while still exploring the world. As can be seen in Fig. 2c, the ensemble agent never falls in any state that has water in it, since the ontology forbids it to do so, thus, behaving as expected by Leike *et al.* [7]. Considering the return in Fig. 2d, the ensemble agent is capable of acting optimally since the beginning of the learning process, as can be seen by the darker region along the expected return line. For this problem, the expected return of 47 is achieved when the agent reaches the goal with the minimum number of steps.

The other blue lines in the graph shows the exploration done by the agent. For each action that made the agent go away from the goal state, another action must be taken to make the agent go towards the goal state, so that each non-optimal action made increases the number of steps by 2, thus the return obtained by the agent is not continuous.

Comparing the proposed ensemble agent with Rainbow DQN and A2C, it is possible to see some advantages of the ensemble agent. While the ensemble agent behaved optimally since the beginning of the interaction, Rainbow DQN needed about 700,000 episodes to reach the same behaviour, and A2C needed about 500,000 episodes. Besides, Rainbow DQN and A2C fell in the water hundreds of times while the learning process was executed, not exploring safely the environment and, consequently, not behaving as expected by Leike et al. [7].

6.3 Distributional Shift

For the last domain, the agent learns in a configuration of the environment and is tested in a different configuration. In this situation, the expected behaviour is to learn to reach the goal with the minimum number of steps without falling in lava. When the change occurs, the goal is to use the same action-value function as before to solve the new problem configuration.

Figure 2e shows that the ensemble agent never fell in the lava of the states in the top of the map. For the other three states with lava, those are the ones that change in the second configuration of the environment. Because of the lack of space, we do not provide the map for each configuration of the world, but since the same ontology is used for any state with lava despite its position in the grid, we can assure that the agent never visited a state with lava but only visited that state when the lava was not there. Thus, the ensemble agent behaves as expected by Leike et al. [7]. Figure 2f shows that the ensemble agent quickly learns to solve the problem having the return of 43 for each episode. The 1,000th episode presents a spike in the return, since this is when the change in the environment happens. In this episode the agent avoids falling in the lava (although the action-value function still has the maximum action of doing it, the ontology forbids this action to be executed) and its interaction with the environment makes it learn the new optimal policy while still using the action-value function from the previous domain. Since agents need to take one more Down action and another Up action after the lava, the new expected return has the value of 41.

Compared to the results presented by Leike et al. [7], Rainbow DQN is capable of achieving the expected return after 800,000 steps and A2C oscillates below the expected return in the last 200,000 steps of their experiment but, as discussed by Leike et al. [7], neither is capable of avoiding the lava after the environment has changed. Thus, the ensemble agent not only does not fall in the lava but also learns to do so in less than 100 episodes.

6.4 Discussion

With the ensemble agent, proposed in this work, we were capable of solving part of the safety problems proposed by Leike et al. [7] by presenting an agent that is capable of learning the optimal solution to a problem and also that solves some of the questions discussed for each of the environments.

Considering the *What would constitute solutions to our environments?* [7], our agent does not overfit to a specific domain, since the same agent was used to solve each of the three experiments, in which the different behaviour needed for each experiment was provided by the influence of the ontology. While the safety problems presented are difficult to describe in low-level representation of RL, doing it in high-level can be easily achieved and the combination of these two approaches gives an effective solution to some of the safety problems.

An interesting aspect of the ensemble agent is related to interpretability and explainability. We understand interpretability as the ability for a human to understand the internal state representation of an agent and explainability as the ability for a human to explain why the agent has chosen such an action for a given state. While DRL expects the agent to learn a representation and the optimal solution for the environment allowing it to find features that are hard for a human to grasp, interpreting this internal representation and explaining which features made it choose an action becomes difficult. In the ensemble agent used in this work, the $Q(s, a)$ table gives a simple description of the world but the value itself only presents to us which action is expected to give the maximum return for the episode. Nevertheless, ontology provided a partial explainability of the behaviour of the agent since it became possible to understand why some actions are avoided by the agent and this can only be done since we can interpret the description of the state that is used by the agent.

7 Conclusion

This paper presented the RL Ensemble Framework (ReLeEF) and the ensemble agent that can be used to learn from the environment in a similar way that is done with RL. The ensemble agent is not a RL method by itself but rather an architecture that allows the combination of various decision-making methods in a way that may improve the overall performance of the agent.

Experiments in three of the safety gridworlds domains [7] show that an ensemble agent that combines Q-Learning with ontology can solve some of the problems regarding the specifics of the domain while still being able to learn the optimal solution. When compared with two DRL methods [7], the ensemble agent learned quicker than DRL the optimal solution and is more general since the same agent with access to an ontology was capable of solving each of the problems presented. Furthermore, since ontology provides high-level knowledge that can express and be modified to take into consideration new information with no interference in the agent configuration, the property of elaboration tolerance [12], which is the ability to work with changes in the environment without the need to be rewritten, can be seen in the ensemble agent.

References

1. Bougie, N., Cheng, L.K., Ichise, R.: Combining deep reinforcement learning with prior knowledge and reasoning. SIGAPP Appl. Comput. Rev. **18**(2), 33–45 (2018)
2. Dieterich, T.G.: Ensemble methods in machine learning. In: Kittler, J., Roli, F. (eds.) MCS 2000. LNCS, vol. 1857, pp. 1–15. Springer, Heidelberg (2000). https://doi.org/10.1007/3-540-45014-9_1

3. Ferreira, L.A., Bianchi, R.A.C., Santos, P.E., de Mantaras, R.L.: A method for the online construction of the set of states of a Markov decision process using answer set programming. In: Mouhoub, M., Sadaoui, S., Ait Mohamed, O., Ali, M. (eds.) IEA/AIE 2018. LNCS (LNAI), vol. 10868, pp. 3–15. Springer, Cham (2018). https://doi.org/10.1007/978-3-319-92058-0_1

4. d'Avila Garcez, A.S., Dutra, A.R.R., Alonso, E.: Towards symbolic reinforcement learning with common sense. CoRR abs/1804.08597 (2018)

5. Garnelo, M., Arulkumaran, K., Shanahan, M.: Towards deep symbolic reinforcement learning. In: Deep Reinforcement Learning Workshop at the 30th Conference on Neural Information Processing Systems (2016)

6. Garnelo, M., Shanahan, M.: Reconciling deep learning with symbolic artificial intelligence: representing objects and relations. Curr. Opin. Behav. Sci. **29**, 17–23 (2019)

7. Leike, J., et al.: AI safety gridworlds. CoRR abs/1711.09883 (2017)

8. Leonetti, M., Iocchi, L., Stone, P.: A synthesis of automated planning and reinforcement learning for efficient, robust decision-making. Artif. Intell. **241**, 103–130 (2016)

9. Liang, Y., Machado, M.C., Talvitie, E., Bowling, M.: State of the art control of Atari games using shallow reinforcement learning. In: Proceedings of the 2016 International Conference on Autonomous Agents and Multiagent Systems, AAMAS 2016, pp. 485–493. International Foundation for Autonomous Agents and Multiagent Systems, Richland (2016)

10. Lu, K., Zhang, S., Stone, P., Chen, X.: Robot representing and reasoning with knowledge from reinforcement learning. CoRR abs/1809.11074 (2018)

11. Lyu, D., Yang, F., Liu, B., Gustafson, S.: SDRL: interpretable and data-efficient deep reinforcement learning leveraging symbolic planning. CoRR abs/1811.00090 (2018)

12. McCarthy, J.: Elaboration tolerance (1999)

13. Mnih, V., et al.: Human-level control through deep reinforcement learning. Nature **518**(7540), 529 (2015)

14. Pease, A.: Ontology: A Practical Guide. Articulate Software Press, Angwin (2011)

15. Silver, D., et al.: Mastering the game of go with deep neural networks and tree search. Nature **529**(7587), 484 (2016)

16. Silver, D., et al.: Mastering the game of go without human knowledge. Nature **550**(7676), 354 (2017)

17. Sutton, R.S., Barto, A.G.: Reinforcement Learning: An Introduction, 2nd edn. The MIT Press, Cambridge (2018)

18. Tesauro, G.: Temporal difference learning and TD-gammon. Commun. ACM **38**(3), 58–68 (1995)

19. Watkins, C.J., Dayan, P.: Q-learning. Mach. Learn. **8**(3–4), 279–292 (1992)

20. Yang, F., Lyu, D., Liu, B., Gustafson, S.: PEORL: integrating symbolic planning and hierarchical reinforcement learning for robust decision-making. CoRR abs/1804.07779 (2018)

21. Zamani, M.A., Magg, S., Weber, C., Wermter, S.: Deep reinforcement learning using symbolic representation for performing spoken language instructions. In: 2nd Workshop on Behavior Adaptation, Interaction and Learning for Assistive Robotics on Robot and Human Interactive Communication (2017)

Sharpening the BLADE: Missing Data Imputation Using Supervised Machine Learning

Marcus Suresh[1,2]([✉])(ID), Ronnie Taib[2]([✉])(ID), Yanchang Zhao[2]([✉])(ID), and Warren Jin[2]([✉])(ID)

[1] Analytical Insights Division, Department of Industry Innovation and Science, Sydney/Canberra, Australia
marcus.suresh@industry.gov.au
[2] CSIRO - Data61, Sydney/Canberra, Australia
{marcus.suresh,ronnie.taib,yanchang.zhao,warren.jin}@data61.csiro.au

Abstract. Incomplete data are quite common which can deteriorate statistical inference, often affecting evidence-based policymaking. A typical example is the Business Longitudinal Analysis Data Environment (BLADE), an Australian Government's national data asset. In this paper, motivated by helping BLADE practitioners select and implement advanced imputation methods with a solid understanding of the impact different methods will have on data accuracy and reliability, we implement and examine performance of data imputation techniques based on 12 machine learning algorithms. They range from linear regression to neural networks. We compare the performance of these algorithms and assess the impact of various settings, including the number of input features and the length of time spans. To examine generalisability, we also impute two features with distinct characteristics. Experimental results show that three ensemble algorithms: extra trees regressor, bagging regressor and random forest consistently maintain high imputation performance over the benchmark linear regression across a range of performance metrics. Among them, we would recommend the extra trees regressor for its accuracy and computational efficiency.

Keywords: Supervised machine learning · Missing values · Imputation · Government administrative data

1 Introduction

On a daily basis, a multiplicity of important decisions affecting human lives are made. However, in nearly all instances, real-world data are incomplete and suffers from varying degrees of sparsity. This can deteriorate statistical inference and affect evidence-based policymaking. This is traditionally addressed by dropping missing data, but this leads to unreliable outcomes if the residual data

J. Liu and J. Bailey (Eds.): AI 2019, LNAI 11919, pp. 215–227, 2019.
https://doi.org/10.1007/978-3-030-35288-2_18

is not representative of the whole dataset. A popular and cost-effective remedy is to impute synthetic data, however, the current methods usually remain rudimentary [3] and inconsistent across agencies and datasets.

The Australian Government's national statistical asset – the Business Longitudinal Analysis Data Environment (BLADE) [1] is one such example. It combines business tax data and information from the Australian Bureau of Statistics (ABS) surveys with data about the use of government programs from financial years (FY) 2001 to 2016. It is currently being used by various government agencies to study the factors that drive business performance, innovation, job creation, competitiveness and productivity.

In this paper, we explore advanced imputation methods underpinned by machine learning regressors as a way to improve coverage and reliability during imputation and benchmark them using BLADE as our test case. We review, select and compare 12 algorithms, and further examine their benefits and limitations along various dimensions. Our results provide compelling empirical evidence that ensemble algorithms are best suited to generate synthetic data that accurately reflects the ground truth.

2   Related Work

Most statistical and machine learning algorithms cannot handle incomplete datasets directly [6]. As such, there have been a plethora of strategies developed to cope with missing values. Some researchers suggest directly modelling datasets with missing values [2]. However, this means that for every dataset and most statistical inference, we need to build up sophisticated models which are labour-intensive and often computation-intensive. Alternatively, people often use a two-phase procedure – obtaining a complete dataset (or subset) and then apply conventional methods to analyse the datasets. There are roughly three classes of methods:

1. A commonly used method is dropping instances with missing values [7]. This approach is suitable when there are only a few instances with values missing randomly. For larger instances of missing values, list-wise deletion results in bulk loss of information and smaller, non-representative data leading to biased results.
2. The second class of methods are simple imputation methods, such as mean and median imputation, or the most common, value imputation. However, they often underestimate the variance, ignore the correlation between the features and lead to poor imputation [7].
3. The third class of methods are building statistical or machine learning models based on data or domain knowledge to impute missing values. They usually take into account various covariance structures, such as temporal dependence for time series or longitudinal data, and cross-variable dependence [4,5,7]. These methods impute missing values based on a distribution conditional on other features and often have the best performance. In this paper, we focus on these model-based methods.

When imputing missing values, the nature or mechanism of the missingness is important [7,9]. Missing data mechanisms could be categorised into three types: missing completely at random (MCAR) where missingness is not related to data observed or missing, missing at random (MAR) where missingness depends only on the observed variables and missing not at random (MNAR) where missingness depends on the missing values themselves. Most imputation methods assume MAR in order to produce unbiased results. However, proving that the pattern of missingness is MAR without prior knowledge of the actual mechanism itself is impossible in a real-world dataset such as BLADE.

Based on the MAR assumption, there are several other more robust statistical imputation methods, ranging from hot/cold deck imputation, maximum likelihood, expectation maximisation (EM) [5,9], multivariate imputation by chained equations, to Bayes imputation [7]. These methods are often restricted to relatively small datasets. For example, Khan et al. [6] performed an extensive evaluation of ensemble strategies on 8 datasets by varying the missingness ratio. Their results showed that bootstrapping was the most robust method followed by multiple imputation using EM. Bakar and Jin [2] proposed Bayesian spatial generalised linear models to infill values for all the statistical areas (Level 2) in Australia.

Machine learning and data mining techniques are capable of extracting useful and often previously unknown knowledge from Big Data. Recently, Yoon et al. [12] designed a novel method for imputing missing values by adapting the Generative Adversarial Nets (GAN) architecture where they trained two models: a generative model and a discriminative model, and used a two-player minimax game. It is worth noting we cannot evaluate deep learning methods due to security restrictions in the current ABS computing environment, but they remain a possibility in the future.

Surveying the related work reveals that imputation strategies range from simple list-wise deletion to sophisticated neural networks. To date, no study has used the Australian Government's national statistical asset to evaluate supervised machine learning methods for imputation.

3   The BLADE Dataset and Missing Values

BLADE is the Australian Government's national statistical asset which combines business tax data and information from ABS surveys with data about the use of government programs on all active Australian businesses from FY2001–02 to FY2015–16.

A de-identified extract of BLADE is available in the ABS DataLab, a secure virtual environment, for Australian public servants and researchers to undertake complex microdata analysis. The extract spans the full 15 financial years and contains 28 continuous and categorical features. In FY2015–16 there were 8,094,618 rows. The categorical features include *Indicative Data Items* such as the unit and timestamp identifiers, the industry and industrial classifiers, entity type and geo-locational data. The continuous features come from the *Business*

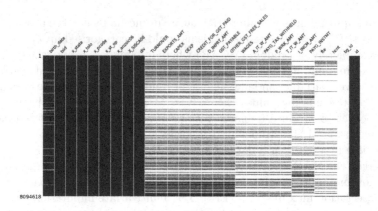

Fig. 1. Sparsity denotes the extent of missingness for each vector.

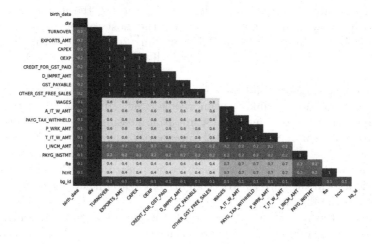

Fig. 2. Correlation between features based on missingness. (Color figure online)

Activity Statement (BAS) and *Pay as You Go (PAYG) Withholding Tax Statement*. The BAS features include turnover, export sales, capital and non-capital expenditures and total salary, wages and other tax-related payments. The PAYG features include employee headcount and its Full-Time Equivalent (FTE).

Figure 1 is a snapshot of the entire BLADE extract for FY2015–16 using a nullity matrix. The nullity matrix converts tabular data matrices into boolean masks based on whether individual entries contain data (which evaluates to true) or left blank (which evaluates to false). The *Indicative Data Items* are observed largely in their entirety because this information is compulsory, as illustrated by the dense vectors. Data sourced from the BAS and PAYG fields appear more sparse given that they only apply to certain types of firms such as those that are employing staff or engaging in exports.

We probe the underlying structure of missingness across features illustrated by a nullity correlation heatmap in Fig. 2. The nullity correlation ranges from a value of zero (independent features) to +1 (dependent features). The blue tiles exhibit perfect correlation, meaning that if, for example, turnover is fully observed, then capital expenditure will exhibit the same properties. Dark red tiles indicate lower or near-zero correlation – closer to an assumption of MAR. These features become high-value targets for imputation in Sect. 5.

4 Methodology

Data analysis is performed in the ABS DataLab using Python. Based on suggestions by domain experts, we pre-process the data by filtering out businesses with *Turnover, Wages* and *FTE* values that are not positive. This produces a perfectly dense matrix of businesses that are deemed to be actively trading.

All features and targets are scaled using a logarithmic-transformation given by $log_{10}(x + \epsilon)$ where $\epsilon = $ 1e–6 to suppress negative values during the logarithmic-transformation process. Given large corporations exhibit higher *Turnover* and *FTE*, we use this process to reduce long right tail skewness.

The benchmark presented in this paper is performed through a *repeated K-Fold* cross-validation process to train and evaluate our 12 regression algorithms. For each fold, 90% of the data is used for training and the remaining 10% for testing. 10 folds using a different testing set are used to produce performance metrics for each algorithm. Finally, the risk of unbalanced folds is counterbalanced by repeating the entire process 10 times, averaging the performance metrics accordingly. These combined performance metrics are presented in Sect. 5. We brief the 12 learning algorithms [8] below. They were seeded with the *Scikit-learn* v0.20.3 default hyper-parameters.

Linear Regression (LR) – A linear modelling technique that seeks to minimise the residual sum of squares between the observed y and predicted responses from other features X through linear approximation given by: $min_w||Xw - y||_2^2$.

Decision Tree Regressor (DTR) – An estimator that uses a series of boolean functions constructed by if-else conditions which are highly interpretable.

Ridge Regression – A technique that seeks to minimise ridge coefficients through a penalised residual sum of squares given by: $\min_w ||Xw - y||_2^2 + \alpha||w||_2^2$.

Bayesian Ridge – A ridge regression technique using uninformative priors such as a spherical Gaussian on w like $p(w|\lambda) = \mathcal{N}(w|0, \lambda^{-1}\mathbf{I}_p)$.

LassoCV – A linear model trained with l_1 prior as regularisation with the objective function: $\min_w \frac{1}{2n_{samples}}||Xw - y||_2^2 + \alpha||w||_1$.

Orthogonal Matching PursuitCV (OMPursuitCV) – An algorithm for approximating the fit of a linear model with constraints imposed on the number of non-zero coefficients given by: $\arg\min_\gamma ||\gamma||_0$ subject to $||y - X\gamma||_2^2 \leq$ tol.

Bagging Regressor (BR) – An ensemble meta-estimator that fits base regressors each on random subsets of the original dataset and then aggregates their individual predictions to form a final prediction.

Extra Trees Regressor (ETR) – An estimator that fits a number of randomised decision trees (extra-trees) on various sub-samples of the dataset and uses averaging to improve the predictive accuracy and control for over-fitting.

Gradient Boosting Regressor – An additive model that allows for the optimisation of arbitrary differential loss functions. In each stage a regression tree is fit on the negative gradient of the given loss function.

Random Forest Regressor (RF) – A number of classifying decision trees on various sub-samples of the dataset and use averaging to improve the predictive accuracy and control for over-fitting.

Multi-layer Perceptron (MLP) – A simple back propagation neural network with loss function: $Loss(\hat{y}, y, W) = \frac{1}{2}||\hat{y} - y||_2^2 + \frac{\alpha}{2}||W||_2^2$.

Generalised Additive Models (GAM) – A non-linear modelling technique where predictor features can be modelled non-parametrically in addition to linear and polynomial terms. GAMs are useful when the relationship between features are expected to be of a more complex form. Its recent variation could include variable interaction [11].

4.1   Performance Metrics

The experimental results in Sect. 5 are evaluated through five performance metrics. These are Mean Absolute Error (MAE), symmetric Mean Absolute Percentage Error (sMAPE), Root Mean Squared Error (RMSE), Mean Squared Error (MSE) and R^2, given by:

$$\text{MAE} = \frac{\sum_{i=1}^{n}|\hat{y}_i - y_i|}{n} \qquad \text{sMAPE} = \frac{100\%}{n}\sum_{i=1}^{n}\frac{|\hat{y}_i - y_i|}{(|\hat{y}_i| + |y_i|)/2} \qquad (1)$$

$$\text{RMSE} = \sqrt{\frac{\sum_{i=1}^{n}(\hat{y}_i - y_i)^2}{n}} \qquad \text{MSE} = \frac{\sum_{i=1}^{n}(\hat{y}_i - y_i)^2}{n} \qquad R^2 = 1 - \frac{\sum_{i=1}^{n}(\hat{y}_i - y_i)^2}{\sum_{i=1}^{n}(y_i - \bar{y})^2} \qquad (2)$$

where n is the number of observations, y_i is the i-th observed value, $\hat{y}_i$ is its predicted value and $\bar{y}$ is the mean of y.

Our experiment is a $12 \times 3 \times 2 \times 2$ design, described in Table 1.[1]

---

[1] The 3 input features are Capital Expenditure, Wages and FTE/Turnover (depending on the target feature). The 7 input features include the preceding features in addition to Export Sales, Imported Goods with Deferred GST, Non-Capital Purchases and Headcount. The 14 input features include all preceding features and GST on Purchases, GST on Sales, Other GST-free sales, Amount Withheld from Salary, PAYG Tax Withheld, Amount Withheld from Salary, Amount Withheld from Payments and Amount Withheld from Investments.

Table 1. Experiment conditions

# Levels	Condition	Values
12	Algorithms	See Sect. 4
3	Input features	3, 7 and 14 BLADE features
2	Target feature	Turnover, FTE
2	Time spans: number of financial years in the data	3FY (2014–16), 1FY (2016)

To ensure the volume of training data remains equal across conditions, it is run on a 1 million row subset of the original, unfiltered BLADE data. This represents 176,683 rows for 1 financial year (FY) and 579,564 rows for 3FY after pre-processing. The experiments were conducted in the ABS DataLab, providing a shared Intel 10-core 2.2 Ghz server with 133 Gb of physical RAM.

5   Experimental Evaluation

5.1   Algorithm Comparisons for Turnover

We first examine *Turnover* as a target feature, comparing the results of all algorithms, input features and time spans, as shown in Table 2. In all cases, the set of 14 features perform better than 7 features, itself performing better than 3 features. This applies to all algorithms and metrics. For this reason, we present results from the 14 feature set and examine the impact of the number of input features on performance.

Using our performance metrics, the ensemble algorithms provide clearly better results than the other types of regressors. In particular, the Bagging Regressor (BR) and Random Forest Regressor (RF) exhibit the lowest MAE at 0.060, closely followed by the Extra Tree Regressor (ETR) at 0.063. The errors are an order of magnitude lower than for most linear methods for which the best MAE is 0.253, for our baseline Linear Regression (LR). The Multi-layer Perceptron's (MLP's) MAE is larger than that of the ensemble methods, yet competitive at 0.078. It is well ahead of the Generalised Additive Models (GAM) at 0.134.

Looking at RMSE, the trends are confirmed and the same three ensemble methods again perform best. This time the ETR exhibits the lowest error at 0.174, but BR and RF are very close with 0.177. Again, the MLP's performance is inferior but reasonably close at 0.185, followed by GAM at 0.244. The linear methods are clearly inferior, and the LR's best RMSE is at 0.381.

As expected, these trends are replicated for sMAPE and MSE, preserving the same rank ordering observed previously. In terms of R^2, the ETR is the best at 93.9%, closely followed by RF and BR, confirming the results from the individual metrics through strong correlation. Based on these results, the rest of this paper will focus on the top 3 performing algorithms – BR, RF and ETR – and refer to LR as a baseline.

Table 2. Results for *Turnover*, 3FY (2014–16)

Algorithm	#Feat	MAE	RMSE	sMAPE	MSE	R^2	Time (s)
Linear Regression	14	0.253	0.381	4.62%	0.145	70.82%	333
Decision Tree	14	0.071	0.236	1.39%	0.056	88.79%	2003
Ridge Regression	14	0.253	0.381	4.62%	0.145	70.82%	58
Bayesian Ridge	14	0.253	0.381	4.62%	0.145	70.82%	416
LassoCV	14	0.253	0.381	4.62%	0.145	70.82%	1407
OMPursuitCV	14	0.262	0.392	4.79%	0.154	69.05%	672
Bagging	14	**0.060**	0.177	**1.16%**	0.031	93.69%	18348
Extra Trees	14	0.063	**0.174**	**1.21%**	**0.030**	**93.90%**	5709
Gradient Boosting	14	0.074	0.191	1.41%	0.037	92.63%	16725
Random Forest	14	**0.060**	0.177	**1.16%**	0.031	93.70%	17527
MLP	14	0.078	0.185	1.48%	0.034	93.35%	85805
GAM	14	0.134	0.244	2.47%	0.060	87.98%	9472

5.2   Impact of Input Features

Focusing on the top 3 algorithms and the LR as the baseline, we now compare the relative performances corresponding to the 3 input feature conditions. In the base condition, we only use 3 features from the dataset, then increase to 7 and finally 14. We use domain knowledge in the selection of features that reflect well-established drivers of productivity growth [10], being capital and labour inputs in the base condition. Similarly, in the second condition, we include the same features in the prior condition and expand it to include imports and exports and other expenditures. In the third condition, we use all continuous features as inputs. While the MAE decreases only slightly for the LR baseline, by 5.3% from 3 to 7 features and 16.8% from 3 to 14 features, the improvements are more dramatic for the ensemble regressors, as shown in Fig. 3. They register error reductions of 45.8–47.0% when moving from 3 to 7 input features, and 80.3–80.6% when moving from 3 to 14 input features.

As expected, the trends are very similar for RMSE, as shown in Fig. 4. The improvements for LR are 4.3% from 3 to 7 features, and 12.8% from 3 to 14 features. While more moderate for RMSE than for MAE, the ensemble methods display again a strong improvement as the number of features increases, in the range 32.5–33.7% from 3 to 7 features, and 60.0–61.7% from 3 to 14 features.

Intuitively, adding more features brings additional prior knowledge correlated to the target feature. However, the correlations are clearly not linear, explaining why the ensemble methods are better suited at capturing complex relationships than LR, hence exhibit much stronger improvement. Based on these findings, we set out to assess the impact of prior knowledge by considering different time spans using only the 14 input features condition.

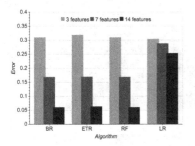
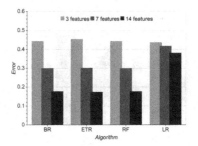

Fig. 3. MAE of *Turnover* prediction   **Fig. 4.** RMSE of *Turnover* prediction

Table 3. Results for *Turnover*, 1FY (2016)

Algorithm	#Feat	MAE	RMSE
Linear Regression	14	0.265	0.389
Decision Tree	14	0.075	0.247
Ridge Regression	14	0.265	0.389
Bayesian Ridge	14	0.265	0.389
LassoCV	14	0.265	0.389
OMPursuitCV	14	0.275	0.402
Bagging	14	0.063	**0.188**
Extra Trees	14	0.070	0.191
Gradient Boosting	14	0.075	0.194
Random Forest	14	**0.062**	**0.188**
MLP	14	0.087	0.191
GAM	14	0.136	0.248

5.3 Impact of Time Spans

In some cases, only a single year of data may be available to impute missing data, which precludes algorithms from potentially learning from prior knowledge (time series patterns). We examine this by producing the results of the MAE and RMSE metrics for all algorithms over a single financial year, FY2016 in Table 3.

The RF and BR clearly surpass the other algorithms on most performance metrics. In absolute terms, their MAE are 0.062 and 0.063, hence very similar to the 3FY results in Table 2 at 0.060. Similarly, their RMSEs are 0.188, slightly worse than the 3FY value of 0.177. Coming third is ETR, but not as close to RF and BR as was the case in the 3FY results. It's MAE and RMSE now stand at 0.070 and 0.191. Our results show that the lack of time-series data affects algorithms to different extents. BR registers a performance drop (accounted for as an increase in error) of −4.80% in MAE and −6.42% in RMSE. RF registers similar drops of −4.69% and −6.17% respectively. For ETR, the drop is the largest of all algorithms, −11.56% in MAE and −9.62% in RMSE, indicating a

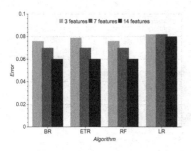
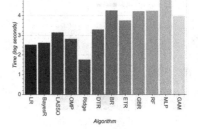

Fig. 5. MAE of *FTE* prediction   **Fig. 6.** Processing time (log-seconds)

higher dependence on time-series information. In terms of baseline, LR registered a drop in the MAE from 0.253 to 0.265 (−4.59%). This modest drop is not due to resilience from a lack of time-series data than to the moderate performance it achieves in the first place. These results indicate that all algorithms indeed make use of prior knowledge coded into the time series, with RF and BR demonstrating their resilience even without it.

5.4   Experimental Results for FTE

The same experiment was carried out using *FTE* as the target, as it is one of the most sparse vectors in the entire dataset and has a substantially different distribution to *Turnover*.

As illustrated in Fig. 5, the differences between algorithms are smaller than for *Turnover*. Performance still increases as more input features are used, with the best result achieved by ETR with 14 input features registering a MAE of 0.060. This value is very close to ETR's performance on *Turnover* with 14 input features (0.063). However, using 3 features only, ETR's performance, 0.079, is superior to 0.316 for *Turnover*.

The same pattern applies to most algorithms and can be looked at in terms of improvement as more features are added. For BR, ETR and RF, moving from 3 to 7 features improves MAE by 8.4–11.5%, while from 3 to 14 features improves MAE by 20.5–24.2%. These ranges are much lower than that observed for the same algorithms applied to *Turnover* (45.8–47.0% and 80.3–80.6%) as we have seen earlier. The improvement for LR is also very modest this time, 0.8% from 3 to 7 features, and 3.0% from 3 to 14 features.

The differences in results obtained across the targets with different distribution help us qualify the resilience of the algorithms and hence their potential applicability to other microdata sets. In essence, the best performing algorithms manage to reach similar levels of performance as more features are added, indicating that using more features are indeed useful. However, in some cases, the gain in performance may be modest, in which case fewer features may be used to decrease processing time.

5.5 Processing Time

Figure 6 shows the elapsed processing time for training and imputation of each algorithm on the 3FY data, testing the 14 input feature condition for the *Turnover* target. The first 5 bars are the linear models which have relatively low processing times ranging from 58 to 1,407 s for Ridge Regression and LassoCV. The ensemble family of algorithms are among the highest performers and orders of magnitude more computationally-intensive, up to 55 times longer than LR. Their processing times range from 2,003 to 18,348 s for DTR and RF. The clear outlier is the MLP at 85,805 s or 4.9 times slower than BR, ETR and RF.

6 Discussion

The experiment presented in this paper demonstrates the benefits of using machine learning-based imputation algorithms on national microdata sets such as BLADE. The high-performance outcomes achieved should encourage statistical and government agencies to reliably improve their imputation for greater data coverage. Our results help practitioners make the best decisions in terms of algorithms and input features, based on their dataset and analysis needs, while understanding the impact of different imputation methods.

Generally speaking, a single simple model, like a decision tree, is sensitive to training data and the results are likely to be overfitting and unstable. Ensemble algorithms, on the other hand, build multiple sub-models with multiple sub-samples of the dataset and produce a set of simple models that are weakly correlated with high variance, combining their results to make the final prediction. The RF, in particular, introduces additional variance by using a random sample of features for each individual sub-model. However, ensemble algorithms come at the cost of longer processing time.

To maximise the generalisability of our findings, we processed two target values with substantially different characteristics. Cross-validation accuracy results for both *Turnover* and *FTE* are seen as high enough to assist analysts using BLADE. The 1.16%–1.2% sMAPE for *Turnover* using BR, ETR and RF indicate imputed values are only slightly off from ground truth. Similarly, as indicated by R^2 values, around 94% variability of the true values were captured by the imputed values of these 3 algorithms.

We also quantified how more input features could substantially improve the imputation performance. Interestingly, the benefits were less pronounced for *FTE*, possibly because (i) less training data are available, only about a third of *Turnover*; and (ii) *FTE* has a more complicated non-linear relationship to input features because part-time effort may not be reflected linearly to *Turnover*.

The main limitation of our work stems from keeping the process simple to ensure easy adoption and higher generalisability. However, tuning the algorithms' hyper-parameters to each dataset could substantially improve imputation performance. It may also dramatically reduce processing time. Another potential limitation lies in using logarithm transformation to address data skewness. Practitioners will need to adapt scaling techniques to the characteristics of their data.

In the future, we plan to perform feature selection to assess the compared benefits of data-driven feature ranking on imputation performance. This may increase the complexity of the process but improve performance and reduce processing time. Also, it would be useful to validate whether using multiple-year feature values for a single business may lead to more reliable or accurate imputation performance as the temporal dependency could be used explicitly. Finally, we plan to further test these methods on other government datasets.

7   Conclusion

We conducted a comprehensive experimental evaluation of machine learning-based imputation algorithms on the Australian Government's national statistical asset – BLADE. Using two target features with distinct characteristics, *Turnover* and *FTE*, we compared 12 machine learning-based imputation algorithms and found that the extra trees regressor, bagging regressor and random forest consistently maintain high imputation performance over the benchmark linear regression across the performance metrics outlined at Sect. 4.1.

We provided detailed results along each algorithm, the number of input features, time spans and processing time conditions. Based on our results, we recommend using extra trees regressor for its overall imputation performance and computational efficiency. This is the most promising algorithm for increasing data coverage within microdata sets containing missing values. This work will help shed some light on novel tools for statistical and government agencies to select and implement supervised machine learning methods for imputation.

References

1. Australian Bureau of Statistics: The Business Longitudinal Analysis Data Environment (BLADE) Standard Product, Australia, 2001–02 to 2015–16. DataLab. Findings based on use of ABS Microdata, Detailed Microdata (2019)
2. Bakar, K.S., Jin, H.: A real prediction of survey data using Bayesian spatial generalised linear models. In: Communications in Statistics-Simulation and Computation, pp. 1–16 (2019)
3. Bakhtiari, S.: Entrepreneurship dynamics in Australia: lessons from microdata. Econ. Rec. **95**, 114–140 (2019)
4. Jin, H., Henderson, B.: Towards a daily soil moisture product based on incomplete time series observations of two satellites. In: Chan, F., Marinova, D., Anderssen, R. (eds.) MODSIM 2011, Perth, Australia, pp. 1959–1965 (2011)
5. Jin, H., Wong, M.L., Leung, K.S.: Scalable model-based clustering for large databases based on data summarization. IEEE Trans. Pattern Anal. Mach. Intell. **27**(11), 1710–1719 (2005)
6. Khan, S.S., Ahmad, A., Mihailidis, A.: Bootstrapping and multiple imputation ensemble approaches for missing data. CoRR abs/1802.00154 (2018)
7. Little, R.J., Rubin, D.B.: Statistical Analysis with Missing Data, vol. 333. Wiley, New York (2014)
8. Pedregosa, F., et al.: Scikit-learn: machine learning in Python. J. Mach. Learn. Res. **12**, 2825–2830 (2011)

9. Rubin, D.: Inference and missing data. Biometrika **63**(3), 581–592 (1976)
10. Solow, R.: A contribution to the theory of economic growth. Quart. J. Econ. **70**, 65–94 (1956)
11. Wood, S.N.: Generalized Additive Models: An Introduction with R. Chapman and Hall/CRC, New York (2017)
12. Yoon, J., Jordon, J., van der Schaar, M.: GAIN: missing data imputation using generative adversarial nets. arXiv preprint arXiv:1806.02920 (2018)

Predicting Financial Well-Being Using Observable Features and Gradient Boosting

Iqbal Madakkatel[✉], Belinda Chiera, and Mark D. McDonnell

Computational Learning Systems Laboratory, School of Information Technology
and Mathematical Sciences, University of South Australia,
Mawson Lakes, SA 5095, Australia
madmy016@mymail.unisa.edu.au,
{belinda.chiera,mark.mcdonnell}@unisa.edu.au

Abstract. Financial well-being and its measurement are well researched topics in personal finance, yet there is no universally agreed definition of financial well-being. Machine learning is proliferating into new application domains. In this study we investigate the use of state-of-the-art gradient boosting methods for predicting subjective levels of financial well-being, using the Consumer Finance Protection Bureau (CFPB) National Financial Well-being dataset. To enable interpretability, we identify the most important observable features required for accurate predictions. These important features are then analysed using factor analysis to understand hidden themes in the data.

Keywords: Personal finance · Financial well-being · Machine learning · Gradient boosting · Decision trees · Exploratory factor analysis

1 Introduction

Personal finance is something concerning everyone, with plenty of resources discussing personal finance concepts and issues. Many studies have been conducted to understand financial well-being of individuals and populations, as a whole, and the components and factors affecting it. However, there is no universally agreed definition or standard way of measuring financial well-being. The Consumer Finance Protection Bureau (CFPB), a U.S. government agency, conducted a systematic study to define and develop a reflexive scale to measure financial well-being. Their definition of financial well-being reflects a concept that is inherently subjective and for that reason it cannot be observed directly [1].

The rigour and the systematic approach to this scale development can be observed from the fact that the final financial well-being scale based on 10 subjective questions (on a five point Likert scale [2]) were arrived at by first conducting 106 interviews to develop the initial pool of candidate items and then three

© Springer Nature Switzerland AG 2019
J. Liu and J. Bailey (Eds.): AI 2019, LNAI 11919, pp. 228–239, 2019.
https://doi.org/10.1007/978-3-030-35288-2_19

rounds of surveys for data collection and scale development. The scale development involved exploratory factor analysis (EFA), confirmatory factor analysis (CFA) and finally developing models based on Item Response Theory (IRT) [3]. As a next logical step, the CFPB fielded the financial well-being questionnaire alongside a number of other survey questions. These questions were intended to capture data pertaining to individual characteristics, household and family characteristics, income and employment characteristics, savings and safety nets, financial experiences and financial behaviours, skills and attitudes. The survey resulted in a dataset of 6,394 samples with 217 features (including some derived features). One of the purposes of making the dataset public was to enable researchers to conduct additional research and produce further insights into financial well-being in the US society[1].

Our aim in this study is to predict financial well-being using observable attributes of individuals, which were captured using the survey and are available in the dataset. Contrary to subjective attributes, these can be measured objectively. For example, the amount of liquid cash that one possesses, whether someone has life or disability insurance, age and whether one has knowledge of financial concepts such as compound interest.

We aimed to answer the following research questions:

1. To what extent financial well-being, an inherently subjective construct, can be predicted by observable features available in the CFPB dataset?
2. If we segregate observable features into three different categories: (1) attributes applicable to participants only, such as current level of savings of participants; (2) attributes applicable to participants and/or any household member(s) such as total household income; and (3) attributes with no control over them (e.g., age, gender), to what extent can these different categories of features predict financial well-being?
3. Which observable features are more important than others? Do such important attributes form one or more latent constructs?

2   Background, Related Work and Motivation

Several attempts have been made to define financial well-being. One of the broadest conceptualisations [4] puts forward the idea that financial well-being is a multi-dimensional concept incorporating several factors that cannot be assessed through one measure. Other studies also show the multi-dimensional aspect of financial well-being [5,6], including a study on Australian financial well-being, which defines three interrelated dimensions with several sub-dimensions in those three dimensions [6]. Another study of financial-wellbeing using a nationally representative survey from Norway presents a definition and identifies three sub-domains of financial well-being [5].

---

[1] National Financial Well-being Survey Public User File User's Guide https://www.consumerfinance.gov/data-research/research-reports/financial-well-being-scale/.

The CFPB devised a model to actually measure financial well-being of individuals and to report it as a number between zero and one hundred[2]. The CFPB defines financial well-being "as a state of being wherein a person can fully meet current and ongoing financial obligations, can feel secure in their financial future and is able to make choices that allow them to enjoy life" [7]. Considering the present and future needs of financial security and freedom of choice, they define four elements and come up with a single measure for financial well-being modelled using 10 subjective questions spanning these four elements, using IRT. It is interesting to note that the same financial well-being score can reflect a diversity of circumstances, conditions, or perceptions. As an example, at all household income levels, financial well-being scores vary widely [8].

Our aim in this work is to investigate whether attributes that are observable (i.e. not subjective) can be used to predict financial well-being and to explain variability in well-being to the extent possible. As pointed out in [9], measuring financial well-being as well as exploring the correspondence and mismatch between objective and subjective financial well-being are very active research areas in personal finance. The possibility of predicting financial well-being using observable features has potential benefits for both individuals and for financial institutions.

We are unaware of any prior research attempting to model and hence understand the effect of observable measures on subjective financial well-being scores, especially using machine learning models. A study with some relevance to the one proposed here is that carried out in [10], which develops two multi-item scales of financial well-being, namely Reported Financial Well-being using self-reported survey data obtained from a subset of clients of a major Australian bank and Observed Financial Well-being using financial-record measures from the banking data of those customers. The study found that there is a positive correlation of 40% between the scales. They treat those scales as two distinct but correlated scales [10]. However, we investigate to what extent observable measures are effective in predicting a subjective scoring and thus linking subjectivity to observable measures. Another study which considers objective measures in measuring financial health is [11]. They define four components of financial health as Spend, Save, Borrow and Plan and two indicators for each component (a total of 8 indicators). The study presents how to measure the indicators using actual data that a financial institution might have and also provides with alternative survey questions in case actual data is not available.

3   Dataset

The CFPB dataset is a US-nationally representative dataset of 6,394 samples. The dataset contains 217 features with their sources as survey item, panel data, or derived variables. In addition to fielding the CFPB financial well-being (FWB) questions, the survey also fielded questions of three other financial scores, namely, Lusardi and Mitchel financial knowledge scale score, Knoll and Houts financial

---

[2] URL: https://www.consumerfinance.gov/consumer-tools/financial-well-being/.

knowledge scale score and Financial skills scale score. The other features provided in the dataset are of select individual and household. These include federal poverty level and demographic characteristics such as race/ethnicity, age, household size, household income from the panel, and survey items belonging to financial behaviour, financial attitudes and experiences[3].

3.1   Pre-processing

There were no missing values as such, as unsubstantiated values $(-5, -4, -3, -2.$ $-1, 8, 98$ and $99)$ were used to fill missing values due to various reasons such as participant refused to provide an answer, participant was not sure of an answer, participant didn't know an answer, participant not in item base or technical issues. In all our experiments we either converted the unsubstantiated values to null values or dropped samples with missing values. Original survey items testing financial knowledge were removed because we included corresponding derived dichotomous variables which indicated whether a participant correctly selected an option or not. Variables were classified as *Subjective* or *Observable*. We further segregated the observable variables into three categories as given in Table 1 and assessed their predictability on the subjective financial well-being reported. We separated those observable features which are applicable to participant and/or one or more household members from those features which are applicable to participant only. Examples of such features include household income, household size, $SNAP$ (Did you or any household member receive SNAP benefits?), $SHOCKS\_1$ (In the past 12 months, did you or any members of your household lose a job?).

Table 1. Distribution of features in the CFPB dataset.

Feature classification	Count
FWB questions	10
Subjective	84
Observable, no control over them	7
Observable, of participant and/or other household member(s)	28
Observable, of participant only	68
Excluded	20
Total	217

The feature *FWBscore* was used for label creation in binary classification and as the score to be predicted in regression experiments. *FWBscore* is a normally distributed variable, rounded to the nearest whole number, on a scale between

---

[3] National Financial Well-Being Survey Public Use File Codebook https://files. consumerfinance.gov/f/documents/cfpb_nfwbs-puf-codebook.pdf.

0 and 100, representing a continuum from severe financial stress to extremely satisfied with one's financial situation. Scores of below 50 are associated with people who are struggling to make ends meet and suffers from material hardships. Binary labels were 1 (Financially stable) for FWBscore $\geq$ 50 and 0 (Financially struggling) for FWBscore $<$ 50.

4   Methods

4.1   Model Development and Testing

Among numerous machine learning techniques available today, gradient boosting decision trees [12] have been found to be very effective in many applications enabling accurate predictions for tabular data [13]. We have chosen a specific gradient boosting decision trees implementation library called CatBoost [14] for our experiments described here. Some of the advantages of the CatBoost implementation include its native support for categorical features. Numeric and categorical variables with missing values can be input to CatBoost. CatBoost guarantees to have a split in decision trees that separates missing values from other values in a variable. In order to ensure that similar results are obtained using another algorithm, we also tried LightGBM [15], another gradient boosting decision tree implementation, on selected experiments.

Binary Classification and Regression. Firstly, we investigated binary classification to predict the broad category of *financially stable* or *financially struggling* and extended the experiments to regression to predict the actual *FWBscore*. The performance of binary classification was assessed using ROC-AUC and Accuracy whereas for regression we used root mean square error (RMSE) and R^2. Confidence intervals were calculated by running 10-fold cross validation on the entire dataset.

Feature Importance. Important features were identified using the built-in capabilities of CatBoost and LightGBM and using *SHAP values*. The default feature importance calculation of CatBoost for classification and regression is *PredictionValuesChange*, in which feature importance is determined by how much prediction value changes on average if the feature in question changes in its values. The bigger the changes in the prediction, the bigger the feature importance. For LightGBM, we used 'gain' for feature importance calculation. In addition to the built-in feature importance calculation of the algorithms, we used feature importance which was determined using *SHAP values* [16], a model agnostic method of finding feature importance with its roots in game theory. The calculation principle for *PredictionValuesChange*[4] and *SHAP values*[5] can be found in the footnotes.

---

[4] URL: https://catboost.ai/docs/concepts/fstr.html.
[5] URL: https://catboost.ai/docs/concepts/shap-values.html.

Ablation Studies. An ablation study was carried out, in which less important features, according to *Prediction Values Change* were removed one by one and a model was trained each time after removal of a feature, with the remaining features to see the performance on the reduced number of important features. After removing a feature, the feature importance of remaining features was recalculated to account for possible surrogate splits.

Exploratory Factor Analysis. Exploratory Factor Analyses (EFA) were carried out on important features identified with the aim of understanding whether they form one or more latent constructs and thus facilitating better explanation. The subset of the data which underwent EFA were tested for additivity, normality, linearity, and homogeneity. Internal consistency was checked using Cronbach's alpha and sampling adequacy was tested using the Kaiser-Meyer-Olkin (KMO) test. The number of factors to be extracted was determined using a combination of parallel analysis and the Kaiser criteria.

5 Results

5.1 Machine Learning Model Results

Learning curves[6] [17, pp. 55] for binary and regression models based on CatBoost with observable features showed that both log loss and ROC-AUC started to plateau at around 2,500 training sample, which is around 40% of the total data. We therefore decided to set the training data to be 60% of the total data. The remaining 40% of the data were split into a validation set and test set equally. As expected all models showed, trivially, that whenever FWB survey questions were added to the input features, then the models could predict the response extremely well. Table 2 shows the comparison of Accuracy and AUC for binary classification under various settings and Table 3 shows the performance of CatBoost regressors under various settings.

Table 2. Performance of CatBoost binary classifiers.

Feature selection	AUC	95% CI	Accuracy	95% CI
FWB questions	0.9981	0.9972–0.9972	0.9781	0.9681–0.9881
Subjective	0.9365	0.9143–0.9586	0.8693	0.8399–0.8987
Observable & Subjective	0.9385	0.9157–0.9613	0.8717	0.8436–0.8997
Observable, no control over them	0.6938	0.6366–0.7509	0.6881	0.6534–0.7227
Observable, shared[a]	0.7806	0.7529–0.8083	0.7378	0.7065–0.7691
Observable, shared/no control	0.7974	0.7670–0.8277	0.7453	0.7168–0.7739
Observable, of participant only	0.8671	0.8385–0.8957	0.8000	0.7737–0.8262
All observable	0.8746	0.8458–0.9034	0.8053	0.7737–0.8368

[a]Observable features of participant and/or other household member(s).

---

[6] Plotting validation metrics against the number of training examples.

Table 3. Performance of CatBoost regressors.

Feature selection	R^2	95% CI	RMSE	95% CI
FWB questions	0.9888	0.9836–0.9924	1.5343	1.2730–1.7957
Subjective	0.7155	0.6832–0.7478	7.4909	6.9570–8.0247
Observable & Subjective	0.7238	0.6846–0.7629	7.3774	6.9081–7.8466
Observable, no control over them	0.1551	0.1053–0.2049	12.9213	11.9478–13.8948
Observable, shared	0.2877	0.2308–0.3445	11.8601	10.9351–12.7851
Observable, shared/no control	0.3269	0.2723–0.3815	11.5257	10.7635–12.2879
Observable, of participant only	0.4875	0.4344–0.5406	10.0548	9.4130–10.6965
All observable	0.5091	0.4481–0.5700	9.8395	9.1952–10.4838

A 5-fold cross validation ablation study found that for the first 7 important features the performance of the binary classifier and regressor with only observable features continuously improved. Figure 1 shows the performance. The performance beyond the first 15 features are minimal, we therefore chose the first 15 important features for factor analyses.

Figure 2 shows the 15 most important features identified using *Prediction ValuesChange* and *SHAP Values* for binary classification and regression. For binary classification, the first 15 features produced a result of AUC of 0.8680, 95% CI 0.8571–0.8788 whereas when all the 102 observable features were used, the model achieved an AUC of 0.8746, 95% CI 0.8458–0.9034. For regression, using the first 15 important features resulted in R^2 as 0.4991, 95% CI 0.4794–0.5188, whereas using all 102 observable features resulted in 0.5091, 95% CI 0.4481–0.5700.

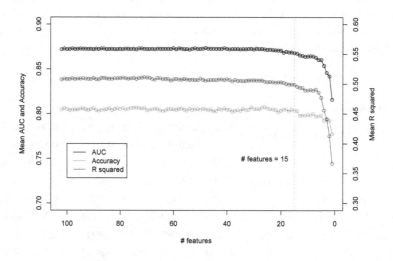

Fig. 1. Ablation study on feature importance.

Binary classification				Regression			
CatBoost	Imp	SHAP	Imp	CatBoost	Imp	SHAP	Imp
SAVINGSRANGES	22.3	SAVINGSRANGES	19.5	SAVINGSRANGES	25.8	SAVINGSRANGES	19.9
MANAGE1_3	10.3	MANAGE1_3	17.7	MANAGE1_3	21.5	MANAGE1_3	16.6
MANAGE1_1	8.9	MANAGE1_1	12.8	MANAGE1_1	10.0	MANAGE1_1	10.5
PPINCIMP	8.3	PPINCIMP	9.2	PPINCIMP	7.5	PPINCIMP	10.4
PPETHM	5.8	COLLECT	6.8	PRODHAVE_6	5.5	PRODHAVE_6	7.7
COLLECT	5.6	EMPLOY1_8	6.2	COLLECT	4.9	agecat	5.8
PPMARIT	5.6	agecat	5.3	agecat	4.3	EMPLOY1_8	5.5
EMPLOY1_8	5.4	SHOCKS_12	5.2	EMPLOY1_8	3.7	COLLECT	5.4
agecat	5.3	PRODHAVE_5	4.9	PPMARIT	3.1	SHOCKS_12	4.3
PPREG9	4.3	KH3correct	4.5	PPREG9	3.0	PRODHAVE_5	4.0
PPREG4	4.0	AUTOMATED_2	2.7	PRODHAVE_5	2.6	PPETHM	2.9
SHOCKS_12	3.9	PPREG4	1.9	HOUSERANGES	2.1	HOUSERANGES	2.4
PRODHAVE_5	3.6	PPETHM	1.6	PPETHM	2.1	SHOCKS_2	2.0
AUTOMATED_2	3.5	PPMARIT	1.0	SHOCKS_2	2.0	PPMARIT	1.3
KH3correct	3.2	PPREG9	0.8	SHOCKS_12	1.9	PPREG9	1.0

not in regression
not in classification

Fig. 2. Top fifteen important features.

Figure 3 shows the direction and magnitude of the 15 most important features for regression. From this, it can be seen that the features $COLLECT$ (Contacted by debt collector in past 12 months), $HOUSERANGES$ (About how much do you pay for your home each month?), $SHOCKS\_2$ (Work hours/pay reduced) are negatively correlated with financial well-being. On the other hand, $SAVINGSRANGES$ (How much money do you have in savings today?), MANAGE1_3 (Paid off credit card balance in full each month), $MANAGE1\_1$ (Paid all your bills on time), $PPINCIMP$ (Household Income), *agecat*, PRODHAVE_6 (Non-Retirement Investments (such as stocks, bonds or mutual funds)),

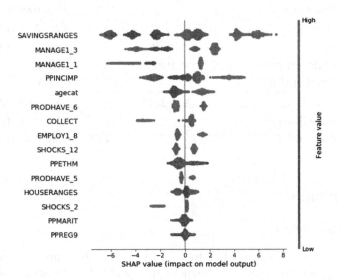

Fig. 3. SHAP summary plot.

EMPLOY1_8 (Retired), $SHOCKS\_12$ (Participant didn't select any of the 11 shocks listed) and $PRODHAVE\_5$ (Pension) are positively correlated.

5.2   Exploratory Factory Analyses

We started EFA with all the 15 important features identified for predicting actual financial well-being score (the column 'CatBoost' under 'Regression' in Fig. 2). Tests prior to EFA for additivity, normality, linearity and homogeneity found the data good for EFA. We dropped the features $PPREG9$ (Census division) and $PPETM$ (Race/Ethnicity) due to low communality and $HOUSERANGES$ due to low consistency. All samples with missing values for any features were removed. Bartlett's test for correlation adequacy was significant (p-value < 0.05). Sampling adequacy was tested using KMO. Overall MSA was 0.77 and none of the feature were below 0.65. Internal consistency tested using Cronback's alpha showed raw alpha as 0.71. The final solution using PCA with verimax orthogonal rotation showed three factors with the loading as shown in Table 4.

Table 4. Exploratory factor analysis – 3 factors solution.

#	Item	Factor_1	Factor_2	Factor_3	h2	u2	com
1	SAVINGSRANGES	0.79			0.70	0.30	1.2
2	PRINCIMP	0.75			0.57	0.43	1.0
3	MANAGE1_3	0.69			0.54	0.46	1.3
4	MANAGE1_1	0.61			0.45	0.55	1.4
5	PRODHAVE_6	0.59			0.40	0.60	1.3
6	COLLECT	−0.52			0.43	0.57	1.9
7	agecat		0.89		0.81	0.19	1.0
8	EMPLOY1_8		0.87		0.78	0.22	1.1
9	PRODHAVE_5		0.62		0.45	0.55	1.3
10	PPMARIT		−0.40		0.35	0.65	2.5
11	SHOCKS_12			0.75	0.56	0.44	1.0
12	SHOCKS_2			−0.69	0.50	0.50	1.1

6   Discussion

6.1   Predictability

Overall, the results suggest that to a great extent observable attributes can be used for predicting subjective financial well-being. The Spearman correlation between predicted values and the actual scores was 0.7213, 95% CI 0.6940–0.7466 and the coefficient of determination was 0.5091 95% CI 0.4481–0.5700. The implication of this is that financial institutions, which are in possession of some of the observable features used (for example, savings level or whether someone paid credit card outstanding in full in each month and so on) could operationalise such actual observed data for measuring financial well-being of their clients to some extent. It is to be noted that the Likert scales used for measuring some of these features can be readily replaced with appropriate equivalents.

6.2   Important Features

The experiment results in highlighting the importance of some of the observable features (such as whether someone paid credit card outstanding in full each month) over other observable features such as household income where the individual participants could be only partially responsible, is worth noting. In a model where all observable features were used, the feature representing the liquid cash someone has was more than three times more important than the feature denoting total household income. Also, observable features where participants having no control (such as gender or where someone lived at the age of 17 or highest level of education by person/people who raised respondent) are not as important as compared to many observable features upon which respondents had full control or some control. However, care should be taken in interpreting these results as the correlation between the subjective financial well-being and the prediction is not very close to 100%.

Figure 3 shows both direction and magnitude of impacts. For instance, SAV-$INGSRANGES$ has highest impact on model output with high values having positive impact. The impact of some features are not symmetrical. For instance, $COLLECT$ is negatively correlated with moderate impact when participant was contacted by debt collector and low impact otherwise. Another example would be $SHOCKS\_2$, with reduced pay/work hours having moderate negative impact and almost nil effect otherwise. It can also been seen that $agecat$ (Age) and $EMPLOY1\_8$ (retirement) are positively correlated with financial well-being.

It appears that first 10 important features out of 102 observable features did not include any features measuring the financial knowledge of a person. There were 14 questions testing financial knowledge. It is likely that, such knowledge or lack of such knowledge was reflected in other features. Out of those 14 questions, $KH3correct$ (Understanding of benefits of diversification) seems to be important as it is the only financial knowledge testing question that appeared in the top 20 important features.

The factor analysis results using the top 15 important features shows three latent factors covering 12 features. It appears that the first factor covering liquid savings, household income, paying credit card in full, paying all bills on time, non-retirement investments and not having contacted by debt collectors, stands for good financial behaviours (saving for present and future needs and keep up with financial discipline). Most of the financial well-being conceptual models present financial behaviours as one of the influential determinants of financial well-being and this result is consistent with them. The second factor covering age, retirement and pension appears to be related to financial well-being at a later stage in the life. The negative correlation of this factor with marital status may indicate different financial situation experienced by someone who is single and never married to someone who is perhaps widowed and may have to pay off partner debts or is experiencing a reduced income compared to their lifestyle. The third factor is related to experience of shocks in life (both financial and non-financial) and it indicates that both (experienced vs did not experience shocks) are equally important. It covers $SHOCKS\_2$ (had work hours and/or pay reduced) and $SHOCKS\_12$ (didn't experience any of the 11 shocks listed in the past 12 months).

6.3   Limitations and Future Work

This study uses only one dataset from the U.S., and even though it is nationally representative in that diverse country, our results may not be applicable in a different society (for instance, Australia) as we used features such as census region, division and SNAP benefits in model development. However, this work can be extended by applying the methodology followed here on other financial well-being datasets containing observable features, as and when they become publicly available. Another way of extending this work would be grouping participants based on attributes such as psychological factors and predicting financial well-being for those groups separately, as long as such grouping results in sufficient amount of data to develop and test machine learning models. Applying on longitudinal datasets would further enable to understand the changes in financial well-being over a period of time with respect to changes in observable and subjective features. This can result in mitigating the effects of confounding features. Another limitation of the study is that it is confined to the 217 features captured through the survey, panel data and derived features. There could be better observable features improving predicting power of models as well opportunities for feature engineering [18] to produce results which are more accurate. Feature engineering has not been explored in this study.

7   Conclusion

This paper explores the possibility of identifying important observable attributes to predict subjective financial well-being and it finds that such a prediction is possible. The study also finds certain observable features such as current savings level, whether people sampled paid all bills on time or paid off credit card outstanding in full each month as important predictors. Many of these attributes could be generated from the databases of financial institutions, enabling them to measure financial-wellbeing of their clients on a continuous basis. The study also finds that observable features which are under the direct control of participants are more effective predictors compared to other observable features which are under no control of them or are applicable to participants and/or any household member(s). As some previous studies [5,6,9,19,20] pointed out, financial behaviours are influential determinants of financial well-being, and our experiments show such influence. Also our study shows that attributes such as financial knowledge or skills are not as important as financial behaviours when it comes to predicting financial well-being.

Acknowledgments. I. Madakkatel acknowledges the support of an Australian Government Research Training Program (RTP) Scholarship.

References

1. CFPB: CFPB Financial Well-Being Scale: scale development technical report (2017)
2. Likert, R.: A technique for the measurement of attitudes. Arch. Psychol. (1932)
3. Embretson, S.E., Reise, S.P.: Item Response Theory. Psychology Press (2013)
4. Joo, S.: Personal financial wellness. In: Xiao, J.J. (ed.) Handbook of Consumer Finance Research, pp. 21–33. Springer, New York (2008). https://doi.org/10.1007/978-0-387-75734-6_2
5. Kempson, E., Finney, A., Poppe, C.: Financial well-being: a conceptual model and preliminary analysis. Final Edition: Project Note, (3) (2017)
6. Muir, K., et al.: Exploring financial wellbeing in the Australian context. Centre for Social Impact & Social Policy Research Centre, University of New South Wales, Sydney (2017)
7. Bureau, C.F.P.: Financial well-being: the goal of financial education. Iowa City, IA (2015)
8. Bureau, C.F.P.: Financial Well-Being in America, Washington, DC (2017)
9. Brüggen, E.C., Hogreve, J., Holmlund, M., Kabadayi, S., Löfgren, M.: Financial well-being: a conceptualization and research agenda. J. Bus. Res. **79**, 228–237 (2017)
10. Comerton-Forde, C., Ip, E., Ribar, D.C., Ross, J., Salamanca, N., Tsiaplias, S.: Using Survey and Banking Data to Measure Financial Wellbeing (2018)
11. Parker, S., Castillo, N., Garon, T., Levy, R.: Eight ways to measure financial health. Center for Financial Services Innovation, Chicago (2016)
12. Friedman, J.H.: Greedy function approximation: a gradient boosting machine. Ann. Stat. 1189–1232 (2001)
13. Olson, R.S., La Cava, W., Mustahsan, Z., Varik, A., Moore, J.H.: Data-driven advice for applying machine learning to bioinformatics problems. arXiv preprint arXiv:1708.05070 (2017)
14. Dorogush, A.V., Ershov, V., Gulin, A.: CatBoost: gradient boosting with categorical features support. arXiv preprint arXiv:1810.11363 (2018)
15. Ke, G., et al.: LightGBM: a highly efficient gradient boosting decision tree. In: Advances in Neural Information Processing Systems, pp. 3146–3154 (2017)
16. Lundberg, S.M., Erion, G.G., Lee, S.I.: Consistent individualized feature attribution for tree ensembles. arXiv preprint arXiv:1802.03888 (2018)
17. Ng, A.: Machine learning yearning (2017). https://www.deeplearning.ai/machine-learning-yearning/
18. Flach, P.: Machine Learning: The Art and Science of Algorithms that Make Sense of Data. Cambridge University Press, New York (2012)
19. Gutter, M., Copur, Z.: Financial behaviors and financial well-being of college students: evidence from a national survey. J. Fam. Econ. Issues **32**(4), 699–714 (2011)
20. Joo, S.H., Grable, J.E.: An exploratory framework of the determinants of financial satisfaction. J. Fam. Econ. Issues **25**(1), 25–50 (2004)

Fast Filtering for Nearest Neighbor Search by Sketch Enumeration Without Using Matching

Naoya Higuchi[1]([✉]), Yasunobu Imamura[2], Tetsuji Kuboyama[3], Kouichi Hirata[1], and Takeshi Shinohara[1]

[1] Kyushu Institute of Technology, Kawazu 680-4, Iizuka 820-8502, Japan
nac24nh@gmail.com, {hirata,shino}@ai.kyutech.ac.jp
[2] System Studio COLUN, Kokubu-machi 221-2, Kurume 839-0863, Japan
imamura.kit@gmail.com
[3] Gakushuin University, Mejiro 1-5-1, Toshima, Tokyo 171-8588, Japan
kuboyama@cc.gakushuin.ac.jp

Abstract. A *sketch* is a lossy compression of high-dimensional data into compact bit strings such as locality sensitive hash. In general, k nearest neighbor search using sketch consists of the following two stages. The first stage narrows down the top K candidates, for some $K \geq k$, using a priority measure of sketch as a filter. The second stage selects the k nearest objects from K candidates. In this paper, we discuss the search algorithms using fast filtering by sketch enumeration without using matching. Surprisingly, the search performance is rather improved by the proposed method when *narrow* sketches with smaller number of bits such as 16-bits than the conventional ones are used. Furthermore, we compare the search efficiency by sketches of various widths for several databases, which have different numbers of objects and dimensionalities. Then, we can observe that wider sketches are appropriate for larger databases, while narrower sketches are appropriate for higher dimension.

Keywords: Similarity search · Nearest neighbor search · Sketch enumeration · Ball partitioning · Hamming distance · Dimension reduction

1 Introduction

One of the most important tasks of similarity search [14] in high dimensional spaces is how to escape from "the curse of dimensionality". Typical approaches use dimension reduction mappings such as principal component analysis (PCA) or K-L transform and Simple-Map [11]. Similar approaches are discussed in the field of pattern recognition [3] by regarding a feature extraction as dimension reduction mapping.

A *sketch* [2,8–10,12], which has been developed for similarity search, is a compact bit sequence representing multidimensional data such as locality sensitive hash (LSH). *Ball partitioning* (BP, for short) is a method to make sketches

© Springer Nature Switzerland AG 2019
J. Liu and J. Bailey (Eds.): AI 2019, LNAI 11919, pp. 240–252, 2019.
https://doi.org/10.1007/978-3-030-35288-2_20

by assigning a bit 0 or 1 to data, such that 0 if it is in a ball and 1 otherwise. BP is also used in vantage point tree [13].

In general, the similarity search using dimension reduction mapping consists of two stages. The first stage selects candidates depending on their priority determined by mapped images, since the dimension reduction mapping cannot preserve the similarity overall. Then, the second stage selects the answer from the candidates. Even if we use a hierarchical spatial index R-tree [4] or M-tree [1], tree construction by clustering based on dimension reduced images improves search efficiency and two stage selection is included.

The proximity for priority of sketches is measured by several ways. The most common one is Hamming distance, that is, the number of mismatched bits. In [5], we proposed other priority measures $score_\infty$ and $score_1$ of sketches, which are defined as aggregations of distance lower bounds by "max" like L_∞, "sum" like L_1, respectively. In order to guarantee a certain level of accuracy at a speed comparable to that of the hierarchical spatial indexing method, the width of the sketch has been considered to be 32-bit or 64-bit. However, we recognized that narrower sketches may provide more efficient search because $score_\infty$ and $score_1$ are more accurate than the conventional Hamming distance.

In the previous work [6], we proposed a method for nearest neighbor search using 16-bit sketch. Since the number of 16-bit patterns is $2^{16} = 65,536$, we can efficiently manage data with bucket method. Note that the number of sketches close to the sketch of a query in the first stage is just a few of 65,536, so the cost for the first stage can be very small. Therefore, if we adopt an algorithm to enumerate sketches in the priority order without performing matching between sketches, then it is possible to increase the speed in practice.

For Hamming distance and $score_\infty$, we presented efficient algorithms to enumerate sketches in priority order. Then, we confirmed the efficiency of the proposed method by using two databases of image features and sound features. However, the first stage for $score_1$ was necessary to naively search all the 2^{16} sketches. Although without implementing efficient enumeration, search speed using $score_1$ was almost the same as that using $score_\infty$ with enumeration.

In this paper, we present an algorithm to enumerate sketches in the priority order according to $score_1$. The enumeration for $score_1$ makes search about two times faster when 16-bit sketch is used. We also investigate the optimal sketch widths for five databases, which have different numbers of data and different dimensionalities. Then, we can observe that wider sketches are appropriate for larger databases and narrower sketches are appropriate for higher dimension.

2   Preliminaries

2.1   Nearest Neighbor Search Using Sketches

Let $\mathcal{U}$ and $db \subseteq \mathcal{U}$ be a data space and a database. We assume that every datum in db is indexed by a natural number from 0 to $n - 1$, so let db be a set $\{x_0, \ldots, x_{n-1}\}$. The dissimilarity between two data x_i and x_j is measured by a given distance $D(x_i, x_j)$. The *nearest neighbor search* (*NN search*, for short) for a query $q \in \mathcal{U}$ is to find a datum $x \in db$ such that $D(q, x) \leq D(q, y)$ for every $y \in db$. We can realize NN search for a query $q \in \mathcal{U}$ using sketches in the following two stages, where s is a function which maps a datum to its sketch and $K \geq 1$ is an arbitrary constant.

1. Preparation stage:
   Compute the sketches $s(x_0), \ldots, s(x_{n-1})$ for every $x_i \in db$.
2. First stage (Filtering using sketches):
   Select K candidates $x_{i_0}, \ldots, x_{i_{K-1}}$ with top K priorities to the sketch $s(q)$.
3. Second stage (NN search using actual distances):
   Select the nearest neighbor datum from the candidates $x_{i_0}, \ldots, x_{i_{K-1}}$.

In the first stage, we conventionally use the Hamming distances as priorities, which are more easily computed using bit operations than the actual distances between features. Since the sketches do not always preserve a metric relation, we use them as a filter. We call the probability that a correct nearest neighbor is obtained the *accuracy* of search. The larger K of the number of candidates in the first stage achieves a more accurate but slower search. Thus, one of the most important subjects on sketches is to achieve more accurate search with smaller K, or equivalently, to speedup search within acceptable error.

2.2   Sketches Based on Ball Partitioning

In this paper, we use sketches based on *ball partitioning* (BP). A pair (p, r) of a point $p \in \mathcal{U}$ and a radius $r \in \mathbb{R}$ is called a *pivot*. A ball partitioning $BP_{(p,r)}$ is defined as follows:

$$BP_{(p,r)}(x) = \begin{cases} 0, & \text{if } D(p, x) \leq r, \\ 1, & \text{otherwise.} \end{cases}$$

A BP based sketch function s_P of *width* w is defined as the bit concatenation for a set $P = \{(p_0, r_0), \ldots, (p_{w-1}, r_{w-1})\}$ of w pivots as follows.

$$s_P(x) = BP_{(p_{w-1}, r_{w-1})}(x) \cdots BP_{(p_0, r_0)}(x)$$

In this paper, we adopt the priority based on distance lower bounds [5] in the first stage, which provides a more accurate search than the Hamming distance. For a query q and a set $P = \{(p_0, r_0), \ldots, (p_{w-1}, r_{w-1})\}$ of w pivots, we define $e_i(q, P)$ as the minimum distance from q to the boundary of partitioning by $BP_{(p_i, r_i)}$, that is,

$$e_i(q, P) = |D(p_i, q) - r_i|.$$

Then, we can obtain the lower bound $b_i(q, s_P(x))$ of $D(q, x)$ as follows:

$$b_i(q, s_P(x)) = \begin{cases} 0, & \text{if } BP_{(p_i, r_i)}(q) = BP_{(p_i, r_i)}(x), \\ e_i(q, P), & \text{otherwise.} \end{cases}$$

We propose priorities using the distance lower bounds $b_i(q, s_P(x))$ as the criteria to select candidates in the first stage. When we adopt the following priority,

$$score_\infty(q, s_P(x)) = \max\{b_i(q, s_P(x)) \mid 0 \leq i \leq w - 1\},$$

we can safely prune some of candidates because it is a distance lower bound. We can also adopt their sum $score_1$ as the priority:

$$score_1(q, s_P(x)) = \sum_{i=0}^{w-1} b_i(q, s_P(x)).$$

Note that $score_1$ is not a distance lower bound, but derives higher accuracy than $score_\infty$. Unfortunately, the reason why $score_\infty$ and $score_1$ give more accurate priority than the Hamming distance is unknown so far.

In experiments in this study, we adopt a heuristic method QBP(Quantization BP) presented in [5] which selects a center for BP from corners of the feature space for pivots by *binary quantization* and minimizes the collision probability as the evaluation index for sketch optimization.

Consider sketch defined by a set of two pivots $P = \{(p_0, r_0), (p_1, r_1)\}$ on a Euclidean plane in Fig. 1. Pivot centers p_0 and p_1 are quantized points of randomly selected data z_0 and z_1 from database using the median *med* as threshold. Two balls divide the space into 4 subspaces A and B, C, D. For any point $x \in A$ or B, C, D, $s_P(x) = 01$, or $00, 10, 11$, respectively. Let q be a query outside of both balls as shown. Then, $s_P(q) = 11$. Priorities for points in subspaces by Hamming distance, $score_\infty$ and $score_1$ for q are summarized in the table. Note that A and C cannot be distinguished by Hamming distances from q, while all subspaces are separated by $score_1$.

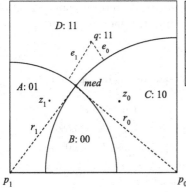

subspace	Hamming	$score_\infty$	$score_1$
A	1	e_1	e_1
B	2	e_1	$e_0 + e_1$
C	1	e_0	e_0
D	0	0	0

med: median of data

Binary Quantization: $z_0, z_1 \rightarrow p_0, p_1$

Order of priorities from query q

$D < A = C < B$ (Hamming)

$D < C < A = B$ $(score_\infty)$

$D < C < A < B$ $(score_1)$

Fig. 1. 2-bit sketch by QBP and priorities

2.3   Fast Filtering by Sketch Enumeration

In actual search process, only a small part of sketches that approximate the sketch of the query is needed. So by using an algorithm that enumerates the sketches in the priority order, it is possible to increase the speed because the first step search becomes almost negligible in cost, when we manage data by bucket method using sketches as keys.

Here, we briefly explain the speedup of the first stage search by using sketch enumeration in Hamming distance order. Before search, we prepare all 16-bit patterns sorted in ascending order of the number of ON bits. Sketches can be enumerated in order of Hamming distance from the sketch of a query by calculating bitwise exclusive or between the sketch of the query and these bit patterns. The second stage search is executed using only initial part of this sequence. By this method, in the first stage search, calculation of the Hamming distance between the sketches becomes unnecessary and almost no search cost is required.

Search algorithms using sketch enumeration for Hamming distance and $score_\infty$ are omitted due to space limitation. They are presented in [6].

Table 1 is a part of experimental results reported in the previous paper, where the average search times (millisecond) for a query are shown with the ratio of K to database size. For 32-bit sketch, the conventional method is used. The search using 16-bit sketch with $score_\infty$ uses the enumeration, while the search using 16-bit sketch with $score_1$ does not use the enumeration. From this table, we can observe that $score_\infty$ and $score_1$ are more accurate than Hamming distance no matter whether the method is conventional wider sketch or narrower sketch. Search using 16-bit sketch is about 10 times faster than the conventional search using 32-bit sketch.

In order to compare search speed, we conducted experiments of full search without using sketches and spatial indexes, and it was found that it takes about 550 ms per query. Therefore, in the search using sketches, in order to maintain high accuracy of 90% or more, the conventional method using 32-bit sketches is only 5 times faster than full search, while the methods using narrow 16-bit sketches are 40 times faster.

Table 1. Image search with accuracy over 90% reported in [6]

Priority	Width = 32-bit	Width = 16-bit
Hamming	139 ms ($K = 2.0\%$)	17.5 ms ($K = 6.5\%$)
$score_\infty$	106 ms ($K = 1.5\%$)	12.8 ms ($K = 5.0\%$)
$score_1$	107 ms ($K = 1.0\%$)	12.0* ms ($K = 2.5\%$)

(* sketch enumeration is not used for $score_1$)
(search time by full search is 550 ms)

3 Fast Search Using Sketch Enumeration in $score_1$ Order

Algorithm 1 illustrates the search method using sketch enumeration for $score_1$. Here, $e[i]$ is set to the following value:

$$e[i] = |D(p_i, q) - r_i|,$$

```
/* x[0], x[1], · · · , x[n − 1]: Array of feature data sorted by sketches.
   id[i]: Data ID of a feature datum x[i].
   f[s]: First position in the array x of data whose sketches are s.
   num[s]: Number of data whose sketches are s.
   K : Number of candidates obtained in 1st stage
       = number of actual distance calculations in 2nd stage.
   w : the width of sketches
   PQ : Priority queue whose elements are triples (score, s, i), where
        score is score₁ of sketch s, i is an integer, and score is used as priority */
```

1 **function** SEARCH($query, s, NN, nearest, checked$)
2   **for** $i = f[s]$ **to** $f[s] + num[s] - 1$ **do**
3   **if** $D(query, x[i]) \leq nearest$ **then** $(NN, nearest) \leftarrow (id[i], D(query, x[i]))$;
4         $checked \leftarrow checked + 1$;
5   **if** $checked \geq K$ **then** $return(NN, nearest, checked)$;
6     $return(NN, nearest, checked)$;

7 **function** SEARCHBYSCORE1($query$)
8   Prepare the minimum distances $e[0], \ldots, e[w-1]$ from $query$ to boundaries of partitioning;
9   Prepare the distance rank order table $bidx[0], \ldots, bidx[w-1]$ for $query$;
10     $(NN, nearest, checked) \leftarrow (\text{"none"}, \infty, 0)$;
11     $s \leftarrow sketch(query)$;
12     $(NN, nearest, checked) \leftarrow$ SEARCH($query, s, NN, nearest, checked$);
13   **if** $checked \geq K$ **then** $return\ NN$;
14     $PQ \leftarrow (e[bidx[0]], s \oplus (1 \ll bidx[0]), 1)$;
15   **while** PQ is not empty **do**
16         $(score, s, i) \leftarrow PQ$;
17         $(NN, nearest, checked) \leftarrow$ SEARCH($query, s, NN, nearest, checked$);
18   **if** $checked \geq K$ **then** $return\ NN$;
19   **if** $i < w$ **then**
20             $s \leftarrow s \oplus (1 \ll bidx[i])$;
21             $PQ \leftarrow (score - e[bidx[i] - 1] + e[bidx[i]], s \oplus (1 \ll (bidx[i] - 1)), i + 1)$;
22             $PQ \leftarrow (score + e[bidx[i]], s, i + 1)$;

23     $return\ NN$;

Algorithm 1. SEARCHBYSCORE1

that is, the minimum distance from a query q to partition boundary for bit position i, and rank order table $bidx$ is prepared such that $bidx[i], \ldots, bidx[w-1]$ are the rearrangement of $0, 1, \ldots, w - 1$ satisfying that:

$$e[bidx[w-1]] \geq \cdots \geq e[bidx[1]] \geq e[bidx[0]].$$

We represent a bitwise exclusive-or operator and a bit left shift operator by $\oplus$ and $\ll$, respectively. Using these operators, for example, the following formula presents a bit pattern obtained by flip the i-th bit of s,

$$s \oplus (1 \ll i).$$

We explain that Algorithm 1 correctly enumerates sketches in $score_1$ order. For simplicity we assume that:

$$e[w-1] \geq \cdots \geq e[1] \geq e[0].$$

In this case, $bidx[i] = i$ for any $i = 0, \ldots, w-1$.

Let $query$ be the query and qs be the sketch of $query$. $MSB(pat)$ is the left most ON bit position of a bit pattern pat. For example, $MSB(1) = 0$, $MSB(10) = MSB(11) = 1$ and $MSB(100) = 2$. We use a priority queue PQ whose elements are triples $(score, s, i)$ of a priority $score$, a sketch s and an integer i satisfying that:

$$score = score_1(query, s) \text{ and } MSB(qs \oplus s) = i - 1.$$

First qs itself is enumerated (line 11). Clearly $score_1(query, qs) = 0$, therefore the first element is correctly enumerated. The next sketch to be enumerated is $qs \oplus 1$, which has the next smallest distance lower bound $e[0]$ as its $score_1$. Since $qs \oplus (qs \oplus 1) = 1$, $MSB(qs \oplus (qs \oplus 1)) = 1$. The first element inserted into PQ is $(e[0], qs \oplus 1, 1)$ (line 14), and it is correctly enumerated from PQ (line 16).

Let $(score, s, i)$ be an element extracted from PQ at line 16. Then, $score = score_1(query, s)$ and $MSB(qs \oplus s) = i - 1$. Let s_1 and s_2 be two sketches inserted to PQ at line 21 and 22, respectively.

$$s_1 = (s \oplus (1 \ll i)) \oplus (1 \ll (i-1)),$$
$$s_2 = s \oplus (1 \ll i).$$

Then, we have

$$score_1(query, s_1) = score - e[i-1] + e[i],$$
$$score_1(query, s_2) = score + e[i].$$

Clearly $MSB(qs \oplus s_1) = MSB(qs \oplus s_2) = i$. Note that for the sketch s extracted from PQ and the sketch qs of $query$,

$$s \oplus qs = 1X,$$

where X is equal to an i-digit binary number and two sketches s_1 and s_2 are $10X$ and $11X$, respectively. From this fact, it is certified that the algorithm generates all the w-bit pattern without repetition. Furthermore, it is guaranteed that the enumeration is done in $score_1$ order by the fact that the scores of s_1 and s_2 are not larger than the score of s.

Algorithm 1 repeats a loop in which it extracts a sketch from the priority queue PQ and inserts two sketches into PQ. The computational costs of insertion and extraction for PQ are both $O(\log m)$, when PQ has m elements. Therefore, the enumeration by Algorithm 1 has $\log m$ delay. On the other hand, the both enumerations for Hamming distance and $score_\infty$ have constant delay, that is, the computational cost between two consecutive enumerations is constant.

The computational cost for enumerating m sketches by Algorithm 1 is $O(m \log m)$, because the number of the insertion is $2m$, the number of extraction is m, and the number of elements in PQ is at most $m+1$. The cost for enumerating sketches in $score_1$ order is larger than those for Hamming distance and $score_\infty$. However, $score_1$ is more accurate than Hamming distance and $score_\infty$, and the search using $score_1$ requires smaller number of candidates in the first stage. We reported that the search speed using $score_1$ without enumeration is almost the same as that using $score_\infty$ with speedup by enumeration [6]. Therefore, we can expect that Algorithm 1 provides faster search than others.

4   Experiments

In this section, we report experiments using 5 databases shown in Table 2, which consist of image feature data extracted as 2D frequency spectrums from video movies. Database 1 is the same as used in the previous paper [6]. Other databases have different sizes or dimensionalities. The dimensional value of the data is the logarithm of the frequency intensity represented by an 8-bit unsigned integer. Data are normalized so that the sum of dimensional values is constant. The degree of difference between data is measured using L_1 distance. Note that Database 2 and Database 3 of lower dimensionality are prepared only for comparison experiments, and their dimensionality may be too low for practical search.

In Database 1, the average distance to nearest neighbors from randomly generated queries is 3,300, while the average distance between two data is 1,650. The typical distance to nearest neighbor is around 200 or 550 for queries extracted from video which has or does not have similar one in Database 1, respectively. Therefore, randomly generated queries are not appropriate for our experiments. We prepare queries by mixing x and y as noise level 5%, 10%, ..., 50% for randomly selected two data x and y from the database. For example, a query with noise level 5% is a sum of x and y with weight 95% and 5%, respectively. The average distance to nearest neighbor from queries with noise level 5% and 50% is 85 and 586, respectively. For each noise level, we prepare 100 queries. Total number of queries is 1,000.

The PC used for the experiments is CPU Intel (R) Xeon (R) CPU E 5 - 2640 2.5 GHz, memory 64 GBytes.

4.1   The Enumeration of Sketches in $score_1$ Order

First we show the improvement by enumeration of sketches in $score_1$ order. Figure 2 shows results for Database 1, where 5 methods are used. The horizontal

Table 2. Databases used in experiments

Database	Database 1	Database 2	Database 3	Database 4	Database 5
Size $(\times 10^6)$	6.9	6.9	6.9	$6.9 \times \frac{1}{4}$	$6.9 \times \frac{1}{16}$
Dimension	64	36	16	64	64

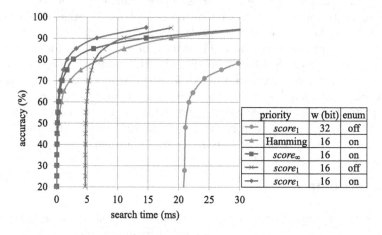

Fig. 2. Search time and accuracy

axis is the average time in millisecond (ms) for query and the vertical axis is the search accuracy. The first one is the conventional method using 32-bit sketch with $score_1$. Others are methods using 16-bit sketch. Methods with Hamming distance and $score_\infty$ use sketch enumeration. For 16-bit sketch with $score_1$, two methods are presented, with and without sketch enumeration. Any method needs more time for higher accuracy as the larger K is needed for accurate search. The main reason of the slowness of the conventional method is caused by the full search at the first stage, which needs at least about 21 ms.

We can see that the sketch enumeration for $score_1$ works very efficiently as expected and the search time about 6 ms for 90% accuracy is as about 100 times faster than 550 ms by full search. The time difference of about 5 ms between methods for $score_1$ with and without enumeration is consumed by matching query sketch with 2^{16} sketches.

4.2   The Optimal Sketch Width for Database 1

For each database and each priority, first we determined the number of candidates for which search accuracy is just 90%. In Table 3, the experimental results using Database 1 are summarized by the following items. In Table 3, we omit results for Hamming distance due to space limitation. We also omit the results on Database 2 to Database 5. All values are the average per query.

- K: the number of candidates (percentage to the database size).
- *sketches*: the number of enumerated sketches.
- *empty*: the number of empty buckets for enumerated sketches.
- *elements*: the average number of elements in enumerated nonempty buckets.
- *time*: the elapsed time (ms) of search
- *unsorted*: the elapsed time (ms) of search without using sorted database.
- *enum*: the elapsed time (ms) consumed for sketch enumeration.
- *sorting effect*: the speedup ratio of *unsorted* to *time* except *enum*.

For any priority of $score_\infty$ or $score_1$, the optimal sketch is width longer than 16-bit in Table 3. In general, the wider the sketches are, the smaller K the numbers of candidates to achieve 90% accuracy are. Although the computational cost for the second stage search is usually considered to be determined by K, the wider sketches do not always result in shorter search times. This phenomenon is considered to be due to the improvement of locality of memory access by sorting data. This is also confirmed by the fact that the best width for search without using sorted database becomes longer. The effect by sorting database becomes smaller when wider sketches are used as shown in sorting effect rows in table. Thus, the best width is determined by the tradeoff between the selectivity of sketch and the improvement of memory locality.

Table 3. Results for Database 1 (Size = 6.9×10^6, Dimension = 64)

	Width	16	17	18	19	20	21	22	23	24
$score_\infty$	$K(\%)$	4.59	4.32	3.77	3.70	3.32	3.02	2.80	2.67	2.47
	Sketches	2,407	4,400	7,383	13,993	23,944	40,742	70,708	126,015	219,453
	Empty	29	174	730	2,899	8,126	19,943	44,396	93,778	181,979
	Elements	133	71	39	23	14	10	7	6	5
	Time (ms)	12.7	11.9	**11.0**	11.7	11.6	12.3	12.9	14.2	16.0
	Unsorted (ms)	38.3	36.5	32.5	32.5	30.2	28.4	**27.7**	28.0	28.3
	Enum (ms)	0.470	0.494	0.498	0.612	0.763	0.978	1.40	2.17	3.25
	Sorting effect	3.09	3.16	3.04	2.87	2.72	2.43	2.29	2.14	1.96
$score_1$	$K(\%)$	2.03	1.75	1.51	1.37	1.22	1.33	1.04	0.94	0.88
	Sketches	862	1,377	2,205	3,630	5,919	9,640	15,589	24,451	40,593
	Empty	4	26	119	454	1,353	3,453	7,696	15,108	29,387
	Elements	163	89	50	30	18	13	9	7	5
	time (ms)	5.74	5.22	**4.97**	5.15	5.56	6.50	8.22	10.5	14.9
	Unsorted (ms)	18.5	16.4	14.3	13.8	**13.3**	13.5	14.3	15.9	20.0
	Enum (ms)	0.309	0.360	0.472	0.699	1.11	1.82	3.09	5.22	9.29
	Sorting effect	3.34	3.29	3.07	2.95	2.75	2.50	2.18	2.02	1.92

4.3   The Effects by Data Dimension and Database Size

Table 4 shows, for each database, the search time (ms) by full search, the best sketch widths and search times (ms) by proposed methods using priorities Hamming distance, $score_\infty$ and $score_1$, with speedup by $score_1$.

Table 4. Optimal sketch widths and speedup by $score_1$ to full search

Database			Full search	Hamming			$score_\infty$			$score_1$			Speedup ($\frac{Full}{score_1}$)
No.	Dim.	Size		w	$K(\%)$	time	w	$K(\%)$	time	w	$K(\%)$	time	
1	64	All	551	19	5.25	16.8	18	3.77	11.0	18	1.51	4.97	111
2	36	All	331	19	2.57	4.43	20	1.29	2.50	19	0.653	1.31	253
3	16	All	136	24	0.538	0.606	27	0.139	0.204	24	0.132	0.179	759
4	64	1/4	136	17	6.92	5.65	16	5.25	4.06	16	2.37	2.02	67.4
5	64	1/16	34.1	15	8.37	1.67	14	6.35	1.21	14	3.00	0.615	55.4

We see the effects by data dimension by comparing experimental results for Database 1, Database 2 and Database 3, which have the same number of data with different dimension. As the dimensionality of the data decreases, the number of candidates for the first stage search decreases, the width of the optimal sketch increases, and the speedup effect by $score_1$ with respect to full search becomes larger. This effect can be considered natural because the distance information included in smaller dimension is small and easily captured by sketches.

We consider the effect by database size by comparing results for Database 1, Database 4 and Database 5, which have data of the same dimension but different size. For any priority, the best width becomes larger when the database size becomes larger. The larger the database size is, the larger speedup by $score_1$ achieves.

5 Concluding Remarks

We proposed an algorithm to enumerate sketches in $score_1$ order, by which the fastest search method is devised. The cost of enumeration in $score_1$ order by the proposed in this paper is small enough but not negligible as those in Hamming distance or $score_\infty$ order proposed in the previous paper [6]. Therefore, in some situation, the search speed by $score_1$ might be slower than that by $score_\infty$. For example, the search time by $score_1$ becomes longer than that by $score_\infty$ for sketch of 27-bit or wider. Because the enumeration algorithm for $score_1$ has $\log m$ delay while that for $score_\infty$ has constant delay. It is an important feature work to find more efficient enumeration algorithm for $score_1$. A challenging subject for $score_1$ and $score_\infty$ is to investigate why they provide more accurate priority than Hamming distance.

We showed that the wider sketch is appropriate for larger database or lower dimension databases. For example, for our image database of about 6.9 million data of dimensionality 64 (Database 1), the search using 18-bit or 19-bit sketch is the fastest. For Database 3 of dimensionality 16, 24-bit or 27-bit sketch is the optimum. Thus, there is a possibility that wider sketches may be suitable. However, if we use very wide sketches, then bucket method cannot be efficiently used, because there are so many empty buckets. Therefore, data manage for wider sketch should be considered.

One of the reasons why we originally focused on the method using narrow 16-bit sketches is that the total number of sketches is small compared to the number of data, and even if all sketches are searched, the first stage search can be done in small constant cost. However, when we use efficient enumeration of sketches in the priority order, it is observed that high efficiency can be obtained using 24-bit and 28-bit sketches for about 6.9 million databases. According to the experimental results using Database 3, in the case of using 28-bit sketches, the speedup effect by sorting is maintained despite the increase of empty buckets. This seems to be due to the fact that the average number of elements of the non-empty bucket visited at the time of search is relatively large. We think that this phenomenon is because high-performance sketches can be created as LSH for low-dimensional data. Therefore, it is an important future work to consider about the method of creating sketches with higher LSH properties for high-dimensional data.

By using AIR, a kind of simulated annealing method, a pivot set of sketches with smaller collision probability than QBP can be obtained, but search accuracy is not improved [7]. It seems necessary to investigate sketch optimization further.

Acknowledgments. This work was partially supported by JSPS KAKENHI Grant Numbers 16H02870, 17H00762, 16H01743, 17H01788, and 18K11443.

References

1. Ciaccia, P., Patella, M., Zezula, P.: M-tree: an efficient access method for similarity search in metric spaces. In: Proceedings VLBD'97, pp. 426–435 (1997)
2. Dong, W., Charikar, M., Li, K.: Asymmetric distance estimation with sketches for similarity search in high-dimensional spaces. In: Proceedings ACM SIGIR'08, pp. 123–130 (2008)
3. Fukunaga, K.: Statistical Pattern Recognition, 2nd edn. Academic Press, Cambridge (1990)
4. Guttman, A.: R-trees: a dynamic index structure for spatial searching. In: Yormark, B. (ed.) Proceedings SIGMOD'84, pp. 47–57. ACM Press (1984)
5. Higuchi, N., Imamura, Y., Kuboyama, T., Hirata, K., Shinohara, T.: Nearest neighbor search using sketches as quantized images of dimension reduction. In: Proceedings ICPRAM 2018, pp. 356–363 (2018)
6. Higuchi, N., Imamura, Y., Kuboyama, T., Hirata, K., Shinohara, T.: Fast nearest neighbor search with narrow 16-bit sketch. In: Proceedings ICPRAM 2019, pp. 540–547 (2019)
7. Imamura, Y., Higuchi, N., Kuboyama, T., Hirata, K., Shinohara, T.: Pivot selection for dimension reduction using annealing by increasing resampling. In: Proceedings LWDA 2017, pp. 15–23 (2017)
8. Mic, V., Novak, D., Zezula, P.: Improving sketches for similarity search. In: Proceedings MEMICS'15, pp. 45–57 (2015)
9. Mic, V., Novak, D., Zezula, P.: Speeding up similarity search by sketches. In: Amsaleg, L., Houle, M.E., Schubert, E. (eds.) SISAP 2016. LNCS, vol. 9939, pp. 250–258. Springer, Cham (2016). https://doi.org/10.1007/978-3-319-46759-7_19
10. Müller, A., Shinohara, T.: Efficient similarity search by reducing I/O with compressed sketches. In: Proceedings SISAP'09, pp. 30–38 (2009)

11. Shinohara, T., Ishizaka, H.: On dimension reduction mappings for approximate retrieval of multi-dimensional data. In: Arikawa, S., Shinohara, A. (eds.) Progress in Discovery Science. LNCS, vol. 2281, pp. 224–231. Springer, Heidelberg (2002). https://doi.org/10.1007/3-540-45884-0_14
12. Wang, Z., Dong, W., Josephson, W., Lv, Q., Charikar, M., Li, K.: Sizing sketches: a rank-based analysis for similarity search. In: Proceedings ACM SIGMETRICS'07, pp. 157–168 (2007)
13. Yianilos, P.: Data structures and algorithms for nearest neighbor search in general metric spaces. In: Proceedings SODA 1993, pp. 311–321. ACM Press (1993)
14. Zezula, P., Amato, G., Dohnal, V., Batko, M.: Similarity Search: The Metric Space Approach. Advances in Database Systems. Springer, Heidelberg (2006). https://doi.org/10.1007/0-387-29151-2

Evaluating the Boundaries of Big Data Environments for Machine Learning

Fathima Nuzla Ismail, Brendon J. Woodford$^{(\boxtimes)}$, and Sherlock A. Licorish

Department of Information Science, University of Otago, Dunedin, New Zealand
ismnu369@student.otago.ac.nz,
{brendon.woodford,sherlock.licorish}@otago.ac.nz

Abstract. Hadoop and Spark are popular open-source Apache projects in the Big Data ecosystem. Due to shortcomings associated with Hadoop MapReduce (Hadoop) Apache Spark had gained prominence in the Big Data environment. However, there is little work aimed at evaluating these two Big Data frameworks to provide understanding for when they could be of most utility for machine learning, for example for when frequently querying large-scale data for input to recommendation systems. To explore the possible best use cases of each platform an experimental analysis between Hadoop and Spark was done and assessed using four criteria in terms of performance, storage, reliability and architecture. Different test environments were created varying memory, cache and volumes of data throughout the experiment, where Impala and Hive were used as query engines on the Hadoop file system against the native Spark query engine. We then conducted analyses along two dimensions. Our outcomes show that Spark performs best with large volumes of data processing compared with other query engines such as Apache Impala and Apache Hive. Findings here suggest that each platform have particular strengths given particular contexts, however, Spark seems to demonstrate most utility overall.

Keywords: Big Data environments · Machine Learning · Apache Impala · Apache Hive

1 Introduction

Data is growing faster than ever before, with recent research done by International Data Corporation (IDC) predicting that by the year 2025 the world will create 180 zettabytes of data annually[1]. This prediction suggests that data growth is much faster than the technological advancement that improves on processing speed. As a solution, parallelizing Big Data involving large clusters will support academia and businesses of all sizes [22]. As an example, recommendation systems are a popular confluence of large-scale data processing and

---

[1] http://www.forbes.com/sites/gilpress/2016/08/05/iot-mid-year-update-from-idc-and-other-research-firms. Retrieved 25 June 2019.

© Springer Nature Switzerland AG 2019
J. Liu and J. Bailey (Eds.): AI 2019, LNAI 11919, pp. 253–264, 2019.
https://doi.org/10.1007/978-3-030-35288-2_21

its application to Data Science (DS), Data Mining (DM) methods and Machine Learning (ML) techniques [17].

To parallelize such Big Data Processing stresses established network programming thus there is a trade-off between determining the appropriate number of computers/node to scale these large data sets whilst reducing the chance of operational execution failure. In extreme cases data node execution does not fail, but reduce its performance and result in system slowness. Increase in the number of nodes can lead to high expense, so a more cost-effective alternative is to write manual programs for each machine which can result in segregated high-level operators leading to improved performance [16]. Another common approach to scaling large data clusters is using Data Flow Engines. As noted by Bu et al. [3], data can be fetched from memory into the CPU where operations are executed, and data is directed from one unit to another. A dataflow can be built using various data sources such as data files or external database tables [8]. Some scalable examples are Pig [11], Hive [29], and Storm [14].

Built on techniques such as Data Flow Engines and Data Nodes for scaling data [8] Apache Hadoop (herein referred to as Hadoop), NoSQL and Apache Spark SQL are considered major platforms for Big Data analytics. However, these technologies have both strengths and weaknesses. Hadoop MapReduce is great at one-pass computation, but incapable of efficient primitives for data and disk storage. Likewise, Big Data technologies have its own restrictions and limitations in processing large volumes of data. Apache Mahout [19] using Hadoop MapReduce can support some common ML tasks but does suffer from slow disk access even though it is an adequate solution for storing and processing data for clustering or document categorization [4]. Apart from that, there are other concerns in Hadoop MapReduce such as performing real-time analysis due to its batch driven nature, which consumes more time in processing data as batches and raises issues in running ad-hoc queries [31] and for online learning [18].

Beating relational databases, NoSQL i.e. non-relational databases, have become popular due to its inbuilt design, scalability, and flexibility. Moreover, its capacity to support nested, semi-structured, and unstructured data is an appealing prospect for ML [18]. Some common NoSQL data stores are MongoDB [7] and Apache HBase [12]. Many NoSQL systems do not support SQL in general; nevertheless, the new emerging query engine such as Impala enables the support of native SQL in a Big Data environment. Impala is the traditional analytics database of Hadoop [21].

Other alternative query engines for Impala would be Apache Hive; data warehousing software which supports querying large distributed data sets on top of Hadoop [29]. Due to the shortcoming of Hadoop Components, Apache Spark (herein referred to as Spark), a data processing framework was introduced for faster data analytics in a distributed computing cluster environment and with the addition of MLlib can efficiently run many ML algorithms [19] sometimes in combination with the Spark SQL query engine [10] which is an alternative to Hadoop Impala and Hive query engines. All the aforementioned technologies have strengths and limitations, thus, research is required for evaluating the boundaries of these Big Data environments for ML, which is the focus of this work. This evaluation has two particular benefits; one, it determines where Hadoop and Spark are of most utility in ascertaining differences in the runtime architecture of each Big Data platform; and two, it explores the possible best uses cases of each platform in terms of resource utilization during task execution (considering: memory, volume of data, query complexity and concurrent query analysis).

The rest of the paper is organized as follows. Related work will be discussed in Sect. 2. Our research setting is then described along with performance measures in Sect. 3. We then present our results, and then detailed discussion in Sects. 4 and 5 respectively. Finally, in Sect. 6 we conclude with a summary of the outcomes, factoring in the threats to validity.

2   Background and Motivation

Hadoop [18] is defined as a framework for distributed processing based on Big Data technologies. This technology comprises four core components: Hadoop MapReduce, Hadoop Utilities, YARN (the resource manager) and a data storage layer known as the Hadoop Distributed File System (HDFS) [25]. More granular Hadoop Utilities also include HBase [12]. Hadoop MapReduce is a programming model which caters for executing programs in parallel with easy scheduling, high fault tolerance and high scalability on commodity clusters. As noted by Zaharia et al. [31], Hadoop MapReduce processes data in two stages, the map and reduce stages. Hadoop is scalable, fault-tolerant, and reliable [25]. It was proven that Hadoop MapReduce is the best fit for Big Data processing, though it returns poor performance for iteration algorithms which numerous ML techniques are based on [32].

Therefore, Zaharia et al. [30] proposed Spark as a streaming engine which is capable of processing large scale data and reduces latency in processing the data. A Spark cluster consists of multiple distributed objects, Resilient Distributed Datasets (RDDs) stored in memory, and it also executes operations in parallel. Spark is considered a substitute for Hadoop MapReduce and is specifically used for data streaming in large scale clusters. Spark's RDD are stored in read only memory which enables this engine to execute operations in parallel. The number of partitions determine the boundary of parallel processes that can be executed [30]. RDD can be created in two ways, by loading a data set from an external source (for example: HDFS), or by running programs in parallel in the driver program that performs the user's main function and executes various parallel operations on a cluster [30]. Depending on which approach is adopted will determine how efficiently fault tolerance can be dealt with. Therefore, Spark does not run operations immediately, but calculates the metadata instead. Spark supports one file system for a specific task and consists of multiple nodes for resource management. For example, if Spark is installed in a Hadoop environment, it needs to enable access for HDFS, whereas, in empty machines it is much easier to start Spark.

Many researchers have examined various techniques for Big Data platform optimization. Examples of data optimization techniques are: adequate resource utilization [20], performance optimization [28] and parallel computation techniques [15].

More specifically, a case study done by Ambrust et al. [1] noted that the main reasons for failure of data flow engines is due to memory management limitations and issues in the networking layer resulting in saturated bandwidth. To address this issue, a custom network module has been built on a low-level Java platform [1].

Other research suggests performing a comparative analysis between Hadoop and Spark to cluster a data set using the k-means algorithm could be useful. Golpani et al. [13] show that the performance of Spark is three times more efficient compared with the Hadoop MapReduce framework. However, there were some fluctuations in the results due to the fact that each initial centroid is chosen randomly, and the value for k must be known in advance. The main issue is the uncertainty of an accurate solution for small iterations. However, with increasing time complexity and iterations, more reliable outputs can be derived [27].

In addition, another study examines a visualization plan as a solution to understand the behavior of the Big Data frameworks [24]. The research is based on a shuffle and caching execution model using two profiling tools. One tool is used to visually correlate the resource utilization for a Big Data framework. Another approach was used to analyze the task execution time behavior. The research outcome shows that Spark is faster than Hadoop MapReduce in every operation such as WordCount (2.5x), k-means (5x), and PageRank (5x) respectively [24].

Apache Impala, (herein referred to as Impala) [21] was built aiming to replace the traditional RDBMS for complex workloads by introducing an analytical Database Management System (DBMS) on top of the Hadoop environment but has its own pros and cons. Impala provides low latency and is able to manage high concurrent workload for data analytics queries on Hadoop [6]. However, Impala shares Hadoop's HDFS resulting in performance loss and the need for increased memory storage when dealing with small files [2]. As an alternative, the Apache Hive (herein referred to as Hive) platform was introduced to process and analyse data stored in Hadoop [29]. Hive can process large volumes of data batch-wise in a distributed storage environment using its own declarative query language called HiveQL which is similar to SQL [29]. Hive is a popular choice for the Big Data industry as evidenced by companies such as Microsoft and Amazon using it [26]. To this end, Impala and Hive are used as query engines on the Hadoop file system in this work, against the native Spark query engine on the Spark platform.

3   Methodology

Compared with previous research where the focus has been on addressing weakness in the platforms' runtime architecture, this work goes one step further than previous studies in analysing the performance of three query engines (Spark, Impala, and Hive) and explores the possible best use cases for both Hadoop and Spark to optimise response times for results of queries which are fed into a recommendation system pipeline. The use case is based on an e-Commerce data set which includes a large volume of customer transactions which occurred throughout a one-year period.

Hence, real world data gives detailed insight into the decision-making process of companies and allows a user to more wisely select a Big Data platform based on specific requirements for application of ML/DS techniques to such Big Data. We answer the following research question:

What are the differences in performance of Hive, Impala, and Spark (for Hadoop and Spark) under various configurations?

3.1   Research Setting

To compare the performance of Hadoop and Spark, laboratory experiments were conducted. The following steps were used in setting up the environment for Hadoop and Spark.

1. Clusters of two shared PCs were connected to a reliable internet connection.
2. Both machines were configured with an Intel Xeon E5-2697 v4 36 core processor running at 3.60 GHz, operating system as Linux CentOS 7, and with 4 GB memory in each machine.
3. A Shared Ethernet connection was used, providing approximately 100 MB/s at the system level.
4. Intel® Distribution for Apache Hadoop* version 3.0.2, Hadoop 2.0.4, Impala 2.6, Spark 2.0, and Hive 2.0 software were installed on the machines.
5. A distributed file system based on HDFDS was created to manage the stored data on disk.
6. Jobs were set manually with a task mapped by the scheduler to all the machines.
7. Hive, Impala, and Spark functions were performed by changing memory, cache and the volume of data according to the process originally proposed by Chang et al. [5].

The following benchmarks were used in analysing the performance of Hive, Impala, and Spark.

1. Using a large-scale version of SSB data, queries were tested across large data sets. SSB data includes e-Commerce details of a retail organization based in Sri Lanka. The e-Commerce site offers a wide range of products (more than 3500), and provides multiple payment options dealing with more than 100 merchants. Out of 13 data sets only five major data sets were used for the experiments. Data used for the experiments were gathered from April 2016 to April 2017. The row counts for each of the database tables are shown in Table 1 below. The following benchmarks were used in analysing the performance of Hive, Impala, and Spark. The 650,107 rows of customer details in

Atg_Customer were used for the first experiment. It was the largest data set of the e-Commerce database used during the experiment.

2. Using an average size data set comprising 8,259 rows (Manufacturer_Details) the performance of Hive, Impala and Spark were evaluated.
3. In a subsequent experiment the concurrency of workload for multiple users were tested.
4. Finally, we analysed the performance of the platforms by changing the memory and cache.

Table 1. The SSB dataset (e-Commerce Dataset 2016–2017).

Table name	No. of rows
Atg_Customer	650,107
Manufacturer_Details	8259
Merchant_Details	1671

Table 2 shows the varied memory and different volume of data sets which were used to conduct the next laboratory experiments. The queries had been designed to simulate the type of common data access tasks required immediately prior to the application of ML algorithms on the resulting answers to the queries.

Table 2. Test environment setup for experiments.

Environment	Memory size	Data set size	Rows	SQL Query	Function
1	2 GB	2 GB	8,259	Query 1	Search function
2	8 GB	8 GB	650,107	Query 2	Comparison condition
3	All	1 MB	1,671	Query 3	Join condition

Each query has been executed three times to avoid practical errors and so an average execution time can be determined. These are defined as follows:

– Q11, Q12, Q13 – Search query on specific period with small number of JOIN conditions and fewer or no GROUP BY conditions. For example, Q11 was:

```
SELECT PRODUCT_ID, P_CATALOG_REF_ID
FROM [PRODUCT_DETAILS] JOIN MANUFACTURER_DETAILS
ON [PRODUCT_DETAILS].MERCHANT_ID = MANUFACTURER_DETAILS.MERCHANT_ID;
```

– Q21, Q22, Q23 – Comparison query with a specific set of Customer/Merchant and date variables. The query includes medium size JOIN conditions with few (one, two, and three) GROUP BY conditions. For example, Q22 was:

```
SELECT ORDER_ID, TOTAL, ORDERSTATUS
FROM FACT_ORDER_ITEM_DETAILS F LEFT JOIN [FACT_ORDER_DETAILS] O
ON O.ORDER_ID = F.ORDER_ID
AND O.ORDERSTATUS LIKE 'COMPLETED'
GROUP BY TOTAL
ORDER BY TOTAL;
```

- Q31, Q32, Q33 – A query that compute a metrics for a specific set of Customer/Merchant and date variables. The query includes large JOIN conditions and many (four, five, and six) GROUP BY conditions.

4 Results

4.1 Large Data Set Analysis

Table 3 shows the comparative performance of Impala, Spark, and Hive for three standard queries against the 650,107 rows of data.

Table 3. Query performance for large data set (fastest execution time for each query is highlighted in bold).

Query	Query execution time (Seconds)		
	Impala 2.6	Spark 2.0	Hive 2.0
Q11	5.6	**4.8**	10.5
Q12	5.0	**3.8**	9.1
Q13	5.6	**3.3**	9.3
Q21	**8.0**	11.8	10.0
Q22	**6.2**	11.0	9.3
Q23	**6.0**	10.6	9.3
Q31	97.3	**64.9**	137.6
Q32	49.1	**30.3**	131.9
Q33	26.8	**19.7**	63.1
Average	23.29 ± 31.5	17.80 ± 19.7	43.34 ± 63.1

Not every Big Data technology performs well for every query. The experiment shows Spark and Impala are comparatively faster than Hive. All the queries tested on the large data set prove that there is no major execution time variation among Impala and Spark. However, there is performance difference with SQL query complexity. For example, when the number of SQL join conditions increases, there is also an increase in query processing time. Also, queries requesting a minimal amount of data filters where there are few WHERE clauses recorded less processing time. Performance increased by more than two times when query selectivity increased for both Spark and Impala. However, Hive did not react much to query selectivity.

4.2   Small Data Set Analysis

Table 4 shows the relative performance of Impala, Spark SQL, and Hive for three standard queries against the 1671 rows of the smallest data set (Merchant_Details). For a small volume of data with the average complexity of SQL queries, our experiments show that both Spark and Impala executed queries with better performance than Hive during data processing. Hive performs less favorably compared with Impala and Spark in both test environments despite the volume of data. Therefore, all three options of query engines in Hadoop are suitable for Big Data processing regardless of the environment and number of variables or columns selected. Hadoop is suitable for Big Data processing regardless of the environment and number of variables or columns selected.

Table 4. Query performance for small data set (fastest execution time for each query is highlighted in bold).

Query	Query execution time (Seconds)		
	Impala 2.6	Spark 2.0	Hive 2.0
Q11	**0.27**	0.48	2.07
Q12	**0.30**	0.48	2.07
Q13	**0.64**	0.70	2.12
Q21	1.64	**1.19**	3.28
Q22	2.57	**1.64**	8.09
Q23	2.13	**1.28**	2.28
Q31	**3.45**	5.58	6.94
Q32	**4.39**	5.38	7.62
Q33	4.39	**2.05**	2.56
Average	2.20 ± 1.58	2.09 ± 2.05	4.11 ± 2.55

4.3   Concurrent Query Analysis

The following experiment was conducted with 13 queries with 10 concurrent users. The smallest data set Merchant_Details (1671 rows) was used considering the time factor to analyze the concurrency of the data flow engines. Figure 1 shows that Hive, Spark and Impala performed consistently with concurrent queries. No query failures resulted for the tested 13 concurrent queries. Failures may result due to multiple reasons such as a permission issue in accessing the HDFS file directory or out of memory exceptions in Spark/Hive server logs [9].

While all query engines performed well in processing small scale data, Impala maintained a better average performance than Spark and Hive in a concurrent workload environment (refer to Fig. 1). In Test Environment-1 the results show

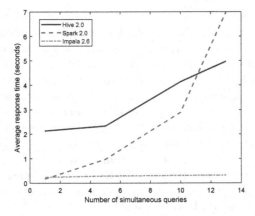

Fig. 1. Concurrent query performance – number of simultaneous queries vs average response time (in Seconds).

that Hive can perform even with the physical memory constraints in the experimental setup, whereas Impala and Spark crashed in the same environment due to the physical memory constraints of 2 GB. Results from Test Environment-2 show that Impala performance is more superior with medium memory capacity.

Finally, in Test Environment-3 it was observed that Spark outperforms Impala and Hive in terms of speed with a fixed memory utility.

Table 5 presents results of the performance of the Big-Data frameworks according to memory size of the computer. It indicates that Hive can run even in constrained memory environment whereas Impala performs consistently in average memory (8 GB) conditions. Given more memory Spark can outperform both Impala and Hive. For all three to perform without any crash, 4 GB (or more) of memory would be sufficient.

Table 5. Performance of the Big-Data frameworks based on memory size.

Memory	Performance
2 GB	Hive can operate but Spark & Impala crashes
8 GB	Impala performs better than Spark & Hive
10 GB	Spark performs better than Impala & Hive

5 Discussion

What are the differences in performance of Hive, Impala, and Spark (for Hadoop and Spark) under various configurations?

Experimental results revealed that all three query engines, Spark, Impala and Hive maintained consistent performance in concurrent query processing environments. However, Impala maintained a better average performance than the other two platforms in small-scale workload which is consistent with the work reported previously [6]. In terms of memory variation, Hive was outstanding when there was lack of memory, while the other platforms crashed in the same environment. In an average memory capacity, Impala performed better than the rest of the platforms, however Spark was fastest in a high memory environment.

In terms of configuration, Hadoop MapReduce is preferred and recommended for varying amounts of data to be processed in batches as per the research done by others [23]; whereas Spark is new to the Big Data environment and it is widely used for complex data analytics purposes [22]. Unlike Hadoop MapReduce, Spark performs well when querying data is in memory and experiments in this study shows that Spark outperforms Hadoop MapReduce on complex queries with similar results with others [24]. Moreover, MapReduce does not support distributed file systems on its own; it clearly depends on Hadoop HDFS. That said, each query-processing engine has its own advantages. For instance, Spark is faster than Hadoop MapReduce for generic queries due to increasing memory consumption. However, Spark is not the best fit for every application because of its asynchronous fine-grained updates. In addition, with limited memory space along with the need for speed, Hadoop MapReduce seems to be the better choice in practice. When there are no restrictions in the consumption of memory and applicability of complex algorithms, Spark demonstrates good performance for any volume of data.

During the process of our experiments, it was identified that Spark was not the easiest tool to work with because of its complex nature in deployment and configuration for custom use cases as presented in the experiments. Therefore, more usability and flexibility aspects should be developed in future work that would help the DS/ML community. Finally, as Hive did not perform well compared with Impala and Spark, more research should be conducted into increasing the performance of Hive queries through further optimizing Hive's current or its more recent Tez execution engine [26].

These findings have implication for a ML pipeline that depends on these tools, and thus practitioners and researchers should take our findings into consideration when planning for such performance outcomes.

6   Conclusion

The objective of this research was to evaluate Big Data environments to assess the utility of each platform for ML applications. Experiments were executed using four use cases as follows: (1) Variation in the volume of data, (2) Query Complexity, (3) Query Parallelization, and (4) Memory Variation. The experiments revealed that Spark and Impala were comparatively faster than Hive regardless of the volume of data. In addition, SQL query complexity directly affected the performance of all the platforms, consuming more processing time with increasing query complexity. In summary, the research outcomes show that Hadoop MapReduce is a good option for day to day research and DS experiments, input to ML applications, and for parallel job processing. It is mainly due to its architecture and the way it performs. Hadoop stores data on disk while Spark stores data in its memory. Moreover, Spark uses resilient distributed data sets to achieve fault tolerance and Hadoop uses data replication mechanisms. However, Spark can run on top of HDFS with existing Hadoop components.

Therefore, based on the operation and resources, these technologies may be wisely used to cater for the requirements and needs of businesses. Moreover, industry experts and researchers can further investigate the trade-offs in both Hadoop MapReduce and Spark in terms of cost models and usability. It is highly recommended that further research commit towards investigating capacity planning using cloud technology.

References

1. Armbrust, M., et al.: Scaling spark in the real world: performance and usability. Proc. VLDB Endow. **8**(12), 1840–1843 (2015)
2. Bende, S., Shedge, R.: Dealing with small files problem in hadoop distributed file system. Procedia Comput. Sci. **79**, 1001–1012 (2016). Proceedings International Conference on Communication, Computing and Virtualization (ICCCV) 2016
3. Bu, Y., Borkar, V., Jia, J., Carey, M.J., Condie, T.: Pregelix: Big(Ger) graph analytics on a dataflow engine. Proc. VLDB Endow. **8**(2), 161–172 (2014)
4. Cai, Z., Gao, Z.J., Luo, S., Perez, L.L., Vagena, Z., Jermaine, C.: A comparison of platforms for implementing and running very large scale machine learning algorithms. In: Proceedings 2014 ACM SIGMOD International Conference on Management of Data, SIGMOD'14, pp. 1371–1382. ACM, New York (2014)
5. Chang, B.R., Tsai, H., Wang, Y., Huang, C.: Resilient distributed computing platforms for big data analysis using Spark and Hadoop. In: Proceedings 2016 International Conference on Applied System Innovation (ICASI), pp. 1–4, May 2016
6. Chen, M., Mao, S., Liu, Y.: Big data: a survey. Mob. Netw. Appl. **19**(2), 171–209 (2014)
7. Chodorow, K., Dirolf, M.: MongoDB - The Definitive Guide: Powerful and Scalable Data Storage. O'Reilly, Sebastopol (2010)
8. Dias, J., Ogasawara, E., de Oliveira, D., Porto, F., Valduriez, P., Mattoso, M.: Algebraic dataflows for big data analysis. In: Proceedings 2013 IEEE International Conference on Big Data, pp. 150–155. IEEE Press, October 2013
9. Floratou, A., Minhas, U.F., Özcan, F.: SQL-on-Hadoop: full circle back to shared-nothing database architectures. Proc. VLDB Endow. **7**(12), 1295–1306 (2014)
10. Frampton, M.: Mastering Apache Spark, 1st edn. Packt Publishing, Birmingham (2015)
11. Fuad, A., Erwin, A., Ipung, H.P.: Processing performance on apache pig, apache hive and MySQL cluster. In: Proceedings International Conference on Information, Communication Technology and System (ICTS) 2014, pp. 297–302. IEEE Press, September 2014
12. George, L.: Hbase: The Definitive Guide, 1st edn. O'Reilly Media Inc., Sebastopol (2011)
13. Gopalani, S., Arora, R.: Article: comparing apache spark and map reduce with performance analysis using K-Means. Int. J. Comput. Appl. **113**(1), 8–11 (2015)
14. Jain, A.: Mastering Apache Storm, 1st edn. Packt Publishing, Birmingham (2017)

15. Kalavri, V.: Performance optimization techniques and tools for data-intensive computation platforms: an overview of performance limitations in big data systems and proposed optimizations (2014). qC 20140605
16. Khan, N., et al.: Big data: survey, technologies, opportunities, and challenges. Sci. World J. **2014**, 1–18 (2014)
17. Kupisz, B., Unold, O.: Collaborative filtering recommendation algorithm based on Hadoop and Spark. In: Proceedings 2015 IEEE International Conference on Industrial Technology (ICIT), pp. 1510–1514. IEEE Press, March 2015
18. Landset, S., Khoshgoftaar, T.M., Richter, A.N., Hasanin, T.: A survey of open source tools for machine learning with big data in the Hadoop ecosystem. J. Big Data **2**(1), 24 (2015)
19. L'Heureux, A., Grolinger, K., Elyamany, H.F., Capretz, M.A.M.: Machine learning with big data: challenges and approaches. IEEE Access **5**, 7776–7797 (2017)
20. Ousterhout, K., Rasti, R., Ratnasamy, S., Shenker, S., Chun, B.G.: Making sense of performance in data analytics frameworks. In: Proceedings 12th USENIX Conference on Networked Systems Design and Implementation, NSDI'15, pp. 293–307. USENIX Association, Berkeley, CA, USA (2015)
21. Russell, J.: Getting Started with Impala, 1st edn. O'Reilly Media Inc., Sebastopol (2014)
22. Salloum, S., Dautov, R., Chen, X., Peng, P.X., Huang, J.Z.: Big data analytics on Apache Spark. Int. J. Data Sci. Anal. **1**(3), 145–164 (2016)
23. Shahrivari, S.: Beyond batch processing: towards real-time and streaming big data. CoRR abs/1403.3375 (2014). http://arxiv.org/abs/1403.3375
24. Shi, J., et al.: Clash of the titans: MapReduce vs. spark for large scale data analytics. Proc. VLDB Endow. **8**(13), 2110–2121 (2015)
25. Shvachko, K., Kuang, H., Radia, S., Chansler, R.: The Hadoop distributed file system. In: Proceedings 2010 IEEE 26th Symposium on Mass Storage Systems and Technologies (MSST), MSST'10, pp. 1–10. IEEE Computer Society (2010)
26. Singh, R., Kaur, P.J.: Analyzing performance of Apache Tez and MapReduce with hadoop multinode cluster on Amazon cloud. J. Big Data **3**(1), 19 (2016)
27. Su, T., Dy, J.: A deterministic method for initializing K-means clustering. In: Proceedings 16th IEEE International Conference on Tools with Artificial Intelligence, pp. 784–786. IEEE Press, November 2004
28. Taneja, R., Krishnamurthy, R., Liu, G.: Optimization of machine learning on Apache Spark. In: Proceedings 2016 International Conference on Parallel and Distributed Processing Techniques and Applications, pp. 163–167. CSREA Press (2016)
29. Thusoo, A., et al.: Hive - a warehousing solution over a map-reduce framework. Proc. VLDB Endow. **2**, 1626–1629 (2009)
30. Zaharia, M., et al.: Resilient distributed datasets: a fault-tolerant abstraction for in-memory cluster computing. In: Proceedings 9th USENIX Conference on Networked Systems Design and Implementation, NSDI'12, p. 2. USENIX Association, Berkeley, CA, USA (2012)
31. Zaharia, M., Chowdhury, M., Franklin, M.J., Shenker, S., Stoica, I.: Spark: cluster computing with working sets. In: Proceedings 2nd USENIX Conference on Hot Topics in Cloud Computing, HotCloud'10, p. 10. USENIX Association, Berkeley, CA, USA (2010)
32. Zhang, Y., Gao, Q., Gao, L., Wang, C.: iMapReduce: a distributed computing framework for iterative computation. J. Grid Comput. **10**(1), 47–68 (2012)

Sequence-to-Sequence Imputation
of Missing Sensor Data

Joel Janek Dabrowski[1(✉)] and Ashfaqur Rahman[2]

[1] Data61, CSIRO, Brisbane, Australia
Joel.Dabrowski@data61.csiro.au
[2] Data61, CSIRO, Hobart, Australia
Ashfaqur.Rahman@data61.csiro.au

Abstract. Although the sequence-to-sequence (encoder-decoder) model is considered the state-of-the-art in deep learning sequence models, there is little research into using this model for recovering missing sensor data. The key challenge is that the missing sensor data problem typically comprises *three* sequences (a sequence of observed samples, followed by a sequence of missing samples, followed by another sequence of observed samples) whereas, the sequence-to-sequence model only considers *two* sequences (an input sequence and an output sequence). We address this problem by formulating a sequence-to-sequence in a novel way. A forward RNN encodes the data observed before the missing sequence and a backward RNN encodes the data observed after the missing sequence. A decoder decodes the two encoders in a novel way to predict the missing data. We demonstrate that this model produces the lowest errors in 12% more cases than the current state-of-the-art.

Keywords: Imputation · Interpolation · LSTM · Encoder-decoder model · Sequence-to-sequence model

1 Introduction and Related Work

From smart cities [1] to personalised body sensor networks [9], sensor data is becoming ubiquitous. This has been fuelled by the rise of the internet of things (IOT), smart sensor networks, and low-cost sensors. Such technologies are however imperfect and their failure may result in *missing data*. Sensors may fail due to hardware or software failure. Communication networks can break down due to low signal level, network congestion, packet collision, limited memory capacity, or communication node failures [14]. Even if sensors and communications prevail, missing data may result from scheduled outages such as maintenance and upgrade routines.

When a data-driven model (such as a machine learning model) uses sensor data for prediction, missing data introduces various challenges in parameterising or training the model. This is especially problematic when the temporal structure of the data is important to the model. To address this problem, various

© Springer Nature Switzerland AG 2019
J. Liu and J. Bailey (Eds.): AI 2019, LNAI 11919, pp. 265–276, 2019.
https://doi.org/10.1007/978-3-030-35288-2_22

methods for imputing or interpolating the missing data have been proposed in the literature.

The Recurrent Neural Network (RNN) has been shown to perform well for missing data recovery [4,5,10,15]. However, there is little research into using the sequence-to-sequence (encoder-decoder) model [12], despite it being considered as a state-of-the-art model in deep learning sequence modelling. The key challenge in applying this model to missing data is that it is designed to use a *single* input sequence to predict some output sequence. However, the missing data problem can be considered to have *two* input sequences that are separated by the missing data. That is, relative to the missing data, the model must take into account data that is observed before and after the missing data sequence.

We propose a novel sequence-to-sequence model that incorporates the data before and after a missing data sequence to predict the missing values of that sequence. For this, two encoders are used: one propagating in the positive time-direction, and one propagating in the negative-time direction. These two encoders feed into a decoder that naturally combines the encoded forward and backward encoders to provide an accurate prediction of the missing data sequence. A key feature of the sequence-to-sequence model is that it can handle arbitrary length input and output sequences. Our key contributions are:

1. The proposed decoder architecture is novel in the way that it merges information from two encoders.
2. We introduce a novel approach to scaling a forward and backward RNN within the decoder according to their proximity to observed data.
3. We demonstrate results which show that our model outperforms the current state-of-the-art methods on several datasets.

The proposed model is particularly applicable in problems where there is no neighbouring data available for imputing across variables at each sequence step. The recovery of the missing data must be determined from temporal information alone. These include univariate problems or multivariate problems where sequences of data are missing across *all* measured variables at the same time. This typically occurs when there is a central system failure, such as the failure of a multi-parameter sensor, the failure of a central communications node in a star-network, or a scheduled outage across a system.

2 Related Work

Various models such as MICE [3] and ST-MVL [13] have been proposed for missing data recovery. We however focus on RNNs, as these are considered to be the state-of-the-art in many missing data recovery applications. Various forms of the RNN have been tested for data imputation. Che et al. [5] use the Gated Recurrent Unit with trainable decays (GRU-D) model for recovering missing data. The decay rates exponentially reduce importance of predictions that are distant from observations. The model however does not consider samples that occur after the missing data sequence.

The M-RNN [15] uses a bidirectional neural network for imputation. The model is a multi-directional RNN that considers temporal information as well as information across sensors to recover missing data. This model thus relies on a subset of data to be available at any time.

The RITS and BRITS [4] model use a RNN to perform one-step ahead forecasting and modelling over sequences. Compared with M-RNN, it trains output nodes with missing data as part of the network. Both this and a bidirectional RNN provide a means learn from data that lies before and after the missing data sequence. Additionally, they use trainable decays similar to the GRU-D. However, like the M-RNN, the RITS and BRITS models perform imputation by considering temporal information as well as information across sensors. Cao et el. [4] do however propose the RITS-I and BRITS-I models as reduced versions of RITS and BRITS which exclude the mechanism used to perform predictions across sensors. These reduced models focus on temporal predictions and are thus used for comparison in this study.

The Iterative Imputing Model (IIM) [17] uses a forward and backward RNN to encode information before and after the missing data. These RNNs could be considered to perform the task of the encoder in the sequence-to-sequence model. However, to predict the missing data, a predict-update loop (similar to the EM algorithm) is used iteratively impute each missing sample. This iterative process is computationally expensive and does not correspond with a decoder in the sequence-to-sequence model.

The SSIM model [16] is the first model to use the sequence-to-sequence approach for recovering missing data. To address the problem of including observations before and after the missing data, SSIM uses a forward and backward RNN together with a variable-length sliding window. A drawback of the model is that it has to "learn" that there is a difference between the observations before and after the missing data [16].

Compared with GRU-D, BRITS, and M-RNN, our model uses the sequence-to-sequence approach, which is the state-of-the-art in applications such as natural language processing. Furthermore, we consider the problem where there is a complete set of data across all sensors or variables. The result is that data recovery is performed on temporal information alone. Compared with IIM, our model uses an arbitrary length decoder that does not require an iterative updating approach. Compared with SSIM, our model naturally stitches the observations before and after the missing data and is thus not required to learn that there is a difference between them. Furthermore, it does not require a variable sliding window to operate.

3   Model

3.1   Architecture

A sequence-to-sequence (encoder-decoder) model is proposed to recover missing time series data. As illustrated Fig. 1, the network comprises a forward encoder, a backward encoder, and a form of bidirectional decoder. The network can be

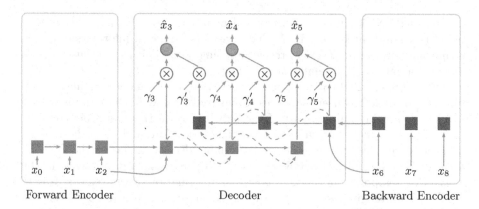

Fig. 1. Illustration of proposed sequence-to-sequence model for missing sensor data imputation. Square nodes denote LSTM cells and circular nodes denote linear output neurons. The circular nodes with the × operator denote element-wise multiplication with the scaling factors γ_t and γ_t'. Observations are provided for x_0, x_1, x_2 and x_6, x_7, x_8. The values for x_3, x_4, x_5 are missing. The forward encoder encodes x_0, x_1, x_2 and the backward encoder encodes x_6, x_7, x_8. The decoder is a bidirectional LSTM that predicts $\hat{x}_3, \hat{x}_4, \hat{x}_5$. Each forward and backward LSTM cell in the decoder predicts the missing data and this prediction is input to the next RNN cell in the sequence as illustrated by the dashed arrows. The LSTMs in the decoder thus perform one-step-ahead forecasting.

viewed as containing two traditional sequence-to-sequence models [12], one in the forward direction, and one in the backward direction. The outputs of the forward and backward RNN cells in the decoder are scaled and merged together in a final output layer in the form of a Multilayered Perceptron (MLP).

The forward and backward decoder RNNs operate by performing one-step-ahead predictions. The prediction of the previous RNN cell is fed to the input of the current cell as illustrated by the dashed arrows in Fig. 1. In a regression problem, the prediction is performed using a MLP with a linear output layer and inputs given by the outputs of the corresponding RNN cell. The forward encoder predictions are denoted by $\hat{x}_t^{\mathrm{FW}}$ and the backward encoder predictions are denoted by $\hat{x}_t^{\mathrm{BW}}$.

The additional outputs at the RNN level are required as all the final output layer's outputs are not available at each sequence step. For example, as illustrated in Fig. 1, computing $\hat{x}_4$ requires the output of the second forward RNN cell and the second backward RNN cell. If the final output layer outputs were fed to the next cell, $\hat{x}_3$ would be fed to the input of the forward RNN at index 4. However, $\hat{x}_3$ also requires the output of the third backward RNN cell, which is not available as the backward RNN has only been processed up to its second cell. To address this dilemma, the forward RNNs and the backward RNNs are first processed over the entire sequence with their local outputs. The results are then passed to the final output layer.

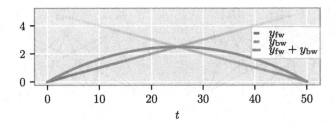

Fig. 2. An illustration demonstrating the principle of the scaling factor approach using two arbitrary linear functions. The variable y_{fw} decays with increasing t (illustrated with a vanishing curve), whereas y_{fw} decays with decreasing t. The prediction is the weighted combination of y_{fw} and y_{bw}. In the proposed model, y_{bw} is the output of the forward decoder RNN, y_{bw} is the output of the backward decoder RNN, and the summation operation in $y_{fw} + y_{bw}$ is a nonlinear operation performed by the output layer of the model.

3.2 Scaling Factors

Before the outputs of the forward and backward decoder RNNs are merged together in the final output MLP, the RNN outputs are scaled with a scaling factor γ_t. In our novel approach, the scaling factor decays as predictions progress further from observed data. The forward RNN outputs in the decoder are scaled according to the linear function

$$\gamma_t = 1 - \frac{t}{T} \tag{1}$$

where T is the length of the missing data sequence and $t = \{1, \ldots, T\}$ is the index of the missing data sequence samples. The backward RNN outputs in the decoder are scaled according to

$$\gamma'_t = 1 - \gamma_t \tag{2}$$

Thus, at time $t = 1$, the forward RNN output is scaled by a factor of $\gamma_1 = 1$. This factor decays to zero as t increases. The opposite is true for the backward RNN, where it is scaled by a factor of $\gamma'_T = 1$ at time $t = T$. This factor decays to zero as t decreases. The result is that the forward decoder RNN is emphasised near the observations associated with the forward encoder and the backward decoder RNN is emphasised near the observations associated with the backward encoder. The principle of this process is illustrated in an example using linear functions in Fig. 2.

Scaling factors have been previously used in RNNs in [5] and [15]. These factors however decay exponentially and are integrated into the RNN network where they can be learned. In our approach, the scaling factors can be viewed as form of a "forced" attention mechanism that favours the RNN outputs that are nearest the observed data. Furthermore, the linear nature of the proposed scaling factors ensures a balanced weighting between the RNNs across the sequence such that $\gamma_t + \gamma'_t = 1 \ \forall t$.

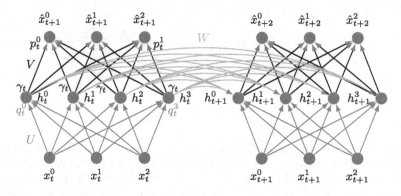

Fig. 3. An illustration of a forward RNN and the output layer in the decoder for the discussion on backpropagation with the scaling factor.

3.3 Backpropagation with Scaling Factors

As the scaling factor scales the predictions, it also scales the derivatives used in backpropagation. This is due to γ_t being a fixed constant. For example, consider the forward decoder RNN (in the form of an Elman network for illustrative purposes) with the output layer as illustrated in Fig. 3. The scaling factor γ_t is applied to each output h_t^j. The variable p_t^k is linear combination of inputs at output neuron k, and q_t^j is the linear combination of inputs at hidden neuron j. The weight matrices U, W, and V are associated with the input-to-hidden, hidden-to-hidden, and hidden-to-output connections respectively.

Following the backpropagation derivation, the derivative of the cost with respect to the weight u_{ij} connecting the ith input to the jth RNN hidden node is given by

$$\frac{\partial \mathcal{L}}{\partial u_{ij}} = \left(\underbrace{\sum_{k=1}^{n_o} \frac{\partial \mathcal{L}}{\partial p_t^k} \frac{\partial p_t^k}{\partial h_t^j}}_{\text{hidden to output}} + \underbrace{\sum_{k=1}^{n_h} \frac{\partial \mathcal{L}}{\partial q_{t+1}^k} \frac{\partial q_{t+1}^k}{\partial h_t^j}}_{\text{hidden to hidden}} \right) \underbrace{\frac{\partial h_t^j}{\partial q_t^j} \frac{\partial q_t^j}{\partial u^{ij}}}_{\text{input to hidden}}.$$

where n_o is the number of output units and n_h is the number of hidden units. The scaling factor affects the link between the hidden layer outputs h_t^j and the output layer linear combination p_t^k. This corresponds to the second factor in the first term. The derivative of this term is computed as

$$\frac{\partial p_t^k}{\partial h_t^j} = \frac{\partial}{\partial h_t^j} \sum_j v_{jk}(\gamma_t h_t^j) + b_{vk}$$

$$= \gamma_t v_{jk}$$

where b_{vk} is a bias. The scaling factor thus affects the derivatives passed back from the outputs to the hidden layers. The result is that, similar to the scaling of the predictions, the backpropagated errors are scaled to emphasise the RNN cells that are near the corresponding encoders. The scaling is thus incorporated into the learning process.

3.4   Output Layer

The scaled forward and backward decoder RNN outputs are passed to a MLP which predicts the missing data. The prediction provided by this output layer at time t is denoted by $\hat{x}_t$. With linear outputs producing the predictions $\hat{x}_t$, $\hat{x}_t^{\mathrm{FW}}$, and $\hat{x}_t^{\mathrm{BW}}$, the cost function is given by

$$\mathrm{loss} = \frac{1}{T} \sum_t \left(\mathscr{L}(x_t, \hat{x}_t) + \mathscr{L}(x_t, \hat{x}_t^{\mathrm{FW}}) + \mathscr{L}(x_t, \hat{x}_t^{\mathrm{BW}}) \right) \tag{3}$$

where x_t is the ground truth value for the missing sample at time t and $\mathscr{L}()$ is the mean squared error loss function (for the regression case).

4   Experiments

Several freely-available datasets are used to evaluate and compare the proposed model. The PM2.5 air quality dataset (from 2014–2015) is used as it is become a benchmark used in several previous studies such as [4,13], and [17]. Note that, imputations are made across time *and* across sensors in these studies. However, in the current study, imputations are made across time only. In addition to this dataset, the Metro Interstate Traffic Volume dataset, the Birmingham Parking dataset [11], and the Beijing PM2.5 Air Quality dataset (from 2010–2014) [8] are used. These datasets are freely available from the UCI Machine Learning Repository[1].

For the PM2.5 dataset, the PM2.5 data for sensor 001001 is used. In Traffic dataset, Temperature and traffic volume are used. Each parking area provides a unique variable in the Parking dataset. Finally, the Dew point, temperature, and pressure variables are used in the AirQuality dataset.

The Mean Absolute Error (MAE) and the Mean Relative Error (MRE) are used as performance metrics. These are given by [4,13,17].

$$\mathrm{MAE} = \frac{1}{N} \sum_i^N |x_{t_i} - \hat{x}_{t_i}|, \qquad \mathrm{MRE} = \frac{\sum_i^N |x_{t_i} - \hat{x}_{t_i}|}{\sum_i^N |x_{t_i}|}$$

where N is the total number of observations.

The proposed model results are compared with results from the RITS-I [4], BRITS-I [4], and the sequence-to-sequence [12] models. In all models, 64 hidden units are used in the Long-Short Term Memory (LSTM) [6] RNN. A linear layer

---

[1] https://archive.ics.uci.edu/ml/index.php.

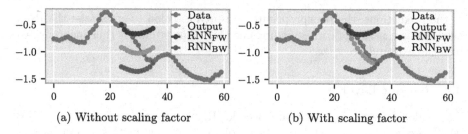

(a) Without scaling factor   (b) With scaling factor

Fig. 4. Demonstration of the scaling factor operation on a Traffic dataset sample. The scaling factor emphasises the forward decoder RNN at the beginning of the prediction and it emphasises the backward decoder RNN at the end of the prediction. The result is a more accurate prediction.

is used in the final output layer. All models are trained using the standard back-propagation approach to minimise (3) with the Adam optimisation algorithm [7]. Early stopping is used to avoid overfitting in the datasets.

The dataset is split into a test and training set such that the last 80% of the dataset is used as a test set. Training and test samples are extracted using a sliding window that is slid across the datasets. Each extracted window is split into a sequence of missing values, a sequence of observed values preceding the missing values, and a sequence of observed values following the missing values. The models are implemented in PyTorch and trained on Dual Xeon 14-core E5-2690 v4 Compute Nodes.

5   Results and Discussion

To demonstrate the scaling factor, a prediction from a Traffic dataset sample is presented. The predictions of the forward decoder RNN, the backward decoder RNN, and the model output are plotted in Fig. 4. The forward and backward RNNs produce significantly differing predictions. If the scaling factor is excluded from the model, the prediction is similar to the average of the forward and backward sequences. As both of these predictions deviate from the ground truth, this final prediction is inaccurate. By including the scaling into the model, the prediction is shifted towards the observed data points, providing a more accurate result.

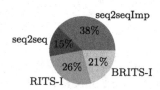

Fig. 5. Pie chart indicating the share over which models produce optimal results.

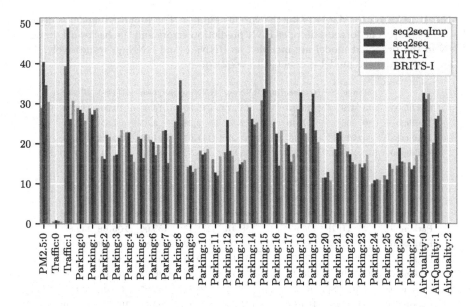

Fig. 6. MRE% results. See Table 1 for detailed MAE results. (The AirQuality results are not visible due to their scale. Refer to Table 1).

Table 1 lists the MAEs and Fig. 6 plots the MREs for the set of models and datasets. The Traffic dataset label indexes index the temperature and traffic volume variables in the dataset. The Parking dataset label indexes index the various parking areas. Finally, the AirQuality dataset label indexes index the dew point, temperature, and pressure variables. For reference, the dataset ranges are included in Table 1. In figures and tables, the proposed model is denoted by seq2seqImp and the sequence-to-sequence model is denoted by seq2seq.

The share of optimal MAEs is presented as a pie chart in Fig. 5. Overall, the proposed model has the highest share with 38% of the lowest MAE results and is 12% higher than the other models. The sequence-to-sequence has the smallest share with 15% lowest errors. This is expected as the model is only provided with data prior to the missing data sequence. The other models are provided with data before and after the missing data sequence.

In the PM2.5 and AirQuality datasets, the proposed model produces significantly lower errors than the other models. For example, considering the proposed model produces MAEs that are a third lower than the competing models. The RITS-I model has the majority of its lowest errors in the Parking dataset. The model is thus well suited to this dataset.

To provide an aggregated representation of the results, Borda counts are used to rank the models through voting. A Borda count ranks a set of N models with integers $(1, \ldots, N)$ such that the model with the highest error is assigned

Table 1. MAE on the datasets for the various models. The proposed model is dented by seq2seqImp. The forward decoder RNN prediction errors and the backward decoder RNN in the proposed model are included as RNN_{FW} and RNN_{BW} respectively. The sequence-to-sequence model is denoted by seq2seq.

	Range	seq2seqImp	RNN_{FW}	RNN_{BW}	seq2seq	RITS-I	BRITS-I
PM2.5:0	[3, 429]	**11.13**	16.27	15.50	16.95	15.50	13.92
Traffic:0	[0, 308]	**1.45**	2.32	2.28	2.35	1.85	1.51
Traffic:1	[0, 7280]	832.33	1027.22	1111.64	1021.09	**621.72**	682.48
Parking:0	[20, 492]	55.82	65.82	66.52	51.25	54.54	**49.70**
Parking:1	[0, 320]	36.45	39.06	42.87	**31.54**	33.71	33.95
Parking:2	[68, 821]	106.73	143.12	127.77	**106.05**	143.84	139.90
Parking:3	[39, 402]	**56.68**	65.11	61.18	58.41	72.29	78.57
Parking:4	[0, 1013]	146.85	163.61	188.61	146.69	110.33	**99.68**
Parking:5	[25, 1197]	136.90	158.31	211.23	133.06	**105.68**	142.88
Parking:6	[15, 612]	53.61	59.70	78.22	50.89	**43.56**	50.70
Parking:7	[30, 470]	50.17	61.18	80.78	54.91	**38.96**	41.62
Parking:8	[2, 220]	**38.77**	51.53	42.93	46.94	54.85	39.51
Parking:9	[170, 678]	62.27	75.78	80.01	65.05	**57.03**	59.27
Parking:10	[55, 845]	**101.60**	124.23	141.86	102.11	103.75	103.80
Parking:11	[156, 723]	74.22	88.79	104.37	61.45	**59.43**	74.16
Parking:12	[53, 503]	62.62	72.78	95.61	75.66	56.69	**52.46**
Parking:13	[155, 413]	**36.69**	42.93	45.09	41.38	43.56	44.47
Parking:14	[4, 246]	30.60	30.41	38.44	27.21	**26.46**	27.70
Parking:15	[46, 593]	**82.45**	92.53	120.29	106.17	104.31	96.41
Parking:16	[48, 689]	73.78	84.67	116.80	73.22	**52.34**	60.43
Parking:17	[77, 2811]	307.67	361.59	451.15	299.45	**236.23**	268.42
Parking:18	[1, 847]	63.88	79.55	84.51	77.57	60.53	**56.34**
Parking:19	[1, 696]	57.90	73.52	79.15	71.45	54.61	**47.50**
Parking:20	[452, 1578]	134.03	166.74	170.08	135.78	151.08	**127.09**
Parking:21	[51, 1534]	**113.36**	153.19	145.35	138.09	142.10	123.52
Parking:22	[524, 3949]	432.00	520.62	576.16	401.78	367.53	**358.83**
Parking:23	[472, 3429]	317.78	462.98	533.55	**313.17**	349.44	362.69
Parking:24	[331, 1444]	**98.10**	134.56	155.27	110.25	113.20	106.14
Parking:25	[224, 1023]	87.47	105.46	109.22	**80.14**	109.43	100.09
Parking:26	[390, 1911]	**142.83**	196.90	193.64	188.51	155.96	152.47
Parking:27	[248, 1561]	155.64	211.38	228.86	**145.20**	158.50	170.15
AirQuality:0	[−33, 28]	**1.52**	2.20	2.18	2.28	2.13	2.19
AirQuality:1	[−19, 41]	**1.32**	1.78	1.83	1.77	1.78	2.00
AirQuality:2	[991, 1046]	**0.64**	1.22	1.19	1.30	1.25	1.09

a value of 1 and the model with the lowest error is assigned a value of N. The sum of Borda counts for the models over all datasets are presented in Table 2. The results show that the proposed model is voted as the highest ranked model.

Table 2. Sum of Borda counts of the models over the datasets. A higher value indicates more points in the voting score. The forward decoder RNN and backward decoder RNN in the proposed model are included as RNN_{FW} and RNN_{BW} respectively.

	seq2seqImp	RNN_{FW}	RNN_{BW}	seq2seq	RITS-I	BRITS-I
MAE	**157**	78	58	131	141	149
MRE	**157**	74	56	138	144	145

6   Conclusion

We propose a novel sequence-to-sequence model for recovering missing sensor data. Our decoder model merges two encoders that summarise the information of data before and after a missing data sequence. This is performed with a forward and backward RNN within the decoder. The decoder RNNs are merged together with a novel overarching output layer that performs scaling of the RNN cell outputs based on their proximity to observed data.

The proposed model is demonstrated on several time series datasets. It is shown that the proposed model produces the lowest errors in 12% more cases than three other state-of-the-art models and is ranked as the best model according to the Borda count.

In future work, it is expected that significant improvement in the results could be achieved by using the attention mechanism [2] between the encoders and the decoder. Furthermore, the scaling mechanism could possibly be improved by parameterising it within the model such that it can be learned. This could be achieved by using a softmax layer such as used in the attention mechanism.

Acknowledgments. The authors thank YiFan Zhang from CSIRO for the discussions around the topic of this study.

References

1. Arasteh, H., et al.: IoT-based smart cities: a survey. In: 2016 IEEE 16th International Conference on Environment and Electrical Engineering (EEEIC), pp. 1–6, June 2016. https://doi.org/10.1109/EEEIC.2016.7555867
2. Bahdanau, D., Cho, K., Bengio, Y.: Neural machine translation by jointly learning to align and translate. In: Proceedings International Conference on Learning Representations (2015). http://arxiv.org/abs/1409.0473
3. Buuren, S.v., Groothuis-Oudshoorn, K.: Multivariate imputation by chained equations: Mice v1.0 user's manual. Technical report. PG/VGZ/00.038, TNO Prevention and Health, Leiden (2000). http://www.stefvanbuuren.nl/publications/MICE
4. Cao, W., Wang, D., Li, J., Zhou, H., Li, L., Li, Y.: BRITS: bidirectional recurrent imputation for time series. In: Advances in Neural Information Processing Systems, pp. 6775–6785 (2018)
5. Che, Z., Purushotham, S., Cho, K., Sontag, D., Liu, Y.: Recurrent neural networks for multivariate time series with missing values. Sci. Rep. 8(1), 6085 (2018). https://doi.org/10.1038/s41598-018-24271-9

6. Hochreiter, S., Schmidhuber, J.: Long short-term memory. Neural Comput. **9**(8), 1735–1780 (1997). https://doi.org/10.1162/neco.1997.9.8.1735
7. Kingma, D., Ba, J.: Adam: a method for stochastic optimization. arXiv preprint arXiv:1412.6980 (2014)
8. Liang, X., et al.: Assessing Beijing's $PM_2.5$ pollution: severity, weather impact, APEC and winter heating. Proc. Roy. Soc. A: Math. Phys. Eng. Sci. **471**(2182), 20150257 (2015). https://doi.org/10.1098/rspa.2015.0257. https://royalsocietypublishing.org/doi/abs/10.1098/rspa.2015.0257
9. Poon, C.C.Y., Lo, B.P.L., Yuce, M.R., Alomainy, A., Hao, Y.: Body sensor networks: in the era of big data and beyond. IEEE Rev. Biomed. Eng. **8**, 4–16 (2015). https://doi.org/10.1109/RBME.2015.2427254
10. Shen, L., Ma, Q., Li, S.: End-to-end time series imputation via residual short paths. In: Zhu, J., Takeuchi, I. (eds.) Proceedings of The 10th Asian Conference on Machine Learning. Proceedings of Machine Learning Research, vol. 95, PMLR, pp. 248–263, 14–16 November 2018. http://proceedings.mlr.press/v95/shen18a.html
11. Stolfi, D.H., Alba, E., Yao, X.: Predicting car park occupancy rates in smart cities. In: Alba, E., Chicano, F., Luque, G. (eds.) International Conference on Smart Cities, vol. 10268, pp. 107–117. Springer, Heidelberg (2017). https://doi.org/10.1007/978-3-319-59513-9_11
12. Sutskever, I., Vinyals, O., Le, Q.V.: Sequence to sequence learning with neural networks. In: Ghahramani, Z., Welling, M., Cortes, C., Lawrence, N.D., Weinberger, K.Q. (eds.) Advances in Neural Information Processing Systems 27, pp. 3104–3112. Curran Associates, Inc. (2014). http://papers.nips.cc/paper/5346-sequence-to-sequence-learning-with-neural-networks.pdf
13. Yi, X., Zheng, Y., Zhang, J., Li, T.: ST-MVL: filling missing values in geo-sensory time series data. In: Proceedings of the Twenty-Fifth International Joint Conference on Artificial Intelligence, IJCAI'16, pp. 2704–2710. AAAI Press (2016). http://dl.acm.org/citation.cfm?id=3060832.3060999
14. Yick, J., Mukherjee, B., Ghosal, D.: Wireless sensor network survey. Comput. Netw. **52**(12), 2292–2330 (2008). https://doi.org/10.1016/j.comnet.2008.04.002. http://www.sciencedirect.com/science/article/pii/S1389128608001254
15. Yoon, J., Zame, W.R., van der Schaar, M.: Deep sensing: active sensing using multi-directional recurrent neural networks. In: Sixth International Conference on Learning Representations (2018)
16. Zhang, Y., Thorburn, P.J., Xiang, W., Fitch, P.: SSIM-a deep learning approach for recovering missing time series sensor data. IEEE Internet Things J. **6**(4), 6618–6628 (2019). https://doi.org/10.1109/JIOT.2019.2909038
17. Zhou, J., Huang, Z.: Recover missing sensor data with iterative imputing network. In: Workshops at the Thirty-Second AAAI Conference on Artificial Intelligence (2018)

The Futility of Bias-Free Learning and Search

George D. Montañez$^{(\boxtimes)}$, Jonathan Hayase, Julius Lauw,
Dominique Macias, Akshay Trikha, and Julia Vendemiatti

AMISTAD Lab, Harvey Mudd College, Claremont, CA 91711, USA
{gmontanez,jhayase,julauw,dmacias,atrikha,jvendemiatti}@hmc.edu

Abstract. Building on the view of machine learning as search, we demonstrate the necessity of bias in learning, quantifying the role of bias (measured relative to a collection of possible datasets, or more generally, information resources) in increasing the probability of success. For a given degree of bias towards a fixed target, we show that the proportion of favorable information resources is strictly bounded from above. Furthermore, we demonstrate that bias is a conserved quantity, such that no algorithm can be favorably biased towards many distinct targets simultaneously. Thus bias encodes trade-offs. The probability of success for a task can also be measured geometrically, as the angle of agreement between what holds for the actual task and what is assumed by the algorithm, represented in its bias. Lastly, finding a favorably biasing distribution over a fixed set of information resources is provably difficult, unless the set of resources itself is already favorable with respect to the given task and algorithm.

Keywords: Machine learning · Inductive bias · Algorithmic search

1 Introduction

Imagine you are on a routine grocery shopping trip and plan to buy some bananas. You know that the store carries both good and bad bananas which you must search through. There are multiple ways you can go about your search. One way is to randomly pick any ten bananas available on the shelf, which can be regarded as a form of unbiased search. Alternatively, you could introduce some bias to your search by only picking those bananas that are neither underripe nor overripe. Based on your past experiences from eating bananas, there is a better chance that these bananas will taste better. The proportion of good bananas retrieved in your biased search is greater than the same proportion in an unbiased search; you used your prior knowledge about tasty bananas. This

Supported by the NSF under Grant No. 1659805, Harvey Mudd College, and the Walter Bradley Center for Natural and Artificial Intelligence.

J. Hayase, J. Lauw, D. Macias, A. Trikha and J. Vendemiatti—Denotes equal contribution.

J. Liu and J. Bailey (Eds.): AI 2019, LNAI 11919, pp. 277–288, 2019.
https://doi.org/10.1007/978-3-030-35288-2_23

common routine shows how bias enables us to conduct more successful searches based on prior knowledge of the search target.

Viewing these decision-making processes through the lens of machine learning, we analyze how algorithms tackle learning problems under the influence of bias. Will we be better off without the existence of bias in machine learning algorithms? Our goal in this paper is to formally characterize the direct relationship between the performance of machine learning algorithms and their underlying biases. Without bias, machine learning algorithms will not perform better than uniform random sampling, on average. Yet to the extent an algorithm is biased toward some target is the extent to which it is biased against all remaining targets. As a consequence, no algorithm can be biased towards all targets. Therefore, bias represents the trade-offs an algorithm makes in how to respond to data.

We approach this problem by analyzing the performance of search algorithms within the algorithmic search framework introduced by Montañez [5]. This framework applies to common machine learning tasks such as classification, regression, clustering, optimization, reinforcement learning, and the general machine learning problems considered in Vapnik's learning framework [6]. We derive results characterizing the role of bias in successful search, extending Famine of Forte results [5] for a fixed search target and varying information resources. Our results for bias-free search then directly apply to bias-free learning, showing the extent to which bias is necessary for successful learning and quantifying how difficult it is to find a distribution with favorable bias for a particular target.

We should note that while bias formally measures how much an algorithm's predisposition towards a fixed outcome causes it's performance to deviate from that of uniform random sampling, we also use that term to refer to the underlying predisposition itself and its causes, which are responsible for that deviance.

2   Related Work

Schaffer's seminal work [11] showed that generalization performance for classification problems is a conserved quantity, such that favorable performance on a particular subset of problems will always be offset and balanced by poor performance over the remaining problems. Similarly, we show that bias is also a conserved quantity for any set of information resources. While Schaffer studied the performance of a single algorithm over different learning classes, Wolpert and Macready's "No Free Lunch Theorems for Optimization" [13] established that all optimization algorithms have the same performance when uniformly averaged over all possible cost functions. They also provided a geometric intuition for this result by defining an inner product which measures the alignment between an algorithm and a given prior over problems. This shows that no algorithm can be simultaneously aligned with all possible priors. In the context of the search framework, we define the geometric divergence as a measure of alignment between a search algorithm and a target in order to bound the proportion of favorable search problems.

While No Free Lunch Theorems are widely recognized as landmark ideas in machine learning, McDermott claims that No Free Lunch results are often misinterpreted and are practically insignificant for many real-world problems [3]. This is because algorithms are commonly tailored to a specific subset of problems in the real world, but No Free Lunch requires that we consider the set of all problems that are closed under permutation. These arguments against the applicability of No Free Lunch results are less relevant to our work here, since we evaluate the proportion of successful problems instead of considering the mean performance over the set of all problems. Furthermore, our results hold for sets of problems that are not closed under permutation, as a generalization of No Free Lunch results.

In "The Famine of Forte: Few Search Problems Greatly Favor Your Algorithm," Montañez [5] reduces machine learning problems to search problems and develops a rigorous search framework to generalize No Free Lunch ideas. He strictly bounds the proportion of problems that are favorable for a fixed algorithm and shows that no single algorithm can perform well over a large fraction of search problems. Extending these results to fixed search targets, we show that there are also strict bounds on the proportion of favorable information resources, and that the bound relaxes with the introduction of bias.

Our notion of bias relates to ideas introduced by Mitchell [4]. According to Mitchell, a completely unbiased classification algorithm cannot generalize beyond training data. He argued that the ability of a learning algorithm to generalize depends on incorporating biases, which equates to making assumptions beyond strict consistency with training data. These biases may include prior knowledge of the domain, preferences for simplicity, restrictions on algorithm structure, and awareness of the algorithm's real-world application. We strengthen Mitchell's argument with a mathematical justification for the need for bias in improving learning performance.

Gülçehre and Bengio empirically support Mitchell's ideas by investigating the nature of training barriers affecting the generalization performance of black-box machine learning algorithms [2]. Using the Structured Multi-Layer Perceptron (SMLP) neural network architecture, they showed that pre-training the SMLP with hints based on prior knowledge of the task generalizes more efficiently as compared to an SMLP pre-trained with random initializers. Furthermore, Ulyanov et al. explore the success of deep convolutional networks applied to image generation and restoration [12]. By applying untrained convolutional networks to image reconstruction with competitive success to trained ones, they show that the impressive performance of these networks is not due to learning alone. They highlight the importance of inductive bias, which is built into the structure of these generator networks, in achieving this high level of success. In a similar vein, Runarsson and Yao establish that bias is an essential component in constrained evolutionary optimization search problems [10]. It is experimentally shown that carefully selecting an appropriate constraint handling method and applying a biasing penalty function enhances the probability of locating feasible solutions for evolutionary algorithms. Inspired by the results obtained from these experimental studies, we formulate a theoretical validation of the role of bias in generalization performance for learning problems.

3   The Search Framework

3.1   The Search Problem

We formulate machine learning problems as search problems using the algorithmic search framework [5]. Within the framework, a search problem is represented as a 3-tuple (Ω, T, F). The finite search space from which we can sample is Ω. The subset of elements in the search space that we are searching for is the target set T. A target function that represents T is an $|\Omega|$-length vector with entries having value 1 when the corresponding elements of Ω are in the target set and 0 otherwise. The external information resource F is a binary string that provides initialization information for the search and evaluates points in Ω, acting as an oracle that guides the search process.

3.2   The Search Algorithm

Given a search problem, a history of elements already examined, and information resource evaluations, an algorithmic search is a process that decides how to query elements of Ω. As the search algorithm samples, it adds the record of points queried and information resource evaluations, indexed by time, to the search history. If the algorithm queries an element $\omega \in T$ at least once during the course of its search, we say that the search is successful. Figure 1 visualizes the search algorithm.

3.3   Measuring Performance

Within this search framework, we measure a learning algorithm's performance by examining the expected per-query probability of success. This measure is more effective than measuring an algorithm's total probability of success, since the number of sampling steps may vary depending on the algorithm used, inflating the total probability for algorithms that sample more. Furthermore, the per-query probability of success naturally accounts for sampling procedures that involve repeatedly sampling the same points in the search space, as is the case of genetic algorithms [1,9]. Thus, this measure effectively handles search algorithms that attempt to manage trade-offs between exploration and exploitation.

The expected per-query probability of success is defined as

$$q(T, F) = \mathbb{E}_{\tilde{P},H}\left[\frac{1}{|\tilde{P}|}\sum_{i=1}^{|\tilde{P}|} P_i(\omega \in T)\,\middle|\, F\right]$$

where $\tilde{P}$ is a sequence of probability distributions over the search space (where each timestep i produces a distribution P_i), T is the target, F is the information resource, and H is the search history. The number of queries during a search is equal to the length of the probability distribution sequence, $|\tilde{P}|$.

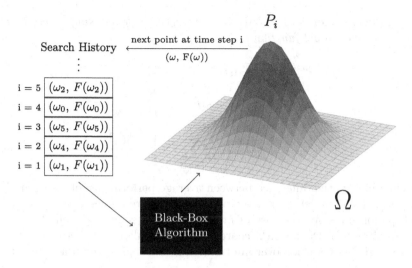

Fig. 1. As a black-box optimization algorithm samples from Ω, it produces an associated probability distribution P_i based on the search history. When a sample ω_k corresponding to location k in Ω is evaluated using the external information resource F, the tuple $(\omega_k, F(\omega_k))$ is added to the search history.

4 Main Results

We present and explain our main results in this section. Note that full proofs for the following results can be found in the Appendix (available online, on arXiv [7]). We proceed by defining our measures of bias and target divergence, then show conservation results of bias and give bounds on the probability of successful search and the proportion of favorable search problems given a fixed target.

Definition 1 *(Bias for a distribution over information resources and a fixed target). Let $\mathcal{D}$ be a distribution over a space of information resources $\mathcal{F}$ and let $F \sim \mathcal{D}$. For a given $\mathcal{D}$ and a fixed k-hot target function t,*

$$\mathrm{Bias}(\mathcal{D}, t) = \mathbb{E}_{\mathcal{D}} \left[t^{\top} \overline{P}_F \right] - \frac{k}{|\Omega|}$$

$$= t^{\top} \mathbb{E}_{\mathcal{D}} \left[\overline{P}_F \right] - \frac{\|t\|^2}{|\Omega|}$$

$$= t^{\top} \int_{\mathcal{F}} \overline{P}_f \mathcal{D}(f) \, \mathrm{d}f - \frac{\|t\|^2}{|\Omega|}$$

where $\overline{P}_f$ is the vector representation of the averaged probability distribution (conditioned on f) induced on Ω during the course of the search, which can be shown to imply $q(t, f) = t^{\top} \overline{P}_f$.

Definition 2 *(Bias for a finite set of information resources and a fixed target). Let $\mathcal{U}[\mathcal{B}]$ denote a uniform distribution over a finite set of information resources*

$\mathcal{B}$. *For a random quantity $F \sim \mathcal{U}[\mathcal{B}]$, the averaged $|\Omega|$-length simplex vector $\overline{P}_F$, and a fixed k-hot target function t,*

$$\text{Bias}(\mathcal{B}, t) = \mathbb{E}_{\mathcal{U}[\mathcal{B}]}[t^\top \overline{P}_F] - \frac{k}{|\Omega|}$$

$$= t^\top \mathbb{E}_{\mathcal{U}[\mathcal{B}]}[\overline{P}_F] - \frac{k}{|\Omega|}$$

$$= t^\top \left(\frac{1}{|\mathcal{B}|} \sum_{f \in \mathcal{B}} \overline{P}_f \right) - \frac{\|t\|^2}{|\Omega|}.$$

We define bias as the difference between average performance of a search algorithm on a fixed target over a set of information resources and the baseline search performance for the case of uniform random sampling. Definition 1 is a generalized form of Definition 2, characterizing the alignment between a target function and a distribution over information resources instead of a fixed set.

Definition 3 *(Target Divergence). The measure of similarity between a fixed target function t and the expected value of the averaged $|\Omega|$-length simplex vector $\overline{P}_F$, where $F \sim \mathcal{D}$, is defined as*

$$\theta = \arccos \left(\frac{t^\top \mathbb{E}_\mathcal{D}[\overline{P}_F]}{\|t\| \|\mathbb{E}_\mathcal{D}[\overline{P}_F]\|} \right)$$

Similar to Wolpert and Macready's geometric interpretation of the No Free Lunch theorems [13], we can evaluate how far a target function t deviates from the averaged probability simplex vector $\overline{P}_f$ for a given search problem. We use cosine similarity to measure the level of similarity between t and $\overline{P}_f$. Geometrically, the target divergence is the angle between the target vector and the averaged $|\Omega|$-length simplex vector. Figure 2 depicts the target divergence for various levels of alignments between t and $\overline{P}_f$.

Theorem 1 (Improbability of Favorable Information Resources). *Let $\mathcal{D}$ be a distribution over a set of information resources $\mathcal{F}$, let F be a random variable such that $F \sim \mathcal{D}$, let $t \subseteq \Omega$ be an arbitrary fixed k-sized target set with corresponding target function t, and let $q(t, F)$ be the expected per-query probability of success for algorithm $\mathcal{A}$ on search problem (Ω, t, F). Then, for any $q_{\min} \in [0, 1]$,*

$$\Pr(q(t, F) \geq q_{\min}) \leq \frac{p + \text{Bias}(\mathcal{D}, t)}{q_{\min}}$$

where $p = \frac{k}{|\Omega|}$.

Since the size of the target set t is usually small relative to the size of the search space Ω, p is also typically small. Following the above results, we see that the probability that a search problem (with information resource drawn from $\mathcal{D}$) is favorable is bounded by a small value. This bound tightens as we increase our minimum threshold of success, $q_{\min}$. Notably, our bound relaxes with the introduction of bias.

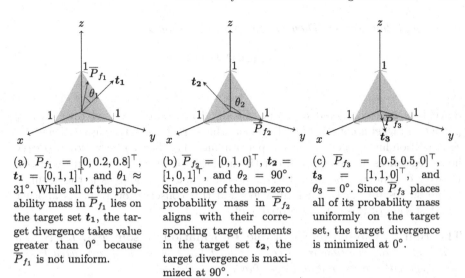

(a) $\overline{P}_{f_1} = [0, 0.2, 0.8]^\top$, $t_1 = [0, 1, 1]^\top$, and $\theta_1 \approx 31°$. While all of the probability mass in $\overline{P}_{f_1}$ lies on the target set t_1, the target divergence takes value greater than $0°$ because $\overline{P}_{f_1}$ is not uniform.

(b) $\overline{P}_{f_2} = [0, 1, 0]^\top$, $t_2 = [1, 0, 1]^\top$, and $\theta_2 = 90°$. Since none of the non-zero probability mass in $\overline{P}_{f_2}$ aligns with their corresponding target elements in the target set t_2, the target divergence is maximized at $90°$.

(c) $\overline{P}_{f_3} = [0.5, 0.5, 0]^\top$, $t_3 = [1, 1, 0]^\top$, and $\theta_3 = 0°$. Since $\overline{P}_{f_3}$ places all of its probability mass uniformly on the target set, the target divergence is minimized at $0°$.

Fig. 2. These examples visualize the target divergence for various possible combinations of target functions and simplex vectors. (b) demonstrates minimum alignment, while (c) demonstrates maximum alignment.

Corollary 1 (Probability of Success Under Bias-Free Search). *When* Bias$(\mathcal{D}, t) = 0$,

$$\Pr(q(t, F) \geq q_{\min}) \leq \frac{p}{q_{\min}}$$

Directly following Theorem 1, if the algorithm does not induce bias on t given a distribution over a set of information resources, the probability of successful search based on an information resource sampled from $\mathcal{D}$ cannot be any higher than that of uniform random sampling divided by the minimum performance that we specify. This bound matches that of the original Famine of Forte [5].

Corollary 2 (Geometric Divergence).

$$\Pr(q(t, F) \geq q_{\min}) \leq \frac{\sqrt{k}\cos(\theta)}{q_{\min}} = \frac{\|t\|\cos(\theta)}{q_{\min}}$$

This result shows that greater geometric alignment between the target vector and expected distribution over the search space loosens the upper bound on the probability of successful search. Connecting this to our other results, the geometric alignment can be viewed as another interpretation of the bias the algorithm places on the target set.

Theorem 2 (Conservation of Bias). *Let $\mathcal{D}$ be a distribution over a set of information resources and let $\tau_k = \{t | t \in \{0, 1\}^{|\Omega|}, \|t\| = \sqrt{k}\}$ be the set of all*

$|\Omega|$-length k-hot vectors. Then for any fixed algorithm $\mathcal{A}$,

$$\sum_{t \in \tau_k} \mathrm{Bias}(\mathcal{D}, t) = 0$$

Since bias is a conserved quantity, an algorithm that is biased towards any particular target is equally biased against other targets, as is the case in Schaffer's conservation law for generalization performance [11]. This conservation property holds regardless of the algorithm or the distribution over information resources. Positive dependence between targets and information resources is the grounds for all successful machine learning [6], and this conservation result is another manifestation of this general property of learning.

Theorem 3 (Famine of Favorable Information Resources). *Let $\mathcal{B}$ be a finite set of information resources and let $t \subseteq \Omega$ be an arbitrary fixed k-size target set with corresponding target function t. Define*

$$\mathcal{B}_{q_{\min}} = \{f \mid f \in \mathcal{B}, q(t, f) \geq q_{\min}\},$$

where $q(t, f)$ is the expected per-query probability of success for algorithm $\mathcal{A}$ on search problem (Ω, t, f) and $q_{\min} \in [0, 1]$ represents the minimally acceptable per-query probability of success. Then,

$$\frac{|\mathcal{B}_{q_{\min}}|}{|\mathcal{B}|} \leq \frac{p + \mathrm{Bias}(\mathcal{B}, t)}{q_{\min}}$$

where $p = \frac{k}{|\Omega|}$.

This theorem shows us that unless our set of information resources is biased towards our target, only a small proportion of information resources will yield a high probability of search success. In most practical cases, p is small enough that uniform random sampling is not considered a plausible strategy, since we typically have small targets embedded in very large search spaces. Thus the bound is typically very constraining. The set of information resources will be overwhelmingly unhelpful unless we restrict the given information resources to be positively biased towards the specified target.

Corollary 3 (Proportion of Successful Problems Under Bias-Free Search). *When $\mathrm{Bias}(\mathcal{B}, t) = 0$,*

$$\frac{|\mathcal{B}_{q_{\min}}|}{|\mathcal{B}|} \leq \frac{p}{q_{\min}}.$$

Directly following Theorem 3, if the algorithm does not induce bias on t given a set of information resources, the proportion of successful search problems cannot be any higher than the single-query success probability of uniform random sampling divided by the minimum specified performance.

Theorem 4 (Futility of Bias-Free Search). *For any fixed algorithm $\mathcal{A}$, fixed target $t \subseteq \Omega$ with corresponding target function $\boldsymbol{t}$, and distribution over information resources $\mathcal{D}$, if* $\text{Bias}(\mathcal{D}, \boldsymbol{t}) = 0$, *then*

$$\Pr(\omega \in t; \mathcal{A}) = p$$

where $\Pr(\omega \in t; \mathcal{A})$ represents the per-query probability of successfully sampling an element of t using $\mathcal{A}$, marginalized over information resources $F \sim \mathcal{D}$, and p is the single-query probability of success under uniform random sampling.

This result shows that without bias, an algorithm can perform no better than uniform random sampling. This is a generalization of Mitchell's idea of the futility of removing biases for binary classification [4] and Montañez's formal proof for the need for bias for multi-class classification [6]. This result shows that bias is necessary for any machine learning or search algorithm to have better than random chance performance, of those representable in our framework.

Theorem 5 (Famine of Applicable Targets). *Let $\mathcal{D}$ be a distribution over a finite set of information resources. Define*

$$\tau_k = \{t \mid t \subseteq \Omega, |t| = k\}$$
$$\tau_{q_{\min}} = \{t \mid t \in \tau_k, \text{Bias}(\mathcal{D}, \boldsymbol{t}) \geq q_{\min}\}$$

where $\boldsymbol{t}$ is the target function corresponding to the target set t. Then,

$$\frac{|\tau_{q_{\min}}|}{|\tau_k|} \leq \frac{p}{p + q_{\min}} \leq \frac{p}{q_{\min}}$$

where $p = \frac{k}{|\Omega|}$.

This theorem shows that the proportion of target sets for which an algorithm is highly biased is small, given that p is small relative to $q_{\min}$. A high value of $\text{Bias}(\mathcal{D}, \boldsymbol{t})$ implies that the algorithm, given $\mathcal{D}$, places a large amount of mass on $\boldsymbol{t}$ and a small amount of mass on other target functions. Consequently, an algorithm is acceptably biased toward fewer target sets as we increase the minimum threshold of bias.

Theorem 6 (Famine of Favorable Biasing Distributions). *Given a fixed target function $\boldsymbol{t}$, a finite set of information resources $\mathcal{B}$, and a set $\mathcal{P} = \{\mathcal{D} \mid \mathcal{D} \in \mathbb{R}^{|\mathcal{B}|}, \sum_{f \in \mathcal{B}} \mathcal{D}(f) = 1\}$ of all discrete $|\mathcal{B}|$-dimensional simplex vectors,*

$$\frac{\mu(\mathcal{G}_{t,q_{\min}})}{\mu(\mathcal{P})} \leq \frac{p + \text{Bias}(\mathcal{B}, \boldsymbol{t})}{q_{\min}}$$

where $\mathcal{G}_{t,q_{\min}} = \{\mathcal{D} \mid \mathcal{D} \in \mathcal{P}, \text{Bias}(\mathcal{D}, \boldsymbol{t}) \geq q_{\min}\}$ and μ is Lebesgue measure.

We see that the proportion of distributions over $\mathcal{B}$ for which an algorithm is acceptably biased towards a fixed target function $\boldsymbol{t}$ decreases as we increase the minimum acceptable level of bias, q_{min}. Additionally, the greater the amount of bias induced by an algorithm given a set of information resources on a fixed target, the higher the probability of identifying a suitable distribution that achieves successful search. However, unless the set is already filled with favorable elements, finding a minimally favorable distribution over that set is difficult.

Theorem 7 (Bias Over Distributions). *Given a finite set of information resources $\mathcal{B}$, a fixed target function t, and a set $\mathcal{P} = \{\mathcal{D} \mid \mathcal{D} \in \mathbb{R}^{|\mathcal{B}|}, \sum_{f \in \mathcal{B}} \mathcal{D}(f) = 1\}$ of discrete $|\mathcal{B}|$-dimensional simplex vectors,*

$$\int_{\mathcal{P}} \mathrm{Bias}(\mathcal{D}, t)\, \mathrm{d}\mathcal{D} = C \cdot \mathrm{Bias}(\mathcal{B}, t)$$

where $C = \int_{\mathcal{P}} \mathrm{d}\mathcal{D}$ is the uniform measure of set $\mathcal{P}$. For an unbiased set $\mathcal{B}$,

$$\int_{\mathcal{P}} \mathrm{Bias}(\mathcal{D}, t)\, \mathrm{d}\mathcal{D} = 0$$

This theorem states that the total bias on a fixed target function over all possible distributions is proportional to the bias induced by the algorithm given $\mathcal{B}$. When there is no bias over a set of information resources, the total bias over all distributions sums to 0. It follows that any distribution over $\mathcal{D}$ for which the algorithm places positive bias on t is offset by one or more for which the algorithm places negative bias on t.

Corollary 4 (Conservation of Bias Over Distributions). *Let $\tau_k = \{t \mid t \in \{0,1\}^{|\Omega|}, ||t|| = \sqrt{k}\}$ be the set of all $|\Omega|$-length k-hot vectors. Then,*

$$\sum_{t \in \tau_k} \int_{\mathcal{P}} \mathrm{Bias}(\mathcal{D}, t)\, \mathrm{d}\mathcal{D} = 0$$

Here we see that the total bias over all distributions and all k-size target sets sums to zero, even if beginning with a set of information resources that is positively biased towards a particular target, as implied by the previous Theorem 7.

5 Examples

5.1 Genetic Algorithms

Genetic algorithms are optimization methods inspired by evolutionary processes [9]. We can represent genetic algorithms in our search framework as follows:

- $\mathcal{A}$ - a genetic algorithm, with standard variation (mutation, crossover, etc.) operators.
- Ω - space of possible configurations (genotypes).
- T - set of all configurations which perform well on some task.
- F - a fitness function which can evaluate a configuration's fitness.
- (Ω, T, F) - genetic algorithm task.

Given any genetic algorithm that is unbiased towards a particular small target when averaged over a set of fitness functions (as in No Free Lunch scenarios), the proportion of highly favorable fitness functions in that set must also be small, which we state as a corollary following directly from Corollary 3.

Corollary 5 (Famine of Favorable Fitness Functions). *For any fixed target $t \subseteq \Omega$ and fixed genetic algorithm unbiased relative to a finite set of fitness functions $\mathcal{B}$, the proportion of fitness functions in $\mathcal{B}$ with expected per-query probability of success at least q_{min} is no greater than $|t|/(q_{min}|\Omega|)$.*

5.2 Binary Classification

We can cast binary classification as a search problem, as follows [5]:

- $\mathcal{A}$ - classification algorithm, such as a decision tree learner.
- Ω - space of possible binary labelings over an instance space.
- $t \subseteq \Omega$ - set of all hypotheses with less than 10% classification error.
- F - set of training examples, where $F(\emptyset)$ is the full set of training data and $F(c)$ is the loss on training data for hypothesis c.
- (Ω, t, F) - binary classification learning task.

In our example, let $|\Omega| = 2^{100}$. Assume the size of our target set is $|t| = 2^{10}$, the set of training examples F is drawn from a distribution $\mathcal{D}$, and that the minimum performance q_{min} we want to achieve is 0.5. Then, by Corollary 1, if our algorithm (relative to $\mathcal{D}$) does not place any bias on the target set,

$$\Pr\left(q(t, F) \geq \frac{1}{2}\right) \leq \frac{p}{q_{min}} = \frac{\frac{2^{10}}{2^{100}}}{\frac{1}{2}} = 2^{-89}.$$

Thus, the probability that we will have selected a dataset that results in at least our desired level of performance is upper bounded by 2^{-89}. Notice that if we raised the minimum threshold, then the probability would decrease—favorable datasets would become more unlikely.

To perform better than uniform random sampling, we would need to introduce bias into the algorithm. For example, predetermined information or assumptions about the target set could be used to determine which hypotheses are more plausible. The principle of Occam's razor [8] is often used, which is the assumption that the elements in the target set are likely the "simpler" elements, by some definition of simplicity. Relating this to our formal definition of bias, if we introduce correct assumptions into the algorithm, then the expected alignment of the target set and the induced probability distribution over the search space increases accordingly.

6 Conclusion

We build on the algorithmic search framework and extend Famine of Forte results to search problems with fixed targets and varying information resources.

Our notion of bias quantifies the extent to which an algorithm is predisposed to a particular fixed target. We show that bias towards any target necessarily implies bias against the other remaining targets, underscoring the fact that no universally applicable form of bias can exist. Furthermore, one cannot perform better than uniform random sampling without introducing a predisposition in the algorithm towards a desired target—unbiased algorithms are useless. Few information resources can be greatly favorable towards any fixed target, unless the algorithm is already predisposed to the target no matter the information resource given. Thus, in machine learning as elsewhere, biases are needed for better than chance performance. Biases must also be correct, since the effectiveness of any bias depends on how well it aligns with the given target actually being sought.

References

1. Goldberg, D.: Genetic Algorithms in Search Optimization and Machine Learning. Addison-Wesley Longman Publishing Company, Boston (1999)
2. Gülçehre, Ç., Bengio, Y.: Knowledge matters: importance of prior information for optimization. J. Mach. Learn. Res. **17**(8), 1–32 (2016)
3. McDermott, J.: When and why metaheuristics researchers can ignore "no free lunch" theorems. Metaheuristics, March 2019. https://doi.org/10.1007/s42257-019-00002-6
4. Mitchell, T.D.: The need for biases in learning generalizations. CBM-TR-117. Rutgers University (1980)
5. Montañez, G.D.: The famine of forte: few search problems greatly favor your algorithm. In: 2017 IEEE International Conference on Systems, Man, and Cybernetics (SMC), pp. 477–482. IEEE (2017)
6. Montañez, G.D.: Why machine learning works. Dissertation, pp. 52–59. Carnegie Mellon University (2017)
7. Montañez, G.D., Hayase, J., Lauw, J., Macias, D., Trikha, A., Vendemiatti, J.: The futility of bias-free learning and search. arXiv e-prints arXiv:1907.06010, July 2019
8. Rasmussen, C.E., Ghahramani, Z.: Occam's Razor. In: Proceedings of the 13th International Conference on Neural Information Processing Systems, NIPS 2000, pp. 276–282. MIT Press, Cambridge, MA, USA (2000)
9. Reeves, C., Rowe, J.E.: Genetic Algorithms: Principles and Perspectives: A Guide to GA Theory, vol. 20. Springer, Heidelberg (2002). https://doi.org/10.1007/b101880
10. Runarsson, T., Yao, X.: Search biases in constrained evolutionary optimization. IEEE Trans. Syst. Man Cybern. Part C Appl. Rev. **35**, 233–243 (2005). https://doi.org/10.1109/TSMCC.2004.841906
11. Schaffer, C.: A conservation law for generalization performance. In: Machine Learning Proceedings 1994, pp. 259–265. Elsevier (1994)
12. Ulyanov, D., Vedaldi, A., Lempitsky, V.: Deep image prior. In: Proceedings of the IEEE Conference on Computer Vision and Pattern Recognition, pp. 9446–9454 (2018)
13. Wolpert, D.H., Macready, W.G.: No free lunch theorems for optimization. Trans. Evol. Comput. **1**(1), 67–82 (1997). https://doi.org/10.1109/4235.585893

WinoFlexi: A Crowdsourcing Platform for the Development of Winograd Schemas

Nicos Isaak[1]([✉])([iD]) and Loizos Michael[1,2]

[1] Open University of Cyprus, Nicosia, Cyprus
nicos.isaak@st.ouc.ac.cy, loizos@ouc.ac.cy
[2] Research Center on Interactive Media, Smart Systems, and Emerging Technologies,
Nicosia, Cyprus

Abstract. The Winograd Schema Challenge, the task of resolving pronouns in certain carefully-structured sentences, has received considerable interest in the past few years as an alternative to the Turing Test. Systems developed to tackle this challenge have typically been evaluated on a small set of hand-crafted collections of sentences, since the development of new sentences by individuals is itself a rather challenging task, requiring care and creativity. In this paper we approach the problem of developing Winograd schemas via the introduction of *WinoFlexi*, a flexible online crowdsourcing system. Our empirical evaluation of the system's performance suggests that *WinoFlexi* allows crowdworkers to develop Winograd schemas of quality similar to that of most typical existing collections.

Keywords: Winograd Schema Challenge · Crowdsourcing

1 Introduction

The Winograd Schema Challenge (WSC) has been proposed as a novel litmus test for machine intelligence. Unlike the Turing Test, which is based on short free-form conversations during which a machine attempts to imitate a human, machines passing the WSC are expected to demonstrate the ability to think without having to pretend to be somebody else [1]. Passing the challenge requires resolving pronouns in certain sentences where shallow parsing techniques seem not to be directly applicable, and where the use of world knowledge and the ability to reason seem necessary [2,3]. Although the challenge is, by design, easy for humans, the development of new Winograd schemas is, itself, too troublesome for humans lacking inspiration and creativity [4].

In this paper, we present *WinoFlexi*, a flexible online collaboration system that allows members of crowdsourcing platforms to collaborate *explicitly* for the development of Winograd schemas. To the best of our knowledge, this is the first work that attempts to use crowdsourcing for this task. We envision the use of this platform as a source of Winograd schemas for use in WSC-based CAPTCHAs

© Springer Nature Switzerland AG 2019
J. Liu and J. Bailey (Eds.): AI 2019, LNAI 11919, pp. 289–302, 2019.
https://doi.org/10.1007/978-3-030-35288-2_24

[5] and in WSC competitions for the evaluation of systems that attempt to pass the challenge [4].

WinoFlexi uses a combination of tools that enhance the schema-development process: *(i)* it is more cheat-proof than existing crowdsourcing platforms, and *(ii)* it uses test questions that are closer to the schema-development process that benefit non-dubious workers and ban dubious ones. Our empirical study with workers from an existing crowdsourcing platform, showed that *WinoFlexi* can be used for the development of Winograd schemas that are comparable to the most typical existing schema collections.

2   The Winograd Schema Challenge

Winograd schemas comprise of two Winograd halves, with each half consisting of a sentence, a definite pronoun or a question, two possible pronoun targets (answers), and the correct pronoun target [1]. The following schema (a pair of halves) illustrates the key characteristics of Winograd schemas: *1. Sentence: Erica called Jennifer on the phone because she was not responding to email. Question: Who was not responding to email? Answers: Jennifer, Erica. Correct Answer: Jennifer. 2. Sentence: Erica called Jennifer on the phone because she was not able to email. Question: Who was not able to email? Answers: Jennifer, Erica. Correct Answer: Erica.*

Given just one of the halves in a schema, the aim is to resolve the definite pronoun in the question to one of its two co-referents. The avoid trivializing the task, the co-referents are of the same gender, and are either both singular or both plural. The two halves differ in a special word or phrase that critically determines the correct answer. Schemas that do not *strictly* follow these rules are called "schemas in the broad sense".

It is believed that the WSC can provide a more meaningful measure of machine intelligence when compared to the Turing Test, exactly because of the presumed necessity of reasoning with commonsense knowledge to identify how the special word or phrase affects the resolution of the pronoun. By extension, it is believed that a system that contains the commonsense knowledge to correctly resolve Winograd schemas should be capable of supporting a wide range of AI applications. Although, as expected from its reliance on commonsense knowledge, English-speaking adults have no difficulty with the challenge, the development of the schemas themselves is a very challenging task [4]. According to Levesque [1] in order to build quality Winograd schemas one needs to avoid two pitfalls: having questions whose answers are in a certain sense too obvious, and (more importantly) having questions whose answers are not obvious enough.

To the best of our knowledge, the availability of Winograd schemas is limited. Currently, only two widely-used WSC collections exist: *(i)* Rahman and Ng's collection [6], which consists of 942 schemas and was developed by students (built under the "broad sense"); *(ii)* Levesque and Davis's [1] collection, which consists of 150 schemas and was developed under the strict rules of the WSC (referred to later as the Winograd-library).

The availability of Winograd schemas seems disproportional to their demand and their potential impact. A recent study [5] showed that the WSC can form the basis of a new type of CAPTCHA, which might encourage more AI researchers to work on the problem of actually trying to tackle the WSC, and perhaps, to help towards the building of machines able to reason with commonsense knowledge. On the other hand, the development of carefully-crafted pronoun resolution tasks towards the development of Winograd schemas is a hard process [4]: it requires creativity and inspiration, and it is too troublesome to be done on a regular basis to support, for instance, competitions on the WSC or the testing of systems that might have been trained on existing collections of Winograd schemas. Perhaps not unrelated to the limited availability of Winograd schemas is the fact that the first and only WSC competition was organized in 2016 [4].

Towards addressing this disparity, we turn to crowdsourcing. Currently, many skilled labor activities are carried out online via crowdsourcing platforms. These platforms can eliminate geographic constraints and help workers to pursue work that they find valuable [7]. This work utilizes such platforms to develop *WinoFlexi*, in an effort to bring together researchers and people from across disciplines, concerned with the acquisition and use of language data in the context of knowledge-based applications like the WSC. The design of appropriate crowdsourcing mechanisms for our particular task and the evaluation of the developed Winograd schemas is the focus of the rest of this paper.

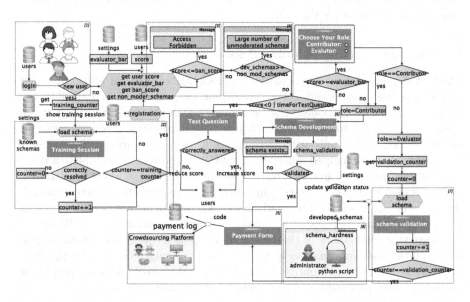

Fig. 1. *WinoFlexi*'s architecture for the development of Winograd schemas. The various parts of the architecture are marked in red rectangles, and are discussed in Sect. 3. (Color figure online)

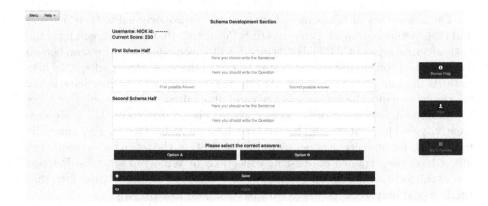

Fig. 2. The contributor dashboard.

3   Crowdsourcing Platform Architecture

We continue to present our platform and its constituent modules (see Fig. 1), and discuss how the crowd collaborates to built schemas under *WinoFlexi*'s evaluation mechanisms. Recognizing that the schema development process is tedious and troublesome, *WinoFlexi* is built to act as an assistant with effective incentive mechanisms for the crowd.

3.1   Registration and Training Session

The first step for each worker is to apply as a Contributor to our platform, where they register their credentials (http://cognition.ouc.ac.cy/mcSchemaBuilder; see *part-1* in Fig. 1). Workers need not be domain experts but need to have a strong command of English to ensure that schemas have no spelling, syntactic, or grammatical errors, and comply with the schema development process. To maximize the quality of the developed schemas, every Contributor has to complete a training task (see *part-2* in Fig. 1). During the training phase workers are familiarized with the development process by being asked to correctly resolve randomly selected schemas from the Winograd-library. The length of the training phase can be increased either by the system administrator or automatically by *WinoFlexi* to ensure that the quality of the produced schemas meets expectations. In particular, if the *auto-training* flag is enabled, then the length of the training phase for every new registered Contributor is determined by how much the number of invalid schemas produced so far exceeds the number of valid ones.

3.2   Contributing and Evaluating

Workers both contribute in the development of schemas, and evaluate their quality.

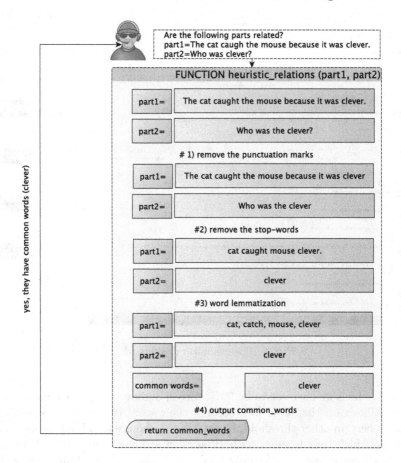

Fig. 3. Heuristic relations to eliminated problems with schema cohesion.

Contributors: Contributors are workers who develop schemas (see *part-6* in Fig. 1), using the dashboard shown in Fig. 2. When a Contributor adds a schema, *WinoFlexi* does some basic checks: *(i)* It checks if each schema half comprises a sentence, a question, and two pronoun targets. *(ii)* It checks if the correct pronoun target of each schema half has been selected. *(iii)* It checks if the sentence, the question, and the two pronoun targets of each schema half are related. *(iv)* It checks if the two halves are related. Relatedness is checked using the heuristic approach shown in Fig. 3 applied to each of the pairs sentence-question, sentence-first_pronoun_target, sentence-second_pronoun_target.

Evaluators: Workers who validate schemas are called Evaluators (see *part-7* in Fig. 1). Contributors are allowed to take on this second role if they meet two requirements: first, the percentage of their valid and approved (by other Evaluators) schemas among those that they have contributed that far exceeds a certain

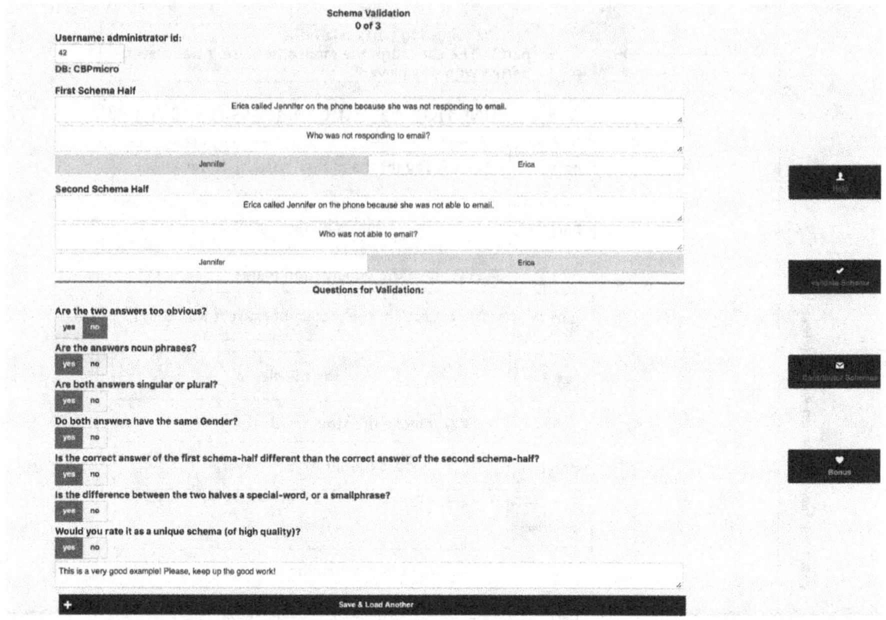

Fig. 4. The evaluator dashboard.

threshold (which we have set to be 90%, corresponding to the bar for *near adult human* abilities on the WSC [3]); second, their score (which we discuss later) is above a certain other threshold. Contributors who are also Evaluators choose the role in which they interact with *WinoFlexi* at login time. At the beginning of the development process, the only Evaluator is the system administrator. The evaluation process comprises of answering a number of yes/no questions using the dashboard shown in Fig. 4. Affirmative responses to all but the first question are necessary to characterize a schema as valid. Additionally, the Evaluators have access to a similarity tool to detect if the Contributors are following a pattern to develop similarly-looking schemas. The tool acts like a *leakage-detector* [7] that queries the WinoFlexi-library and Winograd-library to determine if a newly-contributed schema is "leaked", in that it is significantly similar to an existing schema. Each approved schema increases the Contributor's score and each "leaked" schema decreases it, affecting whether the Contributor will meet the requirements to become an Evaluator.

3.3 Quality-Assurance Measures

Additional mechanisms are used to ensure the quality of the developed schemas.

Test Questions: Many crowdsourcing platforms use tests as a method of assessment, offering their certification mechanisms to verify that a given worker indeed holds a particular skill [7,8]. Previous works indicate that more interactive studies may motivate participants to read instructions more carefully leading to better compliance [9]. Our approach is based on the adaptive interjection of test questions and on rewarding the worker with a positive score for successfully resolving them (see *part-5* in Fig. 1). *WinoFlexi* can be enabled to display test questions as often as necessary, to both Contributors and Evaluators; this can be manually handled by the system administrator, or automatically controlled by the system. By default, a test question has a 10% probability of being displayed after every login. If the *auto-testing* flag is enabled, this probability is adjusted in a manner analogous to how the length of the training phase is adjusted. Test questions are selected from the WinoFlexi-library (validated contributed schemas) and the Winograd-library; both collections include schemas that strictly follow the WSC rules. Correct/wrong answers to test questions increase/decrease a worker's score.

Ban Score: Online certification of skills is still problematic, since dealing with cheating is a major challenge. The *ban-score* mechanism automatically bans workers who have a sufficiently low score (see *part-3* in Fig. 1), with the threshold identified empirically.

Un-Validated Schemas: To prevent workers from entering a large number of potentially invalid schemas, there is a mechanism that limits the number of schemas each worker can develop before they undergo the validation process (see *part-4* in Fig. 1).

Winograd Schema Hardness: *WinoFlexi* leverages existing tools for the WSC to generate feedback to the Contributors (see *part-8* in Fig. 1). Towards this goal, we follow a single-step approach for labeling schemas with a hardness score which indirectly shows if a schema is considered hard to answer by a machine; Winograd schemas are accordingly labeled as such by the computed hardness index. For this purpose we use a recent tool [3] that can take any Winograd schema and output a score that shows its hardness index. The hardness index is presented to the Contributors and the Evaluators. If the majority of a Contributor's schemas are easy (respectively, hard) then our system prompts them to develop schemas that are harder (respectively, easier) to solve.

3.4 Payment and Rewards

Payment Procedure: Most of the microtasks on the crowdsourcing platforms are priced individually, and workers are paid a base rate multiplied by the number of correctly completed tasks. Whatever their motives are, workers want to earn money and seek out tasks to maximize their expected earnings. To make sure that only the workers who developed schemas are going to get paid, we enhanced *WinoFlexi* with a payment verification plug-in (see *part-9* in Fig. 1). Upon each schema development (or validation), Contributors and Evaluators are prompted with a notification message and a code which is automatically generated and inserted into our database. Each worker has to provide the same code on their crowdsourcing platform to receive the actual payment.

Rewards: Workers, recruited through crowdsourcing platforms, must receive a small fixed payment for participating in the experiment, and/or a bonus for high quality results [8]. Past work has shown that the quality of work produced in a crowdsourcing working session can be influenced by the presence of financial incentives, such as bonuses. *WinoFlexi* adopts this philosophy and rewards Contributors based on "relative performance", namely only the worker that performs best receives rewards.

4   Experimental Design and Results

In recent years, a growing number of researchers have been using well-known crowdsourcing platforms [9]. A large body of work has shown **MicroWorkers (MW)** to be a reliable and cost-effective source for various fields and research purposes [8, 9]. Platforms like MW offer a framework that enables the employers to submit individually designed tasks to the crowd. MW has almost 1.5 million subscribed workers, and offers more than 40 million tasks. The MW platform offers many features which can influence the completion time and the results. Moreover, it provides campaign creators with predefined groups of workers from different regions that are organized according to their skills (e.g., best rated countries, writers, workers with certain language qualification tasks). To attract the worker's attention we used a simplified title (*title: Develop Groups of Sentences, Questions & Answers that Meet Certain Criteria*) and promoted it on the MW platform. Workers were given instructions explaining the task directing them to develop schemas without sacrificing accuracy. It was made clear that the development of invalid schemas might ban them from the system. Furthermore, we promoted *WinoFlexi* only under the Hired-Section of *English Speaking Countries + En*, meaning that only members of that group were able to participate. Our selected workers have both English proficiency, and admission tests passed. For our task, we offered a compensation of $1.00 for each developed schema or for the validation of three schemas in a row. We also advertised a bonus for quality schemas without stating the amount.

The experiments ran for one week, and yielded more than 165 schemas (see Table 1), from 50 workers, aged 18 to 65. From the developed schemas, 135 (81%) were valid, and 30 invalid. The highest score of a worker was 250 points and the lowest was −70; the Contributor with the lowest score was automatically banned by *WinoFlexi*. The majority of the workers had a non-negative score, and the top three workers had a score of at least 170, which well-exceeded the second condition for qualifying as an Evaluator. The total cost of our campaign was $258.00. The Contributors were paid $165.00 for the schema development

Table 1. Snapshot of the Contributors' Developed Schemas on *WinoFlexi*.

1	Erica called Jennifer on the phone because she was not responding to email	Who was not responding to email?	Jennifer, Erica
	Erica called Jennifer on the phone because she was not able to email	Who was not able to email?	
2	If Rachel listened to Mrs. Sheila, she would have given her full marks	Who would give full marks?	Mrs. Sheila, Rachel
	Had not Rachel ignored Mrs. Sheila, she would have got full marks	Who would have got full marks?	
3	The martial artist defended himself from the drug dealer because he was violent	Who was violent?	The drug dealer, The martial artist
	The martial artist defended himself from the drug dealer because he was under attack	Who was under attack?	

process, with an additional \$63.00 given as bonuses. On the other hand, \$30.00 were paid to Evaluators for the schema evaluation process.

Our experimental evaluation shows that *WinoFlexi* supports the development of *valid* schemas, with a cost of approximately \$1.91 per schema. Considering the challenge difficulties, we believe that this is a fair cost. Mean response time across all workers was 1.48 min, and the average time for the best worker was 1.66 min. 60% of the bonuses were offered to the top five workers. We believe that our adopted approach leads to more bonus opportunities for workers who submit schemas of good quality.

Evaluators were not observed to show a preference for the evaluation process over the schema design process. Although the evaluation process seems more straightforward, workers might have preferred the schema design process for the following reasons: *(i)* they were more familiar with the schema design process than the evaluation process; *(ii)* through the schema design process they were eligible for rewards, such as cash bonuses; *(iii)* they did not want to leave other Contributors unpaid, or lower their score.

The general picture emerging form the analysis above is that *WinoFlexi* is a platform where workers can collaborate for the schema development process. However, there is a key question when considering this approach that we have not addressed yet: How does the quality of the developed schemas compare to that of schemas in existing collections?

4.1 Quantitative Analysis

Co-reference Resolution: Our baselines are three co-reference resolution systems that were used on the Winograd-library [4], namely the *Stanford-Core-NLP* system, *Wikisense* [10], and *Knowledge-Parser* [2]. Showing a positive correlation of the performance of the three systems on the Winograd-library and the WinoFlexi-library would offer evidence that *WinoFlexi* can be used to develop schemas of good quality. For our experiment, we randomly selected 50 schemas (100 schema-halves) from each library. On the Winograd-library, **Stanford-Core-NLP** correctly resolves 37% schema-halves, incorrectly resolves

39% of them, and does not make any decision on the remaining 23%. On the WinoFlexi-library, it correctly resolves 44% schema-halves, incorrectly resolves 44% of them, and does not make any decision on the remaining 12%. **Wikisense** correctly resolves 59% schema-halves of the Winograd-library, incorrectly resolves 31% of them, and does not make any decision on the remaining 9%. On the WinoFlexi-library, it correctly resolves 56% schema-halves, and incorrectly resolves 44%. **K-Parser** correctly resolves 38% schema-halves of the Winograd-library, incorrectly resolves 36%, and does not make any decision on the remaining 26%. On the other hand, on the WinoFlexi-library, it correctly resolves 37% schema-halves, incorrectly resolves 37% of them, and does not make any decision on the remaining 26%. Comparison of the results shows that the performance of the three systems on the WinoFlexi-library is analogous to their performance on the Winograd-library. According to our results, the two libraries have correlation coefficients of 0.925 (Stanford-Core-NLP), 0.987 (Wikisense), and 0.995 (K-Parser), respectively. The results provide evidence that our developed schemas are of the same or similar quality with the Winograd-library schemas.

Hardness Metric Tool: For the purpose of this experiment, we randomly selected 57 schema-halves of the WinoFlexi-library, and compared their hardness index to that of 57 schema-halves of the Winograd-library taken from a previous work [3]. Figure 5 shows in more detail how the computed hardness index varies across schema-halves, suggesting that indeed, the two sets have comparable average hardness indices and analogous variability in their hardness indices. The general picture emerging from the analysis shows that despite the fact that our workers were not initially familiar with the schema development process, through *WinoFlexi*'s mechanisms they were trained to design schemas of good quality. Furthermore, the data presented here provides evidence that the *WinoFlexi* schemas avoid Levesque's pitfalls, meaning that the questions of the schemas are neither too obvious, nor are their answers not obvious enough.

Schema Structure: Next, we compare the structure of all the crowd-generated schemas (WinoFlexi-library) to that of all the expert-generated schemas (Winograd-library), as a way to determine if using crowdworkers sacrifices quality in exchange for scalability.

For this experiment, we developed a tool that identifies the sentence pattern of each designed schema. Given as input an English sentence, it outputs its pattern/type which can be either a simple, a compound, a complex, or a compound-complex sentence. Simple sentences have only one independent clause (SV; where S = Subject and V = Verb), while compound sentences can have two or more independent clauses (e.g., "SV and SV"). On the other hand, complex sentences can have one independent clause plus one or more dependent clauses (e.g., "SV because SV"), and compound-complex sentences can have two or more independent clauses plus one or more dependent clauses (e.g., "SV and SV because SV."). The connector in each complex sentence shows how the dependent

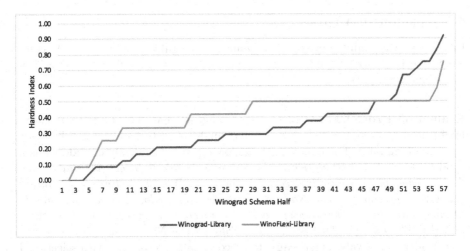

Fig. 5. Hardness index variability across 57 schema Halves of the Winograd-library and 57 schema Halves of the WinoFlexi-library. Each group is sorted based on the hardness index.

clause relates to the independent clause. Based on the typical connectors found in Winograd schemas, we consider the following groupings of connectors for our analysis: *(i)* Cause/Effect: because, since, so that; *(ii)* Comparison/Contrast: although, even though, though; *(iii)* Place/Manner: where, how, however; *(iv)* Possibility/Conditions: if, whether, unless; *(v)* Relation: that, which, who; *(vi)* Time: after, as, before.

The results showed that 9% of the crowd-schemas are based on simple sentences, 8% on compound sentences, and 83% on complex sentences. On the other hand, 41% of the expert-schemas are based on simple sentences, 14% on compound sentences, and 45% on complex sentences. Most of the developed schemas (both expert and crowd) are based on complex sentences. The expert-schemas that were designed with complex sentences had 30% "Cause/Effect", 8% "Comparison/Contrast", 1% "Place/Manner", 4% "Possibility/Condition", 18% "Relation", and 39% "Time" relationships. On the other hand, the crowd-schemas had 52% "Cause/Effect", 1% "Comparison/Contrast", 2% "Possibility/Condition", 1% "Relation", and 44% "Time" relationships. The results provide evidence that with *WinoFlexi*'s help the crowd was able to develop quality schemas that are based on a variety of sentence patterns, similar to the expert developed schemas. Additionally, the fact that crowd-schemas are not based on simple sentences, like the expert-schemas are (41%), might show that the crowd did not sacrifice quality in exchange for scalability. Considering the challenge difficulties, it seems that *WinoFlexi* can motivate and inspire researchers for the faster development of new schemas.

4.2 Qualitative Analysis

Based on the valid developed schemas, and taking into account comments received from Contributors, we present below a qualitative analysis of *WinoFlexi*'s outputs.

Evaluation Procedure: Certain outputs suggest that *WinoFlexi*'s evaluation might need to be optimized, and schemas might need to be evaluated by more than one Evaluator. For instance, the following was mistakenly considered as a valid schema: *1. Sentence: Karen loved going to salons to get her nails done. They always looked so nicely decorated. Question: What looked nicely decorated? Answers: The Salons, The Nails. 2. Sentence: Karen loved going to salons to get her nails done. They always looked so nicely manicured. Question: What looked nicely manicured? Answers: The Salons, The Nails.* This schema cannot be considered as a valid one because the second half is resolvable with selectional restrictions; salons cannot be manicured.

Inspiration and Creativity: One of the problems during schema development is the lack of inspiration and creativity. It seems that the collective intelligence of the crowd is able to mitigate this issue. For instance, the workers developed schemas which are based on a variety of subjects, like cartoon heroes (spiderman, hulk), animals (hyenas, zebras), hospitals (psychiatrists, medications), people in general (fights, burglars), things (cards, drains). The following is an example schema: *1. Sentence: Spiderman spun his web around the Hulk because he was falling. Question: Who was falling? Answers: Hulk, Spiderman. 2. Sentence: Spiderman spun his web around the Hulk because he was annoyed. Question: Who was annoyed? Answers: Hulk, Spiderman.*

Enjoyment and Curiosity: Based on comments that we received, certain workers were motivated by an intrinsic incentive such as enjoyment and curiosity for new knowledge, and not only from potential rewards. Worker *Member0xx*, for example, offered the following comment: *"I am terribly sorry, on my most recent schema I accidentally selected the wrong option. The schema is about putting a shirt in the dryer. I hope it is something you can fix. Thank you for your time and allowing a platform to develop these schemas, I very much enjoy trying to figure out new ways to create a valid schema."*.

5   Conclusion and Future Work

We have presented *WinoFlexi*, an online crowdsourcing system built explicitly for the development of Winograd schemas. Despite the acknowledged difficulty of the task when assigned to individuals, our empirical evaluation offers evidence that online crowd platforms and systems like *WinoFlexi* might offer a viable alternative.

Among possible directions for future research, of interest would be the automation of parts of the process of schema development and validation, without taking humans out of the loop. Sentences upon which schemas could be built, for example, could be automatically detected by crawling the Web, and offered to the *WinoFlexi* crowdworkers for further processing and validation. This human-machine teaming might prove to lead to a more efficient utilization of human time, and might yield a more diverse set of schemas, perhaps expanding the creativity and inspiration of the crowdworkers. In terms of validation, one could attempt to identify heuristics employed by humans when evaluating schemas, and might seek to help Evaluators focus their attention to those aspects of a schema that might be more salient when determining its validity.

Acknowledgments. This work was supported by funding from the EU's Horizon 2020 Research and Innovation Programme under grant agreements no. 739578 and no. 823783, and from the Government of the Republic of Cyprus through the Directorate General for European Programmes, Coordination, and Development. The authors would like to thank Ernest Davis for sharing his thoughts and suggestions on this line of research.

References

1. Levesque, H., Davis, E., Morgenstern, L.: The Winograd schema challenge. In: Proceedings of the 13th International Conference on the Principles of Knowledge Representation and Reasoning (2012)
2. Sharma, A., Vo, N.H., Aditya, S., Baral, C.: Towards addressing the Winograd schema challenge - building and using a semantic parser and a knowledge hunting module. In: Proceedings of the 24th International Joint Conference on Artificial Intelligence, pp. 25–31 (2015)
3. Isaak, N., Michael, L.: A data-driven metric of hardness for WSC sentences. In: Lee, D., Steen, A., Walsh, T. (eds.), Proceedings of the 4th Global Conference on Artificial Intelligence. EPiC Series in Computing, vol. 55, pp. 107–120. EasyChair (2018)
4. Morgenstern, L., Davis, E., Ortiz, C.L.: Planning, executing, and evaluating the Winograd schema challenge. AI Mag. **37**(1), 50–54 (2016)
5. Isaak, N., Michael, L.: Using the Winograd schema challenge as a CAPTCHA. In: Lee, D., Steen, A., Walsh, T. (eds.), Proceedings of the 4th Global Conference on Artificial Intelligence. EPiC Series in Computing, vol. 55, pp. 93–106. EasyChair (2018)
6. Rahman, A., Ng, V.: Resolving complex cases of definite pronouns: the Winograd schema challenge. In: Proceedings of the 2012 Joint Conference on Empirical Methods in Natural Language Processing and Computational Natural Language Learning, Stroudsburg, PA, USA, pp. 777–789. Association for Computational Linguistics (2012)
7. Christoforaki, M., Ipeirotis, P.: Step: a scalable testing and evaluation platform. In: Proceedings of the 2nd AAAI Conference on Human Computation and Crowdsourcing (2014)

8. Hirth, M., Hoßfeld, T., Tran-Gia, P.: Anatomy of a crowdsourcing platform – using the example of microworkers.com. In: Proceedings of the 5th International Conference on Innovative Mobile and Internet Services in Ubiquitous Computing, pp. 322–329. IEEE (2011)

9. Peer, E., Samat, S., Brandimarte, L., Acquisti, A.: In: Diehl, K., Yoon, D.C. (eds.), Beyond the Turk: An Empirical Comparison of Alternative Platforms for Crowdsourcing Online Research. NA - Advances in Consumer Research, vol. 43, pp. 18–22. Association for Consumer Research, MN (2015)

10. Isaak, N., Michael, L.: Tackling the Winograd schema challenge through machine logical inferences. In: Pearce, D., Pinto, H.S. (eds.), STAIRS. Frontiers in Artificial Intelligence and Applications, vol. 284, pp. 75–86. IOS Press (2016)

Detecting Depression in Dyadic Conversations with Multimodal Narratives and Visualizations

Joshua Y. Kim[1]([✉]), Greyson Y. Kim[2], and Kalina Yacef[1]

[1] University of Sydney, Darlington, NSW 2006, Australia
{josh.kim,kalina.yacef}@sydney.edu.au
[2] Success Beyond Pain, Success, WA 6164, Australia
greyson.kim@gmail.com

Abstract. Conversations contain a wide spectrum of multimodal information that gives us hints about the emotions and moods of the speaker. In this paper, we developed a system that supports humans to analyze conversations. Our main contribution is the identification of appropriate multimodal features and the integration of such features into verbatim conversation transcripts. We demonstrate the ability of our system to take in a wide range of multimodal information and automatically generated a prediction score for the depression state of the individual. Our experiments showed that this approach yielded better performance than the baseline model. Furthermore, the multimodal narrative approach makes it easy to integrate learnings from other disciplines, such as conversational analysis and psychology. Lastly, this interdisciplinary and automated approach is a step towards emulating how practitioners record the course of treatment as well as emulating how conversational analysts have been analyzing conversations by hand.

Keywords: Multi-disciplinary AI · Conversational analysis · Visualization · Multimodal data

1 Introduction

When people speak, a lot of information is communicated at several levels. The content, as well as the way the speech is delivered, gives us hints about the emotions and moods of the speaker. To be a good listener in the conversation or a third-party conversation analyst, one must consider a wide range of information, paying attention to the choice of words, attitudes, and emotions, for example.

Analyzing conversations is complex and time-consuming. In specialized settings, such as a clinical psychology setting, expert insights are required to get a sense of what to look out for – both in terms of what was said and how it was said. For example, people who are clinically depressed tend to lose interest in things they were previously interested in [1] (which relates to what was said). Also, while responding, the clients tend to have a longer response time and/or have reduced affect display in facial expression [2, 3] (which relates to how it was being said). As an anecdotal example from one of our authors' experience as a practicing clinical psychologist, his experience is aligned to the aforementioned literature and he also found that during the initial

© Springer Nature Switzerland AG 2019
J. Liu and J. Bailey (Eds.): AI 2019, LNAI 11919, pp. 303–314, 2019.
https://doi.org/10.1007/978-3-030-35288-2_25

treatment, depressed clients tend to employ avoidance coping, such as responding with ambivalence (e.g., I don't know') when they are asked to encounter their inner experience.

In another related discipline, conversational analysis, multimodal information from dialogs have been transcribed using a technical system developed by Jefferson [4]. This system encodes information about how it was being said in addition to what was being said. The challenge is that the manual encoding of such information is very time-consuming and susceptible to human error.

In this paper, we alleviate the manual-intensive problem of representing and visualizing multimodal information. We customize our conversational analysis system so that it takes in temporal multimodal information, weaves them into the verbatim transcript and automatically generates a prediction score for the depression state of the individual. We discuss insights from current practices in the clinical psychology industry to help inform our construction of the multimodal narrative. With the help of current artificial intelligence (A.I.) algorithms, we extract features to accomplish a task that demands both attention and domain-specific expertise. The experiments show that our proposed method performs better than the baseline model. Lastly, we present an example of how the content of a conversation can be visualized and analyzed intuitively by humans.

2   Related Works

2.1   Textual Multimodal Representation

Representations of multimodal information are typically vector-based, i.e., numerical. However, we are proposing a textual form of multimodal representation. There are two closely related tasks in the domain of machine learning – visual question-answering (VQA) [5] and dense video captioning [6] tasks. In these tasks, the model is trained to take in the video input and output a sequence of text that describes the video or answer questions. Our objective differs from these tasks, because our generated text is both used as an intermediary step for downstream models as well as a final product to be used in visualizations. Therefore, our objectives surrounding the generated text are (1) interpretability of the downstream model, and (2) whether the downstream model would be performant. Consequently, we are not concerned with the measures typically used in VQA and dense video captioning tasks to compare against the ground truth. Instead, our objective measure would be on the downstream model performance.

2.2   Detecting Depression with Automated Conversational Analysis

Recently, there has been a growing interest in interdisciplinary research that assesses human conversations automatically. We focus on applications that detect depression and discuss past attempts at detecting depression in conversations. The Audio/Visual Emotion Challenge (AVEC), in the year of 2016, 2017 and 2019, has invited researchers to predict the level of depression severity (measured by the PHQ-8 questionnaire) from audio-visual recordings of a clinical interview. Since our dataset was also used in the AVECs, past attempts in the AVECs are highly relevant.

Although the challenges were about analyzing conversations, we did not find any past accepted papers that were concerned with the textual presentation of the analysis. Many accepted papers did, however, use text as an input. Some used the verbatim transcript in the text format as input into the model. Others extracted numeric features from the transcripts in three main ways – timings, keyword searches, and emotional indices.

3   Data

3.1   Data Collection

We used a publicly available multimodal dataset, Distress Analysis Interview Corpus [7]. It contains interviews of individuals conducted by a virtual human designed to help diagnosis of psychological distress conditions. Self-reported PHQ-8 scores are provided as the dependent variable, with an interval scale from 0 to 24, and larger scores indicate greater severity. In total, there are 219 participants. This dataset was also used in the AVEC 2019 challenge. The organizers have performed the digitization step to extract baseline features [8]. The scripts that replicate the baseline features extraction is publicly available[1]. Of the baseline features, we used the Geneva Minimalistic Acoustic Parameter Set (egemaps) and Facial Action Units (AU).

3.2   Feature Extraction

Using the provided data and features, we extracted more features and classified them into three different levels of inputs. Figure 1 provides an overview of the prediction process and the distribution of the PHQ score. The baseline level of input is the session-level numeric features, followed by a session-level coarse summary. Lastly, the multimodal narrative comprised of both the verbatim transcript and multimodal information at the talk-turn level. The motivation is to produce an interpretable set of features that considers the temporal nature of conversational analyses. In total, there are nine features extracted at the session-level and four features extracted at the talk-turn level.

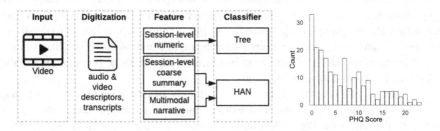

Fig. 1. The high-level architecture of the pipeline (left) and distribution of PHQ score (right).

---

[1] https://github.com/AudioVisualEmotionChallenge/AVEC2019.

3.2.1   Session-Level Numeric Features

We created three families of session-level inputs – *prosody*, *actions*, and *demographics*. Table 1 gives an overview of all features. Summary statistics refer to the maximum, minimum, average, and standard deviation of the feature for the entire session.

Table 1.   Session-level numeric features.

Family	Child	Feature
Demo-graphics	Talkativeness	Total word count & Total distinct word count
	Big 5 Personality	Percentile scores for each of the big 5 personality
	Gender	Predicted Male/Female
Actions	Laughter	Total laughter count
	Facial expression	Summary statistics of the given AU intensity and count values
Prosody	Delay	Summary statistics of time gaps between talk-turns
	Speech rate	Average speech rate

Firstly, for the family of *demographics*, we investigated the effects of *talkativeness*, *Big 5 Personality*, *Gender*. *Talkativeness* is selected because depressed individuals have been found to show reduced response length and poor articulation of distinct words [9].

Of the *Big 5 Personality*, higher neuroticism and lower conscientiousness have been found to correlate with higher depression. In a meta-analysis that reviewed 851 effect sizes based on 175 articles, strong effect sizes have been observed in the correlations between depression and neuroticism ($d = 1.33$), and conscientiousness ($d = -.90$) [10]. Interestingly, it has been found that the *Big 5 Personality* did not correlate with psychomotor retardation, while the *Big 5 Personality* correlates with the negative affect component in depression [11]. Hence, the present study included proxies of depression from both affective (*Big 5 Personality*) and physiological dimensions (*Speech Delay*, *Speech Rate*, *Talkativeness*).

Gender differences exist in the manifestation of depression. Firstly, in a large study using about 80,000 individuals, women tend to report more depressive symptoms than men across all age groups [12]. Secondly, in perpetuating depression, chronic strain, low mastery, and rumination were reported to be more common in women than in men [13]. Therefore, the factor of gender is included to capture these possible systematic differences in depression manifestation.

The method of extracting features for the family of *demographics* is as follows. *Talkativeness* is measured by the total word count and total distinct word count from the supplied transcripts. *Big 5 Personality* is computed using the IBM Watson Personality Insights API, which returns the five percentile scores – one for each *Big 5 personality* – which are used as inputs. *Gender* is predicted by a regularized logistic regression model using the egemaps features supplied. Using all 16 egemaps variables, we obtained an accuracy of 99.1% on the pooled predictions from the cross-validation. We used one-hot encoding to represent gender as a numeric feature.

Secondly, for the family of *actions*, we investigated the effects of *laughter* and *facial expressions*. The reduction in *laughter* frequency has been found to be a symptom of depression, which may be linked to humor deficit and increased feelings of anhedonia observed in depressed patients [14]. *Facial expressions* of emotions are also expected to be reduced with depression [15].

The method of extracting features for the family of actions is as follows. *Laughter* events were detected using the open-source algorithm [16]. We summed up the total number of laughter events per session. As for *facial expressions*, we computed summary statistics for the intensity and count values of each AU. To limit the number of input features, we only computed summary statistics for four AU (AU5, 17, 20, 25) because these have been found to be effective in Yang et al. [17]. The description of each of the four AUs are – AU5: Upper lid Raiser; AU17: Chin raiser; AU20: Lip stretcher; AU25: Jaw drop [18].

Lastly, for the family of *prosody*, we investigated the effects of delay and speech rate. These two features were selected because of the existing literature that suggests the following. Firstly, higher delays in responses (also known as speech pause time) have been found to positively correlate with higher depression scores [2, 3]. Secondly, a lower speech rate has also been found to also correlate with higher depression scores [19].

The method of extracting features for the family of *prosody* is as follows. We computed the summary statistics of time gaps between talk-turns. As for speech rate, the overall average speech rate is computed by dividing the total number of words spoken by the total number minutes of talk-turn duration.

3.2.2 Session-Level Coarse Summary

In addition to numerical inputs, we investigated whether it is possible to represent the inputs in the form of text. The motivation is that in clinical psychology consultations, practitioners are ethically obligated to summarize session-level progress details, to inform subsequent assessments and interventions in the course of treatment (see https://www.psychology.org.au for example). This investigation is a step towards emulating how practitioners record the course of treatment and provides insights on analyzing the session-level coarse summaries. In this section, we first explain the automatic generation of a text representation, then we motivate the extraction of a new family of input features – *comprehension*. The overview of templates for the session-level coarse summary is provided in Table 2.

The method of converting session-level features into text representation involves standardization of the numerical inputs across the training dataset. For each of the numerical inputs, we computed the standardized score (z-score) using the mean and standard deviation obtained from the training fold. Depending on the standardized score, we inserted templates 1 to 7 (except 3), where possible values in the bold-face were "very low" (z-score < -2), "low" (z-score < -1), "high" (z-score > 1) and "very high" (z-score > 2). We did not insert any templates when the z-score was within the normal range of -1 to 1 to keep the narrative succinct. As for template 3, we used the predicted gender from the logistic regression model.

Table 2. Templates for the session-level coarse summary.

Family	Child	ID	Template
Demo-graphics	Talkativeness	1	'number of words **high** number of distinct words **high**'
	Big 5 Personality	2	'openness **very high**'
	Gender	3	The participant is **female**
Actions	Laughter	4	'laughter counts **high**'
	AU	5	'minimum lip depressor **very low** maximum lip depressor **low** average lip depressor **low** variance lip depressor **low**'
Prosody	Delay	6	'minimum delay **very low** maximum delay **low** average delay **low** variance delay **low**'
	Speech rate	7	'speech rate **high**'
Comprehension	Yang et al. [17]	8	See Table 3
	DSM-5	9	See Table 3

Since we are changing the representation of the session from numerical features to text features, we also investigated the addition of a new family of input features – *comprehension*. The recent progress of machine comprehension has prompted the research question of the benefits of using trained machine comprehension models to extract text features for downstream supervised learning. Machine comprehension models take in two inputs – the question and the passage – and return an extracted phrase from the passage that is most related to the question. In our application, we used the model as a targeted summarization tool. The *comprehension* input family consisted of two sets of questions which we discuss in turn. To extract the answers, we used the pre-trained Bidirectional Attention Flow model from AllenNLP [20]. We also set the minimum probability threshold to be 0.1, so that answers that are deemed to be low-confidence by the model are replaced by "not applicable".

The first set of *comprehension* questions were derived from Yang et al. [17], where the authors conducted a content analysis of the transcripts using keywords-matching to identify whether the participant is (a) previously diagnosed, (b) sleeping well, (c) shy or outgoing, (d) feeling bad or good. The second set of *comprehension* questions were derived from the DSM-5 [1]. The DSM-5 is widely used in Australia by psychologists and psychiatrists to make a diagnosis of depression. We present the set of derived questions along with a sample answer extracted from the transcripts in Table 3.

Table 3. Sample *comprehension* features derived.

Yang et al. [17]		DSM-5 [1]	
Question	Sample answer	Question	Sample answer
Am I diagnosed?	no I never been formally diagnosed	Do I feel depressed most of the day?	No lately I've still been pretty depressed
Am I sleeping well?	I have not been sleeping	Do I lose interest?	I was not interested in things that are that I would normally interested in and you know I was sort of withdrawn
Am I shy?	I'm not I'm not extremely shy	Do I feel tired?	Fatigued I'm very tired
How am I feeling lately?	irritated tired lazy	Do I feel worthless?	I feel like invisible
		Do I feel like dying?	I felt like I couldn't cope

3.2.3 Multimodal Narrative

In this section, we also investigated the effects of adding the entire transcripts, annotated with multimodal information. In effect, we added information on *what* was being
said as well as *how* it was being said at a talk-turn level.

At the talk-turn level, we introduced two families of information – *prosody*, and
actions. We weaved this information into the transcript to create the multimodal narrative. Table 4 gives an overview of the templates, the bold-face indicates a variable.

Table 4. Templates for the multimodal annotations

Family	Child	ID	Template
Actions	Laughter	10	'the participant **laughed and** said'
Prosody	Delay	11	'after **two** hundred milliseconds'
		12	'a **long** delay'
	Speech rate	13	'**quickly** said'

The laughter detection algorithm returns the time window of the detected laughter.
Using this time window, we inserted template 10 if the window of the laughter is
completely contained within the time window of the talk-turn.

The method of computing delay is through the provided time window for each talk-
turn in the transcripts. The nominal values (template 11) of delay could be used by the
model to compare the delay lengths across sessions; however the drawback of is that it
does not help the model consider the within-session variation in delay. Therefore, to
tackle this problem, we added template 12 where the template is dependent on the
standardized duration of the delay "long" ($1 \leq$ z-score < 2) and "significantly long"

$(2 \leq$ z-score). The mean and standard deviation of the delay are calculated using all talk-turn delays from the same session. Lastly, we appended template 13 to annotate speech rate variation within the session. Similar to template 12, the possible values of template 13 are dependent on the standardized words per minute for each talk-turn – "very slowly" (z-score < -2), "slowly" (z-score < -1), "quickly" (z-score > 1), and "very quickly" (z-score > 2).

4   Analysis

4.1   Evaluation Metric

To evaluate the performance of the models, the Concordance Correlation Coefficient (CCC) was used, this was also the metric used in the official AVEC 2019 challenges [8]. The CCC is defined by:

$$r_c = \frac{2r\sigma_x\sigma_y}{\sigma_x^2 + \sigma_y^2 + \left(\mu_x - \mu_y\right)^2} \tag{1}$$

where r represents the *Pearson's correlation coefficient (PCC)* between two vectors (ground-truth and prediction), μ represents the mean of each vector, and σ represents the standard deviation of each vector.

4.2   Ablation Test Design

To investigate the benefits of including different families of input features, and different learning algorithms, we designed a series of ablation tests. We discuss the motivations for our ablation test design, as illustrated in Fig. 2. The dotted boxes correspond to the granularity of feature input, as described in Fig. 1. The grey boxes denote the learning algorithm. The white boxes denote the families of inputs that were common to our existing system; whilst the blue boxes denote the families of inputs that are newly added features in this paper. For each model, we start from the left, which uses only *demographic* features. The ablation test setup is such that we add one input family at a time, starting with A, then P and others. We discuss the four motivations for this design.

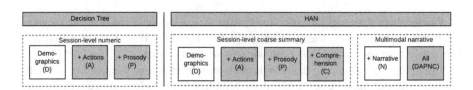

Fig. 2. The high-level architecture of the prediction pipeline.

The first motivation is the ability to compare the differences in performance between the two algorithms, keeping the input configurations similar. Therefore, in Fig. 2, we observe that it is possible to compare the performance of the decision tree versus the HAN for the first three configurations (D, DA, DAP).

The second motivation is the ability to investigate the additional benefits of progressively adding families of input into the configuration. Therefore, we have elected to add one family at a time. We have chosen demographics to be the starting configuration because this family of inputs is always populated for text inputs. In other words, because the other two families (*actions* and *prosody*) are only populated when they contain high standardized values (see Sect. 3.2.2), they are not suitable as the starting configuration.

The third motivation is the ability to investigate the benefits of employing the pre-trained machine comprehension model. Therefore, we have introduced a split at the end of the DAP configuration. On one path, we used the machine comprehension model to perform targeted summarization. On the other path, we used our automatically generated multimodal narrative, which includes both the multimodal information and verbatim transcript.

Lastly, the fourth motivation is the ability to investigate the effects of using all extracted information in the form of text in the DAPNC configuration.

4.3   Regression Tree

The regression tree used is from the rpart package within R. We used the "anova" splitting method to train the regression tree. We tuned the hyperparameters minimum split, maximum depth, and cp through a grid search and the cross-validation. We report in Table 5 the performance metrics using different inputs. The cross-validation is performed on the entire dataset.

4.4   Han

With the text features, each word is represented by the set of Glove word embeddings (300-dimensions). We tuned the learning rate, number of GRU units, recurrent dropout, GRU dropout, and L2 regularization via random-search. We used the Stochastic Gradient Descent optimizer. Batch size is set to 8. The training process consists of 350

Table 5. Cross-validation results for regression tree and HAN. The standard deviation of performance is presented in brackets.

Family	Regression tree	HAN
	CCC	CCC
D	0.144 (0.065)	0.171 (0.027)
DA	0.226 (0.125)	0.200 (0.035)
DAP	0.234 (0.052)	0.239 (0.056)
DAPC	N/A	0.291 (0.118)
DAPN		0.297 (0.132)
DAPNC		0.302 (0.092)

epochs, with no early stopping. We have also clipped the range of the predicted values to be between 0 and 24. The performances of HAN are also presented in Table 5. To facilitate all pairwise comparisons, we also computed whether the performance differences are statistically significant through bootstrapping the CCC differences (N = 1000). At the 0.95 significance level, we found significant differences in two pairs - Tree-D vs. HAN-DAPN, and Tree-D vs. HAN-DAPCN. At the 0.90 significance level, we found a significant difference in one additional pair – Tree-D vs. HAN-DAPC.

5 Discussion

For regression tree, we observe that the CCC cross-validation performance increases significantly from the D configuration (CCC = 0.144) to the DA configuration (CCC = 0.226) and then followed by a small increase in the DAP configuration (CCC = 0.234).

As for the HAN, the increase of CCC is almost linear as we progressively add the session-level inputs – from the D (CCC = 0.171), to DA (CCC = 0.200), and then the DAP configuration (CCC = 0.239). When we added the comprehension features, the performance increases markedly (CCC = 0.291). After that, the performance of the DAPC configuration is similar to DAPN (CCC = 0.297) and the configuration of DAPNC, which contains all text features, is the best (CCC = 0.302).

The DAPC configuration is an efficient way to extract text features for this supervised learning task. This is evident from two observations. Firstly, the performance increase from the DAP to DAPC configuration is high. Secondly, the difference between the DAPC and DAPN configuration is small. However, we posit that the challenge here is asking the machine comprehension model the right questions, which we attempted to overcome by using past research, including the DSM-5.

When we hold the input configuration constant, we found that text representation had the same level of performance as the regression tree when representing session-level inputs (DAP configuration). The CCC performances of other participants of the AVEC 2019 challenge – using the same number of observations and performance metric (CCC) – are not published at the time of writing this paper.

6 HAN Visualization

In the closing section, we demonstrate how the HAN model could be used to support humans analyze conversations, through using the attention weights. We used both the talk-turn as well as word-level attention weights to construct the visualization manually. Here, a talk-turn represents a question (answer) to (from) the machine comprehension model. We extracted and standardized attention weights from all talk-turns within the same session. Having computed the standardized talk-turn-level and word-level weights, we use the following style schemes to construct the visualization.

In the visualization, the numbers on the left indicate the talk-turn number. The analyst could first get a sense of the relative importance of all talk-turns by looking at the talk-turn-level attention weights. Then, the analyst could dive deeper and analyze the relative importance of each word.

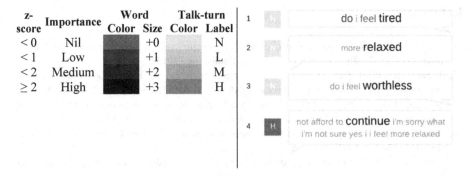

z-score	Importance	Word		Talk-turn	
		Color	Size	Color	Label
< 0	Nil		+0		N
< 1	Low		+1		L
< 2	Medium		+2		M
≥ 2	High		+3		H

Fig. 3. Conversation analysis example.

We picked an example that has the actual PHQ score of 20, and the model predicted a score of 15. In Fig. 3, we illustrate a short extract from the DAPC configuration that has talk-turns with high attention weights. In the extract, we observed that only talk-turn 4 are having high importance in making the prediction score of 15. More interestingly, we noted that the words marked as high importance are concepts semantically related to depression.

7 Conclusion

In this paper, experiments on the DAIC-WOZ dataset [7] were presented, with a focus on the multimodal text representation. Our proposed approach constructs a text narrative and then uses it as input to a model. Finally, both the model and the narrative are used to construct a visualization to analyze the dialog.

We have demonstrated that this approach could accommodate customizations, allowing the researcher to inject research findings from cross-disciplinary literature. In our application, we injected *talkativeness*, *big 5 personality*, *laughter*, *delay*, *speech rate*, *comprehension* information into our multimodal narrative. These selected features are guided by the psychology as well as the conversational analysis literature.

The ablation tests showed that text representations perform just as well as the regression trees. However, the flexibility of text representation makes it possible to extract more information through the pre-trained machine comprehension model and achieve a cross-validation CCC of 0.291. Using all the information, our system achieves a cross-validation CCC of 0.302. For future research directions, we would like to better understand the effectiveness of the produced visualizations and text summaries as well as the time savings from this automated approach through user-studies. There is also future work to improve or widen the multimodal feature extraction to further improve the performance of HAN.

Lastly, the visualization is a step towards emulating the way human conversation analysts analyze conversations, and a step towards emulating how practitioners keep a text record of the course of treatment.

References

1. American Psychiatric Association, et al.: Diagnostic and statistical manual of mental disorders (DSM-5®). American Psychiatric Publishing (2013)
2. Jouvent, R., Widlöcher, D., et al.: Speech pause time and the retardation rating scale for depression (ERD): towards a reciprocal validation. J. Affect. Disord. **6**, 123–127 (1984)
3. Stassen, H.H., Kuny, S., Hell, D.: The speech analysis approach to determining onset of improvement under antidepressants. Eur. Neuropsychopharmacol. **8**, 303–310 (1998)
4. Jefferson, G.: Glossary of transcript symbols with an introduction. Pragmat. Beyond New Ser. **125**, 13–34 (2004)
5. Antol, S., et al.: VQA: visual question answering. In: Proceedings of the IEEE International Conference on Computer Vision, pp. 2425–2433 (2015)
6. Krishna, R., Hata, K., Ren, F., Fei-Fei, L., Carlos Niebles, J.: Dense-captioning events in videos. In: Proceedings of the IEEE International Conference on Computer Vision, pp. 706–715 (2017)
7. Gratch, J., et al.: The distress analysis interview corpus of human and computer interviews. In: LREC, pp. 3123–3128 (2014)
8. Ringeval, F., et al.: AVEC 2019 workshop and challenge: state-of-mind, detecting depression with AI, and cross-cultural affect recognition. arXiv prepr. arXiv:1907.11510 (2019)
9. Buyukdura, J.S., McClintock, S.M., Croarkin, P.E.: Psychomotor retardation in depression: biological underpinnings, measurement, and treatment. Prog. Neuro-Psychopharmacol. Biol. Psychiatry **35**, 395–409 (2011)
10. Kotov, R., Gamez, W., Schmidt, F., Watson, D.: Linking big personality traits to anxiety, depressive, and substance use disorders: a meta-analysis. Psychol. Bull. **136**, 768 (2010)
11. Du, L., Bakish, D., Ravindran, A.V., Hrdina, P.D.: Does fluoxetine influence major depression by modifying five-factor personality traits? J. Affect. Disord. **71**, 235–241 (2002)
12. Angst, J., Gamma, A., Gastpar, M., Lépine, J.-P., Mendlewicz, J., Tylee, A.: Gender differences in depression. Eur. Arch. Psychiatry Clin. Neurosci. **252**, 201–209 (2002)
13. Nolen-Hoeksema, S., Larson, J., Grayson, C.: Explaining the gender difference in depressive symptoms. J. Pers. Soc. Psychol. **77**, 1061 (1999)
14. Fonzi, L., Matteucci, G., Bersani, G.: Laughter and depression: hypothesis of pathogenic and therapeutic correlation. Riv. Psichiatr. **45**, 1–6 (2010)
15. Berenbaum, H., Oltmanns, T.F.: Emotional experience and expression in schizophrenia and depression. J. Abnorm. Psychol. **101**, 37 (1992)
16. Ryokai, K., Durán López, E., Howell, N., Gillick, J., Bamman, D.: Capturing, representing, and interacting with laughter. In: Proceedings of the 2018 CHI Conference on Human Factors in Computing Systems, p. 358 (2018)
17. Yang, L., Jiang, D., He, L., Pei, E., Oveneke, M.C., Sahli, H.: Decision tree based depression classification from audio video and language information. In: Proceedings of the 6th International Workshop on Audio/Visual Emotion Challenge, pp. 89–96 (2016)
18. Ekman, P., Friesen, W.V: Manual for the facial action coding system. Consulting Psychologists Press (1978)
19. Cannizzaro, M., Harel, B., Reilly, N., Chappell, P., Snyder, P.J.: Voice acoustical measurement of the severity of major depression. Brain Cogn. **56**, 30–35 (2004)
20. Gardner, M., et al.: AllenNLP: a deep semantic natural language processing platform (2017)

An Explainable Intelligence Model for Security Event Analysis

Neda AfzaliSeresht[1,2(✉)], Qing Liu[2], and Yuan Miao[1]

[1] ISILC, Victoria University, Melbourne, Australia
{Neda.afzaliseresht,Yuan.Miao}@vu.edu.au
[2] Data61, CSIRO, Hobart, Australia
Q.Liu@data61.csiro.au

Abstract. Huge volume of events is logged by monitoring systems. Analysts do not audit or trace the log files, which record the most significant events, until an incident occurs. Human analysis is a tedious and inaccurate task given the vast volume of log files that are stored in a "machine-friendly" format. The analysts have to derive the context for an incident using the prior knowledge to find relevant events to the incident to recognise why it has happened. Although the security tools by providing visualization techniques and minimizing human interactions have been developed to make the process of analysis easier, far too little attention has been paid to interpret security incident in a "human-friendly" format. Besides, the current detection patterns and rules are not mature enough to recognize early breaches, which have not caused any damage. In this paper, we presented an Explainable AI model that assist the analysts' judgement to infer what is happened from the security event logs. The proposed Explainable AI model includes storytelling as a novel knowledge representation model to present the sequence of the events which automatically are discovered from the log file. For automated discovering sequential events, an aprioriority-like algorithm by mining temporal patterns is utilized. This effort focused on security events to convey both short-life and long-life activities. The experimental results demonstrate the potential and advantages of the proposed Explainable AI model from the security logs that validated on the activities during the security configuration compliance on Windows system.

Keywords: Security events · Storytelling · Periodic frequent item set

1 Introduction

Every day, millions of activities and attempts are recorded in computer systems. Logs, the outputs of the recording process, are usually intended for security and diagnostic purposes; their data can be extremely useful in system audits and forensic investigations. When monitoring systems generate alerts, the first place analysts investigate are the event logs. The log file contains rich information including: when the problem occurred, what applications were running, and which application might have caused the problem. Log file analysis is carried out using a mix of both the powers of machines and the powers of human beings [1, 2]. Machines typically perform simple tasks to tackle the volume and heterogeneity of input data. The human verification on filtered

© Springer Nature Switzerland AG 2019
J. Liu and J. Bailey (Eds.): AI 2019, LNAI 11919, pp. 315–327, 2019.
https://doi.org/10.1007/978-3-030-35288-2_26

data is then required to justify events with minimal false positives. However, what seems to be missing from filtered data is the detail and relevant knowledge. The current approaches apply sufficient context to the data, or have enough intelligence to know why certain classifications are important [3]. Such shortcoming requires human involvement in order to determine the relationship between the events. At the same time, the machine-friendly format of log files is highly challenging for the analysts to extract valuable knowledge [4].

In prior research, automated Cyber Situation Awareness (CSA) tools and models that enhance the cognition and understanding of experts have been proposed [5]. Still, the existing Cyber Situation Awareness systems have not been able to address the challenges practically [5]. A significant impact on the usability of correlation approaches, such as conceptual expressiveness, is achieved through the representation used to model events [6]. Semantic analysis of the log files is also the earlier approach for assistance of forensic investigators and security analysts. Massive volume of the events are not comprehended, thus the researchers focus their effort on the context, and the link to enrich background knowledge [7].

Storytelling is a novel knowledge representation method with high persuasion that can highlight the semantic and implied information from log files into a human-understandable format [8]. The stories generated take advantage of human cognition by building the context around the facts. According to Mackinaly et al. [9], *"Data tells you what is happening. Stories tell you why it matters"*.

The mining algorithm proposed in this paper is similar to the one applied by Khan and Parkinson [10]; however we differ in focus. Although the timespan was used for determining the ordering of event sequences by Khan and Parkinson [10], it was not considered in the mining process for frequent item set. As a result, only the activities that are repeated in the log files are identified as frequent patterns, omitting the short-life activities. Besides, algorithm proposed in [10] deals with different unresolved conflicts through the chain making of the events, that are addressed in this paper. On the other hand, the approach proposed by Mahanta et al. [11], considers the time for partially periodic patterns retrieval, however, the algorithm has only been tested in the market-basket problem [12]. The approach is borrowed for security events.

In this paper, sequence of events from log files is automatically filtered out and presented in a storytelling format. An Explainable AI model for the identification of periodic temporal associations *with timestamps* is proposed. The model is utilised to discover the relationships between events that persist for some duration of time. Since time plays an important role when representing the knowledge among the events, the model is developed to recognise the events within the variation of the association rules over time. Interesting events often occur within a specific period; therefore time aspect is very important factor in log files analysis [13]. By extension of the apriori-like algorithm in the proposed model, the interesting events within the observed period are mined and chains of the sequential events are produced. Furthermore, the interpretation of the sequential events chains in a natural language through the appropriate context enrichment has been proposed. The main contribution of this paper is the story design model for the security events contextualised interpretation to reduce human effort in relevant relationships between the events identification. The rest of the paper is organised as follows. First, we review the apriori-like algorithms from relevant literature, such as frequent item sets and association rules. Then, the proposed AI model is introduced. Finally, the storytelling model is evaluated on a case study, and compared to the algorithm adopted by Khan and Parkinson [10].

2 Terms and Definitions

2.1 Apriori-Like Algorithm

Apriori-like algorithm is a suitable candidate to discover temporal patterns in interval-based data. As the name of the algorithm shows, the main idea of the apriori algorithm is based on the inductive theory. If s ⊂ S, then it can be conducted that the support (S) ≤ support(s). It means that if k-length item set could not be recognised as satisfying pattern, there is no need to check any m-length item set, where m > k [14].

2.2 Frequent Item Set Mining with a Timestamp

The main idea for periodic mining item set is based on the work by Mahanta et al. [11]. According to which the local frequent set is a collection of item sets that are frequent in a specific period. A threshold is used to validate the gap between the current time and the last-seen time of appearance of a particular item set. If the gap exceeds the threshold, it means the last-seen time was the end point of the previous local frequent set, and the current time is the start point of the next period (next set). The minSupport checks the frequency of items in each local set. In other words, the local sets for each candidate are defined if the candidate from start point to end point of the associated time interval is repeated more than the minSupport.

The transaction is set in the time interval [Ti, Tj] if its timestamp occurs inside the interval. The $N_{[T_i,T_j]}$ is the number of transactions that occurred in the time interval [Ti, Tj], and the $N(x)_{[T_i,T_j]}$ is the number of transactions containing item set x. The support of a local item set is calculated as follows (1):

$$\text{support}(x)_{[T_i,T_j]} = \frac{\left|N(x)_{[T_i,T_j]}\right|}{\left|N_{[T_i,T_j]}\right|} \qquad (1)$$

Support amount is calculated in each local frequent set. The item sets may appear in more than one local frequent set. Therefore, the support of item set x is defined based on the average of the local support amounts, where each local support is greater than the minSupport. All k-length item sets are generated and stored as an array. The set of candidates extracted are commonly called CK, where C refers to the candidate, and K refers to the length of the sequence. If the average of local supports is greater than the minSupport, then the item set is added to the sub-sequences of the selected candidates (LK). CK for K > 1 is pruned by dropping the candidates if their item set was not found in the previous LK. All of the time intervals of item set x, when x occurs frequently (more than minSupport), are saved in an array [11].

2.3   Association Rules

"An association rule is an expression of the form x ⇒ y, where x, y are the item sets and x ∩ y = ∅" [15]. Association rules are generated from the discovered frequent item sets to extract useful and understandable patterns from a database. According to the Eq. (2), the support of each association rule is defined as follows:

$$\text{support}(x \Rightarrow y)_{[T_p, T_q]} = \frac{\left| N(x, y)_{[T_p, T_q]} \right|}{\left| N_{[T_p, T_q]} \right|} \tag{2}$$

Where N(x, y) is the number of transactions that contain both x and y in the time interval, the time interval [Tp, Tq] shows the intersection time of item set x and item set y. For generating the association rules, a subsequence called "consequence" is parted from each LK. If the item set from the LK is called as "frequence", then the association is defined according to AR = freq-cons ⇒ cons, and the time interval for each is calculated according to the Eq. (3), based on the TP array.

$$\text{Time (AR)} = \text{TP[freq-cons]} \cap \text{TP[cons]} \tag{3}$$

For each association rule, a confidence value is defined. The confidence of an association rule x ⇒ y is the ratio between the number of transactions that contain x and y and the number of transactions that contain x. The confidence determines the conditional probability of having y contained in a transaction, given that x is contained in that transaction. By defining a rule based on AR, the confidence is estimated using the Eq. (4) based on the support values.

$$\text{Confidence AR}_{\text{Time (AR)}} = \frac{\text{support[freq]}}{\text{support [freqt-conseq]}} \tag{4}$$

An association rule is valid if the confidence in the time interval is greater than the minConf, which is determined by the user. By using the timestamp and finding the local frequent sets, the candidate has great confidence. It means that the timestamps help to select and validate candidates before filtering through the threshold.

3   Related Works

In recent years, many studies present convincing arguments that time plays an important role to identify the knowledge among temporal data since data usually contain time stamping [13]. The timestamp is the main part of a log that conveys the knowledge from what is happened among logs. i.e. logging in a server after the work hours is suspicious activity in many scenarios; however, it is normal if it happens during the work hours. Only time conveys the knowledge.

Retrieving knowledge among the log file by considering the time is also a very important factor for computer forensics investigations to reconstruct the past events and find the relation between them [16]. Digital evidence is built based on computer activates, not only logs [17]. Thus, forensic investigators used software tools for demonstrating the activities through the timeline and compare them with other discovery. According to the limitation of the space, please refer to the survey in [18] for more details.

Semantically analysis the logs are an earlier approach for assisting forensic investigators and security analysts. A Massive volume of events not comprehended; thus, researchers focus on the context and find the linked to rich background knowledge [7]. In [10], a manual pre-defined statuses for activity plan is proposed. The output results used as an automating learning approach from the human. A story from the log file is a novel approach to support the analytical process. There are not much efforts to support analysts by using narrative formats. Simple concepts in sequential sentences are organised in the Explainable AI to discern where the events are headed. It is easier for a human being to find co-relations of events in the log files when they were modelled using storytelling design.

4 The Proposed Explainable AI Model

We used temporal association mining to extract frequent periodical events from log files. The aim of the proposed algorithm is to automatically find chains of the sequence of events in a contiguous subset of log file through time. The main framework of the proposed algorithm is shown in Fig. 1.

1-Extract entities from log file by pre-processing
2-Generate event rules (Figure 2)
3-Generate chain of eventIDs form event rules
4-Generate a story from the chain of sub-sequent events

Fig. 1. The main framework of the proposed algorithm

4.1 Pre-processing

Let $L = \{ID, Timestamp, p_1, p_2,..., p_n\}$ be the log record from a log file in a Windows operation system, where ID and Timestamp are numeric event type IDs of the record and the time of recording respectively. P_i is the event property symbol. The common properties of the Windows event log have been defined by Microsoft. We defined Entity (E), as a set of properties, $E = \{p_i, p_{i+1},..., p_m\}$. The property p_i can be considered as an explicit field of the E such as "User", or an implicit property which is embedded in an explicit property, i.e. "Error-code" from "Message" property in the Windows security events is an implicit property. Both implicit and explicit properties are retrieved from a log record using regular expressions. A short sentence explaining each event is in form of a plain text. The text is part of the message property in the Windows platforms, called as "Short-Description" (implicit property that is extracted from the message property). List of the security event descriptions based on the event IDs can be found in [19].

According to the above model, a log record is L = {(ID, Timestamp), Entity, $(p_{t1},..., p_{tn})$, Short-Description}. The properties from p_{t1} to p_{tn} in the Entity are selected properties from the log record. By using the pre-processing, the Entity is a set of items, and the log file is a database of transactions. Each log record is a transaction with an associated identifier transaction ID (EventID), a timestamp and items. Let T = {t_1, t_2, ..., t_n} be a sequence of timestamps where $t_1 < t_2 < ... < t_n$. The log file is ordered in ascending order of timestamps. By defining the log files and entities based on the market-basket problem [12], using an association mining algorithm for identifying co-occurred properties of log records is easily applicable. The co-occurred properties belong to the relevant events and express happening. In this model, the apriori-like algorithm applied based on the work by Mahanta et al. [11].

## 4.2	Event Rules

The event-based rules are defined by the association rules. According to Sect. 4.1, each log record has eventID corresponding to the Entity, which is used to construct the item sets. Item sets are replaced with the corresponding eventID to construct event-based rules. Figure 2 depicts a procedure to find the log record, which contains all the properties from the item set x and y individually. Then, return the corresponding eventIDs that occurred during the Time (AR) according to Eq. (3). Since log file is ordered based on the timestamps ascending, the retrieval list of eventIDs from each side of the association rules shows the sequential ordering of the event-based rules. It means that each LH and RH in Fig. 2 contains a list of eventIDs that are ordered by time.

```
For x and y in the association-rules
     Item set1=x
     Item set2=y
     SearchinEvents(item set,evenTime,time(association-rule))
          eventID(item)
          if evenTime in interval time(association-rule)
               return eventID
     LH=list of eventIDs for item1
     RH=list of eventIDs for item2
```

Fig. 2. Conversion of association rules to event-based rules.

By considering the timestamps to find the frequent local item set, the sequence of events, which we call as a chain of events is created. It brings improvement in the algorithm proposed by Khan and Parkinson [10]. Since they did not use timestamp for finding the association rules. They proposed an algorithm to order the sequence of eventID and a solution to resolve the conflict in ordering the events, where at least two eventIDs are connected to the same destination. However, the same source and loop conflicts have not been considered. The same source and loop conflicts may happen among the log files since two parallel processes are started, or activity is repeated. Check the security configuration includes repeated activates, which in turn causes loops. For example, a common chain of the actions for checking security configuration is: login from a privileged user, try to login to a system with a blank password by running a script (an administrator defines the blank password for a target user - it is recorded in the log file as a successful or failed login), run the compliance toolkit to set a security baseline (the toolkit checks the blank password – it is recorded in log file as an attempt for finding the blank password), and try to login to a system with a blank password by running the script to validate the security configuration.

4.3   Event Chain to Story

The representation used to model events has a crucial impact on awareness. Generating a story from discovered events is more comfortable for human beings to find correlations of events in the log files. Since making a story requires the annotation to be generated, the short description property (explained in Sect. 4.1) is used for this purpose. Although the short description property interprets the main action (not subject and object), it makes sense for a user who follows-up the event sequence. Each eventID mapped to its corresponding short description causes a chain of subsequence events is translated into a story. While the ordered sequence is kept in the chain and transplantation is based on the order, a loop or the same source conflicts not happened. As Fig. 3 is shown, the event chain includes 5 eventIDs (with loop), the story is generated based on the sequence order without conflicts. Since the order of eventIDs is the same as their appearance in the chain, direction between two sequential eventIDs is only shown by the "→" symbol. By looking up the Table 1, which contains the eventID and its short description property, each event translates to its own description. Table 1 shows a snapshot of the eventID, short description and explanation based on the online source in [19]. The generated story provides a holistic view for better understanding and easier traceability of security events by analysts and forensic investigators. The story from the log files is chucked to M levels, according to Eq. (5), where M is the number of levels that are determined based on the number of association rules, and the interval time threshold that is considered for finding the local set of each item set.

$$M = \frac{N_{\ Association\ Rules}}{Thereshold_{\ TimeInterval}} \tag{5}$$

We suppose that each event in the log file happened 1 s after the previous event. Therefore, story of each local set is explained in one level. The first line of each level shows the start and stop time of period of the story. It helps analysts to make an easier and faster decision about an incident reported by monitoring systems due by referring the relevant story level. The story in each level provides more details about what happened in the period. Sequence of the most important events, which selected based on the frequent item set mining, is demonstrated in a human-understandable format.

Event chain [4717,4625,4688,4797, 4625]

Event by ordered symbol: 4717 → 4625 → 4688 → 4797 → 4625

Lookup the table for finding the short description for each eventID

Generate the story:

system security access was granted to an account → an account failed to log on → A new process has been created →

An attempt was made to query the existence of a blank password for an account → an account failed to log on

Story after using the Template:

From Time x to y (if each event occurred exactly 1 second after the previous one) time is equal to [AR]:

- system security access was granted to an account
- an account failed to log on
- a new process has been created,
- an attempt was made to query the existence of a blank password for an accounts
- an account failed to log on

Fig. 3. Translation of the chain of events into a story.

Table 1. Snapshot of mapping of eventIDs to their descriptions according to [19]

EventID	Short description	Explanation
4717	system security access was granted to an account	This event documents the grant of logon rights such as "Access this computer from the network" or "Logon as a service"
4625	an account failed to log on	It documents each and every failed attempt to logon to the local computer regardless of logon type, location of the user or type of account
4688	A new process has been created	It documents each program that is executed, who the program ran as and the process that started this process
4797	An attempt was made to query the existence of a blank password for an account	this event at least included the process that made the request

5   Experimental Results

In this section, we compare the proposed model with the model introduced by Khan and Parkinson [10], which we call the "StoryPlan". Although authors did not claim the proposal of a story from the log file, their action plans are extracted from the predefined statuses and activities, thus provide a level of understanding and representing the knowledge from the log file. As a result, we add the translation functions to their algorithm instead of their application of automated planning for easier comparison (their action plan is not available). The added function translate the chain of events into the descriptions.

To explain the working of our proposed model and its advantages, we run three scenarios on the Microsoft Windows Server 2012 R2 Base - 64-bit on the AWS[1].

---

[1] Amazon web Server.

The AWS instances are t2.micro type with 1 vCPU and 1 Gigabytes memory. The security event logs are gathered through the period that an administrator checks the security configuration by running PowerShell scripts or Microsoft Security Compliance Toolkit[2]. The aggregated logs are considered as inputs for the Explainable model and StoryPlan. The implicit and explicit properties are extracted based on the regular expressions. The Entity (Sect. 4.1) contains 18 properties as the following:

Entities = {*User, Computer, Event Source Name, Session ID, SecurityID, AccountName,*

AccountDomain, LogonID, LogonType, LogonGUID, ProcessID, ProcesName,

Caller_workstation, TargetAccountName, TargetAccountDomain, WorkstationName,

SourceNetAddress, SourcePort}.

The blank and none value properties are cleared from the data in the pre-processing step. The Date and Time, Event ID, and Short descriptions are extracted properties that stored in the separate tables. The minimum threshold for defining the local set is 300 s or 5 min. According to the experts from the SOC team in the educational institute, whom we work with, 5 min is a reasonable time to trace the incident event in the log files. While each local set is explained in one level of story, the minimum threshold defines the period for tracing events. The minSupport and minConfidence thresholds are considered with the same values in [10], 20% and 70% respectively. Table 2 shows the statistical results of 2 algorithms after running 3 scenarios with different numbers of logs as following:

- *Scenario 1:* login with admin remote user, clear the logs, create 2 accounts, enable auditing policies, run PowerShell scripts to find the blank password and corresponding information, install and run Microsoft Security Compliance Toolkit, run again PowerShell scripts to find the blank password and corresponding information
- *Scenario 2:* login with admin remote user, clear the logs, install and run Microsoft Security Compliance Toolkit, run PowerShell scripts to find the blank password and corresponding information
- *Scenario 3:* login with admin remote user, running the malware simulation tools, changing the auditing policies, install and run Microsoft Security Compliance Toolkit.

By defining local sets through the time, the sequential event rules are generated. As mentioned earlier, the loop and the same source conflicts have not been resolved in [12] for ordering the event rules. As shown in Table 2, events in "StoryPlan" have 5 conflicts in each scenario and the corresponding chain could not be generated. For example, in Scenario 3, there is an event rule that contains both ('4656', '4624') and ('4656', '4672'). No information is provided about which event should be the last one

---

[2] Security Compliance Toolkit (SCT) is a set of tools that allows enterprise security administrators to download, analyze, test, edit, and store Microsoft-recommended security configuration baselines for Windows and other Microsoft products.

in the sequence (the same source conflict). However, in our algorithm, the timestamp in the short period is able to account for the ordering of the events.

The results presented in Table 2 show that the number of association rules in our model is larger than that generated by "StoryPlan" for all scenarios. Since the average confidence for the association rules compared to the average amounts in "StoryPlan" are greater, it means that our proposed algorithm was able to discover the more temporal association items from the log files with better reliant ratio.

Different item set may appear in a log record with the same eventID. Therefore, the same chains may be generated from different item sets. Duplicated chains are deleted for easier understanding at each level. The total number of unique chains and the number of generated sentences are demonstrated in the Table 2. Since duplicated chains can differ from level to level of the story, each level contains various number of sentences.

Table 2. Comparison results from the proposed algorithm vs the proposed model in [10]

Parameters	Explainable AI model			Story plan model [10]		
Scenario	1	2	3	1	2	3
Num of logs	100	1276	4170	100	1276	4170
Num association rules	2509	42920	14982	54	1368	85
Avg confidence	0.9661	0.9663	0.9684	0.9226	0.9573	0.9682
Num unique chains	48	1470	191	6	17	7
Num conflicts	0	0	0	5	5	5
Num sentences	48 in 8 levels	1470 in 143 levels	191 in 50 levels	1	12	2

Figures 4 and 5 show the first generated story from the 2 algorithms in the Scenario 3. In Scenario 3, a malware activity is simulated and ran in the Windows server. The malware is simulated by running an open source tool (malware simulator). Malware simulator created and deleted a file (MalwareSimulator.txt) in all accessible areas. As the Fig. 4 shows, the generated story is started with "A handle to an object was requested". According to the [19], the short description for eventID 4656 is: "A handle to an object was requested". When an application attempts to access the object, a handler to an object is the first recorded event [19]. Therefore, the first event of the malware behaviour correctly is identified by the proposed algorithm.

As Fig. 4 shows, our proposed algorithm has identified the sequential events of the malware behaviour in the chain correctly; (the malware attempts to access different objects and gain the privileges). The story also displays that "An attempt was made to duplicate a handle to an object", which means that another level of access is inherited by the object; for accessing the inner folders. Then the malware updated the scheduled task. After this message, we see some sentences related to windows firewall activities. These is noise that occurred in the real environment, such as where the model was simulated. Our model was not able to ignore all the noise, but it tolerated it and generated a reasonable story with the sequential of events.

From 2019-08-01 07:31:00 to 2019-08-01 07:31:00   Story is:
[['A handle to an object was requested.'] ['The handle to an object was closed.'] ['An object was deleted.'] ['An attempt was made to access an object.'] ['An operation was attempted on a privileged object.'] ['A new process has been created.'] ['A process has exited.'] ['An attempt was made to duplicate a handle to an object.'] ['A scheduled task was updated.'] ['Auditing settings on object were changed.'] ['The state of a transaction has changed.'] ['The Windows Filtering Platform has permitted a connection.'] ['The Windows Filtering Platform has permitted a bind to a local port.']]]

Fig. 4. The first generated story by our proposed algorithm in Scenario 3

The output sentences from the "StoryPlan" is shown in Fig. 5. As the Fig. 5 shows, each translation explains different part of Windows activities that does not make sense in terms of what is the relationships between them; Just a sentence that mentioned "An object a file type, C:\Desktops\Malware.tmp was deleted" related to the malware activity, which attempts to delete a temporary object. Beyond the sequential sentences problem, there is no suggestion for how to pursue the story in "StoryPlan". Our model represents the log file by chucking the story with a specific period as a label. It is easy for users with different preferences to pursue the story through time. It brings an option for analysts to check the specific time for finding what is happened among the log files.

[['A scheduled task was updated.']   ['An object was deleted.']   ['The state of a transaction has changed.']
['An operation was attempted on a privileged object.']   ['An account was successfully logged on.']]]

Fig. 5. The first generated story by "StoryPlan" for Scenario 3 [10]

6 Discussion and Future Works

The disadvantage of the proposed model is a high computation performance since it employs the apriori-like algorithm and iteratively processes various sub-sets of events from a log file. However, the purpose of the model is to assist a human cognition for improved analysis, which takes place offline, after the machine analysis. Log files are analysed in an offline mode. The extracting knowledge is faster and more accurate than a human, who manually analysis and may miss events among the logs. Therefore, the performance can be neglected. In term of future directions, the Explain AI can be tested on more data to show the qualitative and quantities comparison results. Furthermore, to highlight the establishing the novelty of the model, terms such as 'an account', 'a new process', 'a handle', etc., can be translated by an enrichment function; thus makes sense for human and highlight the accuracy of the proposed model.

7   Conclusion

In this paper, Explain AI by automatically extracting the nutshell of cybersecurity events has been proposed. The output of the model reduces a huge amount of log records down to the more understandable sub-sets with chains of sequence and time period of occurrence. The events are translated into their own descriptions. The proposed model has been validated in terms of the effort that is required to convert the log files into the action plans. The proposed model has accomplished the 3 main improvements, i.e. (1) Automatically create chains of subsequent events without pre-defined status, (2) generate more accurate and easily traceable story through the time, and (3) discover the important short and long life span events.

References

1. Liu, S., Wang, X., Liu, M., Zhu, J.: Towards better analysis of machine learning models: a visual analytics perspective. Vis. Inf. **1**(1), 48–56 (2017)
2. CBEST Intelligence-led testing: Understanding cyber threat intelligence operations. Bank of England (2016). https://www.bankofengland.co.uk/-/media/boe/files/financial-stability/finan cial-sector-continuity/understanding-cyber-threat-intelligence-operations.pdf. Accessed 1 Nov 2019
3. Payne, J.: Build a fast, free, and effective threat hunting/incident response console with windows event forwarding and PowerBI (2017). https://blogs.technet.microsoft.com/jepayne/2017/12/08/weffles/
4. Tang, M., Fidge, C.: Reconstruction of falsified computer logs for digital forensics investigations. In: Proceedings of the Eighth Australasian Conference on Information Security, vol. 105, pp. 12–21. Australian Computer Society, Inc. (2010)
5. Albanese, M., Cam, H., Jajodia, S.: Automated cyber situation awareness tools and models for improving analyst performance. In: Pino, R.E., Kott, A., Shevenell, M. (eds.) Cybersecurity Systems for Human Cognition Augmentation. AIS, vol. 61, pp. 47–60. Springer, Cham (2014). https://doi.org/10.1007/978-3-319-10374-7_3
6. Schatz, B., Mohay, G., Clark, A.: Rich event representation for computer forensics. In: Proceedings of the Fifth Asia-Pacific Industrial Engineering and Management Systems Conference (APIEMS 2004), vol. 12, pp. 1–16 (2004)
7. Ekelhart, A., Kiesling, E., Kurniawan, K.: Taming the logs-Vocabularies for semantic security analysis. Proc. Comput. Sci. **137**, 109–119 (2018)
8. Wu, Q., et al.: Internet of things based data driven storytelling for supporting social connections. In: 2013 IEEE International Conference on Green Computing and Communications (GreenCom) and IEEE Internet of Things (iThings/CPSCom) and IEEE Cyber, Physical and Social Computing, pp. 383–390. IEEE (2013)
9. Mackinaly, J., Kosara, R., Wallace, M.: Data storytelling using visualization to share the human impact of numbers (2014). Accessed 5 July 2014
10. Khan, S., Parkinson, S.: Eliciting and utilising knowledge for security event log analysis: an association rule mining and automated planning approach. Expert Syst. Appl. **113**, 116–127 (2018)
11. Mahanta, A.K., Mazarbhuiya, F.A., Baruah, H.K.: Finding calendar-based periodic patterns. Pattern Recogn. Lett. **29**(9), 1274–1284 (2008)

12. Le, D.T., Lauw, H.W., Fang, Y.: Basket-sensitive personalized item recommendation. In: IJCAI (2017)

13. Ghorbani, M., Abessi, M.: A new methodology for mining frequent itemsets on temporal data. IEEE Trans. Eng. Manag. **64**(4), 566–573 (2017)

14. Meamarzade, H., Khayyambash, M.R., Saraee, M.H.: Graph base approaches in mining time interval sequence patterns. Isfahan University White Paper in Persian Language (2009). http://dl.papergram.ir/mobileapp/datamining/pishbini/g272.pdf

15. Aqra, I., et al.: A novel association rule mining approach using TID intermediate itemset. PLoS One **13**(1) (2018). https://doi.org/10.1371/journal.pone.0179703

16. Chabot, Y., Bertaux, A., Nicolle, C., Kechadi, T.: An ontology-based approach for the reconstruction and analysis of digital incidents timelines. Digit. Investig. **15**, 83–100 (2015)

17. Marrington, A., Baggili, I., Mohay, G., Clark, A.: CAT detect (computer activity timeline detection): a tool for detecting inconsistency in computer activity timelines. Digit. Investig. **8**, S52–S61 (2011)

18. Studiawan, H., Sohel, F., Payne, C.: A survey on forensic investigation of operating system logs. Digit. Investig. **29**, 1–20 (2019)

19. Smith, R.F.: Windows security log event id. https://www.ultimatewindowssecurity.com. Accessed 1 Nov 2019

Natural Language Processing and Text Analytics

Using Feature Filtering Metrics as Meta-dimensions in Constructing Distributional Representations

Dongqiang Yang[1(✉)], Yanqin Yin[1], Tonghui Han[2],
and Hongwei Ma[1]

[1] School of Computer Science and Technology, Shandong Jianzhu University,
Jinan 250101, China
dongqiang.yang@gmail.com
[2] Binzhou Polytechnic College, Binzhou, China

Abstract. Feature filtering aims to find useful and relevant features for improvement of machine learning performance, reduction of computation complexity, and disclosure of internal information interaction. We employ some popular filtering criteria as meta-dimensions for the construction of feature space, where a word or a document can be represented with significantly reduced dimensionality. The experiment results show that the meta-feature data representation we proposed requires no extra resources on pre-training to derive word embeddings, and outperforms other traditional frequency-based or learning-based embeddings in the task of sentiment analysis.

Keywords: Feature selection · Text classification · Sentiment analysis

1 Introduction

Feature selection often employs filters, wrappers, and embedded strategies alike to harvest relevant and useful information in data mining. Different from the wrappers and embedded methods where the selection process is directly involved in training classifiers, feature filtering is independent of the classifiers and works in a more fast and effective way of attribute selection. For example in text categorization, feature filtering first converts term distribution in a document collection through metrics like Pointwise Mutual Information (PMI) and Log-likelihood Ratio, among the others into meaningful information units. After ranking these transformed units, the insignificant features can be removed to mitigate the curse of dimensionality. The statistical model induced after feature selection may be more robust and generalize better while interpreting new data.

Motivated by the previous work [1, 2] on using feature filtering to retrieve salient features from data samples, we investigate its effectiveness and efficiency on reconstructing a novel distributional representation for text classification. On assumption that these filtering criteria can be viewed as meta-dimensions or meta-features, we study how to transform the *document-by-word* representation commonly used in text categorization into a *document-by-criterion* one, where the new dimensions only consist of some of typical filtering metrics such as Information Gain (IG), Mutual Information

J. Liu and J. Bailey (Eds.): AI 2019, LNAI 11919, pp. 331–343, 2019.
https://doi.org/10.1007/978-3-030-35288-2_27

(MI), and Odds Ratio (OR). This new data representation can significantly reduce the high dimensionality inherited in the *document-by-word* representation more intuitively. The experiment results also show that the meta-feature representation consistently outperforms the popular frequency-based and the learning-based word embeddings [3] in sentiment classification.

2 Related Work

Feature filtering metrics have been well studied in text categorization and other language engineering tasks such as identifying collocation [4] and collostruction [5], as well as in the non-NLP literature [6]. Their performance on a specific group of homogenous tasks is usually varied and inconsistent depending on unique datasets and methodology employed. For example, Yang and Pedersen [7] revealed that IG and Chi-square test (CHI) worked well above others on k-nearest neighbor (KNN) and a regression-based classifier, whereas Mladenić and Grobelnik [1] concluded that among 11 feature filtering criteria only OR and its variants achieved best results on Naïve Bayes in an unbalanced dataset. Moreover, Forman [2] found that Bi-normal separation and IG frequently outperformed others, after systematically investigating the effectiveness of 12 filtering criteria with 4 classifiers, including Naïve Bayes, Decision Tree, logistic regression, and SVM on 3 benchmark datasets. These metrics demonstrate the distinctive abilities of uncertainty reduction and discrimination power on feature space construction.

In addition to these methods in attempting to find meaningful and authentic information attributes underlying data, a neural language model (NLM) [3, 8–10] can also render a dense and unified word representation, characterized with a lower dimensionality in an unsupervised-learning way. Such learning/predication-based word embeddings can cluster semantically similar words close in a latent feature space, which works effectively in its nature as the matrix factorization of Singular Value Decomposition (SVD) [11].

Among the recent development on NLMs [12] were combining word embeddings with the predefined knowledge resources such as WordNet and Paraphrase databases [13, 14], supplementing word embeddings with syntactic and sentiment information [15], and learning with the deep neural networks (DNN) to induce sentence or document embeddings [16, 17]. The learning-based word embedding is also the cornerstone of the state-of-the-art methods in sentiment classification [18, 19] and other NLP tasks. Another growing research trend is on customizing the unified NLM embeddings [3, 8–10] on a discourse through employing the contextualized embeddings such as CoVe [20], ELMo [21], ULMFiT [22] and BERT [23].

In contrast to the current approaches to developing a feature space, we in the paper aim to use the feature filtering criteria to produce a meta-feature space, through which we design a novel *document-by-criterion* representation specifically for text categorization. To derive such a meta-feature embedding, we first apply feature filtering criteria to calculate a word's relatedness or usefulness in a text collection. We then concatenate these relatedness values sequentially to form the word embedding, which can be further accumulated to form a document embedding. It imposes a similar effect of SVD or NLM on lowering the dimensionality of a vector space model (VSM). Finally, in comparison with the NLM-based and frequency-based embeddings on sentiment classification, we apply some typical classifiers on 3 benchmark product review datasets to systematically evaluate this meta-feature embedding hypothesis. Our proposal on the construction of a meta-feature embedding is essentially different from the previous work on reducing the dimensionality of a *document-by-word* VSM through removing uncorrelated terms or deriving a condensed word embedding with SVD or NLM.

3 Feature Filtering Criteria

We can generally classify the feature selection methods into two groups: one-sided and two-sided in terms of their values' scope [24]. The one-sided measures, such as OR and Correlation Coefficient (CC), only calculate the impact of positive features on feature selection, whereas the two-sided ones, such as IG and CHI, consider both positive and negative ones during estimation of their impact on the class membership. Owing to the unbalanced data distribution and specialty of each application, both groups have been widely used for feature filtering in text categorization.

It is noteworthy that to even cover all of the popular feature filtering methods in this investigation is unrealistic. Since multiple variants of these methods have been studied in the literature, we decide to choose 6 well-known or typical ones from both one-sided and two-sided feature selection groups in the paper: IG and PMI aiming for uncertainty reduction; OR and Probability Ratio (PR) for discriminative power; CC for Pearson correlation coefficient; along with CHI for hypothesis test.

Table 1. A contingency analysis between w and t_i

	t_i $(O|E)$	$\neg t_i (O|E)$	Σ
w	$O_{11}|E_{11}$	$O_{12}|E_{12}$	$O_{11} + O_{12}$
$\neg w$	$O_{21}|E_{21}$	$O_{22}|E_{22}$	$O_{21} + O_{22}$
Σ	$O_{11} + O_{21}$	$O_{12} + O_{22}$	N
$P(w|t_i) = O_{11}/O_{11} + O_{21}$		$P(t_i|w) = O_{11}/O_{11} + O_{12}$	
$P(w|\neg t_i) = O_{12}/O_{12} + O_{22}$		$P(\neg t_i|w) = O_{12}/O_{11} + O_{12}$	
$P(\neg w|t_i) = O_{21}/O_{11} + O_{12}$		$P(t_i|\neg w) = O_{21}/O_{21} + O_{22}$	
$P(\neg w|\neg t_i) = O_{22}/O_{12} + O_{22}$		$P(\neg t_i|\neg w) = O_{22}/O_{21} + O_{22}$	

Given a document d in its collection set D and its corresponding tag t_i in the tag set T for D ($i \in (1, |T|)$), we apply these feature filtering criteria to measure the distinctiveness of a word w in each d. We denote $P(t_i)$ as the probability of the documents tagged with t_i, and correspondingly $P(\neg t_i)$ as the probability without t_i, i.e. $P(\neg t_i) = 1 - P(t_i)$. $P(w)$ is the ratio between the size of the documents containing w and the size of total documents in D, so $P(\neg w)$ is equal to $1 - P(w)$. Table 1 lists the contingence analysis between w and t, and the definitions of probability calculations under different conditions. We calculate those criteria to specify how useful and relevant is w in forecasting t_i for d. We briefly introduce them in the following sections.

3.1 Information Gain

IG, measuring the size of entropy under the condition of w in d or not, indicates the predicting ability of w in classifying d. IG is biased toward features with great values, which is:

$$IG(w) = P(w) \sum_{i=1}^{|T|} P(t_i|w) log P(t_i|w) + P(\neg w) \sum_{i=1}^{|T|} P(t_i|\neg w) log P(t_i|\neg w)$$
$$- \sum_{i=1}^{|T|} P(t_i) log P(t_i)$$

3.2 Pointwise Mutual Information

PMI shows the nonlinear dependence between w in d and its t_i, where PMI = 0 means that w and t_i are independent, otherwise dependent in a variety of degree if PMI > 0. PMI is prone to picking up rare features in text categorization [7]. PMI expresses the degree of reduced uncertainty for a model to induce t_i if w is present in d, which is:

$$PMI(w, t_i) = log(P(w, t_i)/(P(w)P(t_i)))$$

3.3 Odds Ratio

OR measures the strength of association between w and t_i with odds, indicating that when w is present in d, d should be more frequently tagged with t_i. As a relevance two-sided indicator for ranking in feature selection, OR is:

$$OR(w, t_i) = log \frac{P(w|t_i)(1 - P(w|\neg t_i))}{P(w|\neg t_i)(1 - P(w|t_i))}$$

3.4 Probability Ratio

PR is the ratio of the respective rates of true positives and false positives. PR, as a variant of OR, simplifies the calculation of OR. PR can intuitively indicate the preference level of w for the presence or absence of t_i with d, which is:

$$PR(w, t_i) = log(P(w|t_i)/P(w|\neg t_i))$$

3.5 Correlation Coefficient

As a criterion of variable association, CC describes the degree of linear correlation or co-variance shared between w and t_i, which is:

$$CC(w, t_i) = \frac{P(w, t_i)P(\neg w, \neg t_i) - P(w, \neg t_i)P(\neg w, t_i)}{\sqrt{P(w)P(\neg w)P(t_i)P(\neg t_i)}}$$

3.6   Chi-Square

CHI, requiring no normal distribution of variables, can be transformed from correlation coefficient with $X^2 = nCC^2$. It can be regarded as a two-sided CC while taking into account both positive and negative features in counting the class membership. The CHI statistic indicates the significance of dependence between w and t_i, which is:

$$X^2 = \frac{N(O_{11}O_{22} - O_{12}O_{21})^2}{(O_{11} + O_{12})(O_{11} + O_{21})(O_{12} + O_{21})(O_{21} + O_{22})}$$

4   Distributional Representation

In the process of producing a *document-by-word* VSM, feature selection criteria initially cross out redundant or irrelevant words to reduce the sparsity of the VSM. After that, a condensed document embedding is developed and composed of co-occurrence counts of w in d [1, 2, 7]. In contrast to using feature selection criteria to derive such a reduced *document-by-word* feature space, we propose to use the criteria introduced in Sect. 3 as the meta-dimensions/features in data representation, i.e. we reconstruct a condensed *document-by-criterion* embedding for text categorization. In the following, we first introduce the frequency-based and NLM-based word embeddings and then illustrate how to build the meta-feature representation.

4.1   Frequency-Based Representation

Let $|voc|$ be the size of the vocabulary of D. $|d|$ is the size of total words in d. A typical document vector V_d can be represented by its co-occurrence words w with the dimensionality of $|voc|$, and V_d has a corresponding label t_i for d. For such a *document-by-word* model, each dimension of V_d can be valued either with binary or term frequency. Furthermore, according to the Zipfian distribution [25] of word usage, a straightforward way of producing a compressed feature space for d is to apply inverse document frequency (IDF) [26] and the feature filtering criteria [4] on w, or to generate a reduced latent semantic space with SVD [27].

4.2   Learning NLM-Based Representation

After training recurrent NLMs [3, 8–10], each word w is represented with a k-dimensional dense vector V_w, where k's size is varied, say, from 50 to 300, depending on the downstream applications. A sentence or document embedding can be harvested with some simple tensor operations on these words' vectors or with the gramma dependencies among them after parsing the sentence [28]. We can also supply DNN such as convolutional neural networks (CNN) and recurrent neural networks (RNN) with word embeddings to extract more contextual information from a document d [16, 17]. Therefore, instead of a vector V_d, a matrix with a $|d|$ by k dimensionalities can also act as an input of a document's representation into DNN.

4.3   Our Document-by-Criterion Representation

The basic process of developing the novel *document-by-criterion* feature space is illustrated in Fig. 1. For w and t_i across each document in D we first calculate the values of the 6 feature filtering criteria in Sect. 3, as following:

- IG: $\{IG(w)\}$
- PMI: $\{PMI(w,t_1)...PMI(w,t_i)...PMI(w,t_{|T|})\}$
- OR: $\{OR(w,t_1)...OR(w,t_i)...OR(w,t_{|T|})\}$
- PR: $\{PR(w,t_1)...PR(w,t_i)...PR(w,t_{|T|})\}$
- CC: $\{CC(w,t_1)... CC(w,t_i)... CC(w,t_{|T|})\}$
- CHI: $\{X^2(w,t_1)... X^2(w,t_i)... X^2(w,t_{|T|})\}$

Note that we do not calculate the average or maximum of PMI, OR, PR, CC, or CHI; instead we save all the values for each scoring metric and concatenate these values to assemble V_w, i.e. the distributional structure of V_w is composed of IG, MI, OR, PR, CC, and CHI with the dimensionality of $5 * |T| + 1$ ($|T|$ denotes the size of label t_i). Given the diversity of word usage in context, we aim to keep all relevant information between w and t_i.

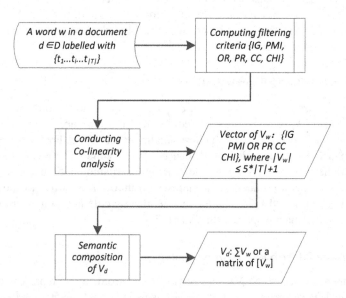

Fig. 1. The workflow for constructing the *document-by-criterion* representation.

To filter out these highly correlated attributes, we supplement a simple co-linearity analysis only using Spearman rank correlation on V_w. Consequently, the dimensionality of the final V_w is much less than $5 * |T| + 1$, depending on word distribution across t_i in D. Note that as for the co-linearity analysis, we did not run any complex heuristic search or the wrapper methods to find the optimal subset of features on V_d for each classifier to avoid the possibility of overfitting. A document's V_d can then be derived with semantic composition through the addition or concatenation of word embeddings (V_w). In line with the NLM-based embeddings, such meta-feature embedding might leverage the reduced dimensionality in text categorization.

5 Sentiment Classification

5.1 Dataset Preparation

We selected 3 benchmark datasets as the test bed for sentiment classification, i.e. IMDB [29] and Yelp2013/14 Dataset Challenges [30]. We kept the same split of training and test data on these datasets in comparison with other models. IMDB has an even distribution of positive and negative reviews (i.e. 25k items for each label), but Yelp 2013 and 14 show severely unbalanced distributions on their 5 labels, with about 12% proportion for the negative and high-negative reviews and over 67% proportion for the positive and high-positive ones.

5.2 Feature Construction

We first preprocessed the datasets with the standard procedure of normalization and stemming, then extracted words above a predefined frequency threshold. We respectively set up the thresholds with 15, 35, and 55 for IMDB, Yelp 2013, and Yelp 2014, according to the size of the datasets. The extracted words, also contained in the sentiment lexicon of MPQA [31], were chosen as candidates for computing filter criteria. Since MPQA was the exclusive lexicon employed in the experiment, it should be fair to compare these data representations in Sect. 4, and we can avoid detrimental effect on using different lexicons on the datasets.

Among the distributional representations introduced in Sect. 4, the frequency-based representation only recorded the co-occurrence frequency. We retrained the word2vec model [32] respectively using the 3 datasets and found that its optimal dimensionality is 40. We also included the original word2vec vectors, pre-trained with CBOW (dimensionality of 300) on 100 billion words from Google News.

In constructing the *document-by-criterion* representation, we followed the workflow framework proposed in Sect. 4.3. After conducting co-linearity analysis in the *document-by-criterion* feature space, we found that IG was one of 5 optimal meta-features for IMDB, together with OR, PMI, PR, and CC that derived on the positive reviews. The optimal meta-feature set consisted of IG, OR, CHI, and CC for Yelp 2013, where OR and CHI were derived on the high-positives and the neutrals; PMI on the negatives; and CC on the high-negatives and the high-positives respectively. The optimal meta-feature set for Yelp 2014 was slightly different from it for Yelp 2013 with

CC derived on the positives rather than on the high negatives. Consequently, only 10 dimensions were used in the *document-by-criterion* space for Yelp 2013/14.

5.3   Sentiment Classification

We employed some typical classifiers, including SVM, Naïve Bayes, and Decision Tree in the experiment. Since we aimed to compare different data representations in Sect. 4, we did not fine-tune these classifiers during each separate training and applied the identical configuration for each classifier on these representations. SVM was configured with a linear kernel; Decision Tree was configured with pruning and the maximum depth of 5.

Apart from these classifiers, we also designed a simplified DNN with 2-layer CNN (each configured with 32 filters, the kernel size of 3, and the *relu* activation), stacked with one max-pooling layer and one flatten layer; one dense layer (with 30 units and the *relu* activation); one output layer (with the *softmax* activation). We did not run grid search to optimize these hyperparameters. As with deep learning, many transfer learning models such as BERT [23] and OpenAI Transformer [33] can be applied to get better results, but using such complicated networks to improve performance was not our purpose in the paper, so we leave that as further work.

6   Results and Discussion

6.1   Sentiment Classification with the Meta-Feature Embedding

As shown in Table 2, the classification results with SVM, Naïve Bayes, and Decision Tree indicated that the meta-feature data representation consistently outperformed other embeddings in Sect. 4 across IMDB and Yelp 2013/14. The reason behind may be that

Table 2. The final test results of different data representations on IMDB and Yelp 2013/14. All accuracy values were reported on the test dataset.

		Counts	NLM: *word2vec* (Google)	NLM: *word2vec* (self-trained)	Meta-feature
SVM	IMDB	0.742	0.83	0.668	**0.84**
	Yelp2013	0.474	0.493	0.411	**0.498**
	Yelp2014	0.445	0.472	0.391	**0.475**
Naïve	IMDB	0.815	0.703	0.59	**0.831**
Bayes	Yelp2013	0.424	0.387	0.357	**0.425**
	Yelp2014	0.401	0.369	0.342	**0.418**
Decision	IMDB	0.639	0.679	0.596	**0.839**
tree	Yelp2013	0.332	0.358	0.321	**0.480**
	Yelp2014	0.323	0.337	0.309	**0.457**
CNN	IMDB	0.792	0.853	**0.876**	0.855
	Yelp2013	0.621	**0.678**	0.673	0.671
	Yelp2014	0.608	**0.672**	0.664	0.67

the meta-features works not only as meaningful dimensions in data representation but also as the sub-models of classifiers for ensemble learning. Given the discrimination power or uncertainty deduction abilities of these feature selection metrics in Sect. 3, each classifier in Table 2 functioned similarly as a stacking ensemble, which could first harvest the pre-selection results of the 6 filters and then generalize better classification outcomes.

As for the simplified DNN we proposed (denoted as CNN in Table 2), the meat-feature representation performed competitively on IMDB with an accuracy of 0.855, although the best results were achieved by the two learning NLM-based (i.e. *word2-vec*). The CNN's performance on Yelp 2013/14 suggested that no significant disparity existed between our proposed method and the two NLM-based embeddings. The results also showed that in terms of ensemble generalization, CNN on the meta-feature embedding did not consistently achieve the equivalent degree of improvements made by the 3 classifiers in Table 2, partly because possible overfitting may exist while using the deep learning on our proposal.

In contrast to the embeddings produced with the learning NLM-based methods, our proposal did not require a significant amount of time on pre-training to achieve competent and stable results. The feature filtering criteria were also relatively easier to calculate than the complex NLM methods. It tends to facilitate disclosing and interpreting internal relationships between a meat-feature and an induced model.

6.2   Related Work on Sentiment Classification

In Table 3 we included the results of state-of-the-art models on the same datasets we used in the experiment for comparison. In contrast to our simple feature filtering method, these models heavily relied on pretraining for sentence or document embedding [34–36], transfer learning [20, 22, 23], designing sophisticated neural architectures with hierarchical attention [38, 39] and adversarial networks [36], and employing DNN-based classifiers [20] in sentiment classification. On the binary classification task of IMDB they (well above an accuracy of 0.91) outperformed our models (an accuracy of 0.855 at best) on the meta-feature representation with significant gains, but their performance was not consistently superior to us on the multiclass classification task of Yelp 2013/2014. We achieved around 0.67 accuracy on Yelp, surpassing paragraph embedding [30, 34], along with CNN or LSTM gated RNN [30], although our model was marginally inferior to two hierarchical attention-based DNN [38, 39]. The results partly implied that the fine-grained sentiment classification is a more challenging task than the coarse-grained even with the adoption of sophisticated DNN in this language understanding task.

On the other side, the robustness of such a "black box" model, derived from the intensively trained DNN, can be problematic. As pointed out by Melis et al. [40] in their evaluation of various recurrent neural language models, the empirical gains of employing sophisticated neural architectures such as recurrent highway networks [41] and reinforcement learning [42] often source from fine-tuning hyperparameters such as dropout and weight decay, whereas the well-regularized vanilla-LSTM can outperform them at no extra cost of deploying the sophisticated architectures. Such issues of designing unnecessarily complicated neural networks were also observed by Lipton

Table 3. Performance of the state-of-the-art methods on IMDB and Yelp 2013/14. The accuracy figures were extracted from their published papers separately. The second column indicates how a document embedding was generated as an input layer to a classifier.

	Document embedding	IMDB
Distributed Memory Model of Paragraph Vectors [34]	Unsupervised training on Feedforward NN for paragraph embedding	0.926
Oh-2LSTMp [35]	One-hot + 3-layer CNN + 2-layer bi-LSTM	0.941
Virtual Adversarial Training [36]	*word2vec* + LSTM (unsupervised pretraining)	0.941
CoVe [20]	Transfer learning: Glove + 2-layer bi-LSTM (attention); Classification: Feedforward NN + bi-LSTM (attention) + 3-layer Maxout NN	0.918
UDA [37]	Transformer model in BERT [23] (large fine-tune) + Unsupervised Data Augmentation	0.958
ULMFiT [22]	Transfer learning: 3-layer bi-LSTM	0.954
		Yelp 2013/14
Paragraph Vector [30, 34]	paragraph embedding	0.577/0.592
Convolutional gated RNN [30]	*word2vec*(self-trained) + CNN + Gated-RNN	0.637/0.655
LSTM gated RNN [30]	*word2vec*(self-trained) + LSTM + Gated-RNN	0.651/0.671
100D structured attention [38]	*word2vec*(self-trained) + 2-layer bi-LSTM with structured attention (on both sentence and document levels)	0.686/na
Hierarchical attention Networks (HAN) [39]	*word2vec*(self-trained) + 2-layer bi-GRU with hierarchical attention (on both word and sentence levels)	0.682/0.705

and Steinhardt [43]. While dealing with billions of parameters commonly generated in DNN, we should be cautious before extending it into different applications; instead the concise subnetworks or "winning tickets" [44] need to be identified and extracted from the initial DNN to improve its generalization and prediction abilities.

7   Limitations and Future Work

In the paper, the feature filtering criteria were used as meta-features/dimensions on the reconstruction of a *document-by-criterion* VSM. Although this meta-feature space only consisted of 5 dimensions for IMDB and 10 dimensions for Yelp, it outperformed the frequency-based or learning NLM-based embeddings in sentiment classification. The noticeable benefit of our proposal was that the dimensionality of VSM can be significantly reduced at no cost of increased complexity on enormous embedding pre-training and sophisticated neural-structure fine-tuning.

Since our purpose was to test the effectiveness of the meta-feature embedding, fine-tuning a DNN model for its better performance on classification is beyond the scope of this paper, and we leave it for future work. We have not conducted the ablation studies on these feature filtering criteria in this experiment as only a limited number of dimensions were reserved after collinearity analysis. Given the growth and richness of feature selection methods, we will further investigate and differentiate their effectiveness on disclosing internal data attributes for embeddings. Moreover, the robustness of the meta-feature embedding needs to be examined for other heterogeneous tasks on text categorization in the future.

Acknowledgement. This research was supported by the National Social Science Foundation of China (Grant No. 17BYY119) and the Humanity and Social Science Foundation of China Ministry of Education (Grant No. 15YJA740054).

References

1. Mladenić, D., Grobelnik, M.: Feature Selection for Unbalanced Class Distribution and Naive Bayes, pp. 258–267 (1999)
2. Forman, G.: An extensive empirical study of feature selection metrics for text classification. J. Mach. Learn. Res. **3**, 1289–1305 (2003)
3. Bengio, Y., et al.: A neural probabilistic language model. J. Mach. Learn. Res. **3**, 1137–1155 (2003)
4. Manning, C.D., Schütze, H.: Foundations of Statistical Natural Language Processing, 680 p. (1999)
5. Wiechmann, D.: On the computation of construction strength: testing measures of association as expressions of lexical bias. Corpus Linguist. Linguistic Theory **4**, 253–290 (2008)
6. Chandrashekar, G., Sahin, F.: A survey on feature selection methods. Comput. Electr. Eng. **40**(1), 16–28 (2014)
7. Yang, Y., Pedersen, J.O.: A comparative study on feature selection in text categorization. In: ICML, pp. 412–420 (1997)
8. Mikolov, T., et al.: Distributed representations of words and phrases and their compositionality. In: NIPS, pp. 3111–3119 (2013)
9. Collobert, R., et al.: Natural language processing (almost) from scratch. J. Mach. Learn. Res. **12**, 2493–2537 (2011)
10. Pennington, J., Socher, R., Manning, C.: Glove: Global Vectors for Word Representation, vol. 14, pp. 1532–1543 (2014)
11. Levy, O., Goldberg, Y.: Neural word embedding as implicit matrix factorization. In: NIPS, pp. 2177–2185 (2014)
12. Baroni, M., Dinu, G., Kruszewski, G.: Don't count, predict! A systematic comparison of context-counting vs. context-predicting semantic vectors. In: ACL, pp. 238–247 (2014)
13. Faruqui, M., et al.: Retrofitting Word Vectors to Semantic Lexicons (2014)
14. Yu, M., Dredze, M.: Improving lexical embeddings with semantic knowledge. In: ACL, pp. 545–550 (2014)
15. Tang, D., et al.: Learning sentiment-specific word embedding for Twitter sentiment classification. In: ACL, pp. 1555–1565 (2014)
16. Kim, Y.: Convolutional Neural Networks for Sentence Classification (2014)

17. Conneau, A., et al.: Very deep convolutional networks for text classification. In: EACL, pp. 1107–1116 (2017)
18. Barnes, J., Klinger, R., Walde, S.S.I.: Assessing State-of-the-Art Sentiment Models on State-of-the-Art Sentiment Datasets (2017)
19. Zhang, L., Wang, S., Liu, B.: Deep learning for sentiment analysis: a survey. Wiley Interdisc. Rev.: Data Mining Knowl. Discov. 8(4), e1253 (2018)
20. McCann, B., et al.: Learned in translation: contextualized word vectors. In: NIPS, pp. 6297–6308 (2017)
21. Peters, M.E., et al.: Deep contextualized word representations. In: NAACL 2018, pp. 2227–2237 (2018)
22. Howard, J., Ruder, S.: Universal language model fine-tuning for text classification. In: ACL (2018)
23. Devlin, J., et al.: BERT: pre-training of deep bidirectional transformers for language understanding. In: NAACL-HLT (2018)
24. Zheng, Z., Xiaoyun, W., Srihari, R.: Feature selection for text categorization on imbalanced data. SIGKDD Explor. Newsl. 6(1), 80–89 (2004)
25. Zipf, G.K.: Human behavior and the principle of least effort: an introduction to human ecology. Facsim. of 1949 ed, 573 p. (1965)
26. Jones, K.S.: Automatic summarising: factors and directions. In: Advances in Automatic Text Summarization (1998)
27. Deerwester, S.C., et al.: Indexing by latent semantic analysis. J. Am. Soc. Inf. Sci. 41(6), 391–407 (1990)
28. Socher, R., et al.: Parsing natural scenes and natural language with recursive neural networks. In: ICML, pp. 129–136 (2011)
29. Maas, A.L., et al.: Learning word vectors for sentiment analysis. In: Proceedings of the 49th Annual Meeting of the Association for Computational Linguistics: Human Language Technologies, vol. 1, pp. 142–150 (2011)
30. Tang, D., Qin, B., Liu, T.: Document modeling with gated recurrent neural network for sentiment classification. In: EMNLP, pp. 1422–1432 (2015)
31. Wilson, T., Wiebe, J., Hoffmann, P.: Recognizing contextual polarity in phrase-level sentiment analysis. In: HLT-EMNLP, pp. 347–354 (2005)
32. Mikolov, T., et al.: Efficient Estimation of Word Representations in Vector Space (2013)
33. Radford, A., et al.: Improving language understanding by generative pre-training (2018)
34. Le, Q., Mikolov, T.: Distributed representations of sentences and documents. In: ICML, pp. 1188–1196 (2014)
35. Johnson, R., Zhang, T.: Supervised and semi-supervised text categorization using LSTM for region embeddings. In: ICML, pp. 526–534 (2016)
36. Miyato, T., Dai, A.M., Goodfellow, I.: Adversarial Training Methods for Semi-Supervised Text Classification (2017)
37. Xie, Q., et al.: Unsupervised Data Augmentation for Consistency Training. eprint arXiv: 190412848 (2019)
38. Liu, Y., Lapata, M.: Learning structured text representations. Trans. Assoc. Comput. Linguist. 6, 63–75 (2018)
39. Yang, Z., et al.: Hierarchical attention networks for document classification. In: HLT-NAACL, pp. 1480–1489 (2016)
40. Melis, G., Dyer, C., Blunsom, P.: On the state of the art of evaluation in neural language models. In: International Conference on Learning Representations (2018)
41. Zilly, J.G., et al.: Recurrent highway networks. In: ICML, pp. 4189–4198 (2017)

42. Zoph, B., Le, Q.V.: Neural Architecture Search with Reinforcement Learning. arXiv e-prints arXiv:161101578Z (2016)
43. Lipton, Z.C., Steinhardt, J.: Troubling Trends in Machine Learning Scholarship. arXiv e-prints arXiv:180703341L (2018)
44. Frankle, J., Carbin, M.: The lottery ticket hypothesis: finding sparse, trainable neural networks. In: ICLR (2019)

The Thin Line Between Hate and Profanity

Kosisochukwu Judith Madukwe[✉] and Xiaoying Gao

School of Engineering and Computer Science, Victoria University of Wellington,
Wellington, New Zealand
{kosisochukwu.madukwe,xiaoying.gao}@ecs.vuw.ac.nz

Abstract. Hate speech can be defined as a language used to demean people within a specific group. Hate speech often contains explicitly profane words, however, the presence of these words does not always mean that the text instance is hateful. In some cases, text instances with profane words are just offensive language and they do not target any specific group, and so cannot be classified as hate speech. In this work, we build on existing studies to find a better demarcation between hate speech and offensive language. Our main contribution is to introduce the use of typed dependency as new features in our feature set. This new feature enables us to consider the relationship between long distance words in a text instance, thereby provides more identifying information than single word-based features. We evaluate our approach using a dataset with the classes: hate, offensive and neither. Comparing our work with existing studies, our feature set is much smaller but we achieve better accuracy and show comparable results in further analysis. Our detailed analysis also showed instances missed by the lexical features that were correctly predicted by the proposed feature set.

Keywords: Hate speech detection · Offensive language · Text classification · Feature extraction

1 Introduction

The task of detecting hate speech instances on social media platforms has become an important and interesting area of research recently. Some of the reasons are the current fragile political environment in several countries and the increasing discussions surrounding religion, immigration, gender identity, sexual orientation among others. A large proportion of these discussions happen online in posts and posts' comment sections on social media and the sensitive nature of these discussions means that some of these posts and comments can contain utterances that are harmful to the lives and properties of the people involved.

Recently, the International Workshop on Semantic Evaluation held a competition, SemEval-2019[1], consisting of several tasks in five different categories.

---

[1] http://alt.qcri.org/semeval2019/.

© Springer Nature Switzerland AG 2019
J. Liu and J. Bailey (Eds.): AI 2019, LNAI 11919, pp. 344–356, 2019.
https://doi.org/10.1007/978-3-030-35288-2_28

One of the categories was Opinion, Emotion and Abusive language detection and it contained 4 different tasks, one of which was OffensEval: Identifying and Categorizing Offensive Language in Social Media[2] with multiple publications from the participants highlighting the various ways they attempted to solve the problem.

Existing studies in this area mostly focus on detecting and distinguishing between hate speech and non-hate speech [8,19] or between the various sub-types of hate speech [1,3,25]. However, an equally important and often overlooked aspect is the difference between a hateful utterance and an offensive or profane one. Most of the existing studies categorize all hateful and profane language into the same category. But, according to the several definitions of hate speech used by legal institutions and organizations like Twitter[3] and Facebook[4]—although a universally accepted definition of hate speech does not exist—the use of profane language does not qualify to be categorized as hate speech.

Fortuna et al. [6] defines hate speech as 'language that attacks or diminishes, that incites violence or hate against groups, based on specific characteristics such as physical appearance, religion, descent, national or ethnic origin, sexual orientation, gender identity or other, and it can occur with different linguistic styles, even in subtle forms or when humour is used'. An example is *'i'll do that if you agree to take your ethiopian starvin looking n*gger[5] as* back to africa'*. Offensive language was defined by [7] as 'text which uses abusive slurs or derogatory terms'. An example is *'these h*es be f*cking all of us n*ggas. i got news for all the monogamous n*ggas, yo bitch f*ck anonymous niggas'*. Offensive language does not meet the criteria outlined in the various definitions of hate speech, in the sense that they do not attack an individual or a group based on protected/specific categories such as ethnicity, race, gender and sexual orientation [6,19,24].

Offensive language has more overlap with hate speech, especially explicit hate speech, thus the false negative rate (with the hate class as the positive class) of existing methods is very high [5,15]. The difficulty of this task has been highlighted in a couple of other studies [7,16,27]. It is difficult to distinguish between offensive language and hate speech because they contain a lot of similar characteristics and the differentiating characteristics are not easy to spot.

In this study, we focus on investigating and improving the distinction between hateful and offensive utterances. Most of the proposed solutions for hate speech detection use profane or pejorative words to detect hate speech, however, a large number of tweets that contain these words are not directed towards an individual or a group of individuals defined by a protected category. In reality, these profane words are used by individuals to be plainly offensive or just show emphasis. There is a thin, blurred line between hateful speech and offensive language. For this

---

[2] https://competitions.codalab.org/competitions/20011.

[3] https://help.twitter.com/en/rules-and-policies/hateful-conduct-policy.

[4] https://www.facebook.com/communitystandards/hate_speech.

[5] The authors have added '*' for public viewing. These were not part of the original tweet.

work, the problem is modelled as a multi-class classification problem supported by a three-class dataset (hate, offensive, neither). We aim to investigate and propose a new feature that can distinguish between the two classes of interest; the Hate class and the Offensive class. We suggest methods that could solve the problems highlighted after an error analysis.

The rest of the paper is structured as follows. In Sect. 2, we discuss existing related studies. Section 3 describes the dataset, presents our methodology and experiments conducted. In Sect. 4, we report and analyse our experimental results. Section 5 concludes the work with suggestions of our proposed next steps to improve on this work and an attempt to answer pending questions from our analysis.

2   Related Work

The task of automatically detecting hate speech has been modelled as a supervised binary classification problem by the majority of the existing studies in literature with the aim of distinguishing between hate speech and non-hate speech. This task is non-trivial however, as has been shown in recent studies [3]; in fact, hate speech is not binary. It contains several subtypes that could overlap or have different identifying features like racism, sexism, religion, disability, gender amongst others. However, all these subtypes can still be classified as hate speech. An often overlooked class that is often lumped together with the hate speech class is the offensive language class. Most existing and public datasets do not distinguish between these two classes (hate class and offensive class).

However, the ternary classification task of accurately differentiating between Hate, Offensive and Neither class has been attempted by a number of researchers. Davidson et al. [5] brought forward the argument that offensive language is not hate speech. For features, they used Tf-Idf weighted token unigrams, bigrams and trigrams, Tf-Idf weighted Parts of Speech (PoS) tags, readability scores derived from Flesch-Kincaid Grade Level and Flesch Reading Ease scores, a sentiment lexicon, hashtags, mentions, retweets, URLs, and number of characters, word and syllables per tweet. They highlighted the difficulty in differentiating between the hate and offensive class by analysing the predictions from their model. The authors highlight the importance of taking context into consideration because tweets without explicit keywords were difficult to classify. We propose to do this with the use of syntactic features that emphasize grammatical dependencies between words in a sentence/tweet.

Malmasi et al. [15], using data made available by Davidson, attempted to distinguish between hate speech and offensive language, using various levels of surface n-grams (word and character) and word skip grams as features for a linear Support Vector Machines (SVM) classifier. Word skip grams are similar to regular word bigrams but skip grams, depending on the selected window size omitting the words that fit into the window immediately after the head word and selecting the word occurring after the window. For example, in this sentence: 'This is an example sentence', a 1-skip gram would generate these features: 'this an', 'is example', 'an sentence' while a bigram would generate these features: 'This is', 'is an', 'an example', 'example sentence'. Word skip grams increase the distance between words thus making them similar to syntactic dependencies [14] and also performs a form of dimensionality reduction to the feature set. The authors report that their features were not effective in correctly distinguishing between hate and offensive language.

The study by Malmasi et al. [15] was extended in [16], where the same authors employed the use of single and ensemble classifiers to discriminate between profanity and hate speech while applying character and word n-grams, skip-grams and Brown clusters. Their results show that 4-character n-grams used for training a single classifier outperformed all other features and also outperformed the ensemble classifiers generated from multiple fusion methods. Furthermore, they conducted a meta-classification experiment using a linear SVM and a nonlinear(rbf) SVM. These classifiers outperformed their previous baselines (single and ensemble classifiers) with the rbf-SVM meta-classifier emerging as the best. However, from their results, it can be seen that the hate class is still grossly misclassified as offensive. A closer analysis of their features showed that obscene words were informative for both the hate and offensive class. They also noted that the different spellings of some words resulted in features for different classes. For example, 'nigger(s)' was a distinguishing feature for hate speech while 'nigga(s)' was one for offensive language. This pattern was initially mentioned by [22], where they highlighted that the second spelling variant was used by a particular ethnic group in daily conversations and music to signify brotherhood and friendship. We might argue that it has been wrongly annotated as offensive because in real life situations, the users do not think it is offensive.

In [7], they report better results for this ternary classification task using an l2 normalized Term frequency-Inverse document frequency (Tf-Idf) weighted n-grams which could be accredited to the fact that they augmented the Davidson dataset thus making the hate class more balanced. Tf-Idf are weights assigned to a word based on the product of its frequency in a document and the inverse of its occurrence across documents or corpus to show the words' importance in that document. A similar data augmentation process was carried out in [27].

We compare our work to [5,15,16] because they used the same dataset, similar classifiers and they have the best results compared to other studies with the same broad aim as ours. These are the major existing studies our work builds on. Our work differs from these in that we used typed dependency as a better syntactic feature over PoS tags. Typed dependencies provide a grammatical relationship between two words in a sentence where one word is syntactically dependent on the other. It produces dependency tags similar to PoS tags, but unlike PoS tags, typed dependencies depict a relationship between dependent words in a sentence. In addition, typed dependencies are more efficient than regular n-grams because they can capture long-distance relationships between words in a sentence.

Typed dependency has been used in literature to represent context in tasks like sentiment classification and document polarity [9,10,23]. It was introduced for hate speech detection and classification in [2,3] and was used in [1] for extracting 'othering' language (language that indicates the divide between an 'us' group and a 'them' group) for cyber-hate classification. The authors in [11–13] used typed dependency as feature, often as an input feature for learning embeddings as opposed to learning embeddings from linear and flat bag of words features. In the area of cyber hate detection, [19] used typed dependency in conjunction with embedding learning to differentiate between hateful and non-hateful text. These studies have shown that embeddings learned using dependency-based context outperforms those learned on regular sequentially ordered text. Deep neural network architectures have also been applied for capturing the order of words in a text as a feature [28].

To the best of our knowledge, this is the first work using typed dependency in conjunction with word and character n-grams for distinguishing between profane language and hate speech. Our hypothesis is that including this dependency feature will improve the classification performance when distinguishing between hate speech and offensive language by capturing dependent words in a sentence separated by a long distance. We investigate two different methods of incorporating the typed dependencies features into our feature set. Also, we use less features compared with existing works but with more potential of distinguishing between our classes of interest.

3   Proposed Methods and Experiment

3.1   Feature Extraction Methods

Here we describe the features used in our classification task and how we extracted them from the tweets in the dataset.

Word and Character N-Grams: As part of our feature set, we use word and character n-grams. Word n-grams are useful in capturing keywords that belong to each of the classes. A word n-gram is a commonly used feature in text classification and has been shown to help improve classification accuracy. The size of the word n-gram varies from 1 to n, however the ideal size depends on the task at hand. Increasing the value of n over a certain threshold might unnecessarily increase the complexity of the feature set. One value of n or a combination of different values can be used to extract features. In this work, we used a combination ranging from 1 to 3 as used in [5]. Since our data is made up of tweets from Twitter which are prone to spelling errors, intentional or unintentional, we used character n-grams to overcome that problem. To reduce noise, we extracted our character n-grams within word boundaries using an n value ranging from 2 to 5. Our n values were based on reports from existing studies. Character n-grams have been shown to improve classification accuracy especially when used with other features. Also the matrix produced by character n-gram is less sparse and thus contains more important data points than that produced by word n-gram [18,26] After extracting the word and character n-grams, we derived their Tf-Idf weights and used that in conjunction with other features as input to our classification algorithm.

Typed Dependency: In order to incorporate syntactic features into our dataset for the purpose of retaining hidden contextual information present in each text instance or tweet, we use typed dependencies. Typed dependency is one way to represent the syntactic structure of a sentence [17]. We employed the use of the SpaCy[6] library (English module) to extract dependency labels from our dataset. The output of the dependency parser gives the syntactic head word (governor), the word that syntactically depends on the head word (dependent) and the dependency tag that joins the governor to the dependent. Figure 1 shows a dependency parse tree for a sentence culled from the dataset *'The Irish in California are all white trash'*. It generates 7 dependency tags, some of which are *nsubj(are, Irish), attr(are, Trash)*. The meaning and function of each tag can be found on the SpaCy[7] website.

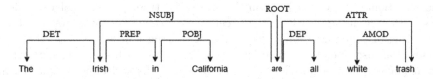

Fig. 1. Dependency parse tree

We experimented with two methods for incorporating the typed dependency feature to the input of the classifiers. First, we use the term frequency weighted dependency tags. We extracted 46 different dependency tags from our corpus which were used to build our feature set. This was concatenated with the word and character n-gram features to form our first syntactic feature set. Next, we used the governor-dependent word pairs. For each tweet in the corpus, we extracted the governor and the dependent words and concatenated each respective governor to its dependent, thereby creating bigram-like pairs. To transform this into a useable feature vector, we calculated the term frequency weight of each word pair, regarding each tweet as a document. The document-term matrix formed was used as an input into the classifier. The results of these experiments are reported in Sect. 4.

3.2   Experiment Design

We aim to improve the detection of hate speech and distinction between hate speech and offensive language by decreasing the false negatives. We employed the traditional pipeline of data gathering and preprocessing and in this section we describe the dataset and the steps taken to preprocesss the data.

---

[6] https://spacy.io/.

[7] https://spacy.io/api/annotation#dependency-parsing.

Dataset: The dataset[8] used in this work was made publicly available by David-son et al. [5] in 2017. They report collecting this data from Twitter using a lexicon from HateBase[9] containing hateful words and phrases. They used a crowdsourc-ing platform (Figure-Eight[10] formerly CrowdFlower) for annotating the tweets into 3 classes (Hatespeech, Offensive and Neither). The annotators were pro-vided with the authors' definitions and specific instructions. They record an inter-rater agreement of 92% as provided by the crowdsourcing platform. The dataset contains 24,802 tweets in English (5.77% labelled as Hatespeech, 77.43% as Offensive and 16.80% as Neither).

Data Preprocessing: We preprocess our data slightly differently from exist-ing works in this research area as a result of the fact that we intend to use typed dependency as a feature extraction method. Therefore, we do not remove the traditional stopwords as it might affect the true grammatical dependen-cies of the remaining words in the tweet. We construct our own stop word list consisting of items like 'amp', 'etc', 'rt', 'ff' amongst others. Using regex, we removed all usernames and mentions including those with an underscore (_) at the beginning, end or middle. We also removed URLs and punctuation marks. Some existing work have used punctuation as a feature because it indicates emo-tion and enthusiasm–more specifically using exclamation marks, question marks and full stops [27]. Nevertheless, we do remove punctuations because the depen-dency parser views punctuation as a token and this increases the dependencies extracted thus inflating the dimensionality of our resulting feature vector. All letters are reduced to their lowercase versions prior to any of the aforementioned preprocessing. Then, using NLTK's WordNetLemmatizer[11], we lemmatized each token in the corpus to return them to their lemmas. We chose this over stem-ming as stemming produces crude results that might have an adverse effect on our extracted features.

Classification Algorithm Design: In order to compare our work to existing studies [5,15] which are SVM based, we use a linear Support Vector Machine (SVM) as a classification algorithm. We used SVM instead of the deep learn-ing algorithms that have been used recently in most tasks because we want to compare our feature sets with existing feature sets using the same classifier. We implemented a stratified 5-fold grid search to discover the best parameters for our problem set, which resulted in $C = 0.1$, penalty $= l2$ and max_iter $= 1000$. We use the One-Vs-Rest approach for our multi-class classification problem and 25% of the dataset to evaluate the performance of our model.

---

[8] https://github.com/t-davidson/hate-speech-and-offensive-language.
[9] https://hatebase.org/.
[10] https://www.figure-eight.com/.
[11] https://www.nltk.org/_modules/nltk/stem/wordnet.html.

4 Results and Analysis

It was noted in [28] that the majority of the existing studies in the area of hate speech detection use the basic classification metrics of Accuracy, Precision (P), Recall (R) and F1-score. They make use of the micro-average scores which could be problematic in hate speech detection and its notoriously unbalanced datasets with the hate class being both the positive class and the minority class. Thus micro-average scores calculated using the total True Positive (TP), False Positive (FP) and False Negative (FN) of all the classes to calculate the P, R and F1-score, is not representative of the actual performance. While [28] suggests the use of macro scores, [25] suggests the use of a weighted F1-score as a metric in order to take into consideration any misclassification of minority classes. The weighted average method is also very similar to the micro-average, hence the misclassification of the minority class will not be noticeable. Since we only have the micro-average results for existing studies reported in their papers, we initially use micro average to compare our results to those studies. But, as pointed out above that these measures are not suitable for unbalanced data, so we also report our macro average scores for all the classes. As a further analysis, we also compared our approach with existing studies using the P, R and F1-score for the hate class.

We experiment with several features and feature combinations but due to a lack of space we report only three combinations. The results are summarized in Table 1. Word+Char represents the lexical features with a combination of Word and Character n-grams. Word+Char+TagDepParse concatenates the dependency parse tags to the previous Word+Char combination. Word+Char+WordPairDepParse concatenates the word pair dependency parses to the Word+Char combination. Table 2 shows precision, recall and F1 score of the hate class alone for our feature sets. The feature set extended with TagDepparse has a better precision than the one extended with WordPairDepParse, however the recall was too low. Considering both Tables 1 and 2, we take the WordPairDepParse feature as our best performing feature set.

Table 1. Classification results for different feature sets.

Features	Accuracy	Macro-P	Macro-R	Macro-F1
Word+Char	0.9	0.75	0.80	0.77
Word+Char+TagDepParse	0.91	0.81	0.67	0.69
Word+Char+WordPairDepParse	**0.90**	**0.75**	**0.79**	**0.77**

Initially, we trained and evaluated our model using the entire extracted feature set but our results showed very low recall for the hate class, and the precision was more than twice the recall. The number of false negative was higher than the true positive with most of the false negative being classified as offensive. We then implemented an embedded feature selection using Logistic Regression

Table 2. Classification results for the **hate speech class** for different feature sets.

Features	Precision	Recall	F1
Word+Char	0.45	0.52	0.49
Word+Char+TagDepParse	0.64	0.18	0.28
Word+Char+WordPairDepParse	**0.47**	**0.49**	**0.48**

as an estimator with penalty set to l2. The cut off threshold value is set the mean of all the feature importance c = scaled by 1.25. Thus we only keep and use features with importance higher or equal to the threshold. This considerably reduced the dimensionality of the feature sets, improved our recall for the hate class and balanced out the recall:precision ratio. We report only the results after feature selection.

Table 3 shows the comparison with existing studies in terms of micro-average scores. We achieve comparable results to Davidson et al. [5] and better results than Malmasi et al. [16], even though we use fewer feature types and only one classifier.

Table 3. Comparison of our best performing results with the baselines

	Accuracy	Micro-precision	Micro-recall	Micro-F1
Davidson et al. [5]	–	0.91	0.90	0.90
Malmasi et al. [15]	0.78	–	–	–
Malmasi et al. [16]	0.798	0.78	0.80	0.79
Ours	**0.90**	**0.90**	**0.90**	**0.90**

We did not include features that represented the readability of the document as used in [5] because tweets are normally filled with spelling mistakes and errors, thus it would not be a good identifying feature. It was corroborated by [21] that these features including the use of mentions and hashtags were not very distinctive. We also refrained from including sentiment features because hate speech and offensive language both have negative sentiments therefore they would not be discriminative.

Table 4 compares results from our hate class with the results of the baselines for the hate class. This shows that with a reduced feature set and a simple linear SVM classifiers, we were able to get comparable results and–in terms of some metrics–better results than the existing studies.

Our further investigation shows that the performance of the syntactic dependence feature set was affected by a couple of factors. One is that dependency parsers are not resilient or robust to misspellings [4], therefore spelling variations of a word will not be recognised as the same word. This increases complexity by increasing the dimensionality of the extracted features thereby causing a

Table 4. Comparison of our best performing results with the baselines' hate class.

	Precision	Recall	F1
Hate class [5]	0.44	0.61	0.51
Hate class [16]	0.59	0.36	0.45
Hate class (Ours)	**0.47**	**0.49**	**0.48**

decrease in performance. Also, a large percentage of the tweets in the dataset contained replies, sometimes more than one. This, after preprocessing, would be converted to one sentence. Hence, a non-hateful tweet with a hateful reply will form one sentence. This can introduce some confusion to the classifier as sentences annotated as offensive or hateful now contain a substantial amount of neutral words with benign meaning.

We made some observations from the error analysis of the misclassified instances. With respect to our feature set, we discovered that the inclusion of typed dependency to the feature set assisted in identifying tweets that were misclassified when using the lexical features alone. For example, '*This kid looks like a retard when he tries hiding his phone... so obvious*' was correctly classified as hateful. However, there are also tweets the extended feature set misclassified that are correctly classified by n-gram features. We discovered that many cases where the word 'f*gg*t' was used were annotated as offensive but were predicted by the classifier to be hateful thus increasing the number of false positives. We also identify problems with human annotation, where some instances were wrongly annotated to be hate speech but were correctly classified as being offensive. Example: '*only fuck niggas would want to continue to mess with these messy ass bitch vs somebody who have been down for them all*' or '*ray j is the perfect example of what happen when you give lame nigga some pussy*'. It can be seen that these examples contain easily offensive words and were predicted to be offensive but have been labeled as hateful. This shows that a better annotation job is needed to provide a dataset for supervised classification.

A lot of factors contribute to this seemingly impossible task of accurately distinguishing between hate and offensive instances. The difficulty of this task cannot be over-emphasized. Recently, the authors in [20] used deep neural network for creating task-specific embeddings and also applied transfer learning to solve this problem. They reported that their models performed worse than the baseline on the Davidson dataset.

5   Conclusion and Future Work

It is of utmost importance to identify and draw the line between hate and profanity. Models built without this distinction, when deployed in real life, can introduce debilitating bias whereby the use of profane words in a plain offensive tweet might be flagged as hateful and the tweet removed. This would have a negative impact amongst social media users. We use typed dependency in conjunction with word and character n-grams for distinguishing between profane language and hate speech. We aimed to reduce the number false negative classification from what was reported in existing studies. To further improve performance, we propose a bias free annotation task to enable the models to be trained with better labels. Also, Twitter data is very noisy and would require a more in-depth preprocessing to get rid of the unnecessary information. We also suggest an investigation into using embeddings learned from the dependency word-pairs.

Disclaimer. This work contains examples of hateful and offensive instances. All examples were obtained from the dataset and do not represent the principles of the authors.

References

1. Alorainy, W., Burnap, P., Liu, H., Williams, M.: The enemy among us: detecting hate speech with threats based 'othering' language embeddings, vol. 9, no. 4, pp. 1–26 (2018). http://arxiv.org/abs/1801.07495
2. Burnap, P., Williams, M.: Hate speech, machine classification and statistical modelling of information flows on Twitter: interpretation and communication for policy decision making. Internet Policy Polit. **9999**(9999), 1–18 (2015). http://orca.cf.ac.uk/id/eprint/65227%0A
3. Burnap, P., Williams, M.L.: Us and them: identifying cyber hate on Twitter across multiple protected characteristics. EPJ Data Sci. **5**(1), 11 (2016). https://doi.org/10.1140/epjds/s13688-016-0072-6
4. Chen, Y., Zhou, Y., Zhu, S., Xu, H.: Detecting offensive language in social media to protect adolescent online safety. In: 2012 International Conference on Privacy, Security, Risk and Trust and 2012 International Conference on Social Computing, pp. 71–80, September 2012. https://doi.org/10.1109/SocialCom-PASSAT.2012.55
5. Davidson, T., Warmsley, D., Macy, M., Weber, I.: Automated hate speech detection and the problem of offensive language (2017). http://arxiv.org/abs/1703.04009
6. Fortuna, P., Nunes, S.: A survey on automatic detection of hate speech in text. ACM Comput. Surv. **51**(4), 85:1–85:30 (2018). https://doi.org/10.1145/3232676
7. Gaydhani, A., Doma, V., Kendre, S., Bhagwat, L.: Detecting hate speech and offensive language on Twitter using machine learning: An n-gram and TFIDF based approach. CoRR abs/1809.08651 (2018). http://arxiv.org/abs/1809.08651
8. Greevy, E.: Automatic text categorisation of racist webpages harassment (August 2004). http://doras.dcu.ie/17275/
9. Hu, M., Liu, B.: Mining and summarizing customer reviews. In: Proceedings of the Tenth ACM SIGKDD International Conference on Knowledge Discovery and Data Mining, KDD 2004, pp. 168–177. ACM, New York (2004). https://doi.org/10.1145/1014052.1014073
10. Kim, E., Sung, Y., Kang, H.: Brand followers' retweeting behavior on Twitter: how brand relationships influence brand electronic word-of-mouth. Comput. Hum. Behav. **37**, 18–25 (2014)

11. Komninos, A., Manandhar, S.: Dependency based embeddings for sentence classification tasks. In: Proceedings of the 2016 Conference of the North American Chapter of the Association for Computational Linguistics: Human Language Technologies, pp. 1490–1500. Association for Computational Linguistics, San Diego, June 2016. https://www.aclweb.org/anthology/N16-1175

12. Levy, O., Goldberg, Y.: Dependency-based word embeddings. In: Proceedings of the 52nd Annual Meeting of the Association for Computational Linguistics, Volume 2: Short Papers, pp. 302–308. Association for Computational Linguistics, Baltimore, June 2014. https://www.aclweb.org/anthology/P14-2050

13. MacAvaney, S., Zeldes, A.: A deeper look into dependency-based word embeddings. In: Proceedings of the 2018 Conference of the North American Chapter of the Association for Computational Linguistics: Student Research Workshop, pp. 40–45. Association for Computational Linguistics, New Orleans, June 2018. https://www.aclweb.org/anthology/N18-4006

14. Malmasi, S., Cahill, A.: Measuring feature diversity in native language identification (July 2015). https://doi.org/10.3115/v1/W15-0606

15. Malmasi, S., Zampieri, M.: Detecting hate speech in social media (2017). http://arxiv.org/abs/1712.06427

16. Malmasi, S., Zampieri, M.: Challenges in discriminating profanity from hate speech. J. Exp. Theor. Artif. Intell. **30**(2), 187–202 (2018). https://doi.org/10.1080/0952813X.2017.1409284

17. de Marneffe, M.C., MacCartney, B., Manning, C.D.: Generating typed dependency parses from phrase structure parses. In: Proceedings of the Fifth International Conference on Language Resources and Evaluation (LREC 2006). European Language Resources Association (ELRA), Genoa, May 2006. http://www.lrec-conf.org/proceedings/lrec2006/pdf/440_pdf.pdf

18. Mehdad, Y., Tetreault, J.: Do characters abuse more than words?, pp. 299–303 (September 2016). https://doi.org/10.18653/v1/w16-3638

19. Nobata, C., Tetreault, J., Thomas, A., Mehdad, Y., Chang, Y.: Abusive language detection in online user content pp. 145–153 (2017). https://doi.org/10.1145/2872427.2883062

20. Rizoiu, M., Wang, T., Ferraro, G., Suominen, H.: Transfer learning for hate speech detection in social media. CoRR abs/1906.03829 (2019). http://arxiv.org/abs/1906.03829

21. Robinson, D., Zhang, Z., Tepper, J.A.: Hate speech detection on Twitter: feature engineering v.s. feature selection. In: ESWC (2018)

22. Stephens-Davidowitz, S.I.: The effects of racial animus on a black presidential candidate: using google search data to find what surveys miss (June 2012). https://ssrn.com/abstract=2050673

23. Tan, L.K.W., Na, J.C., Theng, Y.L., Chang, K.: Phrase-level sentiment polarity classification using rule-based typed dependencies and additional complex phrases consideration. J. Comput. Sci. Technol. **27**(3), 650–666 (2012). https://doi.org/10.1007/s11390-012-1251-y

24. Warner, W., Hirschberg, J.: Detecting hate speech on the world wide web. In: Proceedings of the 2012 Workshop on Language in Social Media (LSM), pp. 19–26 (2012). http://info.yahoo.com/legal/us/yahoo/utos/utos-173.html

25. Waseem, Z.: Are you a racist or am i seeing things? annotator influence on hate speech detection on Twitter pp. 138–142 (2016). https://doi.org/10.18653/v1/w16-5618

26. Waseem, Z., Hovy, D.: Hateful symbols or hateful people? predictive features for hate speech detection on Twitter, pp. 88–93 (2016). https://doi.org/10.18653/v1/n16-2013

27. Watanabe, H., Bouazizi, M., Ohtsuki, T.: Hate speech on Twitter: a pragmatic approach to collect hateful and offensive expressions and perform hate speech detection. IEEE Access **6**, 13825–13835 (2018). https://doi.org/10.1109/ACCESS.2018.2806394

28. Zhang, Z., Luo, L.: Hate speech detection: a solved problem? the challenging case of long tail on Twitter. CoRR abs/1803.03662 (2018). http://arxiv.org/abs/1803.03662

To Extend or Not to Extend?
Context-Specific Corpus Enrichment

Felix Kuhr$^{(\boxtimes)}$, Tanya Braun, Magnus Bender, and Ralf Möller

Institute of Information Systems, University of Lübeck, Lübeck, Germany
{kuhr,braun,m.bender,moeller}@ifis.uni-luebeck.de

Abstract. An agent in pursuit of a task may work with a corpus of documents with linked subjective content descriptions. Faced with a new document, an agent has to decide whether to include that document in its corpus or not. Basing the decision on only words, topics, or entities, has shown to not lead to a balanced performance for varying documents. Therefore, this paper presents an approach for an agent to decide if a new document adds value to its existing corpus by combining texts and content descriptions. Furthermore, an agent can use the approach as a starting point for high quality content descriptions for new documents. A case study shows the effectiveness of our approach given varying types of new documents.

Keywords: Subjective content description · Text mining

1 Introduction

An agent that pursues a defined task or goal may work with a set of documents (corpus) as a form of reference library. A person assembling a range of scientific articles as related work describes such a setting, with the person as the agent, the compiling of related articles as the task, and the articles as the library. From an agent-theoretic perspective, an agent is a rational, autonomous unit acting in a world, perceived through sensors, fulfilling a task, e.g., an agent providing document retrieval services given specific requests from users. For more effective performance, the documents may be annotated with subjective content descriptions (SCDs), which the agents expects to be relevant to its task. The task provides a context in which SCDs add value for the agent. E.g., notes added to specific sentences of an article may provide explanations or references. Thus, SCDs add information relevant for the task or goal and that information has a connection to specific words in the document.

But, what should an agent do if presented with a new document, which typically has no SCDs? Without having thoroughly processed the new document, the question for the agent is: Does that document have anything of value to add in the given context? The problem is a decision making problem: Should the agent extend its reference library with the new document or should it not?

© Springer Nature Switzerland AG 2019
J. Liu and J. Bailey (Eds.): AI 2019, LNAI 11919, pp. 357–368, 2019.
https://doi.org/10.1007/978-3-030-35288-2_29

We aim at providing an approach to making a multi-dimensional decision in the context of the task. We focus on the SCDs in the corpus, which are specific to the task and have links to words in the documents. We model that SCDs generate the words of a document. The links between an SCD and specific words are modelled by a sequence of words in a window, with an SCD located at the center of the window. Words closer to the SCD location are more likely generated by the SCD than words farther away. The key idea for determining if a document adds value to the corpus is to measure how much of a new document without any SCDs can one generate with the existing SCDs in the corpus.

We build an SCD-word distribution for each SCD describing how likely an SCD generates each word of the vocabulary of the corpus. The problem turns into finding most probable SCDs (MPSCDs) for a new document given the SCD-word distributions of the existing SCDs. Given MPSCDs of a new document and their probabilities, an agent decides whether to extend the reference library with that document or not. Solving the problem of finding MPSCDs exactly is infeasible as the vocabulary of a corpus is huge with a large number of annotations. Therefore, we work with the similarity between vectors of SCD-word distributions and vector representations of estimated windows of the new document. We use the cosine similarity because the vectors are sparse and cosine similarity has a low complexity for sparse vectors. An agent identifies those SCDs that have vector representations most similar to the window vectors, assuming that those SCDs are the most probable ones based on the statistics of the corpus. Using the similarities of the chosen SCDs, an agent then computes indicators such as minimum, maximum, and average similarity. Based on that indicators, it decides whether the new document is too similar or too dissimilar compared to the documents in its corpus to contribute anything useful in the context of its task. If the agent decides to extend its library with the new document, it can even choose to retain SCDs with highest similarity, possibly adapting them, and then use them as a basis for further enrichment, automatic [8,15] or manual.

Specifically, the contributions of this paper are: (i) solving the problem of finding MPSCD for a new document by estimating them based on SCD-vector comparisons, (ii) providing a decision making procedure based on MPSCD, and (iii) a case study regarding decision making based on MPSCD given varying new documents. Additionally, we look at two considerations: (i) For large corpora containing documents from various topics, filtering a corpus based on topics decreases the number of documents to consider. (ii) For adapting estimated MPSCDs, an expectation-maximisation approach allows for optimizing window size and positions, e.g., if interested in retaining SCDs for new documents.

The remainder of this paper starts with a look at related work. Then, we specify notations for documents and SCDs. Next, we present our contributions, followed by a case study. The paper ends with a conclusion and future work.

2   Related Work

Over the past 20 years, a considerable number of automatic (semantic) annotation systems have been developed. The systems extract named entities from text of documents and add so-called *semantic annotations* from externally available common-sense knowledge bases, enriching the documents with machine-processable data. Some well-known automatic annotation systems are YEDDA [16], MINTE [4], OpenCalais [12], YAGO [14], KDTA [11], or GATE [5]. Some well-known sources of common-sense knowledge are DBpedia [9], NELL [3], and KnowledgeVault [6]. Named entities represent the link between documents and common-sense knowledge and link prediction is used to identify semantic annotations for an entity. Generally, link prediction describes the task of estimating the likelihood of a link (relation) existing between nodes (entities), given the links and attributes of nodes within a graph [7]. These annotation systems aim at developing a knowledge graph augmented with data from external sources. The systems efficiently solve their underlying problem. However, we investigate a different problem, deciding if a new document provides value to an agent.

Surveying methods of text mining, one can base a decision on different aspects, e.g., (i) similarity of text in the spirit of tf.idf [13], comparing a vector representation of a new document with vector representations of the documents in the corpus, (ii) similarity of topics in the spirit of latent Dirichlet allocation (LDA) [2], comparing an estimated topic distribution of a new document with topic distributions of the documents in the corpus, or (iii) entity matching [10] using named-entity recognition (NER), comparing entities (and relations) retrieved from the new document with entities (and relations) of the SCDs in the corpus. All three approaches carry drawbacks: The first two, based on bag-of-words, ignore SCDs and the order of words. Additionally, they make it hard to model that a document has to add value, i.e., not be a rephrased copy of an existing document or contain only unrelated data. The last approach has the problem that NER tools might not output annotations in the context of the task, which may lead to very few matches with SCDs of the corpus. Additionally, the decision in each case is a one-dimensional decision, based on one feature of the documents. Therefore, we aim at providing an approach to make a multi-dimensional decision that considers the context of the task.

3 Preliminaries

This section specifies notations of the technical framework for this paper and gives a brief overview of LDA, which is used for filtering large corpora (see Sect. 4.4) and is part of our case study in Sect. 5.

3.1 Notation

We define the following terms to formalize the setting of a corpus of documents, each document associated with a repository of additional data, i.e., SCDs.

- A word w is a basic unit of discrete data from a vocabulary $\mathcal{V} = (w_1, \ldots, w_V)$. Each w is represented as a unit-basis vector of length V that has a value of 1 where $w = w_v$ and 0's otherwise.

- A document d is a sequence of words $(w_1, \ldots, w_D)$ where each w_d is from $\mathcal{V}$. The expression $words(d)$ refers to the number of words in d.
- A corpus $\mathcal{D}$ is a set of N documents $\{d_1, \ldots, d_N\}$.
- For each document $d \in \mathcal{D}$ exists a document-specific repository g containing a set of SCDs $\{(t_j, \{\rho_i\}_{i=1}^l)\}_{j=1}^s$. SCDs can take any form. As such, their formats may be highly diverse. A standardized format would be the Resource Description Framework (RDF) but, for our main contributions, the specific format is irrelevant. Each t is associated with a set of positions $\{\rho_i\}_{i=1}^l$ in d where ρ_i refers to the ρ_i'th word in d. Given a document d or repository g, the terms $g(d)$ and $d(g)$ refer to the linked repository and document, respectively. The set of all SCDs of documents in $\mathcal{D}$ is given by $g(\mathcal{D}) = \bigcup_{d \in \mathcal{D}} g(d)$.
- An SCD window $win_{d,t,\rho}$ refers to the words in d that surround the position ρ of $t \in g(d)$, i.e., $win_{d,t,\rho} = (w_{(\rho-i)}, \ldots, w_\rho, \ldots, w_{(\rho+i)})$, $i \in \mathbb{N}$ if ρ marks the middle of the window. The position of a word $w \in win_{d,t,\rho}$ is given by $pos(w, win_{d,t,\rho})$ (0-based numbering). The size of $win_{d,t,\rho}$ is given by $s(win_{d,t,\rho})$, i.e., $s(win_{d,t,\rho}) = 2i + 1$ if ρ marks the middle of the window.
- Each word $w \in win_{d,t,\rho}$ is linked to an influence value $I(w, win_{d,t,\rho})$. The closer a word w is positioned to the position ρ of t, the higher is the influence value $I(w, win_{d,t,\rho})$. The influence value $I(w, win_{d,t,\rho})$ of w is given by the probability of the Binomial distribution at position $pos(w, win_{d',t,\rho})$, i.e.,

$$I(w, win_{d,t,\rho}) = \binom{n}{k} \cdot \pi^k \cdot (1 - \pi)^{n-k}, \tag{1}$$

where $n = s(win_{d',t,\rho}) - 1$, $k = pos(w, win_{d',t,\rho})$, and $\pi = \frac{\rho}{n}$, i.e., $\pi = 0.5$ if t is at the center of $win_{d,t,\rho}$ and influence values to the left and right of ρ should be symmetric. The binomial distribution yields a probability for each word $w \in win_{d,t,\rho}$ that is higher the closer w is to the position of t.

3.2   Latent Dirichlet Allocation

LDA [2], a well-known statistical technique, assumes that documents in a corpus $\mathcal{D}$ represent a mixture of topics where each topic is characterized by a distribution of words from a vocabulary $\mathcal{V}$ of $\mathcal{D}$. LDA generates a topic model from the documents in $\mathcal{D}$, learning latent structures of two forms, (i) a *document-topic distribution* θ for each document $d \in \mathcal{D}$, i.e., the degree to which the content of d relates to each topic in a set of topics and (ii) a *topic-word distribution* ϕ describing the probability of each word from $\mathcal{V}$ occurring in each topic. Both the document-topic distribution and the word-topic distribution depend on the documents in $\mathcal{D}$.

Next, we present the main contributions of this paper, context-specific corpus enrichment based on MPSCDs.

4   Context-Specific Corpus Enrichment

This section provides the theoretical foundations for MPSCDs and presents our approach to estimating MPSCDs. Additionally, it looks into two considerations. This section ends with decision making using MPSCDs.

4.1   Foundations of SCDs

This paragraph formalizes the link between SCDs and the words of a document as a basis for MPSCDs. Specifically, we model that SCDs generate the words of a document. Each document $d \in \mathcal{D}$ has a link to its repository $g(d)$, containing SCDs that themselves are linked to positions in d. Words closer to an SCD location are more likely generated by the SCD than words farther away.

Mathematically, we represent each SCD as a vector of length n, where $n = |\mathcal{V}(\mathcal{D})|$ and each vector entry refers to a word in $\mathcal{V}(\mathcal{D})$. The entry itself is a probability that describes how likely it is that the corresponding SCD generates the word, yielding an SCD-word distribution for each SCD. We represent SCD-word distributions for all m SCDs in $g(\mathcal{D})$ by an $m \times n$ matrix $\delta(\mathcal{D})$, with the SCD-word distribution vectors forming the rows of the matrix:

$$\delta(\mathcal{D}) = \begin{array}{c} \\ t_1 \\ t_2 \\ \vdots \\ t_m \end{array} \begin{bmatrix} w_1 & w_2 & w_3 & \cdots & w_n \\ v_{1,1} & v_{1,2} & v_{1,3} & \cdots & v_{1,n} \\ v_{2,1} & v_{2,2} & v_{2,3} & \cdots & v_{2,n} \\ \vdots & \vdots & \vdots & \vdots & \vdots \\ v_{m,1} & v_{m,2} & v_{m,3} & \cdots & v_{m,n} \end{bmatrix}$$

We can fill $\delta(\mathcal{D})$ based on the documents in $\mathcal{D}$ and their linked SCDs. Using a maximum-likelihood strategy, one counts for each SCD t the number of occurrences of each word w in the windows $win_{d,t,\rho}$ of t over all documents and all positions. The occurrences are weighted by their influence value $I(w, win_{d,t,\rho})$.

Algorithm 1 shows a description of forming matrix $\delta(\mathcal{D})$, in which $\delta(\mathcal{D})[t][w]$ refers to entry at the intersection of the row of t and the column of w. The term $\delta(\mathcal{D})[t]$ refers to the complete row of t. The outer loop (line 3) goes through each SCD with the three inner loops counting the weighted occurrences of words in windows of each document. At the end of each outer loop iteration, the SCD-word distribution of the current t is normalized to yield a probability distribution for each SCD over the complete vocabulary. Formally, normalization is given by

$$v_{i,j} = \frac{v_{i,j}}{\sum_{k=1}^{n} v_{i,k}}. \tag{2}$$

To illustrate line 7 of Algorithm 1, consider the following example. Assume that in document d_1, there is a window $win_{d_1,t_1,\rho}$ for SCD t_1

$$win_{d_1,t_1,\rho} = (w_{21}, w_4, w_8, \underline{w_{15}}, w_{16}, w_{23}, w_{42}) \tag{3}$$
$$(0.015625, 0.09375, 0.234375, \underline{0.3125}, 0.234375, 0.09375, 0.015625) \tag{4}$$

with t_1 positioned at the center (w_{15}, underlined) and the influence values in Eq. 4 based on Eq. 1 with $n = s(win_{d_1,t_1,\rho}) - 1 = 6$, $k \in \{0, \ldots, 6\}$, and entry positions corresponding to positions in Eq. 3. Based on the innermost loop of Algorithm 1, seven entries of $\delta(\mathcal{D})$ are updated, e.g., for w_{21} at position 0:

$$\delta(\mathcal{D})[t_1][w_{21}] \mathrel{+}= 0.015625$$

Algorithm 1. Forming SCD-word distribution matrix $\delta(\mathcal{D})$

```
1: function BUILDMATRIX(Corpus D)
2:     Initialize an m × n matrix δ(D) with zeros
3:     for each t ∈ g(D) do
4:        for each d ∈ D do
5:           for each win_{d,t,ρ} ∈ d do                    ▷ Iterates over ρ
6:              for each w ∈ win_{d,t,ρ} do
7:                 δ(D)[t][w] += I(w, win_{d,t,ρ})          ▷ For I, see Eq. (1)
8:           Normalize δ(D)[t]                              ▷ See Eq. (2)
9:     return δ(D)
```
---

where $\delta(\mathcal{D})[t_1][w_{21}]$ refers to $v_{1,21}$, which is incremented by 0.015625. Algorithm 1 updates $\delta(\mathcal{D})$ for the remaining words and then continues with the next window. When Algorithm 1 is finished with d_1, it moves on to the next document, going through the windows of the next document. After iterating over all documents, Algorithm 1 repeats going through all documents and their windows for the remaining SCDs.

The model behind a SCD-word distribution matrix $\delta(\mathcal{D})$ is generative as one could now choose $M \ll m$ SCDs and sample a new document based on the chosen SCDs. Given the generative nature, we are now interested in the most likely SCDs to have generated words of a new document.

Thus, we look at the problem of finding those SCDs that are most probable given the words of a new document.

4.2   The MPSCD Problem

Generally, the MPSCD problem asks for the M most probable SCDs for a document d' given the SCD-word distribution matrix $\delta(\mathcal{D})$ and the words in d':

$$\underset{t_1,\ldots,t_M \in g(\mathcal{D})}{\arg\max} \quad P(t_1,\ldots,t_M|d',\delta(\mathcal{D})) \tag{5}$$

As we do not model an influence of one SCD on the next and as we place the M windows evenly distributed over d', we can simplify Eq. 5 as follows

$$\underset{t_1 \in g(\mathcal{D})}{\arg\max} P(t_1|win_{d',t_1,\rho},\delta(\mathcal{D}) \cup \cdots \cup \underset{t_M \in g(\mathcal{D})}{\arg\max} P(t_M|win_{d',t_M,\rho},\delta(\mathcal{D})) \tag{6}$$

That is there are M windows $win_{t,d',\rho}$ and for each window individual MPSCDs are estimated. The intuition is as follows: If d' is a document from $\mathcal{D}$ or a close variation of the documents in $\mathcal{D}$, then Eq. 5 yields MPSCDs with high probabilities. If d' is an unknown document, the resulting MPSCDs vary in their probability. If the vocabulary or word composition is very different, the probabilities are very low on average. The closer the vocabulary and word composition of d' get to the characteristics of $\mathcal{D}$, the higher the probabilities are. Determining if a document adds value to a corpus is based on of how much of a new document can one generate with high probability given $\delta(\mathcal{D})$ and what is too much.

Unfortunately, solving the MPSCD problem is intractable as n and m are typically very large, which is why we estimate probability with similarity.

4.3   Estimating MPSCDs

Based on the statistics of the corpus, we estimate Eq. 6 for an SCD t in a window $win_{t,d',\rho}$ by determining the SCD in $\delta(\mathcal{D})$ with the most similar distribution compared to a vector representation of $win_{t,d',\rho}$ using influence values.

The setting is as follows: Given a new document d' and the SCD-word distribution matrix $\delta(\mathcal{D})$, we estimate M MPSCDs. Based on M, M windows $win_{t,d',\rho}$ lie over the text of d' with a window size of $\sigma = \frac{words(d')}{M}$ and positions ρ starting at $\frac{\sigma}{2}$ and incrementing by σ. For each $win_{t,d',\rho}$, the SCD is unknown at the start, i.e., $t = \bot$. As the words in $win_{t,d',\rho}$ have an influence value based on Eq. 1, we can build a vector $\delta(win_{d',t,\rho})$ of length n. The entries $\delta(win_{d',t,\rho})[w]$ are set to 0 for each word $w \in \mathcal{V}$ not in $win_{t,d',\rho}$ and set to $I(w, win_{t,d',\rho})$ otherwise. Using cosine similarity, the SCD t most similar to $\delta(win_{d',t,\rho})$ is given by:

$$\arg\max_{t} \frac{\delta(\mathcal{D})[t] \cdot \delta(win_{d',t,\rho})}{|\delta(\mathcal{D})[t]| \cdot |\delta(win_{d',t,\rho})|}. \tag{7}$$

Algorithm 2 describes estimating MPSCDs for d' using $\delta(\mathcal{D})$ given M. The output is the set of MPSCDs $g(d')$ as well as the windows and similarities for the MPSCDs in $g(d')$. The outer loop (line 3) iterates over the positions of the M SCDs, setting up a window $win_{d',t,\rho}$ and a vector representation $\delta(win_{d',t,\rho})$. Then, Algorithm 2 calculates cosine similarities between $\delta(win_{d',t,\rho})$ and the SCD vectors in $\delta(\mathcal{D})$ based on Eq. 7. It retains the SCD with the highest similarity as MPSCD t for the window $win_{d',t,\rho}$. Our approach rests on the following proposition:

Proposition 1. *Algorithm 2 estimates for a new document d' M (locally) most probable SCDs, i.e., Eq. 7 calculates for each window estimates of Eq. 6.*

We argue that the similarity between the influence distribution over the words in a window and the SCD-word distribution indicates that the SCD is most likely to generate the words in the window. Another SCD generating other words with high probability would not generate the words in the window with a high probability and as such, does not lead to a high similarity.

The MPSCDs represent a local optimum based on the current setting of the windows. If the agent decides on adding the new document to the corpus and using the MPSCDs for additional tasks like query answering or document retrieval, optimizing the initial SCDs of d' might lead to more attuned SCDs.

4.4   Considerations

We look at two considerations, one regarding fine-tuning MPSCDs, e.g., if interested in retaining SCDs for documents, and one regarding large corpora.

Algorithm 2. Estimating MPSCDs

1: **function** ESTIMATEMPSCD(Document d', Number M, matrix $\delta(\mathcal{D})$)

2:    $\sigma \leftarrow \frac{words(d')}{M}$, $\rho \leftarrow \frac{\sigma}{2}$, $\mathcal{W} \leftarrow \emptyset$

3:    **for** $\rho \leftarrow \frac{\sigma}{2}$; $\rho \leq words(d)$; $\rho+ = \sigma$ **do**

4:        Set up a window $win_{d',t,\rho}$ of size σ around ρ with $t = \perp$

5:        $\delta(win_{d',t,\rho}) \leftarrow$ new zero-vector of length n

6:        **for** $w \in win_{d',t,\rho}$ **do**

7:            $\delta(win_{d',t,\rho})[w]+ = I(w, win_{d',t,\rho})$

8:        $t \leftarrow \arg\max_{t_i} \frac{\delta(\mathcal{D})[i] \cdot \delta(win_{d',t,\rho})}{|\delta(\mathcal{D})[i]| \cdot |\delta(win_{d',t,\rho})|}$ in $win_{d',t,\rho}$

9:        $sim \leftarrow \max_{t_i} \frac{\delta(\mathcal{D})[i] \cdot \delta(win_{d',t,\rho})}{|\delta(\mathcal{D})[i]| \cdot |\delta(win_{d',t,\rho})|}$

10:        $\mathcal{W} \leftarrow \mathcal{W} \cup \{(sim, win_{d',t,\rho})\}$

11:        $g(d') \leftarrow g(d') \cup \{t\}$

12:    **return** $g(d')$, $\mathcal{W}$

SCD Window Adjustments. To optimize MPSCDs for a new document d', one can adjust the initial number of SCDs, the corresponding SCD positions, and the window sizes in d' to get MPSCDs with higher overall probability (or similarity).

We require the outputs of Algorithm 2, (repository $g(d')$ for document d', set $\mathcal{W}$ containing the similarities sim and the initial windows $win_{d',t,\rho}$). To optimize the SCDs in $g(d')$, we can iteratively adjust size and position of all windows in $\mathcal{W}$ and update t in each window based on Eq. 7 s.t. the overall similarity of the M influence vectors is maximum, i.e.:

$$\max \sum_{(sim, win_{d',t,\rho}) \in \mathcal{W}} sim. \tag{8}$$

Optimization starts with calculating the overall similarity of the current SCDs in $g(d')$ using the similarities stored in $\mathcal{W}$. Then, it iteratively adjusts windows until it reaches a local optimum for the optimization problem stated in Eq. 8. Each window in $\mathcal{W}$ can be adjusted in the following four different directions: (a) extend left boundary of the SCD-window to the left, (b) extend right boundary of SCD-window to the right, (c) shift left boundary of SCD-window to the right, and (d) shift right boundary of SCD-window to the left. Window adjustments (a) and (b) extend the size of window $win_{d',t,\rho}$, while window adjustments (c) and (d) reduce the size of window $win_{d',t,\rho}$.

Document Clusters. Large corpora contain thousands of documents that may focus on different topics. Identifying documents in a corpus $\mathcal{D}$ having a high topic similarity with a new document d' narrows down the set of possible SCDs for d' by considering only SCDs from similar topics. Therefore, one can form a cluster $\mathcal{C}_{d'}$ of d'-related documents s.t. all $d \in \mathcal{C}_{d'}$ have a Hellinger distance H of their topic distributions θ being smaller than a threshold τ, i.e., $\mathcal{C}_{d'} = \{d \in \mathcal{D} \mid H(\theta_{d'}, \theta_d) < \tau\}$, where $H(\theta_d, \theta_{d'})$ refers to the Hellinger distance between the topic distributions of d and d', respectively. The cluster $\mathcal{C}_{d'}$ takes the place of $\mathcal{D}$ in Eq. 5. The threshold τ decides on the minimum required topic similarity between two documents d' and d, such that $d \in \mathcal{C}_{d'}$. The best value for τ depends on the performance of external applications working with the SCDs in $g(d')$. A smaller τ means a higher similarity between documents in $\mathcal{C}_{d'}$. Next, we build MPSCDs into a decision making procedure for an agent.

4.5   Decision Making

An agent can use the MPSCDs for a new document d' making a decision on adding the new document d' to the corpus or not. Obviously, this decision depends on the goal of the agent. If the agent is interested in similar documents containing new information, it may decide adding documents where half of the SCDs have a high similarity and the other half of the SCDs have a small similarity. Based on the goal of the agent, thresholds have to be set accordingly.

The agent has to decide whether to extend its corpus $\mathcal{D}$ with d' if d' adds value relevant to its task. Document d' may not add value if d' has no or very little connection to $\mathcal{D}$ or if d' does not add new content. SCDs are the connection between documents and context, signalling their value to the task. Thus, the decision incorporates SCDs and the words that are connected to them using the available resources $\mathcal{D}$, $g(\mathcal{D})$, and $\delta(\mathcal{D})$. An agent proceeds as follows if presented with a new document d': (i) Using Algorithm 2, it computes MPSCDs $\{t_1, \ldots, t_M\}$ for d'. As a byproduct, it receives the windows and the maximum similarities of each window in $\mathcal{W}$. (ii) Based on $\mathcal{W}$ and $\{t_1, \ldots, t_M\}$, the agent makes a decision. The decision making is based on a combination of (i) maximum similarity, (ii) minimum similarity, (iii) average similarity, and (iv) maximum and average difference in the similarity between neighbouring windows.

5   Case Study

We present a case study illustrating the potential of the multi-dimensional decision making approach considering the initial question: Should an agent extend its reference library with a new document or should it not? In this case study we use two corpora containing Wikipedia articles. The first corpus contains documents about European largest cities (https://bit.ly/2kOvmwD); the second corpus contains documents about U.S. presidents (https://bit.ly/2Z1v1G9).

We compare for both corpora our multi-dimensional decision making approach with LDA. We do not consider entity matching since entity matching ignores context, which means that unrelated documents can share the same entities and similar documents can have no matches in their entities.

The new documents we test belong to the following four types of documents: (i) Similar documents (d_{sim}); content of new document is very similar to the content of documents in the corpus, e.g., the new document tells about the same event. (ii) Extensions (d_{ext}); content of new document is similar to the content of documents in the corpus and contains additional *information* unavailable in any other document in the corpus, e.g., the new document represents an extension of an article. (iii) Revisions (d_{rev}); the new document represents a revision of

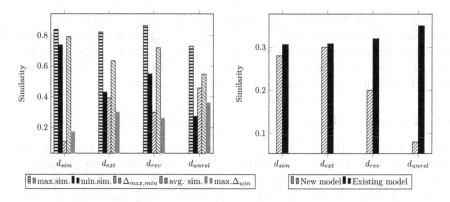

Fig. 1. Representation of the four document types d_{sim}, d_{ext}, d_{rev}, and d_{unrel} using the introduced MPSCD similarity values (left) and topic similarity (right).

another document in the corpus. (iv) Unrelated documents (d_{unrel}); content of new document is unrelated to the content of documents in the corpus. We preprocess all documents by lowercasing characters, stemming words, tokenizing, and eliminating tokens part of the Stanford CoreNLP stop-word list.

Afterwards, we use Stanford OpenIE [1] to automatically extract tuples from the documents acting as SCDs for all documents within the corpus to have roughly the same number of SCDs for all documents that are not influenced by us. The MPSCDs of new documents support agents in their decision making process since MPSCDs of new documents give information about the document type. The MPSCDs are not only suitable to decide if a new document is similar or unrelated to the documents in the corpus, but also if a new document is an extension or a revision of a document in the corpus. We consider the following five indicators to decide on extending a corpus with a new document or not: (i) maximum similarity of all MPSCDs (max. sim.), (ii) minimum similarity of all MPSCDs (min. sim.), (iii) maximum difference between highest and lowest similarity value ($\Delta_{max,min}$), (iv) average MPSCD similarity (avg. sim.), and (v) maximum change between neighbouring MPSCD-windows (max. Δ_{win}).

On the left, Fig. 1 presents the indicators for the MPSCDs for each type of document. On the right, Fig. 1 shows two variants of comparing a new document and the corpus using LDA. The first variant learns a new topic model for the corpus including the new document, yielding a topic distribution for the new document. The second variant infers the topic distribution of the new document using an existing topic model of the initial corpus. Similarity is given by the Hellinger distance between two topic distributions subtracted from the value 1. Infering the topic distribution is significantly faster than calculating a new topic model but makes it impossible to identify the type of a new document since all similarity values are similar. Generating a new topic model allows for distinguishing an unrelated document and a revision from all types but makes it difficult to distinguish a similar document from an extension because both documents share nearly the same topic distribution leading to almost identical similarities. Estimating the MPSCDs for a new document and analysing the five

Table 1. Document type indicator comparision

	City corpus				President corpus			
	d_{sim}	d_{ext}	d_{rev}	d_{unrel}	d_{sim}	d_{ext}	d_{rev}	d_{unrel}
Max Sim	+	+	+	o	+	+	+	o
Min Sim	+	o	o	−	o	o	o	−
$\Delta_{max,min}$	−	o	−	o	−	o	−	o
Avg. Sim	+	o	+	o	+	+	+	o
Max.Δ_{win}	−	o	−	o	−	o	−	o

indicators enables classification of a new document in the context of a given corpus. Generally, the value of indicators slightly change with the corpus.

Table 1 represents the five indicators for all four document types of the city corpus containing articles the largest European cities and the president corpus containing articles about the U.S. presidents. We specify a high similarity (+) for values between 0.7 and 1, an average degree of similarity (o) for values between 0.3 and 0.7 and a low similarity (−) for values below 0.3.

For both corpora new documents of type d_{sim}, d_{ext} and d_{rev} share high values for the maximum similarity. Similar documents (d_{sim}) have a noticeable higher minimum similarity than all other types of documents. Unrelated documents (d_{unrel}) have a smaller maximum similarity value compared all other types of documents and the minimum similarity is small. The maximum similarity change between neighbouring windows ($max.\Delta_{win}$) of document extensions (d_{ext}) is similar to unrelated documents while the maximum similarity change between neighbouring windows of revisions (d_{rev}) is comparable to similar documents.

6   Conclusion and Outlook

If an agent is presented with an unknown document, this paper enables it to answer the question "To extend or not to extend?" in a context-specific way. The decision behind the question has to consider how much added value a document provides within the context of the agent's task. SCDs capture the context and generate the words of documents in introduced model. For a new document, an algorithm allows for estimating MPSCDs based on existing SCDs in the spirit of "how much of the new document can the existing SCDs generate with high probability?" For feasibility, the algorithm uses similarity of vector representations of word distributions. The procedure for making a decision uses the estimated MPSCDs and their similarities. By combining indicators, an agent is able to make a decision about documents with varying value to add.

Future work includes modelling a window sequence with a hidden Markov model to find a most probable sequence of known and unknown segments of a document for decision making. Another aspect is finding a global optimum, trading off better results with more work. Currently, we are further analyzing patterns emerging between windows to extract them for transfer learning and investigate kernel methods to separate the different types of new documents.

References

1. Angeli, G., Premkumar, M.J.J., Manning, C.D.: Leveraging linguistic structure for open domain information extraction. In: Proceedings of the 53rd Annual Meeting of the Association for Computational Linguistics and the 7th International Joint Conference on Natural Language Processing of the Asian Federation of Natural Language Processing, ACL 2015, Beijing, China, Volume 1: Long Papers, 26–31 July 2015, pp. 344–354 (2015)
2. Blei, D.M., Ng, A.Y., Jordan, M.I.: Latent Dirichlet allocation. J. Mach. Learn. Res. **3**, 993–1022 (2003)
3. Carlson, A., Betteridge, J., Kisiel, B., Settles, B., Hruschka, Jr., E.R., Mitchell, T.M.: Toward an architecture for never-ending language learning. In: Proceedings of the Twenty-Fourth AAAI Conference on Artificial Intelligence, AAAI 2010, Atlanta, Georgia, USA, 11–15 July 2010 (2010)
4. Collarana, D., Galkin, M., Ribón, I.T., Vidal, M., Lange, C., Auer, S.: MINTE: semantically integrating RDF graphs. In: Proceedings of the 7th International Conference on Web Intelligence, Mining and Semantics, WIMS 2017, Amantea, Italy, 19–22 June 2017, pp. 22:1–22:11 (2017)
5. Cunningham, H., Tablan, V., Roberts, A., Bontcheva, K.: Getting more out of biomedical documents with gate's full lifecycle open source text analytics. PLoS Comput. Biol. **9**(2), e1002854 (2013)
6. Dong, X.L., et al.: From data fusion to knowledge fusion. PVLDB **7**(10), 881–892 (2014)
7. Getoor, L., Diehl, C.P.: Link mining: a survey. In: SIGKDD Explorations, vol. 7, no. 2, pp. 3–12 (2005)
8. Kuhr, F., Witten, B., Möller, R.: Corpus-driven annotation enrichment. In: 13th IEEE International Conference on Semantic Computing, ICSC 2019, Newport Beach, CA, USA, 30 January 30 – 1 February 2019, pp. 138–141 (2019)
9. Lehmann, J., et al.: DBpedia - a large-scale, multilingual knowledge base extracted from Wikipedia. Semant. Web **6**(2), 167–195 (2015)
10. Newcombe, H.B., Kennedy, J.M., Axford, S., James, A.P.: Automatic linkage of vital records. Science **130**(3381), 954–959 (1959)
11. Papantoniou, K., Tsatsaronis, G., Paliouras, G.: KDTA: automated knowledge-driven text annotation. In: Proceedings of Machine Learning and Knowledge Discovery in Databases, European Conference, Part III, ECML PKDD 2010, Barcelona, Spain, 20–24 September 2010, pp. 611–614 (2010)
12. Reuters, T.: Opencalais. Accessed 16 June 2008
13. Sparck Jones, K.: A statistical interpretation of term specificity and its application in retrieval. J. Documentation **28**(1), 11–21 (1972)
14. Suchanek, F.M., Kasneci, G., Weikum, G.: Yago: a core of semantic knowledge. In: Proceedings of the 16th International Conference on World Wide Web, WWW 2007, Banff, Alberta, Canada, 8–12 May 2007, pp. 697–706 (2007)
15. Braun, T., Kuhr, F., Möller, R.: Unsupervised text annotations. In: Formal and Cognitive Reasoning - Workshop at the 40th Annual German Conference on AI (KI-2017) (2017)
16. Yang, J., Zhang, Y., Li, L., Li, X.: YEDDA: a lightweight collaborative text span annotation tool. In: Proceedings of ACL 2018, System Demonstrations Melbourne, Australia, 15–20 July 2018, pp. 31–36 (2018)

A Machine Learning Benchmark with Meaning: Learnability and Verb Semantics

Csaba Veres[(⊠)] and Bjørn Helge Sandblåst

The University of Bergen, Bergen, Norway
{csaba.veres,bjorn.sandblast}@uib.no

Abstract. Just over thirty years ago the prospect of modelling human knowledge with parallel distributed processing systems without explicit rules, became a possibility. In the past five years we have seen remarkable progress with artificial neural network (ANN) based systems being able to solve previously difficult problems in many cognitive domains. With a focus on Natural Language Processing (NLP), we argue that the progress is in part illusory because the benchmarks that measure progress have become task oriented, and have lost sight of the goal to model knowledge. Task oriented benchmarks are not informative about the reasons machine learning succeeds, or fails. We propose a new dataset in which the correct answers to entailments and grammaticality judgements depend crucially on specific items of knowledge about verb semantics, and therefore errors on performance can be directly traced to deficiencies in knowledge. If this knowledge is not learnable from the provided input, then it must be provided as an innate prior.

Keywords: Machine learning · NLP · Grammar · Learnability ·
Cognition · Benchmarks · Dataset

1 Introduction

Cognitive Science has a long tradition for using ANNs to investigate the nature of mental representation, learning and thought. Perhaps the key driver in the modern era was the 1986 release of Rumelhart and McClelland's two-volume textbook, *Parallel distributed processing: Explorations in the microstructure of cognition*, Volume 1: *Foundations* [20], Volume 2: *Psychological and biological models* [21], which introduced the *Connectionist Paradigm* and brought a sea change in theoretical approaches to cognitive science [7].

A central area of debate concerned the nature of the mental lexicon, how it is represented, learned [19] and accessed [10]. The chapter *On Learning the Past Tenses of English Verbs* [10] showed how a distributed connectionist network could learn lawful linguistic behaviour without learning any explicit rules. The authors presented a system which mimicked key aspects of the human acquisition of the past tense in English, which follows three predictable stages. In

© Springer Nature Switzerland AG 2019
J. Liu and J. Bailey (Eds.): AI 2019, LNAI 11919, pp. 369–380, 2019.
https://doi.org/10.1007/978-3-030-35288-2_30

stage 1 children typically know only a few very high frequency verbs, which are predominantly irregular in their past tense (e.g. *come-came, go-went*). In stage 2 they acquire many of the less frequent verbs, which are predominantly regular (e.g. *wipe-wiped, pull-pulled*). This has been interpreted as learning a rule to add the *-ed* suffix to any verb to obtain the past tense form [2]. Unfortunately at this stage they often add the suffix to irregular verbs they already know, and therefore make mistakes on verbs they had previously used correctly (e.g. *come-comed, go-goed*). Finally in stage 3 children regain the correct use of the irregular forms. The authors showed that a simple two-layer pattern associator network with hand crafted features could not only learn the final rule-like behaviour of past tense formation, but could also learn irregular forms, as well as replicate the three stage process of learning. In the following 20 years the bold attempt to replace rules with connections in the case of past tense learning had resulted in somewhat of a stalemate with over 150 publications both in favour and against the claims [15]. One of the major contributors, Steven Pinker, summarises his view as "denying compositional structure and shoehorning phenomena into a single uniform net" was insufficient to model the processes faithfully [15].

The recent resurgence of connectionist modeling, following the success of deep learning networks in speech recognition, visual object recognition, object detection and many other data intensive domains [28], has given rise to new approaches in language modelling. The past year has seen substantial progress in many NLP tasks, driven by deep learning systems that couple self-supervised learning of a generic language modelling task on massive text corpora, with methods for fine tuning the network to specific target tasks [6,14,18]. This approach immediately resulted in sizeable improvements in many common tasks such as textual entailment, semantic similarity and reading comprehension[1].

On the other hand, the purpose of model construction has changed. Rather than attempting to understand and model knowledge required to perform a task (like forming the past tense of a new verb with rules), the primary aim is to perform as well as possible in standard tasks, no matter what knowledge is required and how it can be acquired. For example during learning, the XLNet network uses bidirectional contexts [27], a wildly implausible method for human language acquisition.

The quest for developing the best performing networks has made it necessary for the community to agree on a common set of tasks and evaluation metrics, both as a source of data to enable development and as a benchmark against which systems can be tested. One current effort which is gaining community traction is the GLUE benchmark project[2] and its successor SuperGLUE [23,24]. The datasets in the suite are designed to include difficult problems such as lexical entailment and problems that require the incorporation of world knowledge in their solution. However the datasets are not primarily motivated by an attempt to understand how humans perform the tasks, or what knowledge they need, but rather to present tasks which humans can solve and machines can emulate.

---

[1] https://openai.com/blog/language-unsupervised/.

[2] https://gluebenchmark.com/.

The problem we suggest is that benchmark tests are not written with the intent to discover what knowledge is attained by a learning system but with the intent to test how well they perform on common tasks, which implicitly rely on the knowledge. The use of insufficiently grounded tasks can additionally lead to spurious errors from unforeseen sources. For example, natural language inference systems can mistakenly judge sentences like "Alice believes Mary" as being entailed by sentences which contain the words as subsequences but not linguistic constituents, such as "Alice believes Mary is lying" [11]. In the premise "Mary" is not the direct object of the verb but rather the subject of the complement "lying", whereas the hypothesis changes the role of "Mary" to direct object of "believes". The mistake can only be discovered when the dataset includes a theory of syntax to semantics mappings.

In this paper we describe our work on a dataset in which the correct classification of entailment relations depends on highly finessed grammatical relations as described in Beth Levin's study on English verbs [9]. The linguistic behaviour of verbs reveals rich semantics which control their behaviour, and the acquisition of this semantic knowledge poses a learnability paradox [17]. The dataset provides a direct test of learnability in artificial neural networks.

2 Related Work

There have been several datasets for NLP tasks that were based on linguistic or cognitive theory. SemEval-2012 Task 2 [8] included a rich variety of sentences for measuring degrees of relational similarity, where the items were based on a category system of relations consisting of 79 categories gleaned from a synthesis of existing psycholinguistic theory [1]. The categories were part of the research framework to understand how students reason in the analogy problems included in the Graduate Record Examinations (GRE), standardized test for admissions to most graduate schools in the United States. Several processing models were proposed for how students solve the analogy tasks with the different types of relations [1]. In other words, not only the task, but the knowledge needed to solve the task, were questions under investigation.

There are two important ways in which this theoretical analysis benefited the dataset and its use in machine learning research. First, the processing models all relied on a dynamic pairwise comparison between the words in the analogy question, at the time of testing. Relations according to this model are not learnt, but computed at time of testing. An implication of this is that single vector-space models in which relational information is encoded within the vector at time of learning, may not be the best approach. The results support this hypothesis since the best machine learning systems used multiple vector spaces to compute similarity with the use of predictive features such as word frequency, positive pointwise mutual information (PPMI), and two measures of co-occurrence in a domain- and function-space [22]. Single vector space models using a recurrent neural network model performed significantly less well [13]. The second important contribution was that results could be further analysed to reveal how the type of relations interacted with the machine learning algorithms. For example some of the classes included relations based on "Class-Inclusion", "Part-Whole", "Similar", "Contrast", "Attribute", "Non-attribute", and "Space-Time". The results showed that systems tended to perform best with the "Similar" category[3] and worst with the "Non-Attribute"[4], but that the "Non-Attribute" examples were also worse than the subtly different "Contrast" examples[5]. Results such as these can be used to investigate the difference in optimal learning scenarios for the different relations.

Models of single word embeddings were subsequently improved with the CBOW and Skip-gram algorithms, and their performance on analogy tasks also improved [12]. Unfortunately the results are not directly comparable because the evaluation of analogical reasoning was not performed with the SemEval task. Instead, a new Google evaluation set was constructed, which was composed of five types of semantic and nine type of syntactic questions. The five semantic relations are "Common capital city", "All capital cities", "Currency", "City-in-state", and "Man-Woman". To the best of our knowledge there is no theoretical justification for these choices, and comparison between categories is difficult, with little theoretical interest. For example the relation "City-in-state" (e.g. Chicago-Illinois) appears to have some semantic overlap with "Common capital city" (e.g. Athens-Greece), but it is not clear if a comparison of results on these classes would be meaningful. The test set was also criticised on the ACL state-of-the-art web site[6] on several grounds, including "In the semantic part, country:capital relation accounts for over 50% of all semantic questions", with the result that the nature of semantic knowledge acquired by CBOW and Skip-gram embeddings is difficult to infer from the test data.

Another dataset which was developed with strong theoretical foundations is the CoLA grammatical acceptability judgement corpus [25]. Acceptability judgements are at the core of modern linguistic theory, which has as its principle goal to discover the grammar capable of generating all and only the acceptable sentences of a language [3]. The goal of the CoLA set was to find evidence concerning the Poverty of Stimulus Argument, which is a claim that the richness of human grammatical knowledge cannot be acquired by purely data driven methods [4]. Sentences were drawn from a pool of texts and technical books about language, and the grammatical status of each sentence was stipulated in the texts. Only three broad classes of violations were included: morphological, syntactic and semantic, and a large range of grammar property violations were looked at. There was no attempt to describe more specific classes of linguistic phenomena.

---

[3] one word represents a different degree or form of the object, action, or quality represented by the other word, e.g. car:auto, buy:purchase, simmer:boil.

[4] one word names a quality, property, or action that is characteristically NOT an attribute of the entity named by the other word, e.g. harmony:discordant, recluse:socialize, famine:plentitude.

[5] one word names an opposite or incompatible of the other word, e.g. alive:dead, old:young, believe:deny.

[6] https://aclweb.org/aclwiki/Google_analogy_test_set_(State_of_the_art).

The experiments showed that state-of-the-art networks were not sufficient to learn the task effectively, with the highest accuracy reaching 0.772. This was taken as evidence for the Poverty of Stimulus Argument.

The test suite SuperGLUE does not use the CoLA set but instead includes grammaticality test from the GLUE diagnostics which use entailment rather than acceptability judgements. The method is based on White et al. who show that it is possible to automatically rewrite classifications into the form of textual entailment pairs [26]. The tasks themselves are not tied to any specific theory of knowledge, however, leaving open the question of what kinds of grammatical knowledge are learnable from text input. We propose a more direct test set in which sentences are constructed to test precisely the knowledge that is required to perform the task. The knowledge itself is based on a linguistic theory which had its roots in the following puzzle about language acquisition.

3   Learnability and Cognition

The puzzle involves verb frames and the possibilities for alternative frames involving the same verb. For example the verb *load* can appear in the following construction (examples taken from [16]).

(1)   Hal is loading hay into the wagon.

In sentence (1) the grammatical subject (Hal) of the verb is the loader, the object is the contents being moved (the hay), and the further object of *into* expresses the container into which the hay is being moved (the wagon). This is called the content-locative construction because the focus of the sentence is the content (hay). The same meaning can be expressed by sentence (2) where the object of the verb is now the container, changing the focus of the sentence. This is called the container-locative construction.

(2)   Hal loaded the wagon with hay.

There are many examples of verbs which behave this way, for example (3). A possible generalisation of this pattern is that verbs appearing in content-locative constructions can also appear in container-locative constructions.

(3)   a.   Jared sprayed water on the roses.
       b.   Jared sprayed the roses with water.

However the generalisation does not hold, as there are many other verbs which result in unacceptable sentences if we try and apply the generalisation. Examples (4) and (5) show that *pour* does not accept the container-locative, and *fill* does not allow content-locative. There does not seem to be a clear way to distinguish the verbs that do, and the ones that don't allow the generalisation. In these examples *pour*, *fill*, and *load* are all verbs which describe someone moving something somewhere.

(4)   a.   Amy poured water into the glass.
      b.   *Amy poured the glass with water.

(5)   a.   *Bobby filled water into the glass.
      b.   Bobby filled the glass with water.

The fact that adult speakers of English can make these distinctions is a learnability paradox. Four conditions summarise the set of relevant facts that lead to the paradox: (a) language speakers generalise from observations, (b) they avoid some possible generalisations, (c) they are not corrected for erroneous generalisations, (d) there is no systematic difference between verbs that allow generalisation and those which do not. Clearly at least one of these statements cannot be correct.

Pinker argues that the fourth condition is where the solution to the paradox lies, and in fact systematic differences do exist. However the differences are described in terms of nonobvious, fine-grained descriptions of semantic structure [16,17]. The research strategy then becomes one of gathering classes of verbs which behave differently with respect to some alternation, and then try to analyse them for subtle semantic variations. Consider examples (6a) and (6b) which show additional verbs that do, or do not accept the locative alternation.

(6)   a.   brush, dab, daub, plaster, rub, slather, smear, smudge, spread, streak, swab
      b.   dribble, drip, drop, dump, funnel, ladle, pour, shake, siphon, slop, slosh, spill, spoon

The core meaning of these verbs all involve getting some substance onto some receptacle. You can, for example, *brush paint onto the floor* or *pour paint onto the floor*. However, Pinker suggests that if we study the physics of the actions, we observe a very different pattern: the (a) list involves actions where the agent applies force to the substance and surface simultaneously by pushing, whereas the (b) verbs allow gravity to do the work [16]. It is the difference between direct action and an enabling action. When you are directly acting on a substance you are in complete control and can therefore *brush the floor with paint* as much as you like, with the desired effect. But you can't *pour the floor with paint*. You can pour the paint out of a container in the direction of the floor, but you cannot control how it lands on the floor. This is a very specific kind of distinction that involves a mental construal about the way the world works. The *Grammatically Relevant Subsystem* hypothesis is that our ability to use verbs correctly hinges on a specific set of shared beliefs about the way the world works, which is somehow intertwined with language [17]. In this case a distinction between direct- and enabling- action.

The Grammatically Relevant Subsystem hypothesis claims that some aspects of human grammar are controlled by semantic knowledge that is not directly observable from the strings of the language. Thus, if a machine learning system differs from a human grammar, then we would conclude that the system was unable to learn the semantic knowledge. This is a better source of evidence for a Poverty of the Stimulus hypothesis than current benchmarks.

Beth Levin performed an extensive analysis of English verbs by grouping them into classes according their behaviour with respect to a large number of possible alternations [9]. The hypothesis is that the syntactic behaviour of verbs is semantically determined, and therefore all verbs in a given class will share some semantic core. Identifying the classes will help identify the core. In her "preliminary investigation" she identifies over 70 distinct alternations. For our initial dataset we selected the 50 alternations where most data was available. Some of these are shown in Table 1, together with example sentences.

This preliminary dataset was constructed following the advice of Dagan et. al. [5] who argue that the Recognizing Textual Entailment (RTE) task is suitable for capturing a variety of semantic inferences. We propose that the semantic relation between alternations can be described as entailment where the text, e.g. "The horse kicked John" entails (or not) the hypothesis "John was kicked by the horse" (see also [26]). The dataset currently contains 311 sentences in which the hypothesis is ungrammatical due to the alternation (e.g. I donated a book to Roy./*I donated Roy a book.), and 306 sentences where the hypothesis is grammatical (e.g. I gave a book to Roy./I gave Roy a book.). Of these 306, there are 102 sentences where the hypothesis is not entailed because the alternation introduces a subtle change in meaning (e.g. This hammer won't break the window/This hammer won't break), and 204 where the hypothesis is entailed. A hypothesis can therefore not be entailed either because of a subtle semantic change, or because it is meaningless.

4   A Preliminary Experiment

We used the AllenNLP system[7] to evaluate each sentence pair for entailment. The package provides a straightforward API for entailment judgements.

Table 2 shows the verb alternation categories that were tested, and whether or not AllenNLP agreed with human judgement on the example sentences. Agreement was defined as at least 70% of the sentences in the category concurring with human judgement[8]. A tick in the first column means that AllenNLP predicted an entailment for grammatical alternations that we judge as semantically equivalent. A tick in the second column means that AllenNLP did not agree. The third column shows results for sentences where the hypotheses are ungrammatical. A tick in this column indicates that AllenNLP predicts a high degree of entailment even though the meaning is not entailed by the alternation. The results show that the system did not perform correctly on any of these cases. In summary the model learns the correct generalization for verbs that allow an alternation, but completely fails to learn verbs that do not.

Since AllenNLP failed completely on this task, we attempted to replicate the results with a more recent XLNet model from the PyTorch-Transformers package[9] tuned on the RTE dataset. However at the time of writing we were

---

[7] https://github.com/allenai/allennlp.

[8] Entailment values exceeding 0.7 for an entailed hypothesis, or below 0.3 for a non-entailed hypothesis.

[9] https://github.com/huggingface/pytorch-transformers.

Table 1. Categories used in the experiment. Categories with a small amount of samples are excluded.

Category	Sample
As Alternations	The president appointed Smith press secretary. / The president appointed Smith as press secretary. The captain named the ship Seafarer. / *The captain named the ship as Seafarer.
Benefactive Alternations	Martha carved a toy out of wood for the baby. / Martha carved the baby a toy out of wood. Martha carved some wood into a toy for the baby. / *Martha carved the baby some wood into a toy.
Body-Part Possessor Ascension Alternations	The horse kicked Penny's shin. / The horse kicked Penny in the shin. The horse broke Penny's shin. / *The horse broke Penny in the shin.
Bound Nonreflexive Anaphor as Prepositional Object	Tamara poured the water over her. / Tamara poured the water over herself. This list includes my name on it. / * This list includes my name on itself.
Causative Alternations	The little boy broke the window./ The window broke. Margaret cut the bread. / * The bread cut.
Characteristic Property Alternations	This hammer won't break the window. / This hammer won't break. This key won't open the lock. / *This key won't open.
Cognate Prepositional Phrase Construction	Kelly buttered the bread. / Kelly buttered the bread with unsalted butter. Kelly buttered the bread. / *Kelly buttered the bread with butter.
Conative Alternations	The mouse nibbled the cheese. / The mouse nibbled on the cheese. The mouse consumed the cheese. / *The mouse consumed on the cheese.
Creation and Transformation Alternations	That acorn will grow into an oak tree. / An oak tree will grow from that acorn. I kneaded the dough into a loaf. / *I kneaded a loaf from the dough.
Dative Alternations	I gave a book to Roy. / I gave Roy a book. I donated a book to Roy. / *I donated Roy a book.
Fulfilling Alternations	The judge presented a prize to the winner. / The judge presented the winner with a prize. The judge offered a prize to the winner. / *The judge offered the winner with a prize.
Instrument Subject Alternations	David broke the window with a hammer. / The hammer broke the window. Doug ate the ice cream with a spoon. / ?The spoon ate the ice cream.
Locative Alternations	The garden is swarming with bees. / Bees are swarming in the garden. The square is seething with people. / *People are seething in the square.
Locative Inversion	A cat jumped onto the table. / Onto the table jumped a cat. A lot of snow melted on the streets of Chicago. / *On the streets of Chicago melted a lot of snow.
Object of Transitive = Subject of Intransitive Alternations	Bill pounded the metal flat. / This metal won't pound flat. Bill pounded the metal. / *This metal won't pound.
Possessor-Attribute Factoring Alternations	I admired his honesty. / I admired him for his honesty. I sensed his eagerness. / *I sensed him for his eagerness.
Preposition Drop Alternations	Martha climbed up the mountain. / Martha climbed the mountain. Sharon came into the room. / *Sharon came the room.
Prepositional Passive	George Washington slept in this bed. / This bed was slept in by George Washington. George Washington slept on Tuesday. / *Tuesday was slept on by George Washington.
Reciprocal Alternations	Brenda and Molly agreed. / Brenda agreed with Molly. Bill and Kathy married. / *Bill married with Kathy.
Resultative Construction	Jasmine pushed the door open. / The door was pushed open. The silversmith pounded the metal flat. / *The silversmith pounded on the metal flat.
Search Alternations	We investigated the area for bombs. /We investigated bombs in the area. We rummaged through the desk for papers. / *We rummaged papers through the desk.
There-Insertion	A flowering plant is on the windowsill. / There is a flowering plant on the windowsill. A lot of snow melted on the streets of Chicago. / *There melted a lot of snow on the streets of Chicago.
Unexpressed Object Alternations	I flossed my teeth. / I flossed. Jennifer craned her neck. / *Jennifer craned.
Verbal Passive	The cook sliced the mushrooms. / The mushrooms were sliced by the cook. The package weighed ten pounds. / *Ten pounds was weighed by the package.

unable to obtain an accuracy greater than 52%, which is below the 88% SOTA, and therefore chose not to report these results.

Another possibility for the poor result is that the ungrammaticality of the hypotheses is not noticed, and the entailment is judged purely on word overlap. We decided to test this possibility with the state-of-the-art XLNet system, to see if it could judge the grammaticality of the hypotheses correctly. We fine tuned XLNet with the CoLA task and obtained the reference results. Table 2 shows the Matthew's correlation coefficient against the sentences in our dataset, where the human grammaticality judgements are taken from Levin's book (and corroborated by the authors).

Table 2. Agreement between AllenNLP and human judgement. Categories with unclear results or insufficient data are indicated with "?". The last column is the Matthew's correlation coefficient against human grammatical acceptability judgement.

Category	Agree	Disagree (grammatical)	Disagree (ungrammatical)	XLNet (grammaticality)
As Alternation			✓	0.333
Benefactive Alternations			✓	0.645
Body-Part Possessor Ascension Alternations	✓		✓	0.654
Bound Nonreflexive Anaphor as Prepositional Object			✓	0.654
Causative Alternations	✓		✓	0.684
Characteristic Property Alternations			✓	1.0
Cognate Prepositional Phrase Construction	✓		✓	1.0
Conative Alternations			✓	0.85
Creation and Transformation Alternations	?			1.0
Dative Alternations	✓		✓	0.658
Fulfilling Alternations	✓		✓	0.632
Instrument Subject Alternations			✓	0.632
Locative Alternations	✓		✓	0.546
Locative Inversion	✓		✓	0.745
Object of Transitive = Subject of Intransitive Alternations	✓			0.786
Possessor-Attribute Factoring Alternations	✓		✓	1.0
Preposition Drop Alternations	✓		✓	0.866
Prepositional Passive	✓		✓	1.0
Reciprocal Alternations	✓		✓	0.480
Resultative Construction	✓		✓	0.654
Search Alternations	✓		✓	0.67
There-Insertion	✓		✓	1.0
Unexpressed Object Alternations	✓		✓	0.715
Verbal Passive			✓	1.0

The acceptability results show that XLNet performs very well on some of the categories, but poorly on others. While the results are more positive towards the machine learning model, the knowledge required for making some acceptability judgements is still lacking. The poorest performing categories were the as-, locative-, reciprocal-, and fulfilling- alternations. For example, the model misjudged sentences like "*The captain named the ship as Seafarer" and "*Bill married with Cathy". However, it correctly judged "*This key won't open" and "*Kelly buttered the bread with butter". This is impressive, and we plan to continue the work by gathering comprehensive human judgements on these sentences to obtain more accurate correlations.

5   Conclusion

This paper proposes a new dataset which is constructed to test the learnability of specific, theoretically motivated knowledge that is relevant for the understanding human language. In this respect it is different from the majority of existing datasets which are task oriented and provide fewer theoretical insights. We claim that current datasets focused on tasks are less useful for scientific discovery. The initial results show evidence for a Poverty of the Stimulus Argument, that current machine learning systems are unable to learn some of the knowledge needed to properly comprehend human language, from linguistic input. In this regard the dataset can be useful for testing new systems, for their ability to learn such knowledge.

But there might be a stronger conclusion. That is, it is possible that systems which learn only from text input are simply unable to learn this knowledge. The implication would then be that machine learning systems will require prior knowledge about causation, duration, tense, aspect, and other concepts implicated by linguistic analyses. One possible implementation could be to include these as semantic features in the training data to be learned alongside the vocabulary. On this view machine learning would serve as an invaluable tool that helps discover the proper set of semantic features in the psycho-linguistic system.

Acknowledgement. This research was supported by the Project News Angler, which is funded by the Norwegian Research Council's IKTPLUSS programme as project 275872.

References

1. Bejar, I.I., Chaffin, R., Embretson, S.: Cognitive and Psychometric Analysis of Analogical Problem Solving. Springer, New York (1991)
2. Berko, J.: The child's learning of English morphology. Word **14**(2–3), 150–177 (1958). https://doi.org/10.1080/00437956.1958.11659661
3. Chmomsky, N.: Syntactic Structures. Mouton (1957)
4. Clark, A., Lappin, S.: Linguistic Nativism and the Poverty of the Stimulus. Wiley, Hoboken (2011)
5. Dagan, I., Glickman, O., Magnini, B.: The PASCAL recognising textual entailment challenge. In: Quiñonero-Candela, J., Dagan, I., Magnini, B., d'Alché-Buc, F. (eds.) MLCW 2005. LNCS (LNAI), vol. 3944, pp. 177–190. Springer, Heidelberg (2006). https://doi.org/10.1007/11736790_9

6. Devlin, J., Chang, M.W., Lee, K., Toutanova, K.: BERT: Pre-training of Deep Bidirectional Transformers for Language Understanding (2018)

7. Gibbons, M.: Attaining landmark status: Rumelhart and McClelland's PDP volumes and the connectionist paradigm. J. Hist. Behav. Sci. **55**(1), 54–70 (2019). https://doi.org/10.1002/jhbs.21946

8. Jurgens, D., Turney, P., et al.: Semeval-2012 task 2: Measuring degrees of relational similarity. In: Proceedings of the First Joint Conference on Lexical and Computational Semantics-Volume 1: Proceedings of the Main Conference and The Shared Task, and Volume 2: Proceedings of the Sixth International Workshop on Semantic Evaluation (2012)

9. Levin, B.: English Verb Classes and Alternations: A Preliminary Investigation. The University of Chicago Press, The University of Chicago (1993)

10. McClelland, J.L.: Parallel distributed processing: explorations in the microstructure of cognition. In: The Programmable Blackboard Model of Reading, vol. 2, pp. 122–169. MIT Press, Cambridge (1986). http://dl.acm.org/citation.cfm?id=21935.42473

11. McCoy, R., Linzen, T.: Non-entailed subsequences as a challenge for natural language inference (2018). arXiv:1811.12112

12. Mikolov, T., Chen, K., Corrado, G., Dean, J.: Efficient estimation of word representations in vector space. arXiv preprint arXiv:1301.3781 (2013). https://scholar.google.com/scholar?cluster=7447715766504981253

13. Mikolov, T., Yih, S.W.t., Zweig, G.: Linguistic regularities in continuous space word representations. In: Proceedings of the 2013 Conference of the North American Chapter of the Association for Computational Linguistics: Human Language Technologies (NAACL-HLT-2013). Association for Computational Linguistics (2013). https://www.microsoft.com/en-us/research/publication/linguistic-regularities-in-continuous-space-word-representations/

14. Peters, M.E., et al.: Deep contextualized word representations. In: Proceedings of NAACL (2018)

15. Pinker, S.: Whatever happened to the past tense debate? (2006)

16. Pinker, S.: The Stuff of Thought: Language as a Window Into Human Nature. Viking, New York (2007)

17. Pinker, S.: Learnability and Cognition: The Acquisition of Argument Structure (1989/2013). MIT Press, Cambridge (2013). New Edition

18. Radford, A., Narasimhan, K., et al.: Improving language understanding by generative pre-training (2018). https://s3-us-west-2.amazonaws.com/openai-assets/researchcovers/languageunsupervised/languageunderstandingpaper.pdf

19. Rumelhart, D.E., McClelland, J.L.: Parallel distributed processing: explorations in the microstructure of cognition. In: On Learning the Past Tenses of English Verbs, vol. 2, pp. 216–271. MIT Press, Cambridge (1986). http://dl.acm.org/citation.cfm?id=21935.42475

20. Rumelhart, D.E., McClelland, J.L., PDP Research Group (eds.): Parallel Distributed Processing: Explorations in the Microstructure of Cognition, vol. 1: Foundations. MIT Press, Cambridge (1986)

21. Rumelhart, D.E., McClelland, J.L., PDP Research Group (eds.): Parallel Distributed Processing: Explorations in the Microstructure of Cognition, vol. 2: Psychological and Biological Models. MIT Press, Cambridge (1986)

22. Turney, P.D.: Similarity of semantic relations. Comput. Linguist. (2006). https://doi.org/10.1162/coli.2006.32.3.379

23. Wang, A., et al.: SuperGLUE: a stickier benchmark for general-purpose language understanding systems (2019)

24. Wang, A., Singh, A., Michael, J., Hill, F., Levy, O., Bowman, S.R.: GLUE: a multi-task benchmark and analysis platform for natural language understanding. In: the Proceedings of ICLR (2019)
25. Warstadt, A., Singh, A., Bowman, S.R.: Neural Network Acceptability Judgments (2018)
26. White, A.S., Rastogi, P., Duh, K., Van Durme, B.: Inference is everything: recasting semantic resources into a unified evaluation framework. In: Proceedings of the Eighth International Joint Conference on Natural Language Processing (2017)
27. Yang, Z., Dai, Z., Yang, Y., Carbonell, J.G., Salakhutdinov, R., Le, Q.V.: XLNet: generalized autoregressive pretraining for language understanding. CoRR abs/1906.08237 (2019). http://arxiv.org/abs/1906.08237
28. Yann, L., Bengio, Y., Hinton, G.: Deep learning **521**(7553), 436–444 (2015). https://doi.org/10.1038/nature14539

Hybrid Words Representation for Airlines Sentiment Analysis

Usman Naseem[1(✉)], Shah Khalid Khan[2], Imran Razzak[1],
and Ibrahim A. Hameed[3]

[1] Advanced Analytics Institue, University of Technology Sydney, Sydney, Australia
engr.usmannaseem87@gmail.com
[2] School of Engineering, RMIT University, Melbourne, Australia
[3] Norwegian University of Science and Technology, Trondheim, Norway

Abstract. Social media sentimental analysis is interesting field with the aim to analyze social conservation and determine deeper context as they apply to a topic or theme. However, it is challenging as tweets are unstructured, informal and noisy in nature. Also, it involves natural language complexities like words with same meanings (Polysemy). Most of the existing approaches mainly rely on clean textual data, however Twitter data is quite noisy in real life. Aiming to improve the performance, in this paper, we present hybrid words representation and Bi-directional Long Short Term Memory (BiLSTM) with attention modeling resulting in improvement in tweet quality by not only treating the noise within the textual context but also considers polysemy, semantics, syntax, out of vocabulary (OOV) words as well as words sentiments within a tweet. The proposed model overcomes the current limitations and improves the accuracy for tweets classification as showed by the evaluation of the model performed on real-world airline related datasets.

Keywords: Natural language processing · Text mining · Sentiment analysis · Hybrid words embedding · Neural networks

1 Introduction

Social media platforms where people share their opinions and views, plays a key role in providing a new approach to collecting the valuable information that allows businesses, researchers, governments, politicians and organizations to know about peoples sentiments which helps for decision making such as improving the services, products, and recommendations for those users. However, it is challenging task as tweet-like social media text is often short, informal and noisy in nature which makes analysis very challenging [23,25]. Although, in recent year, different methods have been presented in literature but still we are not able to fully handle the language complexities with in the content of tweets such as words with different meanings (Polysemy) along with semantics, syntanx, sentiment of words and OOV words [24].

© Springer Nature Switzerland AG 2019
J. Liu and J. Bailey (Eds.): AI 2019, LNAI 11919, pp. 381–392, 2019.
https://doi.org/10.1007/978-3-030-35288-2_31

The language used on social media platforms and blogs is ubiquitous (unstructured and very informal) in nature. Furthermore, tweets are short statements and descriptions. This makes its analysis more challenging for the machines to understand and analyze like human. Every Twitter user post their message in their own style. They use different words, acronyms, emoticons, use URLs to give extra information and sometimes intentionally make spelling mistakes etc. These language imperfections makes the data noisy and an right combination of pre-processing techniques must be applied to improve the quality of text. Furthermore, managing language complexities like human beings also a challenging tasks.

Analysis of social media has attracted the attention of many researchers. Conventional methods for sentiment analysis like lexicon [4] and rule based techniques are easy, simple and not computationally expensive but their dependency on humans for labelling documents, less coverage etc limits them in case of unstructured text. Over the period of time, different researchers claimed that using traditional machine learning and hybrid of lexicon with machine learning improves the classification performance [5].

Recently proposed word representation algorithms like Word2Vec [15] and GloVe [19] have been excessively used for the representation of semantic and syntactical information within the content. Mikolov et al. [15] presented continuous bag of words (CBOW) and skip-gram algorithms for the representation of words which can capture semantics and syntactical information. Similarly, global vectors (GloVe) [19] also deals with semantic and syntactical information but it uses co-occurrence counts to capture this information. Later, deep convolutional neural network (DCNN) was proposed by Jianqiang et al. [10] which gives better accuracy performance by initializing word representation with GloVe whereas, whereas Santos et al. [6] exploited character and word level representations for sentiment classification of short text and fed representation into CNN. All of these methods captures semantic and syntactical information but ignore the issue of polysemy within the content. To address this issue, Liu et al. [13] presented context sensitive embedding which allocate one vector to each word in the context. Similarly, Melamud et al. [14] proposed Context2Vec which utilizes representations from final layer of the model which essentially leave out information from the lower layers which is a major drawback of context2Vec. In recently past, Peters et al. [20] presented deep contextual word representations for learning complex attributes of a word use in a context.

To consolidate the sentiment knowledge into conventional words representation, researchers proposed sentiment specific embedding (SSE). Tang et al. [27] presented several hybrid ranking methods (HyRank), which considers context and sentiment knowledge of words in tweets. Similarly, In another study conducted by Yu et al. [29] where they proposed sentiment embeddings by refining pre-trained embeddings and used intensity score of external resource. Razaeinia et al [21] presented improved word vectors (IWV) by concatenating word representation algorithms, part of speech (POS) and different sentiment lexicons for sentiment analysis. In recent past, Cambria et al. [2] proposed context embeddings by conceptual primitives from data and linked with commonsense concepts and named entities. In our previous work [18] we presented deep intelligent contextual embedding (DICE) which solves the language complexities like polysemy, semantics, syntax, sentiments of words. In this work we improve our model and added character embedding to solve the issue of OOV words along with other language complexities.

Example of word "Like" in Tweets

@united Hmmm...seems like this could be something to be changed to be more #flyerfriendly.

@SouthwestAir @FortuneMagazine I DO like your airlines, congrats! :)

Example of word "Hate" in Tweets

@SouthwestAir please do. Hate having to fly a different airline. You're my fav.

@United is freaking worthless. I hate this airline. http://t.co/dN1if2cGwE

Fig. 1. Examples of research motivation and problems

Figure 1 presents motivation and the problem, we have addressed in this work. It shows the example of tweets where the meaning of words such as *Like* ad *Hate* changes according to its context. Existing word representation models unable to handle this kind of language complexities and assigns same vector to such kind of words which results in low performance. Further, both of these words have some sentiments associated to its meaning which as a human beings we can understand due to our prior knowledge but machines can not. We want to handle this language complexities just like human beings which helps to improve the classification performance [22]. Moreover, unstructured and noisy nature of tweets also results in OOV words. Thus, models which are unable to able handle this kind of language ambiguities and low quality of text results in low performance in case of tweets sentiment classification task. To overcome the aforementioned challenges, in this paper, we present an efficient approach that first improves the quality of tweets followed by handling the natural language complexities defined earlier. Our hybrid word representation model is able to capture polysemy, semantics, syntax, OOV words and words sentiments. We then input our hybrid representations to BiLSTM with attention model which compliments our model to improve the classification performance. We experimented with three Twitter datasets and experimental results proves that classification performance improves significantly when used our proposed model. The **key contribution** of this paper are:

- We improve the quality of tweets like messages by replacing emoticons, acronyms, spell correction, expanding contractions and removing other nose from data. The proposed tweet quality improvement method can be applied to any social media text.
- We improve the representation of text so that it can handle the language complexities and can capture complex language characteristics such as polysemy, semantics, words sentiments, syntax.

– Extensive experiment results on airline datasets showed that proposed approach is able to capture OOV words efficiently which also add to the classification performance.

The rest of the paper is organized as follows. Section 2 describes the architecture of the proposed model. Section 3 highlights evaluation and analysis of the proposed model. Section 4 gives the conclusion of this research.

2   Proposed Model

In this section we describe the proposed tweet classification model which is based on Hybrid Words Representation and Bi-directional Long Short Term Memory (BiLSTM) with Attention. The framework of proposed approach is given in Fig. 2. We have applied five data representation steps to create input vector for LSTM that are (I) POS tagging of word in input tweet (II) language model embedding to extract the vector of each word that consist of polysemy, syntax information as well as provide context embedding. (III) GloVe embedding to create vector of words to capture the word semantic information. (IV) We have also created sentiment score of each word from lexicons in a tweet and create lexicon vector. (V) character embedding to overcome the aforementioned issue of OOV words. Finally, we have concatenated all five input vector and forwarded to BiLSTM with attention for sentiment analysis of tweets. In the below discussion, we have explained each component of proposed hybrid contextual word representation.

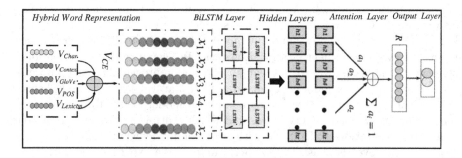

Fig. 2. Hybrid words representation w/ BiLSTM & attention

2.1   Hybrid Words Representation

Tweet classification is challenging task as they are is often short, informal and noisy, and involves language ambiguity such as polysemy. To improve the tweet classification performance, we have applied different data representations to consider both contextual and semantics information. For a given tweet T_i with a sequence of tokens $(t_1, t_2, t_3, ..., t_k)$. Her i are the number of a tweets and k are the number of tokens in a tweet. We applied five data representation on each input tweet that are

Character Embedding: In order to have closer representation among words of same category, the prefix and suffix information of any word provides the character-level features. It does not only helps to deal with the challenge of OOV as well as mitigating issues like unseen words. In our experiment, we have performed character level representations using Bi-LSTMs in order to produce a character-enhanced embedding for each unique word in a tweet [12]. In this experiment, we consider the maximum character length 25 and set forward and backward LSTMs parameters to 25 which results in 50-dimensional embedding vector, $\mathbf{V}_{Char}$.

Context Embedding: The quality of words representation is computed by how it handle polsemy and ad syntax information into the model. This results in improvement semantic word representation. In this work, we have used ELMo.

Deep contextual embeddings are based on ELMo language model learned from Bi language model (BiLM) learned from Bi language model (BiLM) [20]. It considers different aspects of words according to its usage in the context. In training process of BiLMs, we have considered the log-likelihood of each sentence in both forward and backward language models. We have computed the resultant vector by concatenating the hidden representations from both forward language model $\overrightarrow{h}_{n,j}^{LM}$ and backward language model $\overleftarrow{h}_{n,j}^{LM}$, where $j = 1, ..., L$. We can write BiLM as

$$BiLM = \sum_{n=1}^{k}(\log p(t_n|t_1, ..., t_{n-1}; \Theta_x, \overrightarrow{\Theta}_{LSTM}, \Theta_s) + \log p(t_n|t_{n+1}, ..., t_n; \Theta_x, \overleftarrow{\Theta}_{LSTM}, \Theta_s)$$

$$(1)$$

where $\overrightarrow{\Theta}_{LSTM}$ is the forward and $\overleftarrow{\Theta}_{LSTM}$ is the backward BiLSTM parameter. θ_s and θ_x are the softmax and token representation parameters respectively. Both θ_x and θ_s are shared between forward and backward directions. ELMo abstracts the representations learned from intermediate layer and compute the linear combination for each token in a downstream task. BiLM consist of $2L+1$ set of of representations as given below.

$$R_n = (X_x^{LM}, \overrightarrow{h}_{n,j}^{LM}, \overleftarrow{h}_{n,j}^{LM} | \quad j = 1, ..., L)$$
$$= (h_{n,j}^{LM} | \quad j = 0, ..., L)$$

where $h_{n,0}^{LM} = x_n^{LM}$ and $h_{n,j}^{LM} = [\overrightarrow{h}_{n,j}^{LM}, \overleftarrow{h}_{n,j}^{LM}]$ the layer of token and BiLSTM layer respectively. ELMo is the task specific combination of these features where all the layers in M are flattened to single vector, given as

$$ELMo_n^{task} = E(M_n; \Theta^{task}) = \gamma^{task} \sum_{j=0}^{L} s_j^{task} h_{h,j}^{LM} \qquad (2)$$

where s_j^{task} are weights which are softmax normalized for the combination of different layers representations. γ^{task} is a hyper parameter for scaling and optimization of ElMo representation. In this paper, we have used pre-trained ELMo embeddings with the dimensions of 1,024. The pre-trained model is obtained using the 1 Billion Word Benchmark consisting of about 800M tokens of news crawl data from WMT 2011 [3]. In this work, we have computed context vector of 1024 dimensions $\mathbf{V}_{context}$ using ELMo. The resultant vector has the polysemy and syntax information of tweets context.

Glove Embedding: Global Vectors (GloVe) for word representation is an unsupervised learning model to obtain word vector representations through aggregating global word-word co-occurrence statistics by efficiently leveraging the statistical information in a corpus instead of entire sparse matrix i.e. how frequently a word appears in a context [19]. GloVe uses ratios of co-occurrence probabilities. It is favourable to concatenate ELMo embeddings with traditional word embeddings. In this work, we have used pre-trained GloVe embedding (trained on 840 billion token from common crawl) of 300 dimensions. We further compared its performance with Word2Vec and results showed that GloVe provided better performance for tweet classification. The resultant of GloVe embedding model is a vector of 300 dimensions, $\mathbf{V}_{GloVe}$, that consist of word semantics information of tweets.

Lexicon (Sentiment) Embedding: Use of lexicon can be helpful in sentiment analysis, thus in this work, we computed sentiment score from sentiment lexicon. In our case, each lexicon contains a pair of word-sentiment where each words in a tweet has its own sentiment score (-1 <sentiment score> 1). Sentiment score less than zero represents the negative words and sentiment score greater than zero represent the positive words. Selection of semantic lexicon is very important. It could be one or appropriate combination of different lexicons. In this work, we have performed several experiment to select appropriate lexicon and selected the combination 6 different lexicons for extracting sentiments. In case if any token is unavailable in any of these lexicons, we have assigned zero score to that token as well as its outputs $\mathbf{V}_{Lexicon}$ of 6 dimensions. Lexicons used in our experiments are given in Table 1.

Table 1. Lexicons used for Lexicon embedding

(1) SenticNet 5.0 [2]	(4) SemEval Twitter English Lexicon [17]
(2) VADER [9]	(5) NRC Sentiment140 Lexicon [11]
(3) Bing Liu Opinion Lexicon [8]	(6) SentiWordNet [1]

Part of Speech (POS) Embedding: POS tagging is one of the essential processing step for high level text processing of tweet classification in which each word in the context is assigned with an appropriate POS tag. Recently POS has been extensively used and shown promising results in NLP. It provides very useful information about a word, its neighbors and different syntactic categories i.e. nouns, adverbs, verbs, and adjectives etc. In this work, we have generated POS tag through Stanford parser for POS. We have transformed each POS tag token to vector of dimension 50 $\mathbf{V}_{POS}$ of 50 dimensions.

Finally, we concatenated the above vectors to get one vector $\mathbf{V}_{CE}$, which almost free from the aforementioned challenges and consist of word semantics, polysemy, syntax knowledge as well as sentiment knowledge. Equation 3 shows the concatenation of vectors.

$$\mathbf{V}_{CE} = \mathbf{V}_{context} \oplus \mathbf{V}_{Char} \oplus \mathbf{V}_{GloVe} \oplus \mathbf{V}_{POS} \oplus \mathbf{V}_{Lexicon} \tag{3}$$

where element-wise symbol $\oplus$ denotes vectors concatenation. and V_{CE} is the hybrid contextual word vector.

2.2   Attention Based BiLSTM Layer

In this work we have used bidirectional LSTM for the classification of tweets. We have forwarded hybrid words vector to BiLSTM [26] with attention layer for sentiment analysis to capture the information from both directions. The input to BiLSTM is a vector $\mathbf{V}_{CE}$ with a sequence of x_z tokens and produces hidden representation h_i at a given time i by concatenating hidden representations as shown in Eq. 4.

$$h_i = [\overrightarrow{h_i} \parallel \overleftarrow{h_i}] \tag{4}$$

where $\parallel$ denotes the concatenation of outputs from both forward and backward LSTM.

As we know that different words play different role in understanding, thus do not contribute equally in understanding the sentence. In this work, we have further used attention mechanism [28] to enforce the contribution of important words in understanding the sentence. We have assigned weight a_i to each token through a softmax function and finally, representation $\mathbf{R}$ which is a weighted sum of all tokens is computed as shown in Eq. 5.

$$R = \sum_{i=1}^{z} a_i h_i, \tag{5}$$

where,

$$a_i = \frac{exp(e_i)}{\sum_{t=1}^{z} exp(e_t)}, \quad \sum_{i=1}^{z} a_i = 1$$

$$e_i = tanh(W_h h_i + b_h)$$

where W_h and b_h are learned parameters, h_i is the concatenation of the representations of the forward and backward LSTM, introduced in Eq. 4.

2.3 Output Layer

Finally, we used representation **R** generated from an attention layer and forward to fully connected softmax layer to get the class probability distribution. In order to find the optimal parameters, we have used the grid search optimization technique.

3 Experimental Results

In order to validate the performance of proposed approach, we have performed several experiment on benchmark datasets.

3.1 Datasets

In this study, we have used three airline related datasets. Two of these datasets were crawled and labeled by authors whereas third dataset (US airline) is publicly available. Table 2 describes the tweets distribution of each dataset.

US airlines dataset is publicly available at the Kaggle Datasets originally released by CrowdFlower. It consist of 14,640 tweets related to six major US airlines. We filterd out and extracted 11,541 tweets with positive and negative lales only. Furthermore, we have **Three Airlines dataset** consist of 16,454 tweets related to Cathay Pacific, United airline and Singapore airline and annotated positive and negative. In addition to US airline and Three airline datasets, we have also used **Emirates airlines dataset**. It consist of 22,172 and contains tweets related to Emirates airline. The labeling of Three Airline dataset and Emirtes airline dataset are based on guideline by Mohammad et al. [16].

Table 2. Tweets distribution in each dataset

Dataset name	Positive tweets	Negative tweets	Total tweets
US Airlines	2363	9178	11541
Three Airlines	11670	4784	16454
Emirates	17860	4312	22172

3.2 Pre-processing

In this paper, we improved our proposed pre-processing method in our previous work [18] where we consider the noise from unstructured and informal tweets through correction of spelling mistakes. We further performed sentiment aware tokenization (using Potts's tokenizer[1]) i.e. replacing slang words or emotions with possible word and word segmentation of hashtag words. As a results of our pre-processing, we are not only able to capture the basic sentiment related expressions but also able to identify recently used expressions and slangs. In order to correct spell mistake we used Norivig's spell correction technique. Finally, the word segmentation is performed to separate the words in hashtags followed by normalization of all words, removal of punctuation marks, stops words, mentions (@), URLs and special characters.

3.3   Performance Evaluation

Baselines: As a baseline, we compared our proposed model with classic words representation, continuous words representation models and finally, hybrid and sentiment specific words representation models. To be precise, we compared the performance of our model with method proposed by Gao et al. [7] and da Silva et al. [5] where they used weighted word representations TF-IDF with different traditional machine learning based classifiers. From continuous word representation models, we compared our model with (i) deep convolutional neural network[2] (DCNN) where they used GloVe for word representations [10] and (ii) CharSCNN/SCNN[3] [6] utilized character embedding (CharSCNN) and Word2Vec (SCNN) for initializing embedding where resulting embeddings are fed to deep neural networks. Melamud et al. [14] proposed context2Vec to generate context dependent representations. Context2Vec utilizes representations from final layer of the model which essentially leave out information from the lower layers And from the hybrid and sentiment specific word models, We also compared the performance our our proposed model with hybrid word representation model like hybrid ranking [27] (HyRank[4]) and sentiment specific word representation models like refined embeddings Re(*) [29]. Finally, performance of our model was also compared with improved word vectors (IWV) [21] and in last compared the results with our DICE model aswell. We selected those methods because they are the state-of-the-art ones and based on the conducted meta-analysis they exhibit the highest accuracy among the techniques developed so far.

Results: Accuracy results of our model are given in Table 3. As we can see that the accuracy of our model is better than existing methods for sentiment analysis when testing them on three, airline related Twitter datasets. The reasons why our model achieved better results as compared to others are as follows (i) we improve the quality of text by removing noise, learning sentiment aware tokenization and correcting spelling mistakes etc, which helps to learn better representation, and (ii) it hanldes the language ambuiguites by capturing deeper relationships within

---

[1] http://sentiment.christopherpotts.net/code-data/happyfuntokenizing.py.

[2] https://nlp.stanford.edu/projects/glove/.

[3] https://code.google.com/archive/p/word2vec/.

[4] http://ir.hit.edu.cn/dytang/.

Table 3. Comparison of the proposed model

Model\Dataset	US Airlies	Three Airlines	Emirates
TF-IDF SVM	.792	.781	.808
TF-IDF NB	.831	.836	.827
TF-IDF DT	.861	.853	.876
TF-IDF RF	.871	.874	.901
Lexicon Based Classifier	.624	.715	.691
Deep Convolutional Neural Network	.839	.846	.853
Character embedding w/ CNN	.865	.862	.875
Word2Vec Embedding w/ CNN	.836	.842	.861
Context2Vec	.841	.839	.85
Hybrid Rank embedding	.848	.846	.868
Refined Word2vec embedding	.853	.852	.872
Refined GloVe embedding	.860	.859	.875
Improved word vectors w/ BiLSTM	.884	.875	.890
DICE	.936	.931	.939
Proposed	**.942**	**.939**	**.945**

the text. Unlike Word2Vec, GloVe and Fasttext which can not handle words with different meanings in the context (polysemy) whereas our proposed model can capture it. Along with polysemy, our model can also handle the OOV issues and have sentiment knowledge of words which other hybrid model like IMV, Refined embedding, HyRank and DICE fails to capture. Specifically, our proposed model learns high quality representations by adding polysemy, OOV words, sentiment knowledge of words, semantics and syntactical information of words which helps to get better classification results and can be considered as robust solution for sentiment analysis problem.

4 Conclusion

In this paper, we proposed a Hybrid Words Representation model, which handles language complexities for machines within the noisy tweet context. The proposed method handles the issues of polysemy, OOV words, semantics, sentiment and syntax within the tweet context by learning representations from five different embeddings and our pre-processor improves the quality of tweets by removing the noise of informal and unstructured tweets. The experiment shows that our model outperforms different baselines based on traditional word embeddings, contextual, hybrid and sentiment specific word embeddings for sentiment analysis. In future, we plan to explore different ways to incorporate more data characteristics, handle other language complexities and apply our model on different domains.

References

1. Baccianella, S., Esuli, A., Sebastiani, F.: SentiWordNet 3.0: an enhanced lexical resource for sentiment analysis and opinion mining. In: Proceedings of the Seventh Conference on International Language Resources and Evaluation (LREC 2010), Valletta, Malta, May 2010. European Languages Resources Association (ELRA) (2010)
2. Cambria, E., Poria, S., Hazarika, D., Kwok, K.: Senticnet 5: discovering conceptual primitives for sentiment analysis by means of context embeddings. In: AAAI (2018)
3. Chelba, C., Mikolov, T., Schuster, M., Ge, Q., Brants, T., Koehn, P.: One billion word benchmark for measuring progress in statistical language modeling. CoRR, abs/1312.3005 (2013)
4. Chiavetta, F., Lo Bosco, G., Pilato, G.: A lexicon-based approach for sentiment classification of Amazon books reviews in Italian language, pp. 159–170, January 2016
5. da Silva, N.F.F., Hruschka, E.R., Hruschka, E.R.: Tweet sentiment analysis with classifier ensembles. Decis. Support Syst. **66**(C), 170–179 (2014)
6. dos Santos, C.N., de Gatti, M.A.: Deep convolutional neural networks for sentiment analysis of short texts. In: COLING (2014)
7. Go, A., Bhayani, R., Huang, L.: Twitter sentiment classification using distant supervision. Processing, pp. 1–6 (2009)
8. Hu, M., Liu, B.: Mining and summarizing customer reviews. In: Proceedings of the Tenth ACM SIGKDD International Conference on Knowledge Discovery and Data Mining, KDD 2004, pp. 168–177. ACM, New York (2004)
9. Hutto, C.J., Gilbert, E.: Vader: a parsimonious rule-based model for sentiment analysis of social media text. In: ICWSM (2014)
10. Zhao, J., Gui, X.: Deep convolution neural networks for Twitter sentiment analysis. IEEE Access **6**, 23253–23260 (2018)
11. Kiritchenko, S., Zhu, X.-D., Cherry, C., Mohammad, S.: NRC-Canada-2014: detecting aspects and sentiment in customer reviews. In: SemEval@COLING (2014)
12. Lample, G., Ballesteros, M., Subramanian, S., Kawakami, K., Dyer, C.: Neural architectures for named entity recognition. CoRR, abs/1603.01360 (2016)
13. Liu, P., Qiu, X., Huang, X.: Learning context-sensitive word embeddings with neural tensor skip-gram model. In: Proceedings of the 24th International Conference on Artificial Intelligence, IJCAI 2015, pp. 1284–1290. AAAI Press (2015)
14. Melamud, O., Goldberger, J., Dagan, I.: context2vec: learning generic context embedding with bidirectional LSTM. In: CoNLL (2016)
15. Mikolov, T., Sutskever, I., Chen, K., Corrado, G.S., Dean, J.: Distributed representations of words and phrases and their compositionality. In: Burges, C.J.C., Bottou, L., Welling, M., Ghahramani, Z., Weinberger, K.Q. (eds.) Advances in Neural Information Processing Systems, vol. 26, pp. 3111–3119. Curran Associates Inc. (2013)
16. Mohammad, S.: A practical guide to sentiment annotation: challenges and solutions. In: WASSA@NAACL-HLT (2016)
17. Mohammad, S., Kiritchenko, S., Zhu, X.: NRC-Canada: building the state-of-the-art in sentiment analysis of Tweets. In: Second Joint Conference on Lexical and Computational Semantics (*SEM), Volume 2: Proceedings of the Seventh International Workshop on Semantic Evaluation (SemEval 2013), pp. 321–327. Association for Computational Linguistics (2013)

18. Naseem, U., Musial, K.: Dice: deep intelligent contextual embedding for Twitter sentiment analysis. In: 2019 15th International Conference on Document Analysis and Recognition (ICDAR), pp. 1–5 (2019)

19. Pennington, J., Socher, R., Manning, C.: Glove: global vectors for word representation. In: Proceedings of the 2014 Conference on Empirical Methods in Natural Language Processing (EMNLP), pp. 1532–1543 (2014)

20. Peters, M.E., et al.: Deep contextualized word representations. CoRR, abs/1802.05365 (2018)

21. Rezaeinia, S.M., Ghodsi, A., Rahmani, R.: Improving the accuracy of pre-trained word embeddings for sentiment analysis. CoRR, abs/1711.08609 (2017)

22. Saeed, Z., et al.: Whats happening around the world? A survey and framework on event detection techniques on twitter. J. Grid Comput. **17**, 1–34 (2019)

23. Saeed, Z., Abbasi, R.A., Razzak, I., Maqbool, O., Sadaf, A., Xu, G.: Enhanced heartbeat graph for emerging event detection on Twitter using time series networks. Exp. Syst. Appl. **136**, 115–132 (2019)

24. Saeed, Z., Abbasi, R.A., Razzak, M.I., Xu, G.: Event detection in Twitter stream using weighted dynamic heartbeat graph approach. arXiv preprint arXiv:1902.08522 (2019)

25. Saeed, Z., Abbasi, R.A., Sadaf, A., Razzak, M.I., Xu, G.: Text stream to temporal network - a dynamic heartbeat graph to detect emerging events on Twitter. In: Phung, D., Tseng, V.S., Webb, G.I., Ho, B., Ganji, M., Rashidi, L. (eds.) PAKDD 2018. LNCS (LNAI), vol. 10938, pp. 534–545. Springer, Cham (2018). https://doi.org/10.1007/978-3-319-93037-4_42

26. Schuster, M., Paliwal, K.K.: Bidirectional recurrent neural networks. Trans. Sig. Proc. **45**(11), 2673–2681 (1997)

27. Tang, D., Wei, F., Qin, B., Yang, N., Liu, T., Zhou, M.: Sentiment embeddings with applications to sentiment analysis. IEEE Trans. Knowl. Data Eng. **28**(2), 496–509 (2016)

28. Yang, Z., Yang, D., Dyer, C., He, X., Smola, A.J., Hovy, E.H.: Hierarchical attention networks for document classification. In: HLT-NAACL (2016)

29. Yu, L.-C., Wang, J., Robert Lai, K., Zhang, X.: Refining word embeddings using intensity scores for sentiment analysis. IEEE/ACM Trans. Audio Speech Lang. Proc. **26**(3), 671–681 (2018)

Analyzing the Variation Property of Contextualized Word Representations

Sakae Mizuki$^{(\boxtimes)}$ and Naoaki Okazaki

School of Computing, Tokyo Institute of Technology, Tokyo, Meguro-ku, Japan
`sakae.mizuki@nlp.c.titech.ac.jp, okazaki@c.titech.ac.jp`

Abstract. Recent studies have shown that contextualized word representation models are effective on a variety of NLP tasks. However, how these models encode information into representations is not yet well understood because of the insufficient lack of analysis methodologies. To shed light on the behavior of these models, we explore the variation property of word representations produced by the ELMo encoder. More specifically, we analyze how the linguistic, statistical, and semantic features of each word are associated with the variation of its representations. We find that lexical category, word position, the diversity of the contexts, and the diversity of the word senses are the features most closely associated with variation, although the entanglement of word senses in the representation space is also important. In addition, detailed analysis using a randomized ELMo encoder indicates that the word position effect is not a characteristic acquired through the pre-training process but an inductive bias that arises from the ELMo encoder architecture.

Keywords: Representation learning · Contextualized word representation · Analytical study · ELMo

1 Introduction

Contextualized word representation (CWR) models, also known as contextualized encoders, are statistical models that transform each word into a vector by taking the entire words in a sentence as input. This is a clear contrast to traditional static word representation models, which assign a fixed vector to each word regardless of the rest of the sentence. A recent line of works have empirically demonstrated that the CWRs that are trained with large scale corpus using language modeling as a pre-training task such as ELMo [1], BERT [2], and GPT [3], is crucially effective for improving the performance onf a wide range of NLP tasks. Consequently, contextualized encoders are not only becoming a key component of NLP models but are also attracting much attention from researchers, who look to either improve their performance or analyze the mechanisms behind their effectiveness.

The effectiveness of CWRs compared with that of static word representations indicate that contextualized encoders somehow capture useful features that are

© Springer Nature Switzerland AG 2019
J. Liu and J. Bailey (Eds.): AI 2019, LNAI 11919, pp. 393–405, 2019.
https://doi.org/10.1007/978-3-030-35288-2_32

originally represented as the context (surrounding words) of each word. "Probing" is a common approach for analyzing what type of information is encoded in word representations [4]. In this approach, a specific NLP task (e.g., part-of-speech tagging) is typically used as a testbed to evaluate how well it can be predicted using word representations as an input of a classifier, which is trained in a supervised manner. If the performance of the classifier for the task is good, we can argue that a piece of information that is closely related to the target NLP task is embedded in the word representations. A line of research has revealed that linguistic, syntactic, and semantic information can be encoded in CWRs in a convincing manner using carefully designed probing tasks in a convincing manner [5–8].

Previous researchers have already analyzed what is in the CWRs. Now, the next question should be how contextualized encoders encode this information into word representations, because knowing and understanding the behavior of the model is considered to be essential for the development of better methodologies. Unfortunately, analyzing the behavior of contextualized encoders is much more complicated than exploring what is in CWRs because recent models are built on top of deep neural networks, sometimes referred to as "black boxes" [9]. With this in mind, we adopt a simple approach; analyze what word properties affect the variation of the CWRs. The premise behind our analysis is that variation of the representations should be associated with the information that the contextualized encoder encodes. For a specific word, we can quantify to what extent its representation changes depending on the sentence in which it appears by aggregating the sentences in the corpus. Does the scale of the variation differ among words? If it does, what factors or attributes explain the magnitude of these fluctuations? According to the findings of previous probing studies, these plausible explanatory factors should be lexical and contextual properties. However, to the best of our knowledge, no previous studies focused on the variation property.

For these reasons, we analyze which features affect the variation property of CWRs. In concrete terms, we analyze the mutual dependence and correlation between the lexical, statistical, and semantic features and the variance of CWRs. Our final goal is to reason the governing factor of the variation based on our analysis results. Our study provides some interesting insight:

- Association measures, such as mutual information and rank correlation, indicate that lexical category, word position, the diversity of the contexts, and the diversity of the word senses are closely associated with the variance of CWRs.
- The entanglement of word senses in representation space, which is quantified using the soft nearest neighbor loss, also plays an important role in enhancing the connection between the diversity of the word senses and the variance.
- Because of the word position effect, words that mostly appear at the beginning or end of sentences, i.e., title-cased words, exhibit a much smaller variance. The results of an ablation study using *randomized* ELMo strongly indicates

that position awareness is not a characteristic acquired through pre-training but an inductive bias of the recurrent architecture of the ELMo encoder.

2   Methodology

In this section, we explain the details of the methodology we employed to carry out a feature analysis on the variation of CWRs. First, we select a contextualized encoder that we are interested in. Secondly, we define the variation metric which is applied to the CWRs. Thirdly, we introduce a set of features that reflect the lexical, statistical, and semantic properties of each word. Finally, we define association measures that quantify the mutual relatedness between the word features and the variation of the CWRs.

2.1   Contextualized Encoders

In this research, we explore the behavior of the ELMo encoder[1] [1], which is one of the various recently proposed contextual encoders, because ELMo is recommended to use as a feature extractor for downstream tasks, whereas other contextualized encoders, such as BERT, is encouraged to fine-tune for specific tasks. This means that the properties of the CWRs encoded by ELMo directly affect their practical application and thus strengthen the practical interest. We leave the exploration of other contextualized encoders, such as BERT and GPT, for future work.

2.2   Variance of the CWRs

We assume that the empirical distribution of the contextualized representation of a specific word w in the D-dimensional space can be approximated by a Gaussian distribution, whose mean and covariance are $\boldsymbol{\mu}^{(w)}$ and $\boldsymbol{\Sigma}^{(w)}$, respectively. Under this assumption, we define the *variance* of the CWR of a specific word ν_w as the geometric mean of the diagonal elements of the covariance matrix $\boldsymbol{\Sigma}^{(w)}$, where

$$\nu_w = \left(\prod_{d=1}^{D} \Sigma_{d,d}^{(w)} \right)^{\frac{1}{D}} \tag{1}$$

$$\boldsymbol{\Sigma}^{(w)} = \frac{1}{|S_w|} \sum_{s \in S_w} \boldsymbol{g}(w;s) \boldsymbol{g}(w;s)^{\mathrm{T}} - \boldsymbol{\mu}^{(w)} \boldsymbol{\mu}^{(w)\mathrm{T}} \tag{2}$$

$$\boldsymbol{g}(w;s) = \frac{1}{3} \sum_{l=1}^{3} \mathrm{ELMo}_l(w;s) \tag{3}$$

Here, S_w represents the set of sentences that contain a specific word w in the corpus and $\mathrm{ELMo}_l(\mathrm{w};\mathrm{s})$ represents the output of the l-th layer of the ELMo encoder, where a word w in a sentence s is encoded.

---

[1] We obtain the pre-trained model that was pre-trained on a dataset with 5.5B tokens from the author's website at https://allennlp.org/elmo.

Table 1. Summary of the lexical, statistical, and semantic features and their definitions

Type	Feature	Description	Corpus
Lexical	PoS	Most frequently assigned part-of-speech tag	UMBC, SemCor
	PoS-entropy	Diversity of the assigned part-of-speech tags	
Statistical	log-freq	Logarithm of the word occurrence	UMBC
	context-entropy	Diversity of the co-occurring words in the context window	
	position-mean	Average of the relative position in a sentence	
	position-stdev	Standard deviation of the relative position in a sentence	
Semantic	Sense-count	Cardinality of the annotated word senses in the corpus	SemCor
	sense-entropy	Diversity of the annotated word senses in the corpus	
	sense-snnl	Entanglement measure of word senses in representation space	
	adj-sense-entropy	Diversity of the word senses adjusted by the *sense-snnl*	

The ELMo encoder has three layers: two LSTM layers on top of the context-independent character CNN layer. This naturally leads to the arbitrary choice of a pooling function. We follow the standard usage of the ELMo encoder and employ a simple average of all the ELMo layers, as defined in Eq. 3.[2]

2.3   Features

In this study, we distinguish words by their surface form, which means different capitalizations or forms will be considered as different words. Considering this, we assign ten features to each word: two lexical features, four statistical features, and four semantic features. Table 1 shows a summary of these ten features.

For the lexical features, we introduce *PoS* and *PoS-entropy*. **PoS** is the most frequently assigned part-of-speech tag in the corpus. Similarly, **PoS-entropy** is the entropy of the frequency distribution of the assigned part-of-speech tag in the corpus.

For the statistical features, we introduce *log-freq, context-entropy, position-mean*, and *position-stdev*. These features are summary statistics that are computed solely based on the corpus. **log-freq** is the logarithm of the number of occurrences. **context-entropy** is the entropy of the frequency distribution of the co-occurring words within the context window. More specifically, we use a context window size of 5, and we also count the occurrences of special tokens <s> and </s>, which represent the beginning and end of the sentence, mainly to make the feature consistent with the pre-processing methodology of the ELMo encoder. **position-mean** is the average of the relative position within a sentence. The beginning and end of a sentence are represented as 0 and 1, respectively. Similarly, **position-stdev** is the standard deviation of the relative position within a sentence.

For the semantic features, we introduce *sense-count, sense-entropy, sense-snnl*, and *adj-sense-entropy*. These features are calculated using the word sense

---

[2] We conducted a preliminary experiment to investigate which pooling function maximizes the mutual information between the variance and a subset of features. The results showed that a simple average of all the ELMo layers achieved the highest mutual information, which indicates that our methodology is reasonable.

annotated corpus. ***sense-count*** is the cardinality of the word senses annotated in the corpus. Similarly, ***sense-entropy*** is the entropy of the frequency distribution of the annotated word senses.

sense-snnl is the entanglement measure of the word senses in representation space. More specifically, it is the soft nearest neighbor loss [10], which we measure as how close the CWR pairs for the same word sense are and how distant the CWR pairs for the different word senses are. Let the collection of the CWR and annotated word sense pairs of a specific word be $\{\mathbf{x}_i, y_i\}_{i=1}^n$, then the *sense-snnl* of a word $l_{snnl}(.)$ is

$$
l_{snnl}(\{\mathbf{x}_i, y_i\}_{i=1}^n; T) = \frac{1}{n} \sum_{i=1}^n \left\{ \log \sum_{\substack{j \neq i \\ y_j = y_i}} \exp\left(-\frac{||\mathbf{x}_i - \mathbf{x}_j||^2}{T} \right) \right.
$$
$$
\left. - \log \sum_{k \neq i} \exp\left(-\frac{||\mathbf{x}_i - \mathbf{x}_k||^2}{T} \right) \right\},
$$

(4)

where T is the annealing temperature.[3]

adj-sense-entropy is the *sense-entropy* subtracted by *sense-snnl*. Our motivation for introducing this metric can be explained as follows. Intuitively, we expect a positive correlation between the variance of the CWRs and the diversity of the word senses as long as the word senses are reflected on the CWRs. Because *sense-entropy* and *sense-snnl* should respectively capture the former and latter properties independently, we also expect that the difference between these two metrics will act as the diversity of the word senses adjusted by the entanglement of the word senses in representation space.

2.4   Datasets

We use two datasets (corpora) in our experiment; namely, the UMBC corpus [11] as a large-scale text corpus and the SemCor dataset [12] as a word sense-annotated corpus. For the calculation of the lexical and statistical features, we use the 3-billion-word UMBC corpus as a dataset, which is a large-scale collection of paragraphs extracted from the web. We obtain the tokenized version that is available at the SemEval-2018 Task 9: Hypernym Discovery task,[4] and we use the spaCy tokenizer to assign the part-of-speech tags.[5] Note that we limit the vocabulary to words that occur 100 times or more in the corpus in order to decrease the effect of the estimation error. It results in approximately 205 thousand words.

For the calculation of the semantic features, we use the SemCor dataset, which is the manually annotated word sense corpus that contains about 33 K senses in total. More specifically, we use the curated version that was published

---

[3] We use $T = 30$ in our experiment.

[4] Available at: https://competitions.codalab.org/competitions/17119.

[5] We use spaCy version 2.1.0 with **en_core_web_sm** model available at: https://spacy. io.

by Raganato et al. [13]. We also calculated the *PoS* feature to allow for making a comparison between the semantic features and lexical feature in a relative manner. To calculate the *PoS* feature, we use the originally annotated part-of-speech tags as provided. Finally, similarly to the lexical and statistic features, we limit the vocabulary to words that occur 50 times or more in the dataset, which results in 673 words.

2.5   Association Measures

We apply quantitative and visualization methodologies to investigate the effect of each feature on the variation of the CWRs. More specifically, to perform a quantitative analysis, we employ three metrics to quantify the degree of the association between the *variance* and the features: Spearman's rank correlation $\rho(X, Y)$, mutual information $I(X; Y)$, and the mutual information of feature pairs $I(X; Y, Z)$, where X is the *variance* that is defined in Eq. 1 and Y, Z are two of the features that are introduced in Sect. 2.3. Whereas Spearman's rank correlation captures the nonlinear correlation, mutual information captures the dependence on one feature or a pair of features.

We estimate the mutual information $I(X; Y)$ using the Scikit-learn function `mutual_information_regression`. We also estimate the mutual information of feature pairs $I(X; Y, Z)$ by decomposing it into the plain mutual information and conditional mutual information using the chain rule:

$$I(X; Y, Z) = I(X; Z) + I(X; Y|Z) \tag{5}$$

$$I(X; Y|Z) \approx \sum_z I(X; Y|Z = z)\hat{p}(z) \tag{6}$$

where $\hat{p}(z)$ is the empirical distribution of variable Z. When Z is a continuous variable, we convert it into a categorical variable beforehand using K-means clustering with a cluster size of 100.

3   Experimental Results

3.1   Lexical and Statistical Features

In this section, we focus on the experimental results of the lexical and statistical features that are computed on the UMBC corpus.

Table 2 shows the mutual information $I(X; Y)$ and Spearman's rank correlation $\rho(X, Y)$ of each feature. Among the six features, *PoS*, *position-mean*, and *position-stdev* yield a relatively high mutual information compared with *log-freq* and *PoS-entropy*. We also find that the rank correlations of *context-entropy* and *position-stdev* are approximately 0.4, which indicates that these two features have a positive correlation to *variance*.

Table 3 shows the mutual information of the feature pairs $I(X; Y, Z)$. The feature pairs comprising *PoS*, *context-entropy*, *position-mean*, and *position-stdev*

Table 2. Mutual information and Spearman's rank correlation of the lexical and statistical features

Type	Feature name	$I(X;Y)$	$\rho(X,Y)$
Lexical	PoS	0.196	-
	PoS-entropy	0.025	−0.152
Statistical	log-freq	0.028	0.200
	context-entropy	0.091	0.334
	position-mean	0.221	−0.189
	Position-stdev	0.200	0.410

Table 3. Mutual information of the feature pairs $I(X;Y,Z)$

Feature $Y \setminus Z$	PoS	PoS-entropy	log-freq	context-entropy	position-mean	position-stdev
PoS	0.196	0.234	0.292	0.386	0.362	0.334
PoS-entropy	-	0.025	0.073	0.134	0.250	0.236
log-freq	-	-	0.028	0.132	0.287	0.266
context-entropy	-	-	-	0.091	0.329	0.331
position-mean	-	-	-	-	0.221	0.291
position-stdev	-	-	-	-	-	0.200

yield a relatively high mutual information out of all the possible feature pairs. More specifically, the {*PoS, context-entropy*} pair and the {*PoS, position-mean*} pair yield the highest values.

Followed by the quantitative results, we visualize the interaction between the most effective features: *PoS*, *context-entropy*, and *position-mean*. Figure 1 shows a box plot of the *variance* of each *PoS* group. It shows that numerals, proper nouns, and adverbs (NUM, PROPN, ADV) have the largest variance, whereas interjections, determiners, and auxiliary verbs (INTJ, DET, AUX) have the smallest variance. We also verify that the difference between the *PoS* groups are statistically significant.[6]

Figure 2 (left) shows a box plot of the *variance* of each interval of the *position-mean* grouped by *PoS*. As we see the inverted U-shaped figures, the results clearly show that words that frequently appear at the beginning or end of sentences have a smaller variance for most part-of-speech tags. Similarly, Fig. 2 (right) shows a scatter plot of the *variance* versus *context-entropy* grouped by *PoS*. This plot shows that there is a correlation between the *context-entropy* and the *variance* and that the correlation values differ among the various part-of-speech tags.

These experimental results indicate the following properties of the lexical and statistical features. First, part-of-speech type, contextual diversity, and word position are the features most closely related to the variation of the representations. Secondly, the scale of the variation differs among the different part-of-

---

[6] The hypothesis that the median of the variance is the same for all groups was tested using Kruskal–Wallis Test, for which we obtained a p-value of 0.000.

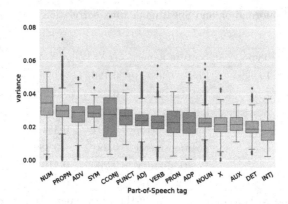

Fig. 1. Differences in the *variance* for the part-of-speech tags

Table 4. Mutual information and Spearman's rank correlation of the semantic features

Type	Feature name	$I(X;Y)$	$\rho(X,Y)$
Lexical	PoS (reference)	0.233	-
Semantic	sense-count	0.063	0.198
	sense-entropy	0.096	0.199
	sense-snnl	0.064	0.131
	adj-sense-entropy	0.172	0.444

speech types. Thirdly, contextual diversity and the variation of the representations have a positive correlation. In other words, words that co-occur with a wide variety of context words tend to have larger variation compared with those that occur in a specific context. Lastly, average word position captures a special effect at either end of sentences. More concretely, words that frequently appear at the beginning or end of the sentence have a smaller variation.

3.2 Semantic Features

In this section, we focus on the experimental results of the semantic features, which are computed on the SemCor dataset.

Table 4 shows the mutual information $I(X;Y)$ and Spearman's rank correlation $\rho(X,Y)$ of each features. Out of the four features, *adj-sense-entropy* yields the largest values for both mutual information and correlation, and all semantic features yield a positive correlation. We also find that the mutual information of *PoS* exceeds that of all other semantic features. These numbers show that the adjustment made using *sense-snnl* enhances the association of the *variance* when using *sense-entropy*.

These experimental results indicate the following properties of the semantic features. First, the higher the diversity of the word senses tends to be, the larger

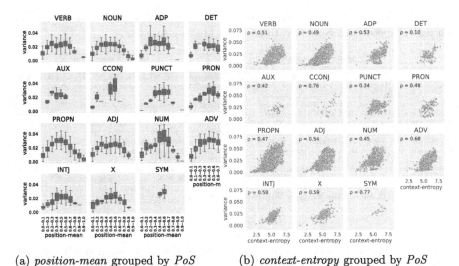

(a) *position-mean* grouped by *PoS*   (b) *context-entropy* grouped by *PoS*

Fig. 2. Interaction between *PoS*, *context-entropy*, and *position-mean*

the scale of the variation of the CWRs is. Secondly, the adjustments made using the degree of the entanglement of word senses in the representation space enhance the dependence and correlation between the diversity measure of the word senses and the scale of variation. The association between the word senses and CWRs is consistent with the findings of (Peters et al. [1]) indicating that CWRs can be used to make predictions for a word sense disambiguation task.

4 Analysis

We reported several experimental results in the previous section. More specifically, we found that the part-of-speech tags, word positions, the diversity of the surrounding words, and the diversity of the word senses are the most closely associated with the variation of CWRs. In this section, we discuss the validity of these findings and the source of some properties.

4.1 Words with Large or Small Variance

In Table 5, we examine some of the top-10 and bottom-10 words for each part-of-speech tag category after sorting from largest to smallest variation, according to the *variance* variable estimated using the UMBC corpus, along with the mean of the variation in each word group[7]. For most part-of-speech tags, the mean of the variation of the top-10 words is two to ten times larger than that for the bottom-10 words, which should be large enough difference for comparing two groups.

---

[7] We excluded words that appeared less than ten thousand times in the corpus and also omitted the part-of-speech tags that did not have a vocabulary size large enough.

Table 5. Words with large variance (right) and words with small variance (left) for each part-of-speech tag. Note that these words are case sensitive.

Part-of	Smallest variance words		Largest variance words	
-speech	Words	Variance	Words	Variance
ADJ	Prerequisite, Such, Many, Numerous, Several, Contrary	0.0054	seventh, long, 9th, sixth, 12th, 7th, 5th, 8th, 6th	0.0488
ADP	Although, Despite, Unlike, Though, Whilst, During	0.0039	vs., Against, of, up, versus, out, en, over, off, per	0.0464
ADV	Additionally, However, Furthermore, Consequently	0.0027	far, much, only, heavily, materially, most, ever	0.0451
CCONJ	But, Yet, Nor, And, Either, Or, Plus, but, neither	0.0162	&, or, +, and, and/or, nor, AND, either, OR	0.0475
DET	These, Each, Some, Both, Those, This, Another	0.0053	all, the, another, no, any, a, both, this, an, some	0.0388
NOUN	Prerequisites, Examples, Anyone, Others, Thousands	0.0066	age, heart, 13th, half, 11th, R, stem, strip	0.0448
NUM	One, Twenty, Two, 1920s, set-up, Three, pop-up, 2020	0.0207	11, 14, 13, 16, 19, 22, 26, 23, 17, 49	0.0517
PRON	They, She, There, We, It, Whatever, Its, Their, He	0.0056	his, its, her, their, himself, it, herself, Me, my	0.0382
PROPN	MR., DR., Sec, Br, Inc, Abstract, Footnote, Fig.	0.0107	de, S., F., D., E., Trade, W., L., Space, G.	0.0615
PUNCT	., ..., ..., ?, !!, !, ..., .3, .2, }	0.0166	-, (, , [, ,, ", , ",],	0.0380
VERB	Depending, Assuming, Posted, According, Founded	0.0049	Left, left, leading, striking, known, passing	0.0429
AUX	Would, Could, Should, Must, Can, MUST, SHOULD	0.0162	Ca, Will, would, can, could, will, might, shall	0.0275
X	etc, etc., , ie, priori, i.e., vitro, se, , hoc	0.0240	la, v, k, <, ex, th, >, facto, z, f	0.0377
INTJ	Id, Please, Tr, Anyway, Okay, Sorry, Sure, Yeah, Well	0.0079	O, ha, yes, id, please, oh, Ah, Hey, yeah, Yes	0.0195

A distinct trend observed is that almost all of the words with small variance are title-cased, which is much less often the case for words with a large variance, except for proper nouns (**PROPN** in the table). Another trend that is observed that, for words that belong to the punctuation category (**PUNCT** in the table), sentence-delimiter symbols, such as the period and the exclamation mark, appear in the small variance group, whereas non-sentence-delimiter symbols, such as brackets and quotation marks, appear in the large variance group. In summary, we can conclude that words/symbols that appear in the small variance groups are those that frequently appear at the beginning or at the end of sentences, which is consistent with the word position effect that we reported in Sect. 3.1.

4.2   Cause of the Positional Effect

Our experimental and analysis results indicate that the ELMo encoder is a position-aware model in terms of the variation of the representations. This is particularly evident at the beginning and end of sentences, which correspond with a decrease in the variation. The plausible explanations of the cause of this behavior are two-fold: the so-called "inductive bias" and the characteristics acquired through the pre-training process. More concretely, the first one corresponds to the recurrent architecture of the LSTM layers, and the second one corresponds to the language modeling task trained using left-to-right and right-to-left directions independently. In this section, we investigate which explanation is more plausible by conducting a feature analysis using *randomized* ELMo in the same manner as the original ELMo.

Randomized ELMo [7] is a pre-trained ELMo model in which all weights above the lexical layer, i.e., all weights in the LSTM layers, are replaced with random values.[8] Intuitively, randomized ELMo is a contextualized encoder that forgets how to process the surrounding words into the representations, which is acquired through language modeling task.

---

[8] We overwrite all linear transformation matrices in the LSTM layers using Glorot initialization [14].

Table 6. Comparison between the results for the randomized and original ELMo

Type	Feature name	$I(X;Y)$		$\rho(X,Y)$	
		Original	Randomized	Original	Randomized
Lexical	PoS	0.196	0.345	-	-
	PoS-entropy	0.025	0.029	−0.152	−0.013
Statistical	log-freq	0.028	0.018	0.200	−0.047
	context-entropy	0.091	0.050	0.334	0.026
	position-mean	0.221	0.388	−0.189	−0.521
	position-stdev	0.200	0.810	0.410	0.877

Table 6 shows the mutual information $I(X;Y)$ and Spearman's rank correlation $\rho(X,Y)$ of the lexical and statistical features obtained using the original and randomized ELMo models. These results show that the randomized ELMo model yields higher values for the positional features, such as *position-mean* and *position-stdev*, whereas the original ELMo yields higher values for the context diversity features, such as *context-entropy* for both metrics. It is noteworthy that *context-entropy* is no longer correlated in the case of randomized ELMo.

The contrast between the two ELMo models strongly suggests that position awareness is not a characteristic acquired through the pre-training process but the inductive bias of the recurrent architecture. Or rather, pre-training seems to reduce position awareness and enhance the effect of the surrounding words so that the model can capture the meaningful contextual information.

5   Conclusion

We study word attributes that are considered to be associated with the variation property of contextualized word representations, namely the outputs of the ELMo encoder. Features that reflect lexical, statistical, and semantic properties are used to quantitatively and qualitatively analyze their dependence and correlation on the variance of the word representations. Among these features, our experimental results show that the lexical category, word position, the diversity of the contexts, and the diversity of the word senses are most closely associated with the variance of CWRs. We also reveal that the entanglement of word senses in representation space is an important property for enhancing the relationship between the diversity of the word senses and the variance. In addition, our analysis strongly indicates that the word position effect, which is evident among words that appear mostly at the beginning and end of sentences, is not caused by the pre-training process but by the inductive bias of the ELMo encoder architecture.

Intuitively, word representations with a large variance may suffer from fine-tuning on downstream tasks if variance acts as a noisy input. Considering this issue, we will investigate the effects of the variation property on downstream tasks and compare different contextualized encoder models in future works.

Acknowledgments. This work was supported by JSPS KAKENHI Grant Number 19H01118.

References

1. Peters, M., et al.: Deep contextualized word representations. In: Proceedings of the 2018 Conference of the North American Chapter of the Association for Computational Linguistics: Human Language Technologies, Volume 1 (Long Papers), pp. 2227–2237 (2018)
2. Devlin, J., Chang, M., Lee, K., Toutanova, K.: BERT: pre-training of deep bidirectional transformers for language understanding. In: Proceedings of the 2019 Conference of the North American Chapter of the Association for Computational Linguistics: Human Language Technologies, NAACL-HLT 2019, Minneapolis, MN, USA, 2–7 June 2019, Volume 1 (Long and Short Papers), pp. 4171–4186 (2019)
3. Radford, A., Narasimhan, K., Salimans, T., Sutskever, I.: Improving language understanding by generative pre-training (2018)
4. Belinkov, Y., Glass, J.: Analysis methods in neural language processing: a survey. Trans. Assoc. Comput. Linguist. **7**, 49–72 (2019). https://doi.org/10.1162/tacl_a_00254
5. Adi, Y., Kermany, E., Belinkov, Y., Lavi, O., Goldberg, Y.: Fine-grained analysis of sentence embeddings using auxiliary prediction tasks. In: 5th International Conference on Learning Representations, ICLR 2017, Conference Track Proceedings, Toulon, France, 24–26 April 2017 (2017)
6. Zhang, K.W., Bowman, S.R.: Language modeling teaches you more syntax than translation does: lessons learned through auxiliary task analysis. CoRR abs/1809.10040 (2018). http://arxiv.org/abs/1809.10040
7. Tenney, I., et al.: What do you learn from context? Probing for sentence structure in contextualized word representations. In: International Conference on Learning Representations (2019)
8. Liu, N.F., Gardner, M., Belinkov, Y., Peters, M.E., Smith, N.A.: Linguistic knowledge and transferability of contextual representations. In: Proceedings of the 2019 Conference of the North American Chapter of the Association for Computational Linguistics: Human Language Technologies, NAACL-HLT 2019, Minneapolis, MN, USA, 2–7 June 2019, Volume 1 (Long and Short Papers), pp. 1073–1094 (2019)
9. Lakretz, Y., Kruszewski, G., Desbordes, T., Hupkes, D., Dehaene, S., Baroni, M.: The emergence of number and syntax units in lstm language models. In: Proceedings of the 2019 Conference of the North American Chapter of the Association for Computational Linguistics: Human Language Technologies, Volume 1 (Long and Short Papers), pp. 11–20 (2019)
10. Frosst, N., Papernot, N., Hinton, G.: Analyzing and improving representations with the soft nearest neighbor loss. In: International Conference on Machine Learning, pp. 2012–2020 (2019)
11. Han, L., Kashyap, A.L., Finin, T., Mayfield, J., Weese, J.: Umbc_ebiquity-core: semantic textual similarity systems. In: Second Joint Conference on Lexical and Computational Semantics (* SEM), Volume 1: Proceedings of the Main Conference and the Shared Task: Semantic Textual Similarity, pp. 44–52 (2013)
12. Miller, G.A., Leacock, C., Tengi, R., Bunker, R.T.: A semantic concordance. In: Proceedings of the Workshop on Human Language Technology, pp. 303–308. Association for Computational Linguistics (1993)

13. Raganato, A., Camacho-Collados, J., Navigli, R.: Word sense disambiguation: a unified evaluation framework and empirical comparison. In: Proceedings of the 15th Conference of the European Chapter of the Association for Computational Linguistics: Volume 1, Long Papers, pp. 99–110 (2017)
14. Glorot, X., Bengio, Y.: Understanding the difficulty of training deep feedforward neural networks. In: Proceedings of the Thirteenth International Conference on Artificial Intelligence and Statistics, pp. 249–256 (2010)

Feature Importance for Biomedical Named Entity Recognition

Hamish Huggard[1]([✉]), Aaron Zhang[1], Edmond Zhang[2], and Yun Sing Koh[1]

[1] University of Auckland, Auckland 1010, New Zealand
{hhug934,azha065}@aucklanduni.ac.nz, ykoh@cs.auckland.ac.nz
[2] Orion Health, 181 Grafton Road, Grafton, Auckland 1010, New Zealand
edmond.zhang@orionhealth.com

Abstract. Within the domain of biomedical natural language processing (bioNLP), researchers have used many token features for machine learning models. With recent progress in word embeddings algorithms, it is no longer clear if most of these features are still useful. In this paper we survey the features which have been used in bioNLP, and evaluate each feature's utility in a sample bioNLP task: the N2C2 2018 named entity recognition challenge. The features we test include two types of word embeddings, syntactic, lexical, and orthographic features, character-embeddings, and clustering and distributional word representations. We find that using fastText word embeddings results in a significantly higher F_1 score than using any other individual feature (0.9142 compared to 0.8750 for the next-best feature). Furthermore, we conducted several experiments using combinations of features, and found that all tested combinations attained a lower F_1 score than using word embeddings only. This indicates that supplementing word embeddings with additional features is not beneficial, and may even be detrimental.

Keywords: Natural language processing · Biomedical NLP · Word embeddings · Feature importance · Named entity recognition

1 Introduction

To achieve biomedical natural language processing (biomedical NLP, or bioNLP) tasks, such as summarising clinical narratives, question answering about patient history, and extracting relations between entities in a health records, many features are conceivably useful[1] For a given token, an algorithm might benefit from any of the following: the syntactic properties of the token, whether the token names a known drug or disease, the orthographic properties of the token, which other tokens tend to co-occur with the token, and so on. At various times, bioNLP researchers have used many features which attempted to capture this kind of information. However with recent advances in word embedding algorithms, it is now conceivable that all previously employed features are now obsolete. Word

---

[1] Our code is available at https://github.com/lajesticvantrashell/N2C2_2018_track_2.

© Springer Nature Switzerland AG 2019
J. Liu and J. Bailey (Eds.): AI 2019, LNAI 11919, pp. 406–417, 2019.
https://doi.org/10.1007/978-3-030-35288-2_33

embeddings are mappings from tokens to fixed dimensional vectors. The mappings should ideally reflect semantic or syntactic information about tokens, so that the vector corresponding to "king" should be similar to that of "monarch". Current word embeddings can take into account semantic, syntactic, morphological [1], and even contextual information [15] about tokens, and have been used to achieve state of the art in several tasks [15]. If it could in fact be verified that current word embedding algorithms render other token features moot, this would be very valuable knowledge for bioNLP researchers. It would simplify the feature engineering task to merely finding the best word embedding.

As a first step towards investigating whether current word embedding techniques obviates the use of other features, we investigate the utility of common bioNLP features in Track 2 of the 2018 National NLP Clinical Challenges (N2C2). This is a named entity recognition (NER) task, in which entities in free medical text relating to drugs and adverse drug events (ADEs) must be annotated. An adverse drug event is defined as an "adverse outcome that occurs while a patient is taking a drug" [5]. Because NER is one of the simplest NLP tasks, this challenge is a natural first domain to investigate feature importance. Our contributions are two-fold. First, we provide a survey of the main features used in bioNLP, with implementations of each feature in our accompanying code. Secondly, we have conducted a feature importance study in which we trained and tested a simple neural network model using each of these features individually on the N2C2 2018 NER challenge. We found that word embeddings produced a significantly higher precision, recall, and F_1 score than any other feature (F_1 of 0.9142 compared to 0.8750 for the next-best feature). We also evaluated several sets of features, and found that supplementing word embeddings with additional features is not beneficial.

This paper is organised as follows. Section 2 discusses related work. Section 3 gives details of our feature importance study method. Section 4 describes the features we use in detail. Section 5 describes the results of our experiments. Section 6 concludes this investigation.

2   Related Work

Many feature engineering or feature importance experiments have been done in the bioNLP domain which used word embeddings. Tang et al. compared several types of word representation features on bioNLP tasks, including Brown clusters, word embeddings, and random indexing [18]. None of these representations was clearly superior to the others, but the combination of all three produced the best results. Liu et al. found that a word embedding feature could achieve better results at drug NER than a traditional drug lexicon-based system [11]. However, the combination of lexical and word embedding features did better than both and achieved state of the art results. Recently, Chen et al. developed an ADE NER system which benefited from lexical features [4]. Much of this research suggests that although word embeddings are useful features, the combination of word embeddings with other conventional features tends to produce the best results.

However, word embedding algorithms have improved significantly since these previous studies were conducted, and it is worth re-examining their conclusions.

Some work has also been done on the best approach to employing word embeddings for bioNLP tasks. Muneeb et al. evaluated different word embedding algorithms on semantic similarity and relatedness tasks in a biomedical context [13], finding that the skipgram implementation of the word2vec was the most accurate. Wang et al. [20] and Wu et al. [23] both compared the performance of word embeddings trained on biomedical corpora versus general corpora on downstream bioNLP tasks. In general, word embeddings trained on biomedical corpora outperformed those trained on general corpora.

It is worth noting that in most actual biomedical NLP applications rule-based systems still dominate [21]. However, given the significant role of neural networks and word embeddings in state-of-the-art natural language processing [12,15], this seems likely to change in the future. We therefore focus on neural network models.

3   Feature Importance Experiment Methodology

Our feature importance study began by dividing the official N2C2 2018 Track 2 training dataset into a training/validation/development partition, which was fixed throughout the study. Then, for each feature we describe in Sect. 4, we trained a simple neural network model on the training set using only that feature, and report the lenient precision, recall, and micro F_1 score of the model on the development set. We also performed a single evaluation of our best feature set on the official N2C2 test set, so that our results could be compared to the official competition outcomes.

3.1   Model Architecture

Because we were primarily interested in studying feature importance, and not creating the most accurate model possible, we elected to use a very simple neural network model for our experiments. However, preliminary experiments with more complex neural network architectures showed no discernible difference in F_1 score. The text was processed in windows of tokens. The features for each token were generated and then concatenated into a single vector per token. These vectors were then fed into a bidirectional LSTM (bi-LSTM). A dense layer with softmax activation then predicted token labels from the bi-LSTM outputs. This simple architecture is illustrated in Fig. 1 and was implemented in `Keras` with `Tensorflow` backend.

A dropout rate of 0.3 was used between layers. In each experiment the model was trained using the Nesterov ADAM optimiser with a batch size of 128. The models were trained for 40 epochs, using early stopping with a patience of 5 epochs. The classification error was given by categorical cross entropy.

We did not perform a formal hyperparameter optimisation for this architecture. However, preliminary testing indicated that the following were sensible options: a token window size of 128, and a latent dimension for the bi-LSTM of 128. At training time the token window had a slide of 32, at test time it was equal to the window size.

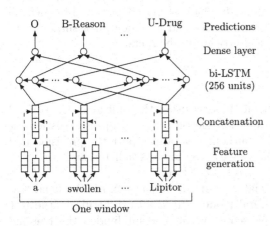

Fig. 1. Our architecture.

Table 1. Effect of training corpora on fastText.

Corpus	Prec.	Recall	F₁
Wikipedia	0.9200	0.8472	0.8821
Pubmed	0.9085	0.8681	0.8878
Wiki-news	**0.9354**	0.8467	0.8889
PMC	0.9312	0.8742	0.9018
MIMIC	0.9353	0.8764	0.9049
Combined	0.9353	**0.8941**	**0.9142**

Table 2. Effect of cluster number on Brown clustering.

#Clusters	Prec.	Recall	F₁
100	0.8933	0.7119	0.7923
200	0.8883	0.7772	0.8290
500	0.9079	0.7824	0.8405
1000	**0.9086**	**0.8231**	**0.8638**

3.2 Dataset

Our models were evaluated using a dataset of nearly 505 clinical narratives provided by Track 2 of the 2018 National NLP Clinical Challenges (N2C2)[2]. The N2C2 dataset is a drawn from the MIMIC-III (Medical Information Mart for Intensive Care III) database [7], with annotations added by domain experts. The annotations consist of entity tags indicating the presence of drug and ADE information. Specifically, the named entities for the N2C2 challenge are "Drug", "Reason", "Strength", "Frequency", "ADE", "Dosage", "Duration", "Form" and "Route".

We used BILOU segment representation for multi-token entities. Under BILOU, for each named entity which spans multiple tokens, the beginning token is labelled with a "B", the last token with an "L", and those tokens inside the named entity (i.e., between the beginning and last token) with an "I". Tokens which are outside of all named entities are labelled with an "O", and named entities consisting of a single (unique) token are labelled "U". So for example, we get the following segment representation: "treated/O with/O vanc/U-Drug for/O the/O septic/B-Reason left/I-Reason knee/L-Reason".

For training certain features we also made use of the following biomedical corpora. The MIMIC III dataset [7] contains de-identified information on 40,000

---

[2] https://portal.dbmi.hms.harvard.edu/projects/n2c2-t2/.

patient encounters in a critical care unit. We extracted the patient summaries and used these to pre-train some of our features. The PubMed Central (PMC) dataset is a repository of biomedical and life sciences journal literature. We downloaded a portion of the articles from the repository for Dec 2018 which contained around 200K articles. The Pubmed dataset is a free search engine primarily accessing the MEDLINE bibliographic database of life sciences and biomedical information. We extracted over 200K articles and abstracts in a snapshot we took by searching for relevant clinical articles or abstracts.

3.3   Evaluation

We evaluated the performance of our models using the official N2C2 track 2 evaluation script. The primary evaluation metric of the competition is lenient micro F_1 (henceforth simply "F_1"), although we also report the precision and recall. "Lenient" here meaning that any overlap in the predicted and true span of a named entity is counted as a correct prediction.

The data is split into 303 official training documents and 202 official test documents. Because we tested several models, to avoid overfitting to the test data and positively biasing our F_1 score, we further subdivided the training data into training, validation, and development dataset, with an 8/1/1 split. The validation set is used for early stopping, and the development set is used for F_1 score evaluation. As a final step in our experiments, we evaluated our most accurate model (according to the development dataset) on the official test set.

4   Features

In this section we list all the features we experimented with in our experiments, aggregated from the literatures on biomedical NLP [3,10,11,18], and general NER [14]. First we considered word representation (WR) features, which can be categorised as word embeddings, cluster-based representations, and distributional representations. We employed two word embedding algorithms: fastText [1] and ELMo [15]. We used Brown clustering as a cluster-based WR, and random indexes as a distribution-based WR. In addition to WRs, we also experimented with character-embedding features, orthographic features, lexical features, and syntactic features.

4.1   FastText

FastText is a word embedding algorithm based on the skipgram model, primarily distinguished from preceding word embedding algorithms in two ways: first, it's computationally much more efficient, and secondly, it generates embeddings at the character n-gram model, as well as at the token level. This allows it to model word morphology, and determine embeddings for tokens which did not appear in the training data. For our experiments, we downloaded two pre-trained fastText embeddings provided by the original authors. Both are trained on general corpora: the first on Wikipedia[3], and the second on both Wikipedia and Google News[4]. We also trained new embeddings on the biomedical corpora MIMIC-III, Pubmed, PMC, and the combination of the three. The results of using fastText embeddings trained on each of these corpora are given in Table 1.

4.2 ELMo

Embeddings from Language Models (ELMo) is a word embedding algorithm which recently debuted by significantly improving the state of the art in six difficult NLP tasks [15]. ELMo is a deep bidirectional language model (biLM), meaning it is composed of several bi-LSTMs stacked on top of one another (imagine Fig. 1 but with the bi-LSTM layer repeated several times). The final word embedding for a token is a learned linear combination of all the LSTM states in a vertical stack. This approach allows ELMo to resolve polysemy - words with multiple meanings - by taking context into account. Due to resource constraints, we did not fine tune ELMo to our task, and simply used out-of-the-box ELMo with TensorFlow Hub[5] to generate 1024-dimensional word embeddings for each token.

4.3 Brown Clusters

Brown hierarchical word clustering is an algorithm designed to allocate classes to tokens, such that the average mutual information between adjacent classes in text is maximised [2]. Because the clustering is hierarchical, clusters may be represented by binary strings denoting the binary tree traversal from the root to the leaf representing the cluster. This is illustrated in Fig. 2, in which we can see that "with" is more closely related to "between" than to "in".

We ran an implementation of Brown clustering [9] over the pre-tokenised MIMIC-III corpus. The number of clusters is a hyper-parameter to be tuned. We considered four different numbers of clusters, and the results of each cluster number are given in Table 2. 1000 clusters were best in our experiments. Examples of the resulting clusters are shown in Table 4. The cluster feature is zero-padded to a fixed length.

4.4 Random Indexing

Random indexing is a distributional word representation method, so tokens which tend to co-occur in documents will have similar representations. Many approaches to distributional word representation - such as latent semantic analysis - rely on a costly dimension reduction step, which must be repeated every time the representation is updated with a new document. Random indexing gets around this problem using the fact that random pairs of sparse, high-dimensional

---

[3] https://fasttext.cc/docs/en/pretrained-vectors.html.

[4] https://fasttext.cc/docs/en/english-vectors.html.

[5] https://tfhub.dev/google/elmo/1.

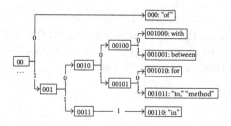

Table 3. Example of syntactic tags produced by the Genia Tagger.

tokens	POS	chunk
The	Determiner	Noun phrase
patient	Noun, singular	Noun phrase
was	Verb, past tense	Verb phrase
tested	Verb, past part	Verb phrase

Fig. 2. Brown clusters illustration [18].

Table 4. Illustration of several features with the text "2.50 mg - Lasix".

tokens	jochem	clusters	shape	short_shape	len	title	upper	lower	numeric	symbol
2.50	False	11110101	0!00	0!0	4	False	0.00	0.00	0.75	0.25
mg	True	1111011	xx	x	2	False	0.00	1.00	0.00	0.00
–	False	11110111101	!	!	1	False	0.00	0.00	0.00	1.00
Lasix	True	1111010000111	Xxxxx	Xx	5	True	0.20	0.80	0.00	0.00

vectors are on average almost orthogonal. This allows a dimension-reduction computation to be approximated by accumulating such vectors onto token representations.

In particular, we adopted the random indexing method described in [16]. Each document D_j was initially assigned an n-dimensional index vector r_j. Index vectors are high dimensional and most elements are zero, with a few elements being $+1$ or -1. Each element of the vector was given by

$$r_{j,i} = \sqrt{s} \begin{cases} -1 & \text{with probability } \frac{1}{2s} \\ 0 & \text{with probability } 1 - \frac{1}{s} \\ 1 & \text{with probability } \frac{1}{2s} \end{cases} \qquad (1)$$

The next step was to generate an n-dimensional context vector v_k for each token w_k in the vocabulary. Initially, $v_k = \mathbf{0}$, and then for each occurrence of w_k in D_j, r_j was added to v_k. In this case we chose $n = 100$, and $s = \sqrt{n} = 10$. These values are indicated to be appropriate in [16]. We trained our random index representation on MIMIC-III.

4.5   Character Embeddings

To capture morphological information about tokens, we used a character-level token representation. Specifically, we used a neural network architecture called CharWNN, which was introduced in [17]. CharWNN produces a representation of each token by convolving over a sequence of character embeddings, and then taking the maximum value at each index of the resulting vectors. We omit the mathematical details here, but we use the same architecture and hyperparameters as [17].

4.6   Lexical Features

Following [11], we checked each token against three popular drug lexica: drugs@FDA[6], DrugBank (version 5.1.2, released 2018-12-20) [22], and Jochem (Erasmus ontollogy) [6]. Each lexicon has a corresponding binary feature, where a value of 1 indicates that the token is present in the lexicon, and 0 indicates it is not. Examples of this token can be seen in Table 4. Each of the entries in these lexica were preprocessed as follows. The entries were tokenised using Spacy, and then each token was lower-cased and stemmed. Any tokens with no alphabetic characters were removed. With this process, 6799 tokens were extracted from drugs@FDA, 14317 tokens were extracted from the 'drug name' and 'active ingredients' columns of the Drugbank database, and 941334 tokens were extracted from Jochem. In addition to a binary feature for each lexicon, we also considered the concatenation of these features as a 3-dimensional feature which we called "all lexica".

4.7   Orthographic Features

We used eight orthographic features to encode information about the *kinds* of characters present in the word. These features are illustrated in Table 4. Firstly, we used a simple orthography feature which gave the proportion of characters in the token which were numeric, uppercase alphabetic, lowercase alphabetic, and symbols, plus a Boolean of whether the token was in title case. We can get a more fine grained picture of the token's orthography by also considering the ordering of character types. This was achieved with word shapes. To obtain the word shape of a token, all uppercase letters were substituted with "X", all lowercase letters were substituted with "x", all numerals were substituted with "0", all symbols were substituted with "!", and all whitespace characters were substituted with "". In addition to the word shapes, short shapes are another feature which summarise the order in which types of characters appear in the token. These were produced by removing consecutive duplicates of the same character type from the word shape. Because there are an unlimited number of possible word shapes and short shapes, all but the 99 most common shapes were replaced with the empty shape "", so that the shape can be encoded in a 100-dimensional one-hot vector.

4.8   Syntactic Features

For syntactic features we used the Genia toolkit[7] to generate part of speech (POS) and chunk tags for each token. Examples of these features are given in Table 3. The Genia toolkit is trained on biomedical texts and has reported high accuracy on several bioNLP tasks [19]. The POS tags used by the Genia toolkit are a variant of the Penn Treebank tags, including 38 POS tags, and 9 other tags

---

[6] https://www.fda.gov/drugs/drug-approvals-and-databases/drugsfda-data-files.

[7] http://www.nactem.ac.uk/GENIA/tagger/.

for punctuation and symbols [8]. The chunking tags indicate where in a syntactic chunk a token resides. These tags combine BIO segment representation (which is the same as BILOU representation, but with B in place of U, and I in place of L), with 28 chunk-type labels. Because the range of possible tags for POS and chunks is relatively small, the tags were simply one-hot encoded.

4.9 Features Not Investigated

In our literature review we encountered several features which we did not investigate - either because they did not seem important enough, or because we could not figure out how to implement them with our architecture. We did not explicitly include any character n-grams, such as suffixes or prefixes. However, the character embedding should in principle capture the same information as character n-grams. We did not use a lexicon of cues denoting contexts in which entities are likely to occur, such as "medication:" indicating that the following token is likely to be a drug. Finally, we did not perform any fuzzy matching with lexica, and we did not use phrase length.

5 Feature Importance Study Results

For each of the individual features described above, we evaluated model accuracy using *only* that feature (using the predetermined train/val/dev datasets described in Sect. 3). The results are given in Table 5. The two word embedding features - fastText and ELMo - achieved the two highest F_1 scores. The best word embedding feature (fastText trained on combined corpus, 0.9142) is significantly better than the highest non-word embedding feature (character embeddings, 0.8750), and even the worst character embedding feature (fastText trained on Wikipedia, 0.8821) is still better than any non-word embedding feature. These and similar observations suggest that the different types of features can be ranked as followed: word embbeddings are the strongest features, followed by other word representations, orthographic features and POS tags come next, and lexical features and chunk tags are the weakest features (although lexical features also have the smallest domains). Drugbank in particular produced a remarkably low F_1 score.

Due to resource constraints we were not able to run a feature selection algorithm over the full set of features. However, we did evaluate the model when the full set of features are used, when only the top-5 most successful features were used, and when the top-2 features were used. We did the latter in two different ways: first, we considered fastText and ELMo as different features, and so used both of them in the top-2 experiment. Second, we considered fastText and ELMo as variations of a "word embedding" feature, and so used only fastText, plus the best non-word embedding feature: character embeddings. Every combination of features resulted in a lower precision, recall, and F_1 score than fastText (combined corpus) by itself. This indicates that not only are word embeddings the most useful feature for this task, but also that supplementing word embeddings with other features is not useful, and is perhaps even detrimental.

To ground our results in the official N2C2 competition outcomes, we also tested our best feature set on the official competition test data. For this final experiment, we kept the previous window size of 128, but reduced the window slide to 16. This is effectively a data augmentation technique which increases the size of the training data, thereby making the final model more accurate, but doubling the memory requirements and training time. For this experiment, the development dataset was added to the training dataset, but otherwise all experimental details were kept the same. The best feature set on the validation set was fastText (combined corpus) only. The final F_1 score achieved with this method was 0.9240. For comparison, the state of the art in this task is 0.9418.

Table 5. Performance of models using subsets of the features. The domains of each of each feature are also included. Binary features are denoted $\mathbb{Z}_2$, n-dimensional real-valued vector features are denoted $\mathbb{R}^n$, one-hot encoded features with n possible values are denoted $\mathbb{Z}_n$.

Feature	Domain	Precision	Recall	F_1
FastText (combined)	$\mathbb{R}^{100}$	**0.9353**	**0.8941**	**0.9142**
ELMo	$\mathbb{R}^{1024}$	0.9190	0.8610	0.8890
Character embedding	$\mathbb{R}^{50}$	0.9162	0.8374	0.8750
Brown clusters	$\mathbb{Z}_2^{15}$	0.9086	0.8231	0.8638
Random index	$\mathbb{R}^{100}$	0.8551	0.7465	0.7971
Orthography	$\mathbb{R}^5 \times \mathbb{Z}_2$	0.9069	0.6006	0.7226
POS	$\mathbb{Z}_{47}$	0.8699	0.5878	0.7016
Word shape	$\mathbb{Z}_{100}$	0.8959	0.5664	0.6941
Short shape	$\mathbb{Z}_{100}$	0.8588	0.5438	0.6660
Length	$\mathbb{Z}$	0.8524	0.5249	0.6497
All lexica	$\mathbb{Z}_2^3$	0.8286	0.5166	0.6364
Drugs@FDA	$\mathbb{Z}_2$	0.7609	0.4173	0.5390
Chunk	$\mathbb{Z}_{27}$	0.8348	0.3798	0.5220
Jochem	$\mathbb{Z}_2$	0.8503	0.3572	0.5030
Drugbank	$\mathbb{Z}_2$	0.5672	0.0425	0.0791
FastText+CE	$\mathbb{R}^{350}$	0.9330	0.8855	0.9086
FastText+ELMo	$\mathbb{R}^{1324}$	0.9329	0.8777	0.9044
Top-5	$\mathbb{R}^{1489}$	0.9192	0.8833	0.9009
All features	$\mathbb{R}^{1873}$	0.9186	0.8848	0.9014
FastText (test set)	$\mathbb{R}^{300}$	**0.9476**	**0.9016**	**0.9240**

6   Conclusion

In accord with past research [20, 23], our experiments indicated that word embeddings trained on biomedical corpera are more useful for bioNLP tasks than those trained on general corpera; as is visible in Table 1. Unlike past research, which found that conjunctions of word embeddings with other word representations were the best feature sets for BioNLP tasks [4, 11, 18], our experiments indicated that best results are obtained by using word embeddings *only*. This discrepancy can be accounted for by the fact that significant progress has been made in word embedding algorithms since these early studies were conducted. These results lend support to the hypothesis that by using state-of-the-art word embedding algorithms, other features which have traditionally been used for bioNLP - such as explicitly syntactic, morphological, and contextual features - can be made redundant. This greatly simplifies the task of bioNLP practitioners, whose feature engineering task is then simplified to merely finding a good word embedding.

There are several caveats to this conclusion. Our experiments only investigated the effect of using different features for a simple neural network model with a single architecture and hyperparameters. Furthermore, we only evaluated the model on a single NER bioNLP task. Further research is therefore required to validate our findings in the broader bioNLP context. On the other hand, our experimental procedure is quite representative of a typical bioNLP scenario: NER is a standard NLP benchmark, and simple recurrent networks - especially biLSTMs - are a popular model choice for natural language problems. Furthermore, in our preliminary experiments we also tested a more complex neural network model, and found very similar results to those reported here.

Acknowledgements. This research was supported by the Precision Driven Health Partnership (www.precisiondrivenhealth.com).

References

1. Bojanowski, P., Grave, E., Joulin, A., Mikolov, T.: Enriching word vectors with subword information. arXiv preprint arXiv:1607.04606 (2016)
2. Brown, P.F., Desouza, P.V., Mercer, R.L., Pietra, V.J.D., Lai, J.C.: Class-based n-gram models of natural language. Comput. Linguist. **18**(4), 467–479 (1992)
3. Campos, D., Matos, S., Oliveira, J.L.: Biomedical named entity recognition: a survey of machine-learning tools. In: Theory and Applications for Advanced Text Mining. IntechOpen (2012)
4. Chen, Y., et al.: Named entity recognition from Chinese adverse drug event reports with lexical feature based BiLSTM-CRF and tri-training. J. Biomed. Inform. **96**, 103252 (2019)
5. Edwards, I.R., Aronson, J.K.: Adverse drug reactions: definitions, diagnosis, and management. Lancet **356**(9237), 1255–1259 (2000)
6. Hettne, K.M., et al.: A dictionary to identify small molecules and drugs in free text. Bioinformatics **25**(22), 2983–2991 (2009)
7. Johnson, A.E., et al.: MIMIC-III, a freely accessible critical care database. Sci. Data **3** (2016). Article number: 160035

8. Kim, J.D., Ohta, T., Teteisi, Y., Tsujii, J.: Genia corpus manual. Technical report, Citeseer (2006)

9. Liang, P.: Semi-supervised learning for natural language. Ph.D. thesis, Massachusetts Institute of Technology (2005)

10. Liu, F., Chen, J., Jagannatha, A., Yu, H.: Learning for biomedical information extraction: methodological review of recent advances. arXiv preprint arXiv:1606.07993 (2016)

11. Liu, S., Tang, B., Chen, Q., Wang, X.: Effects of semantic features on machine learning-based drug name recognition systems: word embeddings vs. manually constructed dictionaries. Information 6(4), 848–865 (2015)

12. Mikolov, T., Chen, K., Corrado, G., Dean, J.: Efficient estimation of word representations in vector space. arXiv preprint arXiv:1301.3781 (2013)

13. Muneeb, T., Sahu, S., Anand, A.: Evaluating distributed word representations for capturing semantics of biomedical concepts. In: Proceedings of BioNLP 2015, pp. 158–163 (2015)

14. Nadeau, D., Sekine, S.: A survey of named entity recognition and classification. Lingvisticae Investig. 30(1), 3–26 (2007)

15. Peters, M.E., et al.: Deep contextualized word representations. arXiv preprint arXiv:1802.05365 (2018)

16. QasemiZadeh, B., Handschuh, S.: Random indexing explained with high probability. In: Král, P., Matoušek, V. (eds.) TSD 2015. LNCS (LNAI), vol. 9302, pp. 414–423. Springer, Cham (2015). https://doi.org/10.1007/978-3-319-24033-6_47

17. dos Santos, C.N., Zadrozny, B.: Learning character-level representations for part-of-speech tagging. In: Proceedings of the 31st International Conference on Machine Learning (ICML 2014), pp. 1818–1826 (2014)

18. Tang, B., Cao, H., Wang, X., Chen, Q., Xu, H.: Evaluating word representation features in biomedical named entity recognition tasks. BioMed Res. Int. 2014 (2014)

19. Tsuruoka, Y., et al.: Developing a robust part-of-speech tagger for biomedical text. In: Bozanis, P., Houstis, E.N. (eds.) PCI 2005. LNCS, vol. 3746, pp. 382–392. Springer, Heidelberg (2005). https://doi.org/10.1007/11573036_36

20. Wang, Y., et al.: A comparison of word embeddings for the biomedical natural language processing. J. Biomed. Inform. 87, 12–20 (2018)

21. Wang, Y., et al.: Clinical information extraction applications: a literature review. J. Biomed. Inform. 77, 34–49 (2018)

22. Wishart, D.S., et al.: DrugBank 5.0: a major update to the DrugBank database for 2018. Nucleic Acids Res. 46(D1), D1074–D1082 (2017)

23. Wu, Y., Xu, J., Jiang, M., Zhang, Y., Xu, H.: A study of neural word embeddings for named entity recognition in clinical text. In: AMIA Annual Symposium Proceedings, vol. 2015, p. 1326. American Medical Informatics Association (2015)

Frequent Semantic Patterns
for Document Relevance Ranking

Hanh Nguyen[(✉)], Yue Xu, and Yuefeng Li

School of Electrical Engineering and Computer Science,
Queensland University of Technology (QUT), Brisbane, QLD 4001, Australia
trandiemhanh.nguyen@hdr.qut.edu.au, {yue.xu,yuefeng.li}@qut.edu.au
http://www.qut.edu.au

Abstract. Modelling user interest has been a challenge for improving
the performance of information filtering systems (IFs). Currently, there
have been term-based, phrase-based, and pattern-based approaches in
modelling user interest [2,5,13]. Patterns have been said to convey more
specific and relevant information in modelling user's interest [5]. However, the existing patterns such as frequent and closed patterns are all
generated based on their statistical features such as frequency. But their
semantic meaning was ignored. This study proposes a new information
filtering model named as Frequent Semantic Patterns for Document Relevance Ranking, shorted as FSPnIF. In particular, a new type of patterns,
called frequent semantic pattern (FSP), is proposed to represent user's
interest. The patterns are representative as they are generated from the
top highly frequent words in the training corpus. These patterns also
convey semantic meanings because they are verified by meaningful concepts in ontology. A new method to measure document relevance based
on FSPs is also proposed to filter relevant documents in IFs. The model
was evaluated in IFs using RCV1 and R8 datasets. The results of extensive experiments show that the new proposed model significantly outperformed all the state-of-the-art baseline models according to five main
evaluating measures.

Keywords: Topic model · LDA · Information filtering · Pattern
discovery · Ontology

1 Introduction

Information Filtering Systems have two main parts which are user interest modelling based on a collection of the user's documents and filtering irrelevant documents from the new incoming document stream based on the user interest model.
Accurately modeling user interest has always been an crucial part in information
filtering systems because the user interest model is used to determine the rel-
evancy of incoming documents. Currently, many term-based and phrase-based
representations have been proposed such as BM25 and TNG in [12,13]. However,
single terms are said to be polysemy and synonymy while phrase-based methods

© Springer Nature Switzerland AG 2019
J. Liu and J. Bailey (Eds.): AI 2019, LNAI 11919, pp. 418–430, 2019.
https://doi.org/10.1007/978-3-030-35288-2_34

encounter the problem of low occurences in documents. Latent Dirichlet Allocation (LDA) has been successfully used to represent users interest as in [2]. However, single topical words are considered to be polysemy as well. Lately, pattern-based topic models (PBTM) can be utilized to generate patterns for representing users' interest effectively [5]. These patterns are said to be more representative and specific to represent topics than terms or phrases generated by term-based topic models such as LDA and phrase-based topic models such as TNG [1,13]. However, the PBTM approach only focuses on structural combination of topical words to generate patterns but ignores the semantic associations between the words in the patterns. Hence, many patterns are not really meaningful.

Patterns have been used for representing documents for decades. Patterns are generated based on co-occurrences, i.e., frequently co-occurring words are generated as patterns. One limitation of patterns is that the semantic meaning of words are ignored, some of the patterns might not be semantically meaningful. It is obvious that topical words are highly frequent words in the training collection. However, some of the topical words might not be meaningful and thus the patterns which are formed from the topical words might not be meaningful. Take a pattern [dutroux, children] as an example, because the word "dutroux" is meaningless and thus the meaning of [dutroux, children] becomes much less meaningful, even meaningless. Unrelated association between topical words is another limitation of generating patterns based on statistical calculation. Moreover, the longer patterns are said to be more specific in terms of meaning as described in [5]. However, this claim is not always true because there are many long patterns which are actually quite ambiguous and thus does not reveal a specific meaning. Longer patterns are not always better than shorter patterns in terms of specificity and meaningfulness. For instance, the pattern [Britain, hotel, growth, industry, percent] is not better than these two shorter patterns [Britain, hotel] and [industry, growth]. Therefore, mining representative and semantically meaningful patterns to represent user's interest in information filtering is important.

In this paper, we develop a novel approach to discover semantically meaningful and statistically frequent patterns called Frequent Semantic Patterns (FSPs), to represent user's interests and use them for document relevance ranking in information filtering systems. The model is named as "Frequent semantic Patterns for Document Relevance Ranking", shorted as FSPnIF. There are three major steps in the new model. In the first step, a method to generate semantic patterns from a topic model is proposed by mapping topics to concepts in an ontology. Secondly, a method to generate FSPs is proposed. Thirdly, a method to rank the relevance of incoming documents based on the frequent semantic patterns is developed for the filtering part in IFs. In the experimental part, we compare results of the proposed model with the state-of-the-art models in information filtering. We found that our proposed model not only outperformed term-based representations and phrase-based representations such as LDA_Words, PLSA_Words and TNG in [2,6,13] but also outperformed pattern-based representations such as PBTM_FP, PBTM_FCP and MPBTM in [5].

This paper has been divided into five parts. The first section is the introduction part. Section 2 presents related works. The proposed model is concerned in the Sect. 3. Section 4 displays the experimental results. The conclusion part is presented in Sect. 5.

2   Related Works

Information filtering systems comprise of two main parts which are user interest modelling and filtering part. In user interest modelling, some conventional methods based on terms, phrases and patterns were utilized to represent users interest. One of the very first models based on terms was reported in BM25 [12]. However, term based representation conveys polysemy and synonymy. Methods of document representation based on phrases were thought to solve the mentioned problems in term based approach such as in [3,13]. Although phrases are considered to be more specific and representative than single words in document representation, phrases still face the problem of low occurrences. For improving the cabability of document representation based on terms, some new approaches have been proposed. The document modelling methods based on word distributions such as PLSA and LDA in [1,6] provided statistic based methods for modelling user's interest in which topical words with high probabilities are used to represent users interest.

In the latest trend in data mining, a considerable amount of literatures have been published on pattern mining [10,11]. A pattern contains a group of words occurring in modelled documents, conveying specific and semantic meanings about things in real world. PBTM approaches in [5] provides a group of effective methods in mining concise patterns. Although these previous pattern discovery approaches could discover highly significant and representative patterns, the semantic aspects of patterns were not explicitly considered. However, our work consider representative and semantic factors of patterns to determine meaningful patterns which is the main difference between our work and the existing pattern based approaches such as the work in [5].

In the next section, an innovative approach to mine frequent and semantic patterns will be proposed, basing on matching topic model to Library of Congress Subject Headings (LCSH) ontology.

3   The Proposed Model

The aim of this paper is to propose a new approach to discover frequent semantic patterns (FSP) for user interest representation and apply the FSPs to information filtering systems. A FSP pattern comprises of a set of words which occur frequently in the modelled corpus and semantically express things in real world. For instance, the patterns "Application software" and "Software" can be considered as semantic patterns because they are meaningful and semantically express specific subdomains in information technology. In addition, the two patterns are also concepts in LCSH ontology. There are three major steps in generating frequent semantic patterns. In the first step, documents are trained to generate a topic model using LDA. The second step discovers all sematic patterns for topics in the topic model by mapping topics generated in the first step and semantic concepts in LCSH ontology. In the third step, a method is proposed for determining the set of frequent semantic patterns from the semantic patterns discovered in the second step. Document relevance ranking is important for many text mining applications such as information filtering and information retrieval. In this paper, we propose a document relevance ranking method based on the frequent semantic patterns and use it to filter out irrelevant documents to satisfy user interest in information. In brief, the process of frequent semantic pattern generation is displayed in Fig. 1 below and explained in Sects. 3.1, 3.2 and 3.3.

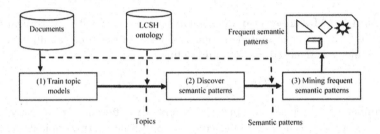

Fig. 1. The process of generating frequent semantic patterns

3.1   Train Topic Models

The process of semantic pattern generation starts by generating topic models from training documents. Topic modelling is a group of algorithms to discover hidden topics in the collection of documents. The basic idea of the technique is to promote high frequent words to represent the topics in the collection. LDA is one of the popularly used techniques for generating hidden topics. Let $D = \{d_1, d_2, ..., d_M\}$ be a collection of M documents. The main idea of LDA is that a document is a multinomial distribution over topics. Each topic is a multinomial distribution over words. At document level, each document is represented by topic distribution $\theta_d = \{V_{d,1}, V_{d,2}, ..., V_{d,v}\}$, $\sum_{j=1}^{v} V_{d,j} = 1$. In the collection level, D is represented by a set of topics. Each topic is represented by a probability distribution over words. For the jth topic, we have $\Phi_j = \{\phi_{j1}, \phi_{j2}, ..., \phi_{jm}\}$, m is the number of words per topic, $\phi_{ji} = P(w_i|z_j)$. Based on the topic model, the probability of word w_i in the document d can be calculated as $P(w_i|d) = \sum_{j=1}^{v} P(w_i|z_j) \times P(z_j|d)$, v is the number of topics. In terms of words, each topic z is represented as a set of words, denoted as $\mathbb{T}(z) = \{w_1, w_2, ..., w_m\}$. After the latent topics are generated by applying LDA, the matched patterns are yielded by mapping the topics and concepts in the ontology. Next section describes the method of generating semantic patterns.

3.2   Semantic Patterns

This section involves how to generate semantic patterns for topic models. The main idea is mapping the topics generated in Sect. 3.1 to concepts in the LCSH ontology for discovering semantic patterns. As mentioned before, concepts in the ontology are semantic phrases generated by human beings such as librarian. For instances, concepts like "Automatic computer" and "univac computer" are meaningful concepts about an electronic equipment. If there is a concept in the ontology, which shares the common information with the examined topic, the concept is called a matched concept. The overlapping part between the concept and that topic is then called a matched pattern or a semantic pattern.

Definition 1 (Ontology): An Ontology can be presented in a tuple $O =<$ $\mathcal{C}, R >$ such that $\mathcal{C}$ is a set of concepts; R is a set of relations.

Definition 2 (Matched concepts): Given a topic z with its topical words denoted as $\mathbb{T}(z)$, a list of matched concepts between the topic z and concepts $\mathcal{C}$ in the ontology is denoted as $\Gamma(z)$ and defined below:

$$\Gamma(z) = \{c|c \in \mathcal{C}, c \cap \mathbb{T}(z) \neq \emptyset\} \tag{1}$$

The number of matched concepts is different for different topics. Normally, a large number of matched concepts contains only one or two topical words, all other words in the concepts are non-topical words. The number of such concepts is much greater than the number of matched concepts which contain more than two topical words. Concepts that contain non-topical words are called partial-matched concepts. There are concepts whose words are all topical words. Those concepts can be classified as full-matched concepts.

Definition 3 (Semantic patterns): The set of semantic patterns of a topic z over matched concepts, denoted as $\mathcal{SP}(z)$, is defined as:

$$\mathcal{SP}(z) = \{p|\forall c \in \Gamma(z), p = c \cap \mathbb{T}(z), p \neq \emptyset\} \tag{2}$$

Each semantic pattern in $\mathcal{SP}(z)$ is the overlapping part between the topic and a matched concept of the topic. Obviously, the minimal length of each pattern is one. If a pattern is the same as a full-matched concept, i.e., $p = c \cap \mathbb{T}(z)$ and $p = c$, that pattern can semantically and strongly explain the topic. In terms of meaning, the shorter patterns convey more general meaning about the things while longer patterns convey more specific meaning about things in real world. In the aspect of topic explanation, a topic can mention about either specific or general meanings. Therefore, both shorter and longer patterns can semantically represent a topic.

3.3   Frequent Semantic Patterns (FSPs)

This section proposes a method to generate frequent semantic patterns for a topic. A frequent semantic pattern is a semantic pattern which consists of topical words and occurs frequently in the training documents. For generating frequent semantic patterns, a transactional dataset is built for each topic of a topic model using the documents in the training collection from which the topic model was built. Then frequent patterns are generated by applying a frequent pattern mining method from the transactional dataset for each topic. A semantic pattern that is frequent according to a pre-specified minimum support is called frequent semantic pattern. In brief, there are two steps to generate the frequent semantic patterns: building transactional dataset for each topic and generating frequent patterns from each transactional dataset.

Transactional Dataset
For a corpus $D = \{d_1, d_2, ..., d_M\}$ and a topic z with its topical words $\mathbb{T}(z)$, a transactional dataset for topic z can be generated based on the topical words in $\mathbb{T}(z)$ and the documents in D. Let $\mathcal{T}^z = \{T_1, T_2, ..., T_M\}$ be the transactional dataset for topic z, each transaction $T_i \in \mathcal{T}^z$ is defined as $T_i = \{w|w \in \mathbb{T}(z), w \in d_i\}$

Example: Given a set of training documents as $D = \{d_1, d_2, d_3, d_4, d_5\}$ over a set of words $Words = \{w_1, w_2, w_3, w_4, w_5, w_6, w_7, w_8, w_9\}$. Assume that there are three possible topics z_1, z_2, and z_3 modelled in D. Then, the transactional datasets called $\mathcal{T}^{z_1}, \mathcal{T}^{z_2}$ and $\mathcal{T}^{z_3}$ for the collection D over the three topics are described as in Table 1 below.

Table 1. Transactional dataset TDS

	z_1	z_2	z_3
T_1	$\{w_1, w_2, w_3\}$	$\{w_1, w_5, w_6\}$	$\{w_1, w_9\}$
T_2	$\{w_3, w_4\}$	$\{w_4, w_5, w_6, w_7\}$	$\{w_6, w_7, w_8\}$
T_3	$\{w_1, w_3\}$	$\{w_2, w_3\}$	$\{w_1, w_9\}$
T_4	$\{w_2, w_3, w_7\}$	$\{w_2, w_3\}$	$\{w_2, w_5\}$
T_5	$\{w_2, w_3, w_4, w_8\}$	$\{w_1, w_2, w_7\}$	$\{w_6, w_8, w_9\}$
TDS	$\mathcal{T}^{z_1}$	$\mathcal{T}^{z_2}$	$\mathcal{T}^{z_3}$

Frequent Semantic Pattern
By applying a frequent pattern mining method such as FP-Growth, for a given minimum support, a set of frequent patterns can be generated from $\mathcal{T}^z$. Let $\mathcal{FP}(z)$ be a set of frequent patterns generated from $\mathcal{T}^z$, the frequent semantic patterns are defined in Definition 4 as below.

Definition 4 (Frequent Semantic Patterns): Given a topic z, let $\mathcal{SP}(z)$ be a set of semantic patterns of z, $\mathcal{FP}(z)$ be a set of frequent patterns of z, the frequent semantic patterns of z is defined as:

$$\mathcal{FSP}(z) = \{p|p \in \mathcal{FP}(z), p \subseteq S, S \in \mathcal{SP}(z)\} \tag{3}$$

3.4   Information Filtering Based on Frequent Semantic Patterns

In this study, the topic model generated from a user document collection is used to represent the user's interest. In the topic model, each topic is represented by the proposed FSPs rather than single topical words as used in LDA. The relevance of an incoming document is assessed based on the significance of topics and topic distribution. The significance of topics in the incoming document is measured based on the significance of the FSPs which represent the topics. In this study, the importance of a pattern is measured based on both its length and the frequency of topical words that make up the pattern. For a new incoming document d, the main idea is to determine the relevance of the document d to the user's interest by aggregating the significances of frequent semantic patterns occurring in d and topic distributions to the training collection.

Let $\mathcal{FSP}(z) = \{p_1, p_2, ..., p_t\}$ be the set of frequent semantic patterns representing the topic z. The significance of a frequent semantic pattern p is calculated by the following formula:

$$sig(p|z) = \left(\frac{1}{|p|} \sum_{i=1, w_i \in p}^{|p|} sig(w_i|z) \right) \times f(p) \times |p|^{0.5} \qquad (4)$$

where $sig(w_i|z)$ is the significance of topical word w_i of topic z, which is defined as $sig(w_i|z) = m_i * P_r(w_i|z), m_i = P_r(w_i|z)/avgP_r(z)$, $P_r(w_i|z)$ is the probability of w_i in topic z. In this study, the topical words with $m_i > 1$ are selected to represent a topic (more detail is given in Sect. 4.3).

This significance of pattern p is measured based on the average of pattern word significance. If the average significance of pattern words w_i is high, the significance of that corresponding pattern is high.

In the filtering stage, let d be a document to be examined and the training corpus is D. We would like to determine whether the document d is relevant to the topic z in the corpus D based on the matched patterns by measuring $sig(z, d)$ as following:

$$sig(z, d) = \sum_{p_t \in \mathcal{FSP}(z), p_t \in d} sig(p_t|z) \qquad (5)$$

Example: Take a topic z_8 in training folder 101 of dataset RCV1 as an example of determining significant patterns for an incoming document d. The topical words of the topic z_8 is listed as:
$z_8 = \{bill, economic, companies, federal, espionage, foreign, house, countries, passed, theft\}$. There are totally 10 FSPs occurring in d. The semantic patterns are listed in Table 2 below.

The pattern $[country, foreign]$ has the same support, 0.571, with the pattern $[country]$ and it also covers the pattern $[country]$. Hence, pattern $[country]$ is not considered as significant pattern while the pattern $[country, foreign]$ is considered as significant pattern. Significant patterns are chosen as: $\{[espionage], [economic, foreign], [company, foreign], [country, foreign], [theft]\}$.

Table 2. List of semantic patterns

Support	Matched patterns
0.857	$[espionage]$
0.571	$[espionage, economic], [country], [country, economic], [economic, foreign],$ $[company], [company, foreign], [theft], [country, foreign], [foreign]$

Document relevance ranking. For a new incoming document d, the relevance score of d over the training collection D with v topics is measured below.

$$rank(d|D) = \sum_{j=1}^{v} sig(z_j, d) \times V_{D,j} \qquad (6)$$

where $V_{D,j}$ is the average topic distribution of all documents in the training collection D, $\theta_D = (V_{D,1}, V_{D,2}, ..., V_{D,v})$, $\sum_{j=1}^{v} V_{D,j} = 1$ and $V_{D,j}$ is calculated as:

$$V_{D,j} = \frac{1}{|D|} \sum_{d \in D} P_r(z_j|d) \qquad (7)$$

4 Experiments

4.1 Dataset

The Library of Congress Subject Headings (LCSH) is available for computer processing as MARC. Concepts in LCSH are meaningful phrases coded by librarians, given another name as subject heading. The subject headings in LCSH have some main relations such as Broader, Narrower, Related, and Variant. In the following experiments, the 498474 topical subject headings in the subject headings database [7] were used as concepts. Two datasets were used in the experiments. The Reuter Corpus Volume 1 (RCV1) dataset [8] was collected by Reuters journals from the year of 1996 to 1997, covering approximately 806,791 documents about various topics. The dataset provides training and testing sets. R8 dataset is a widely used collection for text mining. The data was originally collected and labelled by Carnegie Group, Inc. and Reuters, Ltd. in the course of developing the CONSTRUE text categorization systems [4].

4.2 Baseline Models

The experiments were conducted to evaluate the effectiveness of the proposed model in information filtering against these following baselines. Specifically, there are three groups of document representation methods. The first group comprises of pattern-based representations including MPBTM, PBTM_FCP, and PBTM_FP. Phrase based representation is organized in the second group. Term-based representation methods such as BM25, PLSA_words and LDA_words are organized in the third group.

(1) Pattern based representations

MPBTM [5]: Maximum matched patterns are used to represent users' interest.

PBTM_FP and PBTM_FCP [5]: Frequent patterns and frequent closed patterns generated from LDA topic model are used to represent users' interest.

(2) Phrase based representation

TNG [13]: phrase based topic model, n-grams phrases that are generated by using the TNG model are used to represent users' interest.

(3) Term based representations

BM25 [12]: one state-of-the-art model for representing documents by using terms.

PLSA_Words [6]: topical words in pLSA topic model are used to represent users' interest.

LDA_words [1]: topical words in LDA topic model are used to represent users' interest.

4.3   Experimental Settings

The experiments were conducted to evaluate the effectiveness of ranking documents in document stream based on frequent semantic patterns. For generating topic models, we used MALLET toolkit [9] to train topic models by LDA for the first 50 collections in the RCV1 corpus and 8 collections in dataset R8. The initial parameter settings for LDA are $\alpha = 0.5$; and $\beta = 0.01$. The number of topics is $v = 10$. For different topics, different number of topical words were chosen based on m_i calculated by the probability distribution over words in that topic. The chosen topic words for a topic in our proposed model are words with probabilities higher than the average word probability of that topic. Specifically, the ith topical word in topic z is selected if $P_r(w_i|z) > avgP_r(z)(i.e., m_i > 1)$, where $avgP_r(z)$ is the average word probability in topic z. The minimum support for determining frequent semantic patterns for dataset RCV1 is 0.4 and it is 0.2 for dataset R8.

4.4   Evaluation Measurement

In these experiments, five main evaluation metrics were used to compare performances of the models. The Top-K score evaluates the precision for the first K retrieved documents. In these experiments, Top-10 and Top-20 are used. Mean Average Precision (MAP) measures precision at each relevant document first, and averaging precision over all documents afterwards. MAP metric provides a very succinct summary of the effectiveness of a ranking algorithm. The breakeven point b/p indicates the points where precision and recall are equal. This score measures the effectiveness of the system. The higher this value of b/p, the better the implemented system. $F1$ scores reflect the harmonic average of the precision and recall. $F1$ emphasizes the effectiveness of retrieved documents.

4.5 Results and Discussion

4.5.1 Results

For dataset RCV1, we conducted experiments on our proposed model FSPnIF using different minimum support $\delta = \{0.2, 0.3, 0.4, 0.5\}$ for generating the frequent semantic patterns. $\delta = 0.4$ was chosen based on the experiment results shown in Table 3 where $\delta = 0.4$ leads to the best result. Similar experiments were conducted for dataset R8, $\delta = 0.2$ was chosen for R8 based on the experimental result.

Table 3. Performance of FSPnIF for dataset RCV1

Threshold δ	Top-10	Top-20	B/P	MAP	F1
$\delta = 0.2$	0.584	0.570	0.481	0.504	0.477
$\delta = 0.3$	0.606	0.568	0.483	0.507	0.479
$\delta = 0.4$	0.628	0.573	0.483	0.512	0.481
$\delta = 0.5$	0.640	0.570	0.481	0.509	0.481

Table 4. Performance among methods for dataset RCV1

Methods	Top-10	Top-20	B/P	MAP	F1
FSPnIF	0.628	**0.573**	**0.483**	**0.512**	**0.481**
MPBTM	**0.632**	0.552	0.466	0.477	0.459
PBTM_FCP	0.524	0.489	0.420	0.423	0.422
PBTM_FP	0.522	0.470	0.402	0.427	0.423
%Change	−0.63%	3.80%	3.65%	7.34%	4.79%
TNG	0.468	0.425	0.344	0.354	0.372
%Change	34.19%	34.82%	40.41%	44.63%	29.30%
LDA_Words	0.458	0.433	0.370	0.390	0.401
PLSA_Words	0.444	0.412	0.366	0.371	0.389
BM25	0.348	0.345	0.337	0.330	0.359
%Change	37.12%	32.33%	30.54%	31.28%	19.95%

Comparison with Term-Based Representation. As shown in Table 4, the big improvement was in Top-K score. Obviously, FSPnIF gained 0.628 in Top-10 while the scores of all other term-based methods (i.e., BM25, LDA_words, PLSA_words) were lower than 0.50. This made the improvement changed up to 37.12% against the second best method LDA_words for Top-10 score. Similarly, the change for Top-20 was 32.33% against LDA_words. In Table 5, the change in MAP score between the new model and term-based models was noticable. Specifically, it was 0.701 in FSPnIF while it was 0.432 in LDA_words. This

Table 5. Performance comparison for dataset R8

Methods	Top-10	Top-20	B/P	MAP	F1
FSPnIF	**0.850**	**0.744**	**0.693**	**0.701**	**0.578**
MPBTM	0.750	0.712	0.687	0.676	0.571
PBTM_FCP	0.763	0.719	0.675	0.665	0.567
PBTM_FP	0.763	0.694	0.655	0.668	0.567
%Change	11.40%	3.48%	0.87%	3.70%	1.23%
TNG	0.700	0.619	0.510	0.490	0.455
%Change	21.43%	20.19%	35.88%	43.06%	27.03%
LDA_Words	0.600	0.569	0.462	0.432	0.438
PLSA_Words	0.550	0.550	0.418	0.402	0.372
BM25	0.462	0.412	0.349	0.338	0.347
%Change	41.67%	30.76%	50.00%	62.27%	31.96%

improvement was up to 62.27%. For dataset R8, the Top-10 score in FSPnIF was significantly higher than term-based models, 0.850 in FSPnIF and 0.600 in LDA_words. This improvement gained up to 41.67%.

Comparison with Pattern-Based Representation. As shown in Table 4, the new model FSPnIF performed better than PBTM based models in all five criteria except Top-10 score. The PBTM model was the state-of-the-art model in pattern based representations. In particular, the new model was lower than MPBTM in Top-10 score, which was 0.628 in the new model and 0.632 in MPBTM accordingly. In Top-20 score, the new model achieved 0.573 while it was 0.552 in MPBTM. Similarly, FSPnIF model gained 0.512 in MAP score higher than 0.477 in MPBTM. This made the improvement change 7.34%. For dataset R8, the biggest improvement between the new model and pattern-based model was in Top-10 score. In particular, it was 0.850 in FSPnIF while it was 0.763 in PBTM_FCP. This made the improvement changed up to 11.40%. In MAP score, the new model performed better than all PBTM. Specifically, it was 0.701 in FSPnIF while it was 0.676 in MPBTM.

4.5.2 Discussion

According to the experimental results, it is obvious that the new model FSPnIF performed better than the other models in most of comparison metrics in both datasets RCV1 and R8. The only exception is the Top-10 measure for RCV1, the proposed model is 0.004 less than MPBTM.

In terms of document representations, we can see that FSP patterns can be the best alternative to represent user interest in IFs due to statistical and semantic features of the patterns. Specifically, the patterns are representative as they are generated from the top highly frequent words in the training corpus. These patterns also convey semantic meanings because they are verified by meaningful concepts in the ontology. All of those features contribute to the success of the new model over existing methods based on term, phrase and PBTM representations.

5 Conclusion

In conclusion, this study has proposed a new model named FSPnIF which provides a method of mining FSP patterns from a corpus and how to use them in IFs. For generating FSP, three main steps including topic trainings, semantic pattern generation, and frequent semantic pattern mining, were described in detail. The FSPs were then utilized to represent user's interest in IFs. In the filtering part of IFs, a method of document relevance ranking based on significant FSP patterns was proposed by applying the method to determine significant FSP patterns satisfying user needs in information. The main difference of our model over the existing models in PBTM is that it can discover semantic and representative patterns based on meaningful phrases from knowledge resources. Finally, we apply the proposed model to one of the challenges in information filtering: discovering meaningful and semantic patterns to represent user interest. The experiments were conducted over two large benchmark datasets RCV1 and R8. Experimental results showed that FSPnIF outperformed the existing baseline models. In short, FSPnIF demonstrates a promising methodology to enhance performances of IFs.

References

1. Blei, D.M.: Probabilistic topic models. Commun. ACM **55**(4), 77 (2012). https://doi.org/10.1145/2133806.2133826
2. Blei, D.M., Ng, A.Y., Jordan, M.I.: Latent Dirichlet allocation. J. Mach. Learn. Res. **3**, 993–1022 (2003)
3. Cavnar, W.B., Trenkle, J.M.: N gram based text categorization. Ann Arbor MI **48113**(2), 161–175 (1994)
4. Debole, F., Sebastiani, F.: An analysis of the relative hardness of reuters 21578 subsets. J. Am. Soc. Inform. Sci. Technol. **56**(6), 584–596 (2005)
5. Gao, Y., Xu, Y., Li, Y.: Pattern-based topics for document modelling in information filtering. IEEE Trans. Knowl. Data Eng. **27**(6), 1629–1642 (2015)
6. Hofmann, T.: Probabilistic latent semantic indexing. In: ACM SIGIR Forum, vol. 51, pp. 211–218. ACM (2017)
7. LCSH: Library of congress (2017). https://www.loc.gov/
8. Lewis, D.D., Yang, Y., Rose, T.G., Li, F.: RCV1: a new benchmark collection for text categorization research. J. Mach. Learn. Res. **5**(Apr), 361–397 (2004)
9. McCallum, A.K.: Mallet: a machine learning for language toolkit (2002). http://mallet.cs.umass.edu
10. Pasquier, N., Bastide, Y., Taouil, R., Lakhal, L.: Discovering frequent closed itemsets for association rules. In: Beeri, C., Buneman, P. (eds.) ICDT 1999. LNCS, vol. 1540, pp. 398–416. Springer, Heidelberg (1999). https://doi.org/10.1007/3-540-49257-7_25
11. Roberto, J., Bayardo, J.: Efficiently mining long patterns from databases. SIGMOD Rec. **27**(2), 85–93 (1998). https://doi.org/10.1145/276305.276313

12. Robertson, S., Zaragoza, H., Taylor, M.: Simple BM25 extension to multiple weighted fields. In: Proceedings of the Thirteenth ACM International Conference on Information and Knowledge Management, pp. 42–49. ACM (2004)

13. Wang, X., McCallum, A., Wei, X.: Topical n-grams: phrase and topic discovery, with an application to information retrieval. In: Seventh IEEE International Conference on Data Mining (ICDM 2007), pp. 697–702 (2007). https://doi.org/10.1109/ICDM.2007.86

Optimization and Evolutionary Computing

Optimising Pump Scheduling for Water Distribution Networks

Yanchang Zhao[1]([⊠]), Bin Liang[2], Yang Wang[2], Shaobo Dang[4], Ronnie Taib[4],
Fang Chen[2], Tin Hua[3], Dammika Vitanage[3], and Corinna Doolan[3]

[1] Data61, CSIRO, Canberra, Australia
yanchang.zhao@data61.csiro.au
[2] University of Technology, Sydney, Australia
{bin.liang,yang.wang,fang.chen}@uts.edu.au
[3] Sydney Water Corporation, Sydney, Australia
{tin.hua,dammika.vitanage,corinna.doolan}@sydneywater.com.au
[4] Data61, CSIRO, Sydney, Australia
{shaobo.dang,ronnie.taib}@data61.csiro.au

Abstract. Energy costs can be a major component of operational costs for water utilities. Operational efficiencies including optimising energy costs while maintaining continuity of supply is one area to reduce overall operational costs. To address the challenge, we have proposed an effective optimisation model to minimise the energy cost for water distribution networks. A simulation of the model over a water distribution network in Sydney demonstrated that 15% saving in energy cost could be achieved using this approach, as compared with the existing rule-based method.

Keywords: Optimisation · Pump scheduling · Water distribution networks

1 Introduction

Water utilities supply potable water to customers via a distribution network consisting of reservoirs, pumping stations, control valves and a network of pipes. An example is the Woronora Delivery system in Sydney, Australia, which includes 13 reservoirs sites and supplies on average 80 ML (in summer months) of water per day to approximately 210,000 customers in 30 separate zones. Under normal operating conditions, the majority of raw water is supplied from the Woronora Dam. Within this network, water coming from the dam is filtered and disinfected at the water filtration plant before it travels in the trunk water mains via pumps and valves to the reservoirs and into the reticulation networks to the end users - the customers.

A sub-system of the above water delivery system is shown in Fig. 1, which includes six major sites, two pump stations and four valves. The other sites (shown as cloud) are not included in optimisation, due to data unavailability or incompleteness. However, water flows to those sites, denoted as f_7 to f_{10}, are

© Springer Nature Switzerland AG 2019
J. Liu and J. Bailey (Eds.): AI 2019, LNAI 11919, pp. 433–444, 2019.
https://doi.org/10.1007/978-3-030-35288-2_35

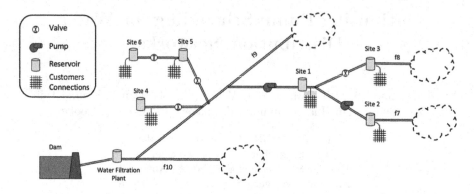

Fig. 1. A water distribution network

included when calculating water demand. Moreover, the methodology used in this work can be easily extended to those sites when data become available.

Energy charges are calculated based on time of use. There are three distinct energy tariff periods, peak hours (2pm–8pm on working weekdays), shoulder hours (7am–2pm and 8pm–10pm on working weekdays) and off-peak hours (all other times). Peak hours are charged with the highest rate and off-peak the least. Moreover, there is a network capacity charge, calculated based on the maximum half-hourly consumption that occur in the peak hours in the last 12 months. Therefore, to reduce energy costs, it is very important to minimise peak-hour and shoulder-hour power consumption, especially during peak hours.

It is critical for water utilities to provide continuous water to customers. However, it is challenging for water utilities to minimise operational costs while guaranteeing the continuity of water supply. Reservoirs should be able to supply enough water for downstream reservoirs and user demand at all times, including peak demand. However, too much water in reservoirs can result in longer water retention time and decreased water quality. In addition, excessive pumping during peak-hours and shoulder-hours will incur higher energy costs. Out of the operational expenditure, pump energy cost can be a major component. For example, the pump energy cost of the above system accounts for 66% of its total operational expenditure [11].

To address this challenge, we have investigated the relationship between water demands, reservoirs, pumping stations and control valves and have proposed a framework for energy saving optimisation, which guarantees the continuity of water supply, minimises energy cost and provides quality water to the customers. At first, a Bayesian probabilistic model was developed to forecast water demand based on historical demand and weather information, which generates a prediction for what the short term (24 to 36 h) future water demand would be. Based on water demand forecasts, an energy saving optimisation model was developed to optimise pump and valve operating schedules, so that water demand is met, reservoir operating window (i.e., lower and upper bounds of reservoir water levels) constraints are satisfied and energy costs are minimised. A simulation over 3 months demonstrated that the proposed method could achieve a saving of 15% in energy cost, compared with the existing rule-based approach.

2   Related Work

There have been several studies on pumping schedule optimisation for water distribution networks and some work on power supply network optimisation, which are relevant to this work. Waterworth et al. [10] compared three methods, dynamic programming, simulated annealing and genetic algorithms, for pump scheduling, but they only applied it to a single reservoir with fixed-speed pumps, used average historic water demand rather than demand forecast and did not consider peak electricity tariff. Moreover, they didn't compare the optimised scheduling or cost against the actual ones.

Kurian et al. [4] proposed a method with linear programming for optimal scheduling of rural water supply schemes, but their work targeted intermittent supply for rural areas to maximise the water delivered to villages in an equitable manner, rather than continuous supply for urban networks.

Castro-Gama et al. [1] proposed a multi-objective optimisation for energy consumption reduction of the water distribution network in Milan, Italy. In their work, the objective functions included Total Energy and Lack of Resilience, an EPANET model was used as hydraulic simulator to estimate the pressures and flows and a genetic algorithm was used to find the optimal solution. Their results showed that the cost saving for the network could be of up to 26%.

Napolitano et al. [6] also studied the problem of pumping schedule optimisation and developed a model to identify optimal decision rules by balancing the risk of water shortages and the cost of pumping stations operating and maintenance. Through scenario analysis, mixed integer programming and quadratic formulation, their developed model could provide the management authority with optimal decision rules, which are reservoirs threshold levels for pumping stations activation.

Another area related to this work is power supply networks, where storage during off-peak hours can be used to meet high demand and save cost during peak hours [2,9]. Garg et al. [2] studied the problem of energy storage management optimisation given short-term predications of demand, prices and renewable power availability and proposed an optimisation algorithm to address online resource allocation problems in terms of Markov Decision Processes with dynamic temporal uncertainty caused by short-term predictions. The method is limited to a single battery, rather than a network of multiple batteries, which cannot work for the optimisation of multiple interconnected reservoirs.

Urgaonkar et al. [9] designed an algorithm for optimally exploiting uninterrupted power supply (UPS) units and delay-tolerance of workloads to minimise the time average cost for data centres. The idea was to store energy within UPS units at a data centre when prices were low and use this to augment the draw from the utility when prices were high. They addressed the above problem with Laypunov optimisation, which enables the design of online control algorithms for time-varying systems.

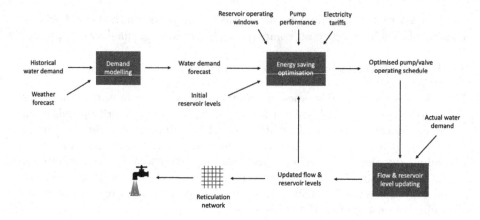

Fig. 2. Energy saving optimisation

To summarise, the problem of optimising pump and valve operations in water supply networks remains unsolved. There is a pressing need for investigating energy saving methodologies for urban water supply networks to meet with the requirements of continuity based on accurate demand forecast.

3   Methodology

Figure 2 shows our proposed framework for energy saving optimisation. At first, historical water demand and weather data are modelled to forecast water demand in the next 24 h. Then demand forecast, together with initial reservoir water levels, operating windows, pump performance and electricity tariffs, are fed into an energy saving optimisation model to produce an optimised pump and valve operating schedule, with which energy cost is minimised.

3.1   Water Demand Forecasting

A prerequisite for optimising network operations, pumping schedules and reducing energy costs is accurately forecasting systems demands within different parts of the network. Water demand forecasting combines with operational data and weather information and generates a prediction of short-term (24 to 36 h) future water demand. Specifically, factor analysis was firstly performed to identify important correlating factors, i.e., past flow, past and forecasted rainfall, past and forecasted temperatures, and a weekday/weekend flag. A Bayesian probabilistic model was then employed to capture forecast uncertainty. Our experimental results demonstrate that the forecasting has a Mean Absolute Percentage Error (MAPE) of around 5%, as compared with the ground truth of historical data. The model can provide operational planners with accurate forecasts of water demand over operational windows, allowing more informed and timely trunk water operational decisions to be made. Details of demand forecasting can be found in our technical report [5].

3.2   Pump Scheduling Optimisation

Based on above water demand forecast, we built a model for optimisation of pump and valve scheduling. The optimisation problem is, given a water distribution network, its initial reservoir water levels and 24-hour water demand forecast, to optimise pump and valve operating schedule, so that continuity of supply is guaranteed and energy cost is reduced. That is,

$$\min \sum_i \sum_t \text{Cost}_i(t),$$

subject to

- water demand satisfaction (see Sect. 4.1),
- reservoir operating windows (see Sect. 4.2),
- pump and valve settings (see Sect. 4.3), and
- other business constraints (see Sect. 4.4),

where $i = 1, 2, 3...$ are site IDs and t denotes time (hour).

$$(1)$$

Note that the number of pumps and their power consumption vary from site to site and the electricity tariff rate is dependent on time of use. The energy cost at site i in hour t can be calculated as

$$\text{Cost}_i(t) = n_i(t)e_i(t)r_i(t), \tag{2}$$

where

- $n_i(t)$ is number of pumps running at site i in hour t,
- $e_i(t)$ is power consumption per pump at site i in hour t, and
- $r_i(t)$ is electricity tariff rate for site i in hour t.

Our experimental results show that, if minimising the above cost function alone, reservoir levels would become close to lower bound at 7am next day, because the optimisation runs daily and only the cost for 24 h is taken into consideration. To minimise the cost for the following days, a penalty function is defined as below make sure that reservoir levels at 7am next day would be close to the upper bound.

$$\text{Penalty} := \sum_i \sum_t b_i(t)v_i(t) \tag{3}$$

where

- $v_i(t)$ is water level of reservoir i at end of hour t, and
- $b_i(t)$ is penalty coefficient and $b_i(t) \leq 0$.

The objective function is finally defined as the sum of above energy cost and penalty.

$$\text{Obj} := \text{Cost} + \text{Penalty} \tag{4}$$

The aim of optimisation is to minimise the above objective function while satisfying all the four types of constraints given in Eq. 1.

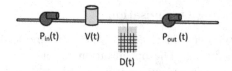

Fig. 3. A single-site model

3.3   A Single-Site Model

To guarantee the continuity of water supply, we use a single-site model (see Fig. 3) to work out the relationship between reservoir water level, pump operation and water demand. Their relationship can be formulated as

$$V(t) = V(t-1) + P_{in}(t) - D(t) - P_{out}(t), \tag{5}$$

where t is time, $V(t)$ is the reservoir water volume of a site, $P_{in}(t)$ is the amount of water loaded through its incoming pumps (or valves), $P_{out}(t)$ is the amount of water flow through pumps (or valves) to downstream sites and $D(t)$ is the water consumption of the reticulation network supplied by the site.

3.4   Extending to Multiple Sites

When there are multiple sites, Eq. 5 can be rewritten as

$$v_i(t) = v_i(t-1) + p_i(t) - d_i(t) - \sum_j \theta_{i,j} p_j(t), \tag{6}$$

where

- $t = 1, 2, ..., 24$ are 24 h, which stand for 7–8am, 8–9am, ... and 6–7am (on the next day),
- $v_i(t)$ is water volume at the end of hour t at site (i.e., reservoir) i, e.g., $v_i(0)$ and $v_i(24)$ are respectively water volume of site i at 7am on a given day and the next day,
- $p_i(t)$ is volume of water flow through pumping station or valve i during hour t,
- $d_i(t)$ is hourly internal water demand (in ML) on site i (excl. water flows to downstream sites) during hour t,
- j is pumping stations or valves that draw water from site i,
- $\theta_{i,j}$ is
    - +1, if pump or valve j draws water from site i,
    - −1, if pump or valve j loads water into site i,
    - 0, if pump or valve j is not connected with site i,

subject to

- reservoir operating windows: $v_i^L \leq v_i(t) \leq v_i^U$, where v_i^L and v_i^U are respectively lower and upper bounds of water level in reservoir i,

– $p_i(t) = \alpha_i(t)n_i(t)$,
– $\alpha_i(t)$: volume of water flow per running pump through pumping station i (or opened valve i) during hour t, and
– $n_i(t)$: number of pumps running at pumping station (or valve) i during hour t.

4 Energy Saving Optimisation for the Woronora Water Distribution Network

In this section, we apply the above generic model to the Woronora network. Specifically, four types of constraints are built according to its network topology and physical settings.

4.1 Constraint I: Water Supply Continuity

This set of constraints define the relationship between reservoir water levels, water flow through pumps and valves, and water demand both from reticulation networks and downstream sites. From Eq. 6 and the Woronora network topology shown in Fig. 1, we can get

$$
\begin{aligned}
v_1(t) &= v_1(t-1) + p_1(t) - d_1(t) - p_2(t) - p_3(t) \\
v_2(t) &= v_2(t-1) + p_2(t) - d_2(t) - f_7(t) \\
v_3(t) &= v_3(t-1) + p_3(t) - d_3(t) - f_8(t) \\
v_4(t) &= v_4(t-1) + p_4(t) - d_4(t) \\
v_5(t) &= v_5(t-1) + p_5(t) - d_5(t) - p_6(t) \\
v_6(t) &= v_6(t-1) + p_6(t) - d_6(t)
\end{aligned}
\tag{7}
$$

where $f_7(t)$ and $f_8(t)$ are water flows to downstream reservoirs from sites 2 and 3, respectively.

The above can be rewritten as

$$
\begin{aligned}
p_1(t) - p_2(t) - p_3(t) + v_1(t-1) - v_1(t) &= d_1(t) \\
p_2(t) + v_2(t-1) - v_2(t) &= d_2(t) + f_7(t) \\
p_3(t) + v_3(t-1) - v_3(t) &= d_3(t) + f_8(t) \\
p_4(t) + v_4(t-1) - v_4(t) &= d_4(t) \\
p_5(t) - p_6(t) + v_5(t-1) - v_5(t) &= d_5(t) \\
p_6(t) + v_6(t-1) - v_6(t) &= d_6(t)
\end{aligned}
\tag{8}
$$

or in short,

$$
AP + BV = D,
\tag{9}
$$

where

- $P = \{p_i(t)\}, i = 1..6, t = 1..24$ and $p_i(t)$ is the volume of water pumped by pumping station (or valve) i during hour t,
- $V = \{v_i(t)\}, i = 1..6, t = 0..24$ and $v_i(t)$ is the volume of water in reservoir i at the end of hour t,
- $D = \{d_i(t)\}, i = 1..6, t = 1..24$ and $d_i(t)$ is the volume of water demand in zone i during hour t,
- A and B are coefficient matrices as above.

4.2 Constraint II: Reservoir Operating Windows

There is a business requirement that reservoirs have to operate within certain water levels. For the Woronora water supply system, the reservoir operating windows are

- $v_1(t) \in [61\%, 94\%] \times 18.3 \, \text{ML}$,
- $v_2(t) \in [50\%, 70\%] \times 14 \, \text{ML}$,
- $v_3(t) \in [76\%, 89\%] \times 9.7 \, \text{ML}$,
- $v_4(t) \in [72\%, 85\%] \times 6.9 \, \text{ML}$,
- $v_5(t) \in [40\%, 50\%] \times 25 \, \text{ML}$, and
- $v_6(t) \in [80\%, 85\%] \times 4.5 \, \text{ML}$,

where, for each site, the percentages in brackets are respectively lower and upper bounds of reservoir water levels and the last number ending with "ML" is the capacity of reservoir. Generally speaking, the wider are the operating windows, the more the energy cost can be reduced and the less frequent will be the start and stop of pumps/valves, which was evidenced by our simulation results (not included in this paper due to limit of space).

4.3 Constraint III: Pump and Valve Settings

In the Woronora network shown in Fig. 1, p_1 and p_2 are two pumping stations, with each having three pumps, and at any time, zero, one, two or all there pumps might be running independently. $p_3, ..., p_6$ are valves and their status are either fully open or closed. Therefore, the range of $n_i(t)$, the number of running pumps (or open valves) at site i during hour t, is

- $0 \leq n_i(t) \leq 3$, when $i \in \{1, 2\}$, and
- $0 \leq n_i(t) \leq 1$, when $i \in \{3, 4, 5, 6\}$.

Note that above constraint are specific for the network in Fig. 1. They need to be adjusted based on the specific network topology if the optimisation model is to be applied to other networks.

4.4   Constraint IV: Minimum Daily Water Flow

There is another business requirement that the daily flow from the Woronora water filtration plant should be no less than 12 ML, that is,

$$\sum_{t=1..24} p_1(t) + p_4(t) + p_5(t) + f_9(t) + f_{10}(t) \geq 12, \tag{10}$$

where f_9 and f_{10} are water flows from the Woronora pipeline to two other water distribution sub-systems (see Fig. 1).

4.5   Implementation

The proposed model is expected to run at 7am every day and, within a few minutes, to produce the optimised pump and valve scheduling for the next 24 h. To build an efficient model, we have chosen linear programming, which is much faster than non-linear programming. The optimisation is implemented with the *symphony* library [8], an open-source mixed-integer linear programming (MILP) solver using branch-and-bound and branch-and-cut methods. The modelling and all above constraints in this work are implemented with R [7] and the *lpsymphony* package [3].

5   Simulation and Results

To validate the effectiveness of optimisation, we ran a simulation over three months from 1 December 2016 to 28 February 2017 to generate optimised pump schedules based on demand forecast and then applied it to the network with actual water demand. The optimised results are compared with the baseline, i.e., the energy cost when business-rule based approach was applied. The above three months are selected because they are high demand seasons and complete data are available for those months. Below is the simulation process, which is also illustrated in Fig. 2.

1. Optimisation for a day. Water demand forecast are fed into the model to find optimised pump and valve operating schedules for the next 24 h starting at 7am.
2. Simulation for the day. Simulate what would have happened if the optimised schedules were applied and actual water demand was extracted from reservoirs.
3. Go to the first step to run optimisation for the next day, until all days within above timeframe have been simulated.

The above process reiterates every day for three months and then the results are compared with actual pump and valve schedules and energy cost. The simulation shows that the method is very quick, taking on average 1.7 s for optimising all six sites for every 24 h, which satisfies business needs.

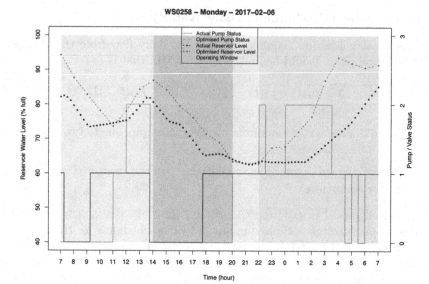

Fig. 4. Optimisation result

Figure 4 shows the optimisation result for the Engadine site on 6 Feb 2017, where the red and blue solid lines show history and optimised pumping schedules, the red and blue dotted lines show history and optimised reservoir levels, and the grey dotted lines show lower and upper bounds of reservoir levels. Please note that the simulation started with the actual reservoir levels at 7am 1 Dec 2016. With the optimised schedule, before 7am of every day, reservoirs are filled with water close to their upper bounds, so that pumping during the following shoulder and peak hours can be reduced. Before 2pm, water is again pumped into reservoirs to ensure that no or little pumping is needed during the following peak hours. The figure clearly shows that peak hour pumping is reduced, with an increase in off-peak-hour pumping.

Comparisons of energy consumption and cost are given in Figs. 5, 6 and 7, where the grey bars (labelled with "Actual") are results of the baseline model with existing business rules and the light-blue bars (labelled with "Optimised") are results of our optimised model. Figures 5 and 6 show energy consumption of two pumping stations during the three months, which demonstrated that pumping during peak and shoulder hours are significantly reduced. Based on electricity consumption, energy cost were calculated and compared against the cost with existing business rules in the three months, which shows that around 15% of energy cost can be saved with our optimisation model (see Fig. 7).

We also studied the impact on water by the optimised pumping schedule (see Fig. 8), which shows that most reservoirs would have better water quality with the optimised pumping schedule. An exception is site 4 and a likely reason is that the reservoir often operated below lower bound in the past and

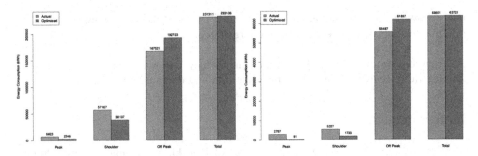

Fig. 5. Energy consumption of site 1 (Color figure online)

Fig. 6. Energy consumption of site 2 (Color figure online)

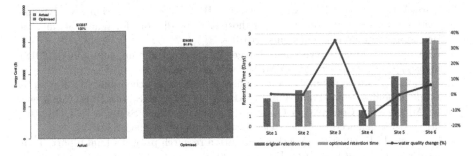

Fig. 7. Total energy cost of all sites (Color figure online)

Fig. 8. Impact on water quality

therefore its reservoir retention time was shorter than that with the optimised pumping schedule. This water quality can be improved with a chemical dosing optimisation model, whose details can be found in our technical report [5].

6 Conclusions

To address the challenge of minimising energy costs while guaranteeing the continuity of water supply in water distribution networks, we have proposed a framework for water supply optimisation and developed an optimisation model for energy saving. Our model has been applied to the Woronora water network in Sydney, Australia and a simulation over three months demonstrated that the model was effective in minimising pumping during peak and shoulder hours and resulted in considerable reduction in energy costs while meeting water demand. The simulation results demonstrated that 15% saving could be achieved with our model.

Future work to extend this research includes running the simulation over a longer period, for example a whole year to cover all seasonal changes, to further validate the impact on network capacity charge, further reducing the likelihood of peak-hour pumping by loading more water into the reservoirs (than forecasted demand) before 2pm, which would be a trade-off between water quality and energy saving, and reducing the number of times of starting/closing pumps and opening/closing valves, especially for large sites.

Acknowledgement. We'd like to thank the Sydney Water Corporation for partially funding this research and also for providing data and domain knowledge.

References

1. Castro-Gama, M., Pan, Q., Lanfranchi, E.A., Jonoski, A., Solomatine, D.P.: Pump-scheduling for a large water distribution network. Proc. Eng. **186**, 436–443 (2017). XVIII International Conference on WaterDistribution Systems, WDSA2016, Milan, Italy
2. Garg, V.K., Jayram, T.S., Narayanaswamy, B.: Online optimization with dynamic temporal uncertainty: incorporating short term predictions for renewable integration in intelligent energy systems (2013)
3. Kim, V.: lpsymphony: symphony integer linear programming solver in R (2018). https://projects.coin-or.org/SYMPHONY
4. Kurian, V., Narasimhan, S., Narasimhan, S.: Optimal scheduling of rural water supply schemes. IFAC-PapersOnLine **51**(1), 142–147 (2018). 5th IFAC Conference on Advances in Control and Optimization of Dynamical Systems ACODS 2018. http://www.sciencedirect.com/science/article/pii/S2405896318301848
5. Li, Z., et al.: Intelligent network optimisation research project - final report. Technical report, Data61, CSIRO, December 2018
6. Napolitano, J., Sechi, G., Zuddas, P.: Scenario analysis for optimization of pumping schedules in complex water supply systems considering a cost-risk balancing problem. Proc. Eng. **89**, 565–572 (2014). https://doi.org/10.1016/j.proeng.2014.11.479
7. R Core Team: R: a language and environment for statistical computing. R Foundation for Statistical Computing, Vienna, Austria (2017). https://www.R-project.org/
8. Ralphs, T., Mahajan, A., Vigerske, S., mgalati13, jpfasano, Bulut, A., anhhz: coin-or/SYMPHONY: version 5.6.16 January 2017. https://doi.org/10.5281/zenodo.248734
9. Urgaonkar, R., Urgaonkar, B., Neely, M.J., Sivasubramaniam, A.: Optimal power cost management using stored energy in data centers. In: Proceedings of the ACM SIGMETRICS Joint International Conference on Measurement and Modeling of Computer Systems, SIGMETRICS 2011, pp. 221–232. ACM, New York (2011). https://doi.org/10.1145/1993744.1993766
10. Waterworth, G., Darbyshire, K.: Comparison of methods of pump scheduling in water supply systems. In: The European Simulation and Modelling Conference, ESM2001, ENGIN-28, June 2001. http://eprints.leedsbeckett.ac.uk/775/
11. Zhao, Y., et al.: An application of energy saving optimisation to water distribution networks. In: OzWater 2019, 7–9 May 2019, Melbourne. Australian Water Association, May 2019

Towards Robust Web Service Composition with Stochastic Service Failures Based on a Genetic Algorithm

Chen Wang[1(✉)], Hui Ma[1(✉)], Gang Chen[1(✉)], and Sven Hartmann[2(✉)]

[1] School of Engineering and Computer Science, Victoria University of Wellington, Wellington, New Zealand
{chen.wang,hui.ma,aaron.chen}@ecs.vuw.ac.nz
[2] Department of Informatics, Clausthal University of Technology, Clausthal-Zellerfeld, Germany
sven.hartmann@tu-clausthal.de

Abstract. Web service composition aims to loosely couple web services to accommodate complex goals, which can not be accomplished by any existing web service. Many researchers have been working on such service composition problems with the aim to find composite services with optimized Quality of Service (QoS) and/or Quality of Semantic Matchmaking (QoSM). Due to the huge search space of this NP-hard problem, Evolutionary Computation techniques have been popularly utilized to search for solutions with near-optimal QoS and QoSM. A majority of these works share a common assumption that QoS of web services seldom or never changes. However, the execution of composite services obtained from the design stage may fail due to unexpected service failures at the execution stage. In this paper, we introduce a robust service composition approach with the goal to build robust composite services that serve as the blueprint/baseline for service execution. These baseline composite services can cope with unexpected interruptions in a robust manner, by applying local search to resume their feasibility while maintaining high quality at the time of execution. Our experiments show that our new approach can significantly outperform a state-of-the-art service composition method (without explicitly considering the robustness) in terms of both effectiveness and efficiency in the event of unexpected service failures.

Keywords: Service composition · QoS optimization · Robust optimization

1 Introduction

Web service composition aims to build a composite service made up of many loosely coupled elementary web services to accommodate more sophisticated users' requirements [13]. This research field has attracted much attention. Many

© Springer Nature Switzerland AG 2019
J. Liu and J. Bailey (Eds.): AI 2019, LNAI 11919, pp. 445–459, 2019.
https://doi.org/10.1007/978-3-030-35288-2_36

works focus on *fully automated service composition* that automatically constructs service workflows supported by carefully selected services to fulfill given functional and non-functional requirements, i.e., *Quality of Semantic Matchmaking* (QoSM) and *Quality of service* (QoS) [13]. In particular, the practical importance of using Evolutionary Computation (EC) techniques to optimize QoS and QoSM of the evolved composite services has been established. Almost all existing works [4,14,19,21–23,26] share the common assumption that the QoS of the elementary web services remains stable. However, such a rigid assumption on the service operating environment is not always satisfied [28].

In the real world, QoS of services are changing dynamically, due to various reasons, e.g., network failures. On the other hand, static data on QoS parameters (such as response time, throughput, failure probability, availability, price and popularity [5]) published by service providers is widely used to match the needs of service requesters. However, this can be very risky because no service provider can guarantee the advertised QoS under all circumstances. Services can fail unexpectedly, causing unforeseeable interruptions to a composite service discovered at the design stage. In fact, a composite service may suffer from various changes. Stochastic service failures constitute the most critical uncertainty because the composite service can become completely useless when any component service fails. For this reason, stochastic service failures are the central focus of this paper.

To design composite services, we must take potential service failures into account to avoid abandoning an ongoing composite service completely. Some existing works [3,12,25] propose to use re-optimization techniques at the service execution stage. Particularly, the frequency of re-optimization is scheduled to cope with changes of the composition environment that are assumed to happen periodically (e.g., every few generations [25] or every time period [3,12]). These re-optimization techniques can also be used to handle stochastic service failures. In fact, [2,10] recommends proactive use of re-optimization techniques in response to anticipated future changes based on historical data.

While re-optimization techniques can help to some extent, these approaches ignore the importance of building robust composite services at the design stage. Moreover, the assumption of periodical changes or sufficient historical QoS data poses noticeable feasibility challenges. In reality, services often fail sporadically in a highly unpredictable manner. Meanwhile, newly registered services may not have sufficient historical QoS data. To address these limitations, we propose a robust service composition approach that consists of two stages, namely, the design stage and the execution stage. In the design stage, our approach constructs baseline composite services by explicitly considering stochastic service failures. At the execution stage, the baseline composite services can cope with unexpected service interruptions in a robust manner with an efficient and effective local search to resume the high quality of the composite services. Genetic Algorithms (GA) are a popular EC technique that has enabled the tackling of several challenging service composition problems [18,19]. Therefore, we will propose a novel GA-based algorithm to generate robust baseline services in this paper.

The overall goal of this paper is to *propose a novel GA-based approach to robust web service composition that can deal with stochastic service failures*, where robust baseline composite services are constructed at the design stage, and can effectively and robustly handle unexpected service interruptions at the execution stage. Driven by this goal, we strive to achieve the following objectives in this paper:

1. We introduce the new model of robust service composition for handling stochastic service failures. Particularly, the robustness of composite services in terms of expected QoS and QoSM is optimized in the event of stochastic service failures. Therefore, optimized composite services can be repaired with an efficient local search technique so that they can be continuously executed with good performance.
2. We introduce two key techniques that jointly form an effective method for searching robust composite services in GA. The first technique is to adopt the Monte Carlo sampling technique [15] to effectively and accurately approximate the robustness of any given composite services. The second technique introduced is an efficient re-optimization technique (i.e., local search) that effectively repairs composite services in response to arbitrary service failures.
3. We conduct experiments to explore the performance of our GA-based approach to robust service composition (henceforth referred to as GA4Robust) and a state-of-the-art GA-based approach (i.e., Fixed Length GA in [19], henceforth referred to as GA) that achieves outstanding performance in finding high-quality solutions. Our experimental results show that GA4Robust can produce baseline composite services with significantly higher robustness. In particular, in the event of service failures at the execution stage, these baselines can continue to work reliably or be easily repaired with negligible impact on quality through fast local search.

2   Related Work

EC techniques have been used to automatically generate composite services with optimized QoS and/or QoSM [4,14,19,21–23,26]. These works can be divided into two groups, namely, static service composition and dynamic web service composition, based on whether QoS for any/all services changes over time or not.

Static service composition is based on the assumption that QoS of web services seldom changes or does not change at all. These works mainly focus on using EC as effective global searching techniques to effectively build composite services with optimized QoS or QoSM. To achieve that, they introduce new and effective representations to encode composite services either directly or indirectly and develop domain-dependent genetic operators to explore large search spaces efficiently. For example, da Silva et al. [16] proposed to represent composite services as DAGs, and developed DAG-based genetic operators to evolve DAGs directly, ensuring the functional correctness of every newly produced DAGs. Some works represent composite services as trees [11,14,17,22,27]. Particularly, different forms of the tree have been proposed to investigate the effectiveness of the tree-based representations. Other works [19,21,23] show strong favor of indirect representations (i.e., a queue of service indexes) for representing composite services. Those indirect representations often reply on some decoding methods that map the indirect representations to service execution workflows. They produce new candidate solutions through the use of "swap"-based genetic operators on the selected parent individuals [19] or sampling techniques based on learned distributions of promising solutions [23].

Dynamic web service composition does not rely on the assumption of static QoS and instead aims to address new problems caused by the changes in QoS. Some works [3,12,25] assume that QoS changes periodically. The re-optimization of composite services is performed after every fixed period of time [3,12,25]. This assumption is the victim of idealization. In reality, this is due to that changes can happen at any time. To ensure the performance of composite services, they need to be re-optimized at running time when QoSs change dramatically or fail. Some recent works [2,10] consider changes of QoS that follow some historical pattern and can be predicted in the future. Unfortunately, these works require sufficient historical data that are not always available for newly registered web services and is not accurate enough. Interesting ideas have also been explored to prevent service failures through distributed service deployment [6,20]. For example, [20] studied the benefits of deploying a sufficient number of distributed service instances for each component service. These works are related but clearly targeted to address a different problem from our paper. In addition, comparing with other existing works [3,12,25] on dynamic service composition, our proposed GA4Robust can handle service sudden failures effectively during running time. Also, our approach does not need to rely on historical data as in [2,10].

3   The Robust Web Service Composition Problem

A *service repository* $\mathcal{SR}$ is a finite collection of services, each service is considered as a tuple $S = (I_S, O_S, QoS_S)$, where I_S is a set of service inputs that are consumed by S, O_S is a set of service outputs that are produced by S, and $QoS_S = \{t_S, c_S, r_S, a_S, pr_S\}$ refer to the response time, cost, reliability, availability, *service failure probability* of S.

In practical service composition, the execution of a composite service is usually confronted with stochastic service failures [5]. A *service failure probability* pr_S can be approximated by dividing the number of failed invocations by the total number of invocations conducted in the past on service S [28]. Also, pr_S of newly published web services can be estimated as the pr_S of web services hosted by the same service providers in the same location. Moreover, for any service in the service repository, its failure probability is assumed to be independent of each other.

A *composition task* from service requestors (also called *service request*) over a given $\mathcal{SR}$ is a tuple $T = (I_T, O_T)$ where I_T is a set of task inputs, and O_T is a set of task outputs. The inputs in I_T and outputs in O_T are parameters that are semantically described by concepts in the ontology $\mathcal{O}$ provided by domain experts.

A *composite service* is often represented in the form of a directed acyclic graph (DAG, denoted as $\mathcal{G}$), where nodes represent web services (also called *component services*) and edges represent robust causal links [9] between two matched services S and S', noted as $S \rightarrow S'$. Other than $\mathcal{G}$, a *composite service* can also be indirectly represented as a permutation $\Pi = (\Pi_0, \Pi_1, \ldots, \Pi_{n-1})$, elements of which are $\{0, 1, \ldots, n-1\}$ such that $\Pi_i \neq \Pi_j$ for all $i \neq j$. Each element in Π represents a unique index id of a web service in the service repository. According to [23], a permutation Π can be further decoded into a $\mathcal{G}$ (denoted as $\Pi \Rightarrow \mathcal{G}$).

The *robustness* of a composite service is defined in the presence of stochastic service failures that create a discrete set of scenarios $\mathbb{Q}$. A *scenario* $Q \in \mathbb{Q}$ corresponds to a set of services $\{S_j\}$ that remain accessible during the execution of a composite service, where $\sum_{Q \in \mathbb{Q}} Pr(Q) = 1$ (i.e., the probabilities of all the scenarios are summed up to 1) and $S_j \in \mathcal{SR}$. Let $\mathcal{L}(\Pi, Q)$ be a local search operator (i.e., an efficient re-optimization technique) that produces a new feasible composite solution Π' for Q through applying local changes to Π. The robustness is defined as the expected quality of a composite service across all possible scenarios and can be directly estimated through Monte Carlo sampling [15] as follows:

$$robust(\Pi) = \sum_{Q \in \mathbb{Q}} f_{cq}(\mathcal{L}(\Pi, Q))Pr(Q) \approx \frac{1}{N} \sum_{i=1}^{N} f_{cq}(\mathcal{L}(\Pi, Q_i)) \qquad (1)$$

where N is the sample size. Particularly, in Eq. (1), Π is evaluated N times based on N sampled Q_i. $f_{cq}(\Pi)$ measures the comprehensive quality of a composite service defined in Eq. (2).

$$f_{cq}(\Pi) = \begin{cases} \hat{MT} + \hat{SIM} + \hat{A} + \hat{R} + (1 - \hat{T}) + (1 - \hat{CT}) & \text{if } \Pi \Rightarrow \mathcal{G} \\ 0 & \text{otherwise} \end{cases} \qquad (2)$$

where the normalized semantic matching type $\hat{MT}$ and the semantic similarity $\hat{SIM}$ are calculated for measuring QoSM, while the normalized availability $\hat{A}$, reliability $\hat{R}$, response time $\hat{T}$, and execution cost $\hat{CT}$ are calculated for measuring QoS, see [23] for more explanations. $\hat{T}$ and $\hat{CT}$ are subtracted from 1 to ensure that higher scores in Eq. (2) correspond to better quality.

Robust web service composition aims to search a baseline solution Π with optimized robustness measured in Eq. (1) for a composition task T over a service repository $\mathcal{SR}$ at the design stage. To search for a solution with optimized robustness, a global search technique will be utilized to find this robust baseline solution offline. When the baseline solution fails at the execution stage due to the unexpected service failures, the baseline solutions Π can be repaired by a local search process to form another solution Π'. This new solution does not depend on any failed component services and is expected to maintain a high-quality level. Due to its efficiency, the same local search operator will be used consistently both at the design and the execution stage.

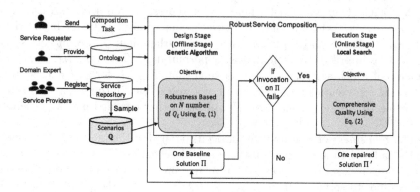

Fig. 1. Two-stage robust web service composition and execution process

Our two-stage robust web service composition and execution process is illustrated in Fig. 1. The process takes three inputs (i.e., a composition task, a service repository, and an ontology of services). At the design stage (also called *offline stage*), GA is utilized to efficiently search for a baseline solution with optimized robustness based on N sampled scenarios using Eq. (1). At the execution stage (also called *online stage*), the baseline solution will be executed if none of its component services fail. Otherwise, this baseline solution will be repaired through a local search technique. This technique produces a repaired solution with good quality as measured in Eq. (2).

4   Our GA-Based Approach to Robust Service Composition

In this section, we present our GA-based method, named GA4Robust, for robust web service composition. We will start with an outline of our approach in Sect. 4.1. Subsequently, we will discuss our simulation-based fitness evaluations for measuring the robustness in Sect. 4.2.

GA has been successfully utilized as a global searching technique for effectively searching service composition with optimized QoS and/or QoSM [19]. However, GA is highly sensitive to the fitness measure used to determine the quality of each evolved composite service. In this paper, we will utilize Eq. (1) to estimate fitness based on a set of randomly sampled scenarios. For each scenario, a local search is used to efficiently repair composite services affected by stochastic failures. For details see Sect. 4.2.

4.1   Outline of Our Method

Our algorithm for evolving robust composite services is outlined in Algorithm 1. GA4Roust follows the state-of-the-art GA-based service composition
approach [19] except Step 2 and Step 6. We begin with initializing population
$\mathcal{P}^0$ with m randomly generated permutations Π_k^g (where $k = 1, \ldots, m$). Note
that each permutation can be interpreted as a DAG thought the use a forward
graph building algorithm in [19,23]. The DAG also allows easy calculations of
fitness in Eq. (2). In step 2, we evaluate the fitness values of each permutation
against N randomly sampled scenarios, see details in Sect. 4.2. The iterative
steps (Steps 4 to 7) will be repeated until the maximum number of generations
is reached. During each iteration, m permutations are produced from genetic
operators (i.e., crossover and mutation operators in [19] are utilized) to form
the next generation $\mathcal{P}^{g+1}$. This newly created population is then evaluated by
following the same process in Step 2. Consequently, the best solution with the
highest fitness is returned after the iteration.

Algorithm 1. GA4Robust method for robust service composition.

Input   : composition task T, Ontology $\mathcal{O}$, service repository $\mathcal{SR}$, sample size N,
            and the number of neighbors n_{nb}
Output: an baseline solution

1: Initialize $\mathcal{P}^0$ with m randomly permutations, each represented as a Π_k^g (where
   $k = 1, \ldots, m$);
2: **Evaluate each permutation in $\mathcal{P}^0$ against the stochastic service failures
   based on N simulations in Eq. (1);**
3: Set generation counter $g \leftarrow 0$;
4: **while** $g < g_{max}$ **do**
5:     Populate $\mathcal{P}^{g+1}$ with m permutations from $\mathcal{P}^g$ through the use of genetic
       operators;
6:     **Evaluate each permutation in $\mathcal{P}^{g+1}$ against the stochastic service
       failures based on N simulations in Eq. (1);**
7:     Set $g \leftarrow g + 1$;
8: Select the best solution Π^{opt} in $\mathcal{P}^g$ as a baseline;

4.2   Simulation-Based Evaluations Using Local Search

Our proposed fitness function in Eq. (1) approximates the robustness of every
candidate solution subject to N randomly sampled scenarios with fast local
search for each scenario. This robustness estimation process is provided in Algorithm 2. Particularly, Step 4 and Step 5 play a crucial role. In Step 4, we produce
another permutation Π' that encodes Π based on each sampled Q. This produced permutation allows some promising component services that belong to
the composite service Π to be re-used by Π'. In this subsection, we will use
Example 1 to demonstrate Step 4. Subsequently, we will define our local search
operator with an example in *Example* 2.

ALGORITHM 2. Simulation-based evaluation with local search (Step 2 or 6 in ALGORITHM 1).

Input : population $\mathcal{P}^g$, the number of neighbor n_{nb} and service repository $\mathcal{SR}$
Output: evaluated $\mathcal{P}^g$

1 **foreach** Π *in* $\mathcal{P}^g$ **do**
2   Sample N scenarios based on pr_S of each S in $\mathcal{SR}$;
3   **foreach** *scenario* Q *in the* N *sampled scenarios* **do**
4   Produce another permutation Π^* that encodes Π based on Q;
5   Generate a size n_{nb} of neighbors from Π^* by local search operator;
6   Identify the best neighbor Π' with the highest fitness based on Eq. (2);
7   Set the fitness of Π as an averaged fitness value of N Π' based on Eq. (1);
8 **return** evaluated $\mathcal{P}^g$;

Example 1. Let us consider a composition task $T = (\{a, b\}, \{e, f\})$ and a service repository $\mathcal{SR}$ consisting of six atomic services. $S_0 = (\{e, f\}, \{g\}, QoS_{S_0})$, $S_1 = (\{b\}, \{c, d\}, QoS_{S_1})$, $S_2 = (\{c\}, \{e\}, QoS_{S_2})$, $S_3 = (\{d\}, \{f\}, QoS_{S_3})$, $S_4 = (\{a\}, \{h\}, QoS_{S_4})$ and $S_5 = (\{c\}, \{e, f\}, QoS_{S_5})$. The two special services $Start = (\emptyset, \{a, b\}, \emptyset)$ and $End = (\{e, f\}, \emptyset, \emptyset)$ are defined by a given composition task T. Figure 2 illustrates one randomly sampled scenario and a process to produce another permutation Π^* that encodes a candidate permutation Π for the sampled scenario.

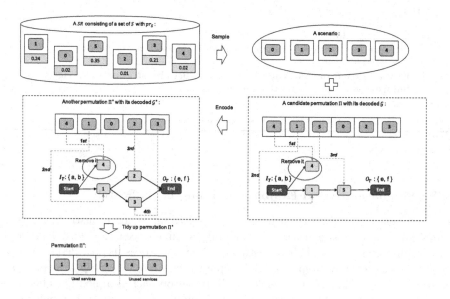

Fig. 2. A new permutation produced based on a sampled scenario

We firstly sample a scenario based on the service failure probability pr_S of each service S in a service repository $\mathcal{SR}$. Let $\{S_0, S_1, S_2, S_3, S_4\}$ be a sampled scenario based on pr_S of each S in $\mathcal{SR}$, so $\{0, 1, 2, 3, 4\}$ is a set of service indexes corresponds to the sampled scenario in Fig. 2. In this example, we also take an arbitrary permutation $\Pi = [4, 1, 0, 2, 3, 5]$ as a candidate solution. For the sampled scenario, we produce another permutation $\Pi^\star$ that encodes permutation Π for the scenario by only removing the service indexes of failed services (i.e., 5) from the permutation. By doing these, the newly produced permutation $\Pi^\star$ can keep some promising component services (e.g., 1) from the candidate Π. We also show two DAGs decoded from Π and $\Pi^\star$ based on the forwarding graph building technique in [19,23], where the DAGs are constructed based on the order of service indexes and node, such as 4, is removed since its outputs are not used in the composition. In the DAG, we can see that the service index 1 of the decoded $\mathcal{G}^\star$ from $\Pi^\star$ is inherited from that of the $\mathcal{G}$ decoded from Π in Fig. 2.

Once the permutation for the sampled scenario is produced, we tidy up this permutation into $[1, 2, 3, |4, 0]$ (| is just displayed for the courtesy of the reader, but not part of the representation) as an input of local search. We produce this permutation by combining two parts, one part $[1, 2, 3]$ is service indexes of component service in $\mathcal{G}^\star$, sorted based on the longest distance from $Start$ to every component services of $\mathcal{G}^\star$ while the second part $[4, 0]$ is indexes of remaining services in simulated permutation not utilized by $\mathcal{G}^\star$.

Let $\Pi^\star = (\Pi_0, \ldots, \Pi_t, |\Pi_{t+1}, \ldots, \Pi_{n-1})$ be the produced permutation in Step 4, elements of the permutation are $\{0, \ldots, t, t+1, \ldots, n-1\}$ such that $\Pi_i \neq \Pi_j$ for all $i \neq j$. Particularly, $\{0, \ldots, t\}$ are service indexes (i.e., id number) of the component services in the corresponding $\mathcal{G}$, and is sorted based on the longest distance from $Start$ to every component services of $\mathcal{G}$. While $\{t+1, \ldots, n-1\}$ be indexes of remaining services in $\mathcal{SR}$ not utilized by the $\mathcal{G}$. Subsequently, we apply a stochastic local search operator (i.e., layer-based constrained one-point swap, see details in [24]) to $\Pi^\star$. To perform this local search, the layer information (i.e., different layers include different web services as layer members based on service inputs) must be utilized. Generally speaking, layer information indicates the order of a service being included into a DAG of a composite service, starting from the input of a composition task I_T. For example, the first layer L_1 includes services that can be immediately executed based on the input of the composition task I_T. The second layer L_2 contains those services that can be executed by using I_T and outputs produced by services in L_1. Other layers can be discovered in a similar way, see the layer discovery technique in [19,24]. Therefore, a neighboring permutation is produced by swapping two selected service indexes Π_a and Π_b in the permutation. Particularly, one service index Π_a, where $0 \leq a \leq t$, is selected, and one layer L_k, where L_k s.t. $\Pi_a \in L_k$, is identified. Afterwards, another service index Π_b is randomly selected from the index set $L_k \cap \{\Pi_{t+1}, \ldots, \Pi_{n-1}\}$.

Example 2. Let us consider a layer-based constrained one-point swap, starting from the produced permutation $[1, 2, 3, |4, 0]$ in *Example 1*. Figure 3 illustrates a process of producing a neighboring permutation from the given permutation.

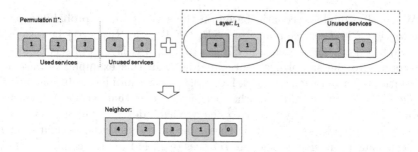

Fig. 3. A neighboring permutation produced from a permutation of a particular scenario

For the permutation $[1, 2, 3, |4, 0]$, one service index (e.g., 1) is firstly randomly selected before the $|$ in the permutation (i.e., 1, 2 or 3). Then we get the layer information of service index 1 (e.g., layer L_1 consists of 1). Afterwards, another service index (e.g., 4) is randomly selected from the intersection set of service indexes in L_1 and the service indexes after the $|$. Consequently, 1 and 4 are swapped to generate a new permutation.

5 Experimental Evaluation

5.1 Experimental Design

We conduct experiments to evaluate the performance of GA4Robust and GA, where GA4Robust and GA aim to generate composite services with optimal robustness and overall comprehensive quality, i.e., Eqs. (1) and (2) respectively. We use five composition tasks with corresponding service repositories for testing. These tasks (i.e., OWL-S TC1 to OWL-S TC5 utilized in [11,14,22]) contain real-world web services and composition tasks originally collected from OWLS-TC [8]. Each service in the service repository is extended with real-world QoS attributes obtained from the QWS dataset [1]. Apart from that, each service is also associated with a separate service failure rate. The failure rate of a service is generated from the normal distribution $\mathcal{N}(\mu, \sigma^2)$ truncated in the interval $[0, 1]$ with mean μ and variance σ^2. According to the failure rates reported in [28] and by using 15 000 failure probabilities observed by 150 users on 100 web services, μ and σ are set to 0.0405 and 0.1732.

To perform the comparisons between GA4Robust and GA, we follow the popular parameter settings in the literature [7,19]: population size is set to 30, crossover and mutation rate are set to 0.95 and 0.05 respectively, tournament size is set to 2 and elitism is set to 2. We set the maximum generation to 100. For Eq. (1), a set of sample size N (i.e., 10, 30, 50, 70 and 90) is to be investigated in Sect. 5.2, and the number of local search steps (i.e., n_{nb}) is set to 10 that empirically produces a good compromise between computation cost and service quality. For Eq. (2), all weights are set to balance quality criteria in both QoSM and QoS, i.e., w_1 and w_2 are set to 0.25, and w_3, w_4, w_5 and w_6 to 0.125 [23] according to the settings in [23]. We have also conducted tests with other weights and parameters and generally observed the same behavior.

We run both GA4Robust and GA 30 times with 30 different random seeds. We then test each baseline composite service obtained by every run of every algorithm over 200 simulated scenarios. Note that, a large number of sampled scenarios (e.g., 200) is taken into account for testing while a small number of sampled scenarios N is used at the design stage. This difference is important for the design stage to remain highly efficient whereas we want to accurately measure the robustness of any composite service during the execution stage. Subsequently, we use two-sample t test with a significance level of 5% to verify the observed difference in the mean fitness values tested on the baselines found by GA4Robust and GA.

5.2 Parameters Sensitivity

To evaluate the impact of N in Eq. (1) on the testing performance, we perform parameters sensitivity tests on OWL-S TC3 using different settings of N in GA4Robust. In Fig. 4, we present a box plot of the testing performance from testing baseline solutions (near-optimal solutions) found by GA4Robust with varied settings of N (i.e., 10, 30, 70 and 90) across 30 independent algorithm runs. It is easy to observe that performance boxes tend to reduce their sizes with increasing N. This observation agrees with our expectation that more accurate fitness evaluation with large N will enhance the reliability of our algorithm. Meanwhile, we can also observe that the medium values in these boxes are also positively correlated to N. This observation further confirms that more accurate fitness evaluations contribute to better algorithm performance. In the all the remaining experiments, we set N to 50 according to Fig. 4, since 50 presents the most ideal trade-off between algorithm performance and sample cost.

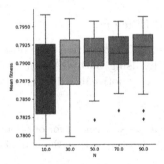

Fig. 4. Mean fitness values tested on near-optimal solutions found by GA4Robust over a set of increasing N for OWLS-TC 03

5.3 Comparison of the Effectiveness

Table 1 shows the mean fitness values and standard deviations obtained from testing on baseline solutions over 30 runs for each task, each run is tested over

200 random scenarios of the execution stage. We verify the significant differences in the fitness values using two-sample t test, and the winner is highlighted in the table.

Table 1. Mean fitness values tested based on the baseline solutions for our approach in comparison to GA (Note: the higher the fitness the better)

Task	GA4Robust	GA [19]
OWL-S TC1	0.922799 ± 0.000304	0.922791 ± 0.000311
OWL-S TC2	0.930779 ± 0.000998	0.929618 ± 0.005009
OWL-S TC3	**0.864505 ± 0.001448**	0.854218 ± 0.00779
OWL-S TC4	**0.790862 ± 0.003172**	0.779121 ± 0.012348
OWL-S TC5	**0.82504 ± 0.005556**	0.812852 ± 0.012388

At the execution stage, GA4Robust can produce composite services that are clearly more robust to stochastic service failures as evidenced by the performance summarized in Table 1. Particularly, baseline solutions produced by GA4Robust achieves significantly higher mean fitness values against 200 random scenarios for 3 out of 5 tasks. Therefore, composite services produced by GA4Robust is more likely to maintain a good quality despite of stochastic service failures. This finding matches well with our new objective at the design stage for GA4Robust.

Moreover, for the two tasks (i.e., OWL-TC1, OWL-TC2), GA4Robust performed similarly as GA. Particularly, both GA4Robust and GA can maintain very high quality across the 200 sampled scenarios with very small standard deviations. This is because the search space of feasible solutions in OWL-TC1, OWL-TC2 is small, and these two methods can always find high-quality solutions through local search in the event of service failures at the execution stage.

5.4   Comparison of the Efficiency

Tables 2 and 3 show two groups of execution time observed for design stage and execution stage, respectively, using both GA4Robust and GA. We keep using two-sample T test to detect any noticeable differences in the experiment results in efficiency.

Table 2. Mean execution time (in s) observed for our approach in comparison to GA at the design stage (Note: the shorter the time the better)

Task	GA4Robust	GA
OWL-S TC1	221.854233 ± 63.968435	**2.279767 ± 0.594116**
OWL-S TC2	51.851 ± 34.814491	**1.502733 ± 0.163235**
OWL-S TC3	27.075967 ± 14.63108	**1.4005 ± 0.132212**
OWL-S TC4	468.054967 ± 342.97007	**13.785767 ± 21.966587**
OWL-S TC5	901.813933 ± 598.884817	**19.577733 ± 71.642104**

Table 3. Mean execution time (in ms) per scenario by local search based on the baseline solutions found by our approach in comparison to GA (Note: the shorter the time the better)

Task	GA4Robust	GA
OWL-S TC1	0.155067 ± 0.06195	0.194944 ± 0.095481
OWL-S TC2	**0.456811 ± 0.323291**	1.173133 ± 1.618681
OWL-S TC3	**0.788439 ± 0.574859**	1.363739 ± 0.892455
OWL-S TC4	9.315556 ± 7.508798	10.824494 ± 5.943972
OWL-S TC5	**12.694856 ± 10.350321**	22.812806 ± 21.672252

For the design stage, we note that GA consistently takes significant less execution time (in seconds) for all the tasks. This is because the fitness evaluation in GA through Eq. (2) is far efficient than GA4Robust through Eq. (1). On the other hand, GA4Robust consistently requires much more execution time. This is because a single evaluation of one candidate solution involves N times of calculations of comprehensive quality against the stochastic service failures using Eq. (1). This observation indicates a sensible trade-off because the frequency of producing baseline solutions by GA4Robust is far less frequent than the that of repairing the baseline solutions by local search. On the other hand, although GA4Robust consumes much longer execution time at the design stage, GA4Robust gains much higher quality against the stochastic service failures at the execution stage, see the previous discussion in Sect. 5.3. The efficiency of evolving robust composite services may be further improved with the help of using surrogate techniques. This will serve as our future work.

For the execution stage, GA4Robust requires significantly less execution time (in milliseconds) than GA for 3 out of 5 tasks per scenario. This observation indicates that baseline solutions produced by GA4Robust are more likely to have useful services, required to build a suitable DAG, to be placed at the very front of the neighbors exploited from them. This can potentially accelerate the process of decoding from permutations to DAGs.

6 Conclusion

In this paper, we proposed a robust service composition method, GA4Robust, for handling stochastic service failures. In particular, we proposed a fitness function using Monte Carlo integration to evaluate the robustness of composition solutions. We then proposed a GA-based method to produce baseline solutions at the design stage. The baseline solutions produced can be used by a local search to find feasible and high-quality solutions to handle situations that some of the component services are not available at the execution stage. Our experimental evaluation shows that GA4Robust can produce more robust composite services compared to a state-of-the-art GA method that merely focuses on searching high-quality solutions. We also investigate the impact of sample size N in our proposed fitness function that plays an important role in making a good balance between the efficiency of evaluations using Monte Carlo integration and the error in the estimation of the robustness. In the future, we will work on improving the efficiency and accuracy of robustness evaluations by proposing a surrogate model for a fast and accurate estimation of the robustness.

References

1. Al-Masri, E., Mahmoud, Q.H.: QoS-based discovery and ranking of web services. In: International Conference on Computer Comm. Networks, pp. 529–534. IEEE (2007)
2. Amin, A., Colman, A., Grunske, L.: An approach to forecasting QoS attributes of web services based on ARIMA and GARCH models. In: IEEE International Conference on Web Services, pp. 74–81. IEEE (2012)
3. Ardagna, D., Pernici, B.: Adaptive service composition in flexible processes. IEEE Trans. Softw. Eng. 33(6), 369–384 (2007)
4. Chen, Y., Huang, J., Lin, C.: Partial selection: an efficient approach for QoS-aware web service composition. In: IEEE International Conference on Web Services, pp. 1–8. IEEE (2014)
5. Daniel, A.M., Menasc, T.: Qos issues in web services. IEEE Internet Comput. 6(6), 72–75 (2002)
6. Geyik, S.C., Szymanski, B.K., Zerfos, P.: Robust dynamic service composition in sensor networks. IEEE Trans. Serv. Comput. 6, 560–572 (2013)
7. Koza, J.R.: Genetic Programming: On the Programming of Computers by Means of Natural Selection, vol. 1. MIT Press, Cambridge (1992)
8. Küster, U., König-Ries, B., Krug, A.: OPOSSum-an online portal to collect and share SWS descriptions. In: 2008 IEEE International Conference on Semantic Computing, pp. 480–481. IEEE (2008)
9. Lécué, F., Delteil, A., Léger, A.: Optimizing causal link based web service composition. In: ECAI, pp. 45–49 (2008)
10. Li, M., Hua, Z., Zhao, J., Zou, Y., Xie, B.: ARIMA model-based web services trustworthiness evaluation and prediction. In: Liu, C., Ludwig, H., Toumani, F., Yu, Q. (eds.) ICSOC 2012. LNCS, vol. 7636, pp. 648–655. Springer, Heidelberg (2012). https://doi.org/10.1007/978-3-642-34321-6_51
11. Ma, H., Wang, A., Zhang, M.: A hybrid approach using genetic programming and greedy search for QoS-aware web service composition. Trans. Large-Scale Data Knowl.-Cent. Syst. 18, 180–205 (2015)
12. Mostafa, A., Zhang, M.: Multi-objective service composition in uncertain environments. IEEE Trans. Serv. Comput. (2015)
13. Rao, J., Su, X.: A survey of automated web service composition methods. In: Cardoso, J., Sheth, A. (eds.) SWSWPC 2004. LNCS, vol. 3387, pp. 43–54. Springer, Heidelberg (2005). https://doi.org/10.1007/978-3-540-30581-1_5
14. Rodriguez-Mier, P., Mucientes, M., Lama, M., Couto, M.I.: Composition of web services through genetic programming. Evol. Intel. 3(3–4), 171–186 (2010)
15. Rubinstein, R.Y., Kroese, D.P.: Simulation and the Monte Carlo Method, vol. 10. Wiley, Hoboken (2016)
16. da Silva, A.S., Ma, H., Zhang, M.: GraphEvol: a graph evolution technique for web service composition. In: Chen, Q., Hameurlain, A., Toumani, F., Wagner, R., Decker, H. (eds.) DEXA 2015. LNCS, vol. 9262, pp. 134–142. Springer, Cham (2015). https://doi.org/10.1007/978-3-319-22852-5_12

17. da Silva, A.S., Ma, H., Zhang, M.: Genetic programming for QoS-aware web service composition and selection. Soft Comput. **20**, 1–17 (2016)
18. da Silva, A.S., Mei, Y., Ma, H., Zhang, M.: A memetic algorithm-based indirect approach to web service composition. In: IEEE Congress on Evolutionary Computation (2016)
19. da Silva, A.S., Mei, Y., Ma, H., Zhang, M.: Evolutionary computation for automatic web service composition: an indirect representation approach. J. Heurist. **24**, 425–456 (2018)
20. Wagner, F., Ishikawa, F., Honiden, S.: Robust service compositions with functional and location diversity. IEEE Trans. Serv. Comput. **9**(2), 277–290 (2016)
21. Wang, C., Ma, H., Chen, A., Hartmann, S.: Comprehensive quality-aware automated semantic web service composition. In: Peng, W., Alahakoon, D., Li, X. (eds.) AI 2017. LNCS (LNAI), vol. 10400, pp. 195–207. Springer, Cham (2017). https://doi.org/10.1007/978-3-319-63004-5_16
22. Wang, C., Ma, H., Chen, A., Hartmann, S.: GP-based approach to comprehensive quality-aware automated semantic web service composition. In: Shi, Y., et al. (eds.) SEAL 2017. LNCS, vol. 10593, pp. 170–183. Springer, Cham (2017). https://doi.org/10.1007/978-3-319-68759-9_15
23. Wang, C., Ma, H., Chen, A., Hartmann, S.: Knowledge-driven automated web service composition—an EDA-based approach. In: Hacid, H., Cellary, W., Wang, H., Paik, H.-Y., Zhou, R. (eds.) WISE 2018. LNCS, vol. 11234, pp. 135–150. Springer, Cham (2018). https://doi.org/10.1007/978-3-030-02925-8_10
24. Wang, C., Ma, H., Chen, G., Hartmann, S.: Memetic EDA-based approaches to comprehensive quality-aware automated semantic web service composition. arXiv preprint arXiv:1906.07900 (2019)
25. Wang, L., Shen, J., Luo, J.: Impacts of pheromone modification strategies in ant colony for data-intensive service provision. In: IEEE International Conference on Web Services, pp. 177–184. IEEE (2014)
26. Yin, H., Zhang, C., Zhang, B., Guo, Y., Liu, T.: A hybrid multiobjective discrete particle swarm optimization algorithm for a SLA-aware service composition problem. Math. Probl. Eng. (2014)
27. Yu, Y., Ma, H., Zhang, M.: An adaptive genetic programming approach to QoS-aware web services composition. In: IEEE CEC, pp. 1740–1747 (2013)
28. Zheng, Z., Zhang, Y., Lyu, M.R.: Investigating qos of real-world web services. IEEE Trans. Serv. Comput. **7**(1), 32–39 (2014)

Bayesian Optimisation for Objective Functions with Varying Smoothness

A. V. Arun Kumar$^{1(\boxtimes)}$, Santu Rana^1, Cheng Li^2, Sunil Gupta^1, Alistair Shilton^1, and Svetha Venkatesh^1

^{1} Applied Artificial Intelligence Institute (A^2I^2), Deakin University, Geelong, Australia
{aanjanapuravenk,santu.rana,sunil.gupta,alistair.shilton, svetha.venkatesh}@deakin.edu.au
^{2} National University of Singapore (NUS), Singapore, Singapore
licheng@comp.nus.edu.sg

Abstract. Bayesian optimisation is a popular method in optimising complex, unknown and expensive objective functions. In complex design optimisation problems, the additional information about the smoothness, monotonicity or the modality of the unknown objective functions can be obtained either from the domain expertise or from the problem environment. Incorporating such additional information can potentially enhance the performance of the optimisation. We propose a methodology to incorporate the aforesaid extra information to have a better fitted surrogate model of the unknown objective function. Specifically, for Gaussian Process regression, we propose a covariance function to encompass varying smoothness across the input space through a parametric function whose parameters are tuned from the observations. Our experiments on both synthetic benchmark functions and real-world applications demonstrate that embodying such additional knowledge accelerates the convergence.

Keywords: Bayesian optimisation · Global optimisation · Gaussian Process · Spatially varying kernels

1 Introduction

The optimisation of real-world complex systems is expensive. Determining the appropriate values for the parameters in the problem environment ensures the success of optimisation. For instance, optimising a complex machine learning model capable of performing classification is a non-trivial task. The selection of right hyperparameters is the key to a good generalisation performance. However, the optimisation of hyperparameters based on a validation set performance can be tedious, if the model to be trained is very complex and training involves a

C. Li—This work was completed during Cheng Li's affiliation with A^2I^2, Deakin University.

© Springer Nature Switzerland AG 2019
J. Liu and J. Bailey (Eds.): AI 2019, LNAI 11919, pp. 460–472, 2019.
https://doi.org/10.1007/978-3-030-35288-2_37

large dataset. As a result, each iteration can be time-consuming and hence finding the optimum parameters in a small number of trials is important. Bayesian optimisation [1], a well-known global optimisation technique addresses the aforesaid issue by offering a theoretically guaranteed fast convergence rate in terms of the number of samples. Recently, the application of Bayesian optimisation has proliferated in many domains. For example, Li *et al.* [10] studied the manufacturing of short polymer fibers with the desired characteristics as an optimisation of a black-box function. Czarnecki *et al.* [3] used Bayesian optimisation for classifying bioactive compounds. Other applications of Bayesian optimisation include circuit designing [18], robot decision making [17] and policy learning in driving simulators [2]. Most of the current Bayesian optimisation methodologies assume the nature of objective function to be completely black-box, *i.e.*, no information about the properties of the objective function is known *apriori*. But, in numerous cases [8,11], the domain experts can reveal some useful knowledge about the function that can be utilised to further boost the performance of Bayesian optimisation. However, embodying the knowledge from experts to improve the performance of the Bayesian optimisation process is not very well explored.

A commonly occurring pattern in complex real-world design problems is that the unknown objective function is mostly flat with low values, except for a few good spots having spikes of high values. Such behaviour is also the reason why in reality finding a good value location can be tricky. It implies that such objective functions have non-stationary behaviour, *i.e.*, the region around a local optimum looks very different from the overall function. Such implicit, but vital prior information originating from the domain experts about the behaviour can contribute to better model accuracy. Previous approaches incorporate prior information either through transfer learning methods [8] to borrow function similarity from the previous tasks or through the incorporation of specific trends [11]. The transfer learning method thrives only when past data is available and cannot enforce any specific knowledge. Methods that can incorporate specific trends are not only problem-specific but also insufficiently flexible to handle the aforesaid common non-stationary pattern that we are interested to exploit.

In Bayesian optimisation, there have been early attempts to account for the objective functions exhibiting non-stationary behaviour. Snelson *et al.* [15] proposed a way to transform the input space of the unknown function learnt using the Gaussian Process (GP) [19]. Dalal *et al.* [4] discussed a general framework for non-stationary covariance functions. Paciorek *et al.* [13] developed a framework for non-stationary GP regression models. Snoek *et al.* [16] devised a methodology to warp the input space of the objective function to a stationary space so that the effects of varying smoothness is eliminated. Martinez-Cantin [12] proposed a methodology to partition the input space into different regions, to model them as separate entities. Gönen *et al.* [7] developed a method to model using multiple kernels instead of one kernel. Many of the aforementioned methods are too general in that it can learn any type of non-stationarity from the data. Learning the non-stationarity from the data offers a more flexible framework, but at the cost of increased demand for the data - a requirement that does not go well with the application of Bayesian optimisation. In contrast, we aim to incorporate a specific kind of non-stationary covariance function to accelerate Bayesian optimisation. For GP based surrogate models, we propose to encode the additional information by considering the length-scale as a parametric function of the input. The parameters of the length-scale function are optimised in the light of data over the iterations. We propose a generic parametric function that can handle objective functions that are mostly flat with only a few good spots. However, our framework is also applicable if there is specific knowledge available about the function's smoothness. The generic prior takes the shape of an inverted Gaussian curve. The mean of the inverted Gaussian is progressively tuned based on the observations. In the experiments, we observe the performance by evaluating our algorithm on different synthetic functions employing both function-specific prior information as well as generic prior information. In our real-world experiments, we use hyperparameter tuning of Support Vector Machines (SVM) [5] and Elastic Nets [21] considering only generic prior length-scale function. We compare the performance of our proposed method against other state-of-the-art Bayesian optimisation algorithms implementing fixed length-scale (FIX) Squared Exponential (SE) kernel [1], Automatic Relevance Determination (ARD) using SE kernel [19] and weighted multiple kernels (MULTI) [7]. The experimental results demonstrate that our proposed method converges faster than the baselines.

2   Bayesian Optimisation

Bayesian optimisation provides an elegant framework for finding the global extrema $(\mathbf{x}^*)$ of an expensive and noisy black-box function $f(\mathbf{x})$, represented as $\mathbf{x}^* = \underset{\mathbf{x} \in \mathcal{X}}{\operatorname{argmax}} f(\mathbf{x})$. The values observed for $f(\mathbf{x})$ is assumed to be noisy, i.e., $y_i = f(\mathbf{x}_i) + \epsilon_i$, where $\epsilon_i \sim \mathcal{N}(0, \sigma_{noise}^2)$ is the Gaussian noise. The central idea behind Bayesian optimisation is to define a prior distribution over the possible set of objective functions and then refine the model sequentially with data. Bayesian optimisation is generally comprised of two main components (i) a Gaussian Process (GP) and (ii) Acquisition Functions [20].

2.1   Gaussian Process Models

A GP is a non-parametric model that provides a flexible framework for placing prior on functions, to find a distribution over the possible functions that are coherent with the observations. Though there exist other popular surrogate models like Student-t process [14], Wiener process [9], GP is still the preferred surrogate model because of its simplicity. The properties of a GP are completely defined by a mean function (μ) and a covariance function (k). If $\mathcal{D}_{1:t} = \{\mathbf{x}_{1:t}, \mathbf{y}_{1:t}\}$ denotes a set of observations, then according to the properties of a GP, the observations $\mathcal{D}_{1:t}$ and a new observation $(\mathbf{x}_{t+1}, y_{t+1})$ are jointly Gaussian. Therefore, the predictive distribution for the new observation is obtained as

$$\mathcal{P}(y_{t+1}|\mathcal{D}_{1:t}, \mathbf{x}_{t+1}) = \mathcal{N}(\mu(\mathbf{x}_{t+1}), \sigma^2(\mathbf{x}_{t+1}))$$

$$\text{where} \quad \mu(\mathbf{x}_{t+1}) = \mathbf{k}^T[\mathbf{K} + \sigma_{noise}^2 I]^{-1}\mathbf{y}$$

$$\sigma^2(\mathbf{x}_{t+1}) = k(\mathbf{x}_{t+1}, \mathbf{x}_{t+1}) - \mathbf{k}^T[\mathbf{K} + \sigma_{noise}^2 I]^{-1}\mathbf{k} \qquad (1)$$

$$\mathbf{k} = [k(\mathbf{x}_{t+1}, \mathbf{x}_1), k(\mathbf{x}_{t+1}, \mathbf{x}_2), \cdots, k(\mathbf{x}_{t+1}, \mathbf{x}_t)]$$

$$\text{and } K_{ij} = k(\mathbf{x}_i, \mathbf{x}_j) \ \forall i, \forall j \in [1, \cdots, t]$$

The covariance function used in a GP plays a vital role in the modelling process, as it incorporates the prior belief about the unknown function being modelled. One of the most commonly used covariance function is the SE kernel function,

$$k(\mathbf{x}, \mathbf{x}') = \sigma_f^2 \exp\left(-\frac{1}{2l^2}||\mathbf{x} - \mathbf{x}'||^2\right) \qquad (2)$$

where l and σ_f^2 correspond to the length-scale and signal variance, respectively. These hyperparameters are collectively represented as $\Theta = \{l, \sigma_f^2\}$. They are estimated by maximising the marginal likelihood, given by the equation

$$\mathcal{L} = p(\mathbf{y}|\mathbf{X}, \Theta) = \int p(\mathbf{y}|\mathbf{f}) \, p(\mathbf{f}|\mathbf{X}, \Theta) \, df \qquad (3)$$

The log marginal likelihood for a GP has a closed-form formulation, given as

$$\log \mathcal{L} = -\frac{1}{2}(\mathbf{y}^T(\mathbf{K} + \sigma_{noise}^2 I)^{-1}\mathbf{y}) - \frac{1}{2}\log|\mathbf{K} + \sigma_{noise}^2 I| - \frac{t}{2}\log(2\pi) \qquad (4)$$

where t corresponds to the number of observations. Traditional global optimisation technique such as a multi-start local optimiser can be used to maximise the log marginal likelihood.

2.2   Acquisition Functions

The posterior distribution obtained from GP is used to pick the next query point that promises to be an optimum. This decision process is characterised by an acquisition function $(\alpha(\mathbf{x}))$ that guides the search for the optimum by balancing the exploration of high variance regions versus the exploitation of high mean regions. The range of acquisition functions that can be employed with GPs is listed in [20]. In our experiments, we have considered the Expected Improvement (EI) acquisition function, which guides the search by taking into account the expected improvement over the current maximum. If $f(\mathbf{x}^+)$ is the best value observed, then the next best point to query is obtained by maximising the EI acquisition function $\alpha_{EI}(\mathbf{x})$, given by

$$\alpha_{EI}(\mathbf{x}) = \begin{cases} (\mu(\mathbf{x}) - f(\mathbf{x}^+)) \, \Phi(Z) + \sigma(\mathbf{x}) \, \phi(Z) \text{ if } \sigma(\mathbf{x}) > 0 \\ 0 \qquad\qquad\qquad\qquad\qquad\quad \text{if } \sigma(\mathbf{x}) = 0 \end{cases} ; \ Z = \frac{\mu(\mathbf{x}) - f(\mathbf{x}^+)}{\sigma(\mathbf{x})}$$

$$(5)$$

where $\Phi(Z)$ and $\phi(Z)$ represent the Cumulative Distribution Function (CDF) and Probability Density Function (PDF) of the standard normal distribution, respectively.

3   Framework

We propose to incorporate the expert knowledge about the unknown function into GPs as a Spatially Varying Length-Scale (SVL). We first discuss the details of the length-scale function and covariance function to be used, followed by the process for estimation of the parameters in the length-scale function. Finally, we provide a Bayesian optimisation algorithm using SVL based covariance functions.

3.1   Spatially Varying Length-Scale

The covariance function $k(\mathbf{x}, \mathbf{x}')$ given by Eq. (2) is the key to incorporate the additional knowledge known *apriori* about the objective function. The length-scale l used in the covariance function $k(\mathbf{x}, \mathbf{x}')$ implies the belief about the smoothness of the objective function. The value selected for this hyperparameter significantly affects the predictions made using the GP Model. A fixed length-scale implies that the smoothness of the objective function is constant across the entire input space. To account for the varying smoothness of the objective function, it is more suitable to have the length-scale l as a function of the input, *i.e.*, $l(\mathbf{x})$. It is important to note that just replacing the fixed length-scale l by a parameterised form $l(\mathbf{x})$ will not result in a valid covariance function $k(\mathbf{x}, \mathbf{x}')$. Therefore, it is of prime importance to carefully select the length-scale function and its range, considering the positive definiteness property of the covariance function.

3.2   Spatially Varying Covariance Function

A valid covariance function $k(\mathbf{x}, \mathbf{x}')$, along with a set of n inputs generates a positive definite covariance matrix $\mathbf{K}(\mathbf{X}, \mathbf{X})$. It is non-trivial to modify a covariance function to accommodate the additional knowledge from the experts. Gibbs [6] derived a valid covariance function by replacing the length-scale l as a positive function of $\mathbf{x}$ without compromising the positive definiteness property of the covariance matrix $\mathbf{K}(\mathbf{X}, \mathbf{X})$. To ensure the positive definiteness of the covariance function $k(\mathbf{x}, \mathbf{x}')$, a network comprised of a set of basis functions $\phi_k(\mathbf{x})$ centered at c_{kd} in each input dimension d is considered. Such basis functions are given by

$$\phi_k(\mathbf{x}) = \prod_{d=1}^{D} \sqrt{\frac{\sqrt{2}}{l(x_d; \theta_d)}} \; \exp\left(-\sum_{d=1}^{D} \frac{(x_d - c_{kd})^2}{l^2(x_d; \theta_d)}\right) \tag{6}$$

where θ_d is the set of parameters in dimension d, *i.e.*, $\Theta = \{\theta_d\}_{d=1}^{D}$. The covariance function capable of embodying varying smoothness by adopting a spatially varying length-scale function is constructed using an infinite number of such

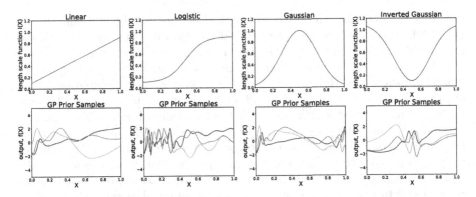

Fig. 1. Samples drawn from the GP prior using different length-scale functions.

networks, each having a fixed set of basis functions $\phi_k(\mathbf{x})$. A positive definite, non-stationary covariance function incorporating spatially varying characteristics of the objective function is given by Eq. (7).

$$k(\mathbf{x}, \mathbf{x}') = \prod_{d=1}^{D} \sqrt{\frac{2\, l(x_d; \theta_d)\, l(x'_d; \theta_d)}{l^2(x_d; \theta_d) + l^2(x'_d; \theta_d)}} \, \exp\left(-\sum_{d=1}^{D} \frac{(x_d - x'_d)^2}{l^2(x_d; \theta_d) + l^2(x'_d; \theta_d)} \right) \quad (7)$$

where $l(x_d; \theta_d)$ is a positive parameterised function of $\mathbf{x}$, with hyperparameters θ_d in the input dimension d. The additional knowledge about the properties of the objective function from the domain experts is captured in the length-scale function $l(x_d)$ mentioned in Eq. (7). Incorporating such extra information about the behaviour of the objective function can boost the performance of the optimisation procedure by improving model accuracy. The length-scale function to be considered in Eq. (7) is chosen carefully, such that the positive definiteness of the covariance matrix is retained. It should also be ensured that the function modelled for $l(x)$ never becomes zero or negative. For instance, if the objective function is expected to exhibit a more jagged behaviour at the beginning of the input space than that of the end, then the length-scale function $l(x_d)$ for modelling such functions can be assumed to vary linearly across the input space. The choice of linear length-scale function results in shorter length-scales at the beginning representing the more wiggly nature and larger values at the end representing greater smoothness. Similarly, if the length-scale function chosen follows the shape of a Gaussian distribution, then the shorter length-scales are observed at the extrema and larger length-scales at the peak of the curve. The inverted Gaussian is used as the generic prior as it provides a sharp function with mostly flat regions. The mean of the inverted Gaussian can be progressively tuned to position it at the global optima of the function. In the case of objective function with multiple modes, we can have a mixture of inverted Gaussian where each mean would go to each mode of the function. However, we see in our experiments that for real-world examples, even using single inverted Gaussian proves quite beneficial. The choice of length-scale function directly impacts GP priors. The variations observed in the GP priors by using different forms for the length-scale function in the spatially varying kernel are depicted in Fig. 1.

The accuracy of the surrogate model generated from GPs plays a significant role in the success of Bayesian optimisation. The posterior distribution for an objective function with identical sets of observed samples using a spatially varying kernel and a fixed length-scale SE kernel is depicted in Fig. 2(a) and (b), respectively. From the posterior obtained using a spatially varying covariance function, it is observed that the portion of input space containing the optimum exhibit larger variances. As a result, the acquisition function concentrates the search for optima in this region. In contrast, posterior from the fixed length-scale kernel predicts the next best sample assuming an equal amount of variations across the entire input space and hence, is focused on the inappropriate region.

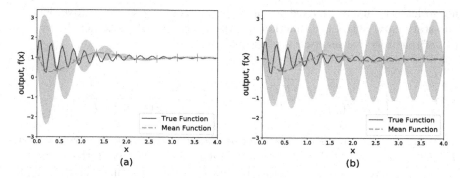

Fig. 2. Posterior distributions obtained using a spatially varying kernel (a) and a fixed length-scale kernel (b). The red markers correspond to the samples observed, the solid blue lines show the true functions, the green dashed lines show the posterior mean function of the GPs and the shaded area covering $\pm 2 \times \sigma$. (Color figure online)

3.3   Optimising Parameters of the Length-Scale Function $l(x)$

The right analytical form for the length-scale function is not sufficient to ensure performance enhancement. The values for parameters in the spatially varying covariance function must be chosen optimally. It is important to restrict the length-scale function from providing invalid length-scale values for the covariance function that can potentially eliminate the positive definiteness of the covariance matrix $\mathbf{K}(\mathbf{X}, \mathbf{X})$. For instance, if a linear function is used as the length-scale function in the given dimension d, then $l(x_d)$ is given by $l(x_d; \theta_d) = a_d \cdot x_d + b_d$, where $\theta_d = \{a_d, b_d\}$. We must ensure that the parameters in θ_d are not such that $l(x_d)$ ever becomes zero or negative within the Bayesian optimisation search bound. We can estimate the optimised values for the hyperparameters θ_d by maximising the log marginal likelihood given in Eq. (4) to obtain

$$\Theta^* = \underset{\theta_d}{\operatorname{argmax}} \log \mathcal{L} \tag{8}$$

To enhance the convergence of the likelihood maximisation, the gradients of the log marginal likelihood are computed and provided to the global optimiser. The general form of the log marginal likelihood gradient is given by Eq. (9).

$$\frac{\partial \log \mathcal{L}}{\partial \Theta} = -\frac{1}{2}\left(\mathbf{y}^\mathsf{T}\mathbf{K}^{-1}\frac{\partial \mathbf{K}}{\partial \Theta}\mathbf{K}^{-1}\mathbf{y}\right) - \frac{1}{2}\mathrm{Tr}\left(\mathbf{K}^{-1}\frac{\partial \mathbf{K}}{\partial \Theta}\right) \tag{9}$$

In our case, gradients of the log marginal likelihood depend on the analytical form of the length-scale function chosen. Therefore, the resulting gradients of the log marginal likelihood are calculated as a Jacobian matrix. For instance, if the length-scale function used is linear, then the Jacobian matrix is given by

$$\frac{\partial \mathbf{K}}{\partial \theta_d} = \left[\frac{\partial \mathbf{K}}{\partial l(x_d)}\cdot\frac{\partial l(x_d)}{\partial a_d} \;,\; \frac{\partial \mathbf{K}}{\partial l(x_d)}\cdot\frac{\partial l(x_d)}{\partial b_d}\right] \text{where,} \; \frac{\partial l(x_d)}{\partial a_d} = x_d \;;\; \frac{\partial l(x_d)}{\partial b_d} = 1 \tag{10}$$

The modified Bayesian optimisation algorithm with the proposed spatially varying length-scale in the covariance function is given by Algorithm 1.

Algorithm 1. Bayesian optimisation with spatially varying covariance function.

Input: Set of Observations $\mathcal{D}_{1:t} = \{\mathbf{x}_{1:t}, \mathbf{y}_{1:t}\}$, length-scale function type $l(x_d, \theta_d)$

1. **For** $t = 1, 2, ..$ **Do**
2.   Optimise hyperparameters to obtain Θ^* using Eq. (8) and Eq. (9)
3.   Use the kernel function in Eq. (7) to update the GP Model with Θ^*
4.   Find the next point to query, *i.e.*, $\mathbf{x}_{t+1} = \underset{\mathbf{x}\in\mathcal{X}}{\mathrm{argmax}}\; \alpha_{EI}(\mathbf{x})$
5.   Query the objective function $f(\mathbf{x})$ to find $y_{t+1} = f(\mathbf{x}_{t+1}) + \epsilon_{t+1}$
6.   Augment the Data $\mathcal{D}_{1:t+1} = \mathcal{D}_{1:t} \cup (\mathbf{x}_{t+1}, y_{t+1})$
7. **end For**

---

4   Experimental Evaluations

We evaluate the performance of the proposed algorithm on various synthetic benchmark functions. Then, we tune the hyperparameters of Support Vector Machines (SVM) with RBF kernel and Elastic Net models, both performing classification task on real-world datasets. We compare the performance of the proposed algorithm (SVL) with the other Bayesian optimisation (BO) algorithms: (i) **FIX** BO with fixed length-scale SE kernel [1], (ii) **ARD** BO with Automatic Relevance Determination (ARD) SE kernel [19] and (iii) **MULTI** BO with multiple weighted kernels [7]. We use Expected Improvement acquisition function $\alpha_{EI}(\mathbf{x})$ to guide the search for the optimum in all our experiments. We plot simple regret, $r_t = f(\mathbf{x}^*) - \underset{\mathbf{x}\in\mathcal{D}_{1:t}}{\max} f(\mathbf{x})$ for the methods mentioned above.

4.1   Synthetic Benchmark Functions

First, we test our algorithm with a benchmark function[1] resembling a damped harmonic oscillator function having multiple local maxima and local minima. This benchmark function is treated as an expensive black-box function in our experiments. The length-scale function is chosen as $l(x_d) = a_d \cdot x_d + b_d$, to model the objective function more accurately. We also present results for other 1D benchmark functions like the Xin-She Yang N.3 function and the Gramacy & Lee function[2]. The results are as shown in Fig. 3.

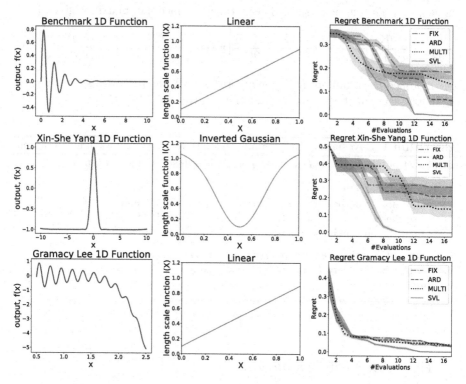

Fig. 3. Simple regret for 1D benchmark functions. The first column depicts the objective function, the second column represents the length-scale function used, and the last column depicts the simple regret over number of iterations.

In the case of higher dimensions, we use the synthetic functions listed in Table 1 for the experiments. The results for the evaluations with 2D benchmark functions are as shown in Fig. 4. For instance, in the case of the Ackley 2D function, the global maximum is found at the origin $O(0,0)$, where it seems to be more wiggly. Therefore we can expect shorter length-scales around this

---

[1] http://infinity77.net/global_optimization/test_functions.html.
[2] https://www.sfu.ca/~ssurjano/optimization.html.

region and larger length-scales, otherwise. This can be achieved by selecting a length-scale function that looks like an inverted Gaussian curve. The shorter length-scales are generated around the origin to concentrate the search around that region and hence the optimum is reached with fewer function evaluations. Likewise, in the experiments with more than three dimensions, we have considered the same inverted Gaussian length-scale function as the generic prior. The main intuition here is that the region around the optimum generally appears to be more jagged than that of the other regions. Therefore, choosing an inverted Gaussian curve and estimating the right value for the mean enables our algorithm to converge quickly. For d dimensional synthetic functions, the convergence results after $10 \times d$ iterations obtained for different algorithms are as shown in Table 2.

4.2   Real-World Dataset

We evaluate the proposed algorithm in tuning hyperparameters of machine learning algorithms operating on Wisconsin Diagnostic Breast Cancer Dataset

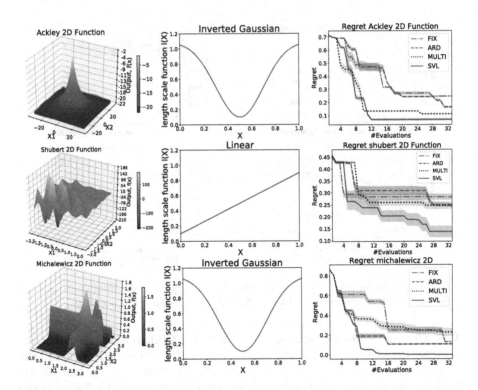

Fig. 4. Simple regret for 2D benchmark functions. The first column depicts the objective function, the second column represents the length-scale function used in both the dimensions, and the last column depicts the regret over iterations.

Table 1. Details of the synthetic benchmark functions.

Function	Range	$f(\mathbf{x}^*)$	$\mathbf{x}^*$
Ackley n-D	$x_i \in [-32.76, 32.76]$	0	$\mathbf{x} = (0, \cdots, 0)$
Shubert 2D	$x_i \in [-5.12, 5.12]$	186.7	$\mathbf{x} = (-1.424, -0.799)$
Michalewicz 2D	$x_i \in [0, \pi]$	1.801	$\mathbf{x} = (2.2044, 1.5692)$
Hartmann 3D	$x_i \in [0, 1]$	3.862	$\mathbf{x} = (0.1146, 0.5556, 0.8525)$
Rosenbrock n-D	$x_i \in [-2.04, 2.04]$	0	$\mathbf{x} = (1, \cdots, 1)$
Hartmann 6D	$x_i \in [0, 1]$	3.322	$\mathbf{x} = (0.201, 0.15, 0.476, 0.275, 0.311, 0.657)$

Table 2. Simple regret for synthetic functions in higher dimensions after $10 \times d$ iterations. Each cell signifies the mean value of regret along with standard error.

Function	MULTI	ARD	FIX	SVL
Hartmann 3D	0.0112 ± 0.00	0.0013 ± 0.00	0.0119 ± 0.00	$\mathbf{0.0002 \pm 0.00}$
Rosenbrock 5D	0.4179 ± 0.00	0.3163 ± 0.01	4.3746 ± 0.07	$\mathbf{0.2119 \pm 0.00}$
Ackley 6D	0.0204 ± 0.00	0.0275 ± 0.00	0.0209 ± 0.00	$\mathbf{0.0144 \pm 0.00}$
Hartmann 6D	0.0153 ± 0.00	0.0172 ± 0.00	0.0200 ± 0.00	$\mathbf{0.0123 \pm 0.00}$

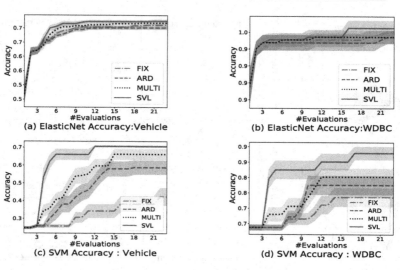

Fig. 5. Hyperparameter tuning for machine learning algorithms. Subfigures (a), (b) depict the accuracy obtained for Elastic Net and (c), (d) for SVM accuracy.

(WDBC) and the Vehicle Dataset, available from UCI data repository[3]. For the SVM, we tune the cost parameter (C) and the width of the RBF kernel in the exponent space of $[-3, 3]$ and $[-5, 0]$, respectively. Next, we tune the Elastic Net hyperparameters, *i.e.*, the Elastic Net mixing parameter (L1 Ratio) in the interval $[0, 1]$ and the penalty parameter in the exponent space of $[-7, -1]$. The results obtained for the hyperparameter tuning are as shown in Fig. 5.

---

[3] https://archive.ics.uci.edu/ml/index.php.

5   Conclusion

We propose a novel method to incorporate additional knowledge from the domain experts about the spatial properties of the objective function to accelerate Bayesian optimisation. We have used a spatially varying kernel to embody the variance in the smoothness of the objective function by representing the length-scale as a function of the input. The added information about the smoothness improves the accuracy of GP surrogate models, thereby ensuring better convergence. We have discussed the valid choices available for the length-scale function and also an approach to estimate its parameters. The experimental results show that our proposed method outperforms other Bayesian optimisation algorithms.

Acknowledgements. This research was partially funded by the Australian Government through the Australian Research Council (ARC). Prof Venkatesh is the recipient of an ARC Australian Laureate Fellowship (FL170100006).

References

1. Brochu, E., Cora, V.M., De Freitas, N.: A tutorial on Bayesian optimization of expensive cost functions, with application to active user modeling and hierarchical reinforcement learning. arXiv preprint arXiv:1012.2599 (2010)
2. Cora, V.M.: Model-based active learning in hierarchical policies. Ph.D. thesis, University of British Columbia (2008)
3. Czarnecki, W.M., Podlewska, S., Bojarski, A.J.: Robust optimization of SVM hyperparameters in the classification of bioactive compounds. J. Cheminformatics **7**(1), 38 (2015)
4. Dalal, C.A., Pavlovic, V., Kopp, R.E.: Intrinsic non-stationary covariance function for climate modeling. arXiv preprint arXiv:1507.02356 (2015)
5. Diehl, C.P., Cauwenberghs, G.: SVM incremental learning, adaptation and optimization. In: 2003 Proceedings of the International Joint Conference on Neural Networks, vol. 4, pp. 2685–2690. IEEE (2003)
6. Gibbs, M.N.: Bayesian Gaussian processes for regression and classification. Ph.D. thesis, Citeseer (1998)
7. Gönen, M., Alpaydın, E.: Multiple kernel learning algorithms. J. Mach. Learn. Res. **12**(Jul), 2211–2268 (2011)
8. Joy, T.T., Rana, S., Gupta, S., Venkatesh, S.: A flexible transfer learning framework for Bayesian optimization with convergence guarantee. Expert Syst. Appl. **115**, 656–672 (2019)
9. Kushner, H.J.: A new method of locating the maximum point of an arbitrary multipeak curve in the presence of noise. J. Basic Eng. **86**(1), 97–106 (1964)
10. Li, C., et al.: Rapid Bayesian optimisation for synthesis of short polymer fiber materials. Sci. Rep. **7**(1), 5683 (2017)
11. Li, C., et al.: Accelerating experimental design by incorporating experimenter hunches. arXiv preprint arXiv:1907.09065 (2019)
12. Martinez-Cantin, R.: Funneled Bayesian optimization for design, tuning and control of autonomous systems. IEEE Trans. Cybern. **99**, 1–12 (2018)
13. Paciorek, C.J., Schervish, M.J.: Nonstationary covariance functions for Gaussian process regression. In: Advances in Neural Information Processing Systems, pp. 273–280 (2004)

14. Shah, A., Wilson, A., Ghahramani, Z.: Student-t processes as alternatives to Gaussian processes. In: Artificial intelligence and Statistics, pp. 877–885 (2014)
15. Snelson, E., Ghahramani, Z., Rasmussen, C.E.: Warped Gaussian processes. In: Advances in Neural Information Processing Systems, pp. 337–344 (2004)
16. Snoek, J., Swersky, K., Zemel, R., Adams, R.: Input warping for Bayesian optimization of non-stationary functions. In: International Conference on Machine Learning, pp. 1674–1682 (2014)
17. Souza, J.R., Marchant, R., Ott, L., Wolf, D.F., Ramos, F.: Bayesian optimisation for active perception and smooth navigation. In: 2014 IEEE International Conference on Robotics and Automation (ICRA), pp. 4081–4087. IEEE (2014)
18. Taddy, M.A., Lee, H.K., Gray, G.A., Griffin, J.D.: Bayesian guided pattern search for robust local optimization. Technometrics $51(4)$, 389–401 (2009)
19. Williams, C.K., Rasmussen, C.E.: Gaussian Processes for Machine Learning, vol. 2. MIT Press, Cambridge (2006)
20. Wilson, J., Hutter, F., Deisenroth, M.: Maximizing acquisition functions for Bayesian optimization. In: Advances in Neural Information Processing Systems, pp. 9884–9895 (2018)
21. Zou, H., Hastie, T.: Regularization and variable selection via the elastic net. J. Roy. Stat. Soc. Ser. B (Stat. Methodol.) $67(2)$, 301–320 (2005)

Bayesian Optimization with Discrete Variables

Phuc Luong$^{(\boxtimes)}$, Sunil Gupta, Dang Nguyen, Santu Rana,
and Svetha Venkatesh

Applied Artificial Intelligence Institute, Deakin University, Geelong, Australia
{pluong,sunil.gupta,d.nguyen,santu.rana,svetha.venkatesh}@deakin.edu.au

Abstract. Bayesian Optimization (BO) is an efficient method to optimize an expensive black-box function with continuous variables. However, in many cases, the function has only discrete variables as inputs, which cannot be optimized by traditional BO methods. A typical approach to optimize such functions assumes the objective function is on a continuous domain, then applies a normal BO method with a rounding of suggested continuous points to nearest discrete points at the end. This may cause BO to get stuck and repeat pre-existing observations. To overcome this problem, we propose a method (named **Discrete-BO**) that manipulates the exploration of an acquisition function and the length scale of a covariance function, which are two key components of a BO method, to prevent sampling a pre-existing observation. Our experiments on both synthetic and real-world applications show that the proposed method outperforms state-of-the-art baselines in terms of convergence rate. More importantly, we also show some theoretical analyses to prove the correctness of our method.

Keywords: Bayesian optimization · Gaussian process · Discrete variables · Hyper-parameter tuning

1 Introduction

Bayesian optimization [11, 12] is an efficient approach to find a global optimizer of expensive black-box functions, i.e. the functions that are non-convex, expensive to evaluate, and do not have a closed-form to compute derivative information. For example, tuning hyper-parameters of a machine learning (ML) model can be considered as an expensive black-box function since it is time-consuming, and there is no explicit mathematical formula that maps the hyper-parameters to the accuracy of the model. Additionally, evaluating the goodness of a hyper-parameter set requires re-training of the model and assessment of the trained model on a validation set, which is expensive especially on large models like deep neural networks. BO can find the best set of hyper-parameters within a reasonable number of iterations because it makes use of observed data to predict a next point where the function should be evaluated. Generally, a BO method

© Springer Nature Switzerland AG 2019
J. Liu and J. Bailey (Eds.): AI 2019, LNAI 11919, pp. 473–484, 2019.
https://doi.org/10.1007/978-3-030-35288-2_38

has two main steps. First, it builds a surrogate model for the objective function and quantifies the epistemic uncertainty of the surrogate model using a Bayesian machine learning technique (e.g. using a Gaussian process). Second, it uses an acquisition function constructed from the surrogate model to decide where to sample the next function evaluation point. A summary of recent research work in BO and its applications in real-world problems can be found in [15].

When optimizing a function, most BO methods assume the input variables to be continuous because BO uses an acquisition function defined only on a continuous domain. In real-world applications, it is common to encounter problems with discrete variables, e.g. the number of trees and depth in tuning a random forest model, the number of layers/hidden units and the batch-size in tuning a neural network. Therefore, applying BO to optimize functions with discrete inputs is a challenging problem. First, when BO samples the next point for function evaluation, it suggests a continuous point that is an invalid input for the function. Second, we have exponentially many combinations of discrete values with respect to the number of variables, which causes the search space to become large and impractical to try all possible values.

Existing Methods. There have been a few prior attempts to develop methods to optimize expensive black-box functions defined on discrete inputs. One of them is the *Transformation* approach of Garrido-Merchán and Hernandez-Lobat [4]. This method is based on BO and assumes that the objective function does not change its values except at discrete points. Although this method can tackle the discrete inputs by simply rounding the inputs of a covariance function, it makes the acquisition function a step-wise function, which is difficult to optimize. Another work is *Sequential model-based optimization for general algorithm configuration* (SMAC) [5], which uses random forest as a surrogate model instead of a Gaussian process. It has a low computational cost and can naturally deal with discrete variables due to the tree-based structure. However, random forest is not a good choice for the surrogate model because it has a limitation in performing extrapolation [9]. Similarly, *Tree-parzen estimators* (TPE) [1] is another tree-based method which estimates the densities of good and bad candidate points in the search space and can cope with discrete variables by randomly sampling candidates from discrete distributions. Unfortunately, TPE requires a large enough number of observations, in the beginning, to model the density distribution efficiently. BO methods for multi-armed bandit [15] can tackle discrete domain. However, they do not incorporate correlation between neighbour discrete values, and they need to sample the same point again to reduce the uncertainty. Because of these disadvantages, the problem of black-box function optimization with discrete variables remains open.

When a standard BO is used to optimize functions with discrete variables, it treats discrete variables as continuous then applies a normal BO method, and finally rounds the suggested continuous point before function evaluations. We call this approach as *BO with naive rounding* (Naive BO). This approach does not have the problems of above-mentioned works e.g. step-wise difficult to optimize acquisition function, extrapolation problems of SMAC, or the density modelling requirement of TPE. However, this approach often starts to repeat the function evaluations at previously tried points due to rounding of a continuous suggestion to the nearest discrete value in the search space. It is illustrated in Fig. 1, and, in this paper, we aim at solving this problem.

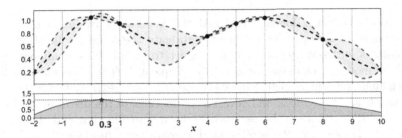

Fig. 1. An illustration of the repetition of pre-existing observations problem of standard BO caused by naive rounding. We can only evaluate at grid locations, and we already evaluated at -2, 0, 1, 4, 5, 6, 8, and 10 indicated by black dots. Using a Gaussian process, we can calculate the predictive mean (dashed line) and variance to build an acquisition function. Maximizing the acquisition suggests a continuous point (red marker) $x = 0.3$ that is invalid to evaluate, so we round to the nearest grid point $x = 0$ which is already observed. (Color figure online)

Our Method. We propose a novel approach, named **Discrete-BO**, to solve the repetition problem in the Naive BO method. In particular, we want the algorithm to sample points that are different from pre-existing observations by shifting the suggested point obtained after maximizing an acquisition function. There are two ways to shift the suggested point. One is to increase the value of the exploration factor of the acquisition function, and another one is to adjust the length scale of the covariance function. To select the optimal values for the exploration factor and length scale, we formalize it as an optimization problem. With these optimal exploration factor and length scale, our proposed method not only suggests valid discrete points but also avoids the repetition of observations.

Our contributions are:

- We propose **Discrete-BO** – a BO method for optimizing expensive black-box functions with discrete inputs.
- We provide theoretical analyses for a deeper understanding of our method.
- We conduct comprehensive experiments on both synthetic functions and real-world applications where our method outperforms state-of-the-art baselines.

2   Background

In this section, we briefly provide basic knowledge of BO with Gaussian process (GP) and the well-known upper confidence bound (GP-UCB) acquisition function since they form the basic framework of our proposed method. A detailed review of BO and acquisition functions can be found in [3,10].

Bayesian Optimization with Gaussian Process. BO is a well-known search strategy for finding the global optimizer of an expensive and noisy black-box function [12]. Specifically, BO finds the optimizer (i.e. the optimal input):

$$x^* = \underset{x \in \mathcal{X}}{\mathrm{argmax}} \, f(x) \tag{1}$$

where $\mathcal{X}$ is a bounded domain in $\mathbb{R}^d$ and $f(x)$ is an objective function.

Normally, it is expensive to directly evaluate the objective function, thus BO builds a surrogate model that is cheaper to sample. One commonly used surrogate model is Gaussian process [13]. Typically, $f(x)$ is assumed to be a smooth function and modelled by a GP, i.e. $f(x) \sim \mathcal{GP}(\mu(x), k(x, x'))$, where $\mu(x)$ and $k(x, x')$ are mean and covariance functions of the distribution. In the context of BO, mean can be assumed to be a zero function and the *squared exponential* kernel (Eq. (2)) is often used for covariance function.

$$k(x, x') = \sigma^2 exp(-\frac{1}{2l^2}\|x - x'\|^2) \tag{2}$$

where σ^2 is a parameter dictating the uncertainty in $f(x)$ and l is a length scale parameter which controls how quickly a function can change.

Let $\mathcal{D} = \{(x_i, y_i)\}_{i=1}^N$ is our observations that contain N inputs x_i and their corresponding function values $y_i = f(x_i) + \epsilon_i$ and $\epsilon_i \sim \mathcal{N}(0, \sigma_\epsilon^2)$. By fitting the observed data into the GP, we obtain the *predictive distribution* of $f(x)$ at any point x in the search space. This predictive distribution is also a Gaussian distribution characterized by the mean and variance as follows:

$$\mu(x) = \mathbf{k}^T(\mathbf{K} + \sigma_\epsilon^2\mathbf{I})^{-1}\mathbf{y}, \quad \sigma^2(x) = k(x, x) - \mathbf{k}^T(\mathbf{K} + \sigma_\epsilon^2\mathbf{I})^{-1}\mathbf{k} \tag{3}$$

where $\mathbf{y} = (y_1, ..., y_N)$ is a vector of the function values we have so far, $k(x, x)$ is the covariance at point x, $\mathbf{k} = [k(x_i, x)]_{\forall x_i \in D}$ is the covariance between the new point x and all other observed points x_i, $\mathbf{K} = [k(x_i, x_j)_{\forall x_i, x_j \in D}]$ is the covariance matrix, $\mathbf{I}$ is an identity matrix with the same dimension as $\mathbf{K}$, and σ_ϵ^2 is the measurement noise.

The posterior mean and variance, calculated from Eq. (3), are used to define an acquisition function $\alpha(x)$, and various types of acquisition function are presented in [3,12]. In our method, we use the well-known GP-UCB because it was theoretically analyzed to have a bounded regret [16].

Upper Confidence Bound Acquisition Function. This acquisition function combines the posterior mean and variance from Eq. (3) as:

$$\alpha_t^{UCB}(x) = \mu(x) + \sqrt{\beta_t}\sigma(x) \tag{4}$$

where β_t is the exploitation-exploration trade-off factor. The author in [16] recommends the value $\beta_t = 2\log\left(t^2 2\pi^2/3\delta\right) + 2d\log\left(t^2 dbr\sqrt{\log\left(4da/\delta\right)}\right)$. Using this β_t, BO algorithm with GP-UCB achieves an upper bound on the cumulative regret with the highest probability, greater or equal to $1 - \delta$, in the search space, which is a subset of $[0, r]^d$ with $r > 0$, and $a, b > 0$ are constants [16].

The acquisition function in Eq. (4) qualifies every point x in the domain so that we can sample the next point x_{t+1} as follows:

$$x_{t+1} = \operatorname*{argmax}_{x \in \mathcal{X}} \alpha_t^{UCB}(x) \tag{5}$$

Acquisition functions differ in the way of balancing exploration and exploitation. The simplest one is the *Probability of Improvement* (PI) [8], which purely exploits the area near the incumbent [3], thus it might easily fall into a local optimum. An alternative is the *Expected Improvement* (EI) [6,7], which incorporates both exploitation and exploration leading to the global solution. Essentially, all acquisition functions mentioned above assume that the objective function $f(x)$ continuous so that the Eq. (5) returns a real-valued point.

3   The Proposed Framework

Given an expensive black-box function $f(x)$ with discrete inputs as illustrated in Fig. 2, our goal is to find the maximum of the function as

$$x^* = \operatorname*{argmax}_{x \in \mathcal{X}} f(x) \tag{6}$$

where $\mathcal{X}$ is **a finite discrete domain** in $\mathbb{R}^d$, and we only have noisy observations in the form $y_i = f(x_i) + \epsilon_i$, $\epsilon_i \sim \mathcal{N}(0, \sigma_\epsilon^2)$.

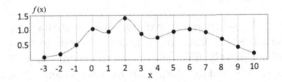

Fig. 2. An example of a black-box function with a discrete variable x. We do not know the form of this function, but we can evaluate it at discrete points in the set $\{-3, ..., 10\}$. Any other values of the variable x are invalid inputs.

The optimization in Eq. (6) is particularly challenging because $f(x)$ is defined only on discrete points. However, since most of the real-world functions may still take correlated values on discrete points in a neighbourhood, one can fit a continuous function passing through these discrete points as shown in dotted line in Fig. 2. We can use a GP to model this continuous function and then use an acquisition function to suggest the next point for function evaluation. Since this point may not be part of the discrete input set, the function is evaluated at the closet point in the discrete set. But as discussed in Sect. 1 (see Fig. 1), this naive approach may repeatedly evaluate the function at the same point making the algorithm become stuck and causing inefficiency in the algorithm.

Before presenting a solution to this problem, we first provide a detail insight into what determines the next sample when using the GP-UCB acquisition function. In particular, since GP-UCB is a combination of $\mu_t(x)$ and $\sigma_t(x)$, its maximum value is determined strictly by one of the three scenarios.

Case 1. $\mu_t(x)$ dominates $\alpha_t(x)$: The maximizer of $\alpha_t(x)$ is determined completely by $\mu_t(x)$, and $\sigma_t(x)$ has no effect on the solution. If the naive rounding scheme experiences repetition of any previously evaluated function values, we can artificially increase the weighting β_t to increase the effect of $\sigma_t(x)$ in determining the maximizer. Although this "artificial" increase of β_t introduces some extra exploration in the optimization, it makes the algorithm going (without repetitions) while ensuring the convergence guarantee [16].

Case 2. $\sigma(x)$ dominates $\alpha_t(x)$: The maximizer of $\alpha_t(x)$ is determined completely by $\sigma_t(x)$, and $\mu_t(x)$ has no effect on the solution. Thus, the repetition is not possible because close to the existing observations, the $\sigma_t(x)$ will be small and will not achieve maximum.

Case 3. $\mu(x)$ and $\sigma(x)$ are balanced: Both $\mu(x)$ and $\sigma(x)$ have influence in determining the maximizer. In the event of any repetition, adjusting β_t can make it $\sigma(x)$ dominated, which will stop repetitions. However, in this case, it may be possible to adjust the GP kernel length scale as an additional control to avoid repetitions as by increasing/decreasing length scale will allow us to not use excessively high values of β_t. We note that changing the length scale may cause slight misspecification of the GP prior, however, the convergence of the algorithm still remains guaranteed.

In three cases, the solution for avoiding the repetitions requires adjusting β_t and/or the kernel length scale. Importantly, it needs to be set to reasonable values as their values directly affect the optimization efficiency. A large value of β causes more exploration, making the algorithm less efficient. Similarly, the length scale l controls the smoothness of a surrogate model, and a large misspecification leads to a requirement of more samples to get accurate function estimation.

Proposed Method

Based on the above observations and analyses, we propose our **Discrete-BO** algorithm. Our idea is to avoid sampling pre-existing observations by increasing the exploration-exploitation trade-off factor β and adjusting the length scale l of the covariance function. In the following we describe an optimal way to adjust the β and the length scale l.

Optimizing β and l. In our proposed algorithm, whenever a suggestion is repeated, we find new values of β and l so that the rounded maximizer of the acquisition function differs from the previously suggested rounded maximizer. Although we can adjust β and l using random search or grid search, it will be computationally expensive to find the appropriate combination of β and l.

Therefore, we take a systematic approach to find the new values of β and l by solving an optimization problem as follows:

$$\beta^*, l^* = \underset{\Delta\beta \in [0,\beta_h], l \in (0,l_h]}{\text{argmin}} g(\beta_t + \Delta\beta, l)$$
$$g(\beta_t + \Delta\beta, l) = \Delta\beta + \|x_{t+1} - x'_{t+1}\|_2 + P(x'_{t+1})$$

(7)

The $\Delta\beta$ is the increment applied on β_t as $\beta_t \leftarrow \beta_t + \Delta\beta$. The x_{t+1} is the point suggested by the original β_t and l_t. The x'_{t+1} is the point suggested by the $\beta_t + \Delta\beta$ and adjusted l. The term $P(x'_{t+1})$ is set to a constant C if $round(x'_{t+1}) \in D_t$, otherwise it is zero. We can manually set the upper limits β_h and l_h.

The optimization problem in Eq. (7) has *three objectives*. The *first* objective is to minimize $\Delta\beta$ since we do not want our new β_t to exceed much more than the original β_t to avoid inefficiency. We can not have negative $\Delta\beta$ as this will take away convergence guarantee of the algorithm [16]. The *second* objective is to minimize the distance between x_{t+1} and x'_{t+1} because the algorithm should suggest a discrete point that is close to the current potential area for exploitation. The *third* objective is to minimize a penalty, which is given to make sure pre-existing observation is not sampled again. The optimization problem in (7) is a continued non-convex problem. We solve it using L-BGFG with multiple random initializations. We summarize **Discrete-BO** in Algorithm 1.

Algorithm 1. Discrete-BO algorithm

Input: GP model, initial data $D_0 = \{(x_0, y_0)\}$, upper limits β_h, l_h

1   **for** $t = 0, ..., n$ **do**
2   β_t is calculated as suggested for GP-UCB, l_t is estimated using D_t
3   Select the next sample $x_{t+1} = \text{argmax}_{x \in \mathcal{X}} \alpha_t^{UCB}(x)$ with β_t, l_t
4     $x_{t+1} = round(x_{t+1})$
5   **if** $x \in D_t$ **then**
6   Find the optimal β^* and l^* using (7): $\beta_t \leq \beta \leq \beta_h$ and $0 < l \leq l_h$
7       $x_{t+1} = \underset{x \in \mathcal{X}}{\text{argmax}} \, \alpha_t^{UCB}(x)$ with β^*, l^*
8       $x_{t+1} = round(x_{t+1})$
9   Query the objective function to obtain y_{t+1}
10   Augment $D_{t+1} = \{D_t, (x_{t+1}, y_{t+1})\}$ and update statistical model GP
11 **end**

---

4   Theoretical Analysis

In this section, we provide a theoretical understanding of our algorithm. We start by providing a definition of the repetition of pre-existing observations.

Definition 1. *In a discrete domain, a sample point is repeated if the following condition holds:* $x_{t+1} = \lfloor \text{argmax}_{x \in \mathbb{R}} \alpha_t(x) \rceil \in D_t$, *where D_t consists of observations up to iteration t.*

The following two Lemmas provide an understanding of the two extreme cases detailed at the start of this section.

Lemma 1. *(μ-dominance) If the BO algorithm repeats an observation due to the dominance of $\mu_t(x)$, there exists an increased β that will lead to a new solution x'_{t+1} of the acquisition function such that $x'_{t+1} \notin D_t$.*

Proof. For μ-dominance case, $\sigma_t(x) \ll \mu_t(x) \ \forall x \in \mathcal{X} \subseteq \mathbb{R}$, then $\max(\alpha) \simeq \max(\mu_t(x))$. Denoting the existing observations up to iteration t as D_t, for any $x_{t+1} \in D_t$, let us assume that x_{t+1} is the rounded value of a continuous value x_a. Also consider another continuous value x_b such that the rounded value of x_b is not in D_t. Then $||x_a - x_{t+1}|| < ||x_b - x_{t+1}||$ and $\sigma(x_a) < \sigma(x_b)$. By sufficiently increasing β_t, we make the effect of $\sigma(x)$ term dominates the $\mu(x)$ term (See $\alpha(x) \triangleq \mu(x) + \sqrt{\beta_t}\sigma(x)$) and thus $\alpha(x_b) > \alpha(x_a)$. Hence, we can always get a solution x_b. Finally, we can recommend the rounded value of x_b to BO. $\blacksquare$

Lemma 2. *(σ-dominance) If the BO algorithm repeats an observation in general, where none of $\mu(x)$ or $\sigma(x)$ dominates, then there exists an increased β and an adjustment in length scale l that will lead to a new solution x'_{t+1} of the acquisition function such that $x'_{t+1} \notin D_t$.*

Proof. For the case where both $\mu_t(x)$ and $\sigma_t(x)$ jointly influence the maximizer of $\alpha_t(x)$, we can always sufficiently increase β_t and tilt the balance such that the problem can become $\sigma_t(x)$ dominated and therefore, no repetition will occur. By adjusting length scale l, it is possible to use a smaller increase in β_t and get the $\sigma_t(x)$ dominance as shown in the proof of Lemma 1. $\blacksquare$

5   Experiments

We conduct experiments to show the performance of our proposed method **Discrete-BO** on both synthetic and real-world applications. We compare our method with existing methods such as BO with naive rounding (Naive BO), Transformation method of Garrido-Merchán and Hernandez-Lobato [4], SMAC [5], and TPE [2]. These baselines are described in Sect. 1.

In our experiments, we use the *squared exponential* kernel and randomly initialize the optimization with $d + 1$ points, where d is the input dimension. The initialized points are kept identical across all methods for a fair comparison. We also use the same *budget* (i.e. the number of iterations), where at each iteration t we report the best function value found so far by each method. We repeat each method 10 times and report the average result along with the standard error.

5.1   Synthetic Applications

We first illustrate our method on synthetic functions. Since most standard benchmark functions are continuous, we need to discretize them. For example, considering the simple 1-dimension Test function in Table 1, it is a continuous function

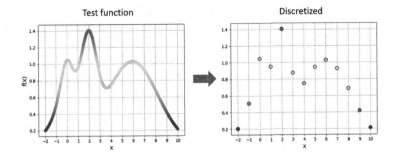

Fig. 3. A discretized version of the Test function in Table 1. It has one global maximum of 1.4 at $x = 2$.

but is discretized, as shown in Fig. 3. Other functions in Table 1 such as Schubert, Eggholder, and Griewank are also discretized, and we multiply them with -1 so that we can find their maximum instead of minimum in their original form.

Table 1. Characteristics of discretized synthetic functions.

Function	Formula	Dim	Range
Test function	$e^{-(x-2)^2} + e^{-\left(\frac{x-6}{10}\right)^2} + \frac{1}{e^{x^2}+1}$	1	$x \in \{-2, \ldots, 10\}$
Schubert	$\prod_{i=1}^{2}\left(\sum_{j=1}^{5} j\, cos((j+1)x_i + j)\right)$	2	$x_1, x_2 \in \{-10, \ldots, 10\}$
Eggholder	$-(x_2 + 47)\, sin\left(\sqrt{\left\|x_2 + \frac{x_1}{2} + 47\right\|}\right)$ $-x_1\, sin\left(\sqrt{\left\|x_1 - (x_2 + 47)\right\|}\right)$	2	$x_1, x_2 \in \{-512, \ldots, 512\}$
Griewank	$\sum_{i=1}^{3} \frac{x_i^2}{4000} - \prod_{i=1}^{3} cos\left(\frac{x_i}{\sqrt{i}}\right) + 1$	3	$x_1, x_2, x_3 \in \{-50, \ldots, 600\}$

Figure 4 shows the optimization results for four functions in Table 1. From the results, we can see that our proposed method **Discrete-BO** is the best method where it significantly outperforms other methods. For example, consider the optimization result of the 1d Test function in Fig. 4(a). Our method and Transformation need only 10 iterations to find the true maximum function value of 1.4. In contrast, TPE requires a double number of iterations (20 iterations) to achieve the same result. Naive BO is unable to find this maximum due to its repetition problem as discussed in Sect. 1. SMAC is better than Naive BO.

When the number of dimensions is increased up to 2 and 3 (Fig. 4(b)–(d)), the optimization becomes a challenging problem due to the large search space. Our method still performs well and it clearly outperforms others. Transformation becomes the second-best method, which can be explained by the fact that the step-wise acquisition function created by Transformation is difficult to optimize on high dimension functions. Interestingly, Naive BO performs much better than TPE and SMAC on the 3d Griewank function.

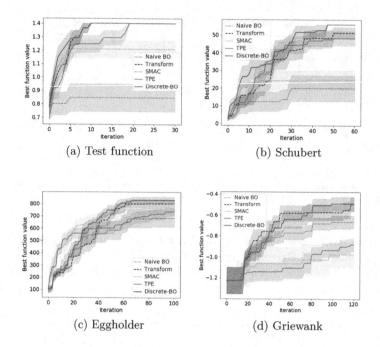

Fig. 4. Results on synthetic functions – best function value (maximum) vs. iteration: (a) Test function, (b) Schubert, (c) Eggholder and (d) Griewank.

5.2 Real-World Applications

The second experiment shows the efficacy of our method in real-world applications: hyper-parameter tuning for a random forest (RF) and a neural network (NN).

Our goal is to find the optimal set of hyper-parameters for two ML models, which achieves the best accuracy in classification. We define the black-box function as a mapping between the hyper-parameters and the classification accuracy on a held-out validation set. For RF, we used the Human Activity Recognition dataset [14], which consists of 10,299 records and 561 features. For NN, we build a network with one hidden layer and train with stochastic gradient descent. We test on the Handwritten Digits dataset [17], which has 1,797 8 × 8 images and 10 labels. The discrete hyper-parameters to optimize are summarized in Table 2.

Figure 5(a) shows the result of hyper-parameter tuning for RF. From the result, we can see that our method **Discrete-BO** and Transformation are the best method. The performances of our method and Transformation are comparable although our method converges slightly faster than Transformation. Compared to SMAC and Naive BO, our method is significantly better. Naive BO is the worst method due to its repetition problem as explained in Fig. 1. TPE is the second-best method and it outperforms SMAC and Naive BO.

Figure 5(b) shows the result of hyper-parameter tuning for NN. Our method clearly outperforms all baselines, needing only 40 iterations to converge to the

Table 2. Hyper-parameters to optimize for Random Forest and Neural Network models. The last column indicates a dataset used to train and test the model.

Model	Hyper-parameters	Dim	Dataset
Random Forest	Estimators $\in \{1,\ldots,100\}$ Min samples in leaf $\in \{1,\ldots,10\}$	2	Human Activity
Neural Network	Hidden units $\in \{1,\ldots,400\}$ Batch size $\in \{1,\ldots,2000\}$ Max iterations $\in \{1,\ldots,1000\}$	3	Handwritten Digits

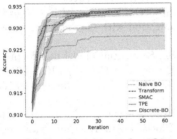

(a) Random forest classifier

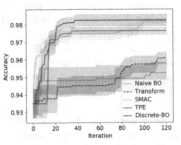

(b) Neural network classifier

Fig. 5. Results of hyper-parameter tuning – best function value (accuracy) vs. iteration for two models: (a) RF and (b) NN.

optimum. Interestingly, Transformation does not perform well whereas SMAC becomes the second-best method; however, SMAC requires 100 iterations (2.5 times larger than ours). TPE is better than Transformation and Naive BO.

6   Conclusion and Future Work

This paper discusses the problem of BO for optimizing black-box functions with discrete variables. The naive rounding BO does not converge since it gets stuck at suggesting pre-existing observations. Our proposed method can improve the vanilla BO in a discrete domain and successfully solves the rounding problem of the vanilla BO without requiring a more complex kernel function. Our experimental results clearly demonstrate the effectiveness of our proposed method.

Acknowledgements. This research was partially funded by the Australian Government through the Australian Research Council (ARC). Prof Venkatesh is the recipient of an ARC Australian Laureate Fellowship (FL170100006).

References

1. Bergstra, J., Yamins, D., Cox, D.D.: Hyperopt: a python library for optimizing the hyperparameters of machine learning algorithms. In: Proceedings of the 12th Python in Science Conference, pp. 13–20. Citeseer (2013)
2. Bergstra, J.S., Bardenet, R., Bengio, Y., Kégl, B.: Algorithms for hyper-parameter optimization. In: Advances in Neural Information Processing Systems, pp. 2546–2554 (2011)
3. Brochu, E., Cora, V.M., De Freitas, N.: A tutorial on Bayesian optimization of expensive cost functions, with application to active user modeling and hierarchical reinforcement learning. arXiv preprint arXiv:1012.2599 (2010)
4. Garrido-Merchán, E.C., Hernández-Lobato, D.: Dealing with categorical and integer-valued variables in Bayesian optimization with Gaussian processes. arXiv preprint arXiv:1805.03463 (2018)
5. Hutter, F., Hoos, H.H., Leyton-Brown, K.: Sequential model-based optimization for general algorithm configuration. In: Coello, C.A.C. (ed.) LION 2011. LNCS, vol. 6683, pp. 507–523. Springer, Heidelberg (2011). https://doi.org/10.1007/978-3-642-25566-3_40
6. Jalali, A., Azimi, J., Fern, X., Zhang, R.: A lipschitz exploration-exploitation scheme for Bayesian optimization. In: Blockeel, H., Kersting, K., Nijssen, S., Železný, F. (eds.) ECML PKDD 2013. LNCS (LNAI), vol. 8188, pp. 210–224. Springer, Heidelberg (2013). https://doi.org/10.1007/978-3-642-40988-2_14
7. Jones, D.R., Schonlau, M., Welch, W.J.: Efficient global optimization of expensive black-box functions. J. Glob. Optim. **13**(4), 455–492 (1998)
8. Kushner, H.J.: A new method of locating the maximum point of an arbitrary multipeak curve in the presence of noise. J. Basic Eng. **86**(1), 97–106 (1964)
9. Lakshminarayanan, B., Roy, D.M., Teh, Y.W.: Mondrian forests for large-scale regression when uncertainty matters. In: Artificial Intelligence and Statistics, pp. 1478–1487 (2016)
10. Lizotte, D.J.: Practical Bayesian optimization. University of Alberta (2008)
11. Mockus, J.: Application of Bayesian approach to numerical methods of global and stochastic optimization. J. Glob. Optim. **4**(4), 347–365 (1994)
12. Mockus, J., Tiesis, V., Zilinskas, A.: The application of Bayesian methods for seeking the extremum. Towards Glob. Optim. **2**(117–129), 2 (1978)
13. Rasmussen, C.E.: Gaussian processes in machine learning. In: Bousquet, O., von Luxburg, U., Rätsch, G. (eds.) ML 2003. LNCS (LNAI), vol. 3176, pp. 63–71. Springer, Heidelberg (2004). https://doi.org/10.1007/978-3-540-28650-9_4
14. Reyes-Ortiz, J.L., Anguita, D., Ghio, A., Parra, X.: Human activity recognition using smartphones data set. UCI Machine Learning Repository; University of California, Irvine, School of Information and Computer Sciences: Irvine, CA, USA (2012)
15. Shahriari, B., Swersky, K., Wang, Z., Adams, R.P., De Freitas, N.: Taking the human out of the loop: a review of Bayesian optimization. Proc. IEEE **104**(1), 148–175 (2016)
16. Srinivas, N., Krause, A., Kakade, S.M., Seeger, M.W.: Information-theoretic regret bounds for Gaussian process optimization in the bandit setting. IEEE Trans. Inform. Theory **58**(5), 3250–3265 (2012)
17. Xu, L., Krzyzak, A., Suen, C.Y.: Methods of combining multiple classifiers and their applications to handwriting recognition. IEEE Trans. Syst. Man Cybern. **22**(3), 418–435 (1992)

Detection of Compromised Models
Using Bayesian Optimization

Deepthi Praveenlal Kuttichira[✉], Sunil Gupta, Dang Nguyen, Santu Rana,
and Svetha Venkatesh

Applied Artificial Intelligence Institute, Deakin University, Geelong, Australia
{dkuttichira,sunil.gupta,d.nguyen,santu.rana,
svetha.venkatesh}@deakin.edu.au

Abstract. Modern AI is largely driven by machine learning. Recent
machine learning algorithms such as deep neural networks (DNN) have
become quite effective in many recognition tasks e.g., object recognition,
face recognition, speech recognition, etc. Due to their effectiveness, these
models are already catering to user needs in the real world. To handle the service requests from large number of users and meet round the
clock demand, these models are usually hosted on cloud platforms (e.g.,
Microsoft Azure ML Studio). When hosting a model on the cloud, there
may be security concerns. For example, during the transit of the model
to the cloud, a malicious third party can alter the model or sometimes
the cloud provider itself may use a lossy compression on the model to
efficiently manage the server resources. We propose a method to detect
such model compromises via sensitive samples. Finding the best sensitive sample boils down to an optimization problem where the sensitive
sample maximizes the difference in the prediction between the original
and the modified model. The optimization problem is challenging as (1)
the altered model is unknown (2) we have to search a sensitive sample
in high-dimensional data space and (3) the optimization problem is a
non-convex problem. To overcome these challenges, we first use a variational autoencoder to transform high-dimensional data to a non-linear
low-dimensional space and then uses Bayesian optimization to find the
optimal sensitive sample. Our proposed method is capable of generating
a sensitive sample that can detect model compromise without incurring
much cost by multiple queries.

Keywords: Cloud service · Sensitive sample · Bayesian optimization

1 Introduction

Machine learning (ML) algorithms have changed the face of problem solving
scenarios of today's world. With the enormous amount of data generated like
medical images, data in social media, images from surveillance cameras and
much more, human analysis of these data is not feasible. ML algorithms analyze
these data to understand useful patterns and perform prediction tasks as good

© Springer Nature Switzerland AG 2019
J. Liu and J. Bailey (Eds.): AI 2019, LNAI 11919, pp. 485–496, 2019.
https://doi.org/10.1007/978-3-030-35288-2_39

as humans in many cases. Consequentially, ML is now being used in many real-world applications such as medical diagnosis, predicting behavioral patterns from posts in social media [16], security systems, autonomous driving and much more. One popular machine learning approach applies Deep Neural Networks (DNN) [12]. A DNN is capable of extracting high-level features from raw data. A DNN has multiple hidden layers, with higher layers learning some high level features from the raw data. In case of images, the low-level features might be some lines or edges. The high-level features might correspond to parts of a face or object. Since they find application in many large-scale problem-solving scenarios and the services are required round the clock, hosting these models locally is not sufficient. Also sometimes training these models requires a lot of computational and storage requirements, which might not be available locally. So these models often use cloud resources. Cloud resources can be used by models in two different ways. The first is to use the resources (e.g. storage space, processing power) to train the model and host it. The second type of usage is to train the model in the local system, then host it in the cloud environment. The former type of cloud service is known as *model training* and the latter is known as *model servicing*. There are many platforms that offer cloud services for training as well as hosting machine learning models. Examples are Amazon Sagemaker, Microsoft Azure ML Studio, and Google cloud ML.

There are certain security threats while hosting a model in the cloud. For example, during the transit of the model to the cloud, a malicious third party can host an attack to modify the model [15]. Also there is a possibility that a dishonest cloud provider might use lossy compression of the original model, at the cost of slight prediction accuracy to save the resources used for hosting. In this situation, the customer ends up paying more than the cost of the actually allocated resources. Other types of attacks target the trained models already hosted on the clouds, like a trojan attack [14], data poisoning attack [3] etc. The common thing about all mentioned types of attacks is that they attempt to adversary modify the *parameters* (aka *weights*) of the model to meet an attack goal.

Detecting if the hosted model is compromised or not is a challenging problem. Once the model is hosted on a cloud, it remains a black-box for the customer. The model can only be queried via the API provide by the cloud service provider. Traditional methods of verification like hashing [10] etc cannot be used. Even if the cloud provider provided an Application Programming Interface (API) to obtain the hash values of the deployed model, it cannot be trusted in case of a dishonest service provider. In the scenario of model servicing, the original model is available in the local machine. In this case a method to detect model compromise is to query the deployed model and look for the mismatch in the prediction of the deployed model (cloud model) and the original model (local model). The attackers usually only slightly modify the model so as to evade detection. So querying with some samples might not detect the compromise. Also querying is costly as payment has to be made for each query. Thus it is imperative to find a sensitive sample that can detect small changes in the model.

A sensitive sample is a sample for which even slight changes in the model, results in different prediction.

Finding a sensitive sample boils down to an optimization problem where the sensitive sample maximizes the difference in the prediction between the original and the modified model. The optimization problem is challenging as (1) the algorithm has to search for a sensitive sample in a high-dimension space and (2) it is a non-convex problem. This requires global optimization. In this paper, we use Bayesian optimization (BO) to efficiently find the sensitive sample. Since the data may lie in a high-dimensional space, we face the challenge of global optimization in high dimension, which is a well known hard problem. Fortunately, for most of the real-world applications, data lie in smaller dimensional manifolds. We use this idea to reduce the data dimension into a non-linear manifold learnt using a variational autoencoder (VAE). We show that the dataset used to train the DNN model is usually sufficient to learn a VAE based data manifold. We then perform the global optimization in the VAE manifold, using a sample efficient global optimizer, widely known as Bayesian optimization. Our proposed method is capable of generating sensitive samples that can detect model compromise without incurring much cost by multiple queries to the cloud.

2 Related Works

Deploying models in clouds poses a risk of being attacked by a third party. Many such attacks have been documented. One such attack is the trojan attack [5,14]. In this technique, the adversary modify the target so as to mis-classify it. Usually this modification is done by adding some kind of trigger (for example, an image where the person wears spectacles). Only the images with triggers will be mis-classified. Another attack technique is data poisoning attack [1,3]. In this method malicious samples are used to tune the parameters of the model to degrade the performance of the system. These integrity breaches pose a major concern in applications such as autonomous driving and user authentication.

There are many works done to verify integrity of the data stored in the cloud [18]. Most of them involve a third party authorization and generating certificates clarifying the integrity of the data. Some traditional integrity checks like hashing are not particularly useful in the cloud scenario. Many cloud service providers do not provide an API to access the hash values. Also, in case of dishonest service providers, these hash values cannot be trusted. A work in integrity checking in cloud scenario has been done by Ghodsi et al. [6]. In this work a framework was proposed to verify the integrity of the cloud provider. This approach struggles to detect some subtle model integrity attacks. Integrity checking by querying the deployed model with sensitive samples has been proposed by He et al. [7]. In this work they query the model with samples that are similar to normal queries but are sensitive to slight changes in the model. They have used a local optimizer to find the sensitive sample.

Bayesian optimization (BO) is an efficient method to optimize expensive functions [2]. It uses the Bayesian technique of setting a prior over the function and using the further observations obtained by evaluation of the function to get the posterior. In order to find the next point of evaluation, it uses an acquisition function that balances the trade-off between exploration and exploitation of the search space. Gaussian process regression (GP) is the most popularly used method for priors in the BO algorithm. Optimization in high dimension is challenging [13]. Finding a representation of high-dimensional data in a low-dimensional manifold is one way to tackle this problem.

VAE is a generative model that consists of an encoder that maps the representation of data in higher dimension to a lower dimension and a decoder that maps the data from latent space to the original dimension [9]. VAE assumes the latent distribution to be a Gaussian distribution. Also the latent space in VAE is continuous. The objective function of VAE ensures that the reconstructed image is similar to the original image and also that the encode representation fall in a Gaussian distribution in the latent space. These two assumptions allow BO to run smoothly in the latent dimension [4].

3   Proposed Method

In the scenario considered for our method, the parameters of the original model is known. The deployed model is a black-box, i.e. the parameters of this model is not known. The parameters usually learned in a DNN model are the weights. Let the parameters of the original model be W and those of the modified black-box model be $W + \Delta w$, where Δw is a perturbation. Let the function of the original model be $y = f(x; W)$ and that of the compromised model be $y' = f(x; W + \Delta w)$. In case of a multi-class problem with r classes, the model function is of the form $y = f(x) = [y_1, y_2, ..., y_r]^T = [f_1(x; W), f_2(x; W), ..., f_r(x; W)]^T$. When a model is compromised, usually the change is in the parameters learned. The goal is to find a sensitive input s similar to x that maximizes the difference between the y and y'. This can be mathematically represented as:

$$s = argmax_x \|y' - y\|_2^2$$
$$= argmax_x \|f(W + \Delta w, x) - f(W, x)\|_2^2 \tag{1}$$
$$= argmax_x \sum_{i=1}^{r} \|f_i(W + \Delta w, x) - f_i(W, x)\|_2^2 \tag{2}$$

Here $\|.\|$ represent l_2 norm of a vector and Δw is the perturbation made by the malicious third party. This perturbation is unknown to us. We do the Taylor expansion of the expression of the Eq. (1) as follows:

$$f_i(W + \Delta w, x) = f_i(W, x) + \frac{\partial f_i(W, x)^T}{\partial W} \Delta w + \mathcal{O}(\|\Delta w\|_2^2) \qquad (3)$$

If Δw is small, we can approximately write

$$\|f_i(W + \Delta w, x) - f_i(W, x)\|_2^2 \approx \left\| \frac{\partial f_i(W, x)^T}{\partial W} \Delta w \right\|_2^2 \qquad (4)$$

When looking at term in Eq. (4), we can ignore the Δw as it does not depend on x. Hence in this case the objective function is of the form $\left\| \frac{\partial f_i(W, x)}{\partial W} \right\|^2$. Here, $f(W, x)$ is the function of the model we have access to. So to find the derivative of this function, we do not need to access the model hosted in the cloud. So the sensitive sample can be found just using the model in hand and can be used to detect multiple model tampering. The derivative of a DNN function w.r.t. weights result in a matrix. The objective function here is the Frobenius norm of the resultant matrix. The objective function also has a constraint that the sensitive sample should fall in the same distribution of the input data. Defining $C(x) \triangleq \left\| \frac{\partial f(W, x)}{\partial W} \right\|_F^2$, the optimization problem can be written as:

$$s = \underset{x \in \mathcal{X}}{\text{argmax}} C(x) \qquad (5)$$

where $\mathcal{X}$ is input data space. For example, in the case of images, the pixel values are in the range between $[0, 255]$. Eq. (5) can be optimized using a local optimizer like Gradient Ascent [7]. However, since Eq. (5) is the gradient of a DNN function and the DNN function is a non-convex function with multiple local minima and maxima, our objective function is also a non-convex function. Using a global optimizer is more suitable for our objective function. Bayesian optimization (BO) is a powerful global optimization method. It is an efficient method to optimize expensive black-box function. When the perturbation Δw is small we can approximate Eq. (1) to a known objective Eq. (5).

3.1 Dimensionality Reduction

Images are high-dimensional inputs. Optimization in high-dimensional space is a challenging problem. Also in our problem, we have to ensure that the sensitive sample lies in the input data distribution. In dimensionality reduction, an assumption is made that for a data distribution in high dimensional space, a representation of the same distribution can be found in a lower-dimensional manifold. To find this lower dimensional representation, various dimensionality reduction techniques like Principal Component Analysis (PCA) and generative models can be used. We have used VAE to achieve this lower dimensional representation.

VAE is a generative model which consists of an encoder and decoder [9]. Encoder maps the observed variable in high-dimensional space to a lower-dimensional latent space. Decoder reconstructs the observed variable from the sample in latent space. VAE is build on the concepts of directed probabilistic graphs. Here the assumption is that for an observed variable x in the high-dimensional space a latent variable z can be inferred in a lower-dimension. In our case the observed variable is the query input. This input is mapped to a latent space by VAE. This latent variable is also assumed to be continuous. The true distribution of the observed variable is a marginal likelihood of x given z which can be expressed as follows:

$$p(x) = \int p(x|z)p(z)dz \qquad (6)$$

The marginal likelihood in Eq. (6) is intractable. The posterior distribution $p_\theta(z|x)$ is also intractable. Thus we use a tractable distribution $q_\Phi(z|x)$ and approximate it to $p_\theta(z|x)$. This approximation is done by minimizing the KL divergence between the two distribution. It can be simplified to the form below:

$$KL(q_\Phi||p_\theta) = log\, p_\theta(x) + \int q_\Phi(z|x)log\, q_\phi(z|x)/p_\theta(z, x) \qquad (7)$$

Here $-\int q_\Phi(z|x)log\, q_\phi(z|x)/p_\theta(z, x)$ is known as the variational lower bound $\mathcal{L}$. Maximizing the lower-bound is equivalent to maximizing the marginal likelihood of the observed variable. Maximizing the lower bound is of the form:

$$\mathcal{L} = -KL(q_\phi(z|x)||p_\theta(z)) + E_{q_\phi(z|x)}\left[log\, p_\theta(x|z)\right] \qquad (8)$$

Equation (8) ensures that the assumed tractable distribution is approximated close to the original latent distribution and the reconstruction error is minimum. Now as the input data distribution is mapped to a latent distribution, we have a latent distribution for our high dimensional input variables. Given a sample x_s in input space the encoding function $q_\phi(.)$ maps the input to latent space to obtain z_s. The decoding function $p_\theta(.)$ maps z_s back to x_s.

3.2   Formulation Using BO

Using BO for high-dimensional data is a challenging problem. Since we have obtained a latent distribution for our input data using VAE, we can use BO in this latent space to obtain a sensitive sample. In BO, since the objective function is assumed to be a black-box function, a Gaussian Process (GP) is used to model the latent function based on observations. We fit a GP in the latent space. The observations are of the form $\{z_j, v_j\}_{j=1}^J$, where J is the number of observations, $v_j = C(p_\theta(z_j)) + \varepsilon_j$ with $\varepsilon_j \sim \mathcal{N}(0, \sigma^2)$, where σ^2 is the measurement noise variance and $p_\theta(.)$ is the decoder function of VAE. Here $C(p_\theta(z_j))$ is the Frobenius norm of the resultant matrix and z_j is the latent variable. For our problem we select a random image from the training dataset, obtain the corresponding representation in the latent space and reconstruct it back in the high-dimensional space to evaluate the objective function and obtain v_j. After using GP to fit the model, we construct an acquisition function to query the next point. Specifically, Gaussian process is a stochastic process where the joint distribution of any point in the domain space is still a Gaussian distribution. Therefore, for a predicted point z_*, its predictive posterior distribution is a Gaussian distribution $\mathcal{N}(\mu(z_*), \sigma^2(z_*))$. With a typical zero-mean assumption for GP mean function, we can write the mean and variance as:

$$\mu(z_*) = \mathbf{k}_{*J}^T (K_{JJ} + \sigma^2 I)^{-1} \mathbf{y}_{1:J}$$
$$\sigma^2(z_*) = k_{**} - \mathbf{k}_{*J}^T (K_{JJ} + \sigma^2 I)^{-1} \mathbf{k}_{*J}$$

where k_{**} is the kernel function, $\mathbf{k}_{*J} = [k(x^*, x_1), \cdots, k(x_{t+1}, x_t)]$ and K_{JJ} is the Gram matrix between $x_{1:J}$. Note that k is the kernel function representing the smoothness of the latent function. The popular choice includes the squared exponential kernel and Matern kernel.

Next based on the built GP, we want an acquisition function to quantify the belief for the next evaluation point. The acquisition function essentially balances between exploration and exploitation. Exploration is when sampling is done from parts of function where we do not have many observations. Exploitation is when we sample near to observed high values of a function. To find the next query point, a natural choice is to use a function to measure the possible improvement over the best observation so far (minimal or maximal). Popular choices include probability of improvement (PI) [11], expected improvement (EI) [8], and GP-upper confidence bound (GP-UCB) [17] have been derived. In our work, we opt for GP-UCB although other acquisition functions are also suitable. We can maximize the acquisition function to obtain the next point and then update Gaussian process and these steps will be repeated. So we propose an algorithm to detect the adversarial compromise of the model using BO, called BO for Compromise Detection (BCD).

4   Experiments

We conduct experiments to show the performance of our proposed method on two real-world datasets, *Olivetti* (aka *AT&T*) and *MNIST*. We compare our method with two popular and recent methods, *Random* and *VerIDeep* [7]. The Random method simply uses a random image chosen from the training set as a *sensitive sample* while the VerIDeep method uses a local optimizer to modify a random image to be a sensitive sample [7].

For VerIDeep, we use the same setting for its hyper-parameters as suggested by the authors. For our BO-based method, we use the *squared exponential* kernel and use the *budget* (i.e. the number of iterations) of 60. We repeat each method 10 times and report the average result along with the standard error.

Algorithm 1. BO for Compromise Dectection (BCD)

---

1. **Input:** $D = \{x_i, y_i\}_{i=1}^n$
2. Train the DNN;
3. The objective function $\left\| \frac{\partial f(W,x)}{\partial W} \right\|_F^2$ is the Frobenius norm of the derivative of DNN;
4. Train the VAE using D;
5. Select a random sample x_s from the Input;
6. Use encoder of VAE q_ϕ to generate $q_\phi(x_s) = z_s$;
7. Use decoder of VAE p_θ to reconstruct z_s in input space and evaluate objective function;
8. The initial observation for BO is $D^{BO} = \{z_i, v_i\}_{i=1}^n$;
9. Fit a GP in z space using initial observation;
10. **For** $t = 1, 2, ...T$ **do**
11.   Recommend z_t by optimizing the acquisition function GP-UCB;
12.   Reconstruct $x_t = p_\theta(z_t)$ to evaluate the objective function;
13.   Augment the initial dataset with the observed points $D_{1:t}^{BO} = D_{1:t-1}^{BO} U\{z_t, v_t\}$ and update GP;
14. **end for**
15. Reconstruct the z_t^* using decoder as the sensitive sample s;

4.1 Dataset Description

In our experiments, we used two standard real-world datasets. The first dataset is the Olivetti dataset. This dataset has 40 labels and 400 data points. These are the facial images of 40 different people, each of who has 10 images under different poses. The second dataset is the MNIST dataset, which has 10 labels and 60,000 digit images, where each image is a gray-scale image of size 28×28. For both datasets, we normalize the data points where we transform the pixel values to the range of $[0, 1]$.

4.2 Architecture of the Model Used

The machine learning model used for our experiment with the dataset Olivetti is a neural network with one hidden layer. The input layer has 4,096 neurons and the hidden layer has 256 neurons with the *relu* activation function. The output layer has 40 neurons with the *softmax* activation function.

For the dataset MNIST, we also use a neural network with one hidden layer. The input layer has 784 neurons, the hidden layer has 256 neurons, and the output layer has 10 neurons. The *relu* function is used as the activation function for the hidden layer while the *softmax* function is used for the output layer.

4.3 Experimental Settings and Results

Since the change in output is mostly influenced by the slight changes in the weights in the last layer [7], we consider only the weights in the last layer as the parameters of interest. For the Olivetti dataset, the original model achieves

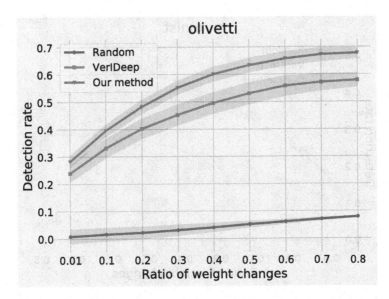

Fig. 1. Detection rate with respect to ratio of weight changes on Olivetti dataset. As the ratio of weight changes increases, the difference between two models (the original model vs. the compromised one) also increases. This allows all methods to detect the compromise easier.

an accuracy of 88.75% and for the MNIST dataset it achieves an accuracy of 97.96%. To compromise the model, we add a Gaussian noise with mean 0 and standard deviation 0.01 to the weights in the last layer. We vary the ratio of the weight changes in the last layer from 0.1% to 80%, the same setting as in [7].

Quantitative Results. Given a *sensitive sample*, if the output given by the original model and the compromised model for that sample is different, we say the sensitive sample has correctly detected the compromised model. For each sensitive sample obtained, we test it against with 500 modified models, and evaluate the *detection rate* calculated as the percentage of times the sensitive sample is able to detect the compromise in the model.

Figure 1 shows the detection rates of the three methods (Random, VerIDeep, and our method) on the dataset Olivetti. From the figure, we can see that our method clearly outperforms the other methods by a large margin. For example, considering the ratio of weight changes at 0.8. Our method is able to detect nearly 70% cases of compromised models whereas the second-best method VerIDeep only achieves an accuracy of 58%. In case the compromised model is just slightly different from the original one (e.g. the ratio of weight changes is just 0.01), our method is still able to detect nearly 30% cases whereas the Random method totally fails in this extreme scenario.

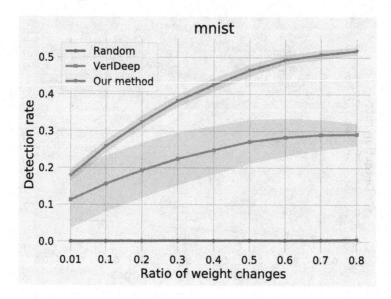

Fig. 2. Detection rate with respect to ratio of weight changes on MNIST dataset. As the ratio of weight changes increases, the difference between two models (the original model vs. the compromised one) also increases.

Figure 2 shows the detection rates of Random, VerIDeep, and our method on the dataset MNIST. Similar to the result on Olivetti, our method is significantly better than the two baselines. Compared to VerIDeep, the gain obtained by our method over VerIDeep is noticeable, around 7–23%.

Qualitative Results. Table 1 shows sensitive-sample images selected randomly by the Random method and those generated by VeriDeep and our method on the dataset Olivetti for 10 runs. Although the quality of images selected by Random is good since these images are original, they are not effective when using them for compromise detection as shown in Fig. 1. This can be explained by the fact that the compromised model is just slightly different from the original model, which often gives the same output for a training image as the original one. Our method is able to generate sensitive-sample images with a comparable quality but they are very sensitive to the model change (i.e. the weight modification). As a result, they are very effective when using for the compromise detection as shown in Fig. 1.

Table 1. Sensitive-sample images selected/generated by each method at each running time on the dataset Olivetti. We remind that the Random method does not generate the sensitive image. Instead, it simply selects a random original image from the training set; thus the image is clearer compared to those generated by VerIDeep and our method.

5   Conclusion

In this paper, we have proposed an efficient method for verifying the integrity of deep models in terms of checking whether the model weights are modified. Our method has two significant advantages. First, it uses a generative model - VAE to transform the high-dimension space of data to a low-dimension space, which allows the searching to perform effectively. Second, it applies BO to find the sensitive sample that achieves the highest sensitivity score w.r.t. to the weights using a global optimization. Our comprehensive experiments on two real-world datasets Olivetti and MNIST show that our method outperforms existing state-of-the-art methods in terms of detection rates.

Acknowledgment. This research was partially funded by the Australian Government through the Australian Research Council (ARC). Prof Venkatesh is the recipient of an ARC Australian Laureate Fellowship (FL170100006).

References

1. Biggio, B., Nelson, B., Laskov, P.: Poisoning attacks against support vector machines. arXiv preprint arXiv:1206.6389 (2012)
2. Brochu, E., Cora, V.M., De Freitas, N.: A tutorial on Bayesian optimization of expensive cost functions, with application to active user modeling and hierarchical reinforcement learning. arXiv preprint arXiv:1012.2599 (2010)
3. Chen, X., Liu, C., Li, B., Lu, K., Song, D.: Targeted backdoor attacks on deep learning systems using data poisoning. arXiv preprint arXiv:1712.05526 (2017)
4. Eissman, S., Levy, D., Shu, R., Bartzsch, S., Ermon, S.: Bayesian optimization and attribute adjustment. In: UAI (2018)
5. Geigel, A.: Neural network trojan. J. Comput. Secur. **21**(2), 191–232 (2013)
6. Ghodsi, Z., Gu, T., Garg, S.: SafetyNets: verifiable execution of deep neural networks on an untrusted cloud. In: NIPS, pp. 4672–4681 (2017)
7. He, Z., Zhang, T., Lee, R.: Sensitive-sample fingerprinting of deep neural networks. In: CVPR, pp. 4729–4737 (2019)
8. Jones, D., Schonlau, M., Welch, W.: Efficient global optimization of expensive black-box functions. J. Global Optim. **13**(4), 455–492 (1998)
9. Kingma, D.P., Welling, M.: Auto-encoding variational bayes. arXiv preprint arXiv:1312.6114 (2013)
10. Kumar, N.G., Rao, K.P.K.: Hash based approach for providing privacy and integrity in cloud data storage using digital signatures. Int. J. Comput. Sci. Inform. Technol. **5**(6), 8074–8078 (2014)
11. Kushner, H.: A new method of locating the maximum point of an arbitrary multipeak curve in the presence of noise. J. Basic Eng. **86**(1), 97–106 (1964)
12. LeCun, Y., Bengio, Y., Hinton, G.: Deep learning. Nature **521**(7553), 436 (2015)
13. Li, C., Gupta, S., Rana, S., Nguyen, V., Venkatesh, S., Shilton, A.: High dimensional Bayesian optimization using dropout. In: IJCAI, pp. 2096–2102 (2018)
14. Liu, Y., et al.: Trojaning attack on neural networks. In: NDSS (2017)
15. Mulazzani, M., Schrittwieser, S., Leithner, M., Huber, M., Weippl, E.R.: Dark clouds on the horizon: using cloud storage as attack vector and online slack space. In: USENIX Security Symposium, San Francisco, CA, USA, pp. 65–76 (2011)
16. Ortigosa, A., Carro, R.M., Quiroga, J.I.: Predicting user personality by mining social interactions in Facebook. J. Comput. Syst. Sci. **80**(1), 57–71 (2014)
17. Srinivas, N., Krause, A., Kakade, S., Seeger, M.: Information-theoretic regret bounds for Gaussian process optimization in the bandit setting. IEEE Trans. Inf. Theory **58**(5), 3250–3265 (2012)
18. Zhang, Y., Juels, A., Oprea, A., Reiter, M.K.: HomeAlone: co-residency detection in the cloud via side-channel analysis. In: IEEE Symposium on Security and Privacy, pp. 313–328. IEEE (2011)

Information-Theoretic Multi-task Learning Framework for Bayesian Optimisation

Anil Ramachandran$^{(\boxtimes)}$, Sunil Gupta, Santu Rana, and Svetha Venkatesh

Applied Artificial Intelligence Institute (A^{2}I^2), Deakin University, Geelong, Australia
{aramac,sunil.gupta,santu.rana,svetha.venkatesh}@deakin.edu.au

Abstract. Bayesian optimisation is a widely used technique for finding the optima of black-box functions in a sample efficient way. When there are concurrent optimisation tasks/functions then it may be possible to transfer knowledge across each other in a multi-task setting and improve the efficiency further. Transferring knowledge requires estimation of task similarity, which in turn requires good knowledge about the objective functions. However, in a multi-task Bayesian optimisation setting the number of observations for all functions can be small, especially at the beginning, making reliable computation of task similarities difficult. In this paper, we propose a novel multi-task Bayesian optimisation method that uses information theory based approach to transfer knowledge across tasks and handle the uncertainty of similarity measurements in an unified framework. Each optimisation task uses contribution from other optimisation task via a mixture model on the location of optima by appropriately combining distribution over optimal locations for each individual task. The probability distribution of the optimal location for individual tasks can be obtained because the objective functions are modeled using Gaussian processes. The weights of the mixture distributions are computed based on the similarities (measured via KL divergence) between two distributions and then appropriately weighting down by the uncertainty in the knowledge. That is, we encourage transfer of knowledge only when two tasks are confident about their high similarity measure and discourage if they are not confident, even if the similarity is high. We evaluate and demonstrate the effectiveness of our proposed method on both synthetic and a set of hyperparameter tuning tests compared to state-of-the-art algorithms.

1 Introduction

Design problems are pervasive in various domains, including scientific studies, engineering design, advertising and banking. These problems are often fraught with complex design choices and parameter settings. The objective of these kinds of problems is to find the optimal design choices and its associated parameter settings via experimentation. In other words, the solution to these problems require to seek the global optima of unknown black box functions, which are

© Springer Nature Switzerland AG 2019
J. Liu and J. Bailey (Eds.): AI 2019, LNAI 11919, pp. 497–509, 2019.
https://doi.org/10.1007/978-3-030-35288-2_40

often expensive to evaluate. A naïve approach is to tune the available choices manually in combination with random or grid search, however the search space is often too vast for the domain experts to navigate effectively. Consequently this approach is expensive in both cost and time. The challenge is to find the optima of such expensive black-box functions in minimum computational cost and time. Bayesian optimisation offers a powerful and sample efficient solution to these kind of problems. Bayesian optimisation is a model based approach in which the experiments are performed sequentially at the optima locations of a computationally cheap surrogate function until an acceptable solution is found. Even though, Bayesian optimisation is an elegant approach towards global optimisation, it faces a "cold start" phase where the algorithm may need a higher number of function evaluations before it reaches a good region. When a new product or process is designed, the experimenter must perform a new optimisation task starting from the scratch and each time he/she experiences this cold start phase. As optimisation model becomes more complex, the cost due to this cold start problem becomes quite high.

There are several settings in which it is possible to partially mitigate the effect of cold start phase. Whilst prior knowledge about functions can be used for this purpose e.g. [10,18], such knowledge may not be available for many scenarios. In absence of any prior knowledge, when one has access to previous similar function optimisations (source), transfer learning can be used to accelerate the current optimisation task (target) [1,4,5,8,12,13,19]. However, transfer learning based methods assume the availability of enough observations in source functions to compute a precise source/target similarity measure. When there are concurrent optimisation tasks, it may be possible to learn from each other in a multi-task setting [17]. In this paper we consider multi-task setting to address the cold start problem. Existing method for multi-task learning using multi-task Gaussian process models [17] has one chief limitation that it completely relies on the relatedness estimate that are usually poor at the beginning of the optimisation due to small number of samples. Additionally, multi-task GP scales poorly with the number of concurrent tasks as it pools all the observations in one single GP. Thus a robust multi-task learning framework for Bayesian optimisation which is capable of estimating task similarities on-the-fly and scalable to large number of tasks is still an open problem.

This paper proposes a multi-task learning framework for Bayesian optimisation that performs simultaneous optimisation of multiple functions by sharing their knowledge about optima locations in the input space. At each iteration, one function is chosen as target in a round robin routine while the remaining as sources. Knowledge about optima locations from a particular source to the target is transferred based on its similarity with the target. From each task-specific Gaussian process the probability distribution on optima location can be obtained via Thompson Sampling. Probability distribution from all sources are combined with that of the target in a mixture model fashion where weights of the target distribution is set as 1 and the weights related to the source distributions are computed via an inverted monotonic transformation of KL-divergence (between source and the target distributions) to keep them between [0 1]. Since all the functions may not have large number of observations available especially in the initial iterations, the optima distribution would be wide and then there is a possibility that the similarities might be measured high, even though this measure is somewhat unreliable as the knowledge itself is uncertain. Therefore, we need to estimate a similarity that can also incorporate a measure of how much each function should rely on the measure. This is obtained by scaling KL-divergence down with the entropy of the source. Following that, a new information-theoretic acquisition function similar to Predictive Entropy Search (PES) is proposed. We validate our multi-task learning framework through application to optimisation of both synthetic and real world experiments and demonstrate the effectiveness by comparing with a well known multi task Bayesian optimisation method, information-theoretic transfer learning method [12] as well as with the generic Bayesian optimisation method.

2 Preliminaries

2.1 Gaussian Process

Gaussian process (GP) is a powerful, non-parametric method to perform non-linear regression in stochastic processes and has earned immense popularity among statistics and machine learning community. Essentially, GP places a flexible prior distribution over the space of continuous functions ($f : \mathcal{X} \to \mathbb{R}$) and is completely specified by a mean function ($\mu : \mathcal{X} \to \mathbb{R}$) and a kernel function ($k : \mathcal{X} \times \mathcal{X} \to \mathbb{R}$). A draw from a GP is a function as $f(\mathbf{x}) \sim \mathrm{GP}(\mu(\mathbf{x}), k(\mathbf{x}, \mathbf{x}'))$. For simplicity, and without loss of generality, we assume the mean to be a zero function which makes the GP fully specified by the kernel function. We also assume that the function measurements as noisy, i.e. $\mathbf{y}_i = f(\mathbf{x}_i) + \epsilon_i$, where $\epsilon_i \sim \mathcal{N}(0, \sigma^2)$ being the measurement noise. Then any finite collection of function observations, $f_{1:n}$ where n is the iteration, follows a multi-variate Gaussian distribution. Given a new query point $\tilde{\mathbf{x}}$, the joint Gaussian distribution between $f_{1:n}$ and $f(\tilde{\mathbf{x}})$ can be written as

$$\begin{bmatrix} f_{1:n} \\ f(\tilde{\mathbf{x}}) \end{bmatrix} \sim \mathcal{N} \left(0, \begin{bmatrix} \mathbf{K} & \mathbf{k} \\ \mathbf{k}^T & k(\tilde{\mathbf{x}}, \tilde{\mathbf{x}}) \end{bmatrix} \right) \tag{1}$$

where $\mathbf{k} = \begin{bmatrix} k(\tilde{\mathbf{x}}, \mathbf{x}_1) \, k(\tilde{\mathbf{x}}, \mathbf{x}_2) \dots k(\tilde{\mathbf{x}}, \mathbf{x}_n) \end{bmatrix}$ and $\mathbf{K}(i, i') = k(\mathbf{x}_i, \mathbf{x}_{i'})$. Using Sherman-Morrison-Woodbury formula [14] we can write the predictive distribution as $p(f(\tilde{\mathbf{x}}) \mid \mathcal{D}_{1:n}, \tilde{\mathbf{x}}) = \mathcal{N}(\mu_n(\tilde{\mathbf{x}}), \sigma_n^2(\tilde{\mathbf{x}}))$, where the predictive mean $\mu_n(\tilde{\mathbf{x}}) = \mathbf{k}^T [\mathbf{K} + \sigma^2 \mathbf{I}]^{-1} f_{1:n}$ and predictive variance $\sigma_n^2(\tilde{\mathbf{x}}) = k(\tilde{\mathbf{x}}, \tilde{\mathbf{x}}) - \mathbf{k}^T [\mathbf{K} + \sigma^2 \mathbf{I}]^{-1} \mathbf{k}$.

2.2 Bayesian Optimisation

Bayesian optimisation is a popular sample-efficient method for the global optimisation of noisy, black-box functions which are expensive to evaluate. Since the objective function is unknown, Bayesian optimisation uses a probabilistic model to express the belief about the function. Typical choices for function modeling are Gaussian process, random forests [7] or Bayesian neural networks [15] as these models are capable of quantifying uncertainty in function values. In this paper, we use Gaussian process to model the unknown objective function due to its tractability. Using this prior and observations so far, a posterior estimate about the true function is derived, which is in turn used to build a cheap surrogate function called acquisition function. The acquisition function is optimised to decide the next promising function evaluation point while keeping a balance between exploitation (sampling regions where function values are likely to be optimal) and exploration (sampling regions where uncertainty about function values are likely to be high) in the search space. Commonly used acquisition functions - Probability of Improvement (PI) [9], Expected Improvement (EI) [11] and GP-UCB [16] are generally constructed using the combination of posterior mean and variance. Another alternate acquisition function called Predictive Entropy Search (PES) [6] recently gained popularity among the practitioners because of its direct approach to reduce uncertainty about the information about the location of the optimum. In this paper, we build a new acquisition function for multi-task learning that is based on predictive entropy search.

2.3   Information-Theoretic Transfer Learning for Bayesian Optimisation

Information-theoretic transfer learning method [12] utilizes the knowledge about global optima locations from different source functions to optimise the target function. A mixture distribution containing global optima samples from both source and target is constructed and is then used to build a new acquisition function based on Predictive Entropy Search (PES). That is, the PES acquisition function (see Eq. (2) in [6]) is modified by constructing a mixture distribution of $p(\mathbf{x}_*)$ from the target and $p^s(\mathbf{x}_*)$ from each source s where $s = 1, \ldots, S$. The proposed mixture distribution is defined as

$$p^{\mathrm{mix}}(\mathbf{x}_*) = \pi_0 p(\mathbf{x}_*) + \pi_1 p^1(\mathbf{x}_*) + \ldots + \pi_S p^S(\mathbf{x}_*) \tag{2}$$

where $\pi_0, \pi_1, \ldots, \pi_S$ are the mixture coefficients. The mixture coefficients are set using the similarity between the target and a source such that $\sum_{s=0}^{S} \pi_s = 1$. The similarity measure ψ_s between the target $p(\mathbf{x}_*)$ and a source $p^s(\mathbf{x}_*)$ is given by as $\psi_s = \exp(-\frac{D_{\mathrm{KL}}(p^s\|p)}{\eta})$ where $\eta > 0$ is a model hyperparameter and $D_{\mathrm{KL}}(p^s\|p)$ is the KL divergence between $p(\mathbf{x}_*)$ and $p^s(\mathbf{x}_*)$. ψ_0 is the similarity of $p(\mathbf{x}_*)$ with itself and is set to 1. Using this similarity measures, the mixture coefficients $\pi_0, \pi_1, \ldots, \pi_S$ is defined as $\pi_s = \frac{\psi_s}{\sum_{s=0}^{S} \psi_s}$. Then PES acquisition function is redefined for the transfer learning setting as

$$\mathbf{x}_{n+1} = \mathrm{argmax}_{\mathbf{x} \in \mathcal{X}} \alpha_n(\mathbf{x}) = \mathbb{H}\left[p(y \mid \mathcal{D}_n, \mathbf{x})\right] - \mathbb{E}_{p^{\mathrm{mix}}(\mathbf{x}_* \mid \mathcal{D}_n)}\left[\mathbb{H}\left[p\left(y \mid \mathcal{D}_n, \mathbf{x}, \mathbf{x}_*\right)\right]\right] \tag{3}$$

The crucial assumption is that the sources have large number of observations, making the measurements of the similarities reliable. In the following we will formulate our proposed multi-task Bayesian optimisation framework using a similar idea where the same $p^{\text{mix}}(x_*)$ is computed for each task but the mixture weights are computed differently because in the small data regimen of the multi-task setting the similarity measurements are unreliable.

3   Proposed Method

We propose a multi-task learning framework for Bayesian optimisation that allows to mutually share the knowledge among different functions and concurrently optimise each function in a dynamic setting. Our framework is based on an information-theoretic acquisition function where we provide a way to incorporate the knowledge from each optimisation task, especially considering the uncertainty of the knowledge.

3.1   The Proposed Multi-task Learning Method

Let us assume there are $t = 1, 2, \ldots, T$ tasks to optimise in a multi-task setting. Our goal is to select (in a round robin routine), at each iteration, a fixed task (let us say t - target) and optimise the same using the knowledge from all other tasks ($\forall t'$ such that $t' \neq t$ - sources). In order to do so, we build a new acquisition function in a manner similar to predictive entropy search that can incorporate the information from every task based on some similarity measure with the target, i.e. we are trying to modify the expectation in (Eq. (3)) for a multi-task setting by constructing a mixture distribution (similar to Eq. (2)) from all the tasks. Since every task faces scarcity in the number of observations especially in the initial iterations, a similarity measure based only on the divergence between optima distributions [12] will be unreliable.

Key Insight: To deal with insufficiency in number of observations while computing the similarity, we incorporate uncertainty in the knowledge for every tasks with the divergence. For a better understanding, we illustrate two different cases of divergence estimation depending on the shape of optima distributions from any two tasks that clearly explains why multi-task learning is different from transfer learning. Before proceeding, let us first denote $p_{t,n}(\mathbf{x}_*)$ as the target optima distribution at time n and $p_{t',n}(\mathbf{x}_*)$ be the same for a source t' at time n. Here we use adaptive kernel density estimation [2] to compute the probability distributions $p_{t,n}(\mathbf{x}_*)$ and $p_{t',n}(\mathbf{x}_*)$ from the available $\mathbf{x}_*$ samples.

Case I (Transfer Learning): Consider a transfer learning scenario where large number of observations from all the sources are already available which translates the sources, $p_{t',n}(\mathbf{x}_*)$ to nearly impulse functions as shown in Fig. 1. Since $p_{t',n}(\mathbf{x}_*)$ is nearly an impulse function, $D_{\text{KL}}(p_{t',n}\|p_{t,n})$ (see Sect. 2.3) between $p_{t',n}(\mathbf{x}_*)$ and $p_{t,n}(\mathbf{x}_*)$ is highly dependent on how much probability mass of $p_{t,n}(\mathbf{x}_*)$ has around the peak of $p_{t',n}(\mathbf{x}_*)$. In Fig. 1a, $p_{t,n}(\mathbf{x}_*)$ has sufficiently high probability mass around the peak of $p_{t',n}(\mathbf{x}_*)$ and therefore the value of $D_{\text{KL}}(p_{t',n}\|p_{t,n})$ will be extremely small. Whereas in Fig. 1b, $p_{t,n}(\mathbf{x}_*)$ has small

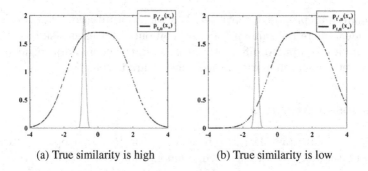

(a) True similarity is high   (b) True similarity is low

Fig. 1. (Transfer learning scenario) Optima distribution of $p_{t',n}(\mathbf{x}_*)$ is densely distributed while the same for $p_{t,n}(\mathbf{x}_*)$ is widely distributed. (a) $D_{\mathrm{KL}}(p_{t',n}\|p_{t,n})$ is extremely small and thus similarity is high. (b) $D_{\mathrm{KL}}(p_{t',n}\|p_{t,n})$ is extremely large and thus similarity is low. Since true similarity for (a) is high and for (b) is low, $D_{\mathrm{KL}}(p_{t',n}\|p_{t,n})$ based similarity is a reliable measure.

probability mass around the peak of $p_{t',n}(\mathbf{x}_*)$ which causes the $D_{\mathrm{KL}}(p_{t',n}\|p_{t,n})$ to take an extremely large value. In both the cases the divergence based measure provides a reliable measure of the underlying similarity as the true similarity in the first case is high and in the second case is low.

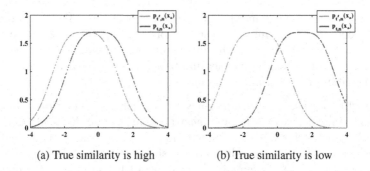

(a) True similarity is high   (b) True similarity is low

Fig. 2. (Multi-task scenario) Optima distribution of $p_{t',n}(\mathbf{x}_*)$ and $p_{t,n}(\mathbf{x}_*)$ are widely distributed. Since $p_{t',n}(\mathbf{x}_*)$ is not sufficiently narrow, $D_{\mathrm{KL}}(p_{t',n}\|p_{t,n})$ will not provide an accurate measure and thus divergence based similarity is undesirable for this case.

Case II (Multi-task Learning): Next consider a scenario of multi-task learning where observations are scarce for both source and target. Hence, both $p_{t',n}(\mathbf{x}_*)$ and $p_{t,n}(\mathbf{x}_*)$ are widely distributed as shown in Fig. 2. Let us assume the true similarity in Fig. 2a is high and in Fig. 2b is low. In both cases, the KL divergence, $D_{\mathrm{KL}}(p_{t',n}\|p_{t,n})$ provide a value which is neither too small nor too large because the source distribution, $p_{t',n}(\mathbf{x}_*)$ is not sufficiently narrow to compute an accurate divergence measure. Therefore, the divergence based measure

---

Algorithm 1. The Proposed Multi-Task Learning Algorithm.

---

1. **Input:** Initial observations from every function: $\left\{\{\mathbf{x}_{t,i}, y_{t,i}\}_{i=1}^{n_0}\right\}_{t=1}^{T}$.
2. **Output:** $\left\{\{\mathbf{x}_{t,n}, y_{t,n}\}_{n=1}^{N}\right\}_{t=1}^{T}$.
3. **for** $n = n_0, \ldots, N$ **do**
   (a) Draw M samples of $\mathbf{x}_*$ from the posterior Gaussian process of each function. Denote them as $\left\{\{\mathbf{x}_*^{t,(j)}\}_{j=1}^{M}\right\}_{t=1}^{T}$.
   (b) Select one function t as target. Compute the KL- divergence $D_{\mathrm{KL}}(p_{t',n}||p_{t,n})$ between t'-th source and the target using samples $\{\mathbf{x}_*^{t',(j)}\}_{j=1}^{M}$ and $\{\mathbf{x}_*^{t,(j)}\}_{j=1}^{M}$. Next compute $\pi_{t',n}$ using Eq. (4).
   (c) Draw $\mathbf{x}_*$ samples from $p_t^{\mathrm{mix}}(\mathbf{x}_*)$ by re-sampling $\{\mathbf{x}_*^{t,(j)}\}_{j=1}^{M}$ and $\{\mathbf{x}_*^{t',(j)}\}_{j=1}^{M}$ in the proportion of $\pi_{t',n}$.
   (d) Use $\mathbf{x}_*$ samples to compute $\alpha_n(\mathbf{x})$ and maximize it as in Eq. (5) to select a new $\mathbf{x}_{t,n}$.
   (e) Evaluate the target function at $\mathbf{x}_{t,n}$: $y_{t,n} = f(\mathbf{x}_{t,n}) + \epsilon_{t,n}$ where $\epsilon_{t,n} \sim \mathcal{N}(0, \sigma^2)$.
   (f) Augment $(\mathbf{x}_{t,n}, y_{t,n})$ to the target observations and update the posterior GP.
   (g) Select the next function as target and when $t = T$, restart the selection.
4. **end for**

---

will provide comparable level similarity for both the cases, which is undesirable. In other words, when the source task itself is not very sure about it's knowledge we should not rely highly on it.

Construction of Multi-task Learning Algorithm: From the multi-task learning scenario, *it is clear that the extent to which a source task should contribute towards the mixture distribution $p^{\mathrm{mix}}(\mathbf{x}_*)$ (see Eq. (2)) should depend on the uncertainty of the $p_{t',n}(\mathbf{x}_*)$.* This will prevent negative transfer from unrelated functions as initially due to the lack of many samples, similarity between any two functions (related or not) can appear high. Here we compute the measure of information contained in any particular source task using an estimate of differential entropy. Differential entropy of a source task t' at time n can be formally written as $\mathbb{H}(p_{t',n}/\mathcal{D}_n) = -\int p_{t',n}(\mathbf{x}) \log p_{t',n}(\mathbf{x})$. We then incorporate this entropy measure with the KL divergence and define the source/target similarity as a product of divergence and entropy. Based on this, the similarity measure $\psi_{t',n}$ between two probability distributions $p_{t,n}(\mathbf{x}_*)$ and $p_{t',n}(\mathbf{x}_*)$ can be written as $\psi_{t',n} = \exp(-\frac{D_{\mathrm{KL}}(p_{t',n}||p_{t,n}) * (\mathbb{H}(p_{t',n}/\mathcal{D}_n)/(r*\log(b-a)))}{\eta})$ where $r > 0$ and $\eta > 0$ are model hyperparameters and are set according to the values of entropy and KL divergence. We also normalize the entropy of $p_{t',n}/\mathcal{D}_n$ using $\log(b-a)$, which is the highest entropy for a bounded distribution with support $[a, b]$. Given the similarity measure, the mixture coefficients can be computed as

$$\pi_{t',n} = \frac{\psi_{t',n}}{1 + \sum_{t'=1, t' \neq t}^{T} \psi_{t',n}} \tag{4}$$

Similarity of $p_{t,n}(\mathbf{x}_*)$ with itself is set to 1. Then the mixture distribution for multi-task learning scenario can be formally written as $p_t^{\mathrm{mix}}(\mathbf{x}_*) = \pi_0 p_{t,n}(\mathbf{x}_*) +$

$\sum_{t'=1,t'\neq t}^{T} \pi_{t',n} p_{t',n}(\mathbf{x}_*)$. Following this, formulation of our proposed multi-task acquisition function is as follows:

$$\mathbf{x}_{n+1} = \underset{\mathbf{x}\in\mathcal{X}}{\operatorname{argmax}} \alpha_n(\mathbf{x}) = \mathbb{H}\left[p(y \mid \mathcal{D}_n, \mathbf{x})\right] - \mathbb{E}_{p_t^{\text{mix}}(\mathbf{x}_*|\mathcal{D}_n)}\left[\mathbb{H}\left[p\left(y \mid \mathcal{D}_n, \mathbf{x}, \mathbf{x}_*\right)\right]\right] \quad (5)$$

The entropies are computed as in [6] (see Eq. (10)).

Note that, in our method, the Gaussian process for each task are built independently. Therefore, the complexity of inverting kernel matrix at iteration n is $\mathcal{O}\left(Tn^3\right)$. This is clearly smaller compared to multi-task Bayesian optimisation [17], which uses multi-task GP and has a complexity $\mathcal{O}\left(T^3 n^3\right)$. This complexity arises due to pooling the observations from all the tasks to build a single GP. Our proposed multi-task learning algorithm for Bayesian optimisation is summarized in Algorithm 1.

4   Experiments

We evaluate our proposed method using both synthetic functions and real data experiments. The synthetic functions are designed to illustrate the behavior of our proposed multi-task learning method in a controlled setting and real data experiments to illustrate the efficacy of our method to tune the hyperparameters of a classification algorithm - Support Vector Machine (SVM). For both synthetic and real experiments, we compare our proposed method with following three baselines:

1. ITTL-BO: This algorithm [12] is a single-task transfer learning method for Bayesian optimisation that assumes the observations from all other functions (sources) are already available. To address multi-task learning, we choose one fixed function (in round robin routine) at each iteration and optimise the same using knowledge from all other functions (sources).

2. MT-BO: This algorithm [17] is the only existing multi-task framework for Bayesian optimisation. In this paper, authors used an approach where the functions are modeled using a multi-task Gaussian process and then each function is optimised using standard Bayesian optimisation. A covariance function that measures the relationship between input-task pairs is fundamental behind multi-task Gaussian process. This covariance function is used to compute predictive mean and variance of each objective function and which is then used with GP-UCB acquisition function to recommend the next function evaluation point.

3. No-Transfer: This baseline does not use any source information and follows the standard predicative entropy search based Bayesian optimisation algorithm [6].

4.1   Experimental Setting

In all the experiments, we use squared exponential kernel for Gaussian process (GP) modeling and maximum a posteriori (MAP) estimate for GP hyperparameter estimation where we used gamma distribution as the prior. All the results are averaged over 20 runs with random initial values.

4.2   Synthetic Experiments

We generated 4 bi-modal Gaussian functions in 3-dimensions with the following form. $f(\mathbf{x}) = 2 - a_1 * \exp\left(-\frac{1}{2}(\mathbf{x} - \boldsymbol{\mu}_1)\boldsymbol{\Sigma}_1^{-1}(\mathbf{x} - \boldsymbol{\mu}_1)^T\right) - a_2 * \exp\left(-\frac{1}{2}(\mathbf{x} - \boldsymbol{\mu}_2)\boldsymbol{\Sigma}_2^{-1}(\mathbf{x} - \boldsymbol{\mu}_2)^T\right)$. For function 1, $\boldsymbol{\mu}_1 = [-1, -1, -1]$ and $\boldsymbol{\mu}_2 = [0.8, 0.8, 0.8]$. For function 2, $\boldsymbol{\mu}_1 = [-0.7, -0.7, -0.7]$ and $\boldsymbol{\mu}_2 = [1.1, 1.1, 1.1]$. For function 3, $\boldsymbol{\mu}_1 = [2.9, 2.9, 2.9]$ and $\boldsymbol{\mu}_2 = [-2.5, -2.5, -2.5]$. For function 4, $\boldsymbol{\mu}_1 = [-2.5, -2.5, -2.5]$ and $\boldsymbol{\mu}_2 = [3, 3, 3]$. For all the five functions $a_1 = 4$, $\boldsymbol{\Sigma}_1 = 0.25 \times \mathbf{I}_{3\times3}$ and $a_2 = 8$, $\boldsymbol{\Sigma}_2 = \mathbf{I}_{3\times3}$. As seen from the values of $\boldsymbol{\mu}_1$ and $\boldsymbol{\mu}_2$, functions 1 and 2 are related to each other while other two functions are unrelated. Figure 3 (first column) shows the immediate regret (IR) obtained for respective functions with respect to iterations. Immediate regret is defined as $\mid f(\tilde{\mathbf{x}}_n) - f(\mathbf{x}_*) \mid$, where $\tilde{\mathbf{x}}$ is the recommended location at time n and $\mathbf{x}_*$ is the location of true global minimum. Each method starts with the same four random observations from $[-4, 4]$ along each dimension. The performance of proposed multi-task method clearly outperforms the baselines for all the functions. Since to draw samples from $p^{\text{mix}}(\mathbf{x}_*)$, we resort to resampling from the samples of $p(\mathbf{x}_*)$ from all the tasks, we can track the number of $\mathbf{x}_*$ samples used from each distribution as the contribution from each distribution. This is shown in Fig. 3 (second and third column) as a function of iteration. From the graphs it is clear that our method selects less number of $\mathbf{x}_*$ samples from all the functions especially in the initial iterations and later when functions get more observations they managed to compute a precise similarity measure and eventually started to have more number of $\mathbf{x}_*$ samples from the related functions. Multi-task baseline is performing worse than No-Transfer in most of the cases because it proceeds by recommending same point to all the functions based on a relationship matrix between input-task pairs. Since there are more number of unrelated functions, evaluating all the functions in a common point might not be a suitable procedure. Since the similarity is not weighted down by the uncertainty in the knowledge, ITTL-BO selects almost equal number of samples from every functions. This causes the degradation in optimisation performance because every function is obtaining large number of samples even from unrelated functions.

4.3   Hyperparameter Tuning: SVM with RBF Kernel

We consider a handwritten digits data set - 'Pen-Based Recognition of Handwritten Digits' - from UCI machine learning repository [3]. The dataset is a multi-class classification dataset consisting of 10 classes (digits 0–9). To demonstrate our multi-class learning method, we consider 4 classes - 'digit 0', 'digit 2', 'digit 4', 'digit 6' and the classifier is realized by training one-vs-all binary classifiers. SVM with RBF kernel has two hyperparameters to tune: cost parameter (C) and kernel parameter (γ). The range for γ is set as $[10^{-4}, 10^3]$ and the same for C is $[2^{-5}, 2^6]$. The multi-task optimisation arises from using one-vs-all scheme for multi-class classification where we build 4 binary classifiers for 4 class problem. Hyperparameter tuning for each binary classifier is one optimisation task. For each binary classifiers, we tuned the two hyperparameters γ and C by

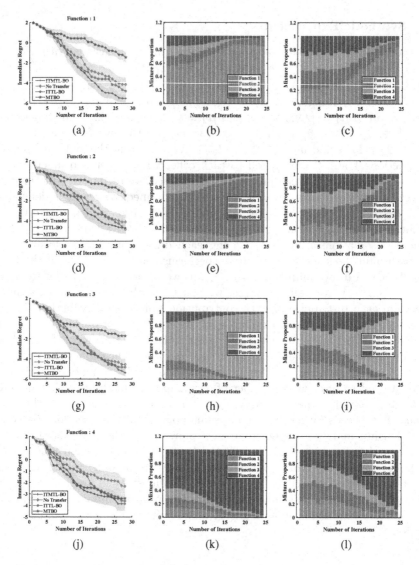

Fig. 3. Synthetic experiments: First column - Immediate Regret vs optimisation iterations for each function, Second column - Proportions of sources and the target in the mixture distribution with respect to optimisation iterations (proposed method), Third column - Proportions of sources and the target in the mixture distribution with respect to optimisation iterations (ITTL-BO). In (b) & (e) at the start of optimisation, the target failed to compute an accurate similarity measure with other functions and thus it relies more on its on x_* samples. Later when all the functions started to get more observations, target identifies the related function and selects more samples from itself while eliminate the influence from other unrelated functions. In (h) and (k) both functions are not related to other functions and when iteration increases the influence from other functions reduce to zero. On the other hand, for ITTL-BO, the similarity is not weighted down by the uncertainty in the knowledge and thus every function share samples almost equally. This causes degradation in the performance.

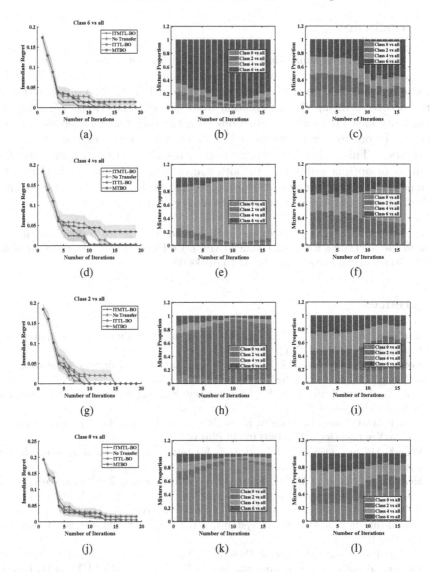

Fig. 4. Hyperparameter tuning for SVM with RBF kernel: First column - Immediate Regret vs optimisation iterations for each function, Second column - Proportions of sources and the target in the mixture distribution with respect to optimisation iterations (proposed method), Third column - Proportions of sources and the target in the mixture distribution with respect to optimisation iterations (ITTL-BO).

optimising the validation performance as a function of hyperparameter values in the exponent space. Figure 4 (first column) shows the immediate regret (1 - AUC) of each function on a held-out validation set. The proportion of contributions from different functions versus iterations is shown in Fig. 4 (second and third column).

5 Conclusion

We proposed a novel multi-task learning algorithm for Bayesian optimisation based on predictive entropy search acquisition function. In a round robin fashion one function is chosen as target at each iteration and the optimisation is performed by utilizing the information from all other functions. We compute a similarity measure of all the functions with the target using their divergence between the optima distributions and scaling it with the entropy of the source distribution. This similarity measure is then used to construct a mixture distribution of optima samples from both source and the target and is used to formulate the new information-theoretic acquisition function. The experiments with diverse optimisation tasks show the ability of our algorithm.

Acknowledgment. This research was partially funded by the Australian Government through the Australian Research Council (ARC). Prof Venkatesh is the recipient of an ARC Australian Laureate Fellowship (FL170100006).

References

1. Bardenet, R., Brendel, M., Kégl, B., Sebag, M.: Collaborative hyperparameter tuning. In: ICML, vol. 2, pp. 199–207 (2013)
2. Botev, Z.I., Grotowski, J.F., Kroese, D.P., et al.: Kernel density estimation via diffusion. The Ann. Stat. **38**(5), 2916–2957 (2010)
3. Dua, D., Karra Taniskidou, E.: UCI machine learning repository (2017). http://archive.ics.uci.edu/ml
4. Feurer, M., Letham, B., Bakshy, E.: Scalable meta-learning for Bayesian optimization. arXiv preprint arXiv:1802.02219 (2018)
5. Feurer, M., Springenberg, J.T., Hutter, F.: Initializing Bayesian hyperparameter optimization via meta-learning. In: AAAI, pp. 1128–1135 (2015)
6. Hernández-Lobato, J.M., Hoffman, M.W., Ghahramani, Z.: Predictive entropy search for efficient global optimization of black-box functions. In: Ghahramani, Z., Welling, M., Cortes, C., Lawrence, N.D., Weinberger, K.Q. (eds.) Advances in Neural Information Processing Systems, vol. 27, pp. 918–926. Curran Associates, Inc. (2014)
7. Hutter, F., Hoos, H.H., Leyton-Brown, K.: Sequential model-based optimization for general algorithm configuration. In: Coello, C.A.C. (ed.) LION 2011. LNCS, vol. 6683, pp. 507–523. Springer, Heidelberg (2011). https://doi.org/10.1007/978-3-642-25566-3_40
8. Joy, T.T., Rana, S., Gupta, S.K., Venkatesh, S.: Flexible transfer learning framework for Bayesian optimisation. In: Bailey, J., Khan, L., Washio, T., Dobbie, G., Huang, J.Z., Wang, R. (eds.) PAKDD 2016. LNCS (LNAI), vol. 9651, pp. 102–114. Springer, Cham (2016). https://doi.org/10.1007/978-3-319-31753-3_9
9. Kushner, H.J.: A new method of locating the maximum point of an arbitrary multipeak curve in the presence of noise. J. Basic Eng. **86**(1), 97–106 (1964)
10. Li, C., et al.: Accelerating experimental design by incorporating experimenter hunches. In: 2018 IEEE International Conference on Data Mining (ICDM), pp. 257–266. IEEE (2018)

11. Močkus, J., Tiesis, V., Žilinskas, A.: The application of Bayesian methods for seeking the extremum. In: Toward Global Optimization, vol. 2, pp. 117–128. Elsevier (1978)

12. Ramachandran, A., Gupta, S., Rana, S., Venkatesh, S.: Information-theoretic transfer learning framework for Bayesian optimisation. In: Berlingerio, M., Bonchi, F., Gärtner, T., Hurley, N., Ifrim, G. (eds.) ECML PKDD 2018. LNCS (LNAI), vol. 11052, pp. 827–842. Springer, Cham (2019). https://doi.org/10.1007/978-3-030-10928-8_49

13. Ramachandran, A., Gupta, S., Rana, S., Venkatesh, S.: Selecting optimal source for transfer learning in Bayesian optimisation. In: Geng, X., Kang, B.-H. (eds.) PRICAI 2018. LNCS (LNAI), vol. 11012, pp. 42–56. Springer, Cham (2018). https://doi.org/10.1007/978-3-319-97304-3_4

14. Rasmussen, C., Williams, C.: Gaussian processes for machine learning. In: Gaussian Processes for Machine Learning (2006)

15. Springenberg, J.T., Klein, A., Falkner, S., Hutter, F.: Bayesian optimization with robust Bayesian neural networks. In: Advances in Neural Information Processing Systems, pp. 4134–4142 (2016)

16. Srinivas, N., Krause, A., Kakade, S.M., Seeger, M.W.: Information-theoretic regret bounds for Gaussian process optimization in the bandit setting. IEEE Trans. Inf. Theory **58**(5), 3250–3265 (2012)

17. Swersky, K., Snoek, J., Adams, R.P.: Multi-task Bayesian optimization. In: Advances in Neural Information Processing Systems, pp. 2004–2012 (2013)

18. Vellanki, P., et al.: Bayesian functional optimisation with shape prior. arXiv preprint arXiv:1809.07260 (2018)

19. Yogatama, D., Mann, G.: Efficient transfer learning method for automatic hyperparameter tuning. Transfer **1**, 1 (2014)

Multi-label Feature Selection Using Particle Swarm Optimization: Novel Initialization Mechanisms

Juhini Desai, Bach Hoai Nguyen[✉], and Bing Xue

School of Engineering and Computer Science, Victoria University of Wellington,
PO Box 600, Wellington 6140, New Zealand
desaijuhi@myvuw.ac.nz, {Hoai.Bach.Nguyen,Bing.Xue}@ecs.vuw.ac.nz

Abstract. In standard single-label classification, feature selection is an important but challenging task due to its large and complex search space. However, feature selection for multi-label classification is even more challenging since it needs to consider not only the feature interactions but also the label interactions. Particle Swarm Optimization (PSO) has been widely applied to select features for single-label classification, but its potential has not been investigated in multi-label classification. Therefore, this work proposes PSO-based multi-label feature selection algorithms to investigate the importance of population initialization in multi-label feature selection. Particularly, the discriminative information is utilized to let the swarm start with more promising feature combinations. Results on eight real-world datasets show that the new strategies can reduce the number of features and improve classification performance over using all features and standard PSO-based multi-label feature selection.

Keywords: Particle Swarm Optimization · Feature selection · Multi-label classification

1 Introduction

Classification is an important task in machine learning, which aims to predict the class labels of unseen instances based on their feature values. In the learning process, a classification algorithm is trained on a set of labeled instances, called a training set. The learned classifier is then applied to classify unlabeled instances, called a test set. The classification performance depends heavily on feature quality. However, many real-world datasets often involve a large number of features which contains irrelevant and redundant features. Classification using a large feature set needs a large number of instances to achieve reliable performance due to the data sparsity, i.e. "curse of dimensionality" [1]. In addition, irrelevant features may blur useful information from the relevant features, which deteriorates the classification performance. Besides, redundant features provide the same information as other features, so they do not provide any more

© Springer Nature Switzerland AG 2019
J. Liu and J. Bailey (Eds.): AI 2019, LNAI 11919, pp. 510–522, 2019.
https://doi.org/10.1007/978-3-030-35288-2_41

useful information and lead to expensive computation time. Feature selection is proposed to address the above problems by removing irrelevant and redundant features, which reduces the training time and improve the classification performance over using all features [2]. However, due to the complex feature interactions and the huge search space, it is challenging to develop an effective feature selection algorithm for datasets with a large number of features [7].

In a standard (single-label) classification problem, each instance is assigned to only one label, resulting in the inability to describe the problem when an instance belongs to multiple labels/classes simultaneously. Multi-label classification deals with the case where one instance is associated with multiple labels simultaneously. Feature selection for multi-label classification is more challenging since the correlation between labels needs to be considered [3,5,6]. A straightforward way is to transform it into many single-label problems, then applying existing single-label feature selection methods to each single-label problem [4]. However, these methods ignore the correlation between labels. This paper proposes a feature selection approach that can directly apply to multi-label problems.

A feature selection approach has two main components: search mechanism—to generate candidate feature subsets, and evaluation—to evaluate the goodness of each candidate subset. Based on the evaluation, feature selection can be classified into three categories: wrapper, embedded, and filter approaches. Wrappers include a classification algorithm as part of the evaluation criterion, while filters operate independently of a learning algorithm [2,7]. Similar to wrappers, embedded approaches also involve a classification algorithm, but the selection process is performed during the classifier's training process. In comparison with the other two approaches, wrappers usually achieve the best classification performance with respect to the wrapped classifier [2,7]. Therefore, this work focus on developing a wrapper-based feature selection algorithm for multi-label problems.

Suppose there are n original features, the total number of possible feature subsets is 2^n which exponentially increases with respect to the number of features. Therefore, feature selection needs an effective search mechanism. Evolutionary Computation (EC) is a population-based optimization family which has been widely applied to feature selection [7]. Among EC techniques, particle swarm optimization (PSO) gains more attention by the feature selection community since it has a natural representation for feature selection. In comparison with other EC techniques, PSO has fewer parameters and is easier to understand. Therefore, we will propose a PSO-based feature selection algorithm for multi-label classification. It has been shown that initialization is an essential step in PSO-based feature selection [7]. Since feature selection has a large and complex search space, a good starting point can help the swarm to avoid local optima, thus improving the quality of the final feature subset. However, there has been no existing work considering the importance of initialization in PSO-based feature selection for multi-label classification.

Goals: The overall goal of this paper is to develop a new PSO based feature selection algorithm for multi-label classification, which selects a smaller number of features and achieves similar or even better classification performance than using all features. In order to achieve this goal, we propose a novel initialization strategy with an expectation that a good starting point can help to improve the selection performance. The proposed algorithm is evaluated on eight real-world benchmark datasets. These datasets are selected from different application areas. They also have different numbers of features, labels, and instances, so they can be good representatives of real-world problems. Specifically, we will investigate:

- whether the proposed PSO-based feature selection algorithm can reduce the number of features and maintain or even improve the classification performance over using all features,
- whether the proposed initialization mechanism can achieve better selection performance than the standard random initialization of PSO, and
- whether the proposed algorithm can outperform two well-known conventional multi-label feature selection methods, RF-BR and RF-LP [6].

2 Related Work

2.1 Multi-label Classification

In many real-world applications, the single-label classification does not fit well [20]. For example, a news document can cover several topics, such as education, health, religion, politics, and finance, at the same time, which is known as multi-label classification. Several standard single-label classifiers have been extended to cope with multi-label classification. Among the proposed multi-label classifiers, Multi-label KNN (ML-KNN) [23] is one of the most common classifiers. In ML-KNN, maximum a posteriori (MAP) principle is employed to determine the label set for an unseen instance based on the statistical information gained from the subset of labels of its neighboring instances. In this work, ML-KNN is used as the wrapped classifier to guide PSO search for the optimal feature subset.

In comparison with single-label classification, multi-label classification needs more complex evaluation metrics, since a label set can be partially correct or fully correct. Therefore, a number of evaluation metrics have been extended to work with multi-label classification. In this work, we use the Hamming loss metric [24], which can be calculated by the following equation:

$$HammingLoss = \frac{1}{mq} \sum_{i=1}^{m} \sum_{l=1}^{q} (I(l \in Z_i \wedge l \notin Y_i) + I(l \notin Z_i \wedge l \in Y_i)) \qquad (1)$$

where m and q are the number of instances and the number of labels, respectively, Z_i and Y_i are the predicted labelset and the correct labelset of the ith instance, I is the indication function, i.e. $I(\text{true}) = 1$, $I(\text{false}) = 0$. The smaller the value of hamming loss the better the performance of algorithm. Ideally, the hamming loss is 0, which indicates all the instances are correctly classified.

2.2   Multi-label Feature Selection

In multi-label feature selection, most existing methods use the problem transformation approach to transform multi-label data into many single-label data and then apply a single-label feature selection algorithm [21]. For example, RF-BR [6] initially transformed the multi-label dataset into q—number of labels—binary-classification datasets and used ReliefF attribute evaluator on each binary datasets. The features with average values greater than or equal to a threshold were selected. RF-LP [6], on the other hand, used the feature importance measured directly on the original multi-label dataset. There are also few feature selection methods which directly dealt with multi-label data [18,25]. Pereira *et al.* [26] presented a multi-label filter adaptation based on the information gain measure. Jungjit and Freitas [27] proposed a new Lexicographic multi-objective Genetic Algorithms (GAs) for Multi-Label Correlation-based Feature Selection (LexGA-ML-CFS). In comparison with GAs, PSO is usually more efficient, but there has been very few works applying PSO to multi-label feature selection.

2.3   Particle Swarm Optimization

Particle swarm optimization (PSO) [8] is a population-based optimization technique, where each particle represents a candidate solution. The particles move in the search space with their own position and velocity vectors, denoted by x and v, respectively. Each particle records its best position, called *pbest*, and the best position discovered by all particles, called *gbest*. Based on the two best positions, the position and velocity of the ith particle can be updated according to the following equations:

$$x_{id}^{t+1} = x_{id}^t + v_{id}^{t+1} \tag{2}$$

$$v_{id}^{t+1} = w * v_{id}^t + c_1 * r_{1i} * (pbest_{id} - x_{id}^t) + c_2 * r_{2i} * (gbest_{id} - x_{id}^t) \tag{3}$$

where t represents the tth iteration, d represents the dth dimension in the search space, c_1 and c_2 are acceleration constants, r_1 and r_2 are random constants in [0, 1], w is the inertia weight. PSO has been widely applied to feature selection [7,28, 29], but very few researches in the literature have focused on PSO for multi-label feature selection. To the best of our knowledge, Zhang et al. [11] proposed the first PSO-based multi-label feature selection, but it considers feature selection as a multi-objective problem. This paper focuses on designing initialization for a PSO-based multi-label feature selection algorithm where feature selection is considered as a single-objective problem.

3   Proposed Approach

3.1   Overall Structure

In the proposed PSO-based feature selection algorithms, a particle's position is represented by a vector of real numbers, where each vector element corresponds to an original feature. The element value at the dth dimension, x_{id}, is in $[0, 1]$, which shows whether the dth feature is selected or not. Particularly, a threshold θ is used to compare with the position value x_{id}. If $x_{id} > \theta$, the dth feature is selected. Otherwise, the dth feature is not selected.

Each candidate feature subset is evaluated by the following fitness function:

$$fitness = weight \times loss + (1 - weight) \times \frac{\#selectedFeatures}{\#oriFeatures} \qquad (4)$$

where $loss$ is the Hamming loss of the feature subset (Eq. (1)), $\#selectedFeatures$ and $\#oriFeatures$ show the number of selected features and original features, respectively, and $weight \in [0, 1]$ is used to control the importance of the two components.

In a standard PSO-based feature selection approach, the candidate solutions are randomly initialized. During the evolutionary process, new candidate solutions are generated based on its best experience ($pbest$) and the swarm's best experience ($gbest$). The candidate solutions are evaluated based on the Eq. (4). The evolutionary process stops when the predefined maximum number of iterations is achieved, and $gbest$ is outputted as the final feature subset. The main contribution of this work is to propose initialization strategies that are specifically designed for multi-label classification. The pseudo-code of the proposed algorithms with new initialization strategies are shown in Algorithm 1 where our contributions are in lines 3–4.

Algorithm 1. PSO using new initialization methods for multi-label FS

---

1 **Input :** Training set, Test set and labels
2 **begin**
3 calculate feature scores;
4 initialize the position and velocity of each particle in the swarm;
5 **while** *Maximum iterations has not been met* **do**
6 | evaluate the fitness of each particle according to Eq. (4);
7 | **for** $i = 1$ to Swarm Size **do**
8 | | update $pbest$ and $gbest$ of particle i;
9 | **end**
10 | **for** $i = 1$ to Swarm Size **do**
11 | | update v_i of particle i according to Eq. (2);
12 | | update x_i of particle i according to Eq. (3);
13 | **end**
14 **end**
15 calculate the training and testing hamming loss of $gbest$;
16 return $gbest$ and its training/testing loss;
17 **end**

3.2   New Initialization Strategies

Standard PSO randomly initializes particles, which means all features have the same chance to be selected at the beginning. However, some features can be more relevant than other features. Therefore, feature relevance can be used to provide a good starting point for PSO, which will be useful, especially for a complex problem like feature selection. During the initialization phase, a set of features are selected to initialize a particle. In the proposed strategy, the probability of choosing a feature depends directly on its relevance, which means the more relevant feature has a higher chance to be selected. The probability of choosing a weaker feature is lower but always greater than zero, so weakly relevant features still have a chance to be selected. This design is important since a combination of weakly relevant features may form a strongly relevant feature subset. Based on the feature relevance, each feature is allocated a slot proportional to its relevance score. Suppose there are n features and their scores are denoted by $w_i > 0 (i = 1, 2, ..., n)$. The selection probability of ith feature is calculated by:

$$p_i = \frac{w_i}{\sum_{i=1}^{n} w_i} \tag{5}$$

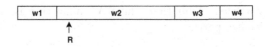

Fig. 1. Selection of a feature among four original features.

In Fig. 1, a line segment of length $\sum_{i=1}^{n} w_i$ out of consecutive slots of length $w_i (i = 1, 2, ..., n)$ is constructed and a random number $R(0 < R < \sum_{i=1}^{n} w_i)$ is generated. The generated random number R is located to the corresponding slot (here, w_2) and hence, the corresponding feature is selected. In the initialization process, each particle is assigned to a feature subset generated by RWS. If a feature is selected, the corresponding element in the particle position is set to a random value greater than the threshold θ. Otherwise, the element is set to a random value smaller than θ. The proposed strategy is inspired by the Roulette Wheel Selection algorithm (RWS) [12].

We propose three novel single feature scoring based initialization strategies which are feature ranking roulette wheel ReliefF Attribute (RF) initialization, feature ranking roulette wheel Correlation Attribute (CR) initialization and single feature ranking roulette wheel (HL) initialization. The three strategies are different in terms of scoring features, which are described as following.

- **Initialization based on Correlation measure (CR):** Correlation attribute evaluator is a filter measure that evaluates features with respect to the target class [16]. Pearson's correlation is used to measure the correlation between a feature and the class label, i.e. the feature relevance. Based on the obtained relevance scores, the probability of selecting each feature is calculated based on Eq. (5). An advantage of the correlation measure is its efficiency and scalability.
- **Initialization based on ReliefF measure (RF):** ReliefF is another popular feature evaluator [13,14]. The key idea is to estimate the feature relevance

according to how well their values distinguish between neighboring instances. For each feature, ReliefF randomly selects an instance R_i and then searches for its nearest neighbor from the same class (a "hit"), and its nearest neighbor from the different classes (a "miss") based on the feature. The feature relevance (score) is updated based on the two nearest "hit" and "miss". The obtained scores for all features are then normalized. Based on the normalized scores, RWS algorithm is applied to select features and initialize particles. Since ReliefF was originally developed for the single-labeled data, we have used label powerset transformation to transform the multi-label problem into a multi-class problem by considering a set of class labels as a single (powerset) label. Such transformation takes the label correlation into account [15].

- **Initialization based on Hamming loss (HL):** In this mechanism, the feature relevance is based on its individual Hamming loss. Each feature is used to classify the training data using the ML-KNN classifier. The obtained Hamming loss is used as the feature score. The more relevant features will have lower loss values. The generated hamming loss values for the individual features are normalized. After that, the RWS algorithm is applied to select features and initialize particles.

The reason for selecting the three measures is how relevant they are to the wrapped classification algorithm, i.e. ML-KNN. Correlation is a filter measure, which is completely independent of ML-KNN. ReliefF is another filter measure, but it is more related to ML-KNN since its mechanism is based on the nearest neighbors. In contrast, Hamming loss can be considered a wrapper-based measure that essentially relies on ML-KNN. We select the three measures to analyze the importance of the consistency between the initialization measure and the evaluation measure.

Table 1. Format of data set

Dataset	Domain	#Feat.	#Labels	#Training instances	#Testing instances
flags	Image	19	7	129	65
cal500	Music	68	174	251	251
emotions	Music	72	6	391	202
yeast	Biology	103	14	1500	917
birds	Audio	258	19	322	323
scene	Image	294	6	1211	1196
enron	Text	1001	53	1123	579
medical	Text	1449	45	333	645

4   Experimental Design

4.1   Benchmark Datasets and Techniques

The popular multi-label repository is maintained in the MULAN website (http://mulan.sourceforge.net/datasets-mlc.html). MULAN [18] is an extension of WEKA [17] for multi-label classification problems. The experiment is conducted on eight multi-label datasets from various application domains such as music, image, biology, audio, and text, which can be seen in Table 1. In the experiment, the performance of the three initialization mechanisms (RF, CR and HL) are compared with using all features and standard PSO-based feature selection that uses the random initialization approach. Furthermore, the performance of HL is compared against two well-known conventional methods, RF-BR and RF-LP [6]. The two methods were implemented in MULAN.

4.2   Parameter Settings

In order to examine the performance of the proposed algorithms, the ML-KNN classification algorithm is used with $K = 9$. Hamming loss is used as the performance measure. The parameters for PSO are set according to common settings proposed by Clerc and Kennedy [19] as follow: inertia weight $w = 0.7298$, acceleration constants $c1 = c2 = 1.49618$, minimum velocity is -0.2, maximum velocity is 0.2, minimum position is 0.0, maximum position is 1.0, population size is 30, maximum number of iterations is 100. The star topology is used. The threshold θ is set as 0.6. For each dataset, the experiment has been conducted for 30 independent runs. The Hamming loss of a selected feature subset is evaluated by 10-fold cross-validation on the training set. After the training process, selected features are evaluated on the test set to obtain the testing Hamming loss as the final performance.

5   Experimental Results and Discussions

Experimental results of the proposed algorithms are shown in Table 2 where the weight is set to 1.0. In the table "All" means that all available features are used, "#Feat." represents the number of selected features. "Ave-Train-loss" and "Ave-Test-loss" represent the average training and test hamming losses of the feature subsets selected by each approach in the 30 runs. The significance test, Wilcoxon test, is performed with the significance level of 0.05. T1 represents the results of the significance test comparing between the three proposed algorithms and using all features. "+"/"="/"−" mean that the proposed algorithms are significantly better/similar/worse than the benchmark algorithms. T2 represents the results of the significance test between HL and the other PSO-based algorithms. The best testing Hamming loss is marked in bold.

Table 2. Experiment results for *weight* = 1.0

Dataset	Method	#Feat.	Ave-Train-loss	Ave-Test-loss	T1	T2	Dataset	Method	#Feat.	Ave-Train-loss	Ave-Test-loss	T1	T2
flags	All	19	0.2337	0.3011				All	260	0.0500	**0.0466**		
	Random	9	0.2388	0.2947		+		Random	96	0.0531	0.0505		=
	RF	9	0.2291	0.2898	+	=	birds	RF	96	0.0513	0.0496	−	−
	CR	11	0.2323	0.2932	+	=		CR	136	0.0524	0.0504	−	−
	HL	9	0.2438	**0.2867**	+			HL	58	0.0528	0.0509	−	
cal500	All	68	0.1345	0.1402				All	294	0.0729	**0.0957**		
	Random	26	0.1339	0.1399		+		Random	106	0.0743	0.1009		−
	RF	37	0.1341	0.1399	+	+	scene	RF	147	0.0746	0.0985	−	−
	CR	39	0.1341	0.1398	+	+		CR	156	0.0736	0.0985	−	−
	HL	21	0.1348	**0.1393**	+			HL	92	0.0782	0.1038	−	
emotions	All	72	0.2758	0.3234				All	1001	0.0452	0.0516		
	Random	24	0.2517	0.3142		=		Random	357	0.0448	0.0509		+
	RF	36	0.2560	0.3169	+	−	enron	RF	511	0.0450	0.0508	+	=
	CR	36	0.2557	0.3183	+	+		CR	529	0.0448	**0.0506**	+	=
	HL	29	0.2520	**0.3128**	+			HL	275	0.0453	**0.0506**	+	
yeast	All	103	0.1802	0.2043				All	1449	0.0148	0.0191		
	Random	45	0.1764	0.2061		=		Random	538	0.0130	0.0153		+
	RF	59	0.1749	**0.2034**	+	−	medical	RF	302	0.0133	0.0169	+	+
	CR	59	0.1760	0.2042	=	=		CR	613	0.0137	0.0174	+	+
	HL	42	0.1761	0.2055	−			HL	279	0.0125	**0.0149**	+	

5.1 Comparison Between the Proposed Algorithms and Using All Features

The results in Table 2 show that on at least five out of the eight datasets, the three PSO-based feature selection algorithms result in significantly lower testing losses than using all features with a much smaller number of selected features. On six out of the eight datasets, the best classification performance is belonged to the three proposed algorithms. On most of the eight datasets, the number of features is reduced by 60–70%. Particularly, on the datasets with large numbers of features such as medical, nearly 80% of the features are removed and hamming loss is also decreased. Thus, the proposed algorithms successfully remove redundant/irrelevant features and at the same time maintain or even improve the classification performance.

5.2 Effect of Different Initialization Mechanisms

On most datasets, RF achieves better Hamming losses than CR. Although both methods use filter measures for initialization, Relief is essentially based on nearest neighbors which is quite close to ML-KNN. Hence, RF usually has better classification performance.

In comparison with RF and CR, HL achieves similar training loss but select significantly smaller numbers of features. The possible reason is that the Hamming loss can distinguish between relevant and irrelevant features, which leads to a few features with high scores while most other features with low scores.

Such behavior allows HL to select relevant features repeatedly (in RWS), so the number of features selected by each particle (at the initialization step) is small. It can be seen that starting with smaller numbers of features enhance the generalization of the feature subsets. On five out of the eight datasets, HL achieves the best Hamming loss on the test set.

The results show that initialization is an essential step in a PSO-based multi-label feature selection. The superiority of HL to the other two algorithms emphasizes the importance of keeping consistency between the initialization step and the evaluation step.

5.3   Effect of Different Weights

The effect of different *weight* values can be seen from Table 3. Setting *weight* to 1 completely ignores the number of selected features, while setting *weight* to 0.99 considers both the number of selected features and the classification performance. It can be seen that when *weight* is set to 0.99, HL usually selects a much smaller number of features than setting *weight* to 1.0. However, setting *weight* to 1.0 usually results in better Hamming loss. The results indicate that *weight* can successfully control the trade-off between the two main objectives of feature selection, which is especially useful when the trade-off is known before.

Table 3. HL with *weight* = 1.0 and *weight* = 0.99

Dataset	weight	#Feat.	Ave-Train-loss	Ave-Test-loss	Dataset	weight	#Feat.	Ave-Train-loss	Ave-Test-loss
flags	w = 1	9	0.2438	0.2867	birds	w = 1	58	0.0528	0.0509
	w = 0.99	8	0.2449	0.2911		w = 0.99	32	0.0524	0.0507
cal500	w = 1	21	0.1348	0.1393	scene	w = 1	92	0.0782	0.1038
	w = 0.99	12	0.1339	0.1394		w = 0.99	91	0.0784	0.1045
emotions	w = 1	29	0.2520	0.3128	enron	w = 1	275	0.0453	0.0506
	w = 0.99	28	0.2520	0.3141		w = 0.99	237	0.0454	0.0505
yeast	w = 1	42	0.1761	0.2055	medical	w = 1	279	0.0125	0.0149
	w = 0.99	37	0.1772	0.2061		w = 0.99	156	0.0125	0.0149

5.4   Further Discussions

Table 4 shows the comparison between two conventional multi-label feature selection algorithms, RF-BR and RF-LP, and the proposed algorithm HL. In the table, "T1" shows the results of the significance test between HL and conventional methods. As can be seen from the table, the conventional methods usually achieve lower Hamming loss on the training set, but they usually select a much larger number of features than HL. It seems that RF-BR and RF-LP tends to overfit the training data by selecting a large number of features. Meanwhile, HL selects a smaller number of features which can generalize better. Therefore, HL achieves significantly better Hamming loss values on the test set.

Table 4. Comparison between HL and two conventional methods

Dataset	Method	Numfeatures	Train-loss	Test-loss	T1	Dataset	Method	Numfeatures	Train-loss	Test-loss	T1
flags	HL	9	0.2438	**0.2867**		birds	HL	58	0.0528	0.0509	
	RF-BR	12	0.2292	0.2945	+		RF-BR	65	0.0500	**0.0464**	–
	RF-LP	19	0.2337	0.3011	+		RF-LP	37	0.0500	**0.0464**	–
cal500	HL	21	0.1348	**0.1393**		scene	HL	92	0.0782	0.1038	
	RF-BR	65	0.1347	0.1397	+		RF-BR	237	0.0765	0.0985	–
	RF-LP	67	0.1344	0.1402	+		RF-LP	232	0.0733	**0.0971**	–
emotions	HL	29	0.2520	**0.3128**		RF-BR	HL	275	0.0453	**0.0506**	
	RF-BR	–	–	–	+		enron	987	0.0456	0.0518	+
	RF-LP	–	–	–	+		RF-LP	1000	0.0451	0.0515	+
yeast	HL	42	0.1761	0.2055		medical	HL	279	0.0125	**0.0149**	
	RF-BR	102	0.181	**0.2033**	–		RF-BR	186	0.0146	0.0178	+
	RF-LP	103	0.1802	0.2043	–		RF-LP	113	0.0146	0.0178	+

6 Conclusions and Future Work

In this work, three new initialization strategies are developed for PSO-based multi-label feature selection. Particularly, the proposed initialization strategies allow PSO to start with more relevant features. The feature relevance is measured by three metrics: relief, correlation, and hamming loss. The results show that PSO can select a small number of features while improving the classification performance over using all features. The three initialization mechanisms can further improve the performance of PSO. In addition, PSO with the proposed initialization mechanisms can select more generalized feature subsets than two conventional multi-label feature selection methods, RF-BR and RF-LP. Among the three initialization mechanisms, using Hamming loss usually results in the best classification performance, which emphasizes the importance of maintaining the consistency between the initialization and the evaluation phases.

Although the proposed algorithms achieve promising results, there is still room for improvement. For example, "premature convergence" is a common problem of PSO, which happens even more frequently in multi-label feature selection due to the large and complex search space. A possible solution is to propose a local search technique to prevent PSO from converging too early.

References

1. Gheyas, I.A., Smith, L.S.: Feature subset selection in large dimensionality domains. Pattern Recogn. **43**(1), 5–13 (2010)
2. Li, J., et al.: Feature selection: a data perspective. ACM Comput. Surv. (CSUR) **50**(6), 94 (2018)
3. Zhang, P., Liu, G., Gao, W.: Distinguishing two types of labels for multi-label feature selection. Pattern Recogn. (2019)
4. Zhang, M.-L., Li, Y.-K., Liu, X.-Y., Geng, X.: Binary relevance for multi-label learning: an overview. Front. Comput. Sci. **12**(2), 191–202 (2018)

5. Pereira, R.B., Plastino, A., Zadrozny, B., Merschmann, L.H.: Categorizing feature selection methods for multi-label classification. Artif. Intell. Rev. **49**(1), 57–78 (2018)
6. SpolaôR, N., Cherman, E.A., Monard, M.C., Lee, H.D.: A comparison of multi-label feature selection methods using the problem transformation approach. Electron. Notes Theor. Comput. Sci. **292**, 135–151 (2013)
7. Xue, B., Zhang, M., Browne, W.N., Yao, X.: A survey on evolutionary computation approaches to feature selection. IEEE Trans. Evol. Comput. **20**(4), 606–626 (2016)
8. Shi, Y., Eberhart, R.: A modified particle swarm optimizer. In: IEEE World Congress on Computational Intelligence, pp. 69–73 (1998)
9. Hu, X., Eberhart, R.: Solving constrained nonlinear optimization problems with particle swarm optimization. In: Proceedings of The sixth World Multiconference on Systemics, Cybernetics and Informatics, vol. 5, pp. 203–206. Citeseer (2002)
10. Lee, J., Kim, D.-W.: Memetic feature selection algorithm for multi-label classification. Inf. Sci. **293**, 80–96 (2015)
11. Zhang, Y., Gong, D.-W., Sun, X.-Y., Guo, Y.-N.: A PSO-based multi-objective multi-label feature selection method in classification. Sci. Rep. **7**(1), 376 (2017)
12. Lipowski, A., Lipowska, D.: Roulette-wheel selection via stochastic acceptance. Phys. A **391**(6), 2193–2196 (2012)
13. Kira, K., Rendell, L.A.: A practical approach to feature selection. In: Machine Learning Proceedings 1992, pp. 249–256. Elsevier (1992)
14. Kononenko, I.: Estimating attributes: analysis and extensions of RELIEF. In: Bergadano, F., De Raedt, L. (eds.) ECML 1994. LNCS, vol. 784, pp. 171–182. Springer, Heidelberg (1994). https://doi.org/10.1007/3-540-57868-4_57
15. Trohidis, K., Tsoumakas, G., Kalliris, G., Vlahavas, I.P.: Multi-label classification of music into emotions. In: ISMIR, vol. 8, pp. 325–330 (2008)
16. Hall, M.A.: Correlation-based feature selection for machine learning (1999)
17. Holmes, G., Donkin, A., Witten, I.H.: WEKA: a machine learning workbench (1994)
18. Tsoumakas, G., Katakis, I., Vlahavas, I.: Data mining and knowledge discovery handbook. Mining Multi-label Data (2010)
19. Clerc, M., Kennedy, J.: The particle swarm-explosion, stability, and convergence in a multidimensional complex space. IEEE Trans. Evol. Comput. **6**(1), 58–73 (2002)
20. Zhang, M.-L., Zhou, Z.-H.: A review on multi-label learning algorithms. IEEE Trans. Knowl. Data Eng. **26**(8), 1819–1837 (2014)
21. Spolaôr, N., Monard, M.C., Lee, H.D.: A systematic review to identify feature selection publications in multi-labeled data. Relatório Técnico do ICMC No **374**(31), 3 (2012)
22. Tsoumakas, G., Katakis, I.: Multi-label classification: an overview. Int. J. Data Warehous. Min. (IJDWM) **3**(3), 1–13 (2007)
23. Zhang, M.-L., Zhou, Z.-H.: ML-KNN: a lazy learning approach to multi-label learning. Pattern Recogn. **40**(7), 2038–2048 (2007)
24. Sorower, M.S.: A literature survey on algorithms for multi-label learning, vol. 18. Oregon State University, Corvallis (2010)
25. Zhang, M.-L., Peña, J.M., Robles, V.: Feature selection for multi-label naive bayes classification. Inform. Sci. **179**(19), 3218–3229 (2009)
26. Pereira, R.B., Plastino, A., Zadrozny, B., Merschmann, L.H.: Information gain feature selection for multi-label classification. J. Inform. Data Manage. **6**(1), 48 (2015)

27. Jungjit, S., Freitas, A.: A lexicographic multi-objective genetic algorithm for multi-label correlation based feature selection. In: Proceedings of the Companion Publication of the Conference on Genetic and Evolutionary Computation, pp. 989–996. ACM (2015)

28. Nguyen, H.B., Xue, B., Andreae, P., Zhang, M.: Particle swarm optimisation with genetic operators for feature selection. In: IEEE Congress on Evolutionary Computation (CEC), pp. 286–293 (2017)

29. Nguyen, H.B., Xue, B., Andreae, P.: PSO with surrogate models for feature selection: static and dynamic clustering-based methods. Memet. Comput. **10**(3), 291–300 (2018)

Genetic Programming for Imputation Predictor Selection and Ranking in Symbolic Regression with High-Dimensional Incomplete Data

Baligh Al-Helali[✉], Qi Chen, Bing Xue, and Mengjie Zhang

School of Engineering and Computer Science, Victoria University of Wellington,
PO Box 600, Wellington 6400, New Zealand
{baligh.al-helali,Qi.Chen,Bing.Xue,Mengjie.Zhang}@ecs.vuw.ac.nz

Abstract. Incompleteness is one of the challenging issues in data science. One approach to tackle this issue is using imputation methods to estimate the missing values in incomplete data sets. In spite of the popularity of adopting this approach in several machine learning tasks, it has been rarely investigated in symbolic regression. In this work, a genetic programming (GP) based feature selection and ranking method is proposed and applied to high-dimensional symbolic regression with incomplete data. The main idea is to construct GP programs for each incomplete feature using other features as predictors. The predictors selected by these GP programs are then ranked based on the fitness values of the best constructed GP programs and the frequency of occurrences of the predictors in these programs. The experimental work is conducted on high-dimensional data where the number of features is greater than the number of instances.

Keywords: Symbolic regression · Genetic programming · Incomplete data · Imputation · Feature ranking

1 Introduction

Genetic programming (GP) is a biological evolution inspired technique for evolving programs to solve a particular task by applying natural-like operations [13]. GP starts with a population of programs generated randomly and applies genetic operators to produce fitter ones through progressively advanced generations [13]. One of the typical applications of GP is symbolic regression. Symbolic regression is the task of discovering mathematical functions in which the dependent variables are expressed in terms of independent variables. The main advantage of symbolic regression over traditional regression methods is the non-requirement of pre-assumptions on the structure of the regression model [4].

Learning from data sets containing missing values is a challenging problem. One way to address this challenge is by applying imputation methods to estimate the missing values and produce complete data that can be used by any

© Springer Nature Switzerland AG 2019
J. Liu and J. Bailey (Eds.): AI 2019, LNAI 11919, pp. 523–535, 2019.
https://doi.org/10.1007/978-3-030-35288-2_42

learning algorithm [10]. Existing imputation methods can be classified into single imputation and multiple imputation [10]. Missing values are categorized into three main types: missing at random, missing completely at random, and missing not at random [10]. The existing research on dealing with missing values mainly focus on classification tasks and only a few studies have been conducted on symbolic regression with incomplete data [2].

Data becomes more and more high-dimensional, i.e. more features, which introduces significant challenges into the field of machine learning [17]. In fact, high-dimensionality can refer to the situation of having more features than instances [14]. Such a situation poses many problems such as curse of dimensionality, spurious correlations, model overfitting, and biased performance estimate [8]. These issues are much more challenging when the data are incomplete due to the risk of having less useful instances and a large number of features. One approach to mitigate the problems related to the high-dimensionality is feature selection [21].

Feature selection is the process of choosing a subset of relevant features [23]. GP performs implicit feature selection as the features involved in a GP program represent a set of selected features. For example, in tree-based GP, the target variable is represented as an expression tree in which the leaf nodes can be chosen from a terminal set that contains the independent features. Any feature appears in the constructed program is considered as a selected feature by this program. GP has been successfully used for feature selection to enhance the performance of different learning tasks such as clustering, classification, and symbolic regression [23]. Feature ranking can be considered as a feature selection method where the features are ranked according to a certain measure and the top-ranked features can be then chosen as a final feature subset [19].

As GP programs can provide mathematical forms to represent the relationships between the input features and a target one, the expressiveness ability of GP makes it suitable for discovering the relationship between predictive features and an incomplete feature in a given data set. To the best of our knowledge, no study has been conducted to investigate feature selection for high-dimensional symbolic regression on incomplete data.

In this work, the main goal is to develop a new GP-based method for predictor selection and ranking to improve the imputation performance. Although GP can select the predictors implicitly, an explicit selection mechanism is imposed into the evolutionary process. Furthermore, the selected predictors are scored and ranked to provide the ability to use different amounts of highly ranked predictors in the learning process. The method is utilized in performing symbolic regression on high-dimensional incomplete data. As high-dimensional data are more likely to contain redundant predictors, the proposed method can improve the performance by using the most relevant predictors. Moreover, using fewer predictors means less computational complexity.

2   Related Work

In symbolic regression research, the most common strategy to deal with incomplete data is to delete the instances having missing values [9]. In [5], GP for symbolic regression method is performed on incomplete data. The missing values are handled through prediction models for the variables. The method employs many heuristics for parameter optimization in the evolutionary process. The experimental results are obtained using synthetic data using a dynamic model called Lorenz attractor system. The main limitation of this method is the enormous computational complexity.

In [22], the missingness is treated as having imbalanced data in certain regions of mathematical functions. A framework for data samples weighting is proposed to take into account the relative importance of each sample. Instead of estimating the missing values, the methods are used to balance synthetic data drawn from mathematical functions. A hybrid method combines GP and KNN to impute missing values for symbolic regression is proposed in [2]. This method works by constructing imputation models for each set of missing values that have the same neighbourhood of complete instances. This approach is time consuming especially on data sets with high instance-based variance.

GP has been successfully used for feature selection and ranking in classification. In [16], the features are scored based on the fitness of the best individuals obtained by multiple GP runs. The frequency of the features is not included and no feature reduction pressure is imposed in the fitness function. A similar fitness-based scoring is presented in [12], where it considers all population individuals in only one GP run. This means that poor individuals may have a high contribution in the scores especially if there are many of such individuals. Moreover, the mutation operator is modified to be biased towards selecting features with higher scores.

In [1], the feature scores are calculated based on the frequency of the features in the best individual of one GP run. Although, scoring the features dose not take into account the fitness value, the fitness function is designed to reduce the number of selected features as in [15]. However, it starts with emphasizing on reducing the features at early generations which may impact the chance of including more useful features from better fitted solutions at later generations.

For high-dimensional symbolic regression, a feature selection method for improving the generalisation ability of GP is proposed in [7]. In [3], artificial bee colony programming is proposed for feature selection in symbolic regression with high-dimensional data. However, these studies used complete data sets. This situation is much more challenging as it needs to consider the treatment of missing values in addition to the dimensionality reduction. This work will develop a feature ranking and selection method for symbolic regression on incomplete high-dimensional data.

3   The Proposed Method

In order to perform symbolic regression on incomplete data, the missing values can be imputed and the resulted complete data are then used. To impute an incomplete feature in a data set, other available features can be used in predicting its missing values. These features are called imputation *predictors* for the incomplete feature to be imputed. The main goal of the proposed method is to select imputation predictors for each incomplete feature and rank them according to their prediction contributions. A good selection of the predictors can improve the imputation performance and reduce the computation time as well.

The Overall System. Figure 1 shows the diagram of the system. It consists of three main processes: the predictor selection and ranking process, the imputation process, and the symbolic regression process. These processes are carried out in two stages, training and testing.

In the process of predictor selection and ranking, the incomplete training data set is used by several GP runs to select a set of predictive features (predictors) for each incomplete feature. Each GP is used to evolve an imputer while reducing the number of used predictors during the evolutionary process. The importance of the selected predictive features is computed based on their contributions in good imputers. The obtained importance is in turn used to score each selected predictor which is then ranked according to the accumulative scores from different runs.

For the imputation process, different sets of highly ranked predictors from the original data are selected for each incomplete feature. Each incomplete is associated with its predictors and this association is fed into an imputation method to be utilized in estimating the missing values. The imputed complete data sets are then used in the symbolic regression process to evaluate the performance of the proposed imputation method.

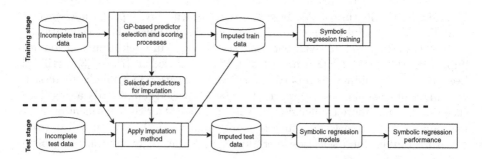

Fig. 1. The overall system.

GP-Based Predictor Selection. Given an incomplete regression data set, D, and an incomplete feature, f, the GP-process is designed to select a set of predictors for this feature. The predictor selection is achieved by enforcing predictor reduction pressure, which is called a selection pressure based on the generation number and the number of selected features as in Eq. (1).

The first factor is the ratio of the number of the current generation, g, to the maximum number of generations, G. When the value of g increases, the importance weight of feature reduction increases monotonically. It is designed in this way to allow including more predictors in the early generations and then in the later generations, where individuals are supposed to be fitter, have more contribution in selecting the predictors.

The other factor is the ratio of the number of selected features, M_{ind} (i.e. the features that are used in the individual), to the number of all available features in the data set, M. If two individuals in a generation have the same prediction value, a lower value is given to the one with fewer features.

$$selection\_pressure_{ind} = \frac{g}{G} * \frac{M_{ind}}{M} \tag{1}$$

Prediction Strategy. The GP prediction strategy is to build GP programs to predict the incomplete features. For an incomplete feature, f, the data set is reformed to consider the feature as the target variable for the GP evolutionary process. The other features (called predictors here) are used in the terminal set. Although all other features including those containing missing values are considered, only the complete instances are used.

The prediction task is performed depending on the data type of the targeted feature. If the incomplete feature is numerical, the prediction process is a regression task and its goodness is measured by the regression error computed using relative squared error (RSE) shown in Eq. (2).

$$RSE = \frac{\sum\limits_{i=1}^{n}(y_i - \hat{y}_i)^2}{\sum\limits_{i=1}^{n}(y_i - \bar{y})^2} \tag{2}$$

where n is the number of instances, y_i ($\hat{y}_i$) is the target value (predicted value) of the ith instance, and $\bar{y}$ is the average of the target values, i.e. $\bar{y} = \frac{\sum_{i=1}^{n} y_i}{n}$.

For the categorical incomplete features, the GP programs are constructed to be classifiers and the prediction error is the classification error rate shown in Eq. (3).

$$Error\_rate = 1 - \frac{\#\text{correctly classified instances}}{\#instances} \tag{3}$$

Following [24], the numerical outputs of GP individuals are translated into class labels using Eq. (4).

$$class(output) = \begin{cases} C_1: & : output \leq 0, \\ C_2: & : T < output \leq 2*T, \\ \dots \\ C_j: & : (j-1)*T < output \leq j*T, \\ \dots \\ C_{n_c}: & otherwise, \end{cases} \quad (4)$$

where C_j , $j = 1, 2, ..., n_c$ are class labels representing the available n_c distinct values in the feature of interest, $output$ is the output of the evolved GP individual, and T is a random positive constant.

Fitness Function. The fitness function for evaluating GP imputation models is proposed to minimise the number of used predictors in addition to minimising the prediction error. As shown in Eq. (5), the fitness function has two parts: the prediction error ($prediction\_error_{ind}$) and the selection pressure ($selection\_pressure_{ind}$). The prediction error measures how accurately the current GP individual fits the incomplete feature, whereas the selection pressure pushes towards using a smaller number of features.

The parameter α is used for controlling the relative importance of features reduction and it is set to be 0.3 because the prediction accuracy is more important. In order to ensure that the selection pressure will not be the dominant part of the fitness function, especially when the prediction error is very small, it is multiplied by the prediction error to be a proportional ratio of the prediction performance.

$$Fitness = prediction\_error_{ind} * (1 + \alpha * selection\_pressure_{ind}) \quad (5)$$

where the $prediction\_error$ is computed as Eq. (6).

$$prediction\_error_{ind} = \begin{cases} \text{Classification error (Eq. (3))}, & \text{for categorical features}, \\ \text{Regression error (Eq. (2))}, & \text{otherwise}. \end{cases}$$

$$(6)$$

GP-Based Predictor Scoring. The scoring of the predictors is based on their frequency in the constructed GP individuals and the fitness values of these models. The score of a predictor, p, for an incomplete feature, f, at a GP run r is denoted as $Score_{r,p,f}$ which is calculated as in Eq. (7).

$$Score_{r,p,f} = \sum_{g=1}^{G} \left(\frac{Freq_{p,g,best\_ind}}{\sum_{\forall q \in P_f} Freq_{q,g,best\_ind}} \right) e^{-fitness_{g,best\_ind}} \quad (7)$$

where $fitness_{g,best\_ind}$ is the best individual fitness value in the gth generation, P_f is the set of all predictors of f, $Freq_{p,g,best\_ind}$ ($Freq_{q,g,best\_ind}$) is the number of times the predictor p (q) appears in this individual, and G is the maximum number of generations.

$Score_{r,p,f}$ is calculated according to the fitness value of the best individual of each generation and the frequency of p in this individual, accumulated across all generations. It is expected to have better fitness in advanced generations or at least not worst (due to the elitism), so the corresponding score is higher in late (mature) generations as the exponential factor $e^{-fitness}$ decreases when the fitness value increases.

The process of scoring predictors is performed R times (the value of R is chosen to be 10 empirically) for each incomplete feature. The scores of the predictors obtained by different runs are accumulated to obtain an overall score of the contribution of the predictor p for the incomplete feature f, $Score_{all,p,f}$, as shown in Eq. (8). The predictors are then sorted according to their total scores and they are given ranks based on their orders after the sorting process.

$$Score_{all,p,f} = \sum_{r=1}^{R} Score_{r,p,f} \tag{8}$$

where $Score_{r,p,f}$ is the score of the predictor p for the feature f in the rth GP run and is computed according to Eq. (7), and R is the number of GP runs.

The predictors that survive in the best individuals in any generation of any GP run represent the set of selected predictors. In fact, these predictors are the ones that have non-zero scores.

4   Experimental Setup

To evaluate the proposed method, four high-dimensional data regression data sets are used. In each data set, the number of features is higher than the number of available instances. The information of the data sets are shown in Table 1 and more details can be found in the data repository OpenML [20]. For each data set, 30 incomplete data sets are generated by imposing 20% missing at random (MAR) probability on 10% of the features. The synthetic incomplete data sets are generated using the R package SIMSEM [18]. In this work, each data set is split randomly with the ratios of 70%, and 30% into a training set, and a test set, respectively.

The goodness of the ranked predictors is evaluated based on their impact on the performance of some widely used imputation methods including linear regression (LR), polynomial regression (PR), random forest (RF), and classification and regression trees (CART). The imputation methods are implemented using the R package MICE [6] with the default settings.

Table 2 shows the settings of GP parameters for both GP-based predictor selection and ranking, and for symbolic regression. The implementation of these methods is carried out under the GP framework provided by distributed evolutionary algorithms in python (DEAP) [11].

Table 1. Statistics of the data sets.

Data set	#Instances	#Features	#Categorical features
Selwood	31	54	0
Pah	80	113	0
Pdgfr	79	321	39
Mtp2	274	1143	55

Table 2. GP settings

Parameter	GP predictor selection	Symbolic regression
Generations	30	100
Population size	256	1024
Crossover rate	0.9	0.9
Mutation rate	0.1	0.1
Elitism	Top-1 individual	Top-5 individual
Selection method	Tournament	Tournament
Tournament size	3	7
Maximum depth	9	9
Initialization	Ramped-half and half	
Function set	$+, -, *$, protected %	
Terminal set	features and constants $\in U(-1, 1)$	
Fitness function	Eq. (5)	Eq. (2)

5 Results and Analysis

5.1 Imputation Performance

To evaluate the impact of using highly ranked predictors on the imputation performance, the results of using four imputation methods are obtained with different ratios of selected predictors. The performance is first evaluated with the highest 10% ranked selected predictors, then with the highest 20%, 40%, 60%, and 80% top-ranked of the selected predictors, then with 100% of the selected predictors referred to *AllS*, which includes all the non-zero scored predictors. The full set of available predictors, denoted as *Full*, is also used for comparisons.

The results of these evaluations are shown in Fig. 2, where the horizontal axis shows the ratio of predictors used in the imputation and the vertical axis shows the average of the imputation error, measured by RSE (Eq. (2)), over 30 runs on the 30 incomplete copies of each data set.

From the shown results, it can be observed that the case of using all predictors doesn't lead to the best imputation performance on any of the used data sets. Moreover, it is worse than any other case on almost all the data sets. On the Selwood data set, all the methods have their best performance when using 20%

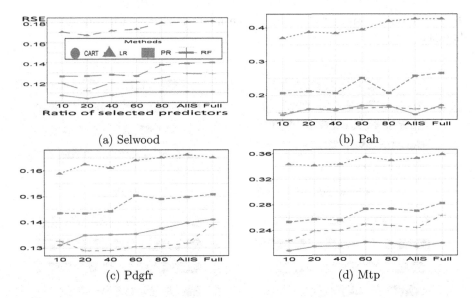

Fig. 2. The imputation performance of using different imputation methods with increasing ratios of top ranked predictors.

of the highly ranked predictors. Compared to any other case, CART and RF can do better by using only 10% top predictors on the Pah data set.

Moreover, the top 10% features are enough to get the lowest error on the Mtp data set with every method. Similar behaviour is observed on the Pdgfr data set for all methods except for the CART method where the best performance is achieved when using the top 20% predictors. The trends in the imputation results reveal that in most cases, using more features could cause a considerable decline in the imputation performance.

5.2 Symbolic Regression Performance

Regarding the symbolic regression performance, after applying each imputation method on each generated incomplete data set, 30 symbolic regression experiments are performed. The symbolic regression is performed by GP using the imputed data provided by imputation methods once with the selected predictors and another one with all available predictors over each incomplete copy of each data set. The used selected predictors are those that have non-zero accumulative scores.

Figure 3 shows the comparisons of the symbolic regression performance. The statistical significance pairwise Wilcoxon test with the significance level of 0.05 is performed to measure the difference in the symbolic regression performance when using each imputation method with and without feature selection. The portion "+" ("−") refers to the number of cases in which the method with selected predictors outperforms (is outperformed by) the same method with all the predictors, whereas "=" refers to the number of cases with no significant difference.

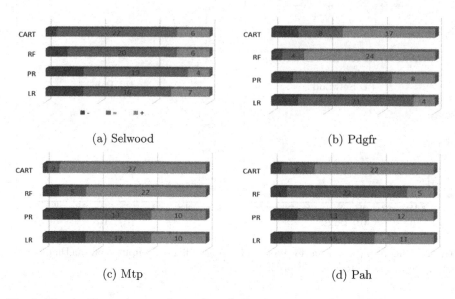

(a) Selwood   (b) Pdgfr

(c) Mtp   (d) Pah

Fig. 3. The significance comparisons of symbolic regression performance between using the selected features and using all the available features.

The results show that the use of the selected features leads to better symbolic regression performance in most of the considered cases. This is particularly true for all the methods on the Mtp data set, and CART and RF on all the data sets. Such results are probably because the selection process gets rid of the noisy predictors which do not contribute towards predicting the missing values. Using all the features as predictors can not obtain the best performance on any data set.

Considering the symbolic regression results along with the imputation results, a correlation between the two evaluations can be found, i.e. the better imputation accuracy, the better symbolic regression performance. For example, the symbolic regression combined with the CART and RF imputation methods leads to better performance than when using LR and PR. In fact, the use of the LR method, which has the poorest imputation accuracy, does not show a significant difference between using the selected predictors and using all predictors.

5.3   Predictor Ranking

To understand the ranking method more, the obtained ranking results in the Selwood data set are analyzed. Table 3 shows the top 20% ranked predictors for the incomplete features in the Selwood data set. The predictors are ordered according to their ranks starting with the highly ranked one.

The shown results are not only useful in improving the imputation performance but also they can be used to discover the relationships between different features, which in turn can be helpful to improve the overall regression performance. It is clear that some features have small numbers of predictors than others. The most frequent feature is oz39, which occurs in the top lists for all the five incomplete features.

Interestingly, some incomplete features are useful for imputing other features. For example, the features oz16 and oz51, which are incomplete features, are ranked among the top 20% predictors to predict other features. They are both appear in the top list for the feature oz38. The feature oz51 is ranked among the top predictors for three incomplete features (viz. oz16, oz25, and oz38). The feature oz16 is the second highly ranked predictor for the feature oz38. Moreover, both features (i.e. oz16 and oz51) have high contributions toward predicting the missing values of each other. This can indicate that there is some shared missingness cause between different features, i.e, the missing values in these features might be due to the same reason.

Table 3. Top 20% predictors for incomplete features in the Selwood data set.

Incomplete feature	Top 20% predictors
oz16	oz7, oz29, oz24, oz17, oz41, oz46, oz51, oz11, oz39
oz25	oz37, oz39, oz38, oz33, oz9, oz45, oz27, oz26, oz1, oz51
oz31	oz52, oz14, oz45, oz24, oz15, oz19, oz39
oz38	oz11, oz16, oz1, oz6, oz39, oz50, oz51
oz51	oz36, oz22, oz38, oz39, oz28, oz19, oz16

6   Conclusions and Future Work

In this work, two challenging problems are addressed: incompleteness and high-dimensionality. A GP-based feature selection and ranking method is proposed and applied to symbolic regression with incomplete data. GP is used to evolve prediction programs for each incomplete feature, select the important predictive features, and score them according to the discovered importance. The method is evaluated on high-dimensional data and the results are promising in improving both the imputation accuracy and the symbolic regression performance.

The main drawback of most single feature ranking methods is considering the importance of individual features without taking into account the interactions with other features. Although the proposed method avoids this limitation by considering the score of the feature in the context of other features, it is difficult to claim which features should be used together. Such a consideration is worth further investigated. Moreover, intensive comparisons with state-of-the-art existing selection methods will be conducted on more data sets from different data repositories. Meanwhile, the applicability of the developed method can also be examined in other machine learning tasks such as classification and clustering.

References

1. Ahmed, S., Zhang, M., Peng, L.: Improving feature ranking for biomarker discovery in proteomics mass spectrometry data using genetic programming. Conn. Sci. **26**(3), 215–243 (2014)
2. Al-Helali, B., Chen, Q., Xue, B., Zhang, M.: A hybrid GP-KNN imputation for symbolic regression with missing values. In: Mitrovic, T., Xue, B., Li, X. (eds.) AI 2018. LNCS (LNAI), vol. 11320, pp. 345–357. Springer, Cham (2018). https://doi.org/10.1007/978-3-030-03991-2_33
3. Arslan, S., Ozturk, C.: Multi hive artificial bee colony programming for high dimensional symbolic regression with feature selection. Appl. Soft Comput. **78**, 515–527 (2019)
4. Austel, V., et al.: Globally optimal symbolic regression. arXiv preprint arXiv:1710.10720 (2017)
5. Brandejsky, T.: Model identification from incomplete data set describing state variable subset only-the problem of optimizing and predicting heuristic incorporation into evolutionary system. In: Zelinka, I., Chen, G., Rössler, O., Snasel, V., Abraham, A. (eds.) Nostradamus 2013: Prediction, Modeling and Analysis of Complex Systems. Advances in Intelligent Systems and Computing, vol. 210, pp. 181–189. Springer, Heidelberg (2013). https://doi.org/10.1007/978-3-319-00542-3_19
6. Buuren, S.V., Groothuis-Oudshoorn, K.: MICE: multivariate imputation by chained equations in R. J. Stat. Softw. 1–68 (2010)
7. Chen, Q., Zhang, M., Xue, B.: Feature selection to improve generalization of genetic programming for high-dimensional symbolic regression. IEEE Trans. Evol. Comput. **21**(5), 792–806 (2017)
8. Clarke, R., et al.: The properties of high-dimensional data spaces: implications for exploring gene and protein expression data. Nat. Rev. Cancer **8**(1), 37 (2008)
9. Dick, G.: Bloat and generalisation in symbolic regression. In: Dick, G., et al. (eds.) SEAL 2014. LNCS, vol. 8886, pp. 491–502. Springer, Cham (2014). https://doi.org/10.1007/978-3-319-13563-2_42
10. Donders, A.R.T., Van Der Heijden, G.J., Stijnen, T., Moons, K.G.: A gentle introduction to imputation of missing values. J. Clin. Epidemiol. **59**(10), 1087–1091 (2006)
11. Fortin, F.A., Rainville, F.M.D., Gardner, M.A., Parizeau, M., Gagné, C.: DEAP: evolutionary algorithms made easy. J. Mach. Learn. Res. **13**(Jul), 2171–2175 (2012)
12. Friedlander, A., Neshatian, K., Zhang, M.: Meta-learning and feature ranking using genetic programming for classification: variable terminal weighting. In: 2011 IEEE Congress of Evolutionary Computation (CEC), pp. 941–948. IEEE (2011)
13. Koza, J.R.: Genetic Programming II, Automatic Discovery of Reusable Subprograms. MIT Press, Cambridge (1992)
14. Liu, X., Wang, H., Ye, W., Xing, E.P.: Sparse variable selection on high dimensional heterogeneous data with tree structured responses. arXiv preprint arXiv:1711.08265 (2017)
15. Muni, D.P., Pal, N.R., Das, J.: Genetic programming for simultaneous feature selection and classifier design (2006)

16. Neshatian, K., Zhang, M., Andreae, P.: Genetic programming for feature ranking in classification problems. In: Li, X., et al. (eds.) SEAL 2008. LNCS, vol. 5361, pp. 544–554. Springer, Heidelberg (2008). https://doi.org/10.1007/978-3-540-89694-4_55

17. Pires, A., Branco, J.: High dimensionality: the latest challenge to data analysis. arXiv preprint arXiv:1902.04679 (2019)

18. Pornprasertmanit, S., Miller, P., Schoemann, A., Quick, C., Jorgensen, T., Pornprasertmanit, M.S.: Package 'simsem' (2016)

19. Tran, B.: Evolutionary computation for feature manipulation in classification on high-dimensional data. Ph.D. thesis, Victoria University of Wellington (2018)

20. Vanschoren, J., Van Rijn, J.N., Bischl, B., Torgo, L.: OpenML: networked science in machine learning. ACM SIGKDD Explor. Newsl. **15**(2), 49–60 (2014)

21. Venkatesh, B., Anuradha, J.: A hybrid feature selection approach for handling a high-dimensional data. In: Saini, H.S., Sayal, R., Govardhan, A., Buyya, R. (eds.) Innovations in Computer Science and Engineering. LNNS, vol. 74, pp. 365–373. Springer, Singapore (2019). https://doi.org/10.1007/978-981-13-7082-3_42

22. Vladislavleva, E., Smits, G., Den Hertog, D.: On the importance of data balancing for symbolic regression. IEEE Trans. Evol. Comput. **14**(2), 252–277 (2010)

23. Xue, B., Zhang, M.: Evolutionary feature manipulation in data mining/big data. ACM SIGEVOlution **10**(1), 4–11 (2017)

24. Zhang, M., Ciesielski, V.: Genetic programming for multiple class object detection. In: Foo, N. (ed.) AI 1999. LNCS (LNAI), vol. 1747, pp. 180–192. Springer, Heidelberg (1999). https://doi.org/10.1007/3-540-46695-9_16

Genetic Programming with Pareto Local Search for Many-Objective Job Shop Scheduling

Atiya Masood[⊠], Gang Chen, Yi Mei, Harith Al-Sahaf, and Mengjie Zhang

School of Engineering and Computer Science, Victoria University of Wellington,
Wellington 6140, New Zealand
{masoodatiy,aaron.chen,yi.mei,harith.al-sahaf,
mengjie.zhang}@ecs.vuw.ac.nz

Abstract. Genetic programming (GP) has been successfully used to automatically design effective dispatching rules for job shop scheduling (JSS) problems. It has been shown that hybridizing global search with local search can significantly improve the performance of many evolutionary algorithms such as GP because local search can directly improve the exploitation ability of these algorithms. Inspired by this, we aim to enhance the quality of evolved dispatching rules for many-objective JSS through hybridizing GP with Pareto Local Search (PLS) techniques. There are two challenges herein. First, the neighborhood structure in GP is not trivially defined. Second, the acceptance criteria during the local search for many-objective JSS has to be carefully designed to guide the search properly. In this paper, we propose a new algorithm that seamlessly integrates GP with Pareto Local Search (GP-PLS). To the best of our knowledge, it is the first time to combine GP with PLS for solving many-objective JSS. To evaluate the effectiveness of our new algorithm, GP-PLS is compared with the GP-NSGA-III algorithm, which is the current state-of-the-art algorithm for many-objective JSS. The experimental results confirm that the newly proposed method can outperform GP-NSGA-III thanks to the proper use of local search techniques. The sensitivity of the PLS-related parameters on the performance of GP-PLS is also experimentally investigated.

Keywords: Many-objective optimization · Genetic programming ·
Pareto Local Search · Evolutionary computation · Job shop scheduling

1 Introduction

Job shop scheduling (JSS) [14] is a classical combinatorial optimization problem which has received a lot of attention owing to its wide applicability in the real world such as cloud computing [16]. A JSS problem deals with a group of tasks or jobs by using different resources or machines. The goal of a JSS problem is to design a schedule, according to which all jobs can be processed as efficiently

© Springer Nature Switzerland AG 2019
J. Liu and J. Bailey (Eds.): AI 2019, LNAI 11919, pp. 536–548, 2019.
https://doi.org/10.1007/978-3-030-35288-2_43

as possible through a set of machines. It is widely mentioned in the literature that JSS by nature presents several potentially conflicting objectives [8], such as makespan, mean tardiness, maximum tardiness and mean flowtime. Therefore, JSS is naturally studied as a many-objective optimization problems (MOaPs) where conflicting objectives require us to find a set of non-dominating solutions, known as the *Pareto front*. The aim of many-objective optimization algorithms is to provide a good representative approximation of the Pareto front.

JSS has been proven to be NP-hard [1] and one of the popular solution approaches to such NP-hard problems is to use dispatching rule heuristics [7]. These rules have some key advantages including being flexible, scalable and efficient, especially when a job shop exhibits high levels of dynamics. Conceptually, a dispatching rule uses a priority function to select the next job in the queue to be processed at each decision point.

Dispatching rules are not universal in nature [13], meaning that no single rule maintains high effectiveness on all problem instances. Particularly, in the manufacturing domain, the underlying properties of the problem often change over time, such as processing time and release dates [9]. Therefore, dispatching rules should be updated frequently according to the condition of the manufacturing environment. It is challenging to design such rules manually because this task relies heavily on human experts and extensive empirical testing to ensure that any newly designed dispatching rules can be used effectively. To circumvent the issues related to manually designing dispatching rules, researchers have proposed various automated design approaches [13]. Among them, Genetic Programming based hyper-heuristic (GPHH) approaches are particularly effective [9,13]. When applied to JSS, GPHH searches for dispatching rules in the heuristic search space. It was shown in [9] that GPHH can evolve much more effective rules than manually-designed rules on many JSS problems. An additional benefit of GPHH comes from the fact that it can integrate easily with many-objective optimization procedures, making it possible to automatically design dispatching rules to simultaneously optimize several conflicting objectives [7].

The literature states that Pareto Local Search (PLS) is a simple and effective local search method for multi-objective optimization tasks [4]. It is a key component of many evolutionary algorithms and has broken performance records in recent years [4]. We can clearly observe from the literature that properly hybridizing global search and local search techniques can often lead to significantly improved performance. This understanding motivates us to integrate GP as a primary global search method with PLS. We face two challenges during the integration. First, the neighborhood structure of a tree (dispatching rule) in GP is not trivially defined. Second, the acceptance criteria during the local search for many-objective JSS has to be carefully designed to guide the search properly. We aim to address both challenges in this paper.

To address the first challenge, we propose to apply a local search driven by restricted mutation to the dispatching rules evolved by GP. The restricted mutation tries to avoid large mutations and prevent the neighborhood rules from being too different from their parent rules. Multiple consecutive local search steps will be performed to encourage the discovery of better rules surrounding an existing one. Meanwhile, the second challenge is tackled by adopting a dominance-based [2] and fitness-guided [6] acceptance strategy. After selecting promising rules obtained by local search, GP with Pareto Local Search (GP-PLS) further adopts the niching mechanism of NSGA-III [3] to evolve a new population of widely distributed dispatching rules that are closer to the Pareto front.

The research objectives of this paper are to: (1) develop a new hybrid approach combining the global search of GP and local search of PLS (GP-PLS) to discover effective dispatching rules for many-objective JSS; (2) compare the proposed GP-PLS algorithm with the current state-of-the-art GP-NSGA-III [8] on a group of benchmark JSS problems since GP-NSGA-III also relies on GP to evolve dispatching rules and the niching mechanism of NSGA-III and (3) analyze the behavior and effectiveness of local search in GP-PLS.

The rest of the paper is organized as follows. Section 2 covers the research background, including the JSS problem, many-objective optimization, and related works. Section 3 introduces GP-PLS. Section 4 describes the experimental design. Section 5 covers the results and discussions. Finally, Sect. 6 concludes this paper and highlights possible future research directions.

2   Research Background

In this section, the JSS problem and many-objective problem will be described first. Then we will discuss some related works.

2.1   Problem Description

Job Shop Scheduling. In a JSS problem, N jobs are to be processed by M machines. Each job J_i includes a series of operations. Each operation O_i^k has a processing time t_i^k and should be processed by machine m_i^k. Any solution to such a JSS problem has to comply with the following three common conditions.

1. An operation is performed on a machine without interruption. This means that all operations are non-preemptive.
2. The operation cannot start until its precedent operation has been completed.
3. Whenever a machine becomes idle (just finished processing an operation), it will be immediately available for processing a new operation.

The goal of JSS is to design a schedule to optimize some objectives such as mean flowtime/tardiness. When using a dispatching rule (e.g. First-Come-First-Serve), the schedule is generated in an online fashion. In JSS, every dispatching rule is represented and evaluated as a GP tree. The GP tree will assign a priority to each pending job in the waiting queue associated with any machine. The job with the highest priority will be processed next.

Fig. 1. The GP tree representation of the 2PT+WINQ+NPT rule.

Many-Objective Optimization. Without loss of generality, in a MaOP, we aim to simultaneously optimize more than three conflicting objectives. In many-objective JSS, the comparison of two dispatching rules/solutions (Δ_1 and Δ_2) is based on the concept of dominance relation [3]. Solution Δ_1 *dominates* Δ_2 if and only if

$$\forall i, 1 \leq i \leq m, f_i(\Delta_1) \leq f_i(\Delta_2) \tag{1}$$

and

$$\exists i, f_i(\Delta_1) < f_i(\Delta_2). \tag{2}$$

If a solution Δ^* is not dominated by any other solution then it is called a *Pareto-optimal* solution. The set of all Pareto-optimal solutions jointly forms the Pareto front (PF) in the objective space and the Pareto set (PS) in the solution space.

2.2 Related Work

Manually designing dispatching rules is a challenging task in an ever-changing manufacturing environment. This issue can be resolved by evolving dispatching rules automatically. In the literature, the most widely explored technique for automatically designing dispatching rules is GPHH [8,10].

GPHH has been widely demonstrated to be an effective learning method for evolving tree-based dispatching rules [9,11]. GPHH not only shows its effectiveness in single-objective JSS problems but can also evolve useful rules for multi-objective and many-objective JSS problems. [12] developed a GPHH method for multi-objective JSS problems involving the optimization of five conflicting objectives. [8] mainly focused on evolving dispatching rules in many-objective JSS problems. However, these methods overlooked the opportunity of enhancing the quality of evolved rules through local search.

Researchers have recently studied the application of PLS to multi-objective evolutionary algorithms [6]. In particular, [6] showed that suitable candidates for local search should be carefully selected based on some scalarization mechanisms. [4] applied PLS and improved the overall quality of the evolved Pareto fronts. However, to the best of our knowledge, no research works have been dedicated to studying PLS in GPHH for many-objective JSS. We are only aware of one existing study on the application of local search to GPHH, but the focus of that research is on single-objective JSS [13]. It is very interesting to investigate the effectiveness of using PLS in GPHH and this is expected to inspire many future studies on PLS in GPHH for many-objective optimization. We aim to achieve this goal in this paper through the development of the new GP-PLS algorithm.

Algorithm 1. The framework of GP-PLS.

    Input   : training set I_{train}
    Output: A set of non-dominated solutions(rules) P^*
1 Initialize of rules and Evaluate the population P_0;
2 $g \leftarrow 0$;
3 **while** $g < g_{\max}$ **do**
4   Apply the Pareto local search $(P_{best})_g = ParetoLocalSearch(P_g)$;
5   Apply genetic operators to $(P_{best})_g$ to generate offspring Q_g;
6   **foreach** $Q \in Q_g$ **do** Evaluate rule Q;
7       $R_g = (P_{best})_g \cup Q_g$;
8   Generate the fronts of R_g: $F = (F1, F2, \ldots)$ by the nondominated sorting;
9   Form the new population P_{g+1} from R_g by the NSGA-III selection;
10      $g \leftarrow g + 1$;
11 **end**
12 **return** *The non-dominated individuals* $P^* \subseteq P_{g_{\max}}$;

---

3 Proposed Algorithm

3.1 Representation of Rules

Consider the popular manually-designed 2PT+WINQ+NPT rule [5]. In the GP tree representation, dispatching rules for JSS are constructed by function nodes and terminal nodes. In Fig. 1, the terminals in the tree are $\{2, PT, WINQ, NPT\}$ (refer to Table 1 for a summary of all terminal types used in this paper) and the functions are $\{+, *\}$.

3.2 General Framework of GP-PLS

Algorithm 1 outlines the framework of GP-PLS. It starts with the initialization by using the ramped-half-and-half method and evaluation (refer to Sect. 3.3) of the dispatching rules. Next, the evaluated rules are processed by the PLS component. PLS features the use of an archive to keep track of candidate rules for local search. The archive initially has either a randomly-selected subset of rules (P_k) in the population or the whole population (P_N). The proposed algorithm iteratively searches through the neighboring solutions of every rule in the archive and stops after a certain number of consecutive local search steps have been performed on each archived rule. In the meantime, GP-PLS keeps track of $(P_{best})_g$. This $(P_{best})_g$ archive represents the best-performing dispatching rules evolved so far. In order to maintain a well-diversified collection of rules in the archive, GP-PLS also adopts the niching mechanism used by NSGA-III. In line with this high-level overview of our algorithmic framework, each key component of GP-PLS will be discussed below.

3.3 Fitness Evaluation

To evaluate the quality of a rule in terms of each objective (lines 1 and 6 of Algorithm 1), it is applied to a set of JSS training instances I_{train} to generate

Algorithm 2. Pareto Local Search

Input : A set of solutions(rules) P_g
Output: A set of best solutions(rules) P_{best}
1 $P_{best} \leftarrow \emptyset$;
2 Randomly select K individuals from P to form $archive$;
3 **foreach** $p \in archive$ **do**
4 | $p_{new} \leftarrow p$;
5 | **for** $step = 1 \rightarrow step_{max}$ **do**
6 | | $p' \leftarrow$ mutate(p);   // neighbors
7 | | evaluate(p');
8 | | **if** p' *is better than* p_{new} **then** $p_{new} \leftarrow p'$;
9 | **end**
10 | **if** p_{new} *is better than* p **then**
11 | | $P_{best} \setminus p$;
12 | | $P_{best} \leftarrow P_{best} \cup p_{new}$
13 | **end**
14 **end**
15 **return** P_{best};

---

schedules for them. Then, for each objective, the quality of a rule p is defined as the average objective value of the schedules generated over the training instances.

3.4 Pareto Local Search

The Pareto local search (PLS, line 4 of Algorithm 1) is described in Algorithm 2. First, PLS randomly selects K individuals from the population to form the archive. Then, for each individual p in the archive, the restricted mutation is used to generate a neighboring rule around p. A maximum of $step_{max}$ neighbors can be generated, and the best neighbors are compared with p. If the neighbor is better than p, then it is added into P_{best}. This local search mechanism will help to enhance the exploitation ability and explore promising rules in the proximity of each selected candidate rule.

Neighborhood Solution. In GP-PLS, a neighboring rule of any given rule p is obtained by using the restricted mutation operator. When the restricted mutation is applied to rule p, we randomly select a node in p whose corresponding sub-tree has a depth of 2. The selected node and its sub-tree are then replaced by a randomly generated sub-tree with the same depth of 2. With the help of this restricted mutation, GP-PLS can effectively prevent a new neighboring rule discovered during the local search process from being significantly different from the original rule.

Exploration. In the local search algorithm, the exploration strategy determines the size of the neighborhood for exploration. One can either explore the

Table 1. Terminal set of GP for JSS.

Attribute	Notation	Attribute	Notation	Attribute	Notation
Processing time of the operation	PT	Ready time of the operation	ORT	Flow due date	FDD
Inverse processing time of the operation	IPT	Ready time of the next machine	NMRT	Work Remaining	WKR
Number of operations in the next queue	NOINQ	Work in the next queue	WINQ	Due Date	DD
Processing time of the next operation	NOPT	Number of operation remaining	NOR	Weight	W
Number of operations in the queue	NOIQ	Ready time of the machine	MRT	Work in the queue	WIQ

neighborhood entirely (best-improvement) [4] or only partially until the termination criterion is met [4]. In this study, the partial strategy is used, since the entire neighborhood is extremely large. Specifically, we randomly sample a neighbor from the neighborhood repetitively until the maximum number of steps ($step_{max}$) is reached, and return the best neighbor sampled so far. The reason of using partial strategy because it is less computationally expensive than the best improvement strategy, especially for a problem with a large number of features.

Comparison. While comparing two rules p' and p_{new} during PLS (e.g. line 8 of Algorithm 2), we consider the following two strategies: (1) the scalarization strategy [6] and (2) the replacement strategy [2]. In the scalarization strategy, the objective vector of each rule is aggregated into a scalar using weighted sum, i.e.,

$$fit(x) = w_1 \cdot f_1(x) + w_2 \cdot f_2(x) + \cdots + w_m \cdot f_m(x), \tag{3}$$

where $\boldsymbol{w} = (w_1, \ldots, w_m)$ is a random weight vector such that $w_i \geq 0$ ($\forall i = 1, \ldots, m$) and $w_1 + \cdots + w_m = 1$.

The replacement strategy is based on the dominance relation. Whenever we compare two rules p_{new} and p', there are three possible outcomes:

- if p_{new} dominates p', p' is replaced by p_{new}.
- if p_{new} and p' are non-dominated by each other, p' is replaced by p_{new}.
- if p_{new} is dominated by p', do nothing.

By replacing rule p with rule p_{new} that dominates it in the archive, we can impose selection pressure on the archive and push it towards the Pareto front.

4   Experiment Design

To verify the effectiveness of GP-PLS, we compare its performance with the current state-of-the-art GP-NSGA-III algorithm. The number of fitness evaluations allowed for running both GP-PLS and GP-NSGA-III is 100000.

4.1 Dataset for JSS

Taillard static (TA) job shop is a widely used static JSS benchmark set [15] and is selected for our experiments. TA consists of 80 JSS problem instances. We group the problem instances with the same number of jobs and machines into the same group. As a result, TA is divided into 8 groups (denoted as TA-1, ..., TA-8). The number of jobs varies from 15 to 100, and the number of machines varies from 15 to 20 across these groups. In the experiments, the total 80 instances were further divided into the *training set* and the *test set*, where each set consists of 40 instances.

4.2 Parameter Settings

In line with the tree-based representation of dispatching rules, the function set in GPHH includes $\{+, -, \times, /\}$ (the protected division operator returns 1 if the denominator is zero), the 2-argument "min" and "max" operators and the 3-argument "If" operator that returns the second argument if the first argument is positive, and the third argument otherwise. Table 1 summarizes the terminals.

For all competing algorithms, the crossover, mutation and reproduction rates are set to 85%, 10%, and 5%, respectively, based on many previous works [8]. The maximal tree depth is set to 8. As a common practice, the population is initialized by the ramp-half-and-half method. In each generation, the parents are selected by the tournament selection method with a tournament size of 7. For GP-NSGA-III, the population size is set to 1000 and the maximal number of generations is set to 100. For GP-PLS, the population size is set to 1000 but a maximal number of generations will be set after the sensitivity analysis (Sect. 4.3). GP-PLS has two additional parameters, size of the archive (K) and the maximum number of local search steps ($Step_{max}$). In our experiment, we aim to minimize four objectives, i.e., the mean flowtime (Obj1), maximal flowtime (Obj2), mean weighted tardiness (Obj3) and maximal weighted tardiness (Obj4). Existing work showed that the four objectives are mutually conflicting [8].

4.3 Sensitivity Analysis

In this experiment, we examined three different combinations of the parameters, $(K, steps_{max}, generations) = (1000, 3, 25), (500, 2, 50), (250, 4, 50)$ for GP-PLS. Sensitivity analysis was applied on both versions (scalarization and replacement) of the PLS. The three-parameter settings have the same total number of fitness evaluations (100000), identical to the number of evaluations in GP-NSGA-III, for a fair experiment comparison. In the sensitivity analysis, for each combination of the parameters, 30 independent runs were performed and obtained 30 final sets of dispatching rules.

Due to the space limit, we summarize our findings without giving detailed results. For the case of (1000, 3, 25), GP-PLS cannot explore the solution space as effectively as GP-NSGA-III due to a limited number of generations. For the case of (500, 2, 50), local search in GP-PLS is weak since only two steps of local

Table 2. The mean and standard deviation over the average HV values of the 30 independent runs on training instances of the compared algorithms. The significantly better results are shown in bold.

HV			IGD		
GP-NSGA-III	GP-PLS-s	GP-PLS-r	GP-NSGA-III	GP-PLS-s	GP-PLS-r
0.688±0.0221	0.690±0.0160	**0.705 ± 0.0130**	0.00125±0.0001	0.00127±0.0001	**0.00120 ± 0.0001**

search can be performed at maximum. In contrast with the first two parameter combinations, (250, 4, 50) obtained much better results due to its balance between better global search (50 generations) and local search (4 steps during the local search) capabilities.

After evaluating the three combinations, we found that the total number of generations and the maximum number of local search steps is highly influential on the performance of GP-PLS. They together provide varied trade-offs between global and local searches in GP-PLS. The result showed that GP-PLS cannot search the solution space extensively with a small number of generations. On the other hand, if GP-PLS cannot perform a sufficient number of local search steps, the power of local search cannot be effectively utilized. In order for GP-PLS to achieve good performance, we select (250, 4, 50) in the subsequent experiments.

4.4 Performance Measures

Inverted Generational Distance (IGD) [17] and Hyper-Volume (HV) [18] are two well-known metrics to evaluate the performance of many-objective algorithms. They measure the algorithms in terms of both convergence and diversity.

In this study, we consider both performance measures. IGD measures the gap between the targeted locations on true Pareto front (PF) and approximated Pareto front (A^*) in the objective space. HV measures the volume of the objective space dominated by evolved Pareto optimal solutions S with respect to a reference point r^*, $r^* = (r_1^*, r_2^*, \ldots, r_m^*)$. The reference point is set to (1.1, 1.1, ..., 1.1). Ideally, a set of non-dominated dispatching rules evolved by GPHH should have high HV and low IGD values.

5 Results and Discussions

For each algorithm in the experiment, 30 GP runs were conducted to obtain 30 sets of dispatching rules. Then, the rules were tested on the 40 test instances.

5.1 Performance of Obtained Dispatching Rules

Table 2 shows the mean and standard deviation of the training performance in terms of HV and IGD of the rules obtained by GP-NSGA-III, GP-PLS-scalarization (GP-PLS-s) and GP-PLS-replacement (GP-PLS-r). Here GP-PLS-s refers to the variation of GP-PLS where the scalarization approach is used for

Table 3. The mean and standard deviation over the HV values on the test instances of the compared algorithms. The significantly better results are shown in bold.

ID	#J_#M	HV			IGD		
		GP-NSGA-III	GP-PLS-s	GP-PLS-r	GP-NSGA-III	GP-PLS-s	GP-PLS-r
1	15_15	.1868(.0368)	.1698(.0125)	**.2723(.0145)**	.0189(.0008)	.0274(.0001)	**.0147(.0001)**
2	15_15	.3296(.0182)	.3070(.0145)	**.4091(.0110)**	.0127(.0005)	.0124(.0004)	**.0117(.0003)**
3	15_15	.2175(.0125)	**.2683(.0125)**	.2508(.0127)	.0173(.0008)	**.0126(.0006)**	.0137(.0002)
4	15_15	.3159(.0183)	.1259(.0133)	**.4561(.0091**	.0162(.0007)	.0260(.0006)	**.0135(.0002)**
5	15_15	.2370(.0202)	.1799(.0302)	**.3479(.0192)**	.0193(.0005)	.0200(.0003)	**.0085(.0007)**
6	20_15	**.4747(.0176)**	.4024(.0186)	.4280(.0139)	**.0079(.0004)**	.0147(.0001)	.0124(.0007)
7	20_15	.2396(.0683)	.2551(.0695)	**.3146(.0683)**	.0250(.0013)	**.0109(.0012)**	.0121(.0014)
8	20_15	.2935(.0201)	**.3201(.0253)**	.2158(.0501)	**.0133(.0001)**	.0156(.0012)	.0147(.0012)
9	20_15	.1787(.0198)	**.3232(.0198)**	.1606(.0219)	.0201(.0001)	**.0108(.0005)**	.0142(.0003)
10	20_15	.3180(.0151)	**.3847(.0141)**	.2743(.0366)	.0129(.0002)	**.0077(.0001)**	.0128(.0003)
11	20_20	.2114(.0038)	.2214(.0138)	**.3087(.0118)**	.0094(.0006)	.0090(.0001)	.0091(.0003)
12	20_20	**.3852(.0133)**	.2452(.0123)	.3206(.0134)	.0217(.0004)	.0168(.0001)	.0147(.0006)
13	20_20	.4540(.0151)	.4541(.0326)	.4550(.0221)	.0155(.0001)	.0112(.0005)	**.0100(.0004)**
14	20_20	.1658(.0110)	.2945(.0140)	**.3318(.0118)**	.0246(.0009)	**.0174(.0005)**	.0216(.0004)
15	20_20	.1742(.0225)	**.1840(.0199)**	.1352(.0125)	**.0191(.0008)**	.0315(.0003)	.0289(.0004)
16	30_15	.2964(.0300)	**.3508(.0234)**	.3198(.0110)	.0111(.0006)	.0090(.0002)	**.0070(.0008)**
17	30_15	.3741(.0096)	.3385(.0229)	**.4076(.0093)**	.0061(.0003)	**.0047(.0008)**	.0077(.0007)
18	30_15	**.3825(.0233)**	.3710(.3032)	.3274(.0103)	.0060(.0006)	.0092(.0008)	.0063(.0007)
19	30_15	**.4353(.0126)**	.3808(.0197)	.3988(.0146)	.0065(.0004)	.0059(.0008)	**.0054(.0007)**
20	30_15	.3800(.0312)	.3801(.0312)	.3762(.0212)	**.0019(.0005)**	.0054(.0003)	.0065(.0002)
21	30_20	.1983(.0657)	**.3340(.0792)**	.2190(.0492)	**.0094(.0022)**	.0097(.0013)	.0125(.00012)
22	30_20	.2385(.0472)	.2954(.0470)	**.3177(.0372)**	.0098(.0010)	.0103(.0006)	**.0095(.0001)**
23	30_20	.2020(.0398)	.2672(.0410)	**.3675(.0294)**	.0077(.0004)	.0074(.0006)	**.0063(.0002)**
24	30_20	.4420(.0503)	**.4652(.0443)**	.4529(.0174)	.0069(.0001)	**.0056(.0001)**	.0085(.0002)
25	30_20	.3372(.0477)	**.3854(.0396)**	.2864(.0427)	**.0056(.0001)**	.0071(.0002)	.0074(.0001)
26	50_15	.4563(.0417)	.4672(.0170)	**.4872(.0270)**	.0057(.0001)	.0058(.00002)	**0054(.0004)**
27	50_15	**.5710(.0361)**	.5685(.0304)	.5555(.0304)	**.0038(.0002)**	.0054(.0001)	.0042(.0004)
28	50_15	.4598(.0398)	**.4966(.0250)**	.4798(.0333)	.0036(.0001)	.0035(.0003)	.0040(.0005)
29	50_15	.5749(.0372)	.5702(.0251)	.4323(.0413)	**0035(.0003)**	.0062(.0003)	.0045(.0003)
30	50_15	.4510(.0406)	.4310(.0333)	**.4732(.0240)**	.0043(.0001)	.0045(.0004)	.0043(.0001)
31	50_20	**.5190(.0424)**	.4477(.0295)	.4870(.0433)	.0047(.0002)	.0046(.0003)	.0052(.0001)
32	50_20	.4354(.0476)	**.5705(.0476)**	.4996(.0375)	.0040(.0001)	.0054(.0002)	.0041(.0001)
33	50_20	.4427(.0266)	.4426(.0838)	**.5165(.0366)**	.0054(.00001)	.0056(.00002)	**.0044(.00008)**
34	50_20	.4108(.0384)	.3945(.0262)	**.4911(.0332)**	.0037(.00005)	.0036(.00008)	**.0033(.00009)**
35	50_20	**.4421(.0349)**	.4138(.0222)	.4140(.0165)	.0032(.00015)	.0032(.00007)	.0031(.00009)
36	100_20	.6054(.0179)	.59169(.0093)	**.6228(.0222)**	.0027(.00020)	.0032(.00001)	**.0021(.00067)**
37	100_20	.6584(.0142)	**.6678(.0101)**	.5857(.0152)	.0034(.00018)	.0031(.00001)	**.0027(.00017)**
38	100_20	.6152(.0196)	.6175(.0136)	.5525(.0111)	.0044(.00028)	**0037(.00004)**	0040(.00008)
39	100_20	.6495(.0185)	.6515(.0191)	**.6695(.0103)**	.0026(.00020)	.0028(.00001)	**.0024(.00067)**
40	100_20	**.6830(.0158)**	.6322(.0100)	.6467(.0104)	**0018(.00001)**	.0019(.00002)	.0022(.00009)

selection in Algorithm 2. On the other hand, GP-PLS-r represents the variation where the replacement strategy is used for selection in Algorithm 2. The Wilcoxon rank-sum test with the significance level of 0.05 is applied to the HV and IGD of the Pareto front evolved by the three compared algorithms. Table 2 reveals that GP-PLS-r performs significantly better than GP-NSGA-III and GP-

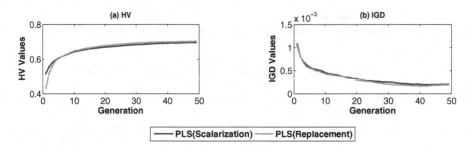

Fig. 2. The curves of the average number of HV and IGD values of the non-dominated solutions on the training set during the 30 independent GP runs.

PLS-s in terms of both HV and IGD. For more detail, Table 3 shows the mean and standard deviation of the test performance on each of the 40 test instances.

In the case of HV, GP-PLS-r performed the best on 16 out of the 40 test instances. GP-NSGA-III performed the best only on 8 instances. GP-PLS-s outperformed the other algorithms on 12 instances. Overall, both GP-PLS-s and GP-PLS-r performed much better than GP-NSGA-III.

Regarding the IGD values, GP-PLS-r performed the best on 16 out of the 40 test instances. In contrast, GP-NSGA-III performed the best on 9 instances. GP-PLS-s outperformed the other algorithms on only 8 instances. Upon taking a closer look at Table 3, we can observe that GP-PLS-r not only performed well on small-scale problem instances but also on larger and more challenging instances. For some test instances (e.g. instances 7, 23 and 36), GP-PLS-r is remarkably better than the other algorithms, especially in terms of HV. This demonstrates the performance advantage of applying PLS to GPHH. Table 3 shows that GP-PLS-r performs significantly better than GP-PLS-s and GP-NSGA-III. This indicates that it is more effective to utilize the dominance relation during local search.

5.2   Further Analysis

To further investigate how PLS affects the GP search process, we plotted (a) the average HV and IGD of the non-dominated solutions evolved by GP-PLS across multiple generations in Fig. 2, and (b) parallel coordinate plots of non-dominated solutions evolved by GP-PLS on one problem instance in Fig. 3.

Figure 2 reveals that GP-PLS-r has better convergence curves in terms of both HV and IGD than GP-PLS-s. Figure 2 also shows that for the first few generations of evolution, both algorithms exhibited similar HV and IGD values. However, after the first ten generations, GP-PLS-r started to outperform. Moreover, in the last few generations, when the solutions were very close to the Pareto front, GP-PLS-r achieved significantly better HV and IGD.

The parallel coordinate plots in Fig. 3 depict the non-dominated set of dispatching rules obtained respectively by GP-PLS (scalarization) and GP-PLS (replacement) on one JSS problem instance. Figure 3 shows that GP-PLS-r obtained better coverage for the third and fourth objectives (i.e. mean weighted

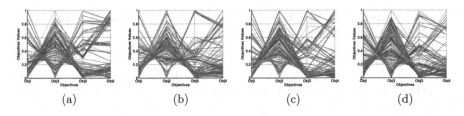

(a)   (b)   (c)   (d)

Fig. 3. Parallel coordinate plot of instance 23 the fitness values of the population (a) GP-PLS-r in generation 10, (b) GP-PLS-r in generation 10, (c) GP-PLS-s in generation 50, and (d) GP-PLS-r in generation 50.

tardiness and maximum weighted tardiness) in generation 10. It can also be seen in Fig. 3 that GP-PLS-r managed to cover a much wider range of values for objective 2 in generation 50 than GP-PLS-s.

6   Conclusions

This paper proposed GP-PLS, which combines GP with Pareto local search for solving many-objective JSS problems. The key idea of this approach is to perform multiple local search steps and effectively explore the neighborhood of non-dominated dispatching rules. GP-PLS features the use of a newly designed restricted neighborhood structure and the partial acceptance mechanism for MOaP. This is the elementary GP with PLS. In this study, we experimentally evaluated two common selection strategies: scalarization and replacement. Our experiment results showed that GP-PLS performs much better than the current state-of-the-art method without local search, in terms of both HV and IGD.

In future studies, we will enhance the performance of our proposed PLS by exploring different local search heuristics. We will develop an intelligent local search operator to guide exploitation based on recently evaluated rules and adaptive selection methods. Furthermore, we will further investigate how GP-PLS search effective dispatching rules. To the best of our knowledge, GP-PLS is the first GPHH method with the local search capability for many-objective JSS. To unleash the great potential of the local search techniques on many-objective GPHH, more investigations are required in the future.

References

1. Błażewicz, J., Domschke, W., Pesch, E.: The job shop scheduling problem: conventional and new solution techniques. Eur. J. Oper. Res. **93**(1), 1–33 (1996)
2. Chen, B., Zeng, W., Lin, Y., Zhang, D.: A new local search-based multiobjective optimization algorithm. IEEE Trans. Evol. Comput. **19**(1), 50–73 (2015)
3. Deb, K., Jain, H.: An evolutionary many-objective optimization algorithm using reference-point-based nondominated sorting approach, part I: solving problems with box constraints. IEEE Trans. Evol. Comput. **18**(4), 577–601 (2014)

4. Dubois-Lacoste, J., López-Ibáñez, M., Stützle, T.: Anytime pareto local search. Eur. J. Oper. Res. **243**(2), 369–385 (2015)
5. Holthaus, O., Rajendran, C.: Efficient jobshop dispatching rules: further developments. Prod. Plan. Control **11**(2), 171–178 (2000)
6. Ishibuchi, H., Murata, T.: A multi-objective genetic local search algorithm and its application to flowshop scheduling. IEEE Trans. Syst. Man Cybern. Part C (Appl. Rev.) **28**(3), 392–403 (1998)
7. Masood, A., Chen, G., Mei, Y., Zhang, M.: Reference point adaption method for genetic programming hyper-heuristic in many-objective job shop scheduling. In: Liefooghe, A., López-Ibáñez, M. (eds.) EvoCOP 2018. LNCS, vol. 10782, pp. 116–131. Springer, Cham (2018). https://doi.org/10.1007/978-3-319-77449-7_8
8. Masood, A., Mei, Y., Chen, G., Zhang, M.: Many-objective genetic programming for job-shop scheduling. In: Proceedings of 2016 IEEE Congress on Evolutionary Computation. IEEE (2016)
9. Nguyen, S.: Automatic design of dispatching rules for job shop scheduling with genetic programming. Ph.D. thesis (2013)
10. Nguyen, S., Mei, Y., Zhang, M.: Genetic programming for production scheduling: a survey with a unified framework. Complex Intell. Syst. **3**(1), 41–66 (2017)
11. Nguyen, S., Zhang, M., Johnston, M.: A genetic programming based hyper-heuristic approach for combinatorial optimisation. In: Proceedings of the 13th Annual Conference on Genetic and Evolutionary Computation, pp. 1299–1306. ACM (2011)
12. Nguyen, S., Zhang, M., Johnston, M., Tan, K.C.: Dynamic multi-objective job shop scheduling: a genetic programming approach. In: Uyar, A., Ozcan, E., Urquhart, N. (eds.) Automated Scheduling and Planning. Studies in Computational Intelligence, vol. 505, pp. 251–282. Springer, Heidelberg (2013). https://doi.org/10.1007/978-3-642-39304-4_10
13. Nguyen, S., Zhang, M., Johnston, M., Tan, K.C.: Automatic programming via iterated local search for dynamic job shop scheduling. IEEE Trans. Cybern. **45**(1), 1–14 (2015)
14. Pinedo, M.L.: Scheduling: Theory, Algorithms, and Systems. Springer, Heidelberg (2012)
15. Taillard, E.: Benchmarks for basic scheduling problems. Eur. J. Oper. Res. **64**(2), 278–285 (1993)
16. Tsai, C.W., Rodrigues, J.J.P.C.: Metaheuristic scheduling for cloud: a survey. IEEE Syst. J. **8**(1), 279–291 (2014)
17. Zhang, Q., Zhou, A., Zhao, S., Suganthan, P.N., Liu, W., Tiwari, S.: Multiobjective optimization test instances for the CEC 2009 special session and competition. University of Essex, Colchester, UK and Nanyang technological University, Singapore, special session on performance assessment of multi-objective optimization algorithms, Technical report, pp. 1–30 (2008)
18. Zitzler, E., Thiele, L., Laumanns, M., Fonseca, C.M., Da Fonseca, V.G.: Performance assessment of multiobjective optimizers: an analysis and review. IEEE Trans. Evol. Comput. **7**(2), 117–132 (2003)

A Biased Random Key Genetic Algorithm with Rollout Evaluations for the Resource Constraint Job Scheduling Problem

Christian Blum[1], Dhananjay Thiruvady[3], Andreas T. Ernst[2(✉)],
Matthias Horn[4], and Günther R. Raidl[4]

[1] Artificial Intelligence Research Institute (IIIA-CSIC), Campus of the UAB,
Bellaterra, Spain
christian.blum@iiia.csic.es
[2] School of Mathematical Sciences, Monash University, Melbourne, Australia
andreas.ernst@monash.edu
[3] School of Information Technology, Deakin University, Geelong, VIC, Australia
Dhananjay.Thiruvady@deakin.edu.au
[4] Institute of Logic and Computation, TU Wien, Vienna, Austria
{horn,raidl}@ac.tuwien.ac.at

Abstract. The resource constraint job scheduling problem considered in this work is a difficult optimization problem that was defined in the context of the transportation of minerals from mines to ports. The main characteristics are that all jobs share a common limiting resource and that the objective function concerns the minimization of the total weighted tardiness of all jobs. The algorithms proposed in the literature for this problem have a common disadvantage: they require a huge amount of computation time. Therefore, the main goal of this work is the development of an algorithm that can compete with the state of the art, while using much less computational resources. In fact, our experimental results show that the biased random key genetic algorithm that we propose significantly outperforms the state-of-the-art algorithm from the literature both in terms of solution quality and computation time.

Keywords: Job scheduling · Genetic algorithm · Rollout evaluation

1 Introduction

The resource constraint job scheduling (RCJS) problem is an *NP*-hard scheduling problem originally motivated by a mineral supply chain application. It involves simultaneously solving multiple single machine scheduling problems subject to a shared resource constraint. In mining supply chains this arises when multiple mines plan their production with a shared rail link that connects the mines to an export port.

Due to the complexity of the RCJS problem, several methods have been developed to solve it. Exact approaches such as integer linear programming [26]

© Springer Nature Switzerland AG 2019
J. Liu and J. Bailey (Eds.): AI 2019, LNAI 11919, pp. 549–560, 2019.
https://doi.org/10.1007/978-3-030-35288-2_44

and constraint programming [15] have been attempted successfully [20,21]. However, these approaches are computationally expensive and can only solve rather small instances. Hence alternatives such as metaheuristics [4] have been explored. Overall, the most effective methods so far are hybrid approaches, e.g., combinations of ant colony optimisation (ACO) and integer programming [22], ACO and constraint programming [7,21], Lagrangian relaxation and particle swarm optimisation (PSO) [9] and column generation and differential evolution [18].

Project scheduling [2,6,8,17], a very well-known class of problems, is closely related to the RCJS problem. There are two main differences: (1) in RCJS jobs must execute on the machine to which they are allocated, and (2) there is only one common shared resource. In addition most variants of project scheduling focus on minimising the makespan rather than tardiness. Brucker et al. [6] categorise project scheduling problem variants. Demeulemeester and Herroelen [8] investigate different heuristic and meta-heuristic approaches for the problem. Neumann et al. [17] tackle project scheduling with time windows and show that genetic algorithms, simulated annealing and exact approaches can be effective. Ballestin and Trautmann [2] explore a problem very similar to the RCJS problem, in which the objective is to minimise the cumulative deviation from the desired completion times of all the tasks. The approach they use is a population-based iterated local search. The studies from [5,23,24] investigate resource constrained project scheduling with the objective of maximising the net present value. Thiruvady et al. [23] show that a Lagrangian relaxation and ACO hybrid finds good heuristic solutions and upper bounds. Brent et al. [5] improve the same hybrid with a parallelisation in a multi-core shared memory architecture. Thiruvady et al. [24] show that a matheuristic derived from construct, solve, merge and adapt and parallel ACO improves upon previous approaches.

Unfortunately, current approaches require a substantial amount of computational resources, both in terms of computation time and in terms of parallel computing facilities. With the aim of deriving a computationally less intensive method, we tackle the RCJS problem in this work by means of a biased random key genetic algorithm (BRKGA). This type of genetic algorithm [16] was first introduced in [11]. Since then, BRKGAs have been shown to obtain excellent results for a substantial range of combinatorial optimization problems, including the maximum quasi-clique problem [19] and the project scheduling problem with flexible resources [1], to name just a few of the more recent applications. Furthermore, parallel and distributed versions of BRKGA have been investigated [10,12]. Júnior *et al.* [12] explore an irregular strip packing problem and the study by Alixandre and Dorn [10] shows good performance on the CEC 2013 benchmark datasets.

2   Resource Constrained Job Scheduling

The RCJS problem consists of a number of nearly independent single machine weighted tardiness problems that are linked by a single shared resource constraint. The problem can technically be described as follows. Each job from a given set $J = \{1, \ldots, n\}$ must execute in a non-preemptive way on one specific machine from a set M of machines. Each job $j \in J$ has the following data associated with it: a release time r_j, a processing time p_j, a due time d_j, the amount g_j required from the shared resource during the jobs execution, a weight w_j, and the machine $m_j \in M$ to which it belongs. The maximum amount of shared resource available at any time is G. Precedence constraints C may apply to two jobs on the same machine: $i \to j \in C$ requires that job i completes before job j starts. The objective is to minimise the total weighted tardiness. Note that this problem is NP-Hard as the single machine weighted tardiness problem is already NP-hard [13].

This problem can be expressed in terms of a time-discretized integer linear program (ILP) as follows. Let $T = \{1, \ldots, t_{\max}\}$ be the set of considered discrete times (with $t_{\max}$ being sufficiently large), and let z_{jt} be a binary variable for all $j \in J$ and $t \in T$ that takes value one if the processing of job j completes at time t or earlier. By defining the weighted tardiness for a job j at time t as $w_{jt} := \max\{0, w_j (t - d_j)\}$, the resulting ILP can be stated as follows:

$$\min \quad \sum_{j \in J} \sum_{t \in T} w_{jt} \cdot (z_{jt} - z_{jt-1}) \tag{1}$$

$$\text{s.t.} \qquad z_{jt_{\max}} = 1 \qquad \forall\, j \in J \tag{2}$$

$$z_{jt} - z_{jt-1} \geq 0 \qquad \forall\, j \in J,\ t \in \{2, \ldots, t_{\max}\} \tag{3}$$

$$z_{jt} = 0 \qquad \forall\, t \in T : t < r_j + p_j,\ j \in J \tag{4}$$

$$z_{bt} - z_{a,t-p_b} \leq 0 \qquad \forall\, (a,b) \in C,\ t \in T : t > r_b + p_b \tag{5}$$

$$\sum_{j \in J^i} z_{j,t+p_j} - z_{jt} \leq 1 \qquad \forall\, i \in M,\ t \in T \tag{6}$$

$$\sum_{j \in J} g_j \cdot (z_{j,t+p_j} - z_{jt}) \leq G \qquad \forall\, t \in T \tag{7}$$

$$z_{jt} \in \{0,1\} \qquad \forall\, j \in J,\ t \in T \tag{8}$$

Equalities (2) ensure that all jobs complete by $t_{\max}$. Inequalities (3) guarantee that once a job completes it stays completed. Equalities (4) account for the release times of jobs. Inequalities (5) ensure that precedence constraints are satisfied and inequalities (6) make sure that at any time only one job is processed on a machine. Inequalities (5) require that the resource constraint on the common resource is satisfied at any time. There are many other ways to formulate this problem, but this is one of the most computationally efficient formulations [20].

3   A BRKGA for the RCJS Problem

A biased random key genetic algorithm (BRKGA) is a steady-state genetic algorithm. The main machinery of the algorithm is problem-independent. Individuals are always coded in terms of random keys, that is, vectors of floating point values in $[0, 1]$. Moreover, the population management and the crossover operator

---

Algorithm 1. BRKGA for the RCJS Problem

1: **input:** a RCJS problem instance
2: **input:** parameter values for p_{size}, p_e, p_m and $prob_{elite}$
3: $P :=$ GenerateInitialPopulation(p_{size})
4: Evaluate(P)
5: **while** computation time limit not reached **do**
6:     $P_e :=$ EliteSolutions(P, p_e)
7:     $P_m :=$ Mutants(P, p_m)
8:     $P_c :=$ Crossover($P, P_e, prob_{elite}$)
9:     Evaluate($P_m \cup P_c$)   {NOTE: P_e is already evaluated}
10:     $P := P_e \cup P_m \cup P_c$
11: **end while**
12: **output:** Best solution in P

---

are problem-independent as well. The only problem-dependent part is the way in which individuals are translated into valid solutions for the specific problem. The problem-independent part of the algorithm is shown in Algorithm 1. It starts by a call to function GenerateInitialPopulation(p_{size}) in order to generate a population P of p_{size} random individuals. Hereby, each individual $\pi \in P$ is a vector of length n (the number of jobs of the RCJS instance). The value of each position j of π (denoted by $\pi(j)$) is randomly chosen from $[0, 1]$. Note that $\pi(j)$ is associated with job j of the RCJS instance. The next step consists of the evaluation of the individuals from the initial population, that is, the translation of the individuals into valid schedules for the RCJS problem, which will be explained in Sect. 3.1. As a consequence, each individual obtains its objective function value denoted by $f(\pi)$. After that, the following actions are performed at each iteration of the algorithm's main loop. First, the best $\max\{\lfloor p_e \cdot p_{size} \rfloor, 1\}$ individuals are copied over from P to P_e (function EliteSolutions(P, p_e)). Second, a set of $\max\{\lfloor p_m \cdot p_{size} \rfloor, 1\}$ so-called mutants—that is, randomly generated individuals—are produced and stored in P_m. Next, a set P_c of $p_{size} - |P_e| - |P_m|$ new individuals are generated by crossover (function Crossover($P, P_e, prob_{elite}$)). The generation of an offspring individual π_{off} by crossover works as follows: (1) an elite parent π_1 is chosen uniformly at random from P_e, (2) a second parent π_2 is chosen uniformly at random from $P \setminus P_e$, and (3) π_{off} is generated on the basis of π_1 and π_2 and stored in P_c. Hereby, value $\pi_{off}(i)$ is set to $\pi_1(i)$ with probability $prob_{elite}$, and to $\pi_2(i)$ otherwise, for all $i = 1, \ldots, n$. After generating all new offspring in P_m and P_c, these new individuals are evaluated in function Evaluate($P_m \cup P_c$). Remember that the individuals in P_e are already evaluated. Finally, the next generations' population is obtained by the union of P_e with P_m and P_c.

3.1   Evaluation of an Individual: The Decoder

The evaluation of an individual π (lines 4 and 9 of Algorithm 1) is the problem-dependent part of the BRKGA. The function that evaluates individuals is called the *decoder*. In our BRKGA implementation for the RCJS problem, the decoder involves the application of a greedy construction heuristic that was introduced in [25]. This greedy heuristic works as follows. It chooses, at each construction step, exactly one of the so-far unscheduled jobs, and provides it with a feasible starting time and, therefore, also with a finishing time. Henceforth, let $J_{done} \subseteq J$ be the set of jobs that are already scheduled, and let s_j denote the starting time of $j \in J_{done}$. At the start of the solution construction process it holds that $J_{done} := \emptyset$. The process stops when $J_{done} = J$.

Let $\max_t := \max_{j=1}^n r_j + \sum_{j=1}^n p_j$ be a crude upper bound for the makespan of any feasible solution. Moreover, let C_j be the set of jobs that – -according to the precedence constraints in C—must be executed before j, and let $M_{m_h} \subseteq J$ be the subset of jobs that must be processed on machine $m_h \in M$. Furthermore, given a partial solution, let $g_t^{sum} \geq 0$ be the sum of the already consumed resource at time t.

Given J_{done}, the set of feasible jobs—that is, the set of jobs from which the next job to be scheduled can be chosen—is defined as follows: $\hat{J} := \{j \in J \backslash J_{done} \mid C_j \cap J_{done} = C_j\}$. In words, the set of feasible jobs consists of those jobs that (1) are not scheduled yet and (2) whose predecessors are already scheduled. A time step $t' \geq 0$ is a feasible starting time for a job $j \in \hat{J}$, if and only if

1. $t' \geq s_k + p_k$, for all $k \in J_{done} \cap C_j$;
2. $t' \geq s_k + p_k$, for all $k \in M_{m_j} \cap J_{done}$ (remember that m_j refers to the machine on which job j must be processed); and
3. $g_t^{sum} + g_j \leq G$, for all $t = t', \ldots, t' + p_j$.

Here T' is the set of feasible starting times for a job $j \in \hat{J}$ and the earliest possible starting time s_j^{min} is defined as $s_j^{min} := \min\{t' \mid t' \in T'\}$. Finally, for choosing a feasible job at each construction step, the jobs from $j \in \hat{J}$ must be ordered in some way. In many scheduling applications, ordering the jobs according to their earliest possible starting times (in an increasing way) is a powerful mechanism. Therefore, our decoder combines the earliest starting time information with the numerical values of π in the following way. It produces an ordered list L of all the jobs j in $\hat{J}$ sorted according to increasing values of $\pi(j) \cdot (s_j^{min} + 1)$. Then, the first job of L—let us call this job j^*—is chosen and added to J_{done}, and its starting time s_{j^*} is fixed to $s_{j^*}^{min}$.

3.2 Applying the Decoder in a Rollout Fashion

Any constructive heuristic can be applied in a so-called *rollout* fashion [3]. In the context of the decoder from the previous sub-section, this works as follows. Instead of ordering the jobs $j \in \hat{J}$ at each construction step according to their $\pi(j) \cdot (s_j^{min} + 1)$ values, the decoder is completely applied to each *partial solution* $J_{done} \cup \{j\}$, for all $j \in \hat{J}$. Hereby, the starting time of j is set to s_j^{min} in each case. This provides us with $|\hat{J}|$ complete solutions whose objective function values— henceforth called the *rollout values*—are then used for producing the ordered list L of all jobs from $\hat{J}$ (in an increasing way). As in the standard decoder, the first job of L—let us call this job again j^*—is chosen and added to J_{done}, and its starting time s_{j^*} is set to $s_{j^*}^{\min}$.

Even though applying the decoder in a rollout fashion provides better evaluations of the individuals, the computational time needed for evaluating an individual increases substantially. Therefore, we make use of the following techniques for shortening the run time:

1. We use an explicit *rollout width* $\text{ro}_{\text{width}} > 0$. In those construction steps in which $\text{ro}_{\text{width}} < |\hat{J}|$, the rollout is only applied to the first ro_{width} jobs from list L (when ordered according to the $\pi(j) \cdot (\text{st}_j^{\min} + 1)$ values). The remaining jobs in L receive a rollout value of ∞. After that, the list L is reorderd according to the rollout values, the first job from L is selected and used to extend J_{done}, before we proceed to the next construction step.
2. The decoder is only applied in a rollout fashion (with a rollout width of ro_{width}) after a number of $n_{\text{noimpr}}^{\max} \geq 0$ consecutive BRKGA iterations without an improvement of the best-so-far solution. After the execution of such a BRKGA iteration in which the decoder is applied in a rollout fashion, the counter for consecutive non-improving BRKGA iterations is re-initialized to zero, as at the start of the BRKGA algorithm.

Clearly, ro_{width} and $n_{\text{noimpr}}^{\max}$ are two important algorithm parameters that control to what extent the decoder is applied in a rollout fashion.

4   Experimental Evaluation

All experiments concerning BRKGA were performed on a cluster of machines with Intel® Xeon® CPU 5670 CPUs with 12 cores of 2.933 GHz and a minimum of 32 GB RAM. As mentioned before, the current state-of-the-art results for the RCJS problem were obtained by a recent hybrid algorithm labelled CG-DE-LS that combines column generation with differential evolution and local search see [18]. Note that, while BRKGA was run in a one-threaded mode with a limit of 3600 s of CPU time for each problem instance, CG-DE-LS was implemented in a parallel framework and each run (limited by 3600 s of wall clock time) was given 16 cores on the Monash University's Campus Cluster. Each machine of the cluster provides 24 cores and 256 GB RAM. Each physical core consists of two hyper-threaded cores with Intel Xeon E5-2680 v3 2.5 GHz, 30M Cache, 9.60GT/s QPI, Turbo, HT, 12C/24T (120W). In summary, consider that a run of CG-DE-LS consumes at least one order of magnitude more computation time than a run of BRKGA.

Problem Instances. The comparison of BRKGA with CG-DE-LS was conducted on 36 instances from a dataset that was originally introduced in [20]. This dataset consists of problem instances with the number of machines ranging from three to twenty, and there are three instances per number of machines. Each machine has to process, on average, 10.5 jobs; that is, an instance with three machines has approximately 32 jobs. Further details concerning the problem instances and their job characteristics (processing times, release times, weights, etc.) can be obtained from the original study.

Tuning of BRKGA. The proposed BRKGA approach has six parameters which require suitable values. In this work we made use of the automatic configuration tool irace [14] for finding such parameter values. More specifically, we aimed at identifying one parameter setting that works well for all 36 test problem instances. For this purpose, we selected six problem instances (having between 3 and 12 machines) from the additional instances provided in [20] which have not been tested in [18]. In addition, we added instances 15–3 and 20–5 from the 36 instances that will be used for the final experimentation, because [20] does not contain any other instances of that size. In total, this makes a set of eight tuning instances. The following parameter value ranges were considered:

- $p_{\text{size}} \in \{10, 50, 100, 200, 500, 1000, 5000\}$.
- $p_e \in \{0.05, 0.1, 0.15, 0.2, 0.25\}$.
- $p_m \in \{0.1, 0.15, 0.2, 0.25, 0.3\}$.
- $prob_{\text{elite}} \in \{0.5, 0.6, 0.7, 0.8, 0.9\}$.
- $\text{ro}_{\text{width}} \in \{2, 3, 5, 10, 20\}$.
- $n_{\text{noimpr}}^{\text{max}} \in \{10, 50, 100, 200, 500\}$.

In total, we allowed a maximum of 5000 experiments—with a computation time limit of 3600 s per run—for tuning. The results provided by irace were as follows: $p_{\text{size}} = 1000$, $p_e = 0.25$, $p_m = 0.15$, $prob_{\text{elite}} = 0.5$, $\text{ro}_{\text{width}} = 3$, and $n_{\text{noimpr}}^{\text{max}} = 200$. These parameter value settings were used for the final experimentation. The parameter settings of CG-DE-LS (for the same set of problem instances) are described in [18].

4.1   Numerical Results

BRKGA was applied ten times to all 36 considered problem instances with a CPU time limit of 3600 s per run. The numerical results—in comparison to those of CG-DE-LS taken from [20]—are presented in Table 1. The first column provides the instance names. The following three columns show the results of CG-DE-LS in terms of the best solution found in 30 runs (column with heading **best**), the average of the values of the 30 solutions found in 30 runs (column with heading **avg**) and the corresponding standard deviation (column with heading **std**). The same three columns (based on tens runs per problem instance) are provided for BRKGA. Two additional columns provide information about the average computation time at which the best solution of each run was found and the corresponding standard deviation. Finally, note that values in columns **avg** are marked in bold font when the corresponding result is better (with statistical significance according to Student's t-test with $\alpha = 0.05$) than the result of the competing algorithm.

The results in Table 1 allow for the following observations:

Table 1. A comparison of BRKGA with CG-DE-LS [18]. Both algorithms were run 30 times on each problem instance and allowed 3600 s of run-time. Statistically significant results at $\alpha = 0.05$ are shown in bold.

Instance	CG-DE-LS			BRKGA				
	best	avg	std	best	avg	*std*	time	std
3–5	505.00	505.00	0.0	505.00	505.00	0.0	2.5	0.5
3–23	149.07	149.29	0.7	149.07	**149.07**	0.0	13.2	30.3
3–53	69.36	69.44	0.2	69.36	**69.36**	0.0	1.0	0.2
4–28	23.81	23.91	0.1	23.81	23.93	0.10	221.5	298.4
4–42	66.73	66.92	0.3	67.64	67.64	0.0	4.4	1.1
4–61	45.96	**45.98**	0.1	45.96	46.47	0.3	696.5	680.2
5–7	252.90	253.79	1.9	253.38	**253.69**	0.4	1827.8	1260.4
5–21	168.63	168.63	0.0	168.63	168.63	0.0	8.9	2.2
5–62	249.68	256.61	2.3	249.50	255.66	2.7	979.8	1016.9
6–10	812.90	**822.45**	6.7	817.10	828.09	6.9	2209.2	1210.7
6–28	218.37	**219.02**	1.6	219.48	228.07	6.6	290.1	556.5
6–58	238.84	242.89	3.3	238.84	**241.33**	1.8	915.7	697.2
7–5	418.06	426.96	7.6	418.06	430.15	10.1	961.7	1027.6
7–23	540.60	**555.17**	5.4	553.40	557.54	4.3	826.3	843.6
7–47	404.09	420.63	7.7	412.41	**418.46**	3.9	1356.8	1116.7
8–3	619.58	634.00	9.2	618.50	**629.76**	8.8	1493.1	1116.6
8–53	449.40	459.16	6.7	442.18	**452.84**	7.4	1345.7	1192.6
8–77	1175.56	1214.36	20.4	1163.78	**1194.32**	20.5	1583.0	1044.6
9–20	871.72	887.18	6.4	877.30	**882.18**	4.5	1626.4	1209.0
9–47	1189.14	1219.74	17.6	1158.25	**1185.53**	17.4	1095.7	1148.8
9–62	1395.08	1449.99	17.5	1382.63	**1399.67**	12.4	1254.2	964.6
10–7	2401.99	2471.82	32.8	2384.04	**2400.26**	13.9	1601.8	1230.1
10–13	2100.96	2148.57	22.1	2082.71	**2106.96**	11.6	1816.7	944.3
10–31	577.54	595.37	8.9	572.03	**586.76**	11.2	2146.8	1193.3
11–21	968.12	1001.94	33.2	964.04	**973.49**	7.2	2037.4	1296.7
11–56	1748.48	1798.08	24.1	1674.49	**1694.78**	15.9	2147.0	1164.4
11–63	1963.26	1994.49	18.1	1887.17	**1912.81**	16.5	2004.2	1004.3
12–14	1670.97	1728.63	26.8	1636.39	**1658.02**	13.0	1693.3	1258.0
12–36	2799.20	2904.02	41.3	2764.17	**2796.94**	28.5	1644.7	1225.5
12–80	2319.92	2372.37	31.5	2226.67	**2258.13**	20.6	1673.1	1032.1
15–2	3797.59	3867.99	41.7	3596.50	**3627.43**	19.8	2191.4	1038.2
15–3	4174.87	4251.49	49.1	3948.22	**3994.25**	40.3	2060.4	1086.1
15–5	3378.38	3433.19	35.4	3234.74	**3275.01**	35.5	1805.3	921.2
20–2	8243.78	8339.35	58.3	7755.29	**7890.49**	66.8	2090.9	1043.8
20–5	13818.30	14120.69	163.3	12899.17	**13123.85**	138.0	2446.2	988.6
20–6	7246.64	7347.18	52.6	6907.80	**6998.20**	74.2	2243.1	742.4

- For the small-medium problem instances (see the first 14 rows of Table 1) there is no a clear pattern, with BRKGA outperforming CG-DE-LS in some cases, and vice versa in others.
- Starting from instance 7–47 (i.e., and all larger instances with 8 machines or more) BRKGA clearly outperforms CG-DE-LS. Hereby, the advantage of BRKGA over CG-DE-LS seems to grow with increasing problem instance size. In the case of the largest 11 instances, for example, the average performance of BRKGA is better than the best solution values found by CG-DE-LS.

In order to better understand the behaviour of BRKGA, we provide graphics about the evolution of the best-so-far solution over time for four rather large problem instances in Fig. 1. More specifically, the graphics show the mean performance of BRKGA over 10 runs, while the grey-shaded area around the curves show, for each time step on the y-axis, the performance of the worst run and of the best run among the 10 runs. Furthermore, the dashed horizontal lines indicate the value of the best solutions found by CG-DE-LS within 30 runs, where each run made use of 16 threads in parallel. Finally, the vertical bars indicate the initiation of iterations with rollout evaluations (in any of the ten runs). In those cases in which such a vertical bar has a white square head, the rollout iteration was successful in the sense that the best-so-far solution was improved. Otherwise—that is, in those cases in which such a bar has a black diamond head—the rollout iteration was not successful. Note that in the context of instances 11–63 and 15–2 (Fig. 1a and b) only the successful rollout iterations are indicated, because showing all rollout iterations would have made these graphics unreadable.

The graphics in Fig. 1 allow us to make the following conclusions:

- First, in all four cases all ten runs of BRKGA improve over the best solution found by CG-DE-LS after a few hundred seconds. This is despite the fact that CG-DE-LS makes use of 16 threads in parallel, while BRKGA is run in one-threaded mode.
- Second, the best moment to make use of rollout iterations seems to be when the algorithm is stuck for quite a while in a local minimum. Remember that the parameter setting was determined by our tuning procedure with IRACE, as described in the third paragraph of Sect. 4. The chosen settings are $ro_{width} = 3$ and $n_{noimpr}^{max} = 200$, that is, a very narrow rollout-width and a rather high number of consecutive non-improving iterations before a rollout iteration is initiated. The effect of this can be nicely seen in the four graphics. In fact, the first rollout iterations are—in all four cases—initiated after the algorithm has already outperformed CG-DE-LS. The reason for making use of rollout iteration in this way is the significant difference in computation time requirements: a standard iteration requires 0.157 s for instance 11–63, 0.34 s for instance 15–2, 0.52 s for instance 20–2, and 0.64 s for instance 20–5. In contrast, a rollout iteration requires 12.7 s for instance 11–63, 41.1 s instance for 15–2, 89.3 s for 20–2, and 115.0 s for 20–5. That is, a rollout iteration consumes about two orders of magnitude more time than a standard algorithm iteration.

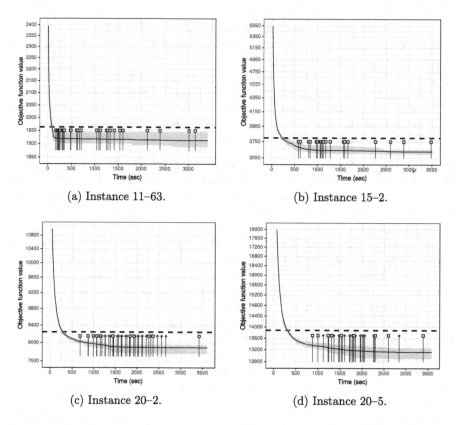

(a) Instance 11–63.

(b) Instance 15–2.

(c) Instance 20–2.

(d) Instance 20–5.

Fig. 1. Evolution of the best-so-far solution of BRKGA for four large problem instances. The curves show the mean performance over 10 runs, while the gray-shaded area behind the curves shows the spread of the 10 runs. The dashed horizontal bars indicate the best result of CG-DE-LS after 30 runs. The vertical bars indicate the initiation of rollout iterations.

Summarizing, we can say that our BRKGA algorithm significantly outperforms the current state-of-the-art algorithm CG-DE-LS, especially with growing problem instance size. Moreover, the algorithm requires much less computational resources than its competitor from the literature.

5   Conclusions and Future Work

We considered the resource constraint job scheduling problem where multiple single machine scheduling problems are linked by one limited shared resource. The objective is to minimize the total weighted tardiness of all jobs. We tackled this problem by means of a biased random key genetic algorithm, which is a quite generic framework. For the problem dependent part of the algorithm—the decoder—we apply a greedy construction heuristic which processes the jobs in an order determined by the jobs' random keys in combination with the earliest starting times. The basic greedy heuristic is further substantially enhanced by applying rollouts in a carefully controlled way in order to obtain a more promising ranking of the jobs. As rollouts are time-expensive, they are only used when the optimization gets stuck with the standard greedy criterion for a certain number of iterations.

Our experimental results show that in particular with growing problem instance size our approach significantly outperforms the leading column generation/differential evolution hybrid from the literature, both in terms of solution quality and computation time.

Acknowledgements. This work was partially funded by the Doctoral Program "Vienna Graduate School on Computational Optimization", Austrian Science Foundation (FWF) Project No. W1260-N35. Moreover, this work was partially supported by the EU H2020 Research and Innovation Program under the LOGISTAR project (Grant Agreement No. 769142).

References

1. Almeida, B.F., Correia, I., Saldanha-da Gama, F.: A biased random-key genetic algorithm for the project scheduling problem with flexible resources. Top **26**(2), 283–308 (2018)
2. Ballestin, F., Trautmann, N.: An iterated-local-search heuristic for the resource-constrained weighted earliness-tardiness project scheduling problem. Int. J. Prod. Res. **46**, 6231–6249 (2008)
3. Bertsekas, D.P., Tsitsiklis, J.N., Wu, C.: Rollout algorithms for combinatorial optimization. Journal of Heuristics **3**(3), 245–262 (1997)
4. Blum, C., Roli, A.: Metaheuristics in combinatorial optimization: overview and conceptual comparison. ACM Comput. Surv. **35**, 268–308 (2003)
5. Brent, O., Thiruvady, D., Gómez-Iglesias, A., Garcia-Flores, R.: A parallel lagrangian-ACO heuristic for project scheduling. In: IEEE Congress on Evolutionary Computation (CEC 2014), pp. 2985–2991. IEEE (2014)
6. Brucker, P., Drexl, A., Möhring, R., Neumann, K., Pesch, E.: Resource-constrained project scheduling: notation, classification, models, and methods. Eur. J. Oper. Res. **112**, 3–41 (1999)
7. Cohen, D., Gómez-Iglesias, A., Thiruvady, D., Ernst, A.T.: Resource constrained job scheduling with parallel constraint-based ACO. In: Wagner, M., Li, X., Hendtlass, T. (eds.) ACALCI 2017. LNCS (LNAI), vol. 10142, pp. 266–278. Springer, Cham (2017). https://doi.org/10.1007/978-3-319-51691-2_23
8. Demeulemeester, E., Herroelen, W.: Project Scheduling: A Research Handbook. Kluwer, Boston (2002)
9. Ernst, A.T., Singh, G.: Lagrangian particle swarm optimization for a resource constrained machine scheduling problem. In: Li, X. (ed.) 2012 IEEE Congress on Evolutionary Computation (CEC), pp. 1–8. IEEE, Institute of Electrical and Electronics Engineers, United States (2012). https://doi.org/10.1109/CEC.2012.6256177
10. de Faria Alixandre, B.F., Dorn, M.: D-BRKGA: a distributed biased random-key genetic algorithm. In: 2017 IEEE Congress on Evolutionary Computation (CEC), pp. 1398–1405 (2017)

11. Gonçalves, J.F., Resende, M.G.C.: Biased random-key genetic algorithms for combinatorial optimization. J. Heuristics **17**(5), 487–525 (2011)
12. Júnior, B., Pinheiro, P., Coelho, P.: A parallel biased random-key genetic algorithm with multiple populations applied to irregular strip packing problems. Math. Probl. Eng. **2017**, 1–11 (2017). https://doi.org/10.1155/2017/1670709
13. Lawler, E.L.: A "pseudopolynomial" algorithm for sequencing jobs to minimize total tardiness. Ann. Discrete Math. **1**, 331–342 (1977)
14. López-Ibáñez, M., Dubois-Lacoste, J., Pérez Cáceres, L., Birattari, M., Stützle, T.: The irace package: iterated racing for automatic algorithm configuration. Oper. Res. Perspect. **3**, 43–58 (2016)
15. Marriott, K., Stuckey, P.: Programming with Constraints. MIT Press, Cambridge (1998)
16. Mitchell, M.: An Introduction to Genetic Algorithms. MIT Press, Cambridge (1998)
17. Neumann, K., Schwindt, C., Zimmermann, J.: Project Scheduling with Time Windows and Scarce Resources. Springer, Berlin (2003)
18. Nguyen, S., Thiruvady, D., Ernst, A.T., Alahakoon, D.: A hybrid differential evolution algorithm with column generation for resource constrained job scheduling. Comput. Oper. Res. **109**, 273–287 (2019)
19. Pinto, B.Q., Ribeiro, C.C., Rosseti, I., Plastino, A.: A biased random-key genetic algorithm for the maximum quasi-clique problem. Eur. J. Oper. Res. **271**(3), 849–865 (2018)
20. Singh, G., Ernst, A.T.: Resource constraint scheduling with a fractional shared resource. Oper. Res. Lett. **39**(5), 363–368 (2011)
21. Thiruvady, D., Singh, G., Ernst, A.T., Meyer, B.: Constraint-based ACO for a shared resource constrained scheduling problem. Int. J. Prod. Econ. **141**(1), 230–242 (2012)
22. Thiruvady, D., Singh, G., Ernst, A.T.: Hybrids of integer programming and ACO for resource constrained job scheduling. In: Blesa, M.J., Blum, C., Voß, S. (eds.) HM 2014. LNCS, vol. 8457, pp. 130–144. Springer, Cham (2014). https://doi.org/10.1007/978-3-319-07644-7_10
23. Thiruvady, D., Wallace, M., Gu, H., Schutt, A.: A lagrangian relaxation and ACO hybrid for resource constrained project scheduling with discounted cash flows. J. Heuristics **20**(6), 643–676 (2014)
24. Thiruvady, D., Blum, C., Ernst, A.T.: Maximising the net present value of project schedules using CMSA and parallel ACO. In: Blesa Aguilera, M.J., Blum, C., Gambini Santos, H., Pinacho-Davidson, P., Godoy del Campo, J. (eds.) HM 2019. LNCS, vol. 11299, pp. 16–30. Springer, Cham (2019). https://doi.org/10.1007/978-3-030-05983-5_2
25. Thiruvady, D., Blum, C., Ernst, A.T.: Solution merging in metaheuristics for resource constrained job scheduling (2019, working paper)
26. Wolsey, L.A.: Integer Programming. Wiley-Interscience, New York (1998)

Image Processing

Efficient 3D Depthwise and Separable Convolutions with Dilation for Brain Tumor Segmentation

Donghao Zhang[1], Yang Song[2(⊠)], Dongnan Liu[1], Chaoyi Zhang[1],
Yicheng Wu[3], Heng Wang[1], Fan Zhang[4], Yong Xia[3],
Lauren J. O'Donnell[4], and Weidong Cai[1]

[1] School of Computer Science, University of Sydney, Sydney, NSW, Australia
[2] School of Computer Science and Engineering, University of New South Wales,
Kensington, Australia
yang.song1@unsw.edu.au
[3] School of Computer Science and Engineering,
Northwestern Polytechnical University, Xi'an, China
[4] Brigham and Women's Hospital, Harvard Medical School, Boston, USA

Abstract. In this paper, we propose a 3D convolutional neural network targeting at the segmentation of brain tumor. There are different types of brain tumors and our focus is one common type named glioma. The proposed network is efficient and balances the tradeoff between the number of parameters and accuracy of segmentation. It consists of Anisotropic Block, Dilated Parallel Residual Block, and Feature Refinement Module. The Anisotropic Block applies anisotropic convolutional kernels on different branches. In addition, the Dilated Parallel Residual Block incorporates 3D depthwise and separable convolutions to reduce the amount of required parameters dramatically, while multiscale dilated convolutions enlarge the receptive field. The Feature Refinement Module prevents global contextual information loss. Our method is evaluated on the BRATS 2017 dataset. The results show that our method achieved competitive performance among all compared methods, with a reduced number of parameters. The ablation study also proves that each individual block or module is effective.

Keywords: Brain tumor segmentation · Magnetic resonance imaging · 3D deep neural network

1 Introduction

Glioma is a common cause of brain tumor, which can be roughly classified into high-grade glioma (HGG) and low-grade glioma (LGG). Once patients are diagnosed as HGG, the average remaining life expectancy can be two years or less. Magnetic resonance imaging (MRI) is routinely applied to diagnose severity of brain tumor [16]. Different imaging modalities shown in Fig. 1 provide complementary information for each other. Automatic segmentation of brain tumor

© Springer Nature Switzerland AG 2019
J. Liu and J. Bailey (Eds.): AI 2019, LNAI 11919, pp. 563–573, 2019.
https://doi.org/10.1007/978-3-030-35288-2_45

from different MRI modalities provides quantitative information for analyzing the anatomical structures, which has a positive influence on the diagnosis, growth rate and future treatment [1]. However, glioma segmentation is still challenging due to the following issues: (1) diffusion of surrounding edema into the tumor region; (2) non-standardized voxel intensity values in MRI unlike the Computed Tomography and X-ray; and (3) irregular shapes and sizes of brain tumors [22].

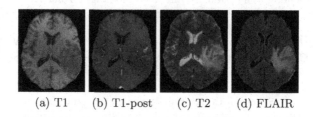

(a) T1   (b) T1-post   (c) T2   (d) FLAIR

Fig. 1. Visualization of different imaging modalities.

Convolutional neural networks (CNNs) have been widely applied to many biomedical related segmentation tasks: neuronal arbours segmentation in 3D microscopic images [15], nuclei segmentation in pathology images [20], prostate segmentation in MR images [5], semantic membrane segmentation in microscopy images [7], retinal vessel segmentation in color fundus retinal images [17] and multiple sclerosis lesions segmentation in MRI images [19]. Recently, many approaches [4,12,14,22,23] have been proposed for brain tumor segmentation. They are typically designed based on the public dataset [10], which provides researchers an opportunity to perform standardized benchmarking and solve the same challenge from different perspectives. Existing segmentation approaches can be roughly categorized into generative models and discriminative models. The generative models try to analyze the probabilistic data distribution. For example, the hierarchical probabilistic framework [14] consists of multi-window Gabor filters and Markov Random Field. The handcrafted features reach their limit of achieving higher accuracy, therefore many recent works use the deep convolutional neural network (CNN). For example, InputCascadedCNN and Two-pathway CNN [4] investigate both global and local contextual features to segment brain tissues, with 2D convolution operations. However, 2D CNNs cannot fully utilize the spatial information, and hence 3D CNNs have been proposed to better address the 3D biomedical image segmentation tasks. For example, one-pass multi-task network [23] shares the feature extraction layers, but independent convolution, classification, and loss layers are applied to effectively solve unique challenges of detection and classification tasks.

Even though most focus has been emphasized on improving the brain tumor segmentation accuracy by customizing the CNN model, there is little work targeting at proposing a lightweight model to improve the efficiency. To the best of our knowledge, the most related work are BiSeNet [18] for semantic segmentation of street scene images and Cascaded 3D lightweight network [9] for brain tumor segmentation, which are proposed to increase the inference speed of semantic segmentation. BiSeNet [18] introduces three novel components: Context Path (CP), Spatial Path (SP), and Feature Fusion Model (FFM) whose backbone is Xception39 with 2D depthwise separable convolutions to reduce the parameters. Unlike the two-stage framework in the Cascaded 3D lightweight network, our proposed model is end-to-end. In addition to the dilated convolutions used in the Cascaded 3D lightweight network, our proposed model also applies 3D depthwise and separable convolutions to reduce the number of parameters.

To address the challenges of glioma segmentation and achieve a balance between efficiency and accuracy, we propose a novel lightweight 3D CNN model. In particular, we design an end-to-end CNN model consisting of Anisotropic Block, Dilated Parallel Residual Block, and Feature Refinement Module. The fundamental building component (Dilated Parallel Residual Block) utilizes efficient 3D depthwise and separable convolutions to reduce the required number of parameters while maintaining the segmentation accuracy. Our method demonstrates competitive performance in segmenting the brain tumor on the MICCAI brain tumor segmentation challenge 2017 dataset (BRATS17).

2 Methods

The proposed network follows an encoder-decoder structure. In the encoder part, there is an Anisotropic Block described in Sect. 2.1 followed by five Dilated Parallel Residual Block series (DPRBs) described in Sect. 2.2. The essential component of the proposed network is DPRB, which consists of independent and parallel Dilated Depthwise Separable Convolution Blocks (DDSCBs) with fewer parameters by depthwise and pointwise convolution compared to the standard convolution. In the decoder part, two additional DPRBs are used to refine the learned feature representations by the encoder and then the processed feature representations are fused together. The fused information is finally processed by Feature Refinement Module in Sect. 2.3 to produce the segmentation output.

2.1 Anisotropic Block

Our design of Anisotropic Block is inspired by kernel decomposition and the existence of some anisotropic image features which can be better learned by anisotropic kernels. In general, 2D kernel with the size of $Q \times Q$ can be decomposed into two adjacent kernels with the size of $Q \times 1$ and $1 \times Q$ respectively to reduce the number of parameters. To extend the 2D kernel decomposition to 3D, there can be several options. For example, a convolution kernel $Q \times Q \times Q$ can be decomposed into several kernels with the size of: (a) $Q \times Q \times 1$, $Q \times 1 \times Q$, and $1 \times Q \times Q$ respectively; (b) $Q \times Q \times 1$, $1 \times 1 \times Q$. In our design, our priority is to balance the accuracy and speed, so option b is chosen for the design of AB. Specifically, $1 \times 7 \times 7$ kernel and $7 \times 1 \times 1$ are used for the left branch. $7 \times 1 \times 1$ kernel and $1 \times 7 \times 7$ kernel are used for the right branch. The middle branch

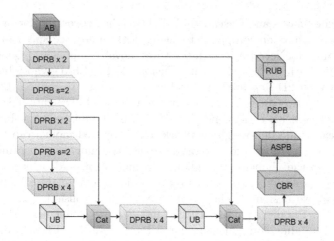

Fig. 2. The encoder of proposed network includes an Anisotropic Block (AB) and five Dilated Parallel Residual Blocks (DPRBs). The decoder consists of 2 Upsampling-Conv Blocks (UBs), 2 Concatenation (Cat) layers, and a Feature Refinement module with Conv-BN-Relu (CBR), Spatial Pyramid Block (SPB), Pyramid Scene Parsing Block (PSPB), and Refine Upsampling Block (RUB). $\times N$ represents the repetition of N times.

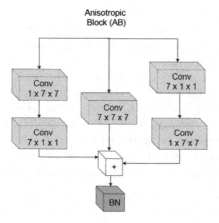

Fig. 3. The architecture of anisotropic block. + and BN stand for the elementwise summation and batch normalization respectively.

uses standard 3D convolution with $7 \times 7 \times 7$ kernel. Three branches are then fused together with batch normalization to produce the output of this AB layer (Figs. 2 and 3).

2.2   Dilated Parallel Residual Block

The main building block for the proposed network is DPRB, which consists of several fundamental components: Dilated Depthwise Separable Convolution Block (DDSCB) and CBR. In order to reduce gridding artifacts, the DPRB is designed to have four parallel DDSCBs to achieve hierarchical information fusion. This design expands the width of DPRB. The DDSCB is motivated by the convolution factorization [18]. It can learn image features representation at different scales with different dilation rates. Different and parallel DDSCBs are incorporated together and the resulted image features are fused by the summation operation to improve the information flow. In addition, DDSCB is also designed to have fewer parameters and lower computational cost compared to the standard convolutional block. We include four DDSCBs in DPRB with the aim of creating a three-level hierarchical feature extraction and fusion mechanism. The first summation of the two middle DDSCBs merges the feature information of different receptive fields. Another DDSCB with the dilation of 2 is further adopted to introduce more global information. The feature maps to be concatenated from left to right are rich in different levels of information. The fusion turns out to be effective enough to learn both the global and local information (Fig. 4).

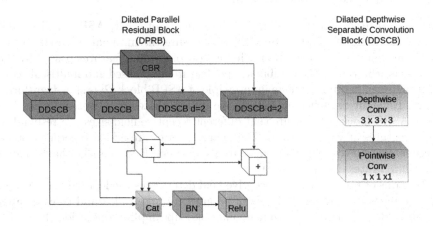

Fig. 4. The architecture of anisotropic block. + and BN stand for the elementwise summation and batch normalization respectively.

In order to better illustrate the difference between the standard 3D convolutional layer and depthwise convolutional layer, the shape of the kernel is simplified as a cube for the following discussion. Assume that the size of input feature map (F) of a standard 3D convolutional layer is $D_F \times D_F \times D_F \times M$ and its corresponding output feature map (G) is $D_G \times D_G \times D_G \times N$, where M and N are numbers of input and output channels respectively. The number of parameters of a standard 3D convolution is then $D_K \times D_K \times D_K \times M \times N$, where D_K depends on the kernel size of convolution operation. In addition, the corresponding computational cost is proportional to $D_K \cdot D_K \cdot D_K \cdot M \cdot N \cdot D_F \cdot D_F \cdot D_F$. Different from the standard 3D convolution, the depthwise convolution performs convolution filter per channel. The computational cost of 3D depthwise convolution is reduced and proportional to $D_K \cdot D_K \cdot D_K \cdot M \cdot D_F \cdot D_F \cdot D_F$. The pointwise convolution helps further reduce the computational cost by using $1 \times 1 \times 1$ convolution filter, and the pointwise convolution can be understood as a linear combination of image features generated by depthwise convolutional layer. The computational cost of pointwise convolution is proportional to $D_K \cdot D_K \cdot D_K \cdot M \cdot N$. The ratio of computational costs between the 3D DDSCB to standard 3D convolution is thus:

$$
\begin{aligned}
R_{cost} &= \frac{D_K \cdot D_K \cdot D_K \cdot M \cdot D_F \cdot D_F \cdot D_F}{D_K \cdot D_K \cdot D_K \cdot M \cdot N \cdot D_F \cdot D_F \cdot D_F} \\
&+ \frac{D_F \cdot D_F \times D_F \times M \times N}{D_K \cdot D_K \cdot D_K \cdot M \cdot N \cdot D_F \cdot D_F \cdot D_F} \\
&= \frac{1}{N} + \frac{1}{D_K \cdot D_K \cdot D_K}
\end{aligned}
\tag{1}
$$

2.3 Feature Refinement Module

The Feature Refinement Module (FRM) consists of CBR, ASPB, PSPB, and RUB. The design motivation of FRM is to ensure the minimal information loss on global contextual information. The process of refining features passed by the encoder is achieved by the combination of feature map based and multiscale convolution based poolings. The main principle of ASPB block [2] is split-transform-merge. Different branches of ASPB have different sizes of receptive fields. The use of ASPB block is to ensure that different receptive field sizes can respond to image features at various scales. The image features are added together instead of concatenation to reduce intermediate parameters. Four branches have dilated convolution rates d = {3, 5, 7, 9}.

In terms of the PSPB, the receptive field determines the learned feature size. Feature maps after different levels of pooling are upsampled and concatenated together. Based on this pyramid pooling and upsampling operation, fixed-size constraint of the network is weakened [21]. The feature maps generated by pyramid pooling at different scales = {0.2, 0.4, 0.6, 0.8} are upsampled to the same size by trilinear interpolation. The upsampled feature maps are concatenated together and are then processed by the RUB module.

The RUB further refines the decoding process by CBR, ASPB, Upsample, LDCB, and Conv. Similar to Depthwise Separable Convolutions, LDCB also balances between speed and accuracy. For LDCB, the entire space might not be fully covered by the manifold of interest because of the non-linear operation. Although it is possible to have lots of channels, the introduction of ReLU might still lead to some information loss. Proved by the Mobilenetv2 [13], the capability of ReLU operation to preserve input manifold information is related to the

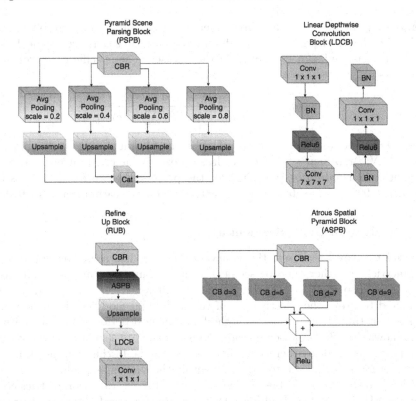

Fig. 5. The architecture of the Feature Refinement Module (FRM) including CBR, ASPB, PSPB, and RUB. s, $+$ and d represent stride value of convolution operation, elementwise summation, and dilation rate for convolution operation, respectively.

coverage of low-dimensional subspace of the input space to the input manifold. Two linear convolutional modules with kernel $1 \times 1 \times 1$ in LDCB are embedded to further improve the capability of preserving input manifold information (Fig. 5).

3   Experimental Results

3.1   Dataset and Parameters Setting

We used the BRATS17 dataset consisting of 210 HGG images for evaluation. The annotated brain tumor regions include complete tumor (necrosis, edema, non-enhancing core, and enhancing core), core region (necrosis, non-enhancing core, and enhancing core), and enhancing region (enhancing core). Ablation study was conducted on a subset containing 58 images for training and 9 images for testing. The remaining images were used for method comparison with 106 images for training and 37 images for testing. The test strategy is to choose the trained model with the highest intersection over union. Data augmentation includes scaling patch size to $144 \times 144 \times 144$, $128 \times 128 \times 128$, $96 \times 96 \times 96$, and flip operation. To be more specific, three different sizes of input are used to train the model. The batch size is 2. The weighted cross-entropy loss is used to deal with the severe class imbalance problem in the dataset. The specific class weight is defined as:

$$classweight[i] = \frac{1}{log(\alpha + hist[i]/(\sum_{j=1}^{N} hist[j]))} \tag{2}$$

where $hist$ is the histogram of class information of brain tumor; total number of classes is N; i represents the specific class type; α is the constant normal value, 1.1. The Adam optimizer is applied for the proposed network where β_1 is 0.9 and β_2 is 0.999; the weight decay is 0.0002. The initial learning rate is 0.0005.

3.2   Analysis of Brain Segmentation

We used the voxel-level sensitivity, specificity, and dice scores as our evaluation metrics. Another type of segmentation measurement metrics, Hausdorff distance, is also used to estimate boundary difference. Ablation studies were conducted to prove the effectiveness of the individual modules of our network. As shown in Table 1, the proposed method had the best performance. In addition, Fig. 6 shows that the proposed method tends to generate a smooth segmentation boundary compared to other state-of-the-art methods. In this example, the proposed method made least errors on segmenting the challenging enhancing region compared to the others. Table 2 shows the quantitative evaluation metrics comparing 3D U-Net, V-Net, HighRes3DNet and the proposed network. We reimplemented 3D U-Net, HighRes3DNet and V-Net for comparison and manually tuned hyperparameters for brain tumor segmentation. The Adam optimizer is also used for fair comparison. The details of comparison methods in experiment setting are referred to [8]. HighRes3DNet has the least parameters among all comparing methods with 811128 trainable parameters only. Regarding with 12 segmentation scores, the proposed method ranked first for 5 metrics. At the same time, the proposed method achieves highest segmentation scores on the Dice-TC, Hausdorff95-TC, Sensitivity-TC, Specificity-ET and Specificity-TC. 3D-UNet has 47772476 parameters which are almost 3 times as the proposed method, and it resulted in the highest performance for only 3 of the metrics. Overall, our proposed method achieves better balance among the number of parameters,

Table 1. Ablation study of the proposed model on the testing images of ablation dataset. The unit of Hausdorff distance is mm. ET, WT, and TC mean enhanced tumor, whole tumor, and tumor core, respectively. w/o stands for without.

Metrics	w/o AB	w/o DPRB	w/o FRM	Proposed
Dice-ET	0.642 ± 0.124	0.319 ± 0.098	0.624 ± 0.355	**0.676 ± 0.179**
Dice-WT	0.820 ± 0.148	0.809 ± 0.103	0.786 ± 0.195	**0.827 ± 0.092**
Dice-TC	0.740 ± 0.198	0.597 ± 0.188	0.717 ± 0.403	**0.775 ± 0.200**

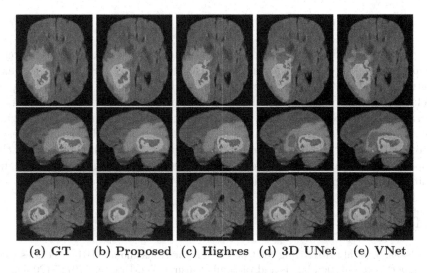

(a) GT   (b) Proposed (c) Highres (d) 3D UNet   (e) VNet

Fig. 6. A visual example from the testing image of the method-comparison set. The first, second, and third rows show axial, sagittal, and coronal views of brain images. Different colors indicate different tumor classes: red (enhancing tumor), yellow (non-enhancing tumor) and green (edema). (Color figure online)

Table 2. Quantitative comparison with 3D U-Net, V-Net, HighRes3DNet, and the proposed method on the method-comparison dataset.

Metrics	3D U-Net [3]	V-Net [11]	HighRes3DNet [6]	Proposed
Parameters	4772476	71049604	811128	1303096
Dice-ET	**0.785 ± 0.204**	0.766 ± 0.214	0.748 ± 0.224	0.753 ± 0.195
Dice-WT	**0.861 ± 0.162**	0.847 ± 0.185	0.801 ± 0.170	0.852 ± 0.174
Dice-TC	0.819 ± 0.222	0.781 ± 0.229	0.800 ± 0.244	**0.839 ± 0.214**
Hausdorff95-ET	11.775 ± 26.048	**6.429 ± 13.749**	20.285 ± 29.927	8.322 ± 20.647
Hausdorff95-WT	11.387 ± 18.092	**6.984 ± 7.910**	36.480 ± 26.326	8.956 ± 16.991
Hausdorff95-TC	14.453 ± 26.825	9.613 ± 13.674	24.967 ± 29.378	**8.151 ± 18.699**
Sensitivity-ET	**0.810 ± 0.210**	0.782 ± 0.231	0.776 ± 0.218	0.759 ± 0.208
Sensitivity-WT	0.890 ± 0.182	0.830 ± 0.215	**0.928 ± 0.169**	0.846 ± 0.201
Sensitivity-TC	0.811 ± 0.249	0.797 ± 0.255	0.808 ± 0.269	**0.816 ± 0.239**
Specificity-ET	0.996 ± 0.009	0.996 ± 0.008	0.996 ± 0.009	**0.997 ± 0.009**
Specificity-WT	0.991 ± 0.008	**0.995 ± 0.004**	0.981 ± 0.013	0.994 ± 0.005
Specificity-TC	0.997 ± 0.003	0.996 ± 0.005	0.997 ± 0.003	**0.998 ± 0.002**

voxel-level and boundary alignment segmentation results. It is noticeable that our proposed method achieves the best performance on the segmentation of the tumor core. This is due to the merging of the multi-scale features. The DPRB series after fusion between encoders and decoders further learn the combination of local spatial information and global contextual information thus resulting in more details being preserved.

4   Conclusion

We propose an efficient 3D brain tumor segmentation encoder-decoder architecture consisting of Anisotropic Block, Dilated Parallel Residual Block, and Feature Refinement Module. The fundamental building block (DPRB) has parallel and residual connections. The 3D depthwise and pointwise convolution operations of DPRB reduce the number of trainable parameters thus saving the computational cost. Ablation studies demonstrated the effectiveness of each individual block or module of the proposed method. Our results show that the proposed method achieves the best balance between trainable parameters and brain tumor segmentation accuracy on the BRATS2017 dataset.

References

1. Bakas, S., et al.: Advancing the Cancer Genome Atlas glioma MRI collections with expert segmentation labels and radiomic features. Sci. Data **4**, 170117 (2017)
2. Chen, L.C., Papandreou, G., Kokkinos, I., Murphy, K., Yuille, A.L.: DeepLab: semantic image segmentation with deep convolutional nets, atrous convolution, and fully connected CRFs. IEEE Trans. Pattern Anal. Mach. Intell. **40**(4), 834–848 (2018)
3. Çiçek, Ö., Abdulkadir, A., Lienkamp, S.S., Brox, T., Ronneberger, O.: 3D U-Net: learning dense volumetric segmentation from sparse annotation. In: Ourselin, S., Joskowicz, L., Sabuncu, M.R., Unal, G., Wells, W. (eds.) MICCAI 2016. LNCS, vol. 9901, pp. 424–432. Springer, Cham (2016). https://doi.org/10.1007/978-3-319-46723-8_49
4. Havaei, M., et al.: Brain tumor segmentation with deep neural networks. Med. Image Anal. **35**, 18–31 (2017)
5. Jia, H., et al.: 3D APA-Net: 3D adversarial pyramid anisotropic convolutional network for prostate segmentation in mr images. IEEE Trans. Med. Imag. (2019)
6. Li, W., Wang, G., Fidon, L., Ourselin, S., Cardoso, M.J., Vercauteren, T.: On the compactness, efficiency, and representation of 3D convolutional networks: brain parcellation as a pretext task. In: Niethammer, M., et al. (eds.) IPMI 2017. LNCS, vol. 10265, pp. 348–360. Springer, Cham (2017). https://doi.org/10.1007/978-3-319-59050-9_28
7. Liu, D., et al.: Densely connected large kernel convolutional network for semantic membrane segmentation in microscopy images. In: 2018 25th IEEE International Conference on Image Processing (ICIP), pp. 2461–2465. IEEE (2018)
8. Liu, D., Zhang, D., Song, Y., Zhang, F., O'Donnell, L.J., Cai, W.: 3D large kernel anisotropic network for brain tumor segmentation. In: Cheng, L., Leung, A.C.S., Ozawa, S. (eds.) ICONIP 2018. LNCS, vol. 11307, pp. 444–454. Springer, Cham (2018). https://doi.org/10.1007/978-3-030-04239-4_40
9. Ma, J., Yang, X.: Automatic brain tumor segmentation by exploring the multi-modality complementary information and cascaded 3D lightweight CNNs. In: Crimi, A., Bakas, S., Kuijf, H., Keyvan, F., Reyes, M., van Walsum, T. (eds.) BrainLes 2018. LNCS, vol. 11384, pp. 25–36. Springer, Cham (2019). https://doi.org/10.1007/978-3-030-11726-9_3
10. Menze, B.H., et al.: The multimodal brain tumor image segmentation benchmark (BRATS). IEEE Trans. Med. Imag. **34**(10), 1993–2024 (2015)

11. Milletari, F., Navab, N., Ahmadi, S.A.: V-Net: fully convolutional neural networks for volumetric medical image segmentation. In: 3D Vision, pp. 565–571 (2016)
12. Pereira, S., Pinto, A., Alves, V., Silva, C.A.: Brain tumor segmentation using convolutional neural networks in MRI images. IEEE Trans. Med. Imag. **35**(5), 1240–1251 (2016)
13. Sandler, M., Howard, A., Zhu, M., Zhmoginov, A., Chen, L.C.: MobileNetV2: inverted residuals and linear bottlenecks. In: CVPR (2018)
14. Subbanna, N.K., Precup, D., Collins, D.L., Arbel, T.: Hierarchical probabilistic gabor and MRF segmentation of brain tumours in MRI volumes. In: Mori, K., Sakuma, I., Sato, Y., Barillot, C., Navab, N. (eds.) MICCAI 2013. LNCS, vol. 8149, pp. 751–758. Springer, Heidelberg (2013). https://doi.org/10.1007/978-3-642-40811-3_94
15. Wang, H., et al.: Segmenting neuronal structure in 3D optical microscope images via knowledge distillation with teacher-student network. In: 2019 IEEE 16th International Symposium on Biomedical Imaging (ISBI 2019), pp. 228–231. IEEE (2019)
16. Wen, P.Y., et al.: Updated response assessment criteria for high-grade gliomas: response assessment in neuro-oncology working group. J. Clin. Oncol. **28**(11), 1963–1972 (2010)
17. Wu, Y., et al.: Vessel-Net: retinal vessel segmentation under multi-path supervision. In: Shen, D., et al. (eds.) MICCAI 2019. Lecture Notes in Computer Science, vol. 11764, pp. 264–272. Springer, Cham (2019). https://doi.org/10.1007/978-3-030-32239-7_30
18. Yu, C., Wang, J., Peng, C., Gao, C., Yu, G., Sang, N.: BiSeNet: bilateral segmentation network for real-time semantic segmentation. In: Ferrari, V., Hebert, M., Sminchisescu, C., Weiss, Y. (eds.) ECCV 2018. LNCS, vol. 11217, pp. 334–349. Springer, Cham (2018). https://doi.org/10.1007/978-3-030-01261-8_20
19. Zhang, C., et al.: MS-GAN: GAN-based semantic segmentation of multiple sclerosis lesions in brain magnetic resonance imaging. In: 2018 Digital Image Computing: Techniques and Applications (DICTA), pp. 1–8. IEEE (2018)
20. Zhang, D., et al.: Panoptic segmentation with an end-to-end cell R-CNN for pathology image analysis. In: Frangi, A.F., Schnabel, J.A., Davatzikos, C., Alberola-López, C., Fichtinger, G. (eds.) MICCAI 2018. LNCS, vol. 11071, pp. 237–244. Springer, Cham (2018). https://doi.org/10.1007/978-3-030-00934-2_27
21. Zhao, H., Shi, J., Qi, X., Wang, X., Jia, J.: Pyramid scene parsing network. In: CVPR, pp. 6230–6239 (2017)
22. Zhao, X., et al.: A deep learning model integrating FCNNs and CRFs for brain tumor segmentation. Med. Image Anal. **43**, 98–111 (2018)
23. Zhou, C., Ding, C., Lu, Z., Wang, X., Tao, D.: One-pass multi-task convolutional neural networks for efficient brain tumor segmentation. In: Frangi, A.F., Schnabel, J.A., Davatzikos, C., Alberola-López, C., Fichtinger, G. (eds.) MICCAI 2018. LNCS, vol. 11072, pp. 637–645. Springer, Cham (2018). https://doi.org/10.1007/978-3-030-00931-1_73

LumNet: A Deep Neural Network for Lumbar Paraspinal Muscles Segmentation

Yingdi Zhang[1,2,3,4,5](✉), Zelin Shi[1,4,5], Huan Wang[6], Chongnan Yan[6], Lanbo Wang[6], Yueming Mu[6], Yunpeng Liu[1,4,5], Shuhang Wu[1,4,5], and Tianci Liu[1,4,5]

[1] Shenyang Institute of Automation, Chinese Academy of Sciences, Beijing, China
zhangyingdi@sia.cn
[2] Institute for Robotics and Intelligent Manufacturing, Chinese Academy of Sciences, Beijing, China
[3] University of Chinese Academy of Sciences, Beijing, China
[4] Key Lab of Opto-Electronic Information Process, Shenyang, China
[5] The Key Lab of Image Understanding and Computer Vision, Shenyang, China
[6] Spine Surgery Department, Shengjing Hospital, Shenyang, China

Abstract. Lumber paraspinal muscles (LPM) segmentation is of essential importance in predicting response to treatment of low back pain. To date, all LPM segmentation methods are manually based instead of automatic. Manual segmentation of LPM requires vast radiological knowledge and experience. Moreover, the manual segmentation usually induces subjective variance. Therefore, an automatic segmentation is desireable. It is challenging to achieve automatic segmentation mainly because the ambiguous boundary of the LPM can be very difficult to locate. In this paper, we present a novel encoder-decoder and attention based deep convolutional neural network (CNN) to address this problem. With the help of skip connections, the encoder-decoder structure can capture both shadow and deep features which represent local and global information. Pre-trained VGG11 in ImageNet performed as encoder. In the decoder part, an attention block is applied to recalibrate the input feature. With the help of attention block, meaningful features are highlighted while irrelevant features are suppressed. To fully evaluate the performance of our proposed network, we construct the first large-scale LPM segmentation dataset with 1080 images and its segmentation masks. Experimental results show that our proposed network can not only achieve a good LPM segmentation result with a high dice score of 0.94 but also outperforms other state-of-the-art segmentation methods.

Keywords: Convolutional neural networks · Attention mechanism · Lumber paraspinal muscles segmentation · Attention mechanism

© Springer Nature Switzerland AG 2019
J. Liu and J. Bailey (Eds.): AI 2019, LNAI 11919, pp. 574–585, 2019.
https://doi.org/10.1007/978-3-030-35288-2_46

1 Introduction

With a lifetime prevalence of up to 84%, low back pain (LBP) affects a massive population [1] and causes enormous economic burden on individuals, families, and governments. To improve the understanding of LBP pathology and develop appropriate treatment strategies, there is a growing interest in investigating the relevance between LBP and lumbar paraspinal muscle morphology and fatty infiltration [2]. Lumbar paraspinal muscles consists of the psoas, quadratus, multifidus and erector spinae. Due to the attachment to the spinal column, lumbar paraspinal muscles influence segmental stability and control of the lumbar spine directly.

Magnetic resonance imaging (MRI) has been used for several years to assess morphology and fatty infiltration of lumber paraspinal muscles [3]. Up to now, the assessment of lumber paraspinal muscle composition consists of qualitative and quantitative methods. Qualitative methods assess the degree of paraspinal muscle fatty infiltration by visual grading schemes [4]. On the other hand, almost all quantitative methods rely on manual segmentation of muscle region of interest [5]. While manual segmentation is relatively precise, it is a time-consuming and subjective procedure. Statistical shape modeling has been used to segment quadratus lumborum muscle [6] and get a dice similarity of 0.87, but it is not able to achieve segmentation of other lumbar paraspinal muscles and cannot achieve a higher segmentation accuracy. Recently, a population-averaged atlas has been proposed for automated image processing and assessments of lumbar paraspinal muscles [7], but it has not achieved automated segmentation. Automated segmentation of muscles especially multifidus and erector spinae is still an urgent problem to be solved. Although automated segmentation of different structures have been successfully explored such as brain, liver and heart [8], there is not an approach to segment lumber paraspinal muscles automatically up to now.

Recently, deep learning methods such as convolutional neural network (CNN) have become popular in computer vision area [9]. Deep neural network learn representations of data with multiple layers automatically. These methods have dramatically improved the state of the art in image classification [10], object detection [11] and so on. Among them, fully convolutional neural network (FCN), a variant of CNN, achieve state of the art in many semantic segmentation tasks [12].

UNet [13], an evolutionary variant of FCN, has achieved excellent performance in many medical image segmentation and other segmentation areas. The UNet architecture consists of an encoder, a decoder and skip connections. The encoder extracts semantic informations through repeated convolution and downsample operations. The decoder achieve precise segmentation with repeated convolution and upsample operations. The key point of UNet is the use of skip connections which combine decoder's deep, semantic, coarse-grained features with encoder's shallow, low-level, fine-grained features.

An architectural component called squeeze & excitation (SE) block has been found effective in image classification task and can be integrated into any CNN model seamlessly [14]. The SE block models dependency among different channels in a feature map, besides, spatial dependency in a feature map can be modeled in a similar way [15]. More generally, the modeling of dependencies of channel dimension and spatial dimension can be categorized as attention mechanism.

In this work, we devise a novel deep neural network for lumbar paraspinal muscle segmentation called LumNet. Inspired by the UNet and attention mechanism, the proposed network architecture consists of three parts: the encoder, the decoder and skip connections. Pre-trained VGG11 is adopted as the encoder. A symmetric structure adopting strategy of repeating attention building blocks performes as the decoder. With the help of skip connections, the low level informations from the encoder which are crucial for locating propagate directly to the decoder which capture contextual informations. The attention blocks in the decoder which models channel and spatial dependency in feature maps plays an important role in precise localizating lumbar paraspinal muscle's ambiguous boundary. Experimental results indicate that our proposed algorithm is effective in lumbar paraspinal muscle segmentation and can improve segmentation accuracy compared to other state-of-the-art methods.

The contributions of this work can be summarized as follows:

1. To study automated lumbar paraspinal muscle segmentation method, we construct the first large-scale lumbar paraspinal muscle segmentation dataset which contains 1080 MRI images and corresponding muscle masks. All muscle masks are acquired by clinical experts. Only multifidus and erector spinae are under consideration in the dataset.
2. A novel attention based deep neural network for image segmentation called LumNet is proposed which achieves automatic segmentation of lumbar paraspinal segmentation for the first time.
3. We evaluate the LumNet on the proposed dataset and compare it with several state-of-the art image segmentation methods. Experimental results show that our network outperforms other methods in a large margin with over 0.94 dice score in multifidus segmentation and over 0.91 dice score in erector spinae segmentation.

2   Methods

2.1   Overall Framework

Figure 1 illustrates the proposed lumbar paraspinal muscle segmentation network. The network takes lumbar paraspinal muscle MRI image as input and outputs the segmentation result in an end-to-end manner. Similiar to UNet [13], the proposed architecture consists of three parts: the encoder, the decoder and the skip connections. The encoder hierarchically subtract semantic features with repeated convolutional, non-linear activation and maxpooling operations. Specifically, we adopt VGG11 [16] as encoder which can be pre-trained on ImageNet [17]. To modify the VGG11 for image segmentation task which was originally

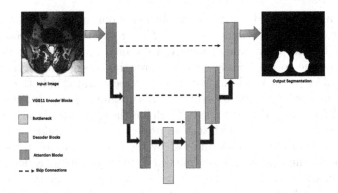

Fig. 1. Illustration of the proposed network architecture. We adopt VGG11 without fully connected layers as encoder, a series of ConvReLU operations and attention blocks as decoder, concatenate and copy operations as skip connections. Input image is progressively filtered and downsampled in the encoder of the network. The decoder merge semantic information from decoding part and contextual information from skip connections to achieve precise segmentation. The attention blocks in decoder helps boost important features and suppress irrelevant features in channel and spatial dimensions. Schematic of the attention block is shown in Figs. 2 and 3.

Table 1. Network configurations

Encoder configuration	Decoder configuration
input(512 × 512 MRI image)	output(512 × 512 segmentation result)
conv3-64	conv1-1
maxpool	convtransposed2d(stride=2)
conv3-128	conv3-192 + attention block
maxpool	convtransposed2d(stride=2)
conv3-256	attention block
conv3-256	conv3-384
maxpool	convtransposed2d(stride=2)
conv3-512	attention block
conv3-512	conv3-768
maxpool	convtransposed2d(stride=2)
conv3-512	attention block
conv3-512	conv3-768
maxpool + conv3-512(bottleneck)	convtransposed2d(stride=2)

designed for image classification, we replace the fully connected layers with a single convolutional layer with ReLU activation operation to serve as bottleneck central part of the network. Symmetrically, the decoder which enables precise localization consists of repeated transposed convolutional operations, ReLU operations and attention blocks. The resolution of output feature is doubled and the number of channels is reduced by half after the transposed convolutional layer. Then the output of transposed convolutional layer is concatenated with the output of the corresponding encoder through the skip connection. After a convolutional layer, the resultant feature map is recalibrated in both channel and spatial dimensions by the attention block. This upsampling procedure is repeated 5 times to output the prediction result which has the same size of the input image. The skip connections in the architecture preserve low level informations which are crucial in segmentation task and lost by the use of maxpool in the encoder. The network configurations are outlined in Table 1. On the decoder of original UNet model, the subsequent component of concatenation operation is a convolutional layer which extract important information directly. In this paper, we suggest model feature dependencies in both channel and spatial dimensions. The proposed attention block which consists of channel attention block and spatial attention block can recalibrate input feature in a meaningful way. After passed into the attention block, the useful channels and spatial locations are magnified and irrelevant ones are suppressed. This helps improving performance.

2.2   Channel Attention Block

The channel attention block recalibrate input feature by channel attention map which models the channel dependency of input feature. As each channel of input feature is considered as a feature detector [15], attention block focus on 'what' is meaningful in input feature.

We describe channel attention block as spatial squeeze and channel excitation, which was proposed in [14]. Consider an input feature map $U \in R^{H \times W \times C}$, $U = [u_1, u_2, \cdots, u_C]$ as an combination of $u_i \in R^{H \times W}$. Spatial squeeze is performed by global average pooling. Vector $z \in R^{1 \times 1 \times C}$ is then produced by global average pooling with its kth element

$$z_k = \frac{1}{H \times W} \sum_{i}^{H} \sum_{j}^{W} u_k(i, j) \tag{1}$$

This operation embeds the global information into channel descriptor z, whose statistics are expressive for the whole image. It is prevalent to exploit feature embeding methods in feature engineering work [15, 18]. In this paper, considering method simplicity and model complexity we apply a simple global average pooling operation as feature embeding approach which can be replaced by other methods such as max pooling.

In order to make use of channel descriptor z which is obtained in the squeeze operation, we propose the second subsequent operation named channel excitation which aims to capture channel-wise dependency. To fulfil this purpose, we employ two fully-connected layers and the ReLU unit:

$$s = F_{ex}(z, W) = \sigma(g(z, W)) = \sigma(W_2 \delta(W_1 z)) \tag{2}$$

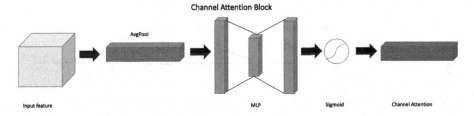

Fig. 2. Schematic of the proposed channel attention block. The channel attention vector is obtained by spatial squeeze (average pool) and channel excitation (multi-layer perception) operations. The sigmoid function make sure the range of channel attention vector is [0.1].

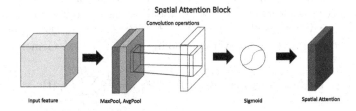

Fig. 3. Schematic of the proposed spatial attention block. The spatial attention vector is obtained by channel squeeze (maxpool, averagepool) and spatial excitation (convolutional operation) operations. The sigmoid function make sure the range of channel attention vector is [0.1].

where δ refers to the ReLU unit [19], σ refers to sigmoid function, $W_1 \in R^{\frac{C}{r} \times C}$ and $W_2 \in R^{C \times \frac{C}{r}}$ being weights of fully-connected layers. The dynamic range of output vector s is $[0, 1]$ due to the using of sigmoid function. The vector s is then used to recalibrate input feature U by channel-wise multiplication:

$$U_{atten} = Channel_{atten}(U) = [s_1 u_1, s_2 u_2, \cdots, s_c u_c] \qquad (3)$$

s_i indicates the importance of the ith channel, which are rescaled.

In the training phase, the weights in channel attention block are adaptively tuned to suppress irrelevant channels and emphasise important ones. In the inference phase, the attention block recalibrate features to propagate more useful informations. The architecture of the module is illustrated in Fig. 2.

2.3 Spatial Attention Block

The spatial attention block recalibrate input feature by spatial attention map which utilize the spatial relationship of the feature. Different from the channel attention block, the spatial attention block focus on 'where' is more important in lumbar paraspinal muscle segmentation task. Similiar to the channel attention block, we describe spatial attention block as channel squeeze and spatial excitation. Consider an input feature map $F \in R^{H \times W \times C}$, $F =$

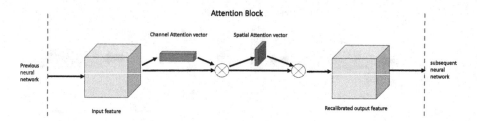

Fig. 4. Schematic of proposed attention block. An input feature is first recalibrated by channel attention vector and then spatial attention vector.

$[f_{1,1}, f_{1,2}, \cdots, f_{1,W}; \cdots; f_{H,1}, f_{H,2}, \cdots, f_{H,W}]$ as a combination of $f_{i,j} \in R^C$. Channel squeeze is performed by both global average pooling and global max pooling. Vector $V^{\max} \in R^{1 \times W \times H}$ and $v^{avg} \in R^{1 \times W \times H}$ are then produced by global maxpooling and global average pooling with its $i * jth$ element

$$v^{\max}{}_{i,j} = \arg\max\left(f_{i,j}\left(t\right)\right); v^{avg}{}_{i,j} = \frac{1}{C}\sum_{t=1}^{t=C} f_{i,j}\left(t\right) \qquad (4)$$

where t represents tth channel in $f_{i,j}$.

After transforming input feature from $F \in R^{H \times W \times C}$ to $V \in R^{1 \times H \times W}$, we obtain two spatial descriptors $V^{\max}$ and V^{avg}. To make full use of spatial descriptors, we concatenate them together in channel dimension to get the final spatial descriptor $[V^{\max}; V^{avg}]$. Then, we apply a convolutional layer and sigmoid function on the spatial descriptor to derive a spatial attention map which encodes where to emphasize or suppress:

$$V = \sigma\left(Conv\left[V^{\max}, V^{avg}\right]\right) \qquad (5)$$

where $[V^{\max}, V^{avg}]$ refers to spatial descriptor, $Conv$ refers to a convolutional layer with the filter size of 7×7, σ refers to sigmoid function. The dynamic range of output vector V is $[0, 1]$ since using of sigmoid function. At last, the spatial attention map is used to recalibrate input feature map by spatial-wise multiplication:

$$F_{atten} = Spatial_{atten}\left(F\right) = [f_{1,1}v_{1,1}; \cdots; f_{H,W}v_{H,W}] \qquad (6)$$

$v_{i,j}$ indicates the importance of the $i * jth$ element in spatial dimension which is used to rescale the corresponding feature. In the training phase, the weights in spatial attention block are adaptively tuned to suppress irrelevant features and emphasis important ones in spatial dimension. In the inference phase, the attention block recalibrate the input feature to transfer more useful informations to the subsequent network. The architecture of the module is illustrated in Fig. 3.

As presented in Fig. 4, given an input feature, channel attention block and spatial attention block recalibrate input feature in a sequential way. Two attention blocks compute complementary attention focusing on 'what' and 'where' respectively.

3   Experiments and Results

3.1   Datasets and Implementation Details

We construct the first lumbar paraspinal muscle segmentation dataset. It contains 1080 MRI images from 120 male patients and corresponding segmentation masks, with the same resolution of 512×512 for all images. All images are splitted into three parts: 756 for training, 216 for validating and 108 for testing.

All the male outpatients, aged from 18 to 35 years, were from the same hospital. The Philips magnetic resonance was used, the repetition time of sagittal scanning is 2500 ms, and that of axial scanning is 24855 ms; the echo time of sagittal scanning is 80 ms, that of axial scanning is 120 ms and that of axial scanning is 4 mm under 3.0T. All the patients' lumbar MR scans included T1/T2 weighted. The sagittal position nearest to the midline was selected as the location image. The axial images corresponding to L3–4, L4–5, L5–S1 discs were scanned. Each disc was divided into three slices. By excluding obvious disc herniation, infection, fracture, tumor and other abnormal changes and incomplete images, T2-weighted axial images of 120 patients were obtained. All images are processed by brightness and contrast adjustment and normalized operation. Five spine surgeons and one imaging surgeon used Photoshop graphics software to label the bilateral erector spine muscles and multifidus muscles in the image manually.

A set of image and corresponding masks are illustrated in Fig. 5. We can deduce from Fig. 5 that the boundaries of multifidus and erector spinae are vague. It is very difficult to locate the border precisely. Besides, more kinds of lumbar paraspinal muscles may be included in the future.

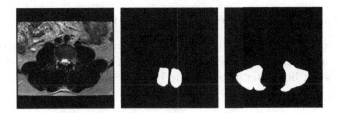

Fig. 5. A set of images in the proposed dataset. From left to right, it is respectively MRI image, corresponding multifidu mask and corresponding erector spinae mask.

All models were implemented based on the deep learning library Pytorch [20]. We use 8 NVIDIA 1080Ti GPUs for training and only one for testing. In the training phase, we adopt Adam algorithm to optimize the network with a batch size of 32. All models were trained for 100 epochs from scratch. The learning rate was initially set to 0.001 in first 70 epochs and decreased to 0.0001 in the subsequent 30 epochs. The original sized images were used as input of network without downsample operation. We performed data augmentation with random brightness, random contrast, random rotation in angle range $[-10, 10]$ and random horizontal flipping. When testing, we apply prediction on the original images.

Loss function indicates optimal update direction in training procedure. To update parameters in an appropriate way, We adopt a hybrid form of loss function which is a combination of binary cross-entropy and dice coefficient. We consider image segmentation task as a pixel classification problem, so the binary cross-entropy loss is defined as:

$$E = -\frac{1}{n} \sum_{i=1}^{n} (y_i \log \hat{y}_i + (1 - y_i) \log (1 - \hat{y}_i)) \tag{7}$$

where y_i is a binary value which is the label of the corresponding pixel i and $\hat{y}_i$ is predicted probability for the pixel. n indicates the total number of pixels in an image. Dice coefficient can be interpreted as similarity measure between two sets X and Y, can be defined as following:

$$D(X,Y) = \frac{2|X \cap Y|}{|X| + |Y|} \tag{8}$$

Considering dice coefficient of true mask and predicted probability heat map as part of loss function, we can rewrite it in the following way:

$$D = 1 - \frac{1}{n} \sum_{i=1}^{n} \left(\frac{2y_i \hat{y}_i}{y_i + \hat{y}_i} \right) \tag{9}$$

Join these expressions, we can generalize the loss function as: $L = E + \omega D$, where ω represents the weight of dice coefficient. In all of our experiments, we set ω equals to 1, which shows applicable in the training process.

3.2 Performance of the Segmentation Task

In this subsection, we empirically show the effectiveness of our proposed method. Some inference results are showed in Fig. 6. As Fig. 6 shows, our proposed method can locate weak boundary pixels properly even when it is a difficult task for human eyes.

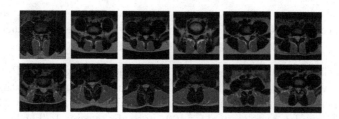

Fig. 6. Multifidus and Erector spinae segmentation results of proposed method. The red region denotes ground truth, and the green region denotes predicting mutifidus mask of our proposed method. Yellow region indicates pixels which are regarded as multifidus or erector spinae by both ground truth and proposed method. (Color figure online)

To demonstrate the advantage of our proposed method, we compare our method with several advanced segmentation methods, including Fully Convolutional Network (FCN) [12], SegNet [21] and the baseline model UNet [13]. We employ several metrics to quantitatively evaluate the segmentation performance of different methods including Dice Similarity Coefficient (Dice Score), Precision and Recall [22].

Table 2 lists the metric result of different method in segmenting multifidus and erector spinae. We can see that our proposed method achieves higher dice score than other state-of-the-art methods. The SegNet works well in precisely locate multifidus but it has a lower recall compared to our proposed method. Our proposed method performs better than the baseline model UNet on nearly all metrics by a large margin, indicating that the using of pre-trained model and attention block brings performance gain.

Table 2. Comparision of Multifidus (MF) and Erector Spinae (ES) segmentation between different methods

Method	Dice score	Precision	Recall
U-Net(MF)	0.900 ± 0.056	0.864 ± 0.082	0.948 ± 0.063
U-Net(ES)	0.865 ± 0.093	0.828 ± 0.126	0.925 ± 0.089
FCN	0.919 ± 0.050	0.889 ± 0.079	0.956 ± 0.042
FCN(ES)	0.899 ± 0.089	0.915 ± 0.097	0.899 ± 0.107
SegNet	0.902 ± 0.059	0.958 ± 0.048	0.860 ± 0.090
SegNet(ES)	0.873 ± 0.084	0.930 ± 0.086	0.837 ± 0.011
Proposed	$\mathbf{0.948 \pm 0.040}$	0.947 ± 0.055	0.951 ± 0.043
Proposed(ES)	$\mathbf{0.912 \pm 0.082}$	0.905 ± 0.102	$\mathbf{0.930 \pm 0.084}$

Table 3. Dice score for different models with and without attention gate in segmenting lumbar paraspinal muscles.

Muscle	With attention block	Without attention block
Multifidus	$\mathbf{0.948 \pm 0.040}$	0.927 ± 0.050
Erector spinae	$\mathbf{0.912 \pm 0.082}$	0.905 ± 0.079

As mentioned above, we propose an attention block which recalibrate features in both channel and spatial dimension to boost important features and suppress irrelevant ones. To evaluate the performance of proposed attention block, we conduct some experiments that make a comparison between with and without attention block in segmenting lumbar paraspinal muscles.

From the results of Table 3 we found that proposed attention blocks improved dice score by 2.1% in multifidus and 0.7% in erector spinae, demonstrating that the use of attention block lead to high-precision segmentation of lumbar paraspinal muscles segmentation.

4 Conclusion

This paper develops a novel encoder-decoder based deep neural network for lumbar paraspinal muscle segmentation in MRI images by harnessing the attention mechanism. The proposed attention block recalibrate features in both channel and spatial dimension which helps decoder to achieve accurate segmentation.

We are the first to realize automated segmentation of lumbar paraspinal muscles, which is a difficult problem because of ambiguous target boundary. To achieve the purpose, we firstly propose a dataset for segmentation of lumbar paraspinal muscles. Experiment results demonstrate that our proposed method can achieve automated segmentation for lumbar paraspinal muscles and outperforms several state-of-the-art segmentation methods. Moreover, experiment results demonstrate that using attention block helps in better locating of the ambiguous boundary. In addition, the proposed method is a general solution and has the potential to be used for other medical image segmentation tasks.

References

1. Balagué, F., Mannion, A.F., Pellisé, F., Cedraschi, C.: Non-specific low back pain. Lancet **379**(9814), 482–491 (2012)
2. Shahidi, B., et al.: Contribution of lumbar spine pathology and age to paraspinal muscle size and fatty infiltration. Spine **42**(8), 616–623 (2017)
3. Beneck, G.J., Kulig, K.: Multifidus atrophy is localized and bilateral in active persons with chronic unilateral low back pain. Arch. Phys. Med. Rehabil. **93**(2), 300–306 (2012)
4. Battaglia, P.J., Maeda, Y., Welk, A., Hough, B., Kettner, N.: Reliability of the Goutallier classification in quantifying muscle fatty degeneration in the lumbar multifidus using magnetic resonance imaging. J. Manipulative Physiol. Ther. **37**(3), 190–197 (2014)
5. Ranson, C., Burnett, A., O'sullivan, P., Batt, M., Kerslake, R.: The lumbar paraspinal muscle morphometry of fast bowlers in cricket. Clin. J. Sport Med. **18**(1), 31–37 (2008)
6. Engstrom, C.M., Fripp, J., Jurcak, V., Walker, D.G., Salvado, O., Crozier, S.: Segmentation of the quadratus lumborum muscle using statistical shape modeling. J. Magn. Reson. Imaging **33**(6), 1422–1429 (2011)
7. Xiao, Y., Fortin, M., Battié, M.C., Rivaz, H.: Population-averaged MRI atlases for automated image processing and assessments of lumbar paraspinal muscles. Eur. Spine J. **27**, 2442–2448 (2018)
8. Mikheev, A., Nevsky, G., Govindan, S., Grossman, R., Rusinek, H.: Fully automatic segmentation of the brain from T1-weighted mri using bridge burner algorithm. J. Magn. Reson. Imaging **27**(6), 1235–1241 (2008)
9. LeCun, Y., Bengio, Y., Hinton, G.: Deep learning. Nature **521**(7553), 436 (2015)
10. Szegedy, C.: Going deeper with convolutions. In: Proceedings of the IEEE Conference on Computer Vision and Pattern Recognition, pp. 1–9 (2015)
11. Ren, S., He, K., Girshick, R., Sun, J.: Faster R-CNN: towards real-time object detection with region proposal networks. In: Advances in Neural Information Processing Systems, pp. 91–99 (2015)

12. Long, J., Shelhamer, E., Darrell, T.: Fully convolutional networks for semantic segmentation. In: Proceedings of the IEEE Conference on Computer Vision and Pattern Recognition, pp. 3431–3440 (2015)

13. Ronneberger, O., Fischer, P., Brox, T.: U-Net: convolutional networks for biomedical image segmentation. In: Navab, N., Hornegger, J., Wells, W.M., Frangi, A.F. (eds.) MICCAI 2015. LNCS, vol. 9351, pp. 234–241. Springer, Cham (2015). https://doi.org/10.1007/978-3-319-24574-4_28

14. Hu, J., Shen, L., Sun, G.: Squeeze-and-excitation networks, vol. 7. arXiv preprint arXiv:1709.01507 (2017)

15. Woo, S., Park, J., Lee, J.-Y., Kweon, I.S.: CBAM: convolutional block attention module. In: Proceedings of European Conference on Computer Vision (ECCV) (2018)

16. Simonyan, K., Zisserman, A.: Very deep convolutional networks for large-scale image recognition. arXiv preprint arXiv:1409.1556 (2014)

17. Deng, J., Dong, W., Socher, R., Li, L.-J., Li, K., Fei-Fei, L.: ImageNet: a large-scale hierarchical image database. In: 2009 IEEE Conference on Computer Vision and Pattern Recognition, CVPR 2009, pp. 248–255. IEEE (2009)

18. Shen, L., Sun, G., Huang, Q., Wang, S., Lin, Z., Wu, E.: Multi-level discriminative dictionary learning with application to large scale image classification. IEEE Trans. Image Process. **24**(10), 3109–3123 (2015)

19. Nair, V., Hinton, G.E.: Rectified linear units improve restricted Boltzmann machines. In: Proceedings of the 27th International Conference on Machine Learning (ICML-2010), pp. 807–814 (2010)

20. Paszke, A.: Automatic differentiation in PyTorch (2017)

21. Badrinarayanan, V., Kendall, A., Cipolla, R.: SegNet: a deep convolutional encoder-decoder architecture for image segmentation. arXiv preprint arXiv:1511.00561 (2015)

22. Chang, H.-H., Zhuang, A.H., Valentino, D.J., Chu, W.-C.: Performance measure characterization for evaluating neuroimage segmentation algorithms. Neuroimage **47**(1), 122–135 (2009)

Semi-supervised Learning Using Siamese Networks

Attaullah Sahito$^{(\boxtimes)}$, Eibe Frank, and Bernhard Pfahringer

Department of Computer Science, University of Waikato, Hamilton, New Zealand
a19@students.waikato.ac.nz, {eibe,bernhard}@waikato.ac.nz

Abstract. Neural networks have been successfully used as classification models yielding state-of-the-art results when trained on a large number of labeled samples. These models, however, are more difficult to train successfully for semi-supervised problems where small amounts of labeled instances are available along with a large number of unlabeled instances. This work explores a new training method for semi-supervised learning that is based on similarity function learning using a Siamese network to obtain a suitable embedding. The learned representations are discriminative in Euclidean space, and hence can be used for labeling unlabeled instances using a nearest-neighbor classifier. Confident predictions of unlabeled instances are used as true labels for retraining the Siamese network on the expanded training set. This process is applied iteratively. We perform an empirical study of this iterative self-training algorithm. For improving unlabeled predictions, local learning with global consistency [22] is also evaluated.

Keywords: Semi-supervised learning · Siamese networks · Triplet loss · LLGC

1 Introduction

The modern world generates vast amounts of data and provides many opportunities to exploit it. However, frequently this data is complex, noisy, and lacks obvious structure. Therefore, explicit modeling of, for example, its distribution is too challenging for a human agent. On the other hand, a human can specify an explicit procedure, i.e., an algorithm, for how to construct such a model. Machine learning (ML) is concerned with algorithms that enable computers to learn from data in this way, especially algorithms for prediction. Many ML algorithms need labeled data for such a task, but it is common that fewer labeled data are available than unlabeled ones. Manual labeling is costly and time-consuming. Hence, there is an ever-growing need for ML methods to work with a limited amount of labeled data and also make efficient use of the side information available from unlabeled data. Algorithms designed to do so are known as semi-supervised learning algorithms.

Supervised learning algorithms employ labeled data to predict class labels for unlabeled examples accurately. Unsupervised learning algorithms search for

© Springer Nature Switzerland AG 2019
J. Liu and J. Bailey (Eds.): AI 2019, LNAI 11919, pp. 586–597, 2019.
https://doi.org/10.1007/978-3-030-35288-2_47

structure in data, which can then be used as a heuristic to infer labels for these examples, on the basis of assumptions about the structure of data. Semi-Supervised learning (SSL) algorithms lie somewhere between supervised and unsupervised learning. SSL methods are designed to work with labeled $L = \{(x_1, y_1), (x_2, y_2), ..., (x_{|L|}, y_{|L|})\}$ and unlabeled instances $U = \{x'_1, x'_2, ..., x'_{|U|}\}$, where X and Y relate to an input space and output space, $x_i, x'_j \in X (i = 1, 2, ..., |L|, j = 1, 2, ..., |U|)$ are examples and $y_i \in Y$ are labels of x_i and $Y = \{1, 2, 3, ..., c\}$, c being the number of classes. Usually, these methods assume a much smaller number of labeled instances than unlabeled ones i.e., $|L| \ll |U|$, because unlabeled instances are more useful when we have a few labeled instances. SSL has proven to be useful especially when we are dealing with anti-causal or confounded problems [15].

Without making any assumptions on how the inputs and outputs are related it is impossible to justify semi-supervised learning as a principled approach [4]. Like the authors in that paper, we make the same three assumptions:

1. If two points x_1, x_2 are close in a high-density region, then their corresponding outputs y_1, y_2 should also be close.
2. If points are in the same structure (referred to as cluster or manifold), they are likely to be of the same class.
3. The decision boundary between classes should lie in a low-density region of input space.

In this work, we will consider a new training method designed to be used with deep neural networks in the semi-supervised learning setting. Instead of the usual approach of learning a direct classification model based on cross-entropy loss, we will use the labeled examples for learning a similarity function between instances, such that instances of the same class are considered similar and those instances belonging to different classes are considered dissimilar. Under this similarity function, which is parameterized by a neural network, the features (embeddings) of labeled examples will be grouped together according to the class labels, in Euclidean space. In addition, we will use these learned embeddings to assign class labels to unlabeled examples. We do this using a simple nearest-neighbor classifier. Following that, confident predictions for unlabeled instances are added to the labeled examples for retraining of the neural network iteratively. In this way, we are able to achieve significant performance improvements over supervised-only training.

2   Related Work

Semi-supervised learning has been under study since the 1970s [12]. Expectation-Maximization (EM) [14] works by labeling unlabeled instances with the current supervised model's best prediction in an iterative fashion (self-learning), thereby providing more training instances for the supervised learning algorithm. Co-training [1] is a similar approach, where two models are trained on two separate subsets of the data features. Confident predictions from one model are then used as labeled data for the other model. Co-EM [2] combines co-training with EM and achieved better results than either of them. Another, graph-based SSL method, LLGC (Local Learning with Global Consistency) [22], works by propagating labels from labeled to unlabeled instances until labels are stable, maintaining local and global consistency.

There is a substantial amount of literature available on SSL techniques using deep neural network based on autoencoders [11,16], generative adversarial networks (GAN) [6,18,20] and based on regularization [9,13,17]. The Pseudolabel [10] approach is a deep learning version of self-learning with an extra loss from regularization and the reconstruction of a denoising autoencoder.

Our method builds on work investigating similarity metric learning using neural networks. [5] used a network with the contrastive loss for face verification in a supervised fashion. [19] suggested network training to be based on triplets of examples. This work was extended to the semi-supervised paradigm [21] for the image classification task. [7] tries to minimize the sum of cross-entropy and ratio loss between class indicators (sampled from labeled examples for each class) and the intra-class distances of instances calculated based on embeddings.

We train our network based on triplets of images and use the triplet margin loss [19]. We found this to perform better than the contrastive loss or the ratio loss in our experiments, while the network is trained in a self-learning fashion. For improving intermediate predictions, we use LLGC [22] in order to get better labels for unlabeled instances in subsequent iterations. Although triplet networks and LLGC are not new, this is the first attempt, to our knowledge, of combining these two approaches for semi-supervised learning.

3   Siamese Networks

Siamese networks [3] are neural networks that are particularly efficient when we have a large number of classes and a few labeled instances per class. Siamese networks can be thought of multiple networks with identical copies of the same function, with the same weights. They can be employed for training a similarity function given labeled data. Figure 1 shows a simple network architecture based on convolutional (CONV) and max-pooling (MP) layers. An input example is passed to the network for computing the embeddings. Different losses are used for training Siamese networks, such as contrastive loss, margin-based loss, and triplet loss. Network parameters are updated according to the loss calculated on embeddings.

3.1   Triplet Loss

The triplet loss [19] has been used for face recognition. A triplet's anchor example a, positive example p, and negative example n are provided as a training example to the network for getting corresponding embeddings. During optimisation of the network parameters, we draw all possible triplets from labeled examples based on class labels. For each mini-batch used in stochastic gradient descent, all valid

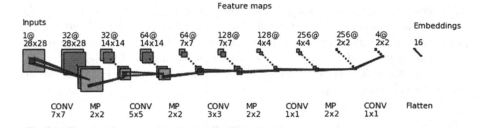

Fig. 1. Network Architecture

triplets(i, j, k) are selected where $labels[i] = labels[j], i \neq j$ and $labels[i] \neq labels[k]$. Then the loss is calculated according to the following equation using the Euclidean distance $d(., .)$ between the embedded examples:

$$\mathcal{L} = max(d(a, p) - d(a, n) + m, 0) \tag{1}$$

where m is the so-called "margin" and constitutes a hyperparameter.

As illustrated in Fig. 2, the triplet loss attempts to push away the embedded negative example n from the embedded anchor example a based on a given margin m and the given positive example p. Depending on the location of the negative example with respect to the anchor and the positive example, it is possible to distinguish between hard negative examples, semi-hard negative examples, and easy negative examples. The latter are effectively ignored during optimisation because they yield the value zero for the loss.

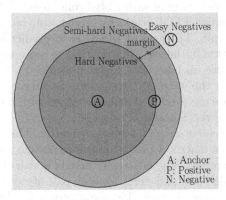

Fig. 2. Triplet loss

3.2 Self-learning Using Siamese Networks

In the first iteration of our semi-supervised learning approach, to be able to label (some of) the unlabeled examples instances, the Siamese network is trained on labeled examples only, using triplet loss. Then the standard nearest neighbor classifier is used to predict labels for the unlabeled examples and a fixed percentage p of unlabeled examples is chosen based on their distance to the labeled instances and added to the set of labeled examples for the next iteration. Throughout, embedded data is used to calculate distances. For more details see the pseudo-code in Listing 1.

Algorithm 1. Proposed approach based on Siamese self-training

---

1: **Input:** Labeled examples (x_L, y_L), Unlabeled examples x_U, number of meta-iterations i and selection percentage p
2: **for** 1 to i **do**
3:     $train\_siamesenetwork(x_L, y_L)$
4:     $embed_U = siamesenetwork(x_U)$
5:     $embed_L = siamesenetwork(x_L)$
6:     $labels_U, dist_U = KNN(embed_U, embed_L, y_L)$
7:     $sorted\_dist_U, sorted\_labels_U = sort(dist_U, labels_U)$
8:     $x_{new}, y_{new} = select\_top(sorted\_dist_U, sorted\_labels_U, p)$
9:     $x_L, y_L = concat((x_L, y_L), (x_{new}, y_{new}))$
10:     $x_U = delete\_from(x_U, x_{new})$
11: **end for**

---

4   Local Learning with Global Consistency (LLGC)

We also investigate local learning with global consistency [22] in addition to the nearest-neighbor classifier. LLGC works by propagating label information to the neighbors of an example. The goal of LLGC is to predict labels for unlabeled instances. The algorithm initializes a matrix $Y_{n \times c}$ to represent label information, where $Y_{ij} = 1$ if example i is labeled as j, and otherwise $Y_{ij} = 0$. We implement a little variation here for the unlabeled examples: instead of using $Y_{ij} = 0$ for all j when i is unlabeled, we use predicted labels obtained with the nearest-neighbour classifier after training the Siamese network.

LLGC is based on calculating an adjacency matrix. This adjacency matrix is then used to establish a matrix S that is applied to update the label probabilities for the unlabeled examples. The adjacency matrix is calculated using Eq. 2 by employing embeddings $f(x_i)$ and $f(x_j)$ for each pair of two examples x_i and x_j, obtained from the Siamese network. The parameter σ is a hyper-parameter.

$$W_{ij} = \begin{cases} e^{-\sigma \times |f(x_i) - f(x_j)|^2}, & \text{if } i \neq j \\ 0 & \text{if } i = j. \end{cases} \tag{2}$$

The matrix S is computed as:

$$S = D^{-1/2} \times W \times D^{-1/2} \tag{3}$$

where D is a diagonal matrix: $D_i = \sum_{j=1}^{n} W_{ij}$. The initial matrix of label probabilities is set to $F(0) = Y$, and the probabilities are updated by:

$$F(t + 1) = S.F(t) \times \alpha + (1 - \alpha) \times Y \tag{4}$$

where $\alpha \in [0, 1)$ is a hyper-parameter for controlling the propagation of label information. The above operation is repeated till convergence. Finally, labels for the unlabeled instances are calculated as:

$$y_i = \underset{j \leq c}{\mathrm{argmax}}\, F_{ij} \tag{5}$$

For efficiently using unlabeled instances, the Siamese network is first trained on labeled examples only, using triplet loss. Then the nearest-neighbor classifier is used to predict labels for unlabeled examples. Then, following that, labeled and unlabeled embeddings along with labels are passed to LLGC. After a certain number of iterations of LLGC, a fixed percentage p of unlabeled examples are chosen based on their LLGC score and added to the labeled examples for the next iteration. For more details see the pseudo-code in Listing 2.

Algorithm 2. Proposed approach based on LLGC self-training

1: **Input:** Labeled examples (x_L, y_L), Unlabeled examples x_U, number of meta-iterations i, selection percentage p, α and σ parameters for LLGC.
2: **for** 1 to i **do**
3:     $train\_siamesenetwork(x_L, y_L)$
4:     $embed_U = siamesenetwork(x_U)$
5:     $embed_L = siamesenetwork(x_L)$
6:     $labels_U = KNN(embed_U, embed_L, y_L)$
7:     $LLGC\_labels, LLGC\_score = LLGC(embed_L, embed_U, [y_L, labels_U], \sigma, \alpha)$
8:     $labels_U = LLGC\_labels[len(x_L):]$
9:     $x_{new}, y_{new} = select\_top(LLGC\_score, p, x_U, labels_U)$
10:     $x_L, y_L = concat((x_L, y_L), (x_{new}, y_{new}))$
11:     $x_U = delete\_from(x_U, x_{new})$
12: **end for**

---

5   Experiments

We consider four standard image classification problems for our evaluation. For all experiments, a small subset of labeled examples was chosen according to standard semi-supervised learning practice, with a balanced number of examples from each class, and the rest were considered as unlabeled. Final accuracy was calculated on the standard test split for each dataset. No data augmentation was applied to the training sets. Siamese networks were trained using triplet loss with margin $m = 0.3$ for all datasets.

A simple convolutional network architecture was chosen for each dataset to ensure performance achieved was due to the proposed method and not the network architecture. For more details about the network architectures, see Table 1. Layer descriptions use (feature-maps, kernel-size, stride, padding) for convolutional layers and (pool-size, stride) for pooling layers. The simple model is used for MNIST, Fashion MNIST, and SVHN, and produces 16-dimensional embeddings, while the CIFAR-10 model produces 64-dimensional embeddings. We trained the networks using mini-batch sizes 50, 100, and 200. We found that batch size 50 was insufficient and 200 did not yield significant improvements compared to batch size 100. Batch size $= 100$ is used for all experiments, with Adam [8] as the optimizer for updating network parameters for 200 epochs. Our proposed approaches Siamese self-training (Algorithm 1) and LLGC self-training (Algorithm 2) respectively were run for 25 meta-iterations. For LLGC, $\alpha = 0.99$ is used in all experiments, while σ is optimized for each dataset. The final test accuracy is computed using a k-NN classifier with $k = 1$ for simplicity. Our results were averaged over 3 random runs, using a different random initialization of the Siamese network parameters for each run and random selection of initially labeled examples except SVHN. We set a baseline by (a) training the network on the small number of the labeled instances only, and by (b) using all the labeled instances. These two baselines should provide good empirical lower and upper bounds for the semi-supervised error rates.

Table 1. Network model

Simple(#parameters $= 163908$)	CIFAR-10(#parameters $= 693792$)
INPUT	INPUT
Conv-Relu(32,7,1,2)	Conv-Relu-BN(192,5,1,2)
Max-Pooling(2,2)	Conv-Relu-BN(160,1,1,2)
Conv-Relu(64,5,1,2)	Conv-Relu-BN(96,1,1,2)
Max-Pooling(2,2)	Max-Pooling(3,2)
Conv-Relu(128,3,1,2)	Conv-Relu-BN(96,5,1,2)
Max-Pooling(2,2)	Conv-Relu-BN(192,1,1,2)
Conv-Relu(256,1,1,2)	Conv-Relu-BN(192,1,1,2)
Max-Pooling(2,2)	Max-Pooling(3,2)
Conv(4,1,1,2)	Conv-Relu-BN(192,3,1,2)
Flatten()	Conv-Relu-BN(64,1,1,2)
	Avg-Pooling(8,1)

We now consider the datasets used in our experiments. The MNIST dataset consists of gray-scale 28 by 28 images of handwritten digits. We select only 100 instances (10 from each class) as labeled instances initially. We apply our algorithms with a selection percentage $p = 10\%$ and the LLGC-based method with $\sigma = 1.8$. Table 2 shows noticeable improvements over the supervised-only approach when compared with the proposed semi-supervised approaches, when using the same number of labeled examples.

Table 2. MNIST Test error %.

# labels	100-Labeled	All (60000)
Supervised-only	9.73 ± 0.74	0.6 ± 0.04
Siamese self-training	$\mathbf{3.24 \pm 0.32}$	–
LLGC self-training	3.50 ± 0.14	–

The Fashion MNIST dataset consists of 28 by 28 gray-scale images showing fashion items. 100 instances are considered as labeled initially. Again, we use selection percentage $p = 10\%$ and $\sigma = 3.2$. Table 3 again shows noticeable improvement over the supervised-only approach when compared with the proposed semi-supervised approaches, when using the same amount of labeled data.

Table 3. Fashion MNIST Test error %.

# labels	100-Labeled	All (60000)
Supervised-only	26.72 ± 1.23	9.66 ± 0.10
Siamese self-training	23.33 ± 0.43	–
LLGC self-training	$\mathbf{23.23 \pm 0.67}$	–

SVHN comprises 32×32 RGB images of house numbers, taken from the Street View House Numbers dataset. Each image can have multiple digits, but only the digit in the center is considered for prediction. The proposed approaches are evaluated using 1000 labeled instances initially, with selection percentage $p = 5\%$, and $\sigma = 2.4$. Table 4 shows noticeable improvement over the supervised-only approach when compared to the proposed approaches when 1000 labeled examples are used. Interestingly, purely Siamese self-training again performs better than LLGC self-training in this case.

The CIFAR-10 dataset contains 32 by 32 RGB images of ten classes. The proposed semi-supervised approaches are evaluated using 4000 labeled instances initially, with selection percentage $p = 5\%$, and $\sigma = 2.4$. Table 5 shows little improvement over the supervised-only approach when compared to the proposed semi-supervised approaches. Siamese self-training performs better than LLGC self-training.

Figures 3, 4, 5 and 6 show a detailed comparison between Siamese self-training and LLGC self-training across three different runs of all four datasets;

Table 4. SVHN Test error %.

# labels	1000-Labeled	All (73275)
Supervised-only	30.33 ± 1.55	12.26 ± 0.52
Siamese self-training	**20.09 ± 3.22**	–
LLGC self-training	27.23 ± 0.99	–

Table 5. CIFAR-10 Test error %.

# labels	4000-Labeled	All (50000)
Supervised-only	40.87 ± 0.56	21.51 ± 0.88
Siamese self-training	**36.56 ± 0.74**	–
LLGC self-training	40.06 ± 0.62	–

MNIST, Fashion MNIST, SVHN, and CIFAR-10. The accuracy curves show definite improvement with respect to the supervised-only version on all datasets using Siamese self-training as well as LLGC self-training. However, CIFAR-10 and SVHN seem to get low or negligible additional improvement from LLGC self-training compared to Siamese self-training only.

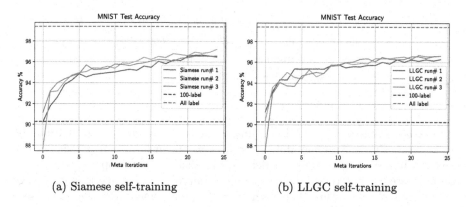

(a) Siamese self-training   (b) LLGC self-training

Fig. 3. MNIST-100 Comparison of Siamese self-training vs. LLGC self-training.

We also tried to visualize the quality of embeddings learned using the proposed method. We trained an additional model by slightly modifying the simple model Table 1. In order to get a 2-dimensional embedding, two feature-maps are used instead of 4 in the last convolutional layer, followed by average-pooling(2,2) before the final flattening layer. For this purpose, we considered MNIST. Figure 7(a) depicts the embeddings for test instances marked in color according to their true class after random initialization of the network. Figure 7(b) depicts the embeddings for test instances after training the Siamese network with only

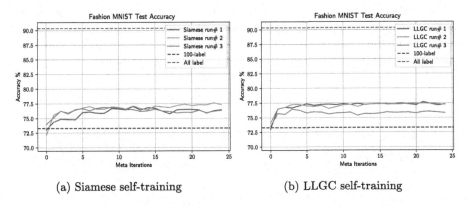

(a) Siamese self-training   (b) LLGC self-training

Fig. 4. Fashion MNIST-100 Comparison of Siamese self-training vs. LLGC self-training.

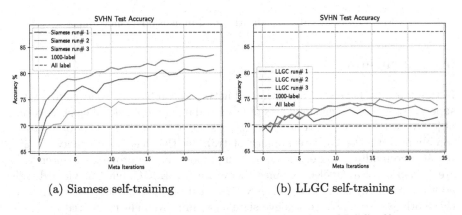

(a) Siamese self-training   (b) LLGC self-training

Fig. 5. SVHN-1000 Comparison of Siamese self-training vs. LLGC self-training.

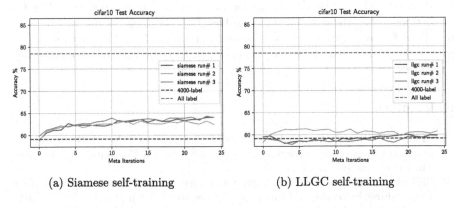

(a) Siamese self-training   (b) LLGC self-training

Fig. 6. CIFAR10-4000 Comparison of Siamese self-training vs. LLGC self-training.

the 100 labeled MNIST instances. It can be seen that the 10000 test examples' embeddings form clusters in Euclidean space after training of the network according to the class labels; test examples' embeddings are largely scattered randomly throughout the 2D space before the network is trained.

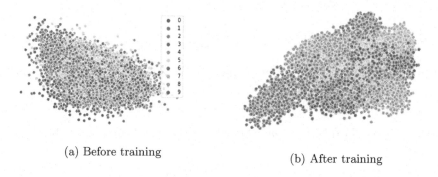

(a) Before training

(b) After training

Fig. 7. MNIST-100: visualisation of 2-dimensional embeddings

6 Conclusion

In this work, we have shown how neural networks can be used to learn in a semi-supervised setting using small sets of labeled data by replacing the classification objective with an objective for learning a similarity function. This objective is compliant with standard techniques of training the deep neural network and requires no modification of the embedding model. For improving the intermediate prediction of unlabeled instances, we evaluated LLGC, but this yielded little additional benefit compared to k-NN classification alone. Using the method in this work, we were able to achieve significant improvement compared to supervised learning only on MNIST, Fashion MNIST and SVHN, when training on a small subset of labeled examples, but obtained little improvement on CIFAR-10. We speculate that instead of a fixed selection of unlabeled instances from LLGC's predictions, a threshold-based selection based on the LLGC score will be more beneficial for subsequent iterations of our meta-algorithm. Also, a more robust convolutional model may help the network in learning distinctive embeddings and achieving state-of-the-art results for the semi-supervised setting.

References

1. Blum, A., Mitchell, T.: Combining labeled and unlabeled data with co-training. In: Proceedings of the Eleventh Annual Conference on Computational Learning Theory, pp. 92–100. ACM (1998)
2. Brefeld, U., Scheffer, T.: Co-EM support vector learning. In: Proceedings of the Twenty-First International Conference on Machine Learning, p. 16. ACM (2004)
3. Bromley, J., et al.: Signature verification using a "SIAMESE" time delay neural network. Int. J. Pattern Recogn. Artif. Intell. **7**, 669–688 (1993)

4. Chapelle, O., Schölkopf, B., Zien, A.: Semi-supervised Learning. Adaptive Computation and Machine Learning. The MIT Press, Cambridge (2006)
5. Chopra, S., Hadsell, R., LeCun, Y., et al.: Learning a similarity metric discriminatively, with application to face verification. In: CVPR, vol. 1, pp. 539–546 (2005)
6. Dai, Z., Yang, Z., Yang, F., Cohen, W.W., Salakhutdinov, R.R.: Good semi-supervised learning that requires a bad gan. In: Advances in Neural Information Processing Systems, pp. 6513–6523 (2017)
7. Hoffer, E., Ailon, N.: Semi-supervised deep learning by metric embedding. arXiv preprint arXiv:1611.01449 (2016)
8. Kingma, D.P., Ba, J.: Adam: a method for stochastic optimization. arXiv preprint arXiv:1412.6980 (2014)
9. Laine, S., Aila, T.: Temporal ensembling for semi-supervised learning. arXiv preprint arXiv:1610.02242 (2016)
10. Lee, D.H.: Pseudo-label: the simple and efficient semi-supervised learning method for deep neural networks. In: Workshop on Challenges in Representation Learning, ICML, vol. 3, p. 2 (2013)
11. Maaløe, L., Sønderby, C.K., Sønderby, S.K., Winther, O.: Auxiliary deep generative models. arXiv preprint arXiv:1602.05473 (2016)
12. McLachlan, G.J.: Iterative reclassification procedure for constructing an asymptotically optimal rule of allocation in discriminant analysis. J. Am. Stat. Assoc. **70**(350), 365–369 (1975)
13. Miyato, T., Maeda, S.I., Koyama, M., Ishii, S.: Virtual adversarial training: a regularization method for supervised and semi-supervised learning. arXiv preprint arXiv:1704.03976 (2017)
14. Nigam, K., McCallum, A., Mitchell, T.: Semi-supervised Text Classification Using EM. Semi-supervised Learning, pp. 33–56. MIT Press, Cambridge (2006)
15. Peters, J., Janzing, D., Schölkopf, B.: Elements of Causal Inference: Foundations and Learning Algorithms. MIT Press, Cambridge (2017)
16. Rasmus, A., Berglund, M., Honkala, M., Valpola, H., Raiko, T.: Semi-supervised learning with ladder networks. In: Advances in Neural Information Processing Systems, pp. 3546–3554 (2015)
17. Sajjadi, M., Javanmardi, M., Tasdizen, T.: Regularization with stochastic transformations and perturbations for deep semi-supervised learning. In: Advances in Neural Information Processing Systems, pp. 1163–1171 (2016)
18. Salimans, T., Goodfellow, I., Zaremba, W., Cheung, V., Radford, A., Chen, X.: Improved techniques for training GANs. In: Advances in Neural Information Processing Systems, pp. 2234–2242 (2016)
19. Schroff, F., Kalenichenko, D., Philbin, J.: FaceNet: a unified embedding for face recognition and clustering. In: Proceedings of the IEEE Conference on Computer Vision and Pattern Recognition, pp. 815–823 (2015)
20. Wei, X., Gong, B., Liu, Z., Lu, W., Wang, L.: Improving the improved training of Wasserstein GANs: a consistency term and its dual effect. arXiv preprint arXiv:1803.01541 (2018)
21. Weston, J., Ratle, F., Mobahi, H., Collobert, R.: Deep learning via semi-supervised embedding. In: Montavon, G., Orr, G.B., Müller, K.-R. (eds.) Neural Networks: Tricks of the Trade. LNCS, vol. 7700, pp. 639–655. Springer, Heidelberg (2012). https://doi.org/10.1007/978-3-642-35289-8_34
22. Zhou, D., Bousquet, O., Lal, T.N., Weston, J., Schölkopf, B.: Learning with local and global consistency. In: Advances in Neural Information Processing Systems, pp. 321–328 (2004)

Intrinsically Motivated Active Perception for Multi-areas View Tasks

Dashun Pei and Linhua Jiang[✉]

Engineering Research Center of Optical Instruments and Systems,
Ministry of Education, Shanghai Key Lab of Modern Optical Systems,
School of Optical-Electrical and Computer Engineering,
University of Shanghai for Science and Technology,
Shanghai 200093, People's Republic of China
honorsir@yandex.com

Abstract. The target recognition of the human eye in real scenes is still far superior to any robot vision system. We believe that there are two major essential reasons. First, humans can observe the environment in which the object is located, get the probability of the object category. Second, human can use foveal to focus on the object and get more object detail features from the high resolution image containing the object and make it easier to identify. This paper proposes a novel method for searching and locating surrounding objects using a monocular Panning/Tilting/Zooming (PTZ) camera with free rotation and zoom functions.

Our system is an active environment-aware vision system based on Intrinsic Motivation and capable of autonomously exploring the surroundings of the camera. At the same time, by combining the visual information of foveal field of view and context field of view, the visual system observes more details and make more accurate prediction, and overcomes the limitation of low-resolution image in target recognition. Finally, our experiment proved that the visual perception system incorporating the curiosity mechanism is superior to the common perception method in terms of time overhead and learning ability.

Keywords: Intrinsic Motivation · Active perception · Computer vision · Intrinsic adaptive curiosity · Developmental robotics

1 Introduction

Future autonomous robots need the ability to perceive the environment autonomously. That is, robots can discern the objects which are worth observing in any unfamiliar environment. However, most robots are still designed to

The research was partly supported by the program for Professor of Special Appointment (Eastern Scholar, 15HJPY-MS02) at Shanghai Institutions of Higher Learning, National Natural Science Foundation of China (No. 61775139).

J. Liu and J. Bailey (Eds.): AI 2019, LNAI 11919, pp. 598–609, 2019.
https://doi.org/10.1007/978-3-030-35288-2_48

perform a specified action after matching a specific condition (a specific target or scene).

The accuracy of the camera perception will be affected by the distance between the perceived camera and the target, small size of the target, and using a low resolution camera especially. Because of above reasons, the targets detection algorithm will classify those targets as backgrounds and ignore them. In order to improve the efficiency of target search and detection in a real environment, robots need to zoom in the image detected area selectively.

The main contributions to this paper are summarized as follows:

1. It studies the autonomous object search and detection of the sensing device in the real indoor environment. We divide the surrounding environment into equal zones, which constitutes 9 perception fields, each containing different visual information. Through the Intrinsic Motivation mechanism enable model to give different values of different perception fields of view are given. The sensing device is capable of autonomously selecting a field of view to observe.

2. We also introduce the foveal field of view to perform secondary verification and further feature learning with richer details, This means more accurate and robust object recognition. But in the past if we wanted to be able to find very small or distant objects, we had to use a higher image resolution camera, now we only need a Panning/Tilting/Zooming (PTZ) camera that can make the part of interest earned a very high resolution.

2   Related Work

In order to effectively analyze the input of the camera's visual modality and interact with objects in a chaotic surrounding environment, the PTZ camera platform relies on attention-based strategy-based visual perception. Today, this idea has been extensively studied and discussed in the perspective of bionics and computer vision [2–4, 22]. In this study, we limit our visual attention to the recognition and localization of objects of interest. This attentional mechanism, through the combination of Intrinsic Motivation and intelligent adaptive curiosity (IAC), achieves curiosity-driven peripherals. Attention to environmental goals.

In the computer vision system with curiosity, the foveated system based on bionics design is a worthy research object. The foveated system usually refers to two types of visual inputs obtained by the camera platform, one is the global field of view of the global, and the other is a partial enlarged view of the object of interest in the field of view. The former is used to grasp the context information and locate the object of interest. The context information can give more reference to the semantic information of the computer vision system. The latter can obtain the target detail features neglected by the context of the target through the high-resolution representation of the target of interest. Minut et al. [5] used the PTZ camera system to learn and locate a target well by learning. Hueber et al. [6] proposed a motion detection and tracking platform for cameras based on integrated foveal field of view and context field of view. Kragg et al. [7] achieved better target recognition by adjusting the zoom level of the camera lens. Ekvall et al. [1] completed a target detection system that introduced a attention-based detection mechanism, which provides a closer view to the target feature matching through the zoom in and pan/tilt-angles of the PTZ camera. However, these researchers form a passive visual perception system through cameras. The system needs to manually set various parameters and types of objects that the sensing system can detect.

Our system is an active environment-aware vision system for the environment. By introducing a curiosity mechanism, the system can dynamically update the attention of various targets in the surrounding environment, effectively improving the progress of the system learning, and at the same time, through the fusion of foveal information makes the observation of each target feature more detailed and accurate.

3   Intrinsically Motivated Active Perception System

Our experimental was developed in the bio-mimetics project, aiming to study and capture some features and habit of the human vision and promote new exploration in the field of robot vision or computer vision strategies, such as recognition, locating, tracking and path planning.

3.1   Physical Hardware

Our camera device is SONY evi-d70p, and shown in Fig. 1. power (W) 12 video port number rs-232 or rs-422 serial control, 216x scaling ratio (18x optical, 12x digital), Angle: +90° to −30° (maximum tilting speed: 90°/SEC), Horizontal resolution: 460 TV cable (evi-d70p); 470 TV cable (evi-d70).

Fig. 1. camera device includes a high-resolution PTZ camera. In our experiments we mount the cameras on a standard tripod instead of using the robotic platform.

3.2   Architecture

The constructed sensorimotor system is defined as a ten-component model **IMAP** $= \{S, A, O, C, V, V_s, L, E_p, E_l, E\}$, the meaning of each element is as follows.

- S: The set of discrete perceived states of IMAP. $\mathbf{S} = \{\mathbf{S}_i \mid i = 1, 2, \dots, n_s\}, \mathbf{S}_i \in \mathbf{S}$. $\mathbf{S}$ is the i-th sense state, and n_s is the number of discreet discrete states.
- A: IMAP action set. $\mathbf{A} = \{\mathbf{A}_i \mid i = 1, 2, \dots, n_s\}, \mathbf{A}_i = \{a_{ij} \mid j = 1, 2, \dots, n_i\}$, a_{ij} represents the j-th optional action of the IMAP in the i-th sense state, and n_i is the number of selectable actions in the i-th state.
- O: IMAP's $perception - motion$ orientation mapping set. $\mathbf{O} = \{\mathbf{O}_i \mid i = 1, 2, \dots, n_s\}, \mathbf{O}_i = diag([o_{i1}, \dots, o_{ij}, \dots, o_{in_i}])_{n_i \times n_i}$, $\mathbf{O}_i$ is the i-th state is a directional mapping matrix of optional actions in this state, $diag$ means that the elements in parentheses are stored diagonally. $o_{ij}(i \in (1, 2, \dots, n_s), j \in (1, 2, \dots, n_i))$ represents a $perception - motion$ map that characterizes the orientation to which the IMAP selects the action m_j in the perceptual state $\mathbf{S}_i \in \mathbf{S}$, or the orientation of perceptual motion of the perceptual state s_i and the action a_{ij}.
- C: Curiosity. $\mathbf{C} = \{\mathbf{C}_i \mid i = 1, 2, \dots, n_s\}$, $\mathbf{C}_i$ is the curiosity of the i-th state of the system. From the perspective of human bionics, the curiosity in a certain state decreases as the number of times the state is explored. Based on this, the curiosity is designed as follows, where: N_i is t The number of times the system explores the state s_i; k, c are the curiosity parameters. The orientation and curiosity are two intrinsic factors that influence the next action of the biological selection.

$$c_i = \frac{1}{1 + e^{k(N_i - c)}} \tag{1}$$

- V: System status orientation. $\mathbf{V} = \{\mathbf{V}_i \mid i = 1, 2, \dots, n_s\}$, The value used to determine the orientation function corresponds to the system's perceived state. Among them, $V_i \in [-1, 1]$, -1 is the state orientation of the worst state, and 1 is the state orientation of the most ideal state.
- V_s: orientation function, $V_s = aV_n + b(V_n - V_o)$, V_o and V_n respectively indicate the state before and after the execution of an action, where $a \geq 0, b \leq 0$ is the parameter of the orientation function, and its value should be selected. The sign of the orientation function does not change the sign of $(V_n - V_o)$, and satisfies $a + b = 1$, which can generally be learned.
- L: Orientation learning matrix. $\mathbf{L} = \{\mathbf{L}_i \mid i = 1, 2, \dots, n_s\}$, The role is to update and adjust the orientation map based on the information provided by the orientation function. Let the system at t time map the orientation in the sensing state s_i to $O_i(t)$. After the action m_j is executed, the orientation map in the sensing state becomes $O_i(t+1)$, and the orientation map updating method is as follows Where $\eta > 0$ is the orientation learning parameter.

$$\begin{cases} p_{ij}(t) = 1 + Sign(V_s(t))(1 - e^{-\eta |V_s(t)|}) + c \times P(t); \\ p_{ik}(t) = 1, k \in (1, 2, \dots, n_i), k \neq j; \end{cases} \tag{2}$$

$$Sign(x) = \begin{cases} 1, & x > 0 \\ 0, & x = 0 \\ -1, & x < 0 \end{cases} \tag{3}$$

$$O_i(t+1) = \frac{O_i(t)L_i(t)}{\sum\limits_{j=1}^{n_i} o_{ij}(t)l_{ij}(t)} \tag{4}$$

- Ep: Predictive entropy of perceptual motion systems. $\mathbf{Ep} = \{\mathbf{Ep}_i \mid i = 1, 2, \ldots, n_s\}$, Determined by the prediction P, the orientation map O, and the action A taken, the prediction P can predict the result update $O(t+1)$ that occurs after the action $A(j)$ is taken under the orientation map $O(t)$ at the moment. the prediction formula is $P(A(j), O(t)) = O(t+1)$. After making the prediction $P(t+1)$ and taking the corresponding action, the robot can measure the actual result $O(t+1)$ and calculate its prediction error $\mathbf{Ep}_i$. The calculation method is $Ep(t) = absoluteValue(P(t+1) - O(t+1))$

$$Ep_i = \left| \frac{k_1 C_i}{\sqrt{\sum\limits_{i=1}^{n_i} (V_i - O_{ij})^2}} - \sum\limits_{j=1}^{num} k_2 \sqrt{(S_i - U_j)^2} \right| \tag{5}$$

- E_l: Learning entropy of perceptual motion systems, $\mathbf{E_l} = \{\mathbf{E_l}_i \mid i = 1, 2, \ldots, n_s\}$, It is used to describe the degree of learning of knowledge in the system, and to characterize the self-learning and self-organizing characteristics of the system. The knowledge entropy of the system t is defined as:

$$E_l(t) = \sum\limits_{i=1}^{n_s} E_{li}(t), \tag{6}$$

$$E_{li}(t) = E_{li}(m_j(t)|s_i) = -\sum\limits_{j=1}^{n_s} o_{ij}(t)\log_2 o_{ij}(t) \tag{7}$$

- E: The comprehensive entropy of the perceptual motion system indicate the degree of the model on the overall macroscopic level of the system. It is calculated by the knowledge entropy E_l and the predicted entropy E_{p_i}: $E = C_1 \times E_{p_i} + C_2 \times E_{li}$ where C_1 and C_2 represent the comprehensive entropy parameters.

Basic working principle is as follows: t time, system to perceive its internal state $i \in S$, calculate the moment of the current status of each action oriented mapping matrix $O_i(t)$ and the state of curiosity $i(t)$; Add curiosity to any action at random and select the action with the largest sum of orientation and curiosity according to the engine mechanism in the system. Perform the action, state transition; After the transition, the foveal visual Angle of each target was twice verified, and the state orientation value and orientation function value of the new state were calculated. According to the information provided by the orientation function, and the orientation mapping matrix is updated to obtain a new $perception - movement$ mapping. Finally, the prediction entropy E_{pi} and knowledge entropy E_{li} of foveal's perspective target in this state are calculated. The experiment ends until the loss falls to a certain value or the learning time is greater than the end time.

3.3   Object Detection

Currently, the most advanced algorithms in the field of target detection are based on deep neural networks. Girshick et al. proposed R-CNN [14], for each region, extract the features with AlexNet with the last softmax layer removed. Subsequently, R. Girshick further optimized the Faster R-CNN [15], designed Region Proposal Networks, the speed is obviously improved. Ren et al. [16] An improved framework was proposed through research that can jointly learn to generate and score object proposals.

Redmon et al. [8,17] proposed YOLO, which generates the probability that the candidate detection box and the per-box target belong to the category, thus achieving good performance. The downside of YOLO is that it is not good for objects that are close to each other, and for small targets, We hope to overcome this problem by introducing foveal vision.

4   Curiosity-Based Learning Algorithm

In Oudeyer's article [10], the effect of independent training between multiple fields of view was achieved by proposing regional experts. Oudeyer [10] used classic Machine learner to make the most appropriate operation, and the Meta Machine learner feeds back to classM based on the result of the operation and the error estimation of classM estimation, for multivariate update classM. Interestingly, it seems that there is a certain degree of similarity with Generative Adversarial Nets (GAN) [21].

Intrinsic motivation [9,18] is one of the indispensable skills in the study of robotic autonomous learning today. But in the early days, intrinsic motivation was paid attention to in the field of psychology [19,20]. In 1938, Skinner [11] first proposed the concept of *operantconditioning*. Rosen et al. [12] used Skinner's proposal achieved the balance control of the inverted pendulum within a certain distance. The system designed by Rosen was After reaching a certain steady state, it is impossible to eliminate the occurrence of small probability events. Shi et al. [13] established a cognitive model of the self-balancing robot perception motion system based on the operator conditioning theory proposed by Skinner, enabling the robot to obtain self-learning in the process of movement The skill of exercise balance, but the action selection mechanism adopted by Shi also causes small probability events to occur.

5   Experimental Results

In the experimental setup, we placed the camera platform in the middle of long tables with some targets to be tested and shown in Fig. 2. The background behind the desk is very complicated. We expect our curiosity mechanism to be very good at avoiding complex background interference. Keep curiosity and attention on the goals on tables.

Fig. 2. The environment around the camera platform during the experiment.

Fig. 3. Foveal perspective of the target of interest in position 4 (pos4).

Fig. 4. Foveal perspective of the target of interest in position 5 (pos5).

The experiment is to observe the current environment by the unconstrained camera platform. After the camera first cycles through the surrounding environment, the convolutional neural network separates each suspected target of the context. The suspected target performs secondary verification and specific feature learning of the foveal field of view one by one and performs curiosity and orientation assignment of the state of view of the environment according to the degree of learning. Figures 3 and 4 shown the feature learning of the foveal field of view separately for targets in different fields of view.

For the surrounding environment, we set up a 3×3 area division, each area is calibrated to a field of view. The state of view of the PTZ camera actively perceived during the exploration process is shown in Fig. 5.

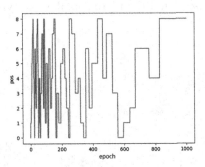

Fig. 5. The state of view of the PTZ camera actively perceived during the exploration process.

We took three groups experiments to study what role the curiosity-based intrinsic motivation strategy play. All experiments set up in the same perception environment, used same perception device, and same loss calculation method. We only change the method that next view field selection. We took a ordinal selection strategy in first experiment, a random selection strategy in second, and a strategy introduced in this paper in third. The pos changes of the three experiments are shown in Fig. 6.

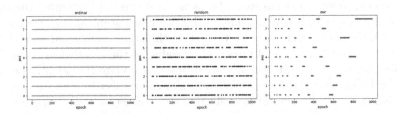

Fig. 6. Camera position(pos) changes of the three experiments. The left: ordinal strategy. The middle: random strategy. The right: curiosity-based intrinsic motivation strategy.

After the completion of the three experiments, for the more intuitive comparison, we retained the display form of the nine field of view states. Figure 7 is a line chart of the results of the curiosity changes of the three experiments in the nine fields of view. It can be seen from the result graph that the green curve representing ordinal in each field of view is stable and uniform, while the blue fold line representing random has a relatively undulating change, and the red fold line representing curiosity is large. The curiosity in a certain state decreases as the number of times the state is explored decreases. The change of curiosity in the nine visual states of the system is shown in Fig. 7. The decline in curiosity represents the learning of the state of vision. The greater the curiosity, the more goals that represent unseen and the more complex the types of goals.

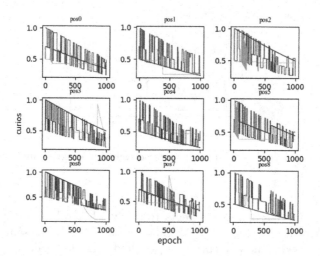

Fig. 7. The line chart of the results of the curiosity changes of the three experiments in the nine fields of view, each field of view in the green lines represent ordinal, blue lines for random, red lines for curiosity. (Color figure online)

The system state orientation value is a value used to determine the orientation function, which corresponds to the perceived state of the system. The orientation value of each state is [0, 1]. 0 is the state orientation value of the worst state, and 1 is the state orientation value of the most ideal state. During the learning process, the camera platform can update the orientation value function by updating the orientation values of the respective states in real time as shown in Fig. 8, thereby further affecting the *perception − motion* orientation mapping set.

The change in loss in the nine fields of view is shown in Fig. 9. The green curve representing the ordinal drops very evenly, and there is no long-term continuous exploration of a particular state. The red curve using the curiosity mechanism will drop sharply at some point in each field of view. When the loss of a certain field of view falls to a certain level at a certain moment, the learning effect of the field of view is improved at that moment. Curiosity will also decline, and the system will automatically jump to other fields of vision to learn, So the process in Fig. 9 is that the moments of the red line breaks in each state are staggered. Loss is the predictive entropy and learning entropy of the perceptual motion system. It can characterize the self-learning and self-organization characteristics of the system.

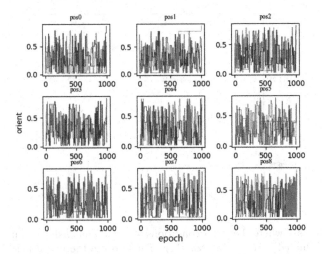

Fig. 8. The line chart of the results of the orient changes of the three experiments in the nine fields of view, each field of view in the green lines represent ordinal, blue lines for random, red lines for curiosity. (Color figure online)

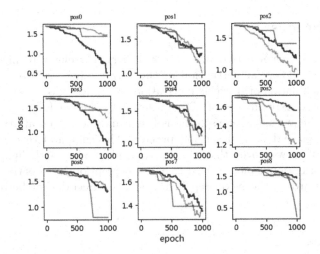

Fig. 9. The line chart of the results of the loss changes of the three experiments in the nine fields of view, each field of view in the green lines represent ordinal, blue lines for random, red lines for curiosity. (Color figure online)

We also introduce the foveal field of view through PTZ camera to perform secondary verification and more detailed feature learning, this means more accurate and robust object recognition. In order to verify the effect of foveal visual field on the active perception system, under the conditions of the same perception environment, we compared the results of using foveal visual field and not using foveal visual field by controlling variables. The experimental results are shown in Fig. 10.

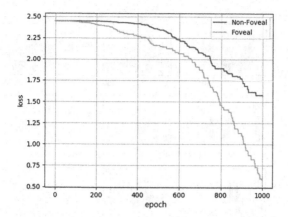

Fig. 10. In the case where the other conditions were not changed, a comparative experiment was conducted by changing whether or not to use the foveal field of view. The results show that the performance of the active sensing process using the foveal field of view is faster, and the Non-Foveal experiment does not detect enough for long-range and small-sized targets, resulting in poor performance.

6   Conclusions

The current research on active-aware robots is fiery, We refer to bionics to imitate the process of biological perception of the surrounding strange environment, using the combination of Intrinsic motivation and convolutional neural network, and the related experiments of active sensing by adding foveal field of view. Experiments show that active sensing is faster and more accurate than random sensing process and ordinal sensing process. The comparative experiment of foveal field of view proves that the foveal field of view with high pixel rich semantic information is more robust to active perception and less time overhead. We look forward to the next step in the visual perception of better research results.

References

1. Ekvall, S., Kragic, D., Jensfelt, P.: Object detection and mapping for service robot tasks. Robotica **25**(2), 175–187 (2007)
2. Borji, A., Itti, L.: State-of-the-art in visual attention modeling. IEEE Trans. Pattern Anal. Mach. Intell. **35**(1), 185–207 (2013)
3. Itti, L., Koch, C.: Computational modelling of visual attention. Nat. Rev. Neurosci. **2**(3), 194 (2001)
4. Frintrop, S., Rome, E., Christensen, H.I.: Computational visual attention systems and their cognitive foundations: a survey. ACM Trans. Appl. Percept. (TAP) **7**(1), 6 (2010)
5. Minut, S., Mahadevan, S.: A reinforcement learning model of selective visual attention. In: Proceedings of the Fifth International Conference on Autonomous Agents. ACM (2001)

6. Hueber, N., et al.: Bio-inspired approach for intelligent unattended ground sensors. In: Next-Generation Robotics II; and Machine Intelligence and Bio-inspired Computation: Theory and Applications IX, vol. 9494. International Society for Optics and Photonics (2015)

7. Young, M.: The Technical Writer's Handbook: Writing with Style and Clarity. University Science Books (2002)

8. Redmon, J., Farhadi, A.: YOLO9000: better, faster, stronger. arXiv preprint (2017)

9. Baldassarre, G., Mirolli, M. (eds.): Intrinsically Motivated Learning in Natural and Artificial Systems. Springer, Berlin (2013)

10. Oudeyer, P.-Y., Kaplan, F., Hafner, V.V.: Intrinsic motivation systems for autonomous mental development. IEEE Trans. Evol. Comput. **11**(2), 265–286 (2007)

11. Skinner, B.F.: An Experimental Analysis. The Behavior of Organisms. BF Skinner Foundation (1990)

12. Rosen, B.E., Goodwin, J.M., Vidal, J.J.: Machine operant conditioning. In: Annual International Conference of the IEEE Engineering in Medicine and Biology Society. IEEE, Piscataway (1988)

13. Tao, S., et al.: A study on autonomous learning mechanism of cognitive robot. In: 2015 27th Chinese Control and Decision Conference (CCDC). IEEE (2015)

14. Girshick, R., et al.: Rich feature hierarchies for accurate object detection and semantic segmentation. In: Proceedings of the IEEE Conference on Computer Vision and Pattern Recognition (2014)

15. Girshick, R.: Fast R-CNN. In: Proceedings of the IEEE International Conference on Computer Vision (2015)

16. Ren, S., et al.: Faster R-CNN: towards real-time object detection with region proposal networks. In: Advances in Neural Information Processing Systems (2015)

17. Redmon, J., et al.: You only look once: unified, real-time object detection. In: Proceedings of the IEEE Conference on Computer Vision and Pattern Recognition (2016)

18. Cangelosi, A., Schlesinger, M.: Developmental Robotics: From Babies to Robots. The MIT Press (2015)

19. Brogden, J.W.: Principles of behavior. J. Consult. Psychol. **8**(5), 330–330 (1944)

20. Berlyne, D.E.: Curiosity and exploration. Science **153**(3731), 25–33 (1966)

21. Goodfellow, I.J., et al.: Generative adversarial nets. In: International Conference on Neural Information Processing Systems. MIT Press (2014)

22. Bajcsy, R., Aloimonos, Y., Tsotsos, J.K.: Revisiting active perception. Auton. Rob. **42**(2), 177–196 (2018)

Author Index